Rita Welck

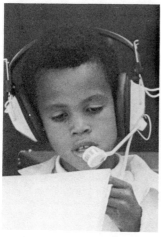

Developing Language Skills
In The Elementary Schools

FOURTH EDITION

4TH
EDITION

Developing Language Skills
In The Elementary Schools

Harry A. Greene

PROFESSOR EMERITUS OF EDUCATION
STATE UNIVERSITY OF IOWA

Walter T. Petty

PROFESSOR OF EDUCATION
STATE UNIVERSITY OF NEW YORK AT BUFFALO

Allyn and Bacon, Inc., Boston

Contents

Foreword   ix

Preface   xi

CHAPTER 1   **The Language Arts and the Professional Teacher   1**

The Language Arts in the School Program   *2*
The Professional Teacher   *4*
The Language Arts Teacher and the Curriculum   *9*
Language and Linguistics   *16*
Linguistics in the Elementary School Program   *27*
Exercises for Thought and Action   *32*
Selected References   *32*

CHAPTER 2   **Planning for Instruction in the Language Arts   34**

Organizing for Instruction   *35*
Pupil Differences in Language Abilities   *43*
Providing for Individual Differences   *45*
A Basic Instructional Approach   *51*
Evaluation in the Instructional Program   *58*
Exercises for Thought and Action   *61*
Selected References   *62*

CHAPTER 3   **Language Development and Early Instruction   63**

Language Development during the Preschool Years   *64*
Factors that Influence Language Development   *67*
Beginning Language Arts Programs   *70*
Kindergarten Language Arts Emphasis   *72*
Instructional Activities in the Kindergarten   *78*
Reading in the Kindergarten   *81*
Exercises for Thought and Action   *83*
Selected References   *84*

CHAPTER 4   **Language Problems of the Societal Disadvantaged   85**

Disadvantages and Deprivations   *86*
Language Development of the Disadvantaged   *91*
Language Characteristics of the Disadvantaged   *95*
The Teacher and the Disadvantaged Child   *98*
Dialects and Teaching Problems   *101*
Additional Teaching Suggestions   *104*
The Problem of the Bilingual Child   *114*
Exercises for Thought and Action   *117*
Selected References   *117*

CHAPTER 5   **The Foundation Program of the Primary Grades   120**

The Language Arts Focus for the Primary Grades   *121*
Activities for Developing Oral Expression   *126*
Helping Children with Listening   *138*
Written Expression in the Primary Grades   *140*
Beginning Reading Instruction   *147*
Exercises for Thought and Action   *150*
Selected References   *150*

CHAPTER 6   **Developing Listening Skills   152**

The Nature of Listening   *153*
Relationship of Other Abilities to Listening   *157*
Types of Listening   *162*
Teaching Listening Skills   *164*
Listening Lessons and Activities   *168*
Evaluating Listening   *178*
Exercises for Thought and Action   *182*
Selected References   *183*

CHAPTER 7   **Teaching Oral Expression   185**

Speech in the School Curriculum   *186*
The Importance of Good Speech Habits   *190*
Developing Oral Language Skills in Special Situations   *199*
Evaluating Oral Language Skills and Products   *226*
Exercises for Thought and Action   *232*
Selected References   *232*

CHAPTER 8   **Teaching Written Expression   234**

Writing: Some Preliminary Considerations   *235*
Motivating Children to Write   *237*
Developing Writing Skills in Special Language Situations   *241*
Teaching the Conventions in Writing   *254*
Written Language Skills in Using Books   *263*
Self-editing and Proofreading   *266*
The Evaluation of Written Expression   *269*
Diagnostic and Remedial Procedures   *274*
Exercises for Thought and Action   *277*
Selected References   *277*

CHAPTER 9   **Fostering Creativity in Language Expression   279**

Creativity and Creative Language Expression   *280*
Conditions Fostering Creative Expression   *287*
The Teacher's Role in Creative Expression   *292*
Getting Expression Started   *296*
Creative Written Expression   *303*
Creative Oral Expression   *310*
Exercises for Thought and Action   *313*
Selected References   *314*
Some Books for Children Helpful in
    Developing Language Expression   *315*

CHAPTER 10   **Skills and Abilities Important to both Oral and Written Language   316**

Dialects, Usage and Grammar   *317*
A Functional Approach to Teaching English Usage   *323*
Developing the Rhetorical Skills   *333*
Promoting Vocabulary Growth   *350*
Using Sources of Information   *357*
Exercises for Thought and Action   *366*
Selected References   *367*

CHAPTER 11   **Grammar in the Elementary School   368**

Grammar and Linguistics   *369*
Developments in the Teaching of Grammar   *371*
Values Attributed to the Teaching of Grammar   *380*
Grammar for Today's Classroom   *383*
Exercises for Thought and Action   *389*
Selected References   *389*

CHAPTER 12   **The Teaching of Spelling   391**

Spelling in the School Curriculum   *392*
Goals of the Spelling Program   *394*
The Instructional Program   *398*
Special Considerations in Spelling Instruction   *404*

Measuring the Results of Spelling Instruction   *417*
Diagnosis and Correction   *422*
Exercises for Thought and Action   *427*
Selected References   *428*

CHAPTER 13   **Improving Children's Handwriting   430**

Handwriting Today   *431*
A Program for Handwriting Instruction   *432*
Instructional Considerations   *437*
Issues and Problems in Handwriting   *447*
Evaluative and Remedial Procedures   *451*
Exercises for Thought and Action   *462*
Selected References   *462*

CHAPTER 14   **Basic Reading Instruction   464**

Reading and Language   *465*
The Objectives of Reading Instruction   *466*
A Modern Reading Program   *467*
Approaches to Reading Instruction   *472*
The Reading Lesson   *477*
Practices and Issues in the Teaching of Reading   *481*
Materials for Reading Instruction   *495*
Evaluation in Reading Instruction   *496*
Exercises for Thought and Action   *500*
Selected References   *500*

CHAPTER 15   **Teaching Literature in the Elementary School   502**

Objectives of the Literature Program   *503*
The Teacher and Literature   *504*
Children's Reading Interests   *506*
Techniques in Teaching Literature   *509*
Special Considerations in the Teaching of Poetry   *523*
Evaluation in the Literature Program
Aids in Book Selection   *529*
Exercises for Thought and Action   *534*
Selected References   *535*

CHAPTER 16   **Textbooks and Workbooks   537**

The Textbooks in the Program   *538*
Using Textbooks in the Language Arts   *543*
The Selection of Language Arts Textbooks   *545*
Workbooks in the Language Arts Program   *549*
The Selection and Use of Workbooks   *555*
Exercises for Thought and Action   *558*
Selected References   *559*

Index 560

Foreword

In a world fraught with anxiety about the survival of humankind it seems especially timely to consider what man's ability to communicate —and particularly to use language—has and has not done to bring us to this state. Certainly information has been exchanged, else the technical skills of the day would not have been accomplished, but have we really learned to talk with one another?

The hope of mankind rests in man's ability to understand his world, his neighbors, and for this he must use language, and he must use it for this purpose and more effectively than he has in the past. Mankind must draw together to survive and live as human beings. We cannot retreat into our nationalistic, racial, or social holes and barricade the entrances, for then we will not be human. A failure to really communicate with one another, however, may force us to that fate.

This book, then, is more than a discourse on the teaching of the English language arts. True, it is that—and we believe it is a good one —but it is a plea also to teachers to understand their children, to help them understand one another, to give them skill and confidence in speaking, writing, listening, and reading so that they may effectively communicate their thoughts and ideas and be receptive to the communication attempts of others. None of us can solve all of the problems of the world, but we can work for understanding and effective communication—a necessary first step.

H. A. G.
W. T. P.

Preface

This fourth edition of *Developing Language Skills in the Elementary Schools* continues to emphasize the authors' belief that language is the basic tool of communication and that the specific skills, abilities, and attitudes needed by children for effective communication must be taught directly and thoroughly. We believe that a child acquires a mastery of language by using it. We believe that the school curriculum must be rich in content and activities which stimulate genuine and extensive language expression and which necessitate meaningful listening and reading. Therefore, the language arts program described is one which avoids contrived experiences and purposeless activities. The focus is upon developing the language proficiency of each child to its maximum and to do so as efficiently as possible.

While language skills need to be taught specifically rather than incidentally, the interrelatedness of all language activities must be recognized. Therefore, in this edition we have given particular attention to integrated language activities, to teaching any language skill whenever the opportunity is presented, and to the transfer of those skills, abilities, and attitudes learned in one language arts area to their related counterparts in other areas.

There is much new content in this edition, particularly in the areas of children's language development, of linguistics, and of teaching the disadvantaged pupil. The matter of dialects is thoroughly discussed, and many suggestions are given as to how best to deal with the instructional problems that are often associated with the dialect differences found in many classrooms. Considerable attention is given to transformational-generative grammar and its relationship to "traditional" and other grammars and to usage problems.

The sections on written expression has been added to greatly in this edition, including new suggestions for relating writing to reading and for sentence building. Activities suggested as useful for teaching listening, spelling, handwriting, creative expression, and vocabulary have also been expanded. While every chapter has been extensively revised, the chapters on listening, grammar, literature, and the disadvantaged have been completely rewritten, and a chapter on language development has been added. Furthermore, the sequence of chapters has been changed to reflect the suggestions of users of the third edition.

An attempt has been made to further strengthen the research orientation of the earlier editions. We try to cite the research evidence that is pertinent to each aspect of the language arts program. We do present a specific point of view, one which we believe is based upon the best available research evidence and upon sound practice, but we have also tried to fairly present points of view which are different from ours.

To the many experienced teachers the authors have known, and to colleagues and students in the institutions in which we have taught, grateful acknowledgment is again expressed for the many contributions they have made directly or indirectly to this book. Particular appreciation is also expressed to Alma Harrington for helping with this edition in many ways; to Donald H. Graves and James J. Mancuso for the photography; to Dr. Mary Montebello, John Dixon, Dr. Freda Chalmers, Fannie Reeves, Marjorie Becking, Dr. Margaret Sawkins, and Marian Gray for their reviews, and the reviews of their students of the third edition; to Julie Schneider for her devoted typing and attention to detail; and to Jennifer Adams for her thorough and interested editing. We also appreciate the frontispiece photograph of Shelley, the junior author's granddaughter, and the skill of her mother-photographer. We are again especially personally and professionally grateful to Dorothy Clem Petty for assistance in all stages of the production of this edition, including major writing contributions in several chapters.

H. A. G.
W. T. P.

Developing Language Skills
In The Elementary Schools

The Language Arts And The Professional Teacher

1

INTRODUCTION

Man has accomplished nothing more wonderful than the development of language. Through language man makes known his feelings and thoughts; through language he is stimulated to action and reaction; through language he acquires understanding, attitudes, ideals; with language he thinks and solves problems; from language he finds inspiration and secures emotional release. Language permeates all that man does. Language is a part of man. Language is an integral part of culture. Language makes possible a society.

The importance of language to mankind is beyond question. In our present fast-moving and changing world effective communication is crucial. Every person needs to be able to express his thoughts and feelings, to learn through seeing, reading, and listening, to consider his own expression thoughtfully, and to react in a like manner to the expression of others. Developing in each child his full capabilities for using language is a major task of the school; it is a task that is ever increasing in importance.

The purpose of this chapter is to introduce the preservice and inservice teacher to language, to the school's program for teaching and developing effective language use, and to a number of teaching concerns of the professional teacher. Specifically, the following topics are discussed:

1. The Language Arts in the School Program
2. The Professional Teacher
3. The Language Arts Teacher and the Curriculum
4. Language and Linguistics
5. Linguistics in the Elementary School Program

Since this is an introductory chapter, the reader is reminded that the above topics are dealt with in an introductory or foundational manner. Thus, while the language arts are defined, the entire book furthers this definition. In a like manner, the subject of linguistics in the elementary school, a topic of increasing concern in language arts instruction, is introduced and briefly discussed, with other chapters making reference in varying degrees of detail to the subject.

The Language Arts in the School Program

Since language is so fundamental to humankind, since it is man's most distinctive human characteristic, a large segment of the school program must be concerned with language. The very extent and diversity of a school program—ranging from the planned to the unplanned—generates a wide use and diversity in language. To develop each child's ability to use his language with maximum proficiency, the language portion of the school program should be, and ordinarily is, organized in a manner designed to teach or to further develop language skills, to foster attitudes important to the most effective use of these skills, and to build appreciation of the role of language in increasing an individual's resources as a human being.

What are the Language Arts? The language arts are usually defined as the *receptive* language activities of reading and listening and the *expressive* language activities of speaking and writing. While "Language Arts" is a term that has rather widespread use, there are other names sometimes given to these receptive and expressive language activities. Traditionally, the aspect of the school program concerned with language has been called "English," and many persons continue to prefer this term. Others favor "The Communicative Arts"; still others use English as a modifier and refer to "The English Language Arts."

Language Arts seems to be the designation which best describes the activities of speaking, writing, listening, and reading and best labels an instructional program which focuses upon developing abilities in these language activities. English, as a designation, tends to narrow the content of the instruction to writing, grammar, and literature.[1] Those who favor the designation *English* believe that a broader concept causes fragmentation and a weakening of the subject area as a discipline. The more limited designation appears to the present writers to be one that does not give proper attention to speaking, listening, and reading and tends to emphasize the content of language and literature to the neglect of developing the skills which make for effective use of language.

[1]*The Basic Issues in the Teaching of English* (Modern Language Association, 1959) defines English as consisting of composition, language, and literature (p. 7).

Certainly the designation that is given to an aspect of the school program tends to determine what is included in it. This designation often becomes the basis for planning, for selecting instructional materials, and for determining objectives. Since speaking, writing, reading, and listening are the activities which use language, and since each is important to every child as well as to society, we believe they should all receive instructional attention.

Even the terms *reading, listening, speaking,* and *writing* are not necessarily defined in the same way by everyone. Thus again one's definitions—or the designation one gives to activities—may determine to a large extent what is taught.

Elements of
the Language
Arts

Writing includes spelling, penmanship, punctuation, capitalization, and matters of convention or custom in the appearance of written discourse for various purposes. Its major element, however, is composition, or the putting together of ideas and information in a coherent and appealing manner. This compositional element is equally important to *speaking.* The instructional emphasis, therefore, must be upon composition, but articulation, pronunciation, and style of delivery are also included in speaking.

Reading and *listening* are both concerned with the reception of information and ideas through language. Both involve the perception and identification of unknown words, in the form of either graphic or oral symbols. Both require using these skills of reception, along with the involvement of experience, in gaining meaning.

All of the language arts are interrelated.[2] The basis for these interrelationships is the common denominator in listening, speaking, reading, and writing: language. Therefore, language itself—how it is structured and how it works—is an element of language arts programs. Grammar, vocabulary, and dialect and usage matters must be given instructional attention. Likewise, a broadly-conceived program, a program which focuses upon developing each child's abilities and resources as they relate to communication—a language arts program—must also include elements tangentially related to receptive and expressive skills: locating information, using a dictionary, proofreading, and so on.

A language arts program does not preclude attention toward language usage differences and communication activities for many varied purposes, or to the esthetic components of these activities. Furthermore,

[2]The interrelatedness of the language arts is discussed on pages 37–40. This interrelatedness is also apparent in the chapters discussing the several elements of the language arts program.

a language arts program regards reading as more than simply a method for gaining meaning from the written word; the opportunity to respond to the literature of mankind is an essential element. In a like sense listening is done for many purposes, and writing is not narrowed to exposition or to "creativeness."

The
Importance of
the Language
Arts

The language arts are the foundation of the school's program. By any criteria that might be devised for determining what is the most essential area of the school curriculum, the language arts would be identified as foremost and critical. In recognition of this fact elementary schools have always emphasized the language arts. In colonial days the first schools developed as reading and writing schools, and this tradition has continued regardless of technological changes because humanity depends upon communication and communication is principally accomplished through language.

In more recent times the language arts curriculum has broadened to include speaking and listening, thus further emphasizing the importance of communication to humanity as well as recognizing the narrowness of the earlier concern with only reading and writing. While educational materials, including curriculum guides, often have not caught up with this recognition—that is, they do not give adequate instructional attention to listening and speaking—and this failure is reflected in teaching practices, the language arts are truly concerned with all aspects of communication through language.

Our time is one of change; and this state is likely to continue. Change is upsetting, frustrating, and even engulfing. It is difficult to live with. Yet throughout our present changes, the need for effective communication has not changed. In fact, change has shown how this need has grown. We need the language arts; children must be competent speakers and writers; they must be thoughful readers and listeners.

The Professional Teacher

In addition to a normal supply of desirable physical, mental, and emotional qualities, every teacher should have extensive professional knowledge and technical skill appropriate to the children in his classroom and to the subject areas he teaches. A professional teacher must have well-founded and defensible opinions on at least four important educational issues: educational purposes, the nature and origin of curriculum content, methods of instruction, and means for evaluation of results. These issues require thoughtful consideration by every person with a genuine interest in the welfare of children and of our schools. No teacher dedicated to his professional task should seek his opinions on these issues casually. Only those opinions which are based upon thoughtful consideration of society, the needs of children, the research evidence that has been accumulated, and his own experiences may be defended.

Consideration of educational purposes is basic to the entire educational enterprise. It raises the question of why. Why is education valued and to what purposes? Why is society devoting resources to its schools? Why teach the language arts? Why must goals for the program be determined?

Educational
Purposes

For most of us the answers to these questions are secured in one of two ways, either by formulating answers from our own critical thinking and experience, or by adopting statements formulated by others who have given them critical thought. The answers we give determine the entire direction and character of our educational program. Without acceptable and clearly defined answers, without an operating point of view, the goals of the instructional program cannot be formulated. The tone and color of the answers determine the goals, and they in turn determine the selection of the skills and subject matter needed to achieve them. The content of the curriculum has a direct bearing both upon the methods of instruction to be used in attaining the goals and upon the methods employed in evaluating the extent to which these purposes have been attained.

The pages of history are filled with examples of the effects of changes in the purposes and outcomes of the educational programs of nations. The glory of Greece was the culmination of a national philosophy, channeled through its educational system, stressing beauty, art, music, and literature. Rome became a world conqueror as a result of a national military service. The rise of Germany as a military power prior to 1914, Nazi Germany under Hitler, Italy under Mussolini, Japan before Pearl Harbor, and Russia under the Communists are all examples of the way in which national philosophies translate themselves into educational programs designed to strengthen specific points of view or purposes. The leaders of all of these nations knew exactly what they were doing when they regimented and controlled the training activities of the youth of their times.

Even within the history of our own nation, social and economic realities have shaped educational philosophy and, in turn, policies and practices in the schools. In our earliest days the religious climate led to objectives based upon religious values. Somewhat later the focus upon the needs of a developing nation led to vocationally-based objectives. Still later examples include the attention to citizenship training in the days of the heavy influx of immigrants, a strong feeling of concern about science instruction immediately after Russia's Sputnik I rose from the earth, and the more recent endeavors toward ensuring equality of opportunity in all facets of life for all citizens.

Throughout every historical period, and after each goal-defining specific event, the most defensible factors in deciding educational purposes should have been those which evolved from a consideration of the needs of individuals as they sought to attain their optimum places in society. Fortunately, with the rise—about 1918—of attempts to make the determination of educational objectives a scientific endeavor, the individual and his role in society have become valued.[3] Even though such things as Sputnik or Rudolf Flesch's *Why Johnnie Can't Read* have caused temporary lapses, the generally operating philosophy of our times is individual-oriented. It holds that the major purpose of education is to prepare the individual in a way that helps him to achieve his optimum place in the societal setting in which he must live. This philosophy leads to the consideration of each child as an individual and of the knowledge, skills, and attitudes that an analysis of society shows he is likely to be called upon to use. It leads to teaching and learning becoming specific rather than general.

This approach to educational purposes gives emphasis to cultural and esthetic values as well as to vocational ones. The nature of needs is very largely determined by the values held by society. Thus many statements have appeared which have attempted to translate the values of the day into definitions of the purposes of education. The following is believed by the authors to be a reasonably acceptable expression of the purpose of education: *education has as its essential purpose the preparation of the individual to do in a better way all the desirable things he will do anyway.*

This statement, gathered from many sources, realistically accepts the school's social responsibility for preparing the individual, within the limits of his ability, to meet the demands which society may make on him as a child and as an adult. It makes no attempt to divert him

[3]Margaret Ammons, "Objectives and Outcomes" in *Encyclopedia of Educational Research,* Fourth Edition, Robert L. Ebel, editor (New York: The Macmillan Company, 1969), p. 909.

from his own fields of interest or to make him something he has no desire to be. It obligates our educational program to prepare the future doctor, lawyer, merchant, teacher, farmer, banker, hewer of logs, or digger of ditches in such a manner that he may perform his functions at his own best level of efficiency.

Determining the knowledge, attitudes, skills, and abilities most needed by the individual and most valued by society is the second of the educational issues which concern the teacher. This raises the question of *what* in education. The acceptance of the purpose of education stated above clearly defines the areas in which the teacher must look for vital elements of the curriculum. Since the individual must be equipped to meet the specific demands of life, the place to look for what he needs must be in life itself. For example, the vocabulary comprising the spelling curriculum should include a limited list of words which the individual needs to use when he writes, not a long list of uncommon words. Logically, the place to look for these words is in the actual written communication used by children and adults in meeting their own expressional needs.

Curriculum
Content

The same may be said about almost every school subject; an effort should be made to include those things which society regards as valuable and useful. It must be admitted, however, that not all of society is agreed upon the specific elements that are of value. Too, there are persons who exert considerable pressure upon those who must determine the curriculum content to include elements which they believe to be valuable but which may have little societal usefulness.

The modernization of the school curriculum in general and of the language arts in particular tends to be slowed by two factors. The first of these is the unwillingness of many educators and teachers to discard curriculum content even though it may have been proved unsound, obsolete, and indefensible in the light of the experimental evidence and changing needs. The second factor is that in many areas of learning, notably the language arts, the complexity of the field itself limits the techniques by which the socially useful skills can be determined.

This difficulty is readily illustrated in the areas of oral and written expression. The evidence shows that while approximately ninety-five percent of all language activity is oral, the instructional emphasis in most language programs is largely on the written skills. Doubtless much of this is a result of the difficulties encountered in research in oral language, and the relative ease of identifying some of the written language skills.

Methods of
Instruction

Educational purposes, the curriculum content, and the currently acceptable principles of learning and child development combine to affect the selection of the specific instructional methods to be used in a given subject. This asks the question of the *how* in education. In general the answer to this question is best found through a critical examination of educational purposes and experimental investigations of learning. The teacher must be well-informed about research and receptive to what it tells him concerning instructional procedures in the classroom. Questionable methods of instruction are more often the results of an obsolete philosophy of education or an out-dated theory of learning than they are of the content of the curriculum itself.

The history of the teaching of the language arts affords good illustrations of both of these points. The primary goal of language arts instruction, that of developing skill and effectiveness in oral and written reception and expression, was as generally accepted by the teacher of forty years ago as it is by the present-day teacher. Many of the desired outcomes would be approved by both groups. Any differences in classroom procedures would be accounted for almost entirely by the different theories of learning involved.

The teachers who believe in a "discipline of the mind" theory of learning—and apparently some still do (though they may label it "learning for learning's sake")—accept formal procedures in instruction. These, by and large, are the teachers who are convinced that the teaching of grammar—of any type—in a formal and structured sense is the best approach for achieving effective language use.

The research evidence long available offers strong support for the use of direct but informal methods rather than formal ones in the teaching of the language arts. Mastery of language use is the result of specific habit formation, rather than the memorizing of rules and generalizations. Modern theory recognizes limitations in the transfer of learning from a generalization to a specific instance. Desirable procedure focuses upon the introduction of activities which stimulate the child to express himself and establishes desired habits by repetition in communication situations.

Evaluating
the Results of
Instruction

The fourth of the fields of information in which a teacher should be well qualified concerns the procedures and the instruments by which the results of instruction may be evaluated. This raises the question of the *how well* in education. It represents an area in which much research has been done and many volumes have been written in the sixty years since the idea of educational evaluation was introduced to the teachers of this country.

The term *evaluation* is used here to include all types of devices and techniques by which the results of classroom instruction may be described. It includes standardized tests and scales ordinarily considered as synonymous with measurement of achievement. In addition, it includes the widely used and often subjective procedures used by teachers in describing such qualities of expression as style, interest, variety, organization, choice of subject matter, and choice of words. Most teachers are convinced that evaluation of the effects of instruction in the language arts involves much more than the use of standardized tests and scales. However, there are times and places for the use of the standardized tests and scales as measures of achievement, status, and growth of individual pupils and classes, as the basis for diagnostic and remedial work, and as a means of evaluating the results of a special instructional or supervisory program. There are also times and places for the use of such instruments as the teacher-made test, the check list for teacher guidance, and the cooperative check list prepared by teacher and pupils for the purpose of setting up standards and for revealing individual pupil and class growth.

The Language Arts Teacher and the Curriculum

The professional teacher makes many decisions in his classroom about what is taught, how it is taught, how the teaching effort should be evaluated, and the purposes of his teaching endeavor. To help this teacher make defensible decisions regarding the content of his language arts program, the sections which follow identify the authors' beliefs concerning the language arts curriculum. These beliefs are the basis for the content of this book and, therefore, are expanded upon in the chapters which follow this one.

The school curriculum in a general sense includes those elements from the experiences of mankind that are considered by society as being worth passing on to succeeding generations. Through the years these experiences have become organized into the various subjects taught in schools. While many persons tend to think of the curriculum as consisting of facts or information, or possibly in terms of the "Three R's," it is much more. There are those who consider the curriculum to be constant and unchanging. Obviously, the curriculum is not static; it is

What is the Curriculum?

also much broader than the "Three R's"; it is more than any amount of subject matter that has been identified. What is presented becomes important only as it becomes a part of the experience of the learner. As one writer has expressed it, "The curriculum exists only in the experience of the children; it does not exist in textbooks, in the course of study, or in the plans and intentions of teachers. . . . In order to evaluate the curriculum of a school, it is necessary to observe carefully the quality of living that goes on in it."[4] Clearly it is the living experience with it that makes subject-matter content real and important to the child.

Determining the Curriculum

The modern school is faced with the almost hopeless task of trying to teach something of everything to everybody. The rapid increase in our school population, combined with the general acceptance of the belief that secondary education and higher education as well as elementary training are the privilege of all, has created a most difficult series of problems. Our educational resources are being taxed to the point that we now know the schools cannot teach everything to everybody. We must, therefore, select what we teach.

Wise and thoughtful men from the time of Confucius down through Herbert Spencer in the last century and John Dewey in the present one quite properly have criticized the schools for their failure to develop the individual to the full measure of his potential. Yet it is only in relatively recent years that steps have been taken to remove some of the major causes of these criticisms. It is virtually inevitable that the curriculum will not coincide with the individual and societal concerns that it should reflect in its activities and experiences. Since changes in life activities must be experienced before their importance can really be evaluated, the school environment in which the young learner finds himself is likely to be unadjusted for some years. In addition to this lag, two other factors contribute to the lack of curricular adjustment. The first is the difficulty in identifying and clarifying the new individual and societal concerns. The second is the educational inertia that insists on retaining in the curriculum much that is obsolete.

The problem of determining which of the current social needs are sufficiently important to justify inclusion in the curriculum is a difficult one to solve. So is the problem of deciding what to drop. For example, when Sir Winston Churchill was chided by his editors for ending a

[4]William B. Ragan, *Modern Elementary Curriculum* (New York: The Dryden Press, Inc., 1953), p. 4.

sentence with a preposition, this able statesman replied: "This is the sort of pedantic nonsense up with which I will not put!" Shall we, then, continue to teach our pupils the rule to which he objected? This is only one of many similar problems that a teacher often must answer. Determining whether to retain or eliminate the teaching of certain information or a skill becomes a difficult problem to solve by objective methods. Too often it becomes a matter of opinion, and frequently a matter of *whose* opinion is involved. Certainly a teacher should consider the needs of his own particular students. Furthermore, he will find it profitable to study the published reports of such groups as the National Council of Teachers of English and the National Conference on Research in English for the best up-to-the-minute thought on these issues.

In 1860 Herbert Spencer condemned rote teaching and "making the pupil a merely passive recipient of others' ideas."[5] He cautioned that knowledge taught would be lost or remain inert if "the art of applying knowledge (was not) cultivated." He advocated further that education should focus upon "knowledge that is of the most worth" and that judgments regarding the selection of such knowledge be based upon the utility the knowledge has in the "preparation for complete living."

The Social Utility Principle

The selection of the elements of the curriculum that are of most worth remains a vital educational problem. It is rather discouraging to note that the social basis for the determination of curriculum content and teaching procedures first stated by Spencer has received only recent acceptance—and even now is being resisted by many forces. Teachers are still inclined to teach *as* they were taught and *what* they were taught. Added to this fact is the inclination of many schools and many teachers to teach the "difficult," the "challenging," rather than the useful.

Certainly the recent growing pains from bulging classrooms and the need for economy of teacher time and effort have compelled schools to eliminate much dead timber from the curriculum. Educational leaders of the present generation and the one just past have aroused an active interest in the application of the social approach to a revitalized curriculum. Skills, knowledge, attitudes, and experiences seeking entrance into the curriculum are challenged by the question: Will their learning better equip the individual to meet the needs of his life and enable him to become a worthy member of society? During

[5]Herbert Spencer, *Education: Intellectual, Moral, and Physical* (New York: D. Appleton and Company, 1860).

this period many elements that were firmly imbedded in the curriculum have also been rooted out by this challenge. Actually the point of view that the skills taught in the school must be those of greatest social need is not confined to the language arts but plays an important part in all modern educational thinking.

Acceptance of the belief that the purpose of the school is the provision of experiences closely allied to those the individual will meet in life situations practically forces the adoption of the social utility principle in the construction of the language arts curriculum. According to this view, decisions regarding what should be taught in the language arts must be based upon an analysis of the attitudes, skills, abilities, and experiences that people encounter and use in life situations.

The evaluation of the social utility of a language skill, ability, activity, or experience is based on the principle that *whatever is taught must fill an important need in life* both inside and outside the school. Importance is determined by analysis of the answers to such questions as these:

1. How frequently is this skill (or ability, etc.) needed and used in life activities?
2. How vital is this value, attitude, skill, or activity when the need for it arises?
3. How universally is this element encountered in all types of life activities?
4. Does this element show evidence of meeting a permanent need of the individual?

No complex or detailed study is needed to convince even the most skeptical of the importance of speaking, writing, reading, and listening. Within each of these language arts there is readily available evidence of the importance of many skills and abilities. For example, few persons would question that the ability to carry on an intelligent conversation with ease is constantly needed in daily activities. The ability to converse is surely a universal need; there is reason to believe that it is as permanent as civilization. On the other hand, many of us as adults may not need to give an oral report on a unit of science or social studies material, or to prepare a detailed topical outline. Yet in the school activities of the child these skills may be extremely crucial as well as frequent. Almost everyone is obliged constantly to write notes and friendly letters, but the need to write a letter of condolence or an answer to a formal invitation may be rare for most of us. The low frequency of the need does not make it any less important for us to be able to meet each of these situations correctly. When the occasion to write a business letter arises, the need is usually great and often crucial, as in the case of a letter of application for employment. An error in form or a mistake in spelling might mean that the application would be discarded. These examples illustrate the way in which the criterion of social utility may be applied in selecting or eliminating content in the language arts curriculum.

The relation of an element's or item's high social frequency to its difficulty of learning seems to be in reverse order. Those that are frequently needed in life situations are usually quite easy to learn. It is not at all clear, however, whether they are easy to learn *because* they are commonly used, or are widely used because they are so easy to learn. The difficulty of making use of a particular element might be enough to exclude it from instruction, but in most cases it merely means that instructional emphasis on it should be postponed until later in the maturity and experience of the learner. Lack of suitability of a skill of reasonably high social frequency, such as the use of slang or profanity, would naturally justify its exclusion from the curriculum.

In spite of the contributions of the social utility point of view to the development of a functional language arts curriculum, there is a danger of too-rigid application. For example, surveys of the language skills, abilities, and knowledge needed in life situations may ignore the benefits of the highest levels of their development, showing only average conditions that are below the capabilities of a great many pupils. Thus, a cross-section analysis may result in the lowering of standards to which the school strives, so that many pupils will not achieve the standard of language usage necessary for the societal aspirations they have.

Limitations of the Social Utility Approach

In addition, surveying the needs of children may show that particular language skills and abilities are needed in situations that may occur very rarely in adult life. Almost invariably these needs arise out of a school-stimulated activity. The fact that they occur as a child need makes them important and, to the child or the children involved, particularly crucial. Children in school take part in plays, entertainments, and other activities seldom engaged in by the average adult. Children make oral and written reports on special school activities. They need to understand and be able to spell the vocabularies of various subject-matter areas. Such activities are of great value in the school curriculum, but the particular skills involved may be associated far more with the child's in-school needs than with his life as an adult. The converse of this is, of course, also true.

The practical application of the social utility principle encounters other serious obstacles. Language is universal; it enters into practically every life activity in which we engage. Even the most comprehensive analysis of language usage must of necessity be based on only a limited sampling of the way it is used in all of life's activities. The samples that have been taken thus far have naturally been those that are easiest to obtain. For example, the frequencies of the words used correctly and in error in friendly letters and notes are relatively easy to obtain by working from copy in which the context has been destroyed. Samples showing context are almost impossible to secure, especially in the important areas of confidential social and business correspondence. Moreover, the samples of letters included in most of these vocabulary studies have been secured from persons who have had some reason to save letters. It is possible that these letters are not truly representative of the countless letters that are written.

Any attempt to record the oral language activities of children or adults assumes a certain artificiality, especially if the persons involved know that their language is being recorded. In most such studies the activities are school-stimulated; this fact takes them out of the desired lifelike setting. Attempts to record oral language activities without the speakers' knowledge introduce many complicated problems. All of these factors make it extremely difficult to obtain samples of oral language for analysis.

Efforts to objectify the written language curriculum have been more successful. These attempts have been of two main types. The first type of investigation has tried to determine the written language needs of persons engaged in various occupations. These data generally have been secured by asking the individuals interviewed to list the written activities they engage in over a specified period of time. From such data have been determined helpful lists of language activities which occur most frequently, and to some extent the activities which are considered most crucial. One special merit of this procedure is the fact that the individuals interviewed reported the actual activities they engaged in, not those they thought they might use in such a situation.

The second type of investigation of written language needs has centered around studies of errors made by many different individuals in their written language activities. For example, hundreds of thousands of running words of the writing of school children at different grade levels, in widely scattered geographical areas, and on systematically controlled topics have been analyzed. These tabulations of usages and mechanical skills have resulted in important information concerning the skills and abilities that occur most frequently, that seem to present the greatest difficulty in written expression, and that by their nature seem most crucial.

The teacher of the language arts in the elementary school faces the very difficult task of creating in the classroom the types of conditions that make the use of language easy and natural. Children have varying backgrounds for understanding, appreciating, and using language, and are different in intellectual, social, and physical maturity. They come from homes of varying economic and social conditions. They are of different races, ethnic groups, and experiential backgrounds. Yet the teacher must accept every child, helping him to develop greater ability in speaking and listening as well as teaching him to read and write. He must encourage the very shy child and give wise guidance to the bold one. He must recognize each child's needs, interests, and potential and seek to provide for his maximum learning.

Each child uses language. It is a tool that is needed constantly in every walk of life. Its effective use is an absolute necessity in the conduct of business and social affairs, in the preservation of ideas and ideals, and in the expansion and growth of societal responsibilities. To teach children to use language effectively requires attention to the content of the curriculum. It also requires consideration of the following points.

1. Learning in the language arts, as in other areas of the curriculum, is essentially an individual matter. Mastery of language comes, not through formal explanation and rules, but as a result of each child's individual activities, effort, and understanding, and its deliberate use in lifelike situations.

2. The language the child brings to school from home provides the basis for the instruction he should receive. The early environment of the child must be respected and dealt with. Changing his habits and attitudes or teaching him new ones must be done in accordance with the principles of learning that operated in the initial learning.

3. Learning the skills, abilities, and attitudes needed for using language effectively is specific rather than general. That is, desirable language usage should be taught directly rather than relying upon learning to transfer from a generalized approach. Further, teaching particular skills and abilities should not be left to those occasions on which they are incidentally encountered.

4. Ability to use language in its expressive aspects and understand it in its receptive aspects is largely a matter of habit. It is acquired through imitation, direct instruction, and use in situations which are meaningful rather than from the teacher's explanation, the learning of rules, or the studying of information unrelated to use.

Language and Linguistics

The fundamental role that language plays in listening, reading, speaking, and writing is understood by every teacher—at least to the extent that he recognizes that language is the basic component of each of these arts. What this component actually is and just what its fundamental role means is less well understood. Because of this lack of understanding, a fact which undoubtedly has influenced many language arts programs, there has been a movement in recent years for the inclusion of *linguistics*—the scientific study of language—in these programs.[6]

Language is defined, its functions discussed, and the role of linguistics in relation to these and to an effective language arts program is examined in the sections which follow.

What is
Language?

What is this basic component of the language arts? What is language? Most people would probably say it is "all the words and sentences we use as we talk with one another." Or they might say "as we communicate verbally with one another," thereby including writing as well as speaking. These are, of course, satisfactory definitions for everyday situations but they are not sufficiently accurate to satisfy the language arts researcher, the linguist, or the teacher of the language arts.

According to the first defining statement in *Webster's Third New International Dictionary,* language is "audible, articulate human speech as produced by the action of the tongue and adjacent vocal organs." A second statement describes language as "any means, vocal or other, of expressing or communicating feeling or thought." The first definition, of course, limits language to a human activity and to vocal sound. The second is more inclusive, implying that the waving of an arm or the furrowing of a brow is language, but at the same time limiting language to a conscious act, thus excluding the instinctive communicative acts one generally associates with animals.

[6]Pose Lamb, *Linguistics in Proper Perspective* (Columbus, Ohio: Charles E. Merrill Publishing Co., 1967), p. 4.

An involuntary cry of pain or fear, the bark of a dog, the wail of a hungry baby—all are sounds that may be heard and may attract the attention of a human being within hearing range, but they are not necessarily language. If the baby wails because he has learned that if he makes enough noise he will be given food, if the dog barks because he has learned that as a result his master will open the door and let him into the house, then these sounds may be considered means for communicating and a kind of language according to the dictionary definition.

The linguist, the true student of language, is precise in his definition of language. Linguists stress certain assumptions concerning language which in effect define language for their studies. The most important is that "the fundamental forms of language activity are the sequences of sounds made by human lips, tongues, and vocal cords. . . ."[7] The linguist says that language is speech, pointing out that speech is as old as human society but that writing is only about seven thousand years old. While the statement of the relative ages is a fact, writing thus being a derivative of speech, teachers and curriculum authorities should not make a fetish of saying that language is speech.[8] Certainly, as will be discussed later, language programs need to give greater attention to oral language than they traditionally have; at the same time, however, the linguistic concerns of written expression must not be ignored. This is not to deny that speech is *the* language, but for school purposes, as opposed to the purposes the linguist has in his studies, it is convenient to refer to oral language and to written language.

The Linguists' Definition of Language

From the basic assumption of the oral nature of language, the linguist moves to identifying certain characteristics. One source lists the five most important of these as follows:[9]

1. *Language is symbolic.* It is a thing of itself, quite distinct from the matter to which it relates. Such a relation is purely arbitrary and may change with time. The nature of the symbol differs in form depending on whether one is speaking or writing.

[7]Archibald A. Hill, *Introduction to Linguistic Structures* (New York: Harcourt, Brace, and World, 1958), p. 1.
[8]David Reed expands on this in "A Theory of Language, Speech, and Writing," *Elementary English,* December, 1965, p. 346.
[9]Taken from Appendix B, *The Language Component in the Training of Teachers of English and Reading: Views and Problems.* Mimeographed material prepared by the Center for Applied Linguistics and the National Council of Teachers of English for a conference at Washington, D. C., April 28–30, 1966.

2. *Language is systematic.* For this reason it can be learned. For the same reason it can be described and must be described in terms of a system. Languages are universally orderly, but there is not, as was once supposed, a universal type of order to which all languages aspire.

3. *Language is human.* It is the most characteristic human activity, completely different in kind from the "language" of animals.

4. *Language is a social instrument.* Our social relationships are achieved by it and through it, on the whole, and their perpetuation is heavily dependent upon it. Social differences and language differences almost invariably go hand in hand.

5. *Language is non-instinctive;* that is, it needs to be learned. The child gains control of the structure of the language in association with parents, brothers and sisters, and playmates. Much of the vocabulary, particularly that reflecting social attitudes, is acquired through the schools.

Linguists usually add the terms *arbitrary* and *complete* to *symbolic,* pointing out that the attachment of words to objects or ideas represents an arbitrary act and that such attachment has been made to express every idea or feeling that the users of the language need. The arbitrary nature of language is illustrated by the symbol attached to the object we know as a dog: In French it is *le chien,* and in English it might as well be *neg* as *dog.* Since the attachment of symbols to things is arbitrary, the attachments must be learned—that is, someone who knows must tell the learner what the symbols are. The complete nature of language is shown in the fact that words and expressions are coined to take care of the language user's needs. For example, the Wichita language of the Oklahoma Indian tribe does not include *nuclear physics* or *celestial navigation,* because the speakers of Wichita have never needed these terms when using their native language.[10] Similarly the word *acrylic* never existed in the English language until the need for it arose.

Most persons realize that language is systematic, even though this knowledge is often unconscious. Because language entities may be arranged in recurrent patterns, a person presented with only part of a pattern can make predictions about the rest of it. He knows, for example, that the *ed* suffix is usually added to form the past tense of a verb. He knows that in the sentence "Bill———s Jim an ———," the first blank must be filled with a verb and the second with a noun. He

[10]Jacob Ornstein and William W. Gage, *The ABC's of Languages and Linguistics* (Philadelphia: Chilton Books, 1964), p. 11.

knows further that not all verbs can be used in the sentence (this one must be third person singular, must end with *s,* and must be able to take both direct and indirect objects) but that words such as *gives, throws, offers,* and *takes* would fit. And he knows that the noun must begin with a vowel (or silent *h*) and takes an article—a noun such as *apple, illustration, orange,* or *example.*

Still another characteristic of language—related both to its symbolic and its systematic nature—is the fact that it changes. Evidence of the change in English is apparent if one compares that used in a page of the King James version of the Bible with one in the works of Shakespeare, the Declaration of Independence, or a modern novel. In addition, we all know that our English has been changed by influxes of people and ideas. Lamb points out that the changes are "not haphazard or accidental," that they "are the hallmarks of a living growing, healthy organism."[11]

Most linguists stress that language is a system of human communication originating in the sound stream produced by the organs of speech.[12] Observers generally believe that animal cries and actions are instinctive and do not constitute language, though the close observer of nature might question this belief as he watches a mother hen call her chicks under her wings at the approach of danger, a colony of ants at work, or a mother quail lure a hunter away from her nest by appearing to be crippled. However, these are instinctive acts—responses to cues, like a dog's responses to a whistle, a pointing finger, or a traffic light. Even the myna bird who says "When do we eat," while obviously vocalizing, is responding instinctively to a cue rather than consciously using language as a result of thought. Therefore, though some might argue that they have conversed with chimpanzees, dolphins, and so forth, most persons agree with the linguists that man alone possesses language.

In a stimulating discussion of the nature and origins of language, Charlton Laird has described man as a "languagized mammal." The following brief quotation will clarify the point made by the writer:[13]

Humanity and Language

[11]Lamb, *Linguistics,* p. 11.

[12]No one—and teachers especially—should overlook non-verbal or "silent" language. We often communicate a great deal by what we do not say, by our actions, by our behavior. See Edward T. Hall, *The Silent Language* (in paperback by Fawcett; first published by Doubleday and Co., 1959).

[13]Reprinted by permission of The World Publishing Company from *The Miracle of Language* by Charlton Laird. Copyright 1953 by Charlton Laird.

A cow may be able to communicate in a cowlike way by bawling and dogs may be able to express themselves by looking soulfully from one end while wagging the other, but man is probably more significantly distinguished from his fellow creatures by his complicated means of communication than by any other differences. In short, man as we know him could not exist without language and until there was a language. Civilization could not exist until there was written language, because without written language no generation could bequeath to succeeding generations anything but its simpler findings. Culture could not be widespread until there was printed language.

Perhaps the notion that language distinguishes man from the other animals is merely man's way of claiming the superiority he desires. On the other hand, using language is largely an unnatural rather than a natural function. The lungs force air through the larynx, causing the vocal cords to vibrate and produce sounds which are varied in quality, volume, and pitch by adjustments of the tongue, jaws, teeth, palate, and lips. This is not an act for which the physical equipment was apparently designed. How then did man learn to use this equipment to produce language? Was there a stage in development that might be called "pre-speech"? And how rapidly was the passage from such a stage to the first words? As one source questions, "Did it take centuries —millennia—from the time he could say, 'I'm hungry,' until he worked himself up to such profundities as, 'Woman, bring me my knotty pine club'?"[14]

No one knows the origin of language. Certainly, language is possible because everyone in a particular culture or setting agrees that certain sounds or combinations of sounds represent things about which they need to communicate with one another. The use of language is such an integral part of our everyday lives that we rarely think of it as something uniquely human. We rarely think of the immense consequences of man's invention of language—by the use of language babies become human beings; without language becoming an adult would mean achieving only an aborted form of fulfillment.[15]

The Purpose for Language

Language is the fundamental means by which ideas, thoughts, feelings, and emotions are communicated. It is a vital part of every human activity. Universally humans talk, and almost invariably they utilize some form of recorded or written expression. The Congo tribes, the

[14]Ornstein and Gage, *ABC's of Languages,* p. 15.
[15]Carl A. Lefevre, "Language and Self: Fulfillment or Trauma?" *Elementary English,* February, 1966, pp. 124–128.

Ecuadorian Indians, the residents of Los Angeles, Brooklyn, London, Moscow, Cairo, Hong Kong, or Tokyo all talk, all communicate by means of language. The language forms used depend entirely upon the culture-area in which the individuals are located. As soon as primitive men began to live together, first in families, and then in tribes, there was a need for some means of making their intentions and desires clear to one another. Warnings of danger had to be given and sources of food reported; orders had to be given for group protection from enemies. Probably the earliest communication was by the use of natural signs— cries, gestures, and facial expressions which at first were made spontaneously in response to natural situations to indicate needs, emotions, feelings. From these early and surely accidental beginnings, meanings were refined for the signs and sounds. Vocal utterances, substituted gradually for manual signs, were found to be more effective, especially in combat and in the dark. Gradually man recognized the need for the creation of graphic symbols (writing) to represent the natural signs. Down through the ages language has been developed and refined until a rather intricate but reasonably effective means of communication has evolved. This development and evolution of our language is still going on and will doubtless continue to do so as long as man's small segment of the universe survives.

The first purpose for language, then, is *communication.* Communication involves at least two persons, one to present the idea or thought by means of speaking or writing, and one to receive the idea or thought by means of reading or listening. The effectiveness with which the actual communication takes place depends entirely upon the knowledge of the language and its skillful use by both of the individuals involved. The individual who has a good command of language and its use for communication will be able to express his ideas and convey the desired meaning to someone else. Likewise, if the reader or listener has an adequate command of language, he will be able to comprehend the intended meaning speedily and correctly.

An integral part of communication that in effect is a second purpose for language is that it is a *vehicle for thinking.* Thinking involves the mental manipulation of symbols which represent certain meanings. The symbols are of two types: mental images and language symbols. Here, again, the development of a fairly complicated primitive society contributed to the early growth and development of language. It was probably not too difficult for primitive man to learn to think in terms of mental images as he planned to go into the jungle to hunt an animal for food. But the process of living with others of his kind brought the need for rules, generalizations, laws, customs—the development of social mores. Such abstractions as truth, honesty, love, honor, courage were not easily expressed or comprehended by means of mental images. As man evolved, his society became more and more complex and new concepts and experiences required the creation of new and more elaborate language symbols to represent them in his mind. These symbols have become the tools by which the individual forms an opinion or draws a conclusion; they are the means by which new meanings and new principles are constructed in his mind.

A third purpose of language is the *transmission of culture.* Many of man's ideas, bright or dull; his thoughts, brilliant or biased; his deeds, heroic or cowardly; his mistakes, stupid or profitable, are accessible to us today as a result of the literature he has left us. This trail has been left principally by language, although art and music, also forms of expression, have made their contributions. *Through recorded language man has shared the accumulation of human experience and conveyed it to posterity.* It would be difficult to imagine what it would be like to live without being able to profit from the experiences and contributions of our ancestors recorded in history and in literature. Without language we would be isolated, we would not be able to share the thoughts and ideas of others living during the same period as ourselves. We would know nothing of history, nothing of the marvelous literature of our own and other cultures. The preservation of the record of man's thoughts and deeds is vitally necessary to education and to the future development of man and society.

What is Linguistics? Linguistics was defined earlier as "the scientific study of language." This is the definition most often found in educational literature, but it is one that needs explanation and extension for most persons. Postman and Weingartner suggest that "any definition of linguistics depends upon who is doing the defining."[16] That is, to many teachers the term linguistics is equated with *grammar;* to others it is the relationship of sound symbols to graphic symbols. To many linguists a definition broadened to include studying the entire culture is most suitable. To the man on the street linguistics may mean the study of dialects or the determining of dictionary definitions.

The Nebraska curriculum guide defines linguistics as "The study of human speech; the units, nature, structure, and modifications of language, languages, or a language including especially such factors as phonetics, phonology, morphology, accent, syntax, semantics, gen-

[16]Neil Postman and Charles Weingartner, *Linguistics, A Revolution in Teaching* (New York: Dell Publishing Co., Inc., 1966), p. 3.

eral or philosophical grammar, and the relation between writing and speech."[17]

Lamb extends her "scientific study of language" with the statement: "Such study may concentrate on the sounds of language (phonology), the origin and changing meaning of words (etymology and semantics), or the arrangements of words in a meaningful context in different languages (syntax-structural or transformational grammar)."[18]

Guth says, "Linguistics is the study, according to rigorously defined methods or principles, *of language as a system.*"[19]

A particularly useful definition of linguistics is that of Postman and Weingartner. They say that "Linguistics is a way of behaving . . . it is a way of behaving while one attempts to discover information and to acquire knowledge about language."[20] They go ahead to discuss the behavior in terms of attitudes and procedures. Their emphasis is upon the inductive approach to learning, a spirit of discovery, a rejection of dogmatism, and the verifying and revising process identified with scientific study.

Linguistic study is done by linguists, though accepting the Postman and Weingartner definition means that anyone, including children in the elementary school, may do linguistic study if it is done in the spirit described. In a more restricted sense, however, linguistics is the study of language by language scientists—the linguists. A linguist may study any language—living or dead—and he may specialize in a particular field of study. He may study the history of a language; he may compare languages, examining such aspects as grammar, phonology, morphology, semantics, or dialects. Linguists subscribe to different theories related to their particular interests. For example, there are a number of widely differing theories—structural and transformational-generative are best known—upon which analyses of language structure are based. The theoretical differences lead to differences in definitions, terminology, and procedures used in language study.

Linguistic study is being extended most recently into language behavior and learning (psycholinguistics), society and language (socio-

Linguistic Study

[17]The Nebraska Curriculum Development Center, *A Curriculum for English: Language Explorations for the Elementary Grades* (Lincoln: University of Nebraska Press, 1966), p. 2.

[18]Lamb, *Linguistics,* p. 4.

[19]Hans P. Guth, *English Today and Tomorrow* (Englewood Cliffs, N.J.: Prentice-Hall, 1964), p. 25.

[20]Postman and Weingartner, *Linguistics, A Revolution in Teaching,* p. 4.

linguistics), and the more totally inclusive "study of mutual relationships between language behavior and other modes of human behavior" (metalinguistics).[21]

Linguistic study in the schools ranges from the study of grammar, usually now a "new" one—in either a formal deductive manner or a functional inductive way—to the somewhat incidental introduction of the concept of language change by "finding new words" and identifying words brought into English from other languages. Later chapters in this book, as well as sections farther along in this chapter, further specify what linguistics means to the school curriculum.

The Study of
Language

The "scientific study of language" has most often been introduced into the school curriculum in the form of a study of language *structure*. That is, the greatest impact has been in the study of the system of language rather than in some other aspect of language study. This interest is undoubtedly related to the traditional role of grammar in schools and the concerns of teachers in helping pupils write "better" and speak "correctly." Because of this interest, brief attention will be given here to the study of language structure. However, detailed examination of the content and procedures of such study will be left to later chapters. Linguistics and the entire question of grammar teaching in the elementary school will be dealt with in Chapter 11. Language learning, including the understanding young children have of the language system, will be discussed in Chapter 3. The matter of the language system and matters of usage—the questions of "correctness" and acceptability —will be discussed in Chapters 4 and 10.

The study of language structure generally starts with *phonology*— the study of the sounds of the language. The basic sounds, called *phonemes* and described as the smallest units of sound by which different meanings may be distinguished, are the core of this study. Most linguists identify twenty-four consonants and nine vowels as constituting the segmental phonemes.[22] That is, through phonation and articulation, the stream of sound uttered by a human is divided into segments that are recognizable as units of meaning. In addition, there are suprasegmental phonemes which also describe the language. These are four degrees of *stress* given to segmental phonemes, three levels of *pitch*, and four *junctures* or interruptions and suspensions in the stream of sound (identified as breaks between words or the greater ones usually signalled in writing by punctuation marks).

[21]*Ibid.*, p. 197.
[22]*Curriculum for English*, p. 18.

The second area of study is usually *morphology*—the study of word forms. Morphology deals with the meaningful groupings of sounds, but with emphasis upon grammatical factors of grouping rather than upon meaning as we commonly think of it. *Morphemes* are described as the smallest meaningful units in language.[23] Thus, the word *hat* is one morpheme, but is made up of three phonemes; *boy* is one morpheme and two phonemes; and *I* is one morpheme and one phoneme. Morphemes include word bases (or roots), prefixes, suffixes, and word form changes or inflections. A *free morpheme* is one that may stand by itself in larger language structures, and a *bound morpheme* is one that must combine with another morpheme. The words above (boy, hat, I) are free morphemes; *pre-* and *-ness* are bound morphemes.

A third concern in studying language structure involves the forms of words. Words, of course, differ in meaning but they also differ in other characteristics. Language study based upon "traditional" or Latin-based grammar classified words according to their meaning (i.e. "A noun is the name of a person, place, or thing") or their function (i.e. "An adjective modifies a noun or pronoun"). Linguists, who do not hold to traditional grammar, classify words in a different way. They speak of *form classes*—which are the traditional parts of speech in English: nouns, verbs, adjectives, and adverbs, although they are sometimes identified by the words Form Class and a number (i.e. Form Class 1 = verbs) instead of by the traditional terms. Words are classified as to form class by testing them in "slots" (see page 346 and Chapter 11), by determining if they will "take" certain suffixes, and by relating the stress given them to other words given like stress in sentences of the same pattern. Related to word form classes is a fourth area of study of the language system known as *syntax* or word order. Syntax is defined as the study of the meaningful combinations of words —the study of the ways that words can be ordered or arranged significantly.[24] This study involves classification of sentences and parts of sentences. *Structural linguists* use several classification systems to categorize sentences. These include relating each sentence to certain basic patterns or sentence skeletons or to the method of expansion of a skeleton by substitution or modification. Syntax can also be studied by a *transformational-generative* approach; this is used by another

[23]Defined in Ornstein and Gage, *ABC's of Languages,* p. 81, as follows: "Roughly speaking, a morpheme is any of the pieces that has a function in a word."

[24]*Curriculum for English,* p. 94.

group of linguists known as transformationalists.[25] Transformational study begins with the assumption that sentences are of two basic types: kernel sentences and transformed sentences.[26] The transformationalist has rules concerning language which show that certain words or phrases can be grammatically moved. The approach is synthetic rather than analytic, as is the approach followed by structuralists. The transformationalist begins with the rules about the phrase structures, the possible transformations, and effects of transformations upon meaning and sound.

Other Linguistic Study

Studying language structure in terms of its phonology, morphology, and syntax is not the only concern of the linguist. As suggested above, the study of language structure (really its grammar) is most likely to receive attention in language arts programs, and for the reasons suggested; however, there are other areas of investigation which interest linguists and are of importance to the language arts.

One area of study is that of language learning by infants and young children.[27] Such study involves a child's first sounds and the progression in his development to words and sentences. Children know their language very well by the time they enter school. They show early skill in ordering words properly and in using inflections. The rate at which young children acquire the basic rules about the system of the language "defies explanation in terms of traditional learning principles, rewarded responses, or imitation."[28]

Another major interest of linguists is *semantics*. Postman and Weingartner say "Perhaps the most important branch of linguistics . . . is semantics."[29] In general, semantics is concerned with meaning. Semanticists make inquiries into varieties of definitions, what really constitutes meaning, and the problems of communication in instances in which "known" words are used.

Of great concern to schools has always been the matter of "correct usage." Linguists study usage, which is essentially the attitudes people have toward variations in their language.[30] The linguist does not pre-

---

[25]A more detailed explanation of transformational grammar, as well as other grammars, is given in Chapter 11.

[26]Paul M. Roberts, *English Sentences,* Teacher's Manual (New York: Harcourt, Brace and World, Inc., 1962).

[27]Early language development is discussed in Chapter 3.

[28]Paul Henry Mussen, John J. Conger, and Jerome Kagan, *Readings in Child Development and Personality* (New York: Harper & Row, 1965), p. 207.

[29]Postman and Weingartner, *Linguistics, A Revolution in Teaching,* p. 122.

[30]See Chapter 10.

scribe what is "right" or "wrong" but simply reports the attitudes people in differing circumstances have about certain words and expressions. The investigations of usage are closely related to dialect studies. Dialect linguists investigate pronunciation, syntax, and vocabulary commonalities that are related to economic, racial, and social groups, to geographical regions, and to migrations of people. In quite recent times many linguists studying dialects have become concerned with learning problems and the relation of a dialect to widespread or "standard" usage.

Linguistic study of the historical development of a language is another appealing area of study—one that has always been of interest in schools and which may have even greater appeal now that "stories about words" are appearing and scholarly works on such word study are more available.[31] Learning that commonplace words, such as *potato, chocolate, canoe, cannibal, barbecue,* etc., moved from the New World to England is of interest to teachers and children. Tracing the origins of many, many words—ranging from *gumbo, yam, chigger,* and *voodoo* to *flabbergast, cab,* and *grovel*—may arouse even greater interest.

Linguistics in the Elementary School Program

The brief discussion of linguistics has been included in this chapter because of the impact linguistics is having upon the curriculum in the language arts in the elementary school and as an introduction to further consideration of aspects of linguistics in later chapters. For some teachers much of the terminology in the preceding discussion may be new. Therefore, they may wish to use the references at the conclusion of this chapter for clarification and further explanation. Considerably more explanation is also provided in Chapter 11.

There are elementary school teachers teaching the terminology (and more) given on the preceding pages. There are others teaching children to work as beginning linguists to discover facts about language, with varying degrees of reference to the terminology. Finally, there are textbooks and curriculum guides being developed by linguists for use in elementary school teaching; these, of course, make much use of terminology new to teachers and to students preparing for teaching.[32]

[31]Books about words suitable for children are listed on page 315.
[32]For example: Paul Roberts, *The Roberts English Series* (New York: Harcourt, Brace, and World, 1966); *Linguistics in the Elementary Classroom* (Los Angeles County Superintendent of Schools Office, 1965); *Curriculum for English.*

What
Linguistics
and How
Much?

Certainly teachers need to be better informed about the language which they use and which they teach to children. Children, too, need to have greater understanding of language, since nothing is more basic to their lives. There is a fundamental issue, however, as to the extent to which the elementary school language arts program should be directed at teaching children to be "junior" linguists, at teaching the terminology of the professional linguist, or at giving particular focus to bringing to the conscious (and verbalizing) level an understanding of the system of the language. Many persons believe that a teacher who follows the suggestions in textbooks and curriculum guides which emphasize linguistic analysis will have a formalized program with little appeal to elementary school children—one which will neither lead to a greater understanding and appreciation of language nor to any greater proficiency in its use. Others believe that understanding and appreciation of language cannot be gained without considerable formal or "disciplined" study and that it is through this kind of understanding and appreciation that greater skill in its use develops. Too often, though, these persons are reflecting on the course of their own careers and on a body of knowledge and its organization rather than upon school children and their needs, interests, and ways of learning.

Further, the question of the relative values of all things proposed for study in the elementary school must enter into any decisions concerning curriculum content. Few linguists attach utility (in the sense of improvement in the child's speaking or writing) to the study of linguistics. O'Donnell, for example, does not believe that linguistics has practical application that "can be achieved by teaching the student a linguistic principle or concept and expecting automatic improvement in communication skills."[33] Some persons preparing materials for children's use—including some linguists—may sometimes hope for such improvement, but there is no research evidence which really supports this hope.[34]

Generally, linguists stress the humanistic value of linguistics and emphasize that traditional concern with grammar should be broadened to a more comprehensive *language* teaching.[35] The teacher in the ele-

[33]Roy C. O'Donnell, "Does Research in Linguistics Have Practical Applications?" *English Journal,* 59:410–412, March, 1970.

[34]For example, see Gleason (H. A. Gleason, Jr., *Linguistics and English Grammar*), pp. 476–477. However, he cautions that a "wooden and prescriptive" teaching of grammar will not lead to the results he hopes for with respect to learning to compose.

[35]*Ibid.,* p. 471. Gleason also says that children in one sense know grammar but that by teaching grammar "we are only teaching how to talk about familiar things."

mentary classroom must, of course, be concerned with helping children use language as effectively as possible to convey their ideas and thoughts and to receive the thoughts of others. The elementary teacher (and those who help him—administrators, parents, textbook writers) must decide how much time is to be devoted to the study of the many things it might be desirable for a child to know. He must also decide what things in terms of children's interests and needs he may teach successfully.

The authors of this book are highly skeptical of the success that may be attained from teaching language by an approach based upon learning terminology and calling for the use of exercises in analyzing sentences or constructing new ones. Further, they are dubious of the importance of much of this knowledge to children even if it could be meaningfully taught. They view much that is being advocated as the reincarnation of the formal teaching of grammar and the fitting out in new dress of an outmoded learning theory.[36] However, closed minds do not lead to progress, so they and the readers of this book should evaluate, weigh, and speculate. Equal open-mindedness, however, should prevail among those in established roles in the teaching profession who are prone to seize upon something new as *the solution* to a complex problem. Everyone concerned with teaching language arts to children in the elementary schools should be interested in experiments which test the effects of teaching language by the various approaches now being advocated or by others which may be proposed.[37] Further, there is undoubtedly much in linguistics of value to many areas of the language arts, especially as consideration is given to linguistics in its broad sense, as is suggested in the following section of this chapter and in other chapters of this book. Perhaps the major value gained from the linguistic "movement" to this point is its effect upon teachers. There surely has been a relaxing of some teachers' attitudes concerning "correctness" of usage, an acceptance of language change, and a greater awareness of the system of the language. Teachers are also realizing that a great deal of linguistics has always been a part of the language arts curriculum. For example, morphology includes what teachers have called "word building"; teachers have taught children rhythm and intonation in reading and choral speaking; sound and symbol relationships have been a part of reading and spelling instruction; children

---

[36]Support for this point of view has also been advanced by linguists. For example, see Wayne A. O'Neil, "Paul Roberts' Rules of Order: The Misuses of Linguistics in the Classroom," *Urban Review,* Vol. 2, No. 7, June, 1968.

[37]Experiments must be carefully designed and controlled, however, since massive "try-outs" and "action research" tend to be inconclusive, often resulting only in opinion—usually reflecting the initial bias of the "experimenter."

have made their own dictionaries and have "looked up" interesting words; and the meanings of affixes and how they work have been learned.

Linguistics and Teaching Children

The authors by no means wish to leave readers with a negative orientation toward linguistics. The content of this book is specifically directed at appreciation of language and its use for many and varied purposes, as well as a true recognition of the language abilities that children possess when they enter school and the ways in which these abilities may best be drawn forth and developed. The value of linguistics in its relationship to the entire domain of language is fully recognized. The cautions suggested have been made in light of the need to keep linguistics within the framework of present knowledge of the ways in which children develop and language is learned. One source expresses this concern in the following way:[38]

> It is easy to get carried away briefly, fascinated by the internal logic of a well-articulated system or impressed by the weight of its scholarship, or intrigued by its refreshing "newness." It is only one step further to let it supplant the children and become the goal.

Linguistics is not the study of how spelling or reading or composition should be taught. As a leading American linguist has said, it is not the tools and techniques of linguistic science that should be brought into the classroom but rather the knowledge derived by linguistic study that should be assimilated and used "to shed new light upon the problems that arise wherever language is concerned.[39] That is, teachers must learn about the linguistic findings and use this knowledge in teaching children. A knowledge of linguistics should lead to the following insights:[40]

> Language is a creative activity of each person.
> Language patterns are well learned by the time a child is five or six.
> He usually knows and uses all the basic structures.
> Language habits, once learned, change slowly.
> Speech is the language; writing reflects the speech.
> The writing system or code of English is alphabetic and has certain inadequacies.

[38]*Linguistics in the Elementary Classroom,* p. 36.
[39]Charles C. Fries, "Advances in Linguistics," *Linguistics—Current Issues* (Champaign, Ill.: National Council of Teachers of English, 1961), p. 37.
[40]*Linguistics in the Elementary Classroom,* pp. 3–4.

Language is continually changing; it has a history.

Language varies with the age, socio-economic group, and geographical region of the speaker. This is his dialect.

The concept of "correctness" is replaced by a concept of alternatives in pronunciation, word choice, phrasing, and construction.

Every language has its own grammar. English grammar is not Latin grammar.

Everyone speaks his native language, to a degree, in his unique way with his particular resources for language. This is his idiolect.

As the elementary teacher understands these concepts, he will find opportunities throughout each school day to make use of them in his teaching. The applications should usually be informal and spontaneous and always directed at helping children to appreciate, understand, and use their language better.

Beyond the informal, spontaneous teaching about language, of course, a teacher may teach much about language specifically and directly. He may even seek to achieve the goals of a program directed (1) toward displaying to children that English is primarily a word-order language, that the structure of English syntax is often of the utmost importance; (2) toward giving children an understanding of the sound (phonology) of the language, its music; (3) toward giving them an understanding of the language's historical dimensions (where our vocabulary came from, etc.) and of the evolution of its spelling system, understandings important not only to spelling, but to reading; and (4) toward giving them an understanding of the extent to which punctuation is a written representation of the suprasegmental features of spoken discourse.[41]

The perceptive teacher will recognize many opportunities for giving attention to linguistics. The following suggestions indicate the kinds of activities and situations which present such opportunities. Further suggestions are included in various other sections of this book.

1. In the primary grades "playing around with" words—rhyming, onomatopoeia, trying out new words—is of interest and will present opportunities to teach about distinctive speech sounds, pitch, and stress.
2. At all grade levels attention can be given to rising and falling inflections in speech and as literature is read orally.
3. Forms of words can be noted at every grade level. For example, in addition to noting physical differences in written symbols (which are

[41]*Curriculum for English,* p. xxii.

important to spelling and reading), greater attention can be given to meaning elements in word form changes, as in *boy-boys, tall-taller-tallest, go-going.*

4. The history of language can be studied, beginning in the intermediate grades. Such study may include searching for the origins of words met in literature, discovering language sources of words incorporated into English, noting words used in English at an earlier time but no longer in use, and noting changes in meaning and spelling.

5. The study of dialects will have great appeal, particularly in the middle and upper grades. Such study should include noting differences in pronunciations, meanings attached to words, and expressions the children hear in their daily activities; observing and comparing dialects in literature study (for example, *Brighty of the Grand Canyon;* Paul Bunyan and Mike Fink tales; Lois Lenski's books; *Sweet Pea* by Krementz; Steptoe's *Stevie,* or Walter's *Lilie of Watts*); and looking at regions of the country and the dialects found in them.

6. In composition teaching, basic activities include the rearranging of information in sentences, the adding of phrases and clauses for greater clarity, and the eliminating of unnecessary words and phrases in sentences. In these activities, attention can be given to sentence patterning, to language system, and to the functional learning of linguistic terminology as it is needed.

Exercises for Thought and Action

1. What do you consider the best way for you as a teacher to acquire a workable educational philosophy?
2. Describe the ways in which educational point of view has influenced the curriculum in schools as you have experienced it.
3. Visit an elementary school classroom and see if you can determine the educational philosophy of the teacher.
4. Illustrate ways in which the content of a specific subject area, such as handwriting, can be directed to meet social needs. Can you as easily illustrate this for an area of the curriculum such as literature?
5. Examine curriculum guides for statements of language arts objectives and how the curriculum content suggested was selected.
6. Look up various theories concerning the origin of language.
7. Examine recently published language arts textbooks for content identified as "historical linguistics," "semantics," and "dialect study." React critically to this material.

Selected References

Blewett, John (editor). *John Dewey: His Thought and Influence.* New York: Fordham University Press, 1960.

Brook, G. L. *A History of the English Language*. New York: W. W. Norton and Co., 1958.

Burns, Paul C. "Linguistics: A Brief Guide for Principals," *The National Elementary Principal*, 45:37–42, September, 1965.

Cain, R. Donald. "What Do We Mean by 'Linguistics'?" *English Journal*, 54:399–404; May, 1965.

Carrol, John B. *The Study of Language: A Survey of Linguistics and Related Disciplines*. Cambridge, Mass.: Harvard University Press, 1959.

Commission on the English Curriculum, National Council of Teachers of English. *The English Language Arts*. New York: Appleton-Century-Crofts, Inc., 1952.

_____. *Language Arts for Today's Children*. New York: Appleton-Century-Crofts, Inc., 1954.

DeBoer, John J. "Earmarks of a Modern Language Arts Program in the Elementary School," *Elementary English*, 31:485–493, December, 1954.

Gleason, H. A., Jr. *Linguistics and English Grammar*. New York: Holt, Rinehart and Winston, Inc., 1965.

Goldstein, Miriam B. *The Teaching of Language in Our Schools*. New York: The Macmillan Company, 1966.

Laird, Charlton. *The Miracle of Language*. Cleveland: The World Publishing Company, 1953.

Lamb, Pose. *Linguistics in Proper Perspective*. Columbus, Ohio: Charles E. Merrill Publishing Company, 1967.

Lefevre, Carl A. *Linguistics and the Teaching of Reading*. New York: McGraw-Hill, Inc., 1964.

Ornstein, Jacob, and Gage, William W. *The ABC's of Languages and Linguistics*. Philadelphia: Chilton Books, 1964.

Petty, Walter T. *Issues and Problems in the Elementary Language Arts*. Boston: Allyn and Bacon, Inc., 1968.

Postman, Neil, and Weingartner, Charles. *Linguistics: A Revolution in Teaching*. New York: Dell Publishing Co., Inc., 1966.

Sauer, Edwin H. *English in the Secondary School*. New York: Holt, Rinehart and Winston, Inc., 1963. Part I, "The Science of Language."

Shane, Harold, and others. *Improving Language Arts Instruction in Elementary Schools*. Columbus, Ohio: Charles E. Merrill Co., 1962.

Squire, James R. "New Directions in Language Learning," *Elementary English*, 39:535–544, October, 1962.

2

Planning For Instruction
In The Language Arts

Every language arts teacher must give thoughtful attention to planning his instructional program. This planning must be based first of all upon the answers he has formulated to the questions of *why, what, how* and *how well* posed in Chapter 1. Of course, these need not be completely answered before planning begins (in fact, even the most experienced teacher should be revising and restating his answers), but considerable thought should have been given to them and at least tentative answers arrived at. In addition to this foundation—and in many ways as an extension of it—the planning must consider the following: (1) the pupils—their needs and abilities, (2) school and classroom organizational plans, (3) the interrelationships among the language arts and the effects of such relationships upon instructional plans, (4) the relationship of the language arts to other areas of the curriculum, (5) various means for giving special attention to individual pupils, and (6) how the pupils will be evaluated and how the results of evaluation will be used.

This chapter presents an overall consideration of the planning that is essential to every language arts program. The content is basic to understanding the specific aspects of the language arts and how they should be taught which are discussed in the remaining chapters. This chapter should be referred to and reread as the other chapters are studied.

The following are the major topics discussed here:

1. Organizing for Instruction
2. Pupil Differences in Language Abilities
3. Providing for Individual Differences
4. A Basic Instructional Approach
5. Evaluation in the Instructional Program

Organizing for Instruction

A teacher must organize a classroom of youngsters, and the subject matter to be taught them, in such a way that the instruction will be effective and the teaching effort efficient. This is not an easy task, nor one that the teacher can do alone. This organization must be based first of all upon the organizational pattern of the school. Traditionally, elementary school classrooms have been self-contained—that is, with one teacher doing all of the teaching for a particular class—but increasingly departmentalized plans of organization are coming into use. Team teaching, modular scheduling, and various grouping plans are also affecting elementary school organization.[1]

Regardless of the particular organizational pattern of the school, however, every teacher in the elementary school has a responsibility for teaching the language arts. Those who are in self-contained classrooms, as well as those who are principally responsible for the language arts in departmentalized systems, must particularly consider how they will organize for teaching the various language skills and abilities, the attitudes which are important to effective communication, and the knowledge about language and literature that is to be included. All teachers—not just those teaching the language arts directly and specifically—must give attention to organizing their teaching and should also consider both the interrelationships among the language arts and the relationships of these arts to their particular teaching concerns. As someone has said, "Teaching children to use their language effectively is too important to be left only to the English teacher."

Educational authorities generally favor relating subject areas to one another as much as possible. There are various plans in modern schools for doing this relating—integration, correlation, unit teaching, and so on. The major difference in the ways for dealing with the subject matter of the language arts is shown in these statements: a *functional* program "provides for closely relating language to work in other areas of study but sets aside some particular periods for systematic work in language . . . ," while in an *integrated* program "language work does not appear

Organizing
Subject
Matter

---

[1]This chapter provides only introductory material regarding organizational plans for a school and a classroom. See a text such as Kenneth A. Hoover and Paul M. Hollingsworth, *Learning and Teaching in the Elementary School* (Boston: Allyn and Bacon, Inc., 1970) for a more adequate discussion.

as a separate subject, but is very closely tied into other areas of study."[2] The difference really is one of degree, since both programs may be functional in that they focus upon children's language arts experiences and integrated in that what the children write, speak or read about, and listen to is derived largely from their study in other curricular areas. Obviously the latter is more easily accomplished in a self-contained classroom.

The best known kind of integrated program is one that makes use of teaching units. A unit, as defined by Beauchamp, is a "means of organizing a series of studies or activities around some central theme or problem."[3] This is not a new concept, as shown by the following, which also illustrates the principle of integration.[4]

> To illustrate, a child may be studying subject matter in connection with a topic in social science, such as *transportation*. He reads geographies or histories or other books to get his information. He may even need to have some practice in how to gather information, how to outline, or how to comprehend what he reads. Thus, reading is related. He may write letters to steamship companies to get additional data. He may summarize the facts he has gathered into a few simple statements. He may find that he needs practice in writing letters or in composing clear summary sentences. Thus, composition is involved. As he writes his sentences, both spelling and penmanship enter in, and needed additional practice in those subjects may be brought to light. Thus, two other fields—spelling and penmanship—are related. He may decide to make a frieze illustrating the progress in types of water transportation. The art teacher comes to the rescue with suggestions on how to make the drawings. A lesson may grow out of this for the whole class on how to label drawings, how to arrange material for a frieze, or on methods of shading or coloring. Thus, another field—art—is related. The object, of course, is not to relate the fields, but to use every means to understand the original problem, *transportation*, and to make it meaningful. This, then, is integration.

It is unrealistic to expect this kind of integration to apply to everything an elementary teacher must teach. Although it is necessary and

[2]Willard F. Tidyman, Charlene Weddle Smith, and Marguerite Butterfield, *Teaching the Language Arts* (New York: McGraw-Hill, Inc., Third Edition, 1969), p. 434.

[3]George A. Beauchamp, *Basic Dimensions of Elementary Method* (Boston: Allyn and Bacon, Inc., Second Edition, 1965), p. 153.

[4]Harry A. Greene and others, *Manual for Building Better English* (Evanston, Ill.: Row, Peterson and Company, 1947), p. 19. Courtesy of Harper & Row, Publishers.

realistic a great deal of the time, some important attitudes, knowledge, skills, and abilities cannot be introduced naturally into certain areas of the curriculum. Failure to recognize this can lead either to an artificial kind of integration in which the relatedness is forced or to the neglect of some things which should be taught.

This problem should be a minimal one in the language arts. Every child must learn that the language skills are the tools by which he receives and transmits ideas and information about all of his daily activities, in school and out. These activities are the content around which a successful language arts program operates. Thus, the language skills can be integrated with every area of the school curriculum—and they should be at every natural opportunity.

As was illustrated in the preceding section, the use of language enters into every area of study. As will be shown later, particular aspects of the total language arts may be separated from the others for purposes of instruction. However, the various aspects or segments are highly interrelated and most are quite strongly related to much other elementary school curricular content. Even the most superficial consideration of the elementary school program leads to the conclusion that subject matter is difficult to separate, that the language arts surely must be taught all day long, and that very rarely does any single language skill or ability function independently of many others.

Inter-relationships Among the Language Arts

The educational literature is replete with statements of the existence of interrelationships among the language arts.[5] Many of these statements are based upon reflection about language arts teaching but, as will be shown later, there is an increasing amount of research becoming available which shows particular relationships. Certainly the inter-relationships are many, varied, and in numerous ways highly intricate. Generally speaking, however, much of the interrelationship is due to the presence of common elements in the areas or facets, and to the fact that an experience affecting one will influence others. For the teaching of language skills such an interrelationship is of basic importance. A teacher who attempts to teach a child to read without recognizing the importance of listening and speaking skills will meet with frustration. A teacher who thoughtfully recognizes the interrelationships of lan-

[5]For example: Virgil Hughes, "A Study of the Interrelationships Among Selected Language Arts Areas and Abilities," unpublished doctoral dissertation, University of Missouri, 1950; Robert Rudell, "Oral Language Skills and the Development of Other Language Skills," *Elementary English,* 43:489–498, May, 1966; and Donald L. Cleland, "The Language Arts Program—A Constellation of Skills," *Education,* 84:323–328, February, 1964.

guage skills may well discover that a reading problem really hinges upon a listening difficulty or an immature speech pattern. Too, the teacher who is sensitive to interrelationships will not wait until confronted by a problem to note the commonness of elements, but will keep the carry-over effects in mind when directing lessons in all of the facets. For instance, a lesson in letter writing will give attention to the skills of spelling, handwriting, and sentence construction, and may call for the use of listening and reading skills.

☐ Listening and Language

The infant's first contact with language is through listening; it is his sole contact for approximately the first year of his life, and it remains a major factor in all of his activities throughout his life. He comes to school with a learned pattern of speech based upon what he has heard, a pattern which is of basic importance in the school's efforts to instruct him in speaking, reading, and writing. For example, recognition that speech habits are learned through imitation—through listening—points up the need for hearing good speech and shows the futility of attempting to make substantial changes in speech by approaches other than listening. The skills of listening are also involved in instruction in the other aspects of language. Instruction in reading, speaking, and writing are often given by the teacher by speaking, and speaking and oral reading by the child call for the use of listening skills by his audience.

Listening and reading are especially close in that they are both receptive aspects of language and that there appears to be a similarity in the particular skills involved.[6] However, the relationship between the skills in the two areas is not so high as might be expected.[7] There are greater intricacies of relationship present than surface appraisal would indicate.

☐ Reading and Language

The second of the receptive aspects of language is reading, which calls for listening, writing, and speaking in both its learning and its teaching.

---

[6]Edward Pratt, "The Experimental Evaluation of a Program for the Improvement of Listening in the Elementary School," unpublished doctoral dissertation, State University of Iowa, 1953.

[7]Harry Goldstein, *Reading and Listening Comprehension at Various Controlled Rates,* Contributions to Education, No. 821 (New York: Columbia University, 1940); Gus P. Plessas, "Reading Abilities and Intelligence Factors of Children Having High and Low Auding Ability," unpublished doctoral dissertation, University of California, 1957.

Reading performance varies significantly with proficiency in oral language. Strickland's study of oral language development and reading achievement showed that children ranking high on measures of comprehension in silent reading make greater use of movables (adverbials or adverbial phrases) and elements of subordination in their oral language than those ranking low on these measures.[8] Loban's extensive studies have also shown positive relationships between language abilities and reading competency.[9] Too, as stated above, reading and listening are positively related. Deficiencies in vocabulary are reflected in reading ability. At the same time, deficiency in reading skill is a limiting factor in the building of vocabulary. However, the process of reading is not necessarily a means for building vocabulary.[10] Certainly what is read is frequently the substance or the point of departure for writing; and any instruction in writing should be built upon the principle that what is written has been written for someone to read.

A particular aspect of writing that is closely associated with reading is spelling. Attention to the form and sounds of words as they are learned in reading assists in the accurate spelling of these words when they are written.[11]

□ Speaking and Language

The linguist says that "speaking is language," but our intent here is to note further the relationships between this facet of the total language arts, or of "language" used as a general term, and the other facets. Speaking is a language skill that develops early in the child's life, preceded only by listening—the facet through which speech is learned. There is a great deal of evidence to indicate that language development depends largely upon the speech experiences of children.[12] Speech is, of course, related closely to the vocabulary development that has been gained by a child through listening and reading. Immaturity in lan-

[8]Ruth G. Strickland, "The Language of Elementary School Children: Its Relationship to the Language of Reading Textbooks and the Quality of Reading of Selected Children," *Bulletin of the School of Education,* Indiana University, 38, July, 1962.

[9]Walter D. Loban, *The Language of Elementary School Children* (Champaign, Ill.: The National Council of Teachers of English, 1963).

[10]Walter T. Petty, Curtis P. Herold, and Earline Stoll, *The State of Knowledge About the Teaching of Vocabulary* (Champaign, Ill.: The National Council of Teachers of English, 1968), p. 84.

[11]Gus P. Plessas and Peggy A. Dison, "Spelling Performances of Good Readers," *California Journal of Educational Research,* 16:14–22, 1965.

[12]Jon Eisenson and Mardel Ogilvie, *Speech Correction in the Schools* (New York: The Macmillan Co., 1963), Chapter 7.

guage development also is a retardant in speaking activities. Again, the skills necessary for effective speaking are many of the same skills needed for effective communication in the other language arts.

☐ **Writing and Language**

A good deal of recent research has pointed to the relationship between effective writing and language maturity. For example, some of this research shows a positive relationship between measures of language growth and such things as clause length, the number of modifications, and the number of words in the T-units (a research "substitute for *sentence*").[13] On the other hand, as is discussed more completely in Chapter 11, evidence continues to accumulate that the systematic study of the system of the language (grammar) does not result in improvement in writing.[14] Yet observation alone leads to the realization that any lack of understanding of the workings of the language very often results in less effective writing than that expressed by a pupil who has greater understanding. Writing and speaking are also obviously interrelated. While writing tends to be more formal than speech, fluency in one affects the other. Particularly is this the case with fluency in writing: what a child writes, and the words he uses, are not likely to go beyond his facility in speaking. Again, this facility is largely a reflection of his language maturity.

Organizing the Classroom Program

The daily and weekly program or schedule by which a classroom operates reflects to some extent the organization of the subject matter —the extent to which the teacher plans to integrate content or to deal with it in separate areas. It does not do so completely, however, since the *integration* of subject matter *takes place in the mind of the learner,* an act that may occur without effort by the teacher. The schedule is a guide to activity and to movement of the pupils—a reminder of things to be done. The listing of each subject may suggest compartmentalization, but the teacher still may use every opportunity to help pupils integrate what they have learned.

Program schedules are often based on directions or suggestions given to teachers by school administrators. These suggestions may

[13]Richard Braddock, "English Composition" in *Encyclopedia of Educational Research,* Fourth Edition, Robert L. Ebel, editor (New York: The Macmillan Co., 1969), p. 452.

[14]Richard Braddock and others, *Research in Written Composition* (Champaign, Ill.: The National Council of Teachers of English, 1963).

reflect the educational interests of the community, but they are more likely to emphasize the value of systematic routine, of limiting the number of distracting tangents, and of assuring that the various aspects of a teacher's task are considered adequately. This emphasis is valid, because reasonable routine saves time and energy for both the teacher and the pupils, while providing a kind of social discipline that develops in the pupils a respect for orderliness and a sense of security.

In the making of a program, consideration must be given to the amount of time available each week and how this time should be allocated. The most recent research known to the authors indicates that the predominant amounts of time allotted to language arts areas are as follows:[15]

> Reading—60 minutes daily
> English—40 minutes daily
> Spelling—20 minutes daily
> Handwriting—30 minutes, twice weekly

An earlier publication lists the following average amounts of time one state devoted to the various areas of the language arts.[16]

			Grade			
	I	II	III	IV	V	VI
Reading	550*	450	350	260	220	200
Language (English)	100	100	100	125	125	140
Spelling	50	75	75	75	70	70
Handwriting	70	75	70	60	40	40
Literature	70	70	70	75	70	60
Library		40	50	45	45	45

*minutes per week—total week 1650 minutes

The preceding are reasonable guides to planning, but no one source of information or set of averages should be the basis for decisions on how much time should be devoted to each part of a program. In some areas, optimum amounts of time have been determined by research. In addition, the special needs of groups of children, the various emphases given in curriculum guides, and the relative importance

[15]Oscar T. Jarvis, "Time Allotments in Elementary Schools—Policies and Practices," *The National Elementary Principal,* 43:64–65, September, 1963.

[16]Taken from table on page 27 in *Resource Ideas for Planning Classroom Programs* (State of Iowa, The Department of Public Instruction, 1955).

attached to the several parts by the teacher and school administrators all may cause differences in the amounts of time allotted.

Many teachers like a program of many short periods, similar to the fourth-grade program illustrated below.

9:00– 9:10	Opening activities
9:10–10:00	Reading
10:00–10:20	Music
10:20–10:30	Recess
10:30–11:05	Mathematics
11:05–11:35	Physical Education (alternating with Art)
11:35–11:50	Spelling
11:50–12:00	Handwriting
12:00–12:50	Lunch
12:50– 1:00	Starting period
1:00– 1:25	Language
1:25– 2:10	Social Studies
2:10– 2:20	Recess
2:20– 2:50	Science–Health (alternating with Library)
2:50– 3:15	Literature (alternating with activity period)
3:15– 3:30	Individual Aid

The following type of program, also popular, lists similar subject matter but divides it into larger blocks of time.

9:00– 9:10	Opening activities
9:10–10:00	Reading
10:00–10:40	Music—two days Science and Health—two days Library—one day
10:40–11:00	Recess
11:00–12:00	Arithmetic—three days Literature—one day Activity—one day
12:00–12:35	Lunch
12:35– 2:00	Language—about 60 minutes three days Spelling—25 minutes three days Art—about 40 minutes two days Physical Education—45 minutes two days
2:00– 2:55	Social Studies
2:55– 3:15	Literature—two days Handwriting—three days

A third program (for the fifth grade) is built around unit study which includes the social studies and the language arts. Reading is included in the unit, since the program presumes that the basic word recognition or decoding skills have been learned. Spelling is excluded, so that the spelling of a basic list of words can be taught efficiently.

9:00–10:30	Unit
10:30–10:50	Recess
10:50–12:00	Unit
12:00– 1:00	Lunch
1:00– 1:15	Spelling
1:15– 2:15	Science—three days
	Library—two days
2:15– 2:40	Physical Education
2:40– 3:30	Mathematics

Other examples of daily and weekly program schedules are available in curriculum guides and textbooks on elementary school organization.

Pupil Differences in Language Abilities

Each child possesses qualities which make him different from all other individuals. Most people consider this true, but observation in the average classroom indicates that many teachers apparently do not take the statement seriously or do not know how to make use of it in their teaching. Many teachers expect the same instructional procedures and standards for achievement to be suitable for all children. Yet, they must know that the children within any given school group differ in mental capacity, sex, physical size and development, motor control, sensitivity of sense organs, amount of pigmentation in the skin, emotional stability, interests, and many other aspects of mental, physical, and emotional development.

In language development, children reveal extremely wide individual differences. Even at the beginning of their school experiences they may, for example, vary by several hundreds or even thousands of words in their vocabularies. Startling ranges of mental ability and school achievement will be found within any given age or school grade. Grouping practices within the classroom may, of course, reduce the range in a single group with respect to certain abilities and knowledge but not with respect to many others. Typically, only about one-third of a class achieve at test norms for the grade level; the other two-thirds are usually about equally divided above and below, with the range increasing as the grade level advances. The teacher faces a hopeless task if he expects to instruct the class so that all members will perform at the same level.

Teacher Identification of Pupil Needs

It is relatively easy to estimate the range of individual differences that may be expected in a classroom, but it is another matter to obtain a clear, detailed picture for each child. General facts regarding individual differences must be interpreted in terms of concrete realities as the teacher works with the children in the various day to day situations. He must deal with each child in his class as a person, not as a statistic.

To determine the specific needs of the members of his class, and the range of differences, the teacher must carry on a continuing program of evaluation and observation. Through this program he can identify the areas of language arts needing initial or further instructional emphasis. Examples of specific methods of determining the needs and differences are the following:

1. Observing and recording speech performance, individual and audience reactions, and specific behavioral elements in selected situations and activities.
2. Making observational notes on individual pupils at regular intervals with respect to nonstandard usage, problems in organizing expression effectively, or lack of ease in speaking.
3. Using a checklist or inventory form for recording skill or lack of skill in particular reading, listening, writing, or speaking situations.
4. Tabulating writing errors made by individual pupils.
5. Using teacher-made and standardized tests in a planned program for measuring growth and achievement in total and specific aspects of language performance.
6. Tabulating departures from standard speech which occur in the children's formal and informal conversation and other language activities in the classroom and on the playground.
7. Making recordings of speech and oral reading and analyzing them for particular problems.
8. Keeping samples of children's written expression for comparison at intervals throughout the school year.

Pupil Identification of Own Needs

Most children realize that everyone must know how to communicate effectively but they may not recognize the importance of the various skills that are essential to effective communication. The extent to which a particular skill seems important varies with each child, as does the degree of mastery of that skill. The problem of getting each child to identify his own deficiences is a major one for the language arts teacher.

Stimulating the pupil to identify his own needs—the skills, abilities, and attitudes on which he particularly needs to work—is a basic motivational procedure and one that will pay rich dividends to the teacher who can do it successfully. He should guide children to use the papers they write, the reading and listening they do, and the talks they give—in all of their classwork—as the bases for judging the progress they are making in using language effectively. By such procedure a child will constantly be working on his own problems, noting his own errors, examining his own papers, and searching out means of improving his skills. The list below indicates ways in which a pupil can identify his own needs.

1. Using a checklist, preferably one that he has helped to devise.
2. Working as one of a pair or as a member of a small group in identifying areas which need improvement by himself, his partner, or others in the group.
3. Looking at the material in a folder which contains samples of his work and records of his achievement.
4. Participating in class discussion of needs, of efforts to meet class-established standards, and of plans for learning activities.
5. Meeting with the teacher to discuss needs.
6. Correcting his own papers, proofreading, and editing his own work.
7. Plotting or recording his own test scores and comparing them with the results of previous testing.
8. Keeping charts of errors made, such as ones made in handwriting.
9. Writing in a notebook things he needs to work on—spelling words, new vocabulary, usage errors.

Providing for Individual Differences

Accepting the reality of individual differences among pupils, and determining the extent of these differences by the means suggested, brings a teacher face to face with the problem of providing appropriate instruction for each pupil. Clymer and Kearney point out a number of needs that must be taken into account in providing for such instruction, although they also indicate that "no prescription can be given" for all such instruction.[17] They list the needs to:

[17]Theodore Clymer and Nolan C. Kearney, "Curricular and Instructional Provisions for Individual Differences," in *Individualizing Instruction,* 61st Yearbook, Part I, National Society for the Study of Education, Nelson B. Henry, editor (Chicago: University of Chicago Press, 1962), p. 276.

1. Know the students
2. Recognize that not all teachers will adjust to individual differences in the same way
3. Provide generous time allotments
4. Plan carefully whatever is to be done in the classroom
5. Work effectively with the group as a whole
6. Move slowly into any type of adjustment to individual differences
7. Accept more noise and more confusion
8. Recognize failure and begin again
9. Accept less than 100 percent adjustment to individual differences
10. Recognize that adjusting to individual differences calls for plain, hard work.

Every elementary school teacher must work with an entire class, with groups within the class, and with individuals. The effort should be made to care for each individual's needs while promoting the greatest amount of growth possible for all the children in the class. In the sections which follow there is a wide variety of suggestions which may provide means for attaining these objectives.

Ability
Grouping

A class can be divided into groups according to abilities or levels of performance. This widely used procedure attempts to simplify the instructional problems by reducing the range of individual differences.[18] In theory this practice is sound; it has been used successfully for reading instruction and, more recently, for the teaching of spelling and handwriting. For some reason, however, the experimental evidence shows that it has not lived up to its theoretical possibilities in the teaching of oral and written expression. Possibly speaking and writing include a more complicated variety of skills than those upon which ability grouping in an area such as reading is based. Part of the difficulty lies in the inadequacy of the means used for possible grouping in the expressional areas. Better identification of the skills and abilities necessary for effective expression may permit more successful grouping practices.

In spite of the shortcomings of grouping for teaching written and oral expression a teacher should group frequently for particular tasks and assignments. For example, one group may be working on storytelling skills, another on improving form in letter writing, and a third on outlining the contents of their reports for social studies class. The

[18]See Chapters 12, 13, and 14 for grouping plans in spelling, handwriting, and reading.

grouping should be flexible and change as the needs and opportunities for its use change.

Organizing schools by grades or levels has been the mode in American education since the days of Horace Mann. Since the late 1940's there has been increasing interest in nongraded schools. The extent of this development is difficult to assess, but published figures indicate that nearly thirty percent of elementary schools have adopted or partially adopted a nongraded plan.[19] The principal feature of the plan is the provision for the continuous academic progress and personal development of pupils without the yearly hurdles of a graded system. The value of the plan for achieving the intended goals is apparently debatable. Dyer reports that "Several researchers have found significant differences in achievement favoring pupils in nongraded groups."[20] However, Anderson and Goodlad concluded that controlled research into the effects of nongrading was almost nonexistent as of 1960.[21] The importance of nongrading to language arts or any other area of the school program was summed up by Goodlad as follows:[22]

> Since school structure is but a shell, dropping the grades and adding or changing nothing else leaves curriculum and instruction —the heart of the educative process—as they were before. *Nongrading is a significant factor in school improvement only as it is seen and used by teachers as means to significant ends they wish to achieve.*

There are many variations in grouping plans. For example, many schools attempt homogeneous grouping of all pupils before children are placed in a classroom. That is, if there is a large enough group of fourth-grade children, for example, to permit having three classes, division of the children may be based on the results of a standardized achievement test. Usually the school tries to get as much homogeneity as possible with this approach, but sometimes definite attempts are made to structure the composition of the classes.

Many school systems also provide for departmentalization of in-

The Nongraded School

Other Variations in Organization

---

[19]National Education Association, *Nongraded Schools,* Research Memo 1965–12 (Washington, D. C.: Research Division, National Education Association, May, 1965).

[20]Prudence Dyer, "Language Arts in the Nongraded School," *Elementary English,* 46:114, February, 1969.

[21]Reported in John I. Goodlad, "Individual Differences and Vertical Organization of the School" (p. 232) in *Individualizing Instruction.*

[22]*Ibid.,* p. 236.

struction, particularly in the upper grades. The value of departmentalization is that it limits the teacher's instruction to fewer subject areas (presumably those he knows best), thus enabling him to give greater attention to the subjects he does teach and to the pupils in these classes. The fault with this plan is that a teacher may be dealing with so many pupils that he knows little about many of them and may provide less individualized instruction than the teacher of a self-contained classroom would.

Team teaching is another method used to give more specialized instruction to a class and possibly to better care for the needs of individuals. The advantages of this procedure over departmentalization are that the several teachers of a team have a smaller group of pupils and that they plan together to care for pupil needs.

Laboratory Instruction

Individual instruction can be given effectively through a laboratory type of program in which each pupil works on his own writing or plans a different speaking occasion. As the writing or planning is taking place, the teacher moves from pupil to pupil, offering help, making suggestions, and encouraging the efforts being made. Each pupil is thus doing something that has purpose for him and the attention of the teacher is given only to the things the child needs to correct or to improve in order to achieve his purpose.

A particular aspect of laboratory instruction accepted by teachers is "Individualized Reading" (see Chapter 14), by which each pupil selects his own materials and progresses at his own rate of reading. The teacher gives him individual attention to assess his growth and instructional needs. At the readiness and beginning reading levels, the teacher frequently uses stories dictated by the pupil and written by the teacher to teach both reading and composition and to encourage expression.

Individualizing Practice

The teacher must provide practice in using the various language skills, taking individual differences into account. As has been stated, both the teacher and the pupil must identify particular instructional needs. If this is done carefully the teacher can provide practice materials which can be distributed as needed and/or pupils can select practice exercises themselves. Children may also be held responsible for using the indexes of textbooks and workbooks to locate practice material. One way to provide practice exercises is to cut up discarded language arts textbooks and workbooks, organizing them according to types of exercises—the particular skills or usages to be practiced. The pages can be placed in envelopes or pasted on stiff paper (particularly if two copies of the textbook or workbook have been cut up) and labeled by type. The exercises can be handed out by the teacher or chosen by pupils who know what skills they need to work on. Pupils may keep records of their use of exercises by signing their names on the envelopes or on the backs of the sheets.

Extensions and modifications of these suggestions can also be made. For example, practice exercises made by teachers (particularly for vocabulary study, spelling, and phonic and analysis activities in reading) can be used instead of pages from textbooks or workbooks. Also, games and enriching activities can be handled in the same way as study exercises. To keep pages clean, exercise pages may be placed in clear plastic envelopes (children can write on them with washable crayons). Furthermore, to emphasize individual evaluation, answers can be placed upon the envelopes or on the backs of pages so that the pupil can check his own work.

Many of the errors pupils make in their written expression are the result of carelessness and the inadequate functioning of desired habits. To remedy these faults teachers must train pupils to proofread their own writing, to see that what they have written conveys the meaning intended and that it is free from mechanical errors. Such training presupposes that the writing is purposeful and that each pupil will genuinely feel the need to do as well as possible.

Proofreading and Self-editing

Habits of proofreading and self-editing of all written work should lead the child logically and directly to the discovery that the complete rewriting of his product invariably results in its improvement. Rewriting should be distinguished from merely recopying the proofread original production, a process which has doubtful value. The pupil will be ready for rewriting when only his best effort will satisfy him. This is a state of mind that the teacher must help to develop.

The fostering of creative expression permits a great deal of individuality in meeting instructional needs. The child who wants to write something of his own, who wants to write imaginatively and with personal feeling, strives to do his best and turns naturally to the teacher for help with his problems. He may also be encouraged to turn to his colleagues for assistance in appropriate situations.

Encouraging Creative Efforts

It is possible to vary the difficulty of individual assignments in the English class, yet have the entire class working on the same general topic (for example, giving reports in social studies). The following example illustrates this procedure:[23]

Varying Assignments

[23]Walter T. Petty, *The Language Arts in Elementary Schools* (Washington, D. C.: The Center for Applied Research in Education, Inc., 1962), p. 8.

... all members of a class might be preparing reports for a social studies unit but the reports might be of differing degrees of difficulty. One child might be seeking information for a report on the foods the pioneers ate; another might be writing the conversation two wagon masters might have had before leaving with their wagon trains; a third might be preparing a critique of a western television show; and a fourth might be tracing routes on a map. The task of each child depends upon his interest and his ability. The child searching for names of foods may have limited reading and writing skills, so he is essentially engaged in finding words and listing them. The child writing conversation must have read extensively, and must be fairly skilled in writing. Each child's task should challenge him, however, and in order to be of value in teaching language skills, should call for the use of some of these skills—particularly those he needs most.

Programmed Instruction

Considerable attention is currently being devoted to programming instruction in a number of areas of the school curriculum. Commercial programmed[24] materials are available in the language arts areas of reading, spelling, and punctuation. The use of these materials, however, is subject to considerable controversy and there appears to be doubt that acceptance will become widespread very soon.

In programs, the information to be taught is separated into fundamental units and then regrouped, or "programmed" into a particular progressive order. The specific items then may be presented mechanically, such as by showing one frame of a film at a time, or in a more or less standard textbook fashion. A programmed textbook (or series of "visuals") differs from regular textbook and film materials in that the learner must finish one step (answer a question, for example) before moving on to the next. The programmed materials are designed for individual use, which is usually not the case with a textbook.

Programmed instruction should have value in teaching particular skills since each step in using the material provides the user with immediate knowledge or immediate responses to questions, thus providing reinforcement for the learning. However, since reading, listening, writing, and speaking make use of many skills (many of which have by no means been adequately identified) which must be assimilated for total performance, programmed materials are not likely to supplant the teacher and the various procedures he may use.[25]

[24]Often spelled with one *m*.
[25]Two volumes, *Programs '62* and *The Use of Programed Instruction in U. S. Schools,* are available from the Superintendent of Documents, Washington, D. C. 20025.

There are many activities which may be engaged in by individual pupils or small groups. Education journals are a good source of ideas which may lead to individualization in classrooms. Here are some activities which have been used.

Special
Activities

1. Having each pupil keep in a notebook for spare time studying a record of words misspelled in his writing.
2. Encouraging children who do good work to help others who are having difficulty.
3. Encouraging children who finish assignments early to make copies of work to be preserved or posted on the bulletin boards.
4. Spelling the difficult words pupils need in writing; that is, writing words on the board that they have not studied but need in their writing.
5. Having children keep individual notebooks for doing unassigned writing of a personal nature with the pupil having the choice of showing it to the teacher or not.
6. Allowing pupils to choose their own topics for reports, their own ideas for stories, and their own roles for dramatizations.
7. Giving incidental individual correction of substandard usage.

Various other chapters in this book suggest other activities which help to provide for individualized instruction. Since the textbook is often responsible for much inattention to individual differences, particular reference should be made to Chapter 16.

A Basic Instructional Approach

A basic plan for teaching the language expressional skills and abilities is suggested in the following sections. While it focuses upon teaching the speaking and writing aspects of the language arts, it is suggestive of a similar approach that might be used for teaching reading and listening. This plan is not intended to provide a complete teaching program, since some areas, such as handwriting and spelling, need direct attention as suggested in Chapters 12 and 13.

The plan calls for two types of lessons: expressional and corrective. Expressional lessons deal mainly with *what* is said or written rather than *how*. Expressional lessons may make use of reading and listening abilities as well as those needed for writing or speaking. An expressional lesson has the purpose of communication and is usually related to subject matter other than the language arts, though the subject of the expression might be literature or language. The correctional lesson is derived from examining the effectiveness of the expressional lesson.

Expressional Lessons

As children discuss plans for a science field trip, converse about some event on the playground, write letters requesting materials for a social studies project, tell a story that they have read or heard, introduce their parents to the teacher or principal, write imaginative stories for pleasure, keep records of class activities, or report answers found to questions in a health unit, the opportunity is present—in each case—for an expressional lesson. An expressional activity requires using language expression for a genuine purpose.

Elements of expressional lessons, with appropriate and applicable techniques, are discussed in the following paragraphs.

□ **Learning by Doing**

Too often teachers assume that children's writing and speaking will improve through discussion of the need for improvement and a program of practice exercises or activities. Nothing could be further from the truth. While practice exercises are of value if their need is understood by children, it is contrary to good psychological practice to expect real improvement except through a program of natural and meaningful writing and speaking experience. The importance of this is summed up in this statement from a United States Office of Education publication:[26]

> Children learn to write by writing. There should be opportunities for every child to write every day in ways that are purposeful. This will not be writing of a formal sort, but rather for many purposes: writing a question on the board, taking notes to answer questions on a problem, writing a letter, ordering merchandise, making an outline for a play, making a bibliography of books containing stories about dogs, writing a fanciful story, or any one of a hundred or more activities that children find interesting and useful.

A similar relationship exists between effective speaking and the opportunity to speak, as expressed in the following:[27]

[26]Helen K. Mackintosh and Wilhelmina Hill, *How Children Learn to Write,* Bulletin 1953, No. 2, U. S. Department of Health, Education, and Welfare (Washington: U. S. Government Printing Office, 1953), pp. 10–11.

[27]Helen F. Olson, "Speech for All." Leaflet 1, *Speech in the English Classroom,* a portfolio published by the National Council of Teachers of English.

People learn to speak by speaking. To improve in speaking, a person needs directions and evaluative techniques by which he can measure his progress toward the goals which he sets for himself. One junior boy complained that his class talked about speeches, they planned speeches, and they hunted information about speeches, but often there was so little time left that only a few of the class had opportunity to give the talks they had prepared. Arranging for guided experience is perhaps the crux of the problem of helping young people to become effective in communicating through speech.

☐ Activity Planning

Both teacher and pupils will profit from planning expressional activities. The teacher should plan carefully for opportunities for such lessons. He should clearly formulate for himself the purposes he hopes to stress and how these purposes will be accomplished, and he must make the purposes known to the pupils. In many activities the planning should be done by the teacher and the children working together. The important point, however, is that children must understand the purpose or purposes to be served by their speaking or writing before they begin to plan what they are going to say or to set down their ideas or the information they have secured. One sixth grade undertook the organization of the school's periodicals, which might otherwise have been discarded. This project illustrates the kind of planning that needs to be done.[28]

> Teacher and pupils planned together from the start. The pupils' activity was directed by repeated questions: How shall we proceed? What shall we do next? What jobs need to be done and who will do them? How much time each week shall we devote to the problem?
> It was decided to limit the work on the problem to three eighty-minute periods a week. The teacher's remark that some record of work and procedure would be needed as the activity broadened brought forth from the class a suggestion that they keep a diary. The pupils agreed to keep a record of the activities in which they participated on large sheets of paper attached to an easel. A guide for writing the diary entries was then set up.

☐ Audience-Reader Consideration

In every expressional lesson it is important that attention be given to the receiver or receivers of the expression. An attentive, interested

[28]The Commission on the English Curriculum of the National Council of Teachers of English, *Language Arts for Today's Children* (New York: Appleton-Century-Crofts, Inc., 1954), pp. 285–286.

audience or an interested reader motivates the child to make his expression as effective as possible. To be well received, an expression must be interesting, appealing, and effectively organized. In oral expression, it must communicate something that the audience wants to know or something in which the audience is likely to become interested. Written expression, also, must attract the reader and hold his attention.

Consideration of the audience or the readers should be a part of the planning. What is the audience like? Is this a subject they will be interested in? Is the information or idea to be told or written something that is new? What is there in this expression that will have appeal?

☐ **The Role of Models**

Children learn much about speaking by observing, listening to, and imitating others. They also learn from seeing models of written products. Thus, if a teacher wants children to write neat letters, to give effective reports, and to tell stories well, he must present models for them to see and hear. In speaking, the teacher or a tape recording may be the model. In writing, pupils may make their own models from samples in textbooks or from one the entire class has worked out on the board.

☐ **Evolving Standards**

The teacher and the pupils, together, should establish standards for each type of expressional activity. These standards may be established after observing a model or they may be the result of a class discussion. The standards should be the pupils' own statements, even if they fall below the goals of the teacher or the textbook, and should be subject to change as the pupils feel the need. If they are too low for one lesson, the pupils will realize this and change them when similar lessons and activities recur. Standards should be recorded in writing, possibly by both the teacher and the pupils. First, the teacher should write them on the board; later he should put them on a chart where they can be seen and referred to. Suggestions for standards may be obtained from textbooks. One book, for example, lists the following standards for storytelling.[29]

1. Stand straight. Do not lean on anything.
2. Speak directly to your audience.
3. Have a good opening sentence.
4. Tell the events of your story in the same order as they happened.

[29]Thomas Clark Pollock, and others, *Using Language*, Book 5 (New York: The Macmillan Co., 1960), p. 217.

5. Speak clearly without hesitating or stringing your sentences together with *and* or *and-uh.*
6. If your story will let you, save the most exciting part until the last for a surprise ending.
7. Imitate as nearly as possible how the characters in your story might speak.

□ Self-editing and Group Criticism

After the first writing has been completed the next step is for the pupil to refer to the standards and check the written product against them. In oral expression this step assumes the form of group criticism of the speaker and his product, since the speaker cannot change his expression after it is given as he may in written expression. This element or step in expressional lessons is particularly important to both speaking and writing situations, however, in that it is the "on the spot" occasion for correction. While correctional lessons focus upon this entirely, there is the need for pupils to immediately have their attention called to improvements that should be made.

Teaching a child to edit his own writing, to really compare his product with the standards, takes time. While a child can learn much in a school year about correcting his own papers, real skill in editing is developed over several years and should be taught by all the teachers in a school.

Criticism comes rather naturally to most persons—perhaps too much so since it often is not constructive. Children are apt to be needlessly harsh or cruel in their comments. For this reason, lessons which are directed particularly at the development of appreciation or enjoyment should not be subjected to criticism by pupils. Frank and friendly discussion of children's expression should sometimes be encouraged. However, the better idea is to focus upon the positive aspects of the expression. These discussions should be controlled by both the children and the teacher. At the beginning of the school year, and at other times with younger children, the teacher should do most of the criticism. The object in discussion is to develop in each child a willingness to accept an evaluation by someone else and to learn to view his own expression critically.

The content for the second basic type of lesson arises from the writing and speaking produced for the expressional lessons. Correctional lessons are designed to bring about individual pupil mastery of the specific knowledge, skills, and abilities required for effective expression. Factors in correctional lessons are discussed in the following paragraphs.

Correctional
Lessons

☐ Evaluation and Diagnosis

By evaluating expressional lessons, the teacher, the class, or both can identify specific errors, bad habits, or special weaknesses. (Such evaluation is often simply an extension of group criticism and self-editing.) The precision of the diagnosis is determined to a large degree by the nature and refinement of the evaluative instruments and procedures. In some language arts areas, such as most oral expression and the composition aspect of written expression, evaluation is largely subjective and hence is dependent upon reference to standards and models, and to the use of checklists by the teacher and the pupils. In other areas, standardized and teacher-made objective tests may be used to diagnose.

☐ Identification of Individual Deficiencies

In order for diagnosis and evaluation to provide a reasonable basis for corrective instruction the exact deficiencies of each pupil must be identified as closely as possible. Moreover, as has been suggested

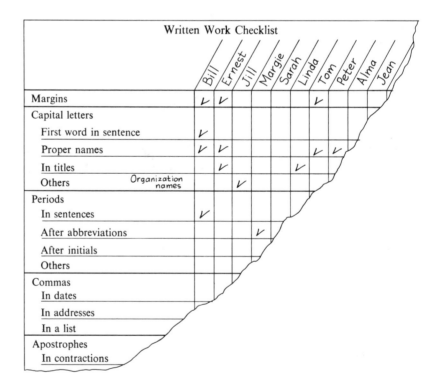

Written Work Checklist	Bill	Ernest	Jill	Margie	Sarah	Linda	Tom	Peter	Alma	Jean
Margins	✓	✓					✓			
Capital letters										
First word in sentence	✓									
Proper names	✓	✓						✓	✓	
In titles			✓				✓			
Others — Organization names				✓						
Periods										
In sentences	✓									
After abbreviations					✓					
After initials										
Others										
Commas										
In dates										
In addresses										
In a list										
Apostrophes										
In contractions										

earlier in this chapter, each child needs to recognize his own weaknesses in order to be properly motivated to remedy them. In addition to the pupil noting his needs, the teacher should record for each pupil the particular errors, habits that need changing, or skills and abilities in need of instruction. This may be done on charts, such as the one shown, so that reference can quickly be made to individual and class needs as instruction is given. Separate charts or other means of recording will be needed to note weaknesses in all of the many expressional activities. Particulars recorded will vary with the grade and ability levels of the children.

☐ **Instructional Drive**

As soon as specific weaknesses of the class and of individual pupils have been identified, the teacher should begin an instructional drive to correct the grossest errors. Errors made last month or even last week are too far in the past to be the subject of a correctional lesson today. The attack on an error made yesterday should have begun yesterday if at all possible. Of course, not all errors, not all poor habits, not all weaknesses, can be attacked at once. If there are common errors for the class or for a large group of children, these may be attended to first. Too, each pupil is likely to have something that he alone needs to work on, and he should receive individual instruction for this. Often he can receive aid from his classmates as well as the teacher, as is suggested in the quotation below.[30]

> The writer has found socialized correction to be an effective means of eradicating individual language weaknesses. Here compositions are copied on the board with all defects and errors duplicated. The pupil-author makes what improvements he can; his classmates then cooperate in suggesting other improvements while this same pupil-author makes revisions on his original paper. He thus is helped to see the exact spots where he needs to make improvement. Usually a lesson in socialized instruction includes a composition with very few errors. This is considered first in order that the entire class have creditable composition practices brought to mind. Then, two or three compositions with typical errors are improved.

This procedure may be accomplished more easily today by showing the papers with an opaque projector or by using copying machines to copy them on transparencies for showing with an overhead projec-

[30]Mildred A. Dawson, *Individualization in the Language Arts,* Language Arts Leaflet Number 3 (Yonkers-on-Hudson: World Book Company, 1949), p. 1.

tor. In any case, the pupil whose paper is being shown is receiving direct and specific instruction, with the other pupils also benefitting.

☐ **Corrective Practice**

After children recognize the individual errors they are making or the particular weaknesses they have, properly designed practice must be provided to establish the new habits or the new learning. The practice should be only upon those things which received instruction, those things for which there is need. Without this emphasis the practice becomes a task that is unrelated to purposes the pupil thinks are important. In some instances the practice occurs as the pupil participates in another expressional lesson; in others—such as punctuation items, for example—practice exercises may be used.

Evaluation in the Instructional Program

Evaluation is concerned with how well instructional goals are being achieved. It seeks to determine the extent to which an entire class and each person in it are growing and the limitations of that growth. In the following sections the role of evaluation in the language arts program is considered, types of evaluative instruments and procedures are identified, and evaluation and the giving of pupil grades is discussed. Specific evaluative techniques and materials and their uses are presented in later chapters.

The Relationship of Evaluation to Instruction

As has often been stated, but is sometimes forgotten, "evaluation procedures are an inherent part of the language program and ... no attempt to separate them in order to justify the use of poor or inadequate instruments for evaluation can change that fact. Certainly the most important factor in the learning situation is the goal of the learner."[31] Evaluation should be a constant element of classroom method at all levels of instruction; it should not be treated lightly or regarded as only a minor or incidental aspect of the program. The importance of evaluation in a typical program of instruction is indicated by an examination of the following steps in such a program:

1. Before starting to teach a particular aspect of the program, ad-

[31]Walter W. Cook, "Evaluation in the Language Arts Program," *Teaching Language in the Elementary School,* Forty-third Yearbook of the National Society for the Study of Education, Part II (Chicago: The University of Chicago Press, 1944), p. 195.

minister initial or inventory tests to determine each child's mastery of it. The instruments used should confront each child with situations calling for responses to the precise abilities or skills included in this aspect of the instructional program. This procedure is used so that the learner does not have to waste time on facts or skills he has already mastered but may focus his learning effort on those elements he personally needs to master.

2. Teach the facts or develop the skills in ways designed to meet each individual's needs so far as possible. Develop the skills by oral presentation, discussion, and demonstration in realistic and lifelike situations.

3. Follow at once with valid and properly motivated opportunities for each individual to repeat the desired reactions correctly. The purpose of this procedure is to fix the facts or skills to the point that the correct responses become habits.

4. Administer a check-test, closely paralleling the content of the inventory test, to determine the extent of each child's improvement.

5. Analyze each check-test to discover each child's remaining difficulties.

6. Reteach any defects identified and give further remedial practice.

7. Retest, and if necessary, reteach.

Evaluation instruments or procedures may be regarded as presenting valid information only to the extent that they themselves are valid. The validity of any evaluation effort depends upon the accuracy with which the instrument or procedure measures what it seeks to measure. Standardized tests usually reflect effort to establish them as valid instruments. However, there are aspects of the language arts which are difficult to measure. Thus, while a test may be a valid measure of a pupil's ability to choose the correct verb form for a sentence from two choices, it is probably not a valid measure of what verb form he would put in the sentence in his natural oral and written expression. Nevertheless, such a test is useful, in that it gives the teacher information he did not have.

Cautions Concerning Evaluation

Evaluation instruments or procedures should also be reliable to be most useful. That is, they must measure consistently whatever they attempt to measure. Most standardized tests are reasonably reliable, as shown by the fact that different forms of the same test usually result in closely comparable test scores. Informal evaluative procedures, however, are often not reliable. Most teachers will admit, for example, that they will not mark a composition the same after a time gap of only a day. Experience, along with adherence to certain criteria, should assist a teacher in marking with greater consistency.

The point here is not to disparage the use of evaluation instruments and procedures. Even though validity and/or reliability may be in question, any effort to measure the results of teaching, to relate achievement to goals, is considerably better than no effort. The purpose is simply to urge that the results and information gained from appraisal procedures be used with proper consideration of the limitations they have. This means that results from different evaluative efforts should not be treated the same; some, by their very objectivity, give far more valid and reliable information than do others. This means also that evaluation instruments should be examined closely for their relationship to the objectives, to the curriculum content, and to the methods of instruction used.

Types of Instruments and Techniques

Measuring instruments and appraisal techniques vary widely in type, structure, and function. Most commonly used are the following: oral questioning (of an individual or a group); essay tests (varying as to length of answers required); objective achievement tests (either commercially produced and standardized or teacher-made); diagnostic or analytical tests (also objective and either commercially or teacher-made but designed to identify individual pupil strengths and weaknesses more specifically); and scales (sample items for comparison with pupil work). Many more generally informal instruments and techniques are designed and/or used by the teacher, the pupils, or both. These include checklists, statements of standards, models, score cards, questionnaires, attitude scales, progress charts, and conferences. Also useful in evaluation are pupil folders, teacher's logs, diaries of pupils, autobiographies, and samples of work.

Many of the instruments and procedures briefly identified above are discussed in later chapters. The reader should also refer to measurement and evaluation textbooks for more information.

Evaluation and Grading

Teachers show more concern about the giving of grades than any other aspect of curriculum and methods. Grading is also a major concern of parents, as witnessed by the frequency with which a school district typically changes its reporting form and procedures.

Evaluation and grading are not the same thing, however. Evaluation is a major factor in the teaching process, while the assigning of grades is a custom that has been established, presumably to report easily to parents and others regarding the pupil's growth and achievement. Proper recognition of this difference should reduce the number of evaluative acts that are graded and increase the proper use of evaluation.

Certainly the assigning of grades (or at least some form of reporting to parents, school authorities, and pupils) must be done, and it is logical to use the results of evaluation as the basis for a grade. However, it is not necessary for the results of every evaluative effort to be graded, nor should a teacher believe that a grade is an adequate report to either the parents or the child.

A teacher, of course, must observe the reporting policies of his school and district, and in the majority of instances this will mean putting grades on a report card. However, he should go further than that in his reporting, even if that is all that is required, by sending home samples of children's work (which have evaluative comments rather than grades), evaluative statements, and explanations of the school program, and by conferring with parents whenever possible.

The following principles of reporting should be observed: Reports should be based upon evidence that can be shown and understood, and is as nearly objective as possible. They should be made in consideration of the child and their effect upon him and his learning; they must be as accurate an assessment of the child's achievement or progress as possible, and as personal as possible, but respectful of the feelings and personalities of all concerned.

Exercises for Thought and Action

1. Find the meanings of integration, fusion, correlation, modular scheduling, differentiated staffing, and teacher-pupil planning, core and unit study, as they are used in educational literature.
2. Secure sample schedules of classroom programs, daily and weekly. Comment upon the suitability of each.
3. Discuss the values and faults of various grouping plans as means of caring for individual differences in instruction.
4. Examine a representative pupil folder kept by a teacher friend. List what is in it. What would you add or subtract from the contents?
5. What is the difference between teaching machines and programmed learning? How are they alike?
6. Visit a nongraded school. What differences, if any, in instructional procedures from those in a graded school did you observe?
7. Evaluate the basic instructional approach presented in this chapter. Record any strengths and weaknesses you believe it to have.

8. Make a recording of children speaking (perhaps in a class discussion situation) and analyze the speech for instructional problems.

9. Find out what tests are given in a classroom in your local school. When are the tests given? For what purposes?

10. Sit with a teacher at a parent-teacher conference and report on what occurred. As an alternative, outline what should occur in such a conference.

Selected References

Ahmann, J. Stanley; Glock, Marvin; and Wardenberg, Helen. *Evaluating Elementary School Pupils*. Boston: Allyn and Bacon, Inc., 1960.

Anderson, Paul S. *Language Skills in Elementary Education*. New York: The Macmillan Company, 1964.

Burns, Paul C., and Lowe, Alberta L. *The Language Arts in Childhood Education*. Chicago: Rand McNally and Co., 1966.

Burton, W. H. *The Guidance of Learning Activities,* Third Edition. New York: Appleton-Century-Crofts, Inc., 1962.

Carbone, Robert F. "A Comparison of Graded and Non-Graded Elementary Schools," *The Elementary School Journal,* 62:82–88, November, 1961.

Garner, Wayne L. *Programmed Instruction*. New York: Center for Applied Research in Education, 1966.

Henry, Nelson B. (ed.). *Individualizing Instruction,* Sixty-first Yearbook, Part I, of the National Society for the Study of Education. Chicago: University of Chicago Press, 1962.

Shane, Harold G., and Mulry, June G. *Improving Language Arts Instruction Through Research*. Washington, D.C.: Association for Supervision and Curriculum Development, 1964.

Thomas, George I., and Crescimbeni, Joseph. *Individualizing Instruction in the Elementary School*. New York: Random House, Inc., 1967.

Thomas, R. Murry, and Thomas, Shirley. *Individual Differences in the Classroom*. New York: David McKay Company, Inc., 1965.

Language Development
And Early
Language Arts Instruction

3

INTRODUCTION

Language arts learning begins with the informal language
expressional and receptional activities of the home. This learning
is certain to take place, but the quality of it is apt to vary greatly from
one child to another. Every child learns the language of his early
environment—for most children, principally that of the home.
This early language learning has increasingly become a national
concern, and much of this concern is the result of the "rediscovery"
of the importance of early childhood education. Psychologists
have rediscovered the work of Jean Piaget, sociologists
have rediscovered that social class affects language learning,
and many of us have rediscovered that being poor implants
an environment on the child that may condition his entire life.

Language development of the child in his infancy and preschool
days is discussed in this chapter. Included is a discussion of the
acquisition of grammatical structure and the factors which
influence language development. The major emphasis in the chapter,
however, is upon beginning school language arts programs—
particularly those of the kindergarten. These major
topics are discussed:

1. Language Development during the Preschool Years
2. Factors that Influence Language Development
3. Beginning Language Arts Programs
4. Kindergarten Language Arts Emphasis
5. Instructional Activities in the Kindergarten
6. Reading in the Kindergarten

Language Development During the Preschool Years

A child's language development begins the moment he hears language. At about four months he will respond to a spoken word by turning his head and before he is a year old will react behaviorally to language. His own vocalization begins at birth and usually develops to the utterance of a word or two by the end of the first year. Shortly after this the child's vocalizing begins to show a language system. This system continues to show development up to and well into the school years, as recent research on indices of language maturity has shown.[1]

Early Experimenting by the Child

Linguistic scientists in recent years have begun to supply a wealth of data on early language development.[2] Recordings of an infant's vocalizations during the first few months of life show little system or little relationship to the language he will later speak.[3] By the third or fourth month, the child's babbling is influenced by the language he hears and he begins to "practice." With this practice comes evidence of control of volume, pitch, and articulation, as shown by his ability to repeat these features.[4]

The child's first "words" may not be words as adults know them but they may be so labeled because he uses them consistently and with reference to some meaning he has attached. He may say "Da-da," which will cause his father's face to glow; it may later fall when the child's experimenting leads him to say "Ma-ma" in a corresponding setting. The child is simply naming things—perhaps someone coming into the room is what "da-da" means. These first "words" are particularly important to the child. They are basic in the development of his phonological (sound) system. As the child says these first words (probably better identified as syllables), he is beginning acquisition of the phonemes (the smallest units of meaningful speech sound). "Phoneme development in general is most rapid during the first year of life; by the age of thirty months the average child possesses approxi-

[1]Kellog W. Hunt, *Grammatical Structures Written at Three Grade Levels,* Research Report No. 3 (Champaign, Ill.: National Council of Teachers of English, 1965).

[2]Susan Ervin-Tripp, "Language Development" in *Review of Child Development Research,* Vol. 2, 1966, Lois Wladis Hoffman and Martin L. Hoffman, editors (New York: Russell Sage Foundation), pp. 55–105.

[3]Ruth H. Weir, *Language in the Crib* (London: Mouton and Co., 1962).

[4]Walter M. MacGinitie, "Language Development" in *Encyclopedia of Educational Research,* Fourth Edition, Robert L. Ebel, editor (New York: The Macmillan Company, 1969), p. 690.

mately 77 per cent of the total adult phoneme production."[5] This rapid acquisition shows the importance of babbling and "practice" to the child; it also reflects the adults' concern with language learning, since in most cultures they have grasped at the child's sounds and invested them with meanings.

Most children say an intelligible word during the second six months of life. Within a few months many are saying many words and "some children go about the house all day long naming things (table, doggie, ball, etc.) and actions (play, see, drop, etc.) and an occasional quality (blue, broke, bad, etc.)."[6] Vocabulary growth is very rapid by the end of the second year of a child's life. Evidence of the rapid growth during the entire preschool period is provided in a study by Smith.[7] She reported that at one year of age the average child had a three-word vocabulary; one year later it was 272. She also noted that the average two-year-old speaks about 80 words during an hour of free play, with more than half of his vocalization comprehensible.

Vocabulary Development

The development of vocabulary in young children clearly shows that generalizing about "the average" may be misleading. Gifted children are advanced in speech and retarded children are slow in developing it. Some children are slow in developing speech because they have received little reinforcement or have had their needs met without having to speak. The wide range in vocabulary was shown by a study of twenty-five two-year-olds that found the children speaking from 6 to 126 words.[8]

Studies of young children show that the children experiment with word order in a manner similar to their experimenting with words. The child who says "No say mama" at age two is trying out word order, but learning the order for his language follows quickly. Furthermore, the young child early learns the classes of words (but, of course, not grammatical names) because he uses many of his first words in various

The Development of Grammatical Structure

[5]William J. Meyer, *Developmental Psychology* (New York: The Center for Applied Research in Education, 1964), p. 60.

[6]Roger Brown and Ursula Bellugi, "Three Processes in the Child's Acquisition of Syntax," *Harvard Educational Review,* Spring, 1964, Vol. 34, No. 2, p. 133.

[7]M. E. Smith "An Investigation of the Development of the Sentence and the Extent of Vocabulary in Young Children," *University of Iowa Studies in Child Welfare,* 1926, 3, No. 5.

[8]M. M. Shirley, *The First Two Years of Life: A Study of Twenty-five Babies,* Vols. I and II (Minneapolis: University of Minnesota Press, Institute of Child Welfare Monographs Series, No. 7, 1933).

contexts, as well as learning to make the inflections our language requires. For example, the following shows some of the sentences spoken by Adam, a 28½-month-old boy:[9]

Here, Mum.	There goes.
Here coffee pot broken, Mum.	There it is.
Want coffee, Mum.	There more block.
Salad, Mum.	There more truck.
Enough, Mum.	There my house.
Here more blocks.	Blanket in there.

This is only a small sample of the language of this child. These sentences show that the child has heard these words, but he has not heard them in all of these sentences. Linguistic researchers point to this fact as evidence that language is not entirely (at least) learned by imitation. Brown and Bellugi include these in their records of model sentences produced by mothers and the imitations produced by children:[10]

Model Utterance	Child's Imitation
Tank car	Tank car
Daddy's brief case	Daddy brief case
He's going out	He go out
That's an old time train	Old time train

These researchers also cite the following as examples of utterances which are not likely to be imitations:[11]

Two foot	You naughty are
A bags	Put on it
A scissor	Cowboy did fighting me
A this truck	Put a gas in

The linguist Chomsky, and many other language scientists, apparently believe that grammatical speech is a built-in human propensity.[12] The extent to which a young child experiments with his language until he gets it organized into a system and the fact that not

[9]Selected from Roger Brown and Colin Fraser, "The Acquisition of Syntax" in *Verbal Behavior and Learning*, C. N. Cofer and Barbara Musgrave, editors (New York: McGraw-Hill, Inc., 1963).
[10]Brown and Bellugi, "Three Processes," p. 137.
[11]*Ibid.*, p. 141.
[12]Noam Chomsky, "Review of B. F. Skinner, *Verbal Behavior*," *Language*, 35:26–58, 1959.

all his speech is direct imitation appear to substantiate this theory. In any case, there is evidence that very young children make great effort to sort out and become proficient in using the language system. Weir's research, based upon the tape-recorded speech of her young son while he was lying in his crib, suggests that language learning is highly motivated by the need to communicate.[13] Any of us might struggle in a manner generally similar to that of the infant if we were thrown into an environment whose language was entirely strange to us.

Because language development is a complex process requiring many years to attain maturity, it is sensitive to environmental conditions. These conditions are particularly important in the first years of a child's life. They affect the development of the child's language—its phonology, vocabulary, and grammar. Many of these environmental conditions, as well as other factors that influence language growth, are considered in the section which follows, and more specifically in the following chapter with respect to the language of the "disadvantaged."

Differences in Language Development

Available evidence indicates that children in all environmental settings and all cultures learn language in the manner briefly described above. Children also learn the language of those humans with whom they interact. Furthermore, each child learns the particular dialect used by those with whom he is in closest contact in his infancy and preschool years. This learning includes the structure and phonology of the dialect, whether that dialect is "standard" or "nonstandard."

Differences in language development of children are reflected in other ways than that of learning a particular language or dialect. These differences are important to teachers because they also carry over to child's entrance in school. They include the rate at which the language is learned, the number of words known, fluency in speaking, and deviations in speech, such as stuttering.

Factors that Influence Language Development

Since using language is a learned activity rather than one that is natural or instinctive, there are factors which affect the learning. These factors include characteristics of both the child and his environment. The child's physical and mental equipment, his family environment, and the kind of stimulation he has for speech all have decided bearing upon language development.

[13]Weir, *Language in the Crib.*

Intelligence and Language

Language ability is generally interpreted as an index of intelligence. Studies show that relationships exist between intelligence and various measures of language—for example, positive correlations between measures of intelligence and the amount of vocabulary, ability to articulate, and language maturity.[14] Of course, since most tests of intelligence are highly dependent upon the use of language, it is difficult to determine what the relationships between measures of language and of intelligence really mean.

There is strong reason to believe, on the other hand, that the level at which language functions is one of the most important determinants of the level of the higher thought processes. Studies of mentally retarded provide very meaningful evidence of this, since they show that the retarded's language facility is generally related to the degree of their retardation. Thus, surely the wide differences in intelligence between the "gifted" and the "retarded" reflect differences in rates at which language is learned and the competencies developed in its use. Of course, there may be common causal factors behind both speech and intelligence retardation.

Physical Equipment of Children

Language acquisition and development depend also upon the child's physical equipment. This equipment includes the speech organs (teeth, tongue, lips, throat, and larynx), the organs for hearing, and the neuromuscular system for receiving and producing sounds. These organs all must work effectively for a child's language development to progress normally. Any handicap to sight and hearing, to the ability to perform neuromuscular acts, or to producing speech sounds is likely to interfere with language development.

Home and Family Influences

The family environment of the child plays the most important part in determining the quality of the language facility he develops and the speed with which he develops it. For instance, an only child tends to have closer association with adults than does one who has brothers and sisters; it is probable, therefore, that he will develop a larger vocabulary and greater facility in expressing himself.[15] Similarly, the child whose parents talk to him a great deal develops facility earlier, while

[14]John Eisenson and Mardel Ogilvie, *Speech Correction in the Schools,* Second Edition (New York: The Macmillan Co., 1963), p. 104.
[15]Edith A. Davis, "The Development of Linguistic Skills in Twins, Singletons with Siblings, and Only Children from Ages Five to Ten Years," unpublished doctoral dissertation, University of Minnesota, 1937.

one who has spent his preschool years in an orphanage may tend to be retarded in language development. Slowest to develop are twins, who often associate so closely with each other that they have a minimum of contact with others.[16]

It is obvious that in order to acquire an extensive vocabulary and new ideas about which to think and talk, the preschool child needs many rich experiences. The child who plays alone or only with other children in his own home has a limited number of opportunities to gain new ideas and concepts. If, however, he goes to the park, visits the zoo, takes vacation trips, travels extensively with his parents, or even accompanies his mother on a shopping expedition, he acquires a wealth of new sights and sounds, and the words that relate to them. The child whose parents talk with him, read to him, and generally interact with him verbally gains greatly in language development.[17] Another major element in a child's home environment which affects language development is the socio-economic status of the family. Numerous studies have shown the relationship between language and social class. Loban, for example, describes educationally important language problems that are related to social class.[18] Similar findings were reported by Templin in an earlier study.[19]

A great deal more might be said about environmental factors that affect language development. Much of this is presented in Chapter 4 as it relates to the "disadvantaged" child; other factors are discussed in Chapter 7 in considering the teaching of oral expression. An environment of economic deprivation, both in the home and in the neighborhood, bears heavily upon a child's language development. The speaking of a dialect which is quite divergent from that spoken in the larger community, or the use of a foreign language in the home, is also an important factor.

Other Factors

Sex differences have long been considered influential in the development of language maturity, with studies pointing to female superiority in vocabulary, articulation, length and complexity of sen-

[16]E. Day, "Development of Language in Twins: Comparison of Twins and Single Children," *Child Development,* 3:179–199, September, 1932.
[17]Robert D. Hess and Virginia Shipman, "Early Experiences and the Socialization of Cognitive Modes in Children," *Child Development,* 36:869–886, 1965.
[18]Walter Loban, *Problems in Oral Language,* Research Report No. 5 (Champaign, Ill.: National Council of Teachers of English, 1966).
[19]Mildred C. Templin, *Certain Language Skills in Children: Their Development and Interrelationships* (Minneapolis: University of Minnesota Press, 1957).

tences, and grammatical correctness up through the age of about ten.[20] However, more recent studies minimize differences which may be attributed to sex, indicating that possibly environmental factors which earlier favored girls—such as more verbal interaction with their mothers—no longer exist.[21]

Beginning Language Arts Programs

Research clearly shows that the first four or five years of a child's life are the period of his most rapid growth in physical and mental characteristics and of his greatest susceptibility to environmental influences. It is in these early years that deprivations are most disastrous in their effects. Attitudes are formed, values are learned, habits are developed, and innate abilities are fostered or retarded by conditions the child meets during these years. Recognition of the importance of the child's early years has led to the extension of schooling downward to meet the young child's needs.

Preschool Programs

The Educational Policies Commission has adopted a position which strongly supports the development of school programs for children of four and five years of age.[22] The Commission stated that the objectives of instruction for these children lie in four major areas—intellectual, emotional, social and physical. In the intellectual area they include the promotion of curiosity, the growth of language, and the development of readiness for the intellectual activities which will come later. The emotional goals are those of promoting children's sense of security and self-respect, while the social goal is to develop concern for and responsibility toward others.

The Commission statement indicates that the objectives and programs suggested have long characterized the practices and programs in many nursery schools. This is true, but the statement nevertheless lends support to the rising concern about the education of young children and to the reactions being made to the mounting evidence of the importance of a child's early years.

The major reaction educationally to preschooling has been the

[20]Dorothy McCarthy, *The Language Development of the Preschool Child*, Institute of Child Welfare Monograph Series No. 4 (Minneapolis: University of Minnesota Press, 1930).

[21]Harris Winitz, "Language Skills of Male and Female Kindergarten Children," *Journal of Speech and Hearing Disorders*, 2:377–385, December, 1959.

[22]Educational Policies Commission, "Universal Opportunity for Early Childhood Education," *NEA Journal*, November, 1966, pp. 8–10.

Head Start program. The Head Start project has sought to expand early childhood education to include children of the lower socio-economic classes. Programs developed at the local level have included free play, language development activities, efforts to build children's self-concept, and experiences to foster cognitive development, creative endeavor, and physical development. The success of Head Start in achieving the goals sought in early childhood education is debatable. A major report criticized the program,[23] yet many teachers and others who have worked in it feel that large numbers of children have overcome many of the effects of an earlier deprivation.[24]

In addition to the involvement of the federal government in the education of young children, there has been a rise in the number of private nursery schools, day care centers, and private and public school kindergartens. With such increase has come attention to teaching practices and other means for achieving the various goals. The educational literature reports on such programs as "The Infant School," "The Bereiter-Englemann Approach," the Montessori "methods and materials," and "The Nimnicht Method."[25] These programs vary greatly —from the informality of the adapted English infant school to the forceful and direct approach of Bereiter-Englemann—but they all reflect the new interest in providing schooling for four- and five-year-old children.

The language arts activities in the preschool provide the foundation for instruction in listening, reading, speaking, and writing in the school program. Children are introduced to literature, given opportunities to communicate with one another and with adults, helped to develop their abilities in visual and auditory discrimination, and provided with experiences which foster vocabulary and concept development and are basic to understanding the written word.

Language Arts
in the
Preschool

The program should be informal, yet organized and genuinely foundational. There should be much looking at and examining of books, pictures, and objects—and talking about them. Many stories should be read, poetry spoken, and language and manipulative games

[23]*The Impact of Head Start: An Evaluation of the Effects of Head Start Experiences on Children's Cognitive and Affective Development* (Washington, D. C.: Westinghouse Learning Corporation/Ohio University, Office of Economic Opportunity, March, 1969).

[24]William F. Brazziel, "Two Years of Head Start," *Phi Delta Kappan,* March, 1967.

[25]Brief descriptions of these are given in *The Grade Teacher,* December, 1969, pp. 51–61.

played. Talking should be further encouraged by many trips—to the corner, to the furnace room, to the bakery, etc.—and many activities, including the sharing of experiences the children have had outside of the classroom.

The language arts activities in the preschool—the nursery school, the Head Start class, the day care center—are further described in the sections which follow, since for many children the kindergarten is the first experience with organized instruction and kindergarten programs generally reflect the preschool objectives.

The Kindergarten Language Arts Emphasis

Most children enter the kindergarten reasonably well equipped to use language orally. They have talked with their families and friends, and through television, radio, and occasional movies they have heard much speech. They normally speak in sentences which are varied in structure. There are, however, wide differences in ability among these children—even if they have attended nursery school. The kindergarten program should fill many gaps in the children's experiences and should strengthen their skill in using language.

Developing Speaking Skills

Many children's speech at kindergarten entrance requires attention. Some have not developed enough flexibility in the articulatory mechanism to produce some sounds accurately and clearly. There are also instances of lisping, baby talk, and perhaps stammering. While much stammering is a normal condition—occurring when a child talks about something of which he has insufficient knowledge, when he lacks the necessary words, when the listener does not respond readily, or when an expression of disapproval is directed at him—it is of concern to the teacher, since it usually reflects particular home conditions and is a practice that is sometimes transmitted to other children in the class.

Kindergarten children enjoy playing with words and sounds, and the teacher can exploit this natural tendency to improve their ability to distinguish among sounds and to enunciate various sound combinations accurately. Children can make up rhymes and songs, make up and repeat nonsense syllables, invent new words, and appreciate and use the words in literature selections such as the "Dr. Dolittle" series or Kipling's "The Elephant's Child," Margaret Wise Brown's *Four Fur Feet,* Virginia Kahl's *The Perfect Pancake,* and Meindert De Jong's *The Last Little Cat.*

Other useful games and activities include:

1. Helping each child with the particular sounds he cannot say. Showing him how to position his lips and tongue to make the sound. Having him listen to the sound in jingles and rhymes and then practice it in easy, monosyllabic words.
2. Having the child say a word as slowly as possible, then as quickly as possible.
3. Making familiar animal sounds (cat, dog, kitten, duck, rooster, pig, etc.) and having children name the animals.
4. Having children imitate sounds (an airplane, a train, a clock, etc.).
5. Choral speaking of simple poetry and rhymes.
6. Arranging for one child or several to name and put objects on a flannel board as they are mentioned in a story which is being read or told.
7. Playing games requiring different types of voices: a young child's tiny voice, a father's big, deep voice, etc.
8. Providing opportunities for dramatic play and simple puppet shows.

The incidence of left-handedness is usually estimated in the current literature as ranging from two to eight percent of the population.[26] There is likely to be a higher percentage in the lower grades, with a falling off as children progress through school and are influenced by pressures for conformity. Teachers of an earlier day were greatly concerned with changing children from left- to right-handedness. For many children, particularly those with firmly established left-hand dominance, learning to write with the right hand was extremely difficult. Recently there has been much concern about the production of emotional upsets and possible speech defects if hand dominance is changed; that is, if a child who is accustomed to performing most tasks with his left hand is suddenly called upon by his teacher to perform a more difficult task than usual with his right hand.

Handedness

The question as to whether a baby is born with a predisposition to either left- or right-handedness has not been answered definitely. In most cases hand dominance is well established by the time the child reaches school age. The teacher certainly should be aware of the dominance of each child but should learn to regard preference for the left hand over the right as no more disturbing than differences in eye or

[26]Betty J. Wills, "Handedness" in *Encyclopedia of Educational Research,* p. 613; E. A. Enstrom ("The Extent of the Use of the Left Hand in Handwriting and the Determination of the Relative Efficiency of the Hand-Wrist-Arm-Paper Adjustments," *Dissertation Abstracts,* 17:1036–37, No. 5, 1957) reports from surveying the opinions of 10,000 teachers that the incidence of left-handedness is slightly over eleven percent.

hair coloring. It follows, too, that a left-hander should be as fluent and skillful in speaking as a right-hander of similar mental and physical endowments. Many cases of speech malfunction do occur, however, due principally either to *physiological* factors (these might be in the nature of a lesion, tumor, or other brain injury in the side of the brain opposite the dominant hand) or to *psychological* factors. Impatient, unscientific, and unsympathetic attempts to change a strong hand preference, as well as similar approaches to other problems of children, may result in mental confusion, instability, and loss of confidence, all of which may affect speech.

The left-handed child should have no more reason for a speech handicap due to physiological factors than would the right-handed child. As to the psychological factors, the story is somewhat different. In a right-handed society, being left-handed is a deviation from the norm. It is easy for a left-handed child to recognize this, and if he receives too much notice from parents, teachers, and classmates, emotional problems are likely to occur.[27] These problems, like any other emotional problem, whatever its cause, may lead to speech problems.

There has been much concern about creating speech defects by forced changes in hand dominance. Particular speech problems, such as stuttering, are most pronounced during the period of establishing dominance. These problems may possibly be caused by procedures used in helping a child establish hand dominance, particularly if the procedure focuses upon changing a dominance that is already present. It is most desirable for the child to develop a dominant handedness at as early an age as possible, since delay in accomplishing this may be a result of some deeper neurological inadequacy which may in itself affect speech.[28] The evidence still seems to agree with the conclusion drawn in 1931 by Ojemann that ". . . under ordinary conditions the danger of producing speech disturbance, after the speech habits have been formed, by training a left-handed child to write with the right hand, is very slight."[29] However, most authorities would not recommend a change where the dominance is strong, the speech habits are not fixed, or emotional problems are already present.

[27]Lawrence T. Dayhaw, "Guiding Handedness in the Development of the Child," *Education,* 74:196–199, 1953.
[28]Margaret M. Clark, *Teaching Left-Handed Children* (New York: Philosophical Library, Inc., 1959), p. 22.
[29]Ralph Ojemann, "Studies in Handedness: III. Relation of Handedness to Speech," *Journal of Educational Psychology,* 22:125, 1931.

Determining hand dominance should not be left to casual observation. Tests such as overarm and underarm throwing movements, putting pegs in holes, locking and unlocking a padlock, cutting with scissors along an irreglar line, winding cord onto a ball, and screwing and unscrewing a top on a bottle or jar, may be used. Eye dominance can be determined readily by rifle-sighting or by the hollow tube test. From such testing, over a period of several attempts with each item, dominance will generally be shown. Hildreth claims that a child ". . . should not be classed as definitely right- or left-handed unless he shows dominance in 75 percent or more of all observations made of his hand usage."[30] If a child has a wavering or weak dominance, he should be encouraged to use his right hand simply because it will be more convenient for him to do so.

The kindergarten environment should give the child much to talk about. In addition, the teacher must foster the spontaneity in expression that some children may lack. Related to spontaneity is vocabulary development. As a child's vocabulary grows and meanings associated with the experiences become fixed, his self-confidence in oral expression develops. A teacher can help by entering into children's conversations, offering friendly comments and suggestions, and giving a great deal of praise.

Fostering Expression and Vocabulary Growth

☐ **Activities**

The best ways to foster expression and help children to make vocabulary growth and learn new concepts are to provide opportunities for interesting experiences through the classroom and school environment and to encourage talking about them. Each day should present rich and varied special experiences in addition to the rhythm, singing, painting, talking, and playing activities of the classroom. Appealing audio and visual materials or the introduction of living things (plants and animals) into the room do much to stimulate language growth. In addition, children will enjoy and profit from visiting special rooms in the school, taking trips to interesting places in the neighborhood, or simply bringing objects to show to the teacher and their classmates.

The activities suggested below can also help a child to grow in language abilities:

[30]Gertrude Hildreth, *Readiness for School Beginners* (Yonkers-on-Hudson: World Book Company, 1950), p. 62.

1. The teacher can make a chart of pictures illustrating fruits, vegetables, furniture, animals, toys, numbers, colors, opposites, etc. The children classify, name, and describe each object.
2. Children may retell stories read by the teacher.
3. Games may be played with words. For example children may be told to walk, skip, sit, listen, hop, etc. Then an adverb is added and they are told to walk slowly, quickly, happily; sit quietly, lazily, sadly, etc.
4. Children may describe objects, each other, clothes, animals, etc.
5. Word games can also require listening and knowledge of concepts. For example, children can be directed to place an object in, on, under, beside, below, above, behind another object.

Developing Perception and Discrimination Abilities

Important in all areas of language learning are the abilities to perceive visual and auditory symbols accurately and to discriminate promptly and correctly among those which are similar in form or sound. All learning requires some ability to discriminate through recognition of likenesses and differences in form and shape, and for reading this ability must be developed to a fairly high degree. Likewise, learning depends upon ability to perceive and distinguish sounds. Learning through both reading and listening requires this ability.

Skill in perceiving and discriminating does not develop to the degree required for the most effective learning in a single stage. A person does not fail to have these abilities and then suddenly have them. Every child entering kindergarten has some ability in recognizing sounds and in telling which sound alike and which are different. Every child entering kindergarten, however, does not have these abilities developed to the degree that they may be developed and to the degree that he needs to make his learning the most effective and efficient.

Kindergarten teachers should continually present opportunities for children to practice perception and discrimination. The following are activities which will help develop the visual skills:

1. Sorting objects or pieces of paper according to shape (circles, squares, triangles, etc.).
2. Matching pieces of paper of different shapes to outlines of shapes drawn on the chalkboard.
3. Assembling form boards or simple puzzles.
4. Sorting according to size tag board objects of the same shape but different size.
5. Sorting pieces of paper of different colors, shapes, and sizes. Children should sort only according to one aspect (color, for instance) at first; later two, and finally all three, aspects may be combined.
6. Matching blocks or beads by size and shape.

Games can combine skills and meaningful interaction

7. Drawing geometric designs placed on the board by the teacher.
8. Telling in what respects objects or drawings are alike or different.
9. Discriminating between two letters of the alphabet or two words as they gain skill in the larger objects and form. The letters and words do not need to be named.

Abilities in auditory perception and discrimination may be developed by the following activities:

1. Showing the children objects which produce different sounds when struck (glass, box, desk, etc.). They close their eyes and try to tell which object was struck.
2. Playing games which call for simple directions.
3. Having children tell whether words rhyme.
4. Pronouncing pairs of words and having children tell whether they begin with the same sound.
5. Having children listen to music and march to various rhythms.
6. Having children listen to records which help teach sounds (see listing in Chapter 6).

Instructional Activities in the Kindergarten

A number of aspects of children's development which should receive attention in a kindergarten language arts program were discussed in the preceding pages. This section presents particular activities which should be included in the language arts curriculum of the kindergarten.

Sharing
Experiences

The child of five likes to talk about himself—things he has and things he has done. The extent to which children will "share" their experiences, however, varies from child to child and, for most children, from situation to situation. The following scale of children's ability to verbalize shows the variation that is possible and must be dealt with.[31]

1. No ideas clearly expressed. Talks very little or far too much. Frequently disorganized or even incoherent. May shrug shoulders, point to an object, or grimace without verbalizing.
2. More advanced than Level 1 but ideas limited and words may be unrelated to one another, inappropriate, incomprehensible, or too few to express an idea adequately.
3. Moderately clear in expression, but sometimes blocked or over-productive. May digress from the subject.
4. Uses words adequately for clear expression of ideas. Apparently says what he wants to say and usually does not talk too much or wander from the subject.
5. Goes beyond Level 4 in showing a desire and ability to include others in a conversational manner in what he has to say.

Children at the lower levels of this scale must receive much understanding and encouragement in the kindergarten—and usually special attention will have to continue into the first and possibly second grades. These children need the background building experiences of a rich kindergarten environment. The children higher on the scale can talk about their pets and their trips, and can bring toys and other objects to show and talk about.

Following
Instructions

Kindergarten children need to learn to follow instructions in order to function in the school setting in which instruction becomes more formalized. Skills needed for following instructions include those of listening, analyzing and seeking clarification of information, remem-

[31]Adapted from Marion Monroe and Bernice Rogers, *Foundations for Reading* (Chicago: Scott, Foresman and Company, 1964), pp. 36–37.

bering any sequence involved, and doing whatever the instructions call for. Teachers must remember that for many children both the school environment and the kinds of instructions that may be given are often puzzling, mysterious, and strange. Therefore, teaching children to follow instructions must be done gradually and without repressing children's curiosity and willingness to talk. A gentle voice, a definite signal for listening (such as a flick of the light switch), and clear and simple wording will help children learn.

All young children love to pretend. A little girl pretends she is "the mother," a boy pretends he is a truck driver or a pilot. Children also imitate animals—a pet dog's bark, the buzzing of a bee, the soaring of a bird. All such dramatic play is a part of children's growing up. It is a part of their life outside of school and will continue in school if it is encouraged and space and materials are provided. The kindergarten room should have blocks of various sizes; play furniture, cooking utensils and equipment, and toys to represent buses and airplanes; a puppet stage with paper bag and stick puppets; and other objects to use for buildings, roads, etc.

Dramatic Play

While dramatic play is essentially impulsive and an activity that the teacher should not direct, there are ways in which such play can provide a great deal of learning. Planning settings, changing settings, getting specific types of equipment or costumes, and considering the context of the activities are all subject to discussion by the group, including the teacher. Talking things over with children leads to much dramatic play, and to more talking while the children are playing.[32]

Storytelling in the kindergarten may include two types of stories— those told by the teacher to the class and those told by children to the teacher and the class. For the first type it is essential for the teacher to have a wide acquaintance with various types of stories. The teacher should select those that have strong appeal to kindergarten children and must know each one well enough to be able to feel the humor or other quality it may possess. He should be skilled in shortening stories and must be able to prepare children for listening to a particular kind of story. For the second type of story, that told by a child, the teacher

Storytelling

[32]Dramatic play and many of the other activities suggested in this section are also discussed in later chapters. Chapter 5, "Language Teaching in the Primary Grades," includes many teaching suggestions and language activities appropriate to the kindergarten. Sources for storytelling activities may be found at the end of Chapter 15.

should see that the child knows his story well before attempting to tell it. This can be determined by quietly questioning the child before he begins and by offering encouragement and suggestion. A story told by a child should be brief and can be one that he has heard the teacher tell.

Group Stories

Most teachers start the kindergarten day with a planning period in which the children are grouped informally around the teacher. He can use this time to have as many of the pupils as possible participate in talking over plans, discussion activities, and reviewing past actions. As the children begin to learn to stick to the point and to sit quietly for a few minutes, the teacher may write a "news" item on the board or on a chart or may ask the children to relate an event without writing it.

Creative Expression

A kindergarten child drew a picture showing the falling of leaves and then dictated to his teacher the following poem:[33]

> The leaves get heavy
> and fall off the tree.
> The stems of the leaves get heavy
> and fall off too.

In another kindergarten the children were suggesting titles for each other's paintings:[34]

> Two pictures in particular inspired picturesque language. For the first, these titles were suggested: "The Diamond," "Under the Sea," "Sea Shells," "Strange Things," "Funny Fishes." "Rainbows Under the Sea" was finally chosen, with the artist's approval. For the second, these: "Star-lighter," "Angel Queen," "In the Night," "Christmas Angel," and finally, "Bless the Tree," which was eventually chosen.

As these examples show, creative expression in the kindergarten is oral. The goal is not a finished poem or story but a real expression of the creative thinking of children. Such creativeness is dependent very largely upon two factors. These are (1) opportunity for experiences which lead to the learning of many new words and expressions to the extent that they are understood and can be used, and (2) provision for many occasions to be creative. These two factors, in a certain sense, represent the main objectives of the language program in all of the pri-

[33]Lynn Smith, 1955–56. Ella School, Marysville, California.
[34]*Communication, A Guide to the Teaching of Speaking and Writing* (Minneapolis: Minneapolis Public Schools, 1953), p. 19.

mary grades, whether evaluated in the long-term practical mastery of the language skills for use in later life, or in the short-term purpose of producing fluency and creativeness in these early years of the child's school life. From either standpoint, it is imperative that the kindergarten teacher follow the proper instructional techniques to attain these goals early in the child's life.

Beyond this point in the child's language experience the teacher's problem is one of coaxing and fanning into flame the small spark of creativeness that may have been generated in the few who are gifted with the necessary abilities and the imagination to express themselves creatively. Of equal importance, of course, is the provision of the fuel of rich experiences and the warm and friendly atmosphere in which the flame may burn unstifled.

Reading in the Kindergarten

The Harvard-Carnegie study of beginning reading practices throughout the United States showed that more than one-fourth of the school systems with kindergartens introduce reading to five-year-old children.[35] In addition, many teachers in school systems which do not have planned, sequential programs in reading in the kindergarten favored offering reading instruction to those children who appeared ready to undertake it. Further evidence of the increasing attention being given to reading in the kindergarten is provided by the experiment in the Denver Public Schools since 1960 and by the comments of a noted educator in describing visits to kindergartens. These comments included the following:[36]

> Tucked under a shelf we can find the picture readiness books and, just to make sure, the phonics booklets. The alphabet is easily viewed above the chalkboard, and wide-lined paper and crayons are ready for the children to use when they copy their names or letters or numbers.
>
> Soon the teacher will use the filmstrip projector to show a picture story, and later the children will re-create the story in their own words. Still later, they will copy it from the chalkboard and read it to the teacher, taking notice of words which are the same.

[35]Mary C. Austin, "Current Reading Practices in the United States" in *Teaching Young Children to Read,* Warren G. Cutts, editor (Washington: U. S. Government Printing Office, 1964).

[36]William D. Sheldon in "A Modern Reading Program for Young Children" (*Teaching Young Children to Read,* p. 31). See also the report on the Denver experiment by Joseph E. Brzeinski in the same publication.

Sources of the Kindergarten-Reading Interest

The age at which children should begin receiving instruction in reading has been a subject of controversy for many years. Until comparatively recently, however, the trend in the United States has been away from teaching reading to young children and, in fact, toward delaying entrance into school as a means of preventing formal instruction from beginning too early. A number of studies have shown, though, that children can be taught to read at an earlier age than the normal first-grade age. Other studies have shown that some children come to school with ability to read, though probably no more than about one percent of children will be able to do so at the beginning of the first grade unless they were given reading instruction in the kindergarten.[37]

Much of the current interest in this country in the teaching of reading in the kindergarten resulted from pressures on educators by the public in its concern (prompted by Sputnik I) with a possible educational lag. Some of this concern was seized upon by misinformed and uninformed critics of schools as a reason to find particular fault with the teaching of reading, including its readiness aspects. More importantly, however, the interest is a reflection of the concern of teachers with giving more than lip service to differences among children and a recognition that many kindergarten programs do not provide as much reading readiness (or readiness for other school learning) as they might with no harmful effects to the children. Ideally, any kindergarten should be able to accommodate the whole range of children and have a satisfying program for every child.

Kindergarten Reading Programs

The Denver experiment included reading activities consisting of these seven steps:[38]

1. Giving children practice in using something spoken to call to mind any word that could come next to make sense.
2. Giving children practice in listening for consonant sounds at the beginning of words spoken to teach what is meant by the beginning of a spoken word.
3. Giving children practice in distinguishing letter forms and learning letter names.
4. Giving children practice in using something spoken and the beginning sound clues to call to mind a word that is omitted.

[37]Dolores Durkin, "Early Readers—Reflections After Six Years of Research," *The Reading Teacher,* 18:3–7, October, 1964.
[38]Joseph E. Brzeinski, "Reading in the Kindergarten" in *Teaching Young Children to Read,* p. 52.

5. Teaching children the letter-sound associations for consonants.
6. Giving children practice in using together something spoken and the beginning consonant letter or letters to call to mind a word that is omitted.
7. Giving children practice in using together something spoken and the beginning consonant letter or letters in a printed word to decide what the word is.

Essentially, this is an oral-visual reading readiness program even though identified as a "beginning reading" one. The intent is undoubtedly to provide specific experiences related to the process of reading rather than the generalized experiences common to many kindergarten programs.

Other kindergarten reading programs are not described as clearly as the Denver program. It is highly probable, however, that many such programs approach the normal first-grade programs, including the emphasis upon "getting children into books" and the use of the typical ancillary materials.

The suggestions in the preceding sections of this chapter constitute pre-reading or readiness activities which should precede other activities more closely related to reading skills. More attention is given to these activities in Chapter 5.[39] At the kindergarten level, however, children must have opportunity to make auditory and visual discriminations and to develop understandings of opposites, relationships, sequence, and left-to-right progression. Perhaps most importantly, the kindergarten readiness program must be broadly conceived in order to care for the learning needs of different children and in recognition of the fact that readiness is a continuing process—with all elements of the program important to reading.

Reading Readiness Activities for the Kindergarten

Exercises for Thought and Action

1. What are some of the major socio-economic factors which seem to affect the child's linguistic progress during the preschool years?
2. What reasons would you advance for not attempting to change the handedness of a child after he reaches the age of school entry?
3. What factors should be considered in deciding to tell a story, rather than to read it, to kindergarten children?

[39]Reading instruction, including that directed at developing reading readiness, is discussed in Chapter 14.

4. Make a list of stories and poetry appropriate for reading to kindergarten children.
5. What would you do as a kindergarten teacher to help a shy "Level I" child talk?
6. Observe a portion of one day in a kindergarten. List the language activities you observe.
7. Make a collection of pictures suitable for use in the kindergarten.

Selected References

Bailey, Matilda, and others. *Language Learnings.* New York: American Book Company, 1960.

Brown, Roger. *Social Psychology.* New York: The Free Press, 1965.

Cutts, Warren G. (editor). *Teaching Young Children to Read.* Bulletin 1964, No. 19, Office of Education, U.S. Department of Health, Education, and Welfare. Washington: U.S. Government Printing Office, 1964.

Dawson, Mildred, and others. *Guiding Language Learning,* Second Edition. New York: Harcourt, Brace, and World, Inc., 1963, Chapter 10.

Frost, Joe L. *Early Childhood Education Rediscovered* (Readings). New York: Holt, Rinehart, and Winston, Inc., 1968.

Lambert, Hazel M. *Teaching the Kindergarten Child.* New York: Harcourt, Brace and Company, 1958.

Lenneberg, Eric H. *The Biological Foundations of Language.* New York: John Wiley & Sons, 1967.

Monroe, Marion, and Rogers, Bernice. *Foundations for Reading.* Chicago: Scott, Foresman and Company, 1964.

Morrison, Ida E., and Perry, Ida F. *Kindergarten-Primary Education.* New York: Henry Holt and Company, 1961.

Robison, Helen F., and Spodek, Bernard. *New Directions in the Kindergarten.* New York: Teachers College Press, Columbia University, 1965.

Todd, Vivian E., and Heffernan, Helen. *The Years Before School.* New York: The Macmillan Company, 1964.

Language Problems Of The
Societal Disadvantaged

4

INTRODUCTION

Increasingly teachers, school administrators, and society in general
are concerned with the educational needs of a large group of
children who have not received the economic and educational benefits
of the majority of their peers or who come to the schools from
cultures different from that of the prevailing "middle class."
These children have been labeled "disadvantaged," "culturally
deprived," "educationally different," "educationally and economically
deprived," "educationally deficient," and so on. As Havighurst has
said, "When we are confronted by a baffling phenomenon, our
first impulse is to name it."[1] The difficulty with such naming in this
case, however, is that any one of the names or labels does not really
describe all of the children who are the focus of this concern.[2]

Regardless of the fallacy in attempts to provide a degree of
homogeneity to the problem by attaching a label to it, there are
definite educational concerns allied with this group of children. It is
the purpose of this chapter to discuss many of these concerns,
particularly those which are related to instruction in the language arts,
and to suggest ways in which the school may help these children
to overcome the disadvantages they have that affect their
achievement in the program. The following areas are included:

1. Disadvantages and Deprivations
2. Language Development of the Disadvantaged
3. Language Characteristics of the Disadvantaged
4. The Teacher and the Disadvantaged Child
5. Dialects and Teaching Problems
6. Additional Teaching Suggestions
7. The Problem of the Bilingual Child

[1]Robert J. Havighurst, "The Educationally Difficult Student," *Bulletin of
the National Association of Secondary School Principals,* March, 1965, p. 110.

[2]Simply for the convenience of the reader and authors, the term "disadvantaged" will be used throughout this chapter.

An effort has been made throughout the chapter to base explanations and suggestions upon research evidence. While a considerable amount of such evidence is available, there are many differences in interpreting the observations made and the research completed, and therefore a great deal of controversy about what should be done in instruction.

Disadvantages and Deprivations

It is futile to look at the large group of children who have experienced many disadvantages and deprivations which may affect their learning in school as a homogeneous group. The concept of individual differences is not lost because children are poor and undernourished, speak a different dialect, live in an urban or a rural slum, grew up in an institution, or are members of a minority racial or ethnic group. Each child is an individual who has had certain advantages and certain disadvantages in life; each one reflects the environmental setting in which he has lived by his language, his behavior, and the values he holds. There are, however, certain social and economic factors which are the basis of many common problems these children have. These factors must be looked at if the problems they cause are to be overcome, and consideration must be given to both common and individual remedies that may be applied.

The Problem of the Disadvantaged
While the "disadvantaged" may be considered a "baffling phenomenon" and our concern with them a reflection of the social concerns of the day, children who have been disadvantaged in one way or another have made up a substantial portion of the school population since the inception of compulsory education. "Economically-, socially-, and educationally-disadvantaged children are not new to American society."[3] However, it is only recently that the schools, the government, and society in general have taken cognizance of the special needs and handicaps of these children. This awareness has resulted from three major causes: (1) increasing urbanization; (2) a proportionate decline in jobs available to those who do not possess the skills which are taught by the schools; and (3) a growing interaction among people because of the mobility they now possess and the instantaneous mass communication they can scarcely escape.

[3]B. Othanel Smith and others, *Teachers for the Real World* (Washington, D. C.: The American Association of Colleges for Teacher Education, 1969), p. 14.

Some forces in society have also begun to realize that the American school system itself complicates the problem and are looking for ways to change the system. The school system is predominantly controlled by business and professional people and labor leaders on boards of education, the majority of whom are white, economically self-sufficient to a large degree, believe in hard work, and value those things American society has always identified as part of the "good" life. They are neither rich nor poor and they somehow want their children to have greater opportunities than they themselves had. They are representatives of the large middle class in society. Teachers and administrators are also of this group, with many of them having struggled to attain this socio-economic status. Thus the school system is a predominantly middle-class oriented institution and one that principally directs its efforts at the majority race. Not only does it teach the values and ideals of the middle class and the conditions of life in the subculture growing from these, but too often it operates as if all the children were from the middle class. Perhaps all of this is inevitable, since the school system has long been a major integrating force in society in terms of the varied backgrounds of immigrants to this country. The more-or-less official ideology has been and continues to be one built upon the will of the majority.

Thus it is natural for many people to think that since education has always been a major road to social advancement and economic success in society, the achievements of the school in dealing in the past with the majority of immigrants' children could be repeated with the children of the poor and the minority racial groups. It is apparent, however, that this is not happening.[4] Perhaps changing the schools—the curriculum, attitudes, and techniques—will help, if such changes can actually be made and can be made in time. Perhaps the problem will only be solved in the larger society—in changing the attitudes, in remedying the conditions which foster poverty and prejudice, and in building a unity of concern and dedication to achieving genuine equalization of opportunity. More likely both will need to happen at the same time if today's disadvantaged are to be helped.

[4]One of many examples that could be cited—if any reader needs to go beyond his own observations—is the statement of Kenneth B. Clark in *Dark Ghetto* (Harper & Row, 1965, p. 124): "It is an ironic and tragic inversion of the purpose of education that Negro children in ghetto schools tend to lose ground in I.Q. as they proceed through the schools and to fall further and further behind the standard for their grade level in academic performance. The schools are presently damaging the children they exist to help."

Who Are the Children? Reams of paper and gallons of ink have been used in the preparation of articles and reports purporting to identify and describe the disadvantaged. Yet no one knows for sure who the disadvantaged are. Certainly, as was suggested earlier, no one label or list of characteristics describes all of the children who are disadvantaged in the school setting and for whom the school system fails partially or completely to provide help. Certainly, too, there is evidence to show that, generally speaking, all of the following groups are disadvantaged in our present society:[5]

1. Blacks, particularly those from the rural South who have migrated recently to the Northern industrial cities and those who are poor—whether they live in urban or rural areas—but all blacks, actually.
2. Poor whites of the South and the Appalachian mountain regions who live in those areas or who have migrated to Northern industrial cities.
3. Puerto Ricans who have migrated to Northern cities.
4. Mexicans who have migrated into the West and Middle West, and to some extent any person with a Spanish surname.
5. American Indians, particularly those living on reservations or in other rural areas.
6. European immigrants with a rural background, from Eastern and Southern Europe.
7. Migrant workers, of whatever race or nationality.

What Are the Disadvantages? The preceding section has suggested that two conditions—economic poverty and cultural difference—are the principal disadvantages with which the children we are concerned about must contend. Many of the children from the groups mentioned above also have to contend with difficult living conditions. (One must keep in mind, however, that some black children and some foreign-born or second-generation children may not come from poor homes or otherwise be "deprived" in an economic or cultural sense). Some of the most common difficulties which these children have to contend with are listed below.[6]

1. Living conditions which are usually crowded and family life that may be somewhat disorganized.
2. A high level of noise caused by outside conditions, a blaring TV, or simply the number of people living together.

[5]Based upon Robert J. Havighurst, "Who Are the Socially Disadvantaged?" *Journal of Negro Education,* Summer, 1964.

[6]For a discussion of these conditions see Harry L. Miller, *Education for the Disadvantaged* (New York: The Free Press, 1967), pp. 31–60.

3. Homes which may be sparsely furnished and with a noticeable absence of reading and "cultural" materials.
4. A family life in which there is no father living at home, but one in which other adults—e.g., a grandmother or an aunt—may be present.
5. Speech in the home which is a nonstandard dialect or sometimes of a language other than English.
6. Language directed toward the child is often minimal, in the form of commands, with few reasons or explanations given. Generally there is little talk between adults and children.

For some, these factors are largely responsible for the appearance of certain psychological and developmental patterns that are different from those of many middle-class children. They may also account for differences in behavior and cultural values. Of course, some of these conditions are faced by children who are generally not identified as disadvantaged. Children with no economic deprivation, no racial prejudice working against them, may live in disorganized homes in which parents bark orders (perhaps in "standard" four-letter words?). Children who have grown up in orphanages have also had to contend with similar factors, with corresponding psychological and developmental patterns emerging.

Every child must contend with the conditions of his environment. For the disadvantaged the difficulties are great and the effects with respect to his learning in school are particularly significant. While all of the following are not effects felt by all disadvantaged children, they do occur with such frequency that teachers must be cognizant of them.

1. The child learns to shut out noise, often developing habits of inattention and a shorter attention span.
2. The child's experiential background is different and perhaps limited in relation to places he has been and the variety of people and conditions he has met; thus his language development may be different from that of the majority of children or may even be curtailed.
3. The child does not develop concepts of time and space. His thinking is generally concerned with the present and the immediate, and his responses are often largely motoric.
4. The child does not learn to relate easily to adults or to look to them as models or as sources of information. The father-image is also weak in families where there is no father or where the mother is the dominant figure.[7]

[7]While the families of white disadvantaged are largely male dominated, the black family is generally matriarchal. See Herbert J. Gans, "The Negro Family: Reflections on the Moynihan Report," *Commonweal,* October 15, 1965, pp. 47–50.

5. The child may have a poor self-image since he is probably one of many and has received little individual attention, especially from adults.

Strengths of the Disadvantaged

The various generalizations listed in the preceding sections are based upon research and observation, and it is to be hoped that they will help schools—and individual teachers—to build programs which will help these children to overcome their disadvantages. But the difficulty with generalizing is pointed out by Watson, who says:[8]

> There may be relatively more fatherless homes in Harlem than Hackensack, but many Harlem children—probably most children —have both father and mother at home. Average reading scores may be low, but some disadvantaged children read voraciously. Not every pupil of Puerto Rican descent is alienated or truant or a discipline problem. Teachers work, not with averages, but with individuals, and the sociological data may or may not help to understand a particular child's needs.

Recent attention to the disadvantaged has led to statements of the positive as well as the negative characteristics of these children.[9] And it is certainly true that they are not lacking in experiences, in values, and in behavioral characteristics that should operate to their advantage. Children in many poor homes are forced by circumstances to develop a great deal of self-reliance. They need to look after younger sisters and brothers, to get meals for working mothers, and to get to places on their own initiative. They frequently have a great deal of practical knowledge about how to get along in their environment. They have learned much about cooperation and the value of mutual aid. They often have learned to value education highly through the urging of their families and through their own observation of conditions about them.

However, as Cuban points out, "It's easy to wax romantic about poverty and exaggerate its 'benefits.' "[10] It is important, then, for teachers to know about studies of the disadvantaged and the conditions which may foster learning problems. It is equally important for them

[8]Goodwin Watson, "A Critical Evaluation of the Yearbook, 1964," *Journal of Negro Education,* 33:343, Summer, 1964.

[9]For example, see Leon Eisenberg, "Strengths of the Inner City Child," *Baltimore Bulletin of Education,* 41:10–16, 1963–64 (Baltimore City Public Schools), and Eugene McCreary, "Some Positive Characteristics of Disadvantaged Learners and their Implications for Education" in *Knowing the Disadvantaged,* Staten W. Webster, editor (San Francisco: Chandler Publishing Company, 1966), pp. 47–52.

[10]Larry Cuban, *To Make a Difference, Teaching in the Inner City* (New York: The Free Press, 1970), p. 20.

to recognize that often schools have simply been ineffective in caring for the individual differences that exist among children generally. Certainly the disadvantaged children are particularly noticeable. But, "They come to school with a broad range of intelligence, aspirations, skill development, and behavior. They happen to be victimized, unfortunately, by poverty and racism."[11] This, more than anything else, signals their difference and their disadvantage.

Language Development of the Disadvantaged

Children who are economically, socially, and educationally disadvantaged in our society have been found to be particularly disadvantaged in the use of language for a number of reasons and in varying degrees. For example, the child who lives in an overcrowded home where everybody has to shout to be heard and where he is always told to shut up, the child who is left alone all day because his mother must work, the child who has nobody to talk to or listen to—each of these is missing the normal give-and-take important to his language and intellectual development as well as the social adjustment needed for success in schools and in society generally.[12] Often the language the child hears is not the standard English[13] of the schools and the verbal communication used is restricted to care for immediate, concrete concerns.[14] Even though the child speaks a dialect that is complete and systematic, the very nature of his environment is frequently not conducive to the development of language in the sense that a middle-class child's environment may be.

An over-crowded home, even if it is neat and clean—though the overcrowding and other factors often preclude this—is not likely to provide a great amount of stimulation for using language beyond that necessary for existence. In many homes there is a lack of variety in shapes and

Environmental Handicaps

---

[11]*Ibid.*, p. 22.

[12]San-su Lin, "Disadvantaged Student? Or Disadvantaged Teacher?" *English Journal*, 56:751–756, May, 1967.

[13]Standard English is a poorly-defined term used to refer to the dialect that has rather widespread acceptance as "the" prestigious or culturally valued form of English. Actually, it varies somewhat from one geographical region to another, but probably is as closely defined by the expression "TV English" as any other. The reader should realize that the use of both "standard" and "nonstandard" in this chapter, as well as in other sections of the book, is a matter of convenience rather than an acceptance of the implied dichotomy.

[14]Basil Bernstein, "Social Structure, Language, and Learning," *Educational Research*, 3:163–176, 1961.

textures, due to the limited number of furnishings. There are few books, pictures, drawing and writing materials, or commercially-made toys. *A program director in one slum area visited thirty-five homes in her area and found only one toy.*[15] True, the deprived child, like any middle-class child, may play with pots and pans and empty boxes, but even the number of these will be limited, and they may be the only playthings he has. For the middle-class teacher, it is virtually impossible to imagine the limitations in vocabulary and ability to verbalize of the child who has never possessed books, crayons, dolls, toy automobiles and trucks, building blocks, stuffed animals, or a pet of his own. When this child enters school, he will not be able to name, describe, compare, contrast, or relate objects in the manner of the middle-class child. He will be totally unfamiliar with many things well-known to the average middle-class child. He may never have had a story read to him, and he may never have seen anyone read a book.[16] He will be woefully unprepared for the verbal experiences in most classrooms.

Experiential Limitations
It is vital for the teacher to be aware of the extent to which the disadvantaged child's experiences have been limited—and will continue to be, unless special provision is made by the school. Not only has this child probably not enjoyed family excursions to the zoo or park, but he may never have traveled more than a few city blocks from his home. A high school teacher in a disadvantaged area of Bakersfield, California, reports that in organizing field trips for students, he discovered that 75 percent of these *high school* students had never been on a freeway, though Bakersfield is on one and is only 85 miles from Los Angeles.[17]

Even the migrant child has limited experience, for he is apt to see only one farm after another, with little varying except the crop that is grown; further, the fact that major highways now frequently bypass urban areas may mean that the child does not even pass through cities on his way from one job to another. The migrant child has the added deficit of attending one school after another, with no educational experience and no opportunity to get special help from the teacher, who

[15]"The Deprived Child: What They Learned About Children of Limited Advantages in New Haven, Connecticut; Dade County, Florida; Baltimore, Maryland," *Grade Teacher* 83:74–79, 180–184, September, 1965.

[16]The authors must comment with a feeling of distress that many parents who are not poor do not read to children or do not read themselves. Reports on book sales attest to the latter statement.

[17]Reported by Mr. James Engel, East Bakersfield High School, Bakersfield, California.

knows that he will soon be moving on and whose class may be swelled and materials strained by his presence.

Obviously, any experiential limitation will have a retardant effect upon vocabulary development and cognitive growth. And while it is true that the disadvantaged child will have had experiences the more economically and socially fortunate child has not had, the breadth and depth of experiences the middle-class child is likely to have had makes "experiential limitations" a valid term.

The deprived child's opportunities for interaction with adults are likely to be fewer than the average middle-class child's for three reasons: (1) the ratio of children to adults is usually greater; (2) parents are often too busy providing the daily necessities of life to be able to spend much time with their children; and (3) the background of parents has usually not oriented them toward the kind of parent-child interaction which encourages language growth and ability to conceptualize.

Deprivation of Adult-Child Interaction

For these reasons the disadvantaged child is denied one of the major sources of language experience, for it is the parent who usually gives the child names for objects and words to describe them; who answers and asks questions; who points out similarities, differences, and relationships; who corrects pronunciation and enunciation; who develops ideas of order and sequence, concepts vital to readiness for learning in school. In addition, the parent of a disadvantaged child generally does not serve as a model for the kind of speech which the child will encounter in school.

The child, of course, will not grow up mute; he will be perfectly able to communicate with siblings and peers—and in adequate and even colorful language. But the kinds of language experiences he has had will ordinarily not be those which will prepare him for success in school. His vocabulary will be restricted, his understanding of variant meanings will usually be inadequate, and his ability to speak or to comprehend standard English structures will be restricted.

The educational literature is replete with contradictory statements regarding verbal deprivation or the lack of such deprivation in the lives of disadvantaged children. Statements of such deprivations are generally made by social psychologists and teachers, while statements attesting to the verbal abilities of these children are made by linguists. For example, Newton says that the disadvantaged black child's language is characterized by:[18] (1) casual observance of standard inflec-

Verbal Impoverishment

[18]Eunice S. Newton, "The Culturally Deprived Child in Our Verbal Schools," *Journal of Negro Education,* 31:185, Spring, 1962.

tions; (2) simple, monosyllabic words; (3) frequently mispronounced words; (4) rare use of descriptive or qualifying terms; (5) the simple sentence or sentence fragment in both oral and written language.

On the other hand, Labov says in speaking of black children,[19]

> The concept of verbal deprivation has no basis in social reality; in fact, Negro children in the urban ghettos receive a great deal of verbal stimulation, hear more well-formed sentences than middle-class children, and participate fully in a highly verbal culture; they have the same basic vocabulary, possess the same capacity for conceptual learning, and use the same logic as anyone else who learns to speak and understand English.

The actual situation is probably somewhere between these two statements. Certainly all children learn a language, including those words that they need to use in their lives. These may or may not be monosyllabic, though short responses to questions and directions are likely to be made with words that are "simple," "basic," and phrased in fragments rather than in sentences. It seems highly unlikely that children hearing a nonstandard dialect will "hear more well-formed sentences" than will children who presumably hear a standard dialect, though of course the sentences of any dialect or any language may be well-formed for that dialect or language. It is probably equally inaccurate to say that there is "casual" observance of standard inflections when the dialect that has been learned does not include such inflections.

The school is a verbal school—perhaps too much so, but the fact remains that if it is to change, the change will be slow—and children must cope with that situation. Not to be able to do so is a disadvantage. And the evidence does seem to weigh rather heavily toward the conclusion that the disadvantaged child is more accustomed to learning "by doing and seeing rather than talking and hearing."[20] In addition, the dialect that he uses "is considered unacceptable by the teacher and the members of the prestigious group who use standard English."[21] Since there is little evidence (see Chapter 10) that teachers are becoming markedly more accepting of nonstandard usages, the child's divergent dialect must be regarded as a disadvantage, if not an impoverishment, as far as school is concerned.

[19]William Labov, "The Logic of Non-standard English." *Monograph Series on Languages and Linguistics*, No. 22, 1969. James E. Alatis, editor (Washington, D.C.: Georgetown University Press), pp. 1–43.

[20]Cuban, *To Make a Difference*, p. 107.

[21]Lin, "Disadvantaged Student?" p. 751.

Language Characteristics of the Disadvantaged

Language represents tremendous social power in any society. To paraphrase a common cliché, "language makes the man." In a society in which those in the mainstream speak one way and those who are outside of that mainstream speak another, the latter are handicapped or disadvantaged. Of course, one can argue that achieving middle-class standards, in language or whatever, is not a goal that should be held above all else, but the fact remains that economic gain, social mobility, and educational achievement are largely controlled by those who have those middle-class standards. Without doubt, one way to describe the disadvantaged child is to say he is someone who is not in a position to successfully achieve the goals established by this majority force in society.

Most Americans do not regard *themselves* as speaking a dialect.[22] Depending upon where they live, they think that someone who comes from the South or Brooklyn or the Midwest or Boston speaks a dialect. The speaker of the dialect may be considered quaint, conceited, uncultivated, parochial, or any number of other things, but he is noticed by those who do not live in his native region. Clearly most people recognize dialect differences and this recognition usually brings forth feelings or attitudes toward their speakers. By many a dialect is regarded as "a corrupt form of language"[23]—an attitude and lack of understanding that is particularly significant in dealing with the problems of the disadvantaged. Shuy says that there are at least three degrees of understanding of what dialects are. The first of these is that "a dialect is something spoken by a white-bearded old man in an out-of-the-way area."[24] The second is an awareness that we all speak a dialect of some sort, and the third is realizing that social layers exist within regional dialect areas. The latter is the important understanding for teachers concerned with the education of the disadvantaged to have. That is, they must realize that well-educated, partly-educated, and uneducated people all may speak a particular dialect, but that they speak different varieties of that dialect.

Dialects:
What They Are

[22]Much of the discussion in this section is based upon Roger W. Shuy, *Discovering American Dialects* (Champaign, Ill.: National Council of Teachers of English, 1967), 68 pp.

[23]Jean Malmstrom, "Dialects—Updated," *The Florida FL Reporter,* Vol. 7, No. 1, Spring/Summer, 1969, p. 47.

[24]Shuy, *American Dialects,* p. 3.

The speakers of a particular dialect may be set off from the speakers of other dialects by certain pronunciations they use, by the meanings attached to some words, by particular choices of words, and by grammatical forms. Most people know that different names are given to identical objects or conditions in different parts of the country:

> pop, soda, soft drink, soda pop, tonic
> corn-on-the-cob, sweet corn, roasting ears
> green beans, snap beans, string beans
> taxi, cab, hack
> bag, poke, sack, toot
> faucet, hydrant, spicket, spigot, tap
> turnpike, toll road, freeway, thruway, expressway

Differences in pronunciation show up when comparing, for example, the Midwesterner's "park the car" with the New Englander's "pahk the cah." Other words whose pronunciations are readily recognized as differing from one region to another are *creek, roof, wash, stomach, this, orange, hog,* and *greasy.*

Differences in grammar are shown in verb tenses, nouns, and word order. For example, some people use *dived* as the past tense of the verb *dive,* while others use *dove.* Some people may say *this is as far as I go;* others will say *this is all the farther I go.* In each case, the usage is "standard"—that is, used by educated people.

Dialects are accounted for by geographical and social differences.[25] Regional dialects have become established by the history of settlement of various immigrant groups, by patterns of population shifts (travel routes, industrialization in cities, prestige of certain cities, and the like), and by geographical conditions (barriers such as rivers and mountains).

Dialects of the Disadvantaged   Studies of dialects show that pronunciation differences may be more related to regions than to education or social class. To a lesser extent, the same is true for vocabulary differences. That is, the speakers of all

[25]Some linguists believe that black speakers of nonstandard English speak a common dialect that is not particularly related to social class or to geographical region. This is not a belief of all students of language, however, but in a sense it is related to the fact that many persons of a particular immigrant stock (Polish, for instance) will have many common features in their dialects, regardless of where they live or the social class to which they belong. For further discussion see William A. Stewart, "Continuity and Change in American Negro Dialects," *The Florida FL Reporter,* Vol. 6, No. 1 (Spring, 1968).

varieties of a particular dialect will generally pronounce many words in the same way (for example, Midland or Southern speakers of all education groups will say *ah'll*[26]) and use words which have the same meaning (e.g., speakers in some sections of the South may call a small stream a *bayou,* while Midwesterners will use *creek*). Thus, as far as the disadvantaged child is concerned, many of his pronunciations are merely reflections of the dialect of his region—a fact that teachers often do not, but should, recognize. The same is true for particular expressions he may use, but of course his vocabulary will be limited by the experiences he has had. As has been pointed out, the disadvantaged child will have a smaller vocabulary than one who has had wider opportunities.

In contrast with differences in pronunciation and vocabulary, differences in grammar are indices of the dialects spoken by the disadvantaged. The following indicate the principal types of grammatical differences:[27]

1. Absence of inflectional endings for noun plurals, noun genitives, third-singular present indicative, past tense, present participle, past participle
2. Analogical forms such as *hisself, theirselves* and the absolute genitives *ourn, yourn, hisn, hern,* and *theirn*
3. Double comparatives and superlatives, such as *more prettier, most lovingest*
4. Omission of the copula *be* with predicate nouns, predicate adjectives, present and past participles.
5. *Be* as a finite verb
6. Differences in the principal parts of verbs, such as *growed, drawed, taken* as a past tense, *rid* as the past participle of *ride, clum* or *clim* as the past tense or past participle of *climb.*

Although all of the characteristics of the language of the disadvantaged—the grammatical features indicated above or particular pronunciations or word usages—will not be present in the speech of any one child, the similarities are such that they should be known by a teacher and serve as the basis for the diagnosis of the language used by children in his classroom. For example, one group of teachers included the following in a listing of language patterns observed in the

[26]Shuy, *American Dialects,* p. 60.

[27]Raven I. McDavid, Jr., "The Sociology of Language," in *Linguistics in School Programs,* Albert H. Marckwardt, ed. The Sixty-ninth Yearbook of the National Society for the Study of Education, Part II (Chicago: University of Chicago Press, 1970), pp. 96–97.

speech of their school—which had a high ratio of disadvantaged pupils:[28]

He be absent ebryday.	Ain't Charlie room nine?
He be absent yistaday.	Me and momma is going to da stoe.
He be's sick.	He big.
He axt her.	Emma pull off her shoes.
How you know?	Da lady come pick me up.
Where he live?	I goes too.
Dey is got it.	How her go?

In another school the teacher and the students included the following in their listing of patterns heard:[29]

Donald he here.	You ain't give me the right change yesterday.
Keith he absent.	I bin seein' Gary last night.
He ain't hit me.	My grandpa done bin work hard all his life.
My sister name Debbie.	She come to school every day.
Debbie she nice.	She always be combing her hair.
She had three sister.	He ax me can I go.

These are simply examples of the speech that might be used by disadvantaged children. The number of nonstandard dialects is probably unknown, but Venezky identifies six (some are groups of dialects rather than single dialects) that a teacher might need to know in order to teach children who speak nonstandard English to read: Northern urban black, Southern Mountain (Appalachian), Spanish-American, American Indian, Hawaiian pidgin, Southern rural (black and white), and Acadian English.[30]

The Teacher and the Disadvantaged Child

A teacher has a particular responsibility to the disadvantaged child and to society because this child is in his class. The teaching methods he employs may not be very different from those used in teaching

[28]From *Language Patterns for the Culturally Disadvantaged* (mimeo), Edison Park Elementary School, Miami, Florida, 1965–1966.

[29]Reported by Mrs. Joan Fickett, linguist doing research in East High School, Buffalo, New York. Mrs. Fickett and her students call the language used "Merican."

[30]Richard L. Venezky, "Nonstandard Language and Reading," *Elementary English,* 47:334–345, March, 1970.

children who are considered nondisadvantaged or "normal" (as is discussed later), but it is vital for him to be sensitive to the needs and aspirations of the disadvantaged child and to the fact that the curriculum may not properly provide for this child's experiential background and cultural values.

While the self-image of every disadvantaged child is not a negative one, there is great danger that the positive aspects of his self-image may be damaged soon after he enters school. This is likely to happen even if his classmates are largely of his own race and/or socio-economic status, for he quickly comes to recognize that his language patterns, his values, his way of living are not those valued by the school or by the dominant middle class whose values it represents. It therefore becomes a vital task of the teacher—even while trying to make him aware of other language patterns and other values than his own—to strengthen his self-concept and make him feel that he is a valuable person who has something to contribute to the society of which he has not been a part. This is not an easy task, but it must be accomplished if the child is to achieve any measure of success in school instead of becoming more and more disoriented from all that it represents.

Accepting the Child

First, the teacher must examine his own values carefully. Does he have any racial bias, however submerged it may be? Does he really believe that each individual is of value, even if that person rejects his standards and beliefs? Does he feel in any way that he is "better" than the people of the subcultures with whom he is dealing, or that his values are "better" than theirs? It is highly unlikely, if he is honest, that he will find himself totally without bias or prejudice, yet children have a "sixth sense" which tells them whether one really likes them or not.

The next task is finding the worth of the children and learning to understand them. The teacher must learn to know the neighborhoods and the families in which they live. Schools would not keep cumulative records for children if it were not important to know something of their backgrounds, problems, and achievements. But for the lower-class child, simply checking the cumulative folder is not enough. The teacher must get to know and respect him as an individual and as a member of a family and a culture. It may help him to recognize why Sammy doesn't follow the lesson closely in class if he knows that the child comes to school regularly without breakfast or sleeps in a bed with four other children. Here the teacher works closely with the counselor and the social worker; however, he must not rely on them to furnish his attitudes and knowledge but must know his children himself.

All this does not imply that the teacher should attempt to replace the parent in the child's affection—or supply the image of an absent parent. He should not create an over-protective and permissive atmosphere; the child's background has in all probability not prepared him for this. In fact, Henderson warns that a teacher must guard against encouraging the child to develop what he calls the *deprived student syndrome;* that is, the feeling by the child that "all I have to do is say my old man came home drunk last night and I can get out of my work."[31]

This child has probably come from a home where, if he has been punished at all, the punishment has been quickly and physically administered. He thus will not be conditioned to protracted reasoning and explanation. Such procedures will likely be regarded as signs of weakness. This does not mean, however, that he will only understand physical punishment. Rather, the discipline of the teacher will be most effective if it is based upon firm management, strict adherence to class-developed rules, and consistent and fair treatment.[32] The emphasis should be upon the positive aspects of each child's behavior and participation. Punishment of the disadvantaged child should not be different from that given to any other child. Every child needs respect, understanding and a fair share of the teacher's time and attention. He does not need maudlin love and over-compensation for actual or supposed deprivations.

Motivating the Learner

Accepting the child and genuinely treating him as an individual of worth will do much toward maintaining or building a positive self-image. This positive direction may be furthered if the teacher shows acceptance of the cultural heritage of each child, including acceptance of his language heritage. This means more than simply not discouraging a child from speaking, from telling about his experiences and the things that are important to him. Efforts must be made to find ways in which his culture, language, or beliefs may contribute to the environment of the school room. This may require a great deal of ingenuity on the part of the teacher, although if he has made a real attempt to discover something about each of the children, the task will not be one of insurmountable difficulty. The Mexican child may help in the singing of a folk song by explaining what certain words mean; the Indian child may

[31]George Henderson. "Pupil Integration in Public Schools: Some Reflections," *Teachers College Record,* 67:276–281, January, 1966.
[32]Frank Reissman. *The Culturally Deprived Child* (New York: Harper and Brothers, 1962), p. 47.

be able to contribute something to the art class or to the history or geography lesson; the slum child may be able to contribute a colorful and unusual metaphor (even though he is unaware that it is one). By using the backgrounds of the children meaningfully, the teacher will help the individual child gain confidence and self-respect, while the entire class will gain both knowledge and a valuable lesson in the meaning of democracy.

Dialects and Teaching Problems

There are three basic approaches to the language problems of disadvantaged children (although there are persons who do not regard the language these children speak as constituting a problem). Shuy has identified and labeled these approaches as follows: (1) eradication, (2) biloquialism, and (3) nonstandard for standard speakers.[33] Eradication, of course, simply means doing away with the nonstandard dialect by substituting a standard one. Biloquialism really means *functional bidialectalism*. That is, there is no attempt made to have the child unlearn his home and neighborhood dialect, but he is taught a school or standard dialect as well. In addition to actually teaching the second dialect, the teacher has the objective of helping a child learn to switch dialects comfortably as the setting he is in changes. The third approach, like the first, is nearly self-explanatory: it advocates that those who speak a standard dialect should learn the nonstandard ones which they encounter either socially or vocationally.

Each of the basic approaches lends itself to a variety of procedures or treatments, the most commonly used of these being enrichment. The focus of this procedure is to surround the child with language experiences appropriate to his age and level of maturation.[34] The emphasis is upon encouraging the child to talk, with much use of conversation, storytelling, dramatic play activities, and group discussion. Many questions are asked, particularly ones which elicit more than a single word or a nod in answering, and the child is expected to use language in seeking to obtain desired goals. Further, he is exposed to seeing much language as well as hearing it.

Enrichment of Language Experiences

[33]Roger W. Shuy, "Bonnie and Clyde Tactics in English Teaching," *The Florida FL Reporter,* Vol. 7, No. 1, Spring/Summer, 1969, pp. 81–83, 160–161.
[34]See Chapters 5 and 7 for further suggestions for providing an enriched oral language program.

The objectives of this procedure are to make up deficiencies and help children to learn standard English through the many new language experiences. While much can be achieved by this approach, the disadvantaged child's lack of many types of experiences handicaps him in achieving the "catching up" required. This procedure is one that has traditionally been used in schools, and since it has not resulted in the kinds of gains hoped for, there is increasing feeling that more direct effort is needed.[35]

Standard English Drills A second procedure is more formal in nature and more specifically directed at speaking rather than at providing language experiences. The drill described by Bereiter and Engelmann is very intensive, is directed at forceful speaking of standard English, and permits no deviation.[36] The objective is the eradication of the nonstandard dialect.

There are many other programs, also structured and formal but usually less intensive, which are directed at teaching standard English through drill.[37] The following illustrates the kind of repetition of patterns of standard usage the children are required to make:[38]

She carry me home.
She takes me home.

He
John
Mrs. Rock   takes me home.
The teacher
Mother

You take me home.

They
The ladies   take me home.

Linguists have given much recent attention to drill or practice activities for teaching standard English by utilizing procedures which

[35]*Language Programs for the Disadvantaged.* The Report of the NCTE Task Force on Teaching English to the Disadvantaged, Richard Corbin and Muriel Crosby, co-chairmen (Champaign, Ill.: National Council of Teachers of English, 1965), pp. 72–73.

[36]Carl Bereiter and Siegfried Engelmann, *Teaching Disadvantaged Children in the Preschool* (Englewood Cliffs, N. J.: Prentice-Hall, Inc., 1966).

[37]For example: Marjorie B. Smiley, "Gateway English: Teaching English to Disadvantaged Students," *English Journal,* 54:265–274 (April, 1965); Charlotte K. Brooks, "Some Approaches to Teaching Standard English as a Second Language," *Elementary English,* 42:728–733 (November, 1964).

[38]*Language Patterns for the Culturally Disadvantaged,* p. 11.

were developed for teaching a second language. These procedures are more structured and more oriented to specific grammatical procedures than the above. For example, Slager includes these exercises:[39]

☐ **Repetition**

Teacher	Class or Pupil
Dick lives on a farm.	Dick lives on a farm.
He doesn't live in Fairfield.	He doesn't live in Fairfield.

☐ **Substitution**

Teacher	Class or Pupil
The Scotts don't live on a farm.	The Scotts don't live on a farm.
Mr. and Mrs. Scott	Mr. and Mrs. Scott don't live on a farm.
Tom Scott	Tom Scott doesn't live on a farm.

☐ **Completion**

She's doing the same thing she always does.
She's reading_____.

☐ **Transformation**

1. Change the affirmative to a negative:
   He lives on a farm. ⟶ He doesn't live on a farm.
2. Change the statement to a yes-no question:
   He lives on a farm. ⟶ Does he live on a farm?
3. Change the statement to a *wh* question:
   He lives on a farm. ⟶ Where does he live?
4. Add a tag question:
   He lives on a farm, ⟶ doesn't he?

It would appear that possibly the best approach to the problem should include a combination of the techniques outlined above. Certainly drill alone would become extremely tedious and boring, nor would it serve to enrich vocabulary to the desired extent or to broaden the experiential background of the child, except in a very limited way. On the other hand, the principle of "learning by doing" suggests that practice in actual use of standard sentence patterns should help children to learn to speak, read, and write more easily. Further, the short attention span of children in general—and of these children in particular—re-

A Combined Approach

[39]William R. Slager, "Effecting Dialect Change Through Oral Drill," *English Journal,* 56:1166–1176, November, 1967.

quires the introduction of as much variety as possible into the program. The sections which follow will suggest techniques for providing both enrichment and practice in a variety of ways.

Additional Teaching Suggestions

The teaching of disadvantaged children may not require unique skills, as does teaching the blind, since the handicap is not inherent in the children themselves but is placed upon them by the situations in which they live and the schools which they attend.[40] However, such teaching does require a great deal of sensitivity and a broad background of experience. Too, particular teaching attention must be given to specific needs, even though the suggestions for giving this attention are not unlike those in later chapters.

Nursery Schools — Since the limited nature of the experiential backgrounds of many children results in language and learning handicaps which prevent their optimum performance in the school situation, there is increased interest in instituting preschool programs as a compensatory measure. The belief that the nursery school is the place to start direct instruction is founded on two fundamental assumptions: (a) The development of skills for learning—such as listening, vocabulary, conceptualization—begins during the preschool years; therefore, the child whose environment has not fostered the growth of these skills is developmentally two to three years behind the middle-class child when he enters school. (b) The awareness that he is behind increases the negative character of the child's self-image, thus psychologically adding to the probability of failure in, and disorientation from, the school situation.

For these reasons federally aided Head Start programs have been developed in many key spots and individual school districts have set up their own preschool programs for the children of disadvantaged areas.[41] The basic objects of such programs are these:

1. To provide experiences which will aid in vocabulary development and in the building of concepts.
2. To provide experiences which will aid in the development of an understanding of relationships: temporal, spatial, cause-and-effect.

[40]Smith, *Teachers for the Real World,* p. 12.

[41]Descriptions of several such programs can be found in "The Deprived Child: What They Learned About Children of Limited Advantages in New Haven, Connecticut; Dade County, Florida; Baltimore, Maryland," *Grade Teacher,* 83:74–79, 180–184, September, 1965. See also Chapter 3.

3. To aid in social development.
4. To develop habits of neatness and cleanliness.
5. To foster the interest of the parents in the school and enlist their assistance in the child's educational development.
6. To prepare the child to use the adult as a source of information and assistance.

Such programs are not intended to copy the experiences the children will have in the regular school program, though certainly they will be similar in many ways to imaginative and progressive kindergartens. The principal objective will be to provide a wealth of experiences—even beyond those that most middle-class children may have had at home or with their families.

The beginning must be simple; the child cannot be taken from a sparsely furnished tenement or shack and plunged into a disconcerting array of experiences that will confuse and frighten him. A few ordinary toys can furnish the groundwork: building blocks, stuffed animals, toy automobiles, dolls. These will begin vocabulary building; conceptualizations of size, shape, relationships; and even the basis for arithmetical learnings. The block is *hard* and has *square* corners so it will not *bounce,* but the ball is made of *rubber* and it will bounce high. This block is *bigger* than that one; therefore, they cannot be placed side by side and another put on top of them. Miguel may play with the yellow car *first,* then Robert will be *second,* and Jackson *third;* tomorrow, Jackson may be first. Color should also be an important factor in the surroundings; decorations should be tasteful but bright and attractive. Children can learn the names of colors and the differences in shade and texture.

From the very beginning the teacher—as well as any adult assistants—gradually assumes the role of listener, helper, and information giver; the doll's arm breaks off and the adult repairs it; he supplies the names of objects and colors; he settles arguments and suggests behavior. As the children become accustomed to their surroundings, new elements may be introduced: crayons, pencils, paper, and picture books. This is their introduction to the materials for reading and writing; they must know many words before they can hope to read them, and certainly they cannot form letters without first making lines, circles, squares, and simple figures—the beginning steps for visual discrimination.

Auditory discrimination can be fostered, too, by nursery rhymes and songs and by the teacher's speech, which should always be clear and distinct, though not artificial. Listening habits can be improved and the attention span increased by the telling of interesting stories, especially with the assistance of hand puppets or other visual aids, and by games that involve questions and answers or responses to visual and verbal clues.

The introduction of a pet or pets for the class can be very productive. Responsibility, regard for routine, and the pride of ownership come from caring for a pet; perhaps even a visit to a pet shop, store, or zoo can be developed as a result of such an addition. Here, again, is the opportunity for vocabulary development, concept building, and observing relationships. The stuffed tiger is a toy, it is soft and furry, and it has buttons for eyes; the kitten looks like the tiger in many ways, but it is a different color and it may scratch if it is not handled gently; the real tiger in the zoo is much bigger than the kitten or the toy tiger, it lives in a cage, and it comes from a far-off place called India. Naturally the geography of India is not immediately introduced to the preschool child who has never been farther from home than this zoo, but a frame of reference has been established for future learning about India.

Many such experiences can be planned: the toy train or bus can lead to a visit to a nearby depot; trips to the beach, a supermarket, or a story hour in the local library will supply new words and concepts. It should be remembered, however, that trips should be short and simple—the four- and five-year-old is not ready for the canning factory or the automobile assembly plant.

The discovery of relationships and the learning of new language should also be actively encouraged by the teacher. The teacher must make a conscious effort to express simple relationships in a variety of ways so that the patterns may become familiar: *"After* the big hand reaches the top of the clock, we will go out to the playground"; *"If* you push the button, the light will go on"; "We will all hold hands and *then* we will dance around in a circle *while* we sing." Verb tenses and the difference between singular and plural may be illustrated in the same way.

It should be remembered, however, that the teacher is a *model,* not a policeman of the child's own speech. If Johnny says "Ain't got no crayon," the teacher may say to Mary "Johnny doesn't have a crayon. Could you let him use one of yours?" This should not be said in a tone that indicates disapproval of Johnny's way of speaking; it is merely a request for something Johnny needs. From this it is hoped that the child will become aware of language differences and the groundwork will be laid for more structured language activities, both those of speaking and of reading.

If the aid of parents can be enlisted, the chances that the child will accept the school are markedly greater. The parent represents whatever the child knows of security, and his support is invaluable—some nursery schools will not accept a child unless the parent agrees to assist in the school at least a few hours per week. They even provide babysitting facilities so that this requirement will not be a financial barrier. Parents can keep materials in order and distribute them, repair broken toys, supervise field trips, etc. Their greatest benefit, of course, is in serving as a link between the child and the school, and if they can be brought to see that the school is truly helping the children, they may even buy a few inexpensive books or see that the child has crayons or pencils at home. Once the parent becomes interested in the child's school experience, he himself may wish to attend night classes, which are often set up as a corollary to the nursery school.

No course of study will fit all preschool programs, even those in the same city; however, a few guidelines, based on the preceding discussion, can be suggested:

1. The program should fit the particular needs of the children involved. Mexican children will not need the same experiences as Indian children, nor slum children the same as rural ones.
2. The success of the program depends upon acceptance of and respect for the child, his family, and his background.
3. Materials and experiences must be simple, the kind experienced by the average middle-class child in the normal course of events. Preschool children are not ready for complex situations.
4. Wherever possible, parents should be involved in the program.

When these criteria are met, the following results may be hoped for: better achievement on readiness tests and a better start in reading; greater language facility and, as a result, better achievement in all aspects of the school situation; fewer adjustment problems and better social adjustment by the children when they start school; a more positive self-image for the children and therefore more probability of success in school; and better home-school relations.

Since nursery or other preschools are still the exception rather than the rule, kindergarten training will probably need to begin with the kinds of materials, activities, and experiences suggested in the preceding section. This is equally true of the first grade when there is no kindergarten.

Kindergarten and Primary

The principal point in regard to the above is that when school-type educational experiences are provided for disadvantaged children (or any children), they must begin at the level of development or readiness for these experiences that the children have. Even after children have been given a great deal of compensatory and broadening experience, and perhaps have begun to learn a standard dialect, they will continue to need added attention from the school. Their home environments will continue to lack enough stimulating experiences, books and toys, and reinforcing adult models. All children must be prepared for the reading experience, of course; however, the disadvantaged child will need particular attention in certain areas.

□ Vocabulary Development

There must be continued planning for vocabulary development. A ride on the bus, a visit to the post office, even a walk around the block or the school yard can furnish opportunities for naming and describing objects, people, experiences, emotions. Storytelling and reading also add vocabulary, and the teacher may furnish synonyms, antonyms, or variant meanings for words.

□ Auditory Discrimination

The children need added practice in auditory discrimination and later in word attack skills. Adult models may have used slovenly speech and mispronunciation, and dialect differences may impose another barrier to reading readiness. The poor Southern child may never have heard the word *you* pronounced in "standard" English, the black child does not *hear* the difference between *kin* and *can* or *sit* and *set,* and the Mexican-American child is not accustomed to hearing the short *a.* This is not to suggest that the teacher should attempt to remove all traces of dialect from the child's speech—such a task would be impossible, in any case.

□ Word Forms, Tenses, and Sentence Patterns

The teacher should give much practice in use of singular and plural forms, verb tenses, and sentence patterns. Children love repetition; a game can be made of such practice, if it is not continued for so long that the children become inattentive. For example, the teacher may ask, "Who knows where the crayons are?" Several children will cry "Me!" The teacher responds, "Louis knows. Who else knows, Louis?" If Louis replies, "Lily know," the teacher repeats, "Yes, Lily knows. Who else knows, Lily?" This may be carried through several repetitions (not too many) and then the teacher may ask, "Who *will get* the crayons?"

This kind of practice may occur throughout the activities of the day, but it should always be purposeful; that is, the activity suggested above should not be initiated unless someone is actually going to get the crayons and they are going to be used by the class. It should also be noted that the teacher does *not* say "we don't say 'Lily *know*' "; he merely supplies the correct form in his repetition. In this child's environment, people do say "He know" or "They knows," but with constant repetition he will discover for himself that at school not only the teacher but also the people in the stories he hears and reads use a different pattern.

☐ **Perceiving Relationships**

Many opportunities for seeing relationships are necessary to prepare pupils for learning in all curricular areas and, especially, to familiarize them with the use of conjunctions, conjunctive adverbs, and prepositions in phrases and in compound and complex sentences. Naturally, the teacher will plan for such occasions, but many will arise from simple, everyday happenings. "What will happen *if* we open the window?" "Why does the rain come in the window *instead* of falling straight down?" "How does the rain feel?" "What does it look like?" "How do you feel *when* it rains?" "Do you feel the same way *when* the sun shines?" "What happens *after* it rains?" Field trips and planning the routine for the day furnish further opportunities for such conceptualizations.

☐ **Muscular Coordination**

The children need much practice in activities involving muscular coordination. Since it has been shown that disadvantaged children are more used to motoric learning than to conceptualization, the teacher might naturally assume that they will be average or even above average in the muscular skills needed for writing, but this is not true, since a lack of toys, writing instruments, and other manipulable objects in their environment may leave them with a deficiency in this area as well.

☐ **Listening Activities**

Listening activities need special attention. The teacher should set an example by listening to what the children say and should expect them to listen in return. Instructions and directions should be simple, short, and clear; perhaps until students learn to listen, they could be asked to repeat directions to be sure they understand them. Reading and telling interesting stories will also help develop listening habits since the children will want to pay attention. Records are an excellent device as there are no visual signals to convey meaning.

Games are both effective and fun; everyone has played the parlor game in which players whisper a message from one to the other and the last player says aloud what he has heard. This game could also be played with teams, the teams competing to see which can reproduce the original statement most accurately. Variations of the Traveler's Game can be used, too: instead of "I went on a trip and took——" the child may say something like "When I was on the playground, I saw ——," with the second child repeating the statement and adding an item, the third adding another, and so on. Children should play this game and others like it in small groups so they will not be too difficult.

In planning the kinds of activities needed to develop skills in the areas mentioned above, the teacher should keep in mind several important considerations.

1. The attention span of many of these children is short, so activities should be varied and not too long in duration. The types of activities which help to teach listening will also help develop a longer attention span, but in the primary grades a variety of activities during the day—or the use of short periods at different times of the day for activities of the same sort—will help to keep the children interested and favorably oriented toward school.

2. When planning the activities for each day, the teacher should list the purpose or purposes of each so that no skill area is neglected. Some activities may have only one primary goal; others may serve several purposes. Role playing, for example, is fascinating to all children and at the same time promotes a number of desirable ends. Listening is encouraged as the children hear a story they are going to enact, language development occurs as they decide what the characters are going to say, and each child's self-image may be improved when he gains the approval of the other students and the teacher for a job well done. Praise, of course, should be liberal.

3. Many of the textbooks on the market and in common use are oriented toward the middle-class child and toward middle-class values, though more are appearing which better fit the concepts and backgrounds of the disadvantaged child.[42] If these are not available, the

[42]These include *Bank Street Readers* (The Macmillan Company), *Chandler Language-Experience Readers* (International Textbook Company), *City Schools Reading Program* (Follett Publishing Company), *SRA Basic Reading Series* (Science Research Associates), and *Sounds of Language Series* (Holt, Rinehart and Winston, Inc.).

teacher may wish to write short sentences, stories, and sketches for the children to read, or to help them write their own stories. The stories can be developed on the chalkboard and then typed on a primary typewriter, duplicated, and made into booklets. The children will take great pride in reading stories which they have helped to write.

4. Many of the techniques used for language development with the ordinary class should, of course, be used, but it should be constantly kept in mind that the disadvantaged child will probably be retarded in most or all areas and will need extra effort.

If a child has received the kind of enrichment and assistance, as well as the sincere interest of his teachers, that has been suggested in the preceding pages, it is quite possible that he will be achieving at or near the level expected by the time he gets to the middle grades. If he has not received special assistance, he will probably be two or more years behind. However, even the child who is achieving at grade level will continue to need special enrichment and assistance, for the reasons mentioned in the preceding sections (see pages 86–90, 91–94). Whether the child is operating at or below grade level, there are a number of techniques which may prove helpful.

Middle Grades

1. Vocabulary building should continue at all levels. Whenever a new experience is to be entered upon, vocabulary pertaining to it should be introduced.

The teacher should search out interesting and unusual word origins, and, especially if some children are of other national origins, the polyglot nature of the English language can be stressed to help build a cultural bridge between them and the language of the school. The usual vocabulary-building activities, such as those concerned with prefixes, common roots, and word families, can also be included.

2. Experience building through field trips, records, movies, and reading by both students and teacher should continue to be a major part of the program. Unless they have had particularly enriched preschool and primary experiences, these children will react far more favorably to the concrete and immediate than to that which is entirely removed from their experience. As they begin to study history in social studies, for example, a visit to a museum is likely to be less stimulating for them than a trip to some local spot which can be connected with their study. Few areas are without places of this sort; there are Indian mounds, old forts, battlegrounds, mining camps, even cemeteries—all of which can help make the past seem real and vital.

With every class, of course, such activities should be thoroughly prepared for, and this is especially important with disadvantaged children. A story, lesson, or series of lessons should lay the groundwork before the trip is announced. Then the expected excursion should be planned and discussed for several days, introducing new words and concepts, listing definite purposes and possible questions to be answered, and stating expected outcomes and follow-up activities. Questions such as the following can be used as guides: (a) Where are we going? What connection has it with what we have been studying? What kind of people lived there and when? (b) What kinds of things will we see? What will they tell us about the people who lived (fought, worked) there? (c) What will we do with this information when we get back?

The answer to the third question should be as specific as possible; everyone should know what is to be expected of him. Perhaps the class will plan to write a group report, or individuals or groups will be assigned to find different kinds of information. This does not mean, naturally, that no unexpected activity may grow out of such a trip. If the children show a desire to write a story, enact a scene depicting a part of what they have seen, or extend the experience by another trip, such experiences can be more productive than those which were planned; however, such activities are more likely to grow from a carefully planned trip than from an unplanned one, for the children will return with more specific information.

Follow-up activities should occur immediately, while the experience is fresh in the children's minds, and opportunity should be provided for questions and clarification of words and concepts not understood. Activities may be both oral and written; some suggestions are the following:

> Individual reports, oral or written
> Group reports, oral or written
> Drawings and murals showing scenes which might have occurred in the place visited
> Poems written by individuals or the entire class
> A play written and enacted by the class

An excellent culminating activity is the preparation of a booklet containing stories, descriptions, or reports written by individual children or groups, pictures drawn by the children or cut from magazines, and perhaps a cover designed by the class. The booklets will be prized by the children as products of their own efforts, will remind them of what they have learned, can aid in showing parents the value of such trips, and can even be used for reading.

3. Experience charts and stories composed by teacher and/or students continue to be valuable devices, both for expression and for reading. The sixth grade child who is reading at second or third grade level is often shamed by the elementary nature of commercial materials; but he can be highly motivated to read a story he has dictated to the teacher or to a tape recorder (which perhaps he can operate by himself even if he is not successful in reading), and which has been typed and returned to him. Groups can compose short selections about things which are familiar to them, and construct questions for testing comprehension; these can be reproduced and exchanged—the students can even make up an entire booklet, to be used in conjunction with books provided by the school.

4. Oral usage drills in groups as well as individual practice with tape recorder or records will help to establish good usage habits or a second dialect. Drills should be frequent, but short in duration. Further practice in establishing usage habits and sentence patterns can be achieved through dramatization of stories read or told by the teacher.

5. Since these children are often reluctant readers, every effort should be made to provide interesting materials at appropriate levels of reading difficulty. The teacher should discover students' interests and activities, then get (from the library and any other available sources) a variety of reading material centered around these interests.[43]

6. It has been pointed out that one of the characteristics of the disadvantaged is their lack of a positive self-image. The teacher should use all his ingenuity to erase this lack. Bulletin board displays can be built around blacks who have achieved success; poems and stories can illustrate the importance of the farmer or laboring man (the teacher can show his own respect for honest labor by treating the school custodian with the same respect he gives to the principal); folk tales of other lands can emphasize the importance of all cultures; Latin-American songs can help the Mexican or Puerto Rican child to feel a part of an important culture.[44]

Holidays are excellent opportunities for introducing customs of other lands and showing how many of these customs have become a part of the American culture; for instance, the Mexican child will glow at the sight of a piñata at a Christmas party.

[43]See Chapter 15 for methods of discovering interests.

[44]Materials related to the contributions of the "disadvantaged" abound in journals today. For example, *Instructor* and *Grade Teacher* give many suggestions. The recent, "The Black Man's Contribution to Social Change" by Dolores Cooper (*Instructor,* March, 1969, pp. 95–105) is one very good article (with pictures).

The Problem of the Bilingual Child

If the language problems of the English-speaking disadvantaged child are sufficient to warrant additional help and concern for his progress in school, the handicap of the child who speaks little or no English requires equal concern. Though such children make up a small minority of the total number of the disadvantaged, there are enough of them to have caused a growing interest in the need for teaching English as a foreign language. The children may be newly arrived immigrants or members of one of several cultural groups who have clung to their own language and customs. Puerto Ricans, Anastasi points out, retain their own language to distinguish themselves from the black, whom they see being treated as a second-class citizen.[45] The Chinese revere their own cultural heritage and do not wish their children to grow up unaware of it. Whatever the reason, some children come to school not knowing a single word of English, and many know very little.

Language Disadvantages of the Bilingual

The language problems of the bilingual are not simple ones. But there are many bilingual children and the teacher in a metropolitan area may find half a dozen children in his class speaking several different foreign languages; one in southern California may have an entire class speaking nothing but Spanish. In either case, the primary task is clear: if these children are to go to American schools and become a part of the American culture, they must be taught to speak, read, and write English. Because their language background and culture are different and because they will probably continue to hear and speak their native tongue at home, the children are likely to have language disabilities greater but not unlike those of the disadvantaged child who speaks only nonstandard English. The bilingual child is likely to have a smaller total vocabulary than the native speaker of standard English because he is learning two languages instead of one. This vocabulary will be mixed, with an intermingling of words from both languages. His English sentences will be short, often incomplete, and seldom of compound or complex forms. Because of differences in the languages he is likely to make errors in inflection, verb tenses, and uses of connectives, articles, and negative forms. Certainly he will tend to misuse idiomatic expression, since translations are apt to be made literally.[46]

[45] Anne Anastasi and Fernando A. Cordova, "Some Effects of Bilingualism Upon the Intelligence Test Performance of Puerto Rican Children in New York City," *Journal of Educational Psychology,* January, 1953, p. 3.

[46] J. Vernon Jensen, "Effects of Childhood Bilingualism," *Elementary English,* February, 1962, p. 135.

In addition to these disadvantages, the bilingual child has other problems. First, he will have difficulty with pronunciation and enunciation. For example, English is one of the few languages which has both the /ð/ (as in *they*) and the /θ/ (as in *thank*) phonemes; therefore, the child whose native language uses neither the /ð/ nor the /θ/ or only one of them will need to be shown the positions of the tongue and lips in forming these and other sounds not familiar to him and will need much practice in using them. Second, the child will need a great deal of practice and experience with the rhythmic patterns of English sentence structure. For these reasons he will need a special program, which has much in common with the language program of the English-speaking child but varies in kind and emphasis.

This program will, in general, follow the design of foreign-language programs in the elementary school. The order of introduction for all items of instruction is *listening, speaking, reading, writing*. The listening and speaking should occupy most or all of the first year, with constant repetition of speech patterns until they become automatic. The reading of words should not be introduced until the children are completely familiar with intonation and sentence patterns and have built up sufficient vocabulary, so that reading does not become a frustrating experience for them.

Words should always be introduced in the kinds of patterns in which they are commonly used, not in isolation. The teacher pronounces the pattern and shows how the word is formed, if necessary; then the children repeat the pattern together and singly until it is familiar. A good starting point is with phrases of greeting: "Hello," "My name is Mr. Barton. What is your name?" The children may make a game of this, greeting each other with "My name is Jose. What is your name?" The answer is not simply "Maria," but rather "My name is Maria." Later, the progression is made to "Is your name Maria?" with the answer, "No, my name is not Maria," or "Yes, my name is Maria." Activities should be varied so that the children do not tire of them, and practice periods should be short. Songs, games, dialogs, storytelling—all these may add variety and provide opportunities for learning. Audio-visual aids should be plentiful, too; records, pictures, three-dimensional figures, puppets, and objects that they can handle and name are excellent for getting the children to respond. They should be chosen carefully; for example, pictures should not show so many different things that they are confusing. They should picture clearly identifiable objects and should be attractively mounted.

Ideas should always be presented as clearly as possible. For instance, the teacher may show a ball, saying, "This is a ball." Then perhaps a second and even a third ball may be shown, each with the repetition of the statement, "This is a ball." He may then proceed to asking the children "What is this?" When they have practiced answering "It is a ball," the next step may take place. The concept of size could be introduced, using the phrases "a big ball" and "a little ball," with appropriate gestures accompanying the presentation, and questions and answers following. *Question:* "Is this a big ball?" *Answer:* "No, it is not a big ball," or "Yes, it is a big ball."

When the pattern has been established by the teacher-led question-and-answer period, the children may question one another. Many kinds of word games can be devised. The names of colors can be learned with the use of colored cards which the children exchange upon request. A "pretend" grocery store may be set up in which children practice asking for various food items. The teacher may tell stories, using a flannel board and simple figures to illustrate the events. All these activities must be planned and prepared with new words and concepts always being introduced singly and in orderly sequence. And constant repetition and practice should accompany each new concept or pattern until responses can be supplied automatically and without conscious thought.[47]

The Role of
the Teacher

The success of any program for non-English-speaking or bilingual students depends in large measure on the teacher. Like any good teacher, he must be genuinely fond of his students and interested in their welfare, but more specific qualifications are equally important. Ideally, the teacher should know the native language of the children in the class so that he can recognize possible trouble spots and make the children feel less strange in their new surroundings by speaking to them in their own tongue. If he does not know the language, he should familiarize himself with its structural and pronunciation patterns—again for the purpose of identifying possible "trouble spots." He should also know and respect the culture of his students and be familiar with its customs. This will help him to understand his students and will give him points of reference in introducing the students to the school culture. The teacher must remember that his purpose is to introduce the children to a new language and culture, *not* to erase the old. The new ones are not better; they are simply different. Particularly in the middle grades,

[47]Many suggestions for songs and games, as well as a complete plan for telling a story to non-English-speaking students can be found in *Teaching Young Students English as a Foreign Language,* by Faye L. Bumpass (New York: American Book Company, 1963).

the bilingual child's self-concept can be strengthened by stories showing how members of his own culture have contributed to the American
heritage or to the world.

Many materials can and should be prepared by the teacher for use
with particular groups or in particular situations. The student or the
teacher can get ideas for constructing his own teaching aids from
commercial and other materials. These include the following:

Materials and Books

1. The *American English Series,* D. C. Heath and Company.
2. The *We Learn English Series,* American Book Company.
3. The *English for Today Series,* McGraw-Hill, Inc.
4. *The Michigan Oral Language Series,* Michigan Migrant Primary Inter-
   disciplinary Project, Michigan Department of Education, Ann Arbor.
5. A variety of texts, charts, tapes, and records, available through the
   Latin American Institute Press, 200 Park Avenue South, New York,
   New York.

Exercises for Thought and Action

1. Suppose that your district has neither nursery school nor kindergarten.
   As a primary teacher, what language activities would you plan for disadvantaged children?
2. Plan the telling of a story for non-English-speaking children at a grade
   level of your choice. Outline the entire procedure, including visual aids
   to be used.
3. Suggest ways in which you might help members of a particular minority group to improve their self-concept.
4. Work out a word game which could be used for vocabulary building at
   the kindergarten level.
5. Plan a field trip for the middle grades which would serve both the
   social studies and the language areas. Include both preparatory and
   follow-up activities.
6. Defend or refute the thesis that education for disadvantaged children
   should begin at three or four instead of five or six years of age.
7. List the ways in which the disadvantaged child is unready for ordinary
   reading activities and suggest ways for helping to develop readiness.

Selected References

American Education and the Search for Equal Opportunity. Educational
   Policies Commission of the National Education Association and the
   American Association of School Administrators. Washington, D.C.:
   NEA, 1965.

Anastasi, Anne, and Cordova, Fernando A. "Some Effects of Bilingualism upon the Intelligence Test Performance of Puerto Rican Children in New York City," *Journal of Educational Psychology,* 44 (January, 1953), pp. 1–19.

Bellack, Arno A., and others. *The Language of the Classroom.* New York: Teachers College Press, 1967.

Black, Millard H. "Characteristics of the Culturally Disadvantaged Child," *Reading Teacher,* 18 (March, 1965), pp. 465–470.

Booker, Simeon. *Black Man's America.* Englewood Cliffs, N.J.: Prentice-Hall, 1964.

Bumpass, Faye L. *Teaching Young Students English as a Foreign Language.* New York: American Book Company, 1963.

Chavez, Simon J., and Erickson, Twila Lee. "Teaching American Children from Spanish Speaking Homes," *Elementary School Journal,* 57 (January, 1957), pp. 198–203.

Corbin, Richard, and Crosby, Muriel. *Language Programs for the Disadvantaged.* Champaign, Illinois: National Council of Teachers of English, 1965.

Cuban, Larry. *To Make a Difference, Teaching in the Inner City.* New York: The Free Press, 1970.

Dale, Edgar. "Vocabulary Development of the Underprivileged Child," *Elementary English,* 42 (November, 1965), pp. 778–785.

Davis, Allison, *Social Class Influences upon Learning.* Cambridge: Harvard University Press, 1962.

Deutsch, Martin. "Some Psychological Aspects of Learning in the Disadvantaged," *Teachers College Record,* 67 (January, 1966), pp. 260–265.

―――――. *The Disadvantaged Child and the Learning Process: Some Social, Psychological, and Developmental Considerations.* Paper prepared for Ford Foundation Work Conference on Curriculum and Teaching in Depressed Urban Areas, Columbia University, New York, 1962.

Frank, Virginia. *New Curricular Materials and the Teaching of the Disadvantaged* (Project Report/One). Washington, D.C.: The NDEA National Institute for Advanced Study in Teaching Disadvantaged Youth, May, 1968.

Frost, Joe L., and Hawkes, Glenn R. (eds.). *The Disadvantaged Child.* Boston: Houghton Mifflin Company, 1966.

Green, William D. "Language and the Culturally Different," *English Journal,* 54 (November, 1965), pp. 724–733.

Jensen, J. Vernon: "Effects of Childhood Bilingualism," *Elementary English,* 39 (February, 1962), pp. 132–143, 358–366.

John, Vera P. "The Intellectual Development of Slum Children: Some Preliminary Findings," *American Journal of Orthopsychiatry,* 33 (October, 1963), pp. 813–822.

Johnson, Kenneth R. "Language Problems of Culturally Different Negro Students," *California English Journal,* 2 (Spring, 1966), pp. 28–33.

Kohl, Herbert. *36 Children*. New York: New American Library, 1968.

Kvaraceus, William C., and others. *Negro Self-Concept: Implications for School and Citizenship*. New York: McGraw-Hill, Inc., 1965.

Labov, William, and others. *A Study of the Non-Standard English of Negro and Puerto Rican Speakers in New York City*. Final Report, Cooperative Research Project No. 3288, Office of Education, Washington, D.C., 1968.

Lund, Betty Faye. "The Dilemma of the California Indian," *CTA Journal*, October, 1965, pp. 20–23.

Metz, F. Elizabeth. "Poverty, Early Language Deprivation, and Learning Ability," *Elementary English*, 43 (February, 1966), pp. 129–133.

Miller, Harry L. (ed.). *Education for the Disadvantaged*. New York: The Free Press, 1967.

Newton, Eunice S. "The Culturally Deprived Child in Our Verbal Schools," *Journal of Negro Education*, 31 (Spring, 1962), pp. 184–187.

_____. "Verbal Destitution: The Pivotal Barrier to Learning," *Journal of Negro Education*, 29 (Fall, 1960), pp. 497–499.

Passow, Harry. *Education in Depressed Areas*. New York: Teachers College Press, 1965.

Ponder, Eddie G. "Understanding the Language of the Culturally Disadvantaged Child," *Elementary English*, 42 (November, 1965), pp. 769–774.

Potter, Robert R. *Developing Original Materials in Reading*. Hunter College of the City of New York: Project English Curriculum Study Center, n.d.

Shuy, Roger W. (ed.). *Social Dialects and Language Learning*. Champaign, Ill.: National Council of Teachers of English, 1964.

Thompson, Hildegard. "Teaching English To Indian Children," *Elementary English*, 43 (April, 1966), pp. 333–340.

Webster, Staten (ed.). *The Disadvantaged Learner*. San Francisco: Chandler Publishing Company, 1966.

Witty, Paul A. (ed.). *The Educationally Retarded and Disadvantaged*. The Sixty-sixth Yearbook of the National Society for the Study of Education, Part I. Chicago: The University of Chicago Press, 1967.

The Foundation Program
Of The Primary Grades

5

INTRODUCTION

The language arts program of the primary grades continues the transitional program of the nursery school and kindergarten in bridging the gap between the child's first language learning activities and those which are more directly designed to give him genuine skill and assurance in communication. The program in the primary grades seeks also to build a firm foundation for the more direct and specific instruction he will receive in the middle and upper grades of the elementary school and beyond. The emphasis in the primary years should be first of all upon oral expression—developing spontaneity, fluency, and social awareness in speaking and skill and courtesy in listening. The program also emphasizes teaching children to read, helping them to discover the satisfaction to be gained from reading, and providing instruction in written expression.

This chapter extends the suggestions made in Chapter 2, provides detail about an effective primary language arts program, and introduces the expressional and receptive language teaching procedures and learning activities presented in later chapters. The following topics are discussed:

1. The Language Arts Focus for the Primary Grades
2. Activities for Developing Oral Expression
3. Helping Children with Listening
4. Written Expression in the Primary Grades
5. Beginning Reading Instruction

The teaching suggestions in this chapter are only some of those which are applicable for use with children in the primary grades. The teacher of the primary grades has children of a wide range of abilities, so consideration must also be given to techniques and procedures presented in later chapters.

The Language Arts Focus for the Primary Grades

The language arts are the core of the elementary school program, and nowhere is this fact more evident than in the primary grades. Good primary school education is that which focuses upon life-like, genuine needs for communication and provides for those needs by bringing forth from each child the verbal expression of his feelings and thoughts. However, even a lesser program would have much communication, much use of language. Language is a part of most activities and its use cannot be long denied. The experienced teacher of the primary grades is well aware of this fact and capitalizes upon it in recognition of the transitional and foundational nature of these years in every child's life. This capitalization leads to an effective program.

While due recognition must be given to the experiences each child has had prior to coming to school—experiences which have been significantly responsible for the learning he has acquired and the habits, attitudes, emotions, and interests which make up his personality—the building of further background is important to all children. Too often this provision for "intake" is neglected in the hurry to foster expression and teach children to read and write.[1] In this day of television and ease of travel, children have had a wider range of experiences than in the days of the horse and wagon (or even the days when only radio brought in the outside world), but each child has different experiences; classroom learning must be built on a foundation of common experience. Few children's "mental bank accounts" can be drawn on interminably for ideas on which to base the expressive aspects of the language program.

The Enrichment of Experiential Backgrounds

Children enter school with widely different capacity, maturity, and experience. These differences remain present throughout the entire school experience. Not only do children differ from each other but the same child may reveal surprising differences in readiness and interest in different fields of activity. He may love color and form and be skillful with his hands in art but show no interest in learning to read or to write. He may be relatively mature in his understanding vocabulary, yet immature in making certain speech sounds. He may have skill in telling a story and in holding an audience, yet speak in nonstandard

[1]The term *intake* has been used in the literature on language arts teaching primarily by Mildred Dawson. See, for example, *Guiding Language Learning* (New York: Harcourt, Brace and World, Inc., second edition, 1963).

ways. The language arts program, particularly in the primary grades, must recognize these individual differences at the outset and meet them with experiences designed to develop the skills, attitudes, and abilities the child will need to relate himself properly to the learning activities in the school curriculum.

An effective program is built into a framework of communication for genuine purposes. It is a continuing process of receiving ideas and information and expressing thoughts generated by them. Thus, no experiences can be "banked" interminably.

The "intake" aspect of the primary language arts program should include many opportunities for firsthand observation and participation —the bringing into the classroom of objects, live and inanimate; the taking of trips (even only into the school yard); the making of plans; the playing with toys and the using of equipment; and the working and playing together of small groups. It should include a classroom environment that is attractive and which fosters investigation as well as looking. It should include the sharing of knowledge and thoughts, by both teacher and pupils. Most of all, it should consist of the provision for many kinds of vicarious experiences—reading and telling stories, looking at picture books, viewing films and filmstrips, listening to recordings, listening to poetry, and reading and discussing textbooks.

The Objectives of Fostering Expression

Since the language arts program in the primary grades is informal and since children enter school with widely varying backgrounds of readiness and experience, it is impossible to assign specific skills for mastery at particular grade levels. The result is that all primary grade teachers emphasize much the same language skills, though with proper recognition of the development that has taken place. However, general objectives that are important to all phases of language learning—listening and reading as well as speaking and writing—must receive major attention. These general objectives are discussed in the paragraphs which follow:

☐ Spontaneity of Expression

At the top of any list of objectives in the teaching of language to young children should be the development of fluency and naturalness in expression. While the desire to express themselves is instinctive in children, quite often their willingness to do so must be encouraged by providing satisfying experiences which require expression. No matter how many ideas a child may have or how much language skill he may possess, there must be a desire to impart these ideas to others. The experiences must foster this desire, above all else. Beyond this, the key element in the development of fluency and spontaneity in expression is an abundance of experiences that will genuinely provide children with things to talk about; thus the need for the "intake" aspects of the program is clear.

□ Socialization

A second major objective is the socialization of the child. Each child, particularly at the kindergarten level and continuing into the first grade, is in every sense of the word an "individual." Many children at this level will be little interested in listening to others, in taking turns talking, or in trying to learn to feel comfortable while talking to an audience. In fact, some children will have had little social contact with other children and will know little about behavior appropriate to membership in a group.

The young child progresses through three distinct phases in his socialization that are discernible in his language: (1) egocentric speech, in which he talks to himself; (2) parallel speech in which several children playing together talk at the same time, no one either giving response or expecting it from another; (3) socialized speech, in which children speak and respond *to* one another. There is a great deal of overlap in these phases, of course, but the third phase needs to be reached before instruction in many aspects of the school program can be given. It is the task of the primary teacher to help children reach this phase—to guide them in learning to talk freely and easily, to listen courteously to others, and to acquire habits of using socially accepted phrases such as "thank you" and "excuse me." The children must learn to share ideas, as well as materials, and to develop a sense of responsibility, both as individuals and as members of groups.

□ Enunciation and Voice Control

A third objective is the development of ability to enunciate words properly and to achieve voice control. Baby talk, lisping, stuttering, and incomplete enunciation retard reading and writing learning and are definite handicaps in mastering language usage and acquiring skill and ease in speaking. Too, if they are allowed to persist, they may become definite sources of embarrassment. Indistinctness and an unpleasingly high voice are also major handicaps in developing ability and fluency in language. The early language program should work toward the development of an easy, pleasant manner in speaking, good voice control both in volume and tone, and accurate articulation and clear enunciation when speaking.

☐ Organization of Thought

An extremely important objective is the development of skill in the organization of ideas for expression. Organization is necessary to the effective presentation of ideas in sentences and paragraphs in oral as well as in written form. Early in his school experience the child should learn to arrange pictures in the correct order to tell a story. Later he should use sentences to relate a story or an experience in sequential order. This kind of organizing should be brief and simple in the early grades and gradually include more items and details as the child matures in his ability to arrange the thoughts and ideas into an organized plan, eliminate extraneous information, and relate new information to that already acquired.

☐ Standard Usage

The establishment of acceptable habits of language usage is an important objective of the language program in the primary grades as well as one of the major objectives throughout the school's program. Since many children come to school speaking dialects which include non-standard usages, it is important that the teacher begin at once to eliminate gross errors and socially handicapping usages.[2] Naturally, the teacher must not attempt to "correct" every item of usage that he regards as an "error," or the child may become overly self-conscious and grow fearful of expressing himself. Consequently, this objective—while important—must not receive a teacher's single or most prominent attention.

Other Basic Objectives   There are other objectives which the teacher must consider. Again, some children will have achieved these in whole or in part, but other children will not have made even a beginning—or so it may seem.

☐ Effective Listening

A fundamental factor in the achievement of several of the objectives identified above and those which follow is the skill a child has in listening effectively. Problems in enunciation and voice control are often traceable to children's not hearing how they, themselves, sound or how other persons sound. The problem of changing children's usage is affected by the success children have in accurately hearing the usage being taught. Of particular importance, too, is the role of listening in

[2]This is the point of view of the authors and is one held rather widely. As was suggested in Chapter 4, however, there are others whose views are contrary to this.

learning to read. Children not only must learn what to listen to and what to screen out as they concentrate on the printed page, but also must sharpen the skills needed to listen to and discriminate among differences in sounds. Most of all, children need to improve their listening abilities. They must learn to listen to directions, to information and ideas from other children, and to stories being read to them. They must listen to gain knowledge from virtually all communication activities.

☐ Visual Discrimination Skill

The teacher of young children must be concerned with their developing skill in focusing their eyes for the visual tasks they face in learning to read and write. The visual abilities of children in the early grades vary greatly, partly because of physical differences and partly because of the different experiences the children have had. Some children have developed habits of careful observation of details, while others have learned to react only to gross differences. Of course, a teacher cannot force physical development, but most children who have difficulty with the visual tasks called for in initial language learning activities simply need practice in moving from the gross visual discrimination tasks to those requiring the finer judgments of shape, size, place relationships, and arrangements necessary for reading.

☐ Rhythmic Movement and Creativity

Bodily movement and language expression are related—both provide for showing thoughts and feelings. It is very often through bodily movement that a child first expresses his creativity. As with other abilities that young children have, there is great variation in the control they have of their bodies and in the freedom and creativity they express with them. As was stated above, physical development cannot be speeded, but children can learn to use their bodies to the extent that their development permits. Thus the primary teacher gives attention to rhythmic activities, to play which calls for bodily movement and expression. In a like manner, creative expression, by both body and voice, is also encouraged.

☐ Vocabulary Development

Children enter the primary grades understanding a considerable number of words, but an enlivened classroom will evoke new interest in vocabulary. There is evidence that children in the first grade may have an understanding of as many as 24,000 words.[3] However, this does

[3]Mary K. Smith, "Measurement of the Size of General English Vocabulary through the Elementary Grades and High School," *Genetic Psychology Monographs*, 24:311–345, 1941.

not mean that they can use nearly that many in their speaking and, of course, they have had little or no experience in writing words or in recognizing them in written forms. All the new activities of school add to the children's background of experiences and ideas. With each new experience must come new meanings and new words to describe and explain it. Since the knowledge of words and word meanings is essential in both the expressive and receptive aspects of language, vocabulary building is vitally important to the early language program. Therefore, all activities of the children should be utilized to furnish both additional words and new meanings for familiar words.

Growth in using language in both its receptive and expressive forms is a gradual and continuous process of development. Every primary teacher knows that some of the more able pupils in a given class may be far ahead of some pupils in the grade above who have been slower to develop—particularly in some areas of development. The teacher also knows that within a given class the rates of development of the children differ and that for each child there may be great variations in learning and development in different curricular areas. For this reason only the major language objectives for the primary grades' instructional program have been stated in this chapter; specific objectives are discussed in the chapters concerned with the teaching of oral expression, written expression, listening, spelling, and so forth. These specific objectives are appropriate teaching goals for the primary teacher as individual children or groups of children are ready for them, and many of the suggestions which follow in this chapter relate to these objectives.

Activities for Developing Oral Expression

The interest young children have in learning, the curiosity they express if given the opportunity, and their freedom from the inhibitions related to working with others that they will later develop make the providing of worthwhile language arts activities in the primary grades relatively easy. These activities may vary widely and no one listing should be regarded as conclusive. The sections which follow indicate the kinds of activities which interest children and which provide opportunities for achieving the objectives of the program.

Play and
Activity
Periods

The primary child spends more time each day playing informally and taking part in other informal activities outside of school than he does in the formal and informal school program. The school can do little about teaching language in situations over which it has no control or direction. However, it can do something about the informal language situations that are part of the school program. The play periods at school are usually under the direction of a teacher. The teacher thus has as great a responsibility for developing language attitudes and skills at those times as he has at any other time during the school day. The same responsibility holds for music, physical education, and art periods, which are much less formal than other parts of the program. Language habits are not produced in the language period alone; they must be taught at all times when the teacher is with the children.

This does not mean that he should stop a game to have a pupil change a particular usage. For one thing, in many instances it would be virtually impossible to call a halt to the activity because of the enthusiasm and spontaneity of the children. The teacher should, however, note the errors made, and whenever possible the child making the error as well. This can be done on a regular chart in many instances; in others the teacher will need to rely on his mental notes until such time as written notes can be made.

The noting of departures from standard usage, faults in sentence construction, and improprieties in the social use of language is of particular importance in the primary grades; since only a few things should be selected to receive instructional emphasis, they should be the most serious errors that are made with the greatest frequency by the majority of the children in a class.

Most improvement in primary children's use of language will come through the use of an audience situation, the children's imitation of the teacher, and incidental individual correction. Since spontaneity of expression is the first consideration in teaching language during these years, attempts at correction of errors in many language activities will have to be done in such ways as to avoid embarrassment to the child. Spontaneity will probably not be inhibited by suggestions for improvement that are given in a kindly and unobtrusive manner. For example, the teacher may remark on the side to Tom, "You *saw* it, Tom. Say, 'I *saw* the dog.' "

While children have many opportunities for using language in their informal activities, there must be an abundance of planned experiences for children to talk about. Naturally a teacher should stress firsthand observation and participation in all such activities. These planned observations and activities may take the form of field trips throughout the neighborhood and into the school yard or they may occur in the classroom or on the way to and from school. Children with very little

Personal Experience Activities

encouragement will bring butterflies, worms, Indian relics, rocks, and innumerable other objects into the classroom.

Some activities that will lead to subjects of conversation, reporting, and discussion may be found in nature. Such continuing projects as keeping an aquarium or terrarium, keeping indoor gardens of various kinds, caring for classroom pets, keeping weather charts, and helping in planning daily activities are all subjects interesting and real to children. Many other activities are seasonal in nature or occur as the subject matter of social studies changes throughout the year. The following is a representative list of opportunities for personal experiences that will lead to much more language activity:

1. Noting temperature differences in sunshine and shade.
2. Collecting leaves of different kinds.
3. Looking at frost under a magnifying glass.
4. Watching flying formations of birds.
5. Feeding birds in winter.
6. Collecting nuts, rocks, seeds, etc.
7. Observing soil erosion.
8. Planning and obtaining the contents for Junior Red Cross boxes.
9. Making puppets to play out a story.
10. Observing variations in growth of different seeds.
11. Caring for a classroom pet.
12. Daily observing of an ant house or a termite box.
13. Feeling various materials, such as velvet, fur, aluminum foil, and sand.
14. Tasting substances, such as berries, nuts, pickles.

Informal Conversing and Discussing

In the primary grades there are many times during the school day when children can use somewhat more formal language than they use in play activities or in telling about experiences. Particularly there are occasions for conversing about class activities, discussing things that have happened, or making plans for things to do. Many primary grade teachers start the day with a "Talking Time" in which matters of interest are discussed. Here is an opportunity to help children practice the amenities and skills of good conversation, and if the topic of interest goes beyond the conversational stage (see Chapter 7 for distinctions made between conversation and discussion), to help them stick to the point and to take turns in discussing.

Sometimes the morning "Talking Time" will take the form of a "newspaper" in which children report items of interest to the group and the teacher serves as the reporter by writing the news on the chalkboard. At such times teaching largely consists of making decisions as to content—whether what is being reported is of general interest, whether it is news or already known, and whether the item is appropriate for "their newspaper." Opportunity is also present at such a time for the teacher to provide individual incidental attention to language usage, to help a child phrase his thoughts and organize them in a systematic way, and to call attention to certain aspects of written language by saying such things as, "Who can tell me what I need to put at the end of this sentence?" "Tell us that again, but one sentence at a time," and, "That's a big word. What letter do you suppose it begins with?"

Throughout the school day there are many occasions for planning. Children and teacher must plan for games and activities on the playground, for cleaning up after the art period, for various daily housekeeping tasks, for activities for part of the group while the others are working with the teacher, and for numerous special events, excursions, and changes in the daily schedule. There are also many occasions for conversation and discussion that arise relative to extending and clarifying concepts. A new word met in a reading lesson may lead to a considerable exchange of ideas; some knowledge gained in science may need clarifying. The above are merely suggestive of the many opportunities in the primary program which utilize conversation and discussion and which may serve the teacher in guiding language development.

In the primary grades this oral language activity usually takes place under the names "Show and Tell" and "Sharing." Time provided for oral reporting gives each child opportunity to tell about things of interest to him, thus fostering the major objective of spontaneity of expression. The period also provides the teacher with an occasion to focus attention upon the expressional facility of each child and to help him with his most perplexing language problems.

Oral
Reporting

The "Show and Tell" activity has a very great advantage over simply "sharing" in that the child who is showing something—a new sweater, a turtle, a sea shell, a book—has something on which to direct his attention and thus keeps from thinking about himself and any hesitancy he may feel about talking. Then too, the act of showing something tends to make the oral expression organized; when something has been shown and features of it mentioned, there is no need to ramble on, as is sometimes the case with "sharing."

Not all "showing and telling" and "sharing" must be prefaced by the child first marching to the front of the room. Sharing may occur quite informally if the classroom climate is one of mutual respect. Children may show or share things with only a small group; they may show and share with only the teacher. The teacher, however, should strive continually to achieve with each child the objectives of spontaneity of expression, socialization, enunciation and voice control, correct usage, and organization of thought. Oral reporting which is not being directed at the achievement of one or more of these objectives should be avoided.

Principles for the primary teacher to observe in teaching oral reporting include the following:

1. The child should be encouraged to talk to the group, not to the teacher.
2. Each child should report on or show only one thing.
3. Questions and comments on the report should be encouraged.
4. Attention and good listening must be insisted upon. The teacher must listen too.
5. Adequate time should be provided for each child to report.
6. The scheduling of "turns" should not be too formalized; some scheduling is necessary, but special occasions should always be provided for.
7. As a child progresses in achieving spontaneity, greater attention may be given to usage and organization of the content of the expression.

It is generally a good idea not to interrupt a child when he is speaking. In order to correct an error in usage such as "I *seen* him last night," the teacher may say after the report is concluded, "We are glad you *saw* him, so you could tell us about it." More direct help may also be given to the child in private. After the reporting period the teacher may simply take the child aside and after pointing out positive aspects of his report, restate correctly the sentence in which the error occurred and have him repeat it several times. When this has been done, the child should then be complimented on his new achievement.

Storytelling

Storytelling in the primary grades includes (1) the telling of stories the child has heard (or read), (2) the relating of imaginative stories created by the child, and (3) the telling of stories derived from the child's personal experiences. In the third sense it is virtually identical to "Show and Tell" and "Sharing." Relating personal experiences represents for the younger child the most potent approach to more advanced forms of storytelling.

The development of good taste in literature is an objective of storytelling that should receive particular attention. Furthermore, storytelling gives the teacher an opportunity to serve as a model for the children in speaking. The stories should be told with interest and en-

Children enjoy sharing stories and pictures

thusiasm: The teacher should choose, from a wide acquaintance with various types of children's stories, those that are suitable to the backgrounds and interests of the class.[4]

After listening to a wide variety of stories and reproducing many of them in dramatic form, the children themselves will begin to tell stories they have read or heard. This activity helps to develop such desirable language skills as recalling events in proper sequence, using descriptive words and phrases, speaking loudly and distinctly enough for all to hear, and avoiding fragmentary and run-on sentences. In addition, it will help children learn to make changes in voice for emphasis or to express characterizations and to speak fluently and without distracting self-consciousness.

The creative quality of expression may appear early in various phases of the child's language development, and it will grow in extent

[4]See bibliography for suggestions of sources. See also Chapters 7 and 15.

and effectiveness if given encouragement. It must be developed through the use of familiar personal experiences. The child relives his experiences and interprets them if he has the opportunity to express his own thoughts and feelings. Jimmie is giving vent to personal feelings as he tells his fellow first-graders about George. He calls his story "The Bad Pussy":

> This cat is sort of grey and funny looking. He does silly things and gets in trouble. He's got a spool that he spins and tosses, and sometimes he sits in the big chair. One time he caught a mouse. Then what do you think he did? He ran away!
>
> Yesterday George put his paw in his milk and spilled it. Boy, did he get into trouble!

Jimmie has learned by the time he tells about George that a story has a title. In the kindergarten, Donald hasn't learned about titles, but his story has sequence and he's telling about something with which he is familiar:

> Once upon a time, on a rainy day, two cows were outside and the crops were all ready. The farmer picked his crops and took them to town to sell because he needed some money to buy a new horse. His old horse had a broken leg and was sleeping in the barn.

Some stories told by primary children are longer than others and more fanciful. Margaret May, a seven-year-old, has considerable storytelling ability. Her story reflects her experiences:

> There was a queen in a big castle. She had lots of things, but she wasn't happy. The king tried to make her happy, but she wouldn't be.
>
> One day he gave her some awfully pretty jewels. She said, "Thank you, but I'm still not a bit happy."
>
> So the king brought some Hawaiian girls to dance for her. But she didn't like that either.
>
> So the king brought some funny old clowns, too. They did silly things. But she didn't like that either.
>
> The king didn't know what to do.
>
> That night a fairy came with a map. She said there were some nice kids that had no homes and if the queen had some kids, she would be happy. [Margaret explained that the map showed where the children could be found.]
>
> The king brought the kids to the castle. Boy, when the queen saw all those kids she was so glad she clapped her hands.

Some children need much encouragement and stimulation to tell original stories or experiences. Creating a pleasant atmosphere in a room filled with things of interest to children is a major first step in leading them into relating their experiences. Having an object or pictures to show as they talk may also be very helpful to children in telling an original story.

Perhaps the most common form of storytelling in the lower grades is the retelling of stories which the children have been told, most often by the teacher. It is important to emphasize again that successful teaching of storytelling can best be accomplished informally. If possible, children should gather in an informal group, very often sitting on the floor, with evident expectancy that something pleasant is about to happen. There should be no feeling of a standardized way of doing things, no emphasis upon technicalities and memorization of details. The teacher should always remember that a child tells a story because he is enthusiastic about something interesting that he wishes to share with others, and that an audience listens to stories for the purpose of enjoyment.

Brief dramatizations of stories children read, hear, or tell should be an important part of the oral language program in the primary grades. Dramatization is a natural outgrowth of children's thinking about their particular interests, and they engage in it in their play, both at home and in school.[5]

Dramatization

Kindergarteners enjoy dramatizing Mother Goose Rhymes and short stories about animals. Often simple masks are used; this delights and encourages the shy child to take part. First show a filmstrip of Mother Goose or a familiar story. Talk about the story as it is presented. Reshow the filmstrip and let different children participate in describing what is happening on the screen.

At the first-grade level children are interested in choosing the characters whom they would like to represent. Many, of course, want to be the same character. This calls for taking turns, and in some cases, for dramatizing only a part of a story or doing the entire story in segments.[6]

[5]*Language Arts Guide for Yolo County* (Woodland, Calif.: County Superintendent of Schools, 1953), p. 7.
[6]*Learning Through Action* (Aberdeen, S. Dak.: Aberdeen City Schools, no date), p. 42.

The first grade children were reading a story, "The Funny House." They decided that they should play the story. After the characters were chosen, a house was constructed by placing a blanket over a heavy cord and this was dropped over the children. Each child played a role and one was chosen as the narrator.

Dramatization or less-structured dramatic play will not arise without opportunities for them to do so. As one state guide points out: "A lush environment with opportunities for varied experiences invites dramatic play. Trips, sensory experiences, manipulative materials, reading and listening to poetry and stories, and listening to selected radio programs encourage this form of expression. Encouraging children to use their imaginations will free them to 'use their wings.' A costume box adds to the fun and effectiveness of dramatic play. Teachers tell how donning a mask, throwing a rug or a skin over the head, or handling a simple property seems to help the child lose his identity and interpret the part he is playing with an unanticipated vigor and reality."[7]

Dramatization in the primary grades should not be done solely for the purpose of performing for parents or others. While occasionally a dramatization may be performed for an audience, the emphasis is upon the development of language skills that it provides and the pleasures it affords to the children who participate. At this level, the audience is the group itself; it is an audience with which the child is familiar and not one which may inhibit his expression. If a dramatization seems to be such that it would appeal to children in another grade or to parents, and if the idea of performing for others appeals to the children, it may be polished up to be presented. This does not mean learning lines and parroting them verbatim on cue, but rather getting the "feel" of the dramatization and a particular part. When children have the feel of what they are doing, it will go well and the interpolating and ad libbing will be normal and natural.

Speaking and Hearing Poetry

While most people enjoy the feeling of saying poetry and of hearing it spoken, this is particularly true of young children. They enjoy hearing their teacher read poetry about things with which they are familiar and poetry that stimulates the senses and stretches the imagination.

The teaching of poetry is discussed fully in Chapter 15 but special attention is given to it here because of its importance to the young child. Not only does he greatly enjoy poetry, but it is a valuable means

[7]*Language Arts for the Elementary Schools of Utah* (Salt Lake City: Utah State Department of Public Instruction, February, 1954), pp. 204–205.

of helping him to learn to use his language effectively. As May Hill Arbuthnot says in *Time for Poetry:*[8]

> Undeniably, poetry with its emphatic melody and rhythm has the power of evoking in its hearers strong sensory imagery and emotional responses. The happenings of everyday life are lifted out of the commonplace by the small perfect frame of words that poetry gives them. The child finds in verse what the adult finds—an exhilaration that comes from the compatibility between ideas and the movement of lines, and from the little shiver of delight that these qualities induce. More than any other type of literature, poetry trains the child's ears to the cadence of words and develops his sensitivity to the power and music of the English language.

Poetry is read to children to give them a feeling for our language, to help them appreciate that it may have rhythm and rhyme. Poetry, if carefully chosen and well read, teaches the child to listen carefully and appreciatively. It teaches him new words, new ways of saying things, and new ideas and feelings for his own expression.

One first grade teacher tells her children to close their eyes and listen carefully to see how many lovely things they can "see" as she reads this poem.[9]

> Of speckled eggs the birdies sing
> And nests among the trees
> The sailor sings of ropes and things
> In ships upon the seas.
> The children sing in far Japan
> The children sing in Spain
> The organ, with the organ man,
> Is singing in the rain.

The children then tell all the lovely things they saw. They tell them in words and phrases, but some will use sentences. The children may repeat the poem in unison with the teacher. Sometimes an individual child will say a line or two of the poem.

The qualities of poems that appeal to young children are similar to the qualities of stories they enjoy: plot, action, humor, mystery, and surprise. Young boys and girls imagine they are the child who says:[10]

[8]From *Time for Poetry,* May Hill Arbuthnot, ed. Copyright, 1951, by Scott, Foresman and Company, Chicago.

[9]From *Arts and Skills of Communication for Democracy's Children,* Vol. 1 (San Bernardino, Calif.: San Bernardino County Schools, no date), p. 72.

[10]From *The Poetry of Robert Frost,* edited by Edward Connery Lathem. Copyright 1939, © 1967, 1969 by Holt, Rinehart and Winston, Inc. Reprinted by permission of Holt, Rinehart and Winston, Inc.

I'm going out to fetch the little calf
That's standing by the mother. It's so young
It totters when she licks it with her tongue.
I shan't be gone long.—You come too.

Children like poems that paint pictures for them. For the children to see the pictures the poems paint, the poems must not be too far removed from their experiences. Not all young children see the subtle comparison in Carl Sandburg's "Fog" but those living near the ocean would see it.[11]

The fog comes
on little cat feet.
It sits looking
over harbor and city
on silent haunches
and then moves on.

In the early grades before facility with the mechanics of writing is developed, poems can be written as a joint effort of teacher and children. This example, from a first grade, describes how this may be done.

Teacher:	Isn't the snow beautiful? What's it like? Like—what?
Children (in turn):	Tissue paper stars, woolly sheep, little popcorn balls, millions of pearls, white angels flying, white ferns, fairies dancing, fuzzy—and so on.
Teacher (recording):	Tell me now in sentences what it looks like to you.
Pupil 1:	When the snow falls out of the sky it's kind of fuzzy.
Pupil 2:	The branches on the tree look wrapped in lamb's wool.

And so on. Later the children's impressions were put down in free verse as follows:[12]

A Snowy Day
One day we looked out of the window.
We saw the beautiful snow falling.
It fell like rain upon the drain.

---

[11]From *Chicago Poems* by Carl Sandburg. Copyright 1916 by Holt, Rinehart and Winston, Inc. Copyright 1944 by Carl Sandburg. Reprinted by permission of Holt, Rinehart and Winston, Inc.

The rain turned to snow.
It fell on the trees.
The snow was like diamonds.
The snow glistened and sparkled.
It sparkled like stars in the sky.
It looked like stars falling.
The trees were weary and cold.
And the snow covered them like a white blanket.
The snow was white as a polar bear.
It was white as a sheep's coat.
When people walked on the white snow
It s-cr-unched down.
We could make a snowman.
We could make a snow bunny.
I loved the snow when it fell.
It was so nice and white.

Children naturally love to play with words, to feel their power and rhythm, to experiment with using them. Not all of this needs to be done by the group. One kindergartener composed this "Slide Song" and his teacher wrote it for him:

Down, down
Yellow and brown.
Here comes someone down the slide!

Young children enjoy repeating poetry in unison. Group reading or choral speaking helps to improve voice quality and clear speech. It also provides opportunities for the shy to participate without embarrassment. A teacher has to read or repeat a poem to primary children only once or twice, allowing them to say as much as they can after each reading, and they will know it. Children sometimes enjoy solo parts instead of repeating the entire selection in unison.

Pussy-Cat, Pussy-Cat

All:	Pussy-cat, pussy-cat, where have you been?
Solo:	I've been to London to visit the queen.
All:	Pussy-cat, pussy-cat, what did you there?
Solo:	I frightened a little mouse under the chair.

Such a poem may be repeated several times with different children taking the solo part, boys taking the first line, girls the third.

[12]*Communication: A Guide To the Teaching of Speaking and Writing* (Minneapolis: Minneapolis Public Schools, 1953), p. 19.

Helping Children with Listening

The fact that every communicative act requires reception as well as expression should always be kept in mind by a teacher. The presence of an audience of one or more persons who are really desirous of hearing the expression is the most effective motivation possible. Most young children, while interested in themselves and what they are doing and saying, can be taught to listen and be good members of an audience.

Readiness for Listening Instruction

There are many activities which may be used quite naturally and informally in the primary grades to help children learn to listen effectively. A number of these were suggested in Chapter 3 (see page 77); others which may be used are the following:

1. Having the children say nursery rhymes in unison. Good ones to use, for example, are *Jack Be Nimble; Little Boy Blue; Hickory, Dickory, Dock.*
2. Giving oral directions, one step at a time, for cutting and folding paper or for drawing something.
3. Saying groups of words and asking the children to say the word that begins with a different sound from the others in the group. For example, *mice, fish, money, mouse; fire, fat, dog, fence.*
4. Having the children supply missing words in simple rhymes. For example: *We traveled far/in our new ———. He saw a cat/who was very ———.*
5. Talking about loud and soft sounds as they occur in activities, using the terms *louder* and *softer, loudest* and *softest.*

Being a Good Listener

Good audience behavior is a form of social courtesy which should be practiced and learned. Children themselves are interested in audience standards and readily cooperate in setting up proper standards of audience behavior. Such standards will emphasize listening courteously and attentively, expressing enjoyment and appreciation, avoiding interruption, and offering constructive criticism or asking intelligent questions.

One second grade developed these standards:

A Good Listener
Looks at the person talking
Keeps hands quiet
Doesn't talk
Thinks about what is said

An audience that feels a need for listening has the ability to do so effectively, and in having its need met will behave in the manner desired. The key is making certain that the activity is a genuinely communicative one.

Children can be helped to listen more effectively if the teacher gives attention to the following principles:

Teaching Principles

1. Readiness for the listening activity must be established. The stage must be set by deciding upon the purpose and relating the attainment of this purpose to previous learning and experience. The stage-setting phase may include creating a need to listen through the use of materials and situations which secure the pupils' attention. A teacher may gain attention for the stage setting by using puppets, charts, pictures, sudden noises, or an unusual action. Sometimes the stage may be set for listening simply by discussing what to listen for. Usually more prompting is necessary. The teacher may need to say, "How many of you have heard this story?" Or, "The words in this song are sung very fast. See if you can hear every word."

2. Appraisal of the speaking is necessary. Usually this may be in terms of purpose and may be in the form of questions—in the same manner as following the reading of a story—using such questions as, "Did you think that would happen? What did Bill tell us? Can you name the three games Mary said they played? What do you suppose would have happened if . . .?"

3. Recognition should be given to an audience which has listened effectively. Praise should be given the children when they have listened carefully and perceptively.

4. The teacher himself must demonstrate good listening and audience participation. In doing so it is necessary to avoid giving faked attention (which pupils easily detect), demanding pupil attention, and making repeated statements when such repetition is needless.

The teaching of listening is discussed more fully in Chapter 6 in connection with oral language activities in the elementary grades above the primary level; however, the following suggestions from one language guide suggest appropriate listening activities for the primary grades.[13]

Instructional Suggestions

[13]Selected from *Language Arts Curriculum Guide, K-6,* Jefferson County Public Schools, Lakewood, Colorado, 1960.

1. *Remembering action words.* After the children have listened to a story, have them list certain action words that help tell the story. For example, after one story the children may recall the following words and tell what they remember about the story: bark, running, rumbling, jumped, piled, raced, fell.
2. *Summarize a story.* The teacher reads a short story to the group and has the pupils retell the plot in one sentence. Use stories on the reading level of the group.
3. *What happens next?* Read aloud part of a story which is unknown to the pupils and have them suggest what will happen next.
4. *Telling back.* Read a story to the group and ask the children to retell it in their own words.
5. *Following directions.* The group may be divided into two or three teams. The teacher gives a series of directions, perhaps three or four specific things to do. A child is then selected from each group to carry out the directions. Each child who can follow the directions accurately and in order scores one point for his team.
6. *Listening to conversation.* Reading aloud the conversational parts of a story may help children to listen for dialogue or for characterizations.
7. *Taping a story.* If a tape recorder is available, children may be asked to record stories they have made up themselves. The class will then listen to the stories and ask questions.

Written Expression in the Primary Grades

Writing in the primary grades is a natural and gradual outgrowth of the oral language activities. A program in written expression is limited, however, by the children's lack of mastery of the mechanics of spelling and handwriting. It may be further limited if the fostering of spontaneity in oral expression has been neglected and if little attention has been given to helping children organize their thinking.

Limitation does not mean that there should be no program. It does mean that recognition must be given to the limitations and that the maturation of each child must be respected. It means, also, that in the beginning stages of the program the teacher should do the writing for the children. In addition, the program should seek to develop in children a recognition of how writing serves adults and how it can serve them; the desire to use writing to meet their needs, as well as for pleasure; the attitude that writing is a satisfying means of self-expression; the oral vocabulary and forms of spoken expression which later can be transferred into writing; and the visual-muscular coordination requisite for handwriting.

Writing should be taught when the children are ready to learn it; that is, when they have achieved the muscular coordination necessary for letter formation, when they feel a need to write their thoughts, and when they have the necessary emotional and mental maturity for learning the skills. Most children in the first grade have sufficient physical, mental, and emotional maturity to begin to learn some form of handwriting. There are exceptions, of course, and the child who is not ready should not be forced into writing. Children must be motivated by a need to write in order to learn handwriting. Therefore the presence or absence of this need is a major factor in deciding when handwriting should be introduced. Up to this point children have become accustomed to having their needs satisfied through the use of vocal language. Parents and teachers answer their questions and supply them with physical needs; this is satisfactory to most children. While there is interest in writing, developed from hearing about school, a real need to learn to write as a means of communication has often not been felt. The teacher, then, must create this need; otherwise neither the necessary readiness for learning the skill nor the mastery of the skill itself will be achieved.

Handwriting Instruction

Primary teachers correctly stress activities that aid in the development of the children's control of the larger muscular systems in their bodies. Teachers must also recognize that many of the smaller muscles, such as some of those required in writing, develop slowly and need time to mature. Accordingly, only general manual activities should be undertaken at first. For training in coordinating the movements of their hands and eyes, children may write with crayons or pencils with large soft leads.

Manuscript writing is generally the form recommended for teaching to children initially.[14] The following reasons are usually advanced in support of this practice:

1. Print script, or manuscript writing, is easier than cursive writing for the beginner to learn. Only simple curves and straight lines are required in the formation of letters.
2. The normal six-year-old lacks the motor coordination necessary to do connected, or cursive writing. This motor control develops later.
3. The formation of letters in manuscript writing is similar to the form of letters and words encountered in reading.
4. Print script is typically more legible than cursive writing.

[14]See Chapter 13 for samples of manuscript form and for teaching suggestions.

5. Primary pupils derive great satisfaction from their rapid progress in mastering manuscript writing.
6. The use of manuscript writing appears to contribute to achievement in reading and spelling.
7. Primary grade pupils using manuscript writing produce more and better written language products.

The introduction of cursive writing may properly take place in the latter part of the second grade or in the beginning of the third grade. The transfer from manuscript to cursive writing form can usually be made in six to ten weeks. The social utility of cursive writing is sufficient reason for its inclusion in the curriculum as soon as the children develop the necessary motor coordination to master it economically.

Spelling Instruction
Systematic instruction in spelling may begin in the first grade but more often begins in the second. In any case, instruction should not begin until the children are ready for it. The child who is interested in writing and is ready to do it feels the need to spell the words he wishes to use. As a child reaches this point, instruction in spelling should begin.

The first stage of the spelling program in the primary grades should consist of teaching children to listen accurately and to learn to discriminate among sounds. The second stage should be the relating of sounds to letters representing the sounds in words the children wish to use in their writing. A beginning program should also teach children the most commonly used words in writing as shown from research studies. In addition, a teacher should always help the beginning writer with his spelling by writing the word he needs on the board or, preferably, on a slip of paper for him to look at, copy, and retain for future use. Misspelled words that a child has not had an opportunity to learn may be pointed out, without criticism or penalty, in order to emphasize the importance of correct spelling.[15]

Written Expression as a Group Production
The first form of writing in the primary grades should be that in which the teacher is the scribe, with all the children helping to dictate what to write. In later first grade, the children can begin to work in groups, giving their ideas to the teacher for recording and organization. Later still the children can compose individually, with the teacher helping only in selecting words that are easy to write and in keeping the sentences short but continuing to do the writing.

Group composition is widely used in all of the primary grades. It

[15]See Chapter 12 for teaching suggestions.

gives the children experience in finding ways to express ideas in written work, and of course, in its beginning stages, satisfies the children's desire to express themselves while they are handicapped by lack of skill in the mechanics of writing.

☐ **Dictated Stories**

Stories dictated by the group usually precede or follow closely some group activity such as a trip, a film, a party, a visit from someone, or even a story, song, or something a little different that takes place in the classroom. If the class is planning a field trip, the teacher might think it wise to discuss class behavior before leaving. The suggestions again should be recorded by the teacher. These rules should guide the children on the trip; since they are written, they are likely to be remembered better than if they were just talked about. If the children are taking a trip to the dairy, they might have questions about cows, milk, and how the milk gets to their doorsteps in the mornings. The teacher might record their questions on chart paper.

> Where does milk come from?
> How does it get in the cartons?
> How does it get to the store?
> How does it get on our doorstep?

After the trip the children will have much rich experience to draw upon for writing activities. In the discussion following, they should find the answers to their questions and the teacher should record this information, perhaps in story form. In addition to finding answers to the initial questions, the children will probably learn about milking machines, pasteurization, and the sterilization of containers. Thus many new words and concepts will be learned and will be included in the group stories that are written.

If the children in the example cited above are early first-graders, the teacher probably would have to point out the need for writing down questions and possibly make suggestions as to what might be written; the children could then make selections from his suggestions. The same would be true in the composing of stories after the trip.

Children need guidance in the composition of group stories. If they are going to write about what they saw at the dairy, the teacher will usually guide the story's development with questions: "Where did we go first?" "Where are the cows kept?" "What does the milking machine do?" etc. In recording the children's responses and putting them into story form, the first writing may not be well organized. The teacher may need to say, "Let's go back over this and decide which sentences we need to keep in our story and how they should be arranged." Every effort should be made to make the final story the product of the children's thinking rather than of what the teacher wants, although with good guidance and stimulation of thinking the two may be the same.

Some attention should be paid in group writing, even from the very first productions, to the mechanical skills. As the teacher uses a capital letter, he may say, "I'm making a capital letter to begin my sentence." Later he may say, "How do I begin this sentence?" The same approach may be used with periods and other punctuation and with margins, position of title, and, with less direct attention, the spelling of words.

Sometimes the teacher may make copies of stories written and give one to each child so that he may put his name on it and identify it as "his" story. Primary children may be satisfied just to have the story read back to them or to read it themselves after it is written, but sometimes they want their own copies of a story such as this one:

> *Our Halloween Party*
> We had a Halloween party.
> We had cookies and milk
> Mothers sent the cookies.
> Thank you, Mothers.
> Some visitors came.
> We had fun!

Many group stories should be written on chart paper rather than on the chalkboard so that they may be kept hanging in the room. This practice will help to fix vocabulary, give opportunity for learning the spelling of words, and of course aid in the teaching of reading. When stories are duplicated as suggested above, or if the stories are copied by the children, many of these should also be kept and placed in story booklets.

☐ **Dictated Summaries and Reports**

When children have achieved some ability in using manuscript form and some knowledge of the uses of capitalization and punctuation, they will be ready to write directly from teacher dictation of a story, report, or summary. Generally this will occur in the mid-second grade. The first step is again one of group production. The teacher writes on the board the composition of the children. Attention is called to the spelling of words that are unfamiliar, to the punctuation needed to give the meaning desired, to the necessary capitalization, and to the order of the composition for clarity, exactness, and interest.

After the composition has been written it should be read over carefully by the teacher while the children listen for the organization of the story or report. Next, the sentences should be read one at a time while the children pay particular attention to spelling, punctuation, and capitalization. After this initial familiarization procedure is completed, the children should write each sentence—or possibly each phrase if a sentence is long—immediately after repeating the sentence read by the teacher. The teacher should inspect pupils' papers immediately after each sentence is written to be certain that it has been written accurately. When an error is found, it should be discussed with the pupil immediately and then corrected by him.

Within a few weeks after learning to write from this type of dictation, some of the children will be able to write a dictated story that they have not composed or seen. This procedure will not be suitable for use with all second-graders, but those who are capable should be given this type of training.

☐ Copying Letters, Notes, Invitations

In slightly more advanced group composition, particularly in the first and second grades, children should compose brief letters and notes, make lists, write invitations and news notices, and engage in other similar practical writing. Teacher guidance will be needed in selecting words that are easy to write and in keeping sentences short. Such compositions will be limited generally to three or four lines, but may be longer if required by the content. At the time of the children's copying the note, letter, or other composition, the teacher should rewrite the original copy, presenting it word by word or phrase by phrase as the children write. By doing this, the teacher is given another opportunity to call attention to punctuation, capitalization, paragraphing, and other similar writing skills.

Sometimes some individuality in the written message may be provided when the children are able to do the handwriting without close teacher guidance. For example, several messages may be suggested by the children as appropriate for "get-well" cards being sent to an absent classmate: "Get well soon," "Come back soon," "I miss you," "We miss you at school." From the suggestions which the teacher has written on the board the child may select the one he likes and write it on his card.

Copy work can take many forms, from copying a simple label or name in the kindergarten or early first grade to copying a report of possibly two short paragraphs in the second grade. In all copy work, the standard of work should be absolute accuracy in the reproduction.

Moving Toward Independent Writing

The first independent writing children do should be simple enough for successful completion. For example, a story of three lines can be composed by the group and written by the teacher, with the children copying and individually adding a fourth line, as in the following:

> *Our Trip*
> We visited the zoo.
> We went on the bus.
> It was fun riding that far.

Different children might add to this "We saw elephants and lions," "We had fun," "I liked the monkeys," and so on.

Other independent writing that may be done includes story titles, captions for pictures or charts, one word or phrase to complete a sentence, names, and numbers. The emphasis in such writing should be upon making the child think while minimizing the actual writing he has to do.

Throughout the period of transition to independent writing (which should vary from child to child) pupil dictation to the teacher and the copying of group productions should continue. Pupil dictation will ordinarily include experience stories, letters, news items, records of the weather, directions for plant or animal care, and rules for games. Copywork may include short poems, brief letters, Christmas and Valentine messages, sentences in booklets, labels, and short stories.

Opportunities for Independent Writing

Each school day brings many opportunities for different kinds of writing that are meaningful to pupils. Children enjoy writing about experiences they have had and making up stories, particularly if the classroom climate encourages such expression and if their achievements are recognized. There is need for them to write answers to questions, write short reports, and make various kinds of listings; such writing is a part of study activities they willingly do. Primary children also enjoy writing directions for doing various activities, keeping records of classroom events, making booklets, writing rhymes and jingles, and writing the many kinds of friendly letters and notes. The teaching of this writing is discussed fully in Chapter 8, with special attention to creative writing given in Chapter 9. It is important for the primary grades teacher, however, to remember that interest and success in writing begins in the primary grades. It is in the primary grades, too, that compositional skills are learned or not learned, setting the pattern for later writing.[16] Teachers should help children to organize their thinking before they begin writing, to develop sentence sense, and to regard writing as a communicative act which requires that the reader be considered.

Beginning Reading Instruction

Learning to read is a lifelong task, with development occurring in stages along a continuum from no reading ability to highly skilled maturity. The rate of progress along this continuum fluctuates in each person as well as varying from person to person. Each stage reached grows out of those that have preceded it and points toward those that are to follow. A successful reading program must recognize this process of learning to read. It must take into account the differences among pupils as to position upon the development continuum, the differences in speed in moving along it, and the factors which may cause a pupil to slow down or to accelerate. It must recognize the need for a continuing program of readiness for each pupil to keep him moving, to keep him learning.

Children come to school eager to learn to read. They expect to learn and their parents expect them to. While parents sometimes expect actual instruction in reading to begin at once, the children usually remain eager throughout the period of preparatory activities—unless it is extended beyond the point at which they are ready for the first formal stages of reading instruction.

Almost all children need a pre-reading program, though the character and length of the program should vary with the individual child and with the materials and methods available. The objectives suggested earlier in this chapter are important to each child in learning to read. Each child needs spontaneity and considerable fluency in oral expression before he encounters the printed word. Each child must make satisfactory social adjustment to the classroom, to working with other children and the teacher, to accepting direction, and to working independently upon assigned tasks. Further, every child must have an adequate experience background before instruction in reading begins.

---

[16]See Chapter 10 for suggestions for teaching compositional skills.

This background of experience must, of course, relate to the content of the materials they will meet in the initial reading activities.

As has been stated, children come to school eager to learn to read. However, this eagerness is not shared among all pupils equally, nor are all children equally familiar with what reading is. Until a child knows what reading is and what it does, he cannot begin to learn how to do it. For such children the teacher should provide opportunities for becoming aware of reading. This means that many stories should be read, and that reading should be made important in the classroom by having notices on the bulletin board, by using name cards, by displaying picture books, by having a pupil from the next grade level read to the children, and by the writing of experiences and news for teacher reading and "reading" by the pupils.

Activities for Developing Initial Readiness

There is no sharp line of demarcation between the beginning readiness program and initial experiences in reading. Many of the readiness activities which may be used in developing readiness for beginning reading need to be continued throughout the primary grades. The following activities are suggestive of many others that may be used by primary teachers:

1. For building experiential backgrounds a teacher may have field trips (including discussing them and writing about them), discuss the toys and other objects that children are encouraged to bring to school, show pictures and films, have children listen to stories, show picture books, and spend much time talking to children and listening to them talk about things they are interested in.

2. For developing verbal expression a teacher may have children describe objects and events; dramatize words like walked, ran, crept, etc.; put on puppet shows; talk about experiences; and discuss things that occur in the classroom. In addition, the teacher needs to provide a model for the pupils in his speech. Other activities include choral speaking, conversation time, dramatic play, and talking individually with children.

3. To build awareness of left-to-right progression, a teacher may have pupils arrange pictures in proper sequence in telling a story, react to directions which use "left" and "right," play games requiring left and right movements, and work exercises which require left-to-right eye movement. The teacher should also call attention to the left-to-right movement in his writing, in stories he reads, and in using pictures in storytelling—such as by placing them in left-to-right sequence on a flannelboard.

4. To develop good listening habits a teacher may develop standards with the children, establish purposes for listening experiences, and give directions which increase in complexity as the pupils' skills develop.

Using a flannelboard for reading preparation and storytelling.

5. For developing ability in auditory perception and discrimination, a teacher may have children distinguish among sounds—such as pencil tapping, striking a glass object, and dropping small objects. This kind of perception and discrimination activity should progress as rapidly as possible to listening for rhyming words, distinguishing likenesses and differences between beginning sounds of words, and associating sounds and letters.

6. For further ability in making visual discriminations, a teacher may have pupils note likenesses and differences among geometric shapes, pictures, and objects. As children show abilities in making these discriminations, a teacher should provide experiences in noting likenesses and differences among letters and words.

As children show signs of readiness to understand the meaning of written symbols, they should be introduced to actual reading. At first this should be the reading of experience charts and the "big books" commonly a part of basal reading series. This is followed by beginning books which recognize the importance of the readiness activities that

have preceded their use. The teaching of reading is discussed further
in Chapter 14.

1. Can you think of other objectives for the language arts program in the
   primary grades? What would you add? How should a teacher go about
   achieving this (or these)?
2. Discuss the need for developing the experiential backgrounds of pupils.
   Is the need as great today as in times before the advent of television,
   mobility of the population, etc.?
3. List objects which primary pupils might bring to the classroom for
   "Show and Tell."
4. What should be the teacher's attitude toward the correction of pupils'
   expressional errors?
5. Plan a flannelboard story for telling to primary children. Include the
   collecting or making of pictures you will need.
6. Collect stories written by primary children. Note the differences in
   children that these stories reflect.
7. Write a hypothetical experience story a pupil might dictate to you.
   Write it on chart paper. Keep in mind that it is a model for the children.
8. Evaluate the significance of the instructional activities in oral language outlined in this chapter. Discuss fully the three you consider
   most important.
9. Outline steps you as a teacher may take to make creative expression
   really productive in the primary grades.

Selected References

Applegate, Mauree. *Easy in English*. Evanston, Ill.: Row, Peterson and
Company, 1960.

Bailey, Matilda, and others. *Language Learnings*. New York: American
Book Company, 1960.

Bureau of Elementary Education, Department of Education. *Teachers
Guide to Education in Early Childhood*. Sacramento: California State
Department of Education, 1956.

Carrillo, Lawrence W. *Informal Reading-Readiness Experiences*. San Francisco: Chandler Publishing Company, 1964.

Cutts, Warren G. (editor). *Teaching Young Children to Read*. Washington, D.C.: U.S. Office of Education, Government Printing Office,
1964.

Dawson, Mildred A., and Newman, Georgianna C. *Language Teaching in
Kindergarten and the Early Primary Grades*. New York: Harcourt,
Brace and World, Inc., 1966, Chapter 5.

Gans, Roma, and others. *Teaching Young Children.* Yonkers-on-Hudson: World Book Company, 1952, Chapter 8.

Huey, J. Frances. *Teaching Primary Children.* New York: Holt, Rinehart and Winston, Inc., 1965.

Logan, Lillian M., and Logan, Virgil G. *A Dynamic Approach to Language Arts.* Toronto: McGraw-Hill Company of Canada, Limited, 1967, Chapters 1–3.

Morrison, Ida E., and Perry, Ida F. *Kindergarten-Primary Education.* New York: Henry Holt and Company, 1961.

Shane, Harold G.; Reddin, Mary E.; and Gillespie, Margaret C. *Beginning Language Arts Instruction with Children.* Columbus: Charles E. Merrill Books, Inc., 1961.

Strickland, Ruth G. *Guide for Teaching Language in Grades 1 and 2.* Boston: D. C. Heath and Company, 1962.

6

Developing Listening Skills

INTRODUCTION

Listening has recently been called the "Johnny Come Lately" of
the language arts program; therefore it is well to discuss the teaching
of listening at an early point in this book. Listening has always
been a component of teaching, but until relatively recent years most
teachers have assumed that its teaching does not require separate
planning and that children will simply acquire the skill as they
progress in other directions.

Probably the major reason for the interest now shown in
teaching listening has been the growing realization of the amount
of time people spend in listening. As early as 1928, a study by
Rankin showed that, of the time people spend in communicating,
approximately 45 percent is devoted to listening, 30 percent to
speaking and the rest to reading and writing.[1] This study had some
effect, but as pointed out by Taylor, 90 percent of the listening
research has been done since 1952.[2]

Even today, in spite of the importance of listening and the
amount of research done, too little genuine attention is being given
to lessons on listening. While apparently no one is advocating the
addition of another course to an already crowded elementary school
curriculum, it is just as apparent that children do not learn to
listen well either by growing up or by simply listening. Listening must
be taught, and most properly is taught through relating it to the
other language arts.[3] Unfortunately the failure to do more teaching
of this valuable skill is related to the fact that textbooks

[1]Paul T. Rankin, "The Importance of Listening Ability," *English Journal,*
college ed., 17:623-630, October, 1928.

[2]Stanford E. Taylor, *What Research Says to the Teacher: Teaching Listening*
(Washington, D.C.: National Education Association, April, 1964), p. 1.

[3]*Ends and Issues: 1965–1966; Points of Decision in the Development of
the English Curriculum* (Champaign, Ill.: National Council of Teachers of
English, 1966), pp. 29–30.

continue to give little attention to listening, a recent survey showing that less than 1 percent of the content of textbooks is devoted to listening lessons.[4]

This chapter presents discussion on the following topics and gives specific suggestions for making the teaching of listening a functioning part of the curriculum:

1. The Nature of Listening
2. Relationships of Other Abilities to Listening
3. Types of Listening
4. Teaching Listening Skills
5. Listening Lessons and Activities
6. Evaluating Listening

The Nature of Listening

Listening involves more than just hearing or paying attention. Effective listening requires active and conscious attention to the sounds heard for the purpose of gaining meaning from them. We may listen to an interesting speaker, to the music of a fine orchestra, or to traffic sounds as we drive. In each of these cases, if we are really listening, we react to what we hear.

The writers of one textbook identify four steps in the listening process: (1) hearing, (2) understanding, (3) evaluating, and (4) responding.[5] First, a series of sounds is *heard*—the actual words and sentences. Second the meanings of these words and sentences are *understood* in the context in which they are heard. Third, the meanings gained are *evaluated* and the total communication accepted or rejected. Finally, a *response* is made to what was heard—by further thought, bodily movement, facial expression, or audible reaction.

While listening is the term generally given to the total act of receiving communication by auditory means, some researchers prefer to think of the total act as having three distinguishable stages: hearing, listening, and auding.[6] From this point of view, *hearing* is the process by which sound waves are received and modified by the ear, *listening* is the process of becoming aware of the sound components and recognizing

Listening Defined

---

[4]Kenneth L. Brown, "Speech and Listening in Language Arts Textbooks," *Elementary English,* 44 (Part I, 336–341, April, 1967; Part II, 461–465, May, 1967).

[5]John Erwin and Marjorie Rosenberger, *Modern Speech* (New York: Holt, Rinehart, and Winston, Inc., 1961), p. 42.

[6]Taylor, *Teaching Listening*, pp. 5-6.

these components in sequences which have meaning, while *auding* is the process by which the flow of sound sequences of speech is translated into meaning.

Nichols and Lewis, on the other hand, do not use "auding" (avoiding the term is a customary practice, since *auding* has received little popular acceptance), but essentially they emphasize the same process.[7] They say that hearing and listening are obviously not identical and should be thought of as two distinguishable phases: the receiving of sound and the interpreting of sound. The first phase (hearing) requires a perception of sounds and discrimination among them; the second phase (listening) requires the attachment of meaning to these sounds.

Listening and Hearing

Since hearing is basic to listening, attention must be given to factors which affect hearing. These include auditory acuity, binaural hearing, auditory perception and discrimination, the masking of communication by other sounds, and auditory fatigue. Problems with any of these, or a combination of two or more of them, may reduce hearing effectiveness and thus listening ability.

Auditory acuity is the ability to receive sound waves of various frequencies (tones) at various intensities (levels of loudness).[8] The inability to respond to normal frequencies and intensities represents a hearing loss. Such losses range from minor to serious, with an estimated 5 to 10 percent of children being so handicapped. Many of these losses are discovered through audiometer tests given to most school children; others are found because children cup the ear and lean forward when spoken to. Teachers should also closely observe children who typically speak too loudly or too softly or who seem to have difficulty with pronunciation and articulation and difficulty with rhyming and other phonetic exercises.

Binaural hearing problems may be related to problems of depth perception in vision. With adequate binaural hearing, a listener can locate the speaker he wants to listen to if he is in the presence of two or more conversations. Recent studies have shown that less capable listeners have difficulty with this task.[9] Related to this problem, but with no physical base, are masking and auditory fatigue. *Masking* occurs from the superimposition of sounds which interfere with those

---

[7]Ralph G. Nichols and Thomas R. Lewis, *Speaking and Listening* (Dubuque, Iowa: William C. Brown Company, 1965), p. 6.

[8]Taylor, *Teaching Listening,* p. 6.

[9]*Ibid.,* p. 8.

being listened to, while *auditory fatigue* is simply a temporary hearing loss, often caused by a monotonous tone or droning voice. Under either condition listening effectiveness is impaired.

The importance of normal hearing to effective listening should not be minimized, nor should poor listening habits be excused on the basis of hearing losses. Neither should a genuine hearing loss be confused with inattention, boredom, or indifference. Masking and auditory fatigue are sometimes so confused.

Some children who have excellent hearing may have difficulty in *discriminating between sounds.* Still others may hear well but have difficulty in *retaining auditory expressions.*[10] Of course, every child who can speak has some ability in perceiving sounds and discriminating among them or he would not have learned to speak. However, studies have shown that children with speech problems—and these may range from articulation difficulties to unfamiliarity with standard dialect— have inferior auditory discrimination ability. The importance of adequate auditory perception and discrimination, and their relationship to speech, is reflected in the Eisenson and Ogilvie report of a study which found that a number of children with hearing losses had not been identified by their teachers, even though their slightly inarticulate speech should have been a clue to problems with auditory perception and discrimination.[11]

Even with normal hearing ability there are conditions which affect a listener's reception of sounds and his reactions to them. These include the factors of attention and concentration, the means or ways an individual has for identifying and attaching meaning to sounds, and the rate at which sounds flow. In addition, listening is influenced most importantly by the experience and background of the listener and his capacity to use language.

Factors Which Influence Listening

Attention and concentration are affected by the tone, style, and manner of the speaker, the content of his message, the organization of that message, and the listening environment—temperature, the presence or absence of distractions, acoustics, etc. Attention is not necessarily shown by quietness, nor is concentration reflected only in facial expression. On the other hand, distractions of noise, movement, and the speaker himself do affect attention and the concentration required for effective listening.

[10]Jon Eisenson and Mardel Ogilvie, *Speech Correction in the Schools* (New York: The Macmillan Company, 1963), p. 196.
[11]*Ibid.,* p. 190.

In the listening process sounds must be identified in order for meaning to be gained from what is heard. Usually this identifying is done automatically because the sound is known; it has been heard before. It is a sound or word that the listener has heard many times and immediately recognizes. This automatic condition is not always present, however. New words, new sounds are heard and must be identified; some meaning must be attached to them or the entire communication is lost to the listener. The principal means a listener has for identifying unknown sounds is using the total context of what he is hearing, and particularly that context which is adjacent to the unknown. This context may supply clues helpful to identification, but of course the effectiveness of this depends upon the skill of the listener, the content of the message, and factors affecting concentration. Clues to unknown sounds are also supplied by the manner of delivery and by the mood created by both the setting and the speaker.

While much of the above suggests that listening is affected by the skill of the listener, this generalized *skill* needs to be thought of in terms of its components: the *skills* of listening. Effective listening does not just happen. It is the result of clear-cut identification of the needed skills and practice in using them.

The Listening Skills

Listening skills take many forms, depending upon the purpose of the activity. In the English program we are principally concerned with the skills necessary for the accurate and thoughful reception of speaking, although the program may also include listening to music and to sounds for the setting of moods for creative expression. The identification of the skills needed for different types and levels of listening is not yet complete. Broadly speaking, however, the necessary skills may be put into two classifications: (1) those concerned with accuracy of reception, and (2) those concerned with reactions to what was received. Pratt and Greene further identify these skills as follows:[12]

1. Word perception
   a. Recall of word meanings
   b. Deduction of meanings of unknown words
2. Comprehension of ideas
   a. Noting details
   b. Following directions

[12]Edward Pratt and Harry A. Greene, *Training Children to Listen*. A Monograph for Elementary Teachers, No. 80 (Evanston, Ill.: Row, Peterson and Company, 1955).

    c. Organizing into main and subordinate ideas
    d. Selecting information pertinent to a specific topic
    e. Detecting clues that show the speaker's trend of thought
3. *Using ideas to build understandings*
    a. Evaluating an expressed point of view or fact in relation to previous learning
    b. Making justifiable inferences

    Other listings of skills are usually related to the above but sometimes include statements which imply that more skills are needed. For example, the following may suggest other skills or subskills:

1. Listening to answer questions
2. Determining the speaker's purpose
3. Selecting items for summary
4. Separating fact and opinion
5. Recognizing emotional appeal
6. Detecting bias, prejudice, or propaganda
7. Responding to mood or setting
8. Understanding use of gestures, asides, satire, voice inflection
9. Creating visual images of verbal descriptions

Relationship of Other Abilities to Listening

    The relationship of listening to other factors is of concern in planning an instructional program for teaching listening. Since listening is a part of so many situations, in school and out, and so much learning is dependent upon it, listening is related to many other abilities. The relationship of listening to three other factors is discussed in this section.

    Since any language activity—expressive or receptive—is a thinking activity, most teachers assume a strong relationship between listening and intelligence. This assumption is supported by correlations reported by a number of researchers. Ross found a correlation of .76 between listening scores and verbal intelligence scores;[13] Brown found .82 at the fourth-grade level and .76 at the fifth-grade level;[14] Anderson and

Listening and
Intelligence

    [13]Ramon Ross, "A Look at Listeners," *Elementary School Journal,* 64:369–372, April, 1964.
    [14]Charles T. Brown, "Three Studies of the Listening of Children," *Speech Monographs,* 32:129–138, June, 1965.

Baldauf reported a coefficient of .58.[15] It is well to remember, however, that a high correlation does not mean a cause-and-effect relationship. As has been pointed out by researchers, the high correlations between listening and intelligence are probably somewhat spurious due to the common factors found in tests used to measure listening and intelligence.[16]

There is some evidence that children who have above average *nonlanguage* intelligence scores are better listeners than they are readers.[17] This evidence is supported by the indication in another study that students of below average intelligence tend to possess larger listening vocabularies than they do reading vocabularies.[18] Thus it appears that the "nonverbal" child, because this factor affects his intelligence test score, might learn better from listening than from reading, though he probably would not learn as effectively from either means as his classmate who scored higher on the intelligence test.

Listening and Reading

As individual sounds—the phonemes—are received by a listener, they are almost simultaneously translated into words and larger units of language. As the listener assimilates this flow of language, he must respond with understanding or no communication is occurring. The listener must bring into play all of his experience, all of his background, and all of the thinking processes he is capable of using in order to gain meaning. This total process is similar to the one used by a reader; therefore, we think of reading and listening as the receptive language arts.

The relationship between listening and reading has been investigated by many researchers. For example, Lundsteen reported a correlation of .52 between critical listening and reading achievement at the fifth-grade level;[19] Plessas reported correlation coefficients ranging from .27 to .80 between scores on listening tests and various aspects

[15]Harold M. Anderson, and Robert J. Baldauf, "A Study of a Measure of Listening," *Journal of Educational Research,* 57:197–200, December, 1963.

[16]Edwin E. Vineyard and Robert B. Bailey, "Interrelationships of Reading Ability, Listening Skill, Intelligence and Scholastic Achievement," *Journal of Developmental Reading,* 3:174–178, 1960.

[17]Robert O. Hall, "An Exploratory Study of Listening of Fifth Grade Pupils," unpublished doctoral dissertation, University of Southern California, 1954.

[18]Stanley B. Kegler, "A Comparative Study of the Size and Nature of Reading and Listening Vocabularies," unpublished doctoral dissertation, University of Minnesota, 1958.

[19]Sara Lundsteen, "Teaching Abilities in Critical Listening in the Fifth and Sixth Grades," unpublished doctoral dissertation, University of California, 1953.

of reading achievement;[20] and Devine reported a correlation of .65 from a study of high school listening.[21]

Further evidence has been provided by Hampleman, who compared the listening and reading comprehension of fourth- and sixth-grade pupils.[22] He found that (1) sixth-grade pupils were superior to fourth-grade pupils in both listening and reading comprehension, (2) listening comprehension was superior to reading comprehension in both grades, and (3) boys were superior to girls in listening comprehension of difficult materials. Hampleman suggested the need for more intensive investigation into the specific kinds of subject matter best suited to auditory presentation—the kind of informal investigation that could be done by a teacher without waiting for the researcher. His findings, which suggest the need for revising the method by which material in the curriculum is presented to some pupils, have been supported by other studies.[23]

There is conflicting evidence on both the improvement of reading by the teaching of listening and the improvement of listening by the teaching of reading.[24] Because of the similarity of the receptive skills in both reading and listening, sound principles of transfer of learning would appear to operate (a viewpoint generally accepted by authors and publishers of basal reading materials and one that teachers should observe). That is, both reading instruction and listening instruction should be directed at improvement of the skills common to both, as well as at the particular skills important to each.

Knowing the similarities between reading and listening skills is essential for such teaching. The listing of listening skills earlier in this

[20]Gus P. Plessas, "Reading Abilities and Intelligence Factors of Children Having High and Low Auding Ability," unpublished doctoral dissertation, University of California, 1957.

[21]Thomas G. Devine, "The Development and Evaluation of a Series of Recordings for Teaching Certain Critical Listening Abilities," unpublished doctoral dissertation, Boston University, 1961.

[22]Richard S. Hampleman, "Comparison of Listening and Reading Comprehension Ability of Fourth and Sixth Grade Pupils," *Elementary English,* 35:49–53, January, 1958.

[23]Harry Goldstein, "Reading and Listening at Various Controlled Rates," *Contributions to Education,* No. 821, Bureau of Publications, Teachers College, Columbia University (New York: Columbia University Press, 1940).

[24]For example: Paul M. Hollingsworth, "A Study to Compare the Effects of Two Listening Programs on Reading Achievement and Listening Comprehension," unpublished doctoral dissertation, University of Arizona, 1963; and Paul J. Seymour, "A Study of the Relationship between the Communication Skills and a Selected Set of Predictors and of the Relationship among the Communication Skills," unpublished doctoral dissertation, University of Minnesota, 1965.

chapter suggests the extent of the similarity. In addition, the following parallelisms between listening and reading may be helpful:

1. Certain elements are common to both areas—vocabulary, sentence patterns, organizational structures.
2. Both require relating to past experiences; that is, the ideas or concepts in the materials read or listened to must be partly familiar.
3. Both may be done more efficiently when their purposes have been clearly defined. Questions such as these might be discussed by the teacher and pupils in order to understand purposes for reading or listening.
   a. How does listening affect school work?
   b. What part does a listener play in conversation?
   c. What can hinder good listening?
   d. Why do we want others to listen to us?
   e. How does listening affect speaking?
4. In both, the word is usually not the unit of comprehension but it affects understanding of the phrase, sentence, or paragraph. Children must hear or read certain key words accurately, and they must understand the meanings of individual words in the contexts in which they are used.
5. Both require attention to "signals"—punctuation marks in writing and pauses and intonations in speech.
6. Both involve critical and creative interpretation of material. Pupils must consider the source of the material, its relevancy, and the emotional power of words.

It must not be assumed because of the many similarities that reading and listening are identical or that skill in one means that equal skill will be held in the other. Listening does not permit "going back," taking time to look up a word in a dictionary, controlling the speaker's rate of delivery, or pausing to absorb what has just been heard. On the other hand, reading is done without the personal contact often present in listening situations, including the voice inflections, gestures, and facial expressions.

Reviewing the research on listening, Witty and Sizemore considered the relative value of oral and visual presentation of material.[25] The most important of their findings are summarized below and show, further, the relationship between listening and reading.

1. Listening, as a way of learning, is more effective than reading in early childhood.

[25]Paul A. Witty and Robert A. Sizemore, "Studies in Listening: I. Relative Values of Oral and Visual Presentation," *Elementary English,* 35:538–552, December, 1958.

2. Listening seems less effective than reading as an adult way of learning certain materials, particularly if critical discrimination and analysis are involved.
3. Listening is often reinforced by the simultaneous use of visual and kinaesthetic approaches to the subject.
4. Success in learning through listening, as with other sensory approaches, depends to a considerable degree on the individual's experiences with it.

Listening and speaking are obviously related, but the nature of the relationship has not been established by research. Some studies have shown positive correlations between children's abilities in listening and their abilities in speaking, while others have reported relationships of a similar extent between the structure of children's language and listening.[26] For example, Strickland stated, "The structure of children's oral language as measured by the fluency of use of the common structural patterns was more closely related to listening comprehension than to any other variable."[27]

Listening and Speech

There is little doubt that listening can be done at a more rapid rate than that at which the human speech organs are capable of producing speech. This fact probably accounts in part for the loss of attention that speakers sometimes note in their audiences even when there is general interest in what is being heard.[28] A number of experiments have been made using compressed speech (silences between sounds in recorded speech taken out by mechanical means) as well as some in which the rate of speaking has simply been increased.[29] These have consistently shown that listening power is not overly taxed by the increased rates as long as the compression or the speeding of speech remains intelligible.

Some researchers have suggested that the development of listening skill in an individual "probably plays an important role in the ultimate development of his skill as a speaker in being able to order verbal

[26]Joel Stark, "An Investigation of the Relationship of the Vocal and Communicative Aspects of Speech Competency with Listening Comprehension," *Speech Monographs,* 24:98–99, June, 1957.

[27]Ruth G. Strickland, *The Language of Elementary School Children: Its Relationship to the Language of Reading Textbooks and the Quality of Reading of Selected Children,* Bulletin of the School of Education, Vol. 38, No. 4 (Bloomington, Indiana: Indiana University, 1962), pp. 85–86.

[28]John Cohen, and others, "Mind Wandering," *British Journal of Psychology,* 47:61–62, 1956.

[29]Sam Duker, "Listening," in *Encyclopedia of Educational Research,* Fourth Edition, Robert L. Ebel, editor (New York: The Macmillan Company, 1969), pp. 747–758.

behavior."[30] Others have reported that the organization of a speech or the manner in which it is delivered has no effect on its comprehension.[31]

Types of Listening

Both in school and out, each child does various types of listening. These types set levels for the listening done. The types suggest the need for a teacher to consider the nature of listening and the particular skills necessary for communication to take place in different situations. At some time or other, each child listens for information, for directions, for pleasure; he listens to gain new insights, to explore new ideas. For the different types of listening he does he performs at the following levels:

1. Hearing sounds or words but not reacting beyond bare recognition of them.
2. Intermittent listening, with the mind wandering in between.
3. Half-listening or listening only closely enough to know when it is his turn to do something.
4. Listening passively with little or no response.
5. Listening narrowly, missing significant parts but accepting that which is familiar or agreeable to him.
6. Listening and forming associations with related items from his own experiences.
7. Listening closely enough to get the organization of the material heard —to get the main ideas and supporting details.
8. Listening critically, including asking for more data on statements made.
9. Appreciative and creative listening with genuine mental and emotional response.

Rather than considering levels of listening, the Commission on the English Curriculum has defined the various types of listening as follows:[32]

[30]Reed Lawson, "Verbal Sequencing Without Mediation," *Journal of Communication,* 14:98–104, June, 1964.
[31]David B. Orr, and others, "Trainability of Listening Comprehension of Speeded Discourse," *Journal of Educational Psychology,* 56:148–156, 1965.
[32]Commission on the English Curriculum, National Council of Teachers of English, *Language Arts for Today's Children* (New York: Appleton-Century-Crofts, Inc., 1954), p. 80.

A Puppet's View of Language Enjoyment: Puppets provide opportunities for a variety of language use

Passive or *marginal listening* is prevalent today as many children study with the radio on. In fact, there is often a deliberate "tuning out" of what is heard with just enough consciousness of the language or sound to bring the child back to attention when a favorite radio personality comes on. Similarly, in classroom or home the tone of voice of teacher or parent may flash the danger signal which alerts the child whose attention has been wandering. The way one listens to background music while reading differs markedly from the type of listening one does when evaluating critically a proposed plan for action which affects one personally or professionally.

Appreciative listening is involved when the hearer settles down to enjoy a dramatization, a story, or a poem. The process of developing new or original solutions to problems presented through the spoken word may be termed *creative listening* or the act of entering imaginatively into the experiences, the setting, and the feelings of the characters in a story which is being told orally or produced on screen or stage.

Attentive listening is needed in situations in which accuracy of comprehension is involved, as in directions, announcements, and introductions. Probably there is a different mind set in situations in which the hearer participates, such as in conversation and discussion; this might be called *responsive listening*.

Analytical listening takes place, for example, when the listener weighs what is heard against personal experience and is alert to attempts of the speaker to sway his opinion by the devices of propaganda. This kind of listening must be developed by older elementary and high school pupils in order that they may evaluate what they hear.

There are other classifications of types of listening which might be made, such as appreciational, informational, and critical;[33] or attentive, purposeful, critical, and responsive.[34] Regardless of the classification that might be made, or whether one listens at different levels, the point of concern is that listening requires specific abilities and skills. It is obvious that we listen to particular sounds, for particular purposes; we do not *just* listen.

Teaching Listening Skills

While an ever-increasing number of teachers are now aware of the need to do something about teaching listening, too few know exactly what should be done, too few take advantage of the opportunities occurring daily for such teaching, and too few go beyond simply demanding silence and the paying of attention. This situation can be remedied, however, and Duker has identified a large number of studies and expository articles which will provide assistance in such an attempt.[35] These are concerned with the teaching of listening at all school levels, and there is considerable agreement among all of them that listening skills can be taught and that the results of such teaching can be measured. One study that takes exception to this conclusion was done by Petrie, who critically examined the previous research and argues from this examination and his experiment with college freshmen that too little is known about listening skills or testing listening ability to do any instruction.[36] The National Council of Teachers of English, however,

[33]Ralph B. Nichols, "Ten Components of Effective Listening," *Education,* 75:292–302, January, 1955.

[34]Earl J. Dias, "Three Levels of Listening," *English Journal,* 36:252–253, May, 1947.

[35]Sam Duker, *Listening Bibliography* (Scarecrow Press, 1964), 221 pp.

[36]Charles R. Petrie, "An Experimental Evaluation of Two Methods for Improving Listening Comprehension Abilities," unpublished doctoral dissertation, Purdue University, 1961.

has stated that listening should be taught because it is the most used of the language arts and is often poorly done.[37]

A number of writers who have given thoughtful attention to the teaching of listening suggest that a teacher first examine his own listening habits and the listening situation in his classroom. For example, Berry[38] urges the teacher to begin with (1) a frank analysis of his own listening experiences, (2) a thoughtful study of the listening situation in the classroom, (3) a fostering of concern in children for the development of their own listening competence, and (4) a development of listening instruction in relation to communication.

This kind of analysis should lead to the identification of specific instructional tasks. The first of these tasks should be to make the children aware of the importance of listening. Children must learn that skillful listening is important to them in school, on the playground, and at home. They must also learn that listening is important to adults in almost every life activity. They must learn that listening skills can be developed, that they result from the formation of good habits which are easily learned, and that this mastery will reward them with a richer, more meaningful life.[39]

As a second step the teacher should stimulate the sense of hearing, or auditory acuity, in the children. For example, the teacher might ask individuals in the class to name all the sounds they can remember hearing at a circus, in a hospital, or at an airport or bus station. Each sound may be written on the board as it is mentioned, for the class to think about. Perhaps some pupils will be interested in writing a story which is based on the activities suggested by the words on the board. These pupils can read their stories to the class when they are completed. Similar exercises based on familiar situations will contribute to the development of a keen appreciation of the sense of hearing, and make children more alert to sounds they have previously taken for granted.

The third step is the provision of opportunities for meaningful listening. A wide variety of opportunities for listening experiences must be introduced into the classroom if the children are to learn to adapt the kind of listening they do to the type that will best serve the purpose

[37]National Council of Teachers of English, *Ends and Issues*, p. 29.

[38]Althea Berry, "Experiences in Listening," *Elementary English,* 28:130–132, March, 1951.

[39]Robert Canfield, "A Study of the Effects of Two Types of Instruction on the Listening Comprehension of Fifth Grade Children." unpublished doctoral dissertation, Syracuse University, 1960.

of the activity.[40] Thus, the program should call for listening to music, to poetry, to stories, to reports, to descriptions, etc. It should call for listening for specific purposes: for appreciation, for information, and for critical evaluation.

Related to the above is the fourth task, that of teaching children the specific skills needed for various listening purposes. The emphasis in this teaching should be upon the development of the skills through specific teaching situations and lessons rather than upon simply giving attention to such things as "paying attention." Thus the skills must be known by the teacher and, in a general way, by the pupils. The teacher must also know procedures for developing each needed skill.[41]

A fifth responsibility of the teacher is to give the children many opportunities to talk about things that interest them. As they share experiences, hobbies, books, and information that are of genuine interest, with encouragement they will see the point of practicing the skills of listening as others practice the skills of speaking.

A final step involves the teacher himself. He must teach the children to listen to him. This does not mean that he should "out-shout" them or speak in such a low voice that he is inaudible. It does mean that his tone should be low enough to force youngsters to stay alert in order to keep up with what is going on. It is advisable, too, to warn the children that the practice of not repeating instructions, explanations, or announcements will be followed in the class. In addition, the teacher should make every effort to ensure that classroom activities are so interesting that all the children will want to listen.

The example a teacher sets for his pupils is of major importance. The teacher should "pay attention," "show courtesy to the speaker,"

[40]Good sources of ideas for listening situations are David H. Russell and Elizabeth F. Russell, *Listening Aids Through the Grades* (New York: Bureau of Publications, Teachers College, Columbia University, 1959) and Guy Wagner, Max Hosier, and Mildred Blackman, *Listening Games* (Darien, Connecticut: Teachers Publishing Corporation, 1962).

[41]As mentioned in several sections of this chapter, a good many studies of the teaching of listening have required the development of listening lessons. Some examples of the most recent of these studies are the following: Annabel Fawcett, "The Effect of Training in Listening upon the Listening Skills of Intermediate Grade Children," *Elementary English*, 43:473–476 (May, 1966); Sue E. Trivette, "The Effect of Training in Listening for Specific Purposes," *Journal of Educational Research*, 54:276–277 (March, 1961); Marcus Allenger, "A Study of the Effectiveness of Teaching Listening Through a Planned Daily Program," unpublished master's thesis, Texas Technological College, Lubbock, 1963; Helene I. Collins, "A Program for the Improvement of Auding Skills in a Fifth Grade Classroom," unpublished master's thesis, Central Connecticut State College, New Britain, 1966; Ramon Ross, "Teaching the Listener, Old Mistakes and a Fresh Beginning," *Elementary School Journal*, 66:239–244 (February, 1966).

and observe all the other practices that teachers are inclined to urge children to use. Many teachers are engrossed in *telling*—a practice that may not be teaching—and thus simply are not doing the listening that they should. It might be well for every teacher to answer honestly such questions as the following:[42]

1. Is it because of *me* that children do not pay attention? Could they be shutting out my voice for some reason?
2. Am I defeating good listening by talking too much?
3. Do I realize that children have difficulty listening attentively for a long period of time and that they can be encouraged to listen by being given fresh, original motivation?
4. Do I use changes in pitch, loudness, and rate in my own speaking?
5. Do I expect children to concentrate upon too many items at one time? Perhaps they need time to think about each one.
6. Do I give children time to think when I ask questions—to find the answer to one question before another is asked?
7. Are my explanations clearly presented and correctly timed? Do I repeat an assignment the necessary number of times? Do I get the full attention of the class before giving an assignment?
8. Do I try not to repeat what each child says but rather require the group to concentrate on the speaker?
9. Am I taking too much time in explaining to one child while others lose interest?
10. Do I have a democratic type of discipline in my room, knowing that children work better when there is neither an atmosphere of chaos nor one of strict authoritarianism?
11. Am I relaxed and unhurried in my speaking and in my movements?
12. Do I try not to repeat phrases or expressions so often that they become ineffective and monotonous?
13. Do I express appreciation for what children say? Are their opinions treated with respect?
14. Do I make myself available for listening? Do children feel free to come to me with their problems and know that they will have my undivided attention?
15. Am I setting a good example by being an attentive listener?

In addition to the teaching tasks suggested and the cautions a teacher might observe about his own listening, there are a number of practices and principles which should receive attention in an instructional program for listening.[43]

Further Suggestions

[42]Checklist used at Scenic View School, Englewood, Colorado.

[43]See also Sam Duker, "Goals of Teaching Listening Skills in the Elementary School," *Elementary English,* 38:170–174 (March, 1961); P. M. Hollingsworth, "Teaching Listening in the Elementary School," *Education,* 89:103–104 (November, 1968); and Gloria L. Horrworth, "Listening: A Facet of Oral Language," *Elementary English,* 43:856–864, 868 (December, 1966).

1. Considerable flexibility is needed in the activities provided, since children differ widely in listening abilities and since different types of listening are appropriate to different occasions.

2. With the help of the children, a teacher must plan for a wide variety of oral language situations. These should be for genuine purposes of communication, as well as being lessons and activities directed at teaching particular listening skills. The oral language situations may include informal conversation, sharing, reporting, social courtesies, telephoning, planning, reacting to films, storytelling, making announcements, giving directions, interviewing, and dramatizations.

3. Readiness increases the amount of learning that can be gained from listening. The teacher and pupils should discuss the purpose for the listening activity and make preparations in terms of previous experiences, new vocabulary, and the type of listening required.

4. Listening should be *for* rather than *at*. The purposes should be such that they are understood by the pupils.

5. Listening may be used as a change of pace—a chance for relaxation or pleasure as well as a way of getting information.

6. Children profit from formulating standards—both for the speaker and the listener—and in giving attention to these in the planning, in the activity itself, and in the evaluation.

Listening Lessons and Activities

While every listening situation is an opportunity for developing listening skills and fostering good listening habits, an organized instructional program—planned for in some detail and evaluated with adequate attention to objectives—should be a part of every classroom. A planned program will include specific lessons designed to teach listening skills and calling for the several types of listening identified earlier in this chapter. A planned program will also provide activities which build interest in learning to listen well and which foster good listening habits.

A Listening Lesson

The following procedures, primarily related to teaching a listening lesson of an appreciational type, are suggestive of those which should be used in other types of listening lessons.

Clearly Defining the Purpose of the Listening Experience. The purpose of the listening activity should be one that the children will understand and appreciate. For example, the teacher might make this introductory statement of purpose: "We have talked about river steamers and have seen pictures of them; now let's listen to this recording of music played on river steamers and see if this is the kind of music we would expect to hear on a steamboat."

Giving Preliminary Attention to Unfamiliar Vocabulary. The teacher should know the vocabulary that is used in the material to be heard. Unusual words that possibly will be heard by these children for the first time should be discussed and related to known words and previous experiences. This, of course, must be done with care, for it can be carried too far. For example, to appreciate a lovely poem, to derive meaning and pleasure from listening to it, a person does not require a complete understanding of each word. The sounds of the new words may, for some children, be the greatest source of pleasure in the activity.

Giving Preliminary Attention to the Recall of Related Experiences. The teacher should attempt to relate what is to be heard to something that is known. This is really only a stage in making assignments that good teachers have always used. However, in listening for enjoyment and appreciation this must be handled with caution, for children may derive real enjoyment without complete understanding of all of the subtle elements involved.

Using Guides as Aids in Attaining the Listening Purpose. Listening guides directing the attention of the children to particular features of the material may sometimes be prepared in advance and given to the pupils shortly before the listening lesson begins. Such devices should not be used often, however, for they tend to over-formalize this type of listening activity.

Providing for Follow-up. The listening act is not complete without reaction: there must be some response, preferably one directly related to the purposes for listening which were established prior to the lesson. Thus, a necessary step is that of follow-up: What reactions were there? Was the purpose of the listening experience achieved? What is the evidence that the purpose was accomplished?

Re-Listening for Added Emphasis or Another Purpose. A second listening to a musical selection, an exciting tale, a stirring speech, or a marvelous poem often brings out elements of appreciation and thought not gained the first time. The value of this procedure may be brought home to the children by setting new purposes and seeing if these are accomplished. Replaying, of course, can be overdone and is usually most successful when the listening is directed at some appreciational elements.

The following report of a portion of a listening experience designed to aid in developing creative writing ability illustrates the points presented above.[44]

Presentation. Read aloud and discuss Walt Whitman's *I Hear America Singing.* Listen to recording of *Ballad For Americans* in order to discuss the things people do to earn their living.

Discuss the fact that we are living in an American city, where many wheels are turning and many people are busy turning those wheels, and that we can hear the sounds of people and machines at work from our windows. Plan to write an original verse or paragraph describing how the city sounds to us and our feelings about it.

Exploration. Listen to the sounds from the schoolroom. (There should be a minute of listening, then naming of sounds heard.) As the children name the sounds, the teacher writes the words on the chalkboard. Then there should be another listening period for purposes of further identification.

Procedure. The ideas are shared and enlarged upon during a discussion period. When the time comes for individual writing, each child develops the idea that appeals to him and tries to express it in his own way. During this writing time, there is no interchange of ideas. However, the teacher should make the children feel free to ask for individual assistance if they need it. Since this writing should be a joyful and spontaneous experience, the children should not be forced to write. Those who do not write should engage in a quiet activity.

Stenographic Report of the Lesson

Children:	Rumble, rattle, roar, purr, slither, squeak, roll, chug, whistle, skid, sizzle, hiss, squeal, whiz, zoom, hum, sigh, squawk, scream, call, shout, chime, ring, clang, whine
Teacher:	Now let's listen again for a minute. We may hear more. (All listen for a minute.) What things made the sounds we heard? What did we hear these things do?
Children:	Cars—rumble, rattle, roar, purr, slither Trains—roll, chug, whistle Tire—skid, sizzle, hiss, squeal, squeak Planes—whiz, roar, zoom, dash Buses—hum, signal, squeak, groan, whisper Trucks—rumble, roar, thump, rattle, pound, clatter Pneumatic drills—rat-a-tat

[44]*A Guide for the Teaching of Language Arts: Kindergarten–Eighth Grade* (San Francisco: Elementary School Division, San Francisco Unified School District, 1955), p. 82.

	Sea gulls—mew, squawk, scream
	People—call, shout
	Children—shriek, scream, bubble, whoop, yell, cry, wail
	Signals—clang, clatter, toot, screech, wail, squawk
	Boats—whistle, toot
	Bells—ring, chime, clang, clatter
	Electric saw—whine
Teacher:	What adjectives can we use to describe these sounds?
Children:	*Low* rumbles, *loud* roar, *soothing* purr, *high* squeak, *steady* click, *loud* squawk, *steady* roll, *mournful* whistle, *impatient* chug, *fast* squeak, etc.

In teaching attentive, analytical, and critical listening, supplemental activities such as notetaking, outlining, writing summaries, and using reference sources to check on the reliability of the material heard will help pupils to organize their thinking and to remember what they have heard.

Simply asking children to listen to a selection does not identify for them particular listening skills nor teach habits that they need to learn. A teacher should have no difficulty in constructing his own lessons if he gives attention to purposes and designs each lesson so that one or more of the listening skills will be taught by the lesson. The following are sample lessons of the kinds that can be constructed.[45] It must be emphasized that these are examples. A teacher must consider the experiences the children in his class have had or are having in choosing content for such lessons.

Other Examples of Listening Lessons

☐ **Listening for Details**

The teacher asks the children to listen for details about what Father and Mother do and then reads the following paragraph:

Every morning Father goes to work by bus. He usually leaves the house about seven o'clock. In rainy weather Mother drives him to the bus station. When the bus reaches the city at seven forty-five, Father goes to the general office of his company. An elevator

[45]Further suggestions are available in Stanford E. Taylor, *Teaching Listening*. See also footnotes earlier in this chapter and many of the recently published basal reading textbooks. For example, Houghton Mifflin Company publishes *Listening and Learning* (1969) and *Listen and Do* (1963)—both with lp recordings and guide books for teaching—as parts of their reading program.

carries him to the eighth floor. His important job takes hours of extra time, and many evenings he doesn't arrive home until late. Joe and Betty are disappointed when he works at night, for he frequently helps them with their lessons. Then, too, if there is time after dinner for games, he often plays with them before they begin to study.

Following the reading the teacher asks questions such as these:

(1) What times does Father leave the house in the morning?
(2) What does Mother do for Father when it is raining?
(3) On what floor is Father's office?
(4) How does Father help Joe and Betty when he is home?
(5) When does Father play games with them?

☐ Listening for the Main Idea

The teacher writes these sentences on the board and covers them.

The burro is a very gentle animal.
Children ride on their burros.
The burro is a favorite pet in Mexico.
The children give names to their burros.

The teacher asks the children to listen carefully to what they are about to hear and to think of the one thing it tells about. This paragraph is then read:

Many children in Mexico have burros for pets. The burro is so gentle that a small child can take care of him. The children enjoy riding on their burros. Sometimes the children ride them in parades. They call their pet burros by name, and talk to them just as they talk to one another. Often a boy will carry sugar in his pocket. His burro will follow him, sniffing in his pocket to get the sugar.

The teacher then uncovers the sentences and reads them aloud. He then asks the children to write the sentence which is the main idea of the paragraph.

☐ Listening to Follow Directions

The teacher distributes to each pupil one sheet of lined paper and says, "Today we are going to have a game to see how well you can listen to directions. Have your pencils ready, and be sure to do exactly what my directions say. I shall give each direction only once." The following is then read:

(1) Write your first and last name in the upper right-hand corner of the paper.
(2) At the left-hand margin, on every other line, write the numbers from one to ten for answers to ten directions.
(3) After number 1 write the words *from, with, at.*
(4) If California is south of Oregon, write the word *south.*
(5) Listen to these numbers and write the largest of them 6-2-7-5-1-8-3.
(6) Draw a square and put the number 3 in the lower right hand corner of it.

The directions could be continued for as long as the teacher wishes, and the pupils are motivated to listen. Answers should be checked.

☐ **Listening for Word Meaning from Context**

The teacher writes the following words on the board: *exalt* and *ravine.* He asks the pupils if they know the meanings of them. He writes the meanings they give and then asks them to listen to the following to find out if they were right:

> A little way off, to the left, stood a small house; and to the right was another, before which stood the wagons belonging to his father. Directly in front was a wide expanse of rolling prairie, cut by a deep ravine. To the north, beyond the small farm which was fenced, a still wider region rolled away into unexplored and marvelous distance. Altogether is was a land to exalt a boy who had lived all his life in thickly settled Wisconsin.[46]

Following the reading the meanings of the words should again be discussed and looked for in a dictionary if necessary.

☐ **Listening to Distinguish the Relevant from the Irrelevant**

The teacher asks the pupils to listen to a selection and to be ready to tell which sentences are needed to gain the meaning and which do not really relate to the remainder of the selection. The following is read:

> There were six boys beside the campfire. The dry sticks blazed and the heavy logs glowed with the heat. It was almost time to put the fish in the frying pan. Already they had poked the potatoes in their foil wrappings and they were softening. Jim's older brother had stayed at home. He was going to college this fall. All the boys were hungry and were anxious to eat. Bill put on more wood and Bob got the frying pan.

[46]From Hamlin Garland, *Boy Life on the Prairie* (New York, Frederick Ungar Publishing Co., Inc., 1959).

The teacher asks the pupils to tell which sentences do not relate to the remainder of the paragraph and why they are not relevant.

☐ **Listening to Draw Inferences**

The teacher tells the pupils to listen to the following to answer some questions which can only be answered by listening "between the lines."

> The air was crisp and clear but a wet snow had pelted the windows last night. I breathed deeply, glanced toward the snow-covered cars parked along the curbing, and thought "What a beautiful day." Suddenly I came down with a bump on the sidewalk.

The teacher then asks these questions and the meaning of making inferences is discussed:

(1) Why did the speaker fall?
(2) Does the speaker live in town or in the country?
(3) Has the snowing stopped?

Listening Activities

Every school day abounds with opportunities for teaching children to be more effective listeners. Not all of these opportunities need to be converted to listening lessons as specific as the ones previously suggested, although a good many of them can be, but variety may be injected and still give effective attention to listening. The suggestions below may be used as bases for developing others.

1. Read a description of a scene to the class. Have the pupils draw pictures depicting what they heard.
2. Read descriptions of well-known people—perhaps persons studied in social studies—and have the pupils guess their names.
3. Select written material that contains words unfamiliar to the students and list the words on the chalkboard. Read the material aloud after asking the pupils to listen to determine the meanings of the words from the context.
4. After a child's oral report ask questions of the pupils. For example: What did Jim talk about (main idea)? What did he say first, next, and last (details and sequences)?
5. Use directions with several parts. For example: "Write your last name first, then your first name, in the upper right hand corner of your paper. Under this write the date."
6. Tape record a short radio or TV newscast that presents facts without commentary. Also record a new commentator who broadcasts his own opinions along with the facts. Play the two recordings to the class and ask the pupils to point out the differences between the two recordings.

7. Have the pupils keep TV and radio logs of listening habits. Have the logs discussed, including giving attention to standards for choosing programs.

8. Play a tape recording of a talk. Cut it off before the conclusion and ask the pupils to state what the speaker's conclusion will be. Such recordings may vary in difficulty, and progression should be made from the simple to the more difficult.

9. Prepare tape recordings of materials and have pupils listen for signals which guide their gaining of meaning. Language signals may be such phrases as "three reasons for this plan . . . ," "the following are . . . ," and "my major concern is . . . ," or transition words and phrases such as "on the other hand," and "on the contrary."

10. Have oral messages carried from class to class, giving children opportunity to practice retention of ideas.

11. Read sentences to the children, omitting one or more words in each sentence. Have them tell the missing words. Make some of the sentences the kind that requires the children to "listen on" (similar to "read on") in order to determine the words.

12. Oral arithmetic is also useful for teaching listening skills. For example, you might say "Let's see if you can follow a number trail. Add 13 and 3, take away 6, multiply by 5, and divide by 2. What do you have?"

13. When children are absent from class, give those present the assignment of summarizing and passing on orally the instructions missed by the absentees. Make certain that you check these.

14. Speak the last syllable of a word to the class ("ick," for example). Ask the pupils to speak aloud as many words as possible ending in the same sound (*lick, tick, sick, pick, etc.*) without repeating any words.

15. Read a short poem to the class and ask the pupils to guess the title, or to make up a title. Encourage the children to give reasons for their choices.

16. Have the pupils finish tall tales or other stories told or read to them. Encourage them to continue the story theme, thus requiring careful listening in order not to have the story take a new direction.

17. Give tests orally; that is, instead of writing questions on the chalkboard read them to the class. This works well for questions with short answers, such as true or false.

18. Read stories with an occasional word missing. Have the pupils supply the missing words.

19. Have the pupils listen to appealing articles related to social studies or science which have unknown words but which provide some context clues. Illustrate for the pupils before they listen that clues to unknown words may be provided by synonyms, by summary statements which explain, by statements which provide definitions, and so forth.

20. Have the pupils listen to classmates read to see if they can determine the punctuation. They may also evaluate the reader in terms of his reading with feeling, his ability to "capture" his audience, his intonation, etc.

Individualizing
Listening
Instruction

Many teachers are profitably making use of tape and disc recorders fitted with single or multiple sets of earphones so that listening can be done by one or more pupils while the remainder of the class is engaged in other activities. The listening can be done at desks (if they are so wired), in a corner of the room, or in a section partially screened off and called a *Listening Center*. Many things can be recorded for children to listen to—literature selections, directions for paper and pencil activities, spelling lessons, vocabulary work, and specific listening lessons of the types suggested in the preceding section. The effec-

Many listening activities may be individualized

tiveness of this procedure, including the fact that even very young children can work independently, has been reported by a number of writers.[47]

There are many audio-visual aids, including books, which present worthwhile content in literature, social studies, science, and so on that can be used to teach listening. Some have been commercially prepared especially for this purpose. Many may be used by individual pupils, as suggested above, as well as with a group or the entire class.

Aids to
Listening
Instruction

☐ Records and Tapes

Many single records and albums, and an increasing number of tapes, present literature narrations, historical accounts, folk tales and songs, instrumental music, and music directed at rhythmic activities. Some records call for identification of sounds. These include the following: *Sounds Around Us* (3 records, Scott, Foresman & Co.); *The Downtown Story, The Sounds of Camp, Sounds of My City, Sounds of Animals, Sounds of Insects,* and *Sounds of the Satellites* (Folkways/Scholastic Records); and *Let's Listen* (Ginn). Records related to reading and listening include *Listening Skills for Pre-Readers* and *Sounds for Young Readers* (Kimbo Records), and *Listening Time* (3 records, Educational Record Sales), which also provides ear training. The tape series for upper elementary grades, *Listen: Hear* (Paul S. Amidon and Associates) is more specifically directed at the listening skills, as is *The Listening Skills Program* (Science Research Associates). The *American Landmarks* records (Enrichment Teaching Materials) provide historical dramatizations useful for teaching listening because of the motivation they provide. Literature records include the following: *Hans Christian Andersen Fairy Tales* (7 records), *Just So Stories* (2 records), *Old Possum's Book of Practical Cats, You Know Who* (Encyclopedia Britannica); *Poetry Time* (Scott Foresman & Co.); *Prose and Poetry Enrichment* (album, Enrichment Teaching Materials); and the tape series which includes *Stories are Fun, Open the Door,* and *Land of Make Believe* (National Tape Recording Repository).

☐ Films and Filmstrips

Most films can provide worthwhile listening experiences. Some of the most appealing films for listening are the following, by Encyclopedia

---

[47]For example: M. P. Hickey, "They Really Listen Now That They Have a Listening Center," *Instructor,* 76:85 (October, 1966); Miriam Hoffman, "Our Listening Center Livens Language Arts," *Elementary School Journal,* 63:381–385 (April, 1963); Gloria L. Horrworth, "Listening: A Facet of Oral Language," *Elementary English,* 43:856–864, 868 (December, 1966).

Britannica: *The Loon's Necklace, The Bear and the Hunter, Adventures of a Baby Fox, Morning Star, Let's Go to the Circus, Gray Gull the Hunter, The Hunter and the Forest* (has sounds but no words), and *Korochan, the Little Bear.* Coronet Films has similar films and one, *Listen Well, Learn Well,* was prepared specifically for the teaching of listening. The filmstrip series *How to Listen* (Society for Visual Education) is also particularly useful, as is their *Listening and Reading Skills.*

☐ **Books**

Selections can be made from particularly appealing or informative books for the content of listening lessons. Most of the basal reading series provide for some listening lessons, particularly in the primary grades, and relate them to the reading skills in the text. There are also books such as those for the primary grades by Margaret Wise Brown (*The City Noisy Book, The Winter Noisy Book,* etc.), Helen Borton's *Do You Hear What I Hear?,* Paul Showers' *The Listening Walk,* and Don Safier's *The Listening Book,* which have great appeal and develop listening abilities. The SRA Laboratories include *Listening Skill Builders* in their programs. Materials such as the Gates-Peardon *Practice Exercises* (Macmillan) and the Reader's Digest *Skills Builder* can readily be used to teach listening skills.

Evaluating Listening

With listening now recognized as an area of the language arts important to the curriculum and one that requires teaching, instruments for the appraisement of listening ability are beginning to appear. Few of these instruments are standardized tests, so that much of the task of measuring children's listening abilities and determining the levels of achievement of listening skills still falls upon the teacher.[48]

Standardized Tests

One standardized test of listening that may be used in the elementary school is provided in the *Sequential Tests of Educational Progress* (the STEP test).[49] This test, available in forms for several levels (primary, and grades 4-6, 7-9, 10-12, 13-14), attempts to measure simple

---

[48]O. W. Kopp, "The Evaluation of Oral Language Activities: Teaching and Learning," in *Research in Oral Language,* Walter T. Petty, editor (Champaign, Ill.: The National Council of Teachers of English, 1967).

[49]Educational Testing Service, Princeton, New Jersey, 1967.

comprehension, interpretation, evaluation, and application. The test is based upon an oral presentation by the teacher with the pupil giving one of four optional answers to each question. The pupils have copies of the questions and the four options, hence certain elements of reading ability are involved.

The items on the test relate to the following skills, which have been identified by research: identifying main ideas, remembering significant details, remembering simple sequences of information, seeing bias and prejudice in what the speaker says, judging the validity of information, distinguishing fact from fancy, judging the relevance of details to an idea, determining the organization of the spoken context, and recognizing what the speaker wants the listener to do and believe. The test results are a useful guide to a teacher in evaluating his listening program.

A second standardized test is the *Durrell Listening-Reading Series,* which "is designed to provide a comparison of children's reading and listening abilities."[50] The test series seeks to measure both vocabulary knowledge and comprehension ability, with tests at three levels: grades 1-3.5, grades 3.5-6, and grades 7-9. The tests are administered orally by the teacher, including the reading of option responses so that the pupil does no reading.

Teachers may use a standardized listening test as a model for the construction of an informal test. They may also use listings of listening skills such as those given earlier in this chapter or those provided in reports of research directed at teaching listening. For example, Brown lists the following skills as important to consider in developing listening tests:[51]

Teacher-made Tests

1. Identification and recall of details presented orally.
2. Ability to follow the sequence of details in the form of oral directions.
3. Retention of details long enough to answer questions about them.
4. Ability to listen reflectively for the purpose of identifying the central idea of the statement given orally.
5. Ability to draw inferences from the supporting facts presented in the statement.

[50]Donald D. Durrell and others, *Durrell Listening-Reading Series* (New York: Harcourt, Brace and World, Inc., 1969).

[51]James I. Brown, "The Construction of a Diagnostic Test of Listening Comprehension," *Journal of Experimental Education,* 18:139–146, December, 1949. See also: David H. Russell, "A Conspectus of Recent Research on Listening Abilities," *Elementary English,* 41:262–265, March, 1964.

6. Ability to distinguish relevant from irrelevant materials.
7. Use of contextual clues to word meanings.
8. Recognition of transitional elements in sentences.

Pupil-developed Standards

Involving pupils directly in evaluation is very important. Even in the early primary grades children can formulate standards for listening and judge whether or not their performances meet their own standards. Such standards in the early grades should focus upon proper audience behavior and should emphasize listening courteously and attentively, expressing enjoyment and appreciation, avoiding interruption, and offering constructive criticism or asking intelligent questions.

One second grade developed these standards:[52]

A Good Listener
Looks at the person talking
Keeps hands quiet
Doesn't talk
Thinks about what is said

Standards, of course, should change as the children mature and learn. They should be more advanced at the end of the year than at the beginning. Upper elementary children should be capable of developing and evaluating their own listening by standards such as the following:[53]

Do I hold the thread of the talk or discussion in mind?
Do I listen to content even though it does not affect me directly?
Am I aware of transitional phrases and what they mean?
Do I discount, when forming a judgment, possible bias in what a speaker says?
Have I disagreed with the speaker in a courteous manner?
Do I reserve judgment until I have heard different viewpoints?
Do I show in what I say that I have considered the ideas of others?

Lack of courtesy is often displayed by listeners—a fact that suggests the listening is less effective than it should be. The most important courtesy is being attentive. Attentiveness is more than

[52]West Acres School, West Sacramento, Calif. Mrs. Morley, teacher.
[53]Adapted from listing in Stanley B. Kegler, "Techniques in Teaching Listening for Main Ideas," *English Journal*, 45:30–32, January, 1956.

merely appearing to listen; it is becoming involved in such a way with the speaker that his every phrase, inflection, and gesture is noted and reacted to. This reaction—as insignificant as it might be with respect to physical movement—is sensed by the speaker; hence no one can really appear to listen and not actually do so. The following suggestions for pupils, based upon courtesy and attentiveness, also may be used to evaluate the pupils as listeners.[54]

1. Relax and be comfortable.
2. Try to determine the plan or organization of the talk. Listen for the cue words or phrases, for example:
   (a) There are three main points . . . ."
   (b) The most important problem is . . . ."
3. Listen for a summary of the talk or discussion.
4. Take notes on informational material.
5. Ask speakers for more information on certain points or for clarification of a point.
6. Compare what is being heard with what is already known about the subject.

Pupils can keep logs of their listening activities and analyze these in terms of what they have learned and which were most effective. This practice will be helpful in evaluating many listening experiences but should not be carried beyond the point where pupils are interested in it. Related to keeping logs is charting the flow of discussion, an activity which will help pupils to recognize the importance of being both speakers and listeners. As with the logs, the charts (kept by a pupil or the teacher) can be analyzed and pupils helped to relate the record to their own performances as listeners. In an even more informal manner, pupils and the teacher may simply discuss listening in their classroom, the particular skills involved, and how effective their listening is.

Further Suggestions for Evaluating Listening

Any of the above procedures have assessment value, but they should be supplemented by some kind of written record of specific listening behaviors and attainments. A checklist such as the one below is probably the best written record since it forces the pupil to react to direct questions. Most statements of standards can be effectively translated into checklists.[55]

[54]Ursula Hogan, "An Experiment in Improving the Listening Skills of Fifth and Sixth Grade Pupils," M.A. Seminar Study, University of California, Berkeley, June, 1953.
[55]Adapted from Kopp, "Evaluation of Oral Language Activities."

Checking up on My Listening

	Yes	No
1. Did I remember to get ready for listening?	___	___
(a) Was I seated comfortably where I could see and hear?	___	___
(b) Were my eyes focused on the speaker?	___	___
2. Was I ready to concentrate on what the speaker had to say?	___	___
(a) Was I able to push unrelated thoughts out of my mind for the time being?	___	___
(b) Was I ready to think about the topic and call to mind the things I already knew about it?	___	___
(c) Was I ready to learn more about the topic?	___	___
3. Was I ready for "take-off"?	___	___
(a) Did I discover in the first few minutes where the speaker was taking me?	___	___
(b) Did I discover his central idea so that I could follow it through the speech?	___	___
4. Was I able to pick out the ideas which supported the main idea?	___	___
(a) Did I take advantage of the speaker's clues (such as first, next, etc.) to help organize the ideas in my mind?	___	___
(b) Did I use my extra "think" time to summarize and take notes—either mentally or on paper?	___	___
5. After the speaker finished, did I evaluate what had been said?	___	___
(a) Did this new knowledge seem to fit with the knowledge I already had?	___	___
(b) Did I weigh each idea to see if I agreed with the speaker?	___	___

If you marked questions *NO*, decide why you could not honestly answer them *YES*.

Exercises for Thought and Action

1. Keep a log of the listening activities you engage in during a single day. Record the amount of time spent actually listening.

2. Explain various ways in which tape recorders could be used in the teaching of listening.

3. Discuss the relative social significance of the four types of listening emphasized in this chapter. Are there other types that should also receive teaching attention?

4. Look in the curriculum guides for other listening activities. See how many additional activities you can think of. Add all you have found and thought of to the list in this chapter.

5. Write a lesson plan for teaching a lesson in critical listening for the grade level of your choice.

6. How important are physical conditions in listening effectively? Can high humidity, excess warmth, or nearby movement actually prevent listening?
7. Observe in an elementary school classroom for at least an hour. List the occasions for pupil listening, teacher listening. Classify the listening by types.
8. Ask a teacher friend what he or she considers the major skills needed by pupils for effective listening. Compare the answer with the listing of skills in this chapter.
9. Try listening to the same content at different speeds. What do you conclude about the rate at which you can listen?

Selected References

Anderson, Rhea; Minshall, Lucille; and Comfort, Iris Tracy. "How to Teach Better Listening." *N.E.A. Elementary Instructional Service Leaflet.* Washington, D.C.: National Education Association, 1962.

Beery, Althea. "Teaching Listening Comprehension," *Journal of Communication,* 3:127–130, November, 1953.

Brown, Charles T. "Studies in Listening Comprehension," *Speech Monographs,* 26:288–294, November, 1959.

Canfield, Robert, "How Useful Are Lessons for Listening?" *The Elementary School Journal,* December, 1961, pp. 147–151.

Denby, R. V. "NCTE/ERIC Report on Research in Listening and Listening Skills," *Elementary English,* 46:511–517, April, 1969.

Devine, Thomas G. "Reading and Listening: New Research Findings," *Elementary English,* 45:346–348, March, 1968.

Duker, Sam. "Goals of Teaching Listening Skills in the Elementary School," *Elementary English,* March, 1961, pp. 170–174.

————. *Listening Bibliography.* Scarecrow Press, 1964. 211 pp.

Ernest, Carole H. "Listening Comprehension as a Function of Type of Material and Rate of Presentation," *Speech Monographs,* 35, No. 2, June, 1968.

Hall, Edward T. "Listening Behavior: Some Cultural Differences," *Phi Delta Kappan,* 50, No. 7, March, 1969.

Hall, Robert Oscar. "Listening: Questions and Problems," *Quarterly Journal of Speech,* 33:83–86, February, 1947.

Keller, Paul W. "Major Findings in Listening in the Past Ten Years," *Journal of Communication,* 10:29–38, March, 1960.

Monaghan, R. R., and Martin, J. G. "Symbolic Interaction: Analysis of Listening," *Journal of Communication,* 18:127–130, June, 1968.

Neville, Mark A. "Listening is an Art: Practice It," *Elementary English,* April, 1959, pp. 226–233.

Petty, Walter T. "Listening: Directions for Research," *Elementary English,* October, 1962, pp. 574–577.

Reddin, Estoy. "Characteristics of Good Listeners and Poor Listeners," *The Journal of the Reading Specialist,* 7:109–113, March, 1968.

Ross, Ramon. "A Look at Listeners," *Elementary School Journal,* 46:369–372, April, 1964.

Lundsteen, Sara W. "Language Arts in the Elementary School," in *Teaching for Creative Endeavor,* W. B. Michael, ed. Bloomington: Indiana University Press, 1968.

Russell, David H. "A Conspectus of Recent Research on Listening Abilities," *Elementary English,* March, 1964, pp. 262–267.

Schwartz, Sheila. "What Is Listening?" *Elementary English,* April, 1961, pp. 221–224.

Smith, Dora V. "Learning to Listen—Learning to Learn in the Elementary School," *NEA Journal,* 47:100–101, February, 1958.

Taylor, Stanford. *What Research Says to the Teacher: Teaching Listening.* Washington, D.C.: National Education Association, 1964.

Wilt, Miriam. "A Study of Teacher Awareness of Listening as a Factor in Elementary Education," *Journal of Educational Research,* 43:626–636, April, 1950.

Teaching Oral Expression

7

The development of skill in speaking is the result of a carefully planned and purposeful program of teaching. While the ability to speak, to give expression to one's needs and feelings orally, has been acquired by children before they come to school, this is only a foundation for the mastery of the skills necessary for effective oral communication. Systematic and continuous instruction must be provided in order to develop and reinforce this foundation.

The need for a planned oral language program in the schools is strongly supported by the fact that many individuals, even though they may have sound and constructive ideas, are unable to express them effectively. Many are actually afraid to stand before a group of their associates and read an announcement, make a report, or present an opinion. Such persons may be seriously handicapped in their social effectiveness and in their business or professional activities. It is vital, therefore, that the school provide a well-organized program which fosters oral expression and teaches children to speak effectively.

In addition to this practical and personal need of individuals, a strong program in oral expression is required as the basis for the development of other expressional and receptive language abilities. The work of linguists in emphasizing the primacy of speech tells us much about the role of oral language in relation to writing, to listening, and to reading. Linguistic science has also shown teachers that oral language is not an entity relating equally to all children. Dialect differences, social class and racial influences upon the child and his language, and differences in sensitivity to language are all becoming increasingly recognized as matters with which the school must deal, and the oral language program of necessity becomes the heart of the concern the school shows.

The content of this chapter is an extension of that in earlier chapters. An attempt has been made to avoid repetition, except for the emphasis the authors felt necessary. Therefore, the program for teaching oral expression in the kindergarten and primary grades is not repeated, although teachers in those grades should be able to make use of many of the suggestions in this chapter. This chapter is also especially related to Chapter 10, which discusses the teaching of skills common to both oral and written expression. The major topics to be discussed here include the following:

1. Speech in the School Curriculum
2. The Importance of Good Speech Habits
3. Developing Oral Language Skills in Special Situations
4. Evaluating Oral Language Skills and Products

Speech in the School Curriculum

The school program has traditionally given a considerable amount of teaching attention to written expression, but it is only in recent years, perhaps no more than thirty or forty, that the teaching of oral expression has been recognized as deserving of similar attention. Even now there is an awareness on the part of many educational leaders that recognizing the need for teaching oral language skills does not mean that school programs reflect the amounts of time and instructional effort really necessary.[1]

Certainly many schools and many teachers are making special efforts to provide opportunities for a wide range of oral language activities, but still the traditional cliché "the good classroom is the quiet classroom" hovers as a convenient threatening cloud over others more content to live with tradition. And even in classrooms which have much oral expression there is too little actual instruction being given that develops the skills, abilities, and attitudes important to effective speaking.

Speech and the Other Language Arts

There is little doubt that oral expression is particularly related to all means and modes of expression and reception which make use of the tool and process of language. One report says, "Research evidence available strongly suggests a high degree of interrelatedness among the various communication skills. The functional understanding of vocabulary and the ability to comprehend relationships between elements of vocabulary in structural patterns appear to encompass common communication components in the language arts."[2]

[1]Helen K. Mackintosh (editorial chairman), *Children and Oral Language.* Published by the Association for Childhood Education International, Association for Supervision and Curriculum Development, International Reading Association, and National Council of Teachers of English, 1964.
[2]Robert B. Ruddell, "Oral Language and the Development of Other Language Skills," *Research in Oral Language,* Walter T. Petty, editor (Champaign, Ill.: The National Council of Teachers of English, 1967), p. 16.

Statements as to the interrelatedness of the language arts are repeatedly encountered in educational literature.[3] In all of these statements there is a high degree of consistency: oral language development is an underlying base for the development of reading and writing abilities; measures of listening and speaking achievements correlate highly; language maturity is related to reading ability; and so on.

In practical terms all of this simply means that the focus of teaching in most classrooms should be upon oral language. Children must be permitted to express themselves, to "talk out" their ideas and feelings, and to have their willingness to talk fostered rather than inhibited. The teacher must recognize that the child who lacks maturity in oral expression is not ready to tackle tasks in reading and writing which require even greater language maturity to accomplish them successfully. It also means that special effort should be made to capitalize upon the interrelationships in all teaching endeavors, to show how what is said can be written, what is read silently can be spoken, and what is spoken is meant to be heard. The capitalization can go further by relating similar receptive skills of reading and listening and similar expressive skills of writing and speaking. Language itself is the basis of the relationships, and the maturity in and the facility with language that a child has is first and foremost shown in his oral expression. This must be realized by teachers if full utilization is to be made of the learning transfer potential in all language skills.

Oral language is very much related to the personal and social development of the child. "While research evidence appears not to be available to support the viewpoint that language ability directly affects the personality and social development of every person, adequate substantiation of the interrelatedness of language ability, environmental and physical and interpersonal factors, personality, and several behavioral tendencies such as the expression of anxiety has been shown."[4]

Speech and Individual Development

Certainly the effects of differences in the personalities of children upon the oral language activities in the classroom have been observed by many teachers. The aggressive child tends to assume a great deal of classroom leadership, and it naturally follows that he tries to monopolize speaking activities. On the other hand, it could be

[3]For example: Mildred A. Dawson, "Interrelationships Between Speech and Other Language Arts Areas," *Elementary English,* 31:223–233 (April, 1954); A. Sterl Artley, "Research Concerning Interrelationships Among the Language Arts," *Elementary English,* 27:527–537 (December, 1950); and Mackintosh, *Children and Oral Language.*

[4]Walter T. Petty and Roberta J. Starkey, "Oral Language and Personal and Social Development" in *Research in Oral Language,* p. 7.

that his assurance in speaking has fostered the aggressive behavior. Likewise, the shy, retiring child may behave that way because he lacks language maturity—or it may be that because he is shy, his confidence in speaking has been retarded. The cause and effect relationships are clearer in considering anxiety and speech. Anxieties children have are reflected in their speech, the most observable example being shown by children who stutter.

The effects of differences in individual development upon oral language are also shown by many children with handicaps—physical, mental, and cultural. Research indicates that children experiencing hearing loss, articulatory difficulty, parental rejection, or environmental deprivation tend to be less effective in using oral language than children without such handicaps.[5]

Teachers must teach the children in their classrooms, knowing and respecting the personalities of all. They must foster the development of speaking ability in the shy child, teach the overly-aggressive child to respect the rights of others, attempt to reduce the anxieties of the insecure child, and try to provide compensations for the children who are handicapped. Every teacher should watch for special interests and abilities of children and build upon these in developing an oral language instructional program.

Environmental Factors and Speech

Each child's language is in large part the product of his environment. The effects of environment—the home, neighborhood, and school—are many and varied. Some of these environmental forces have been discussed earlier, particularly those related to the learning of language before a child comes to school and during his first school years (see pages 64–70) and those bearing upon the language of the disadvantaged child (pages 86–94). In this section some environmental influences provided by the teacher and the peer group are briefly discussed.

There is some research evidence that young children tend to imitate a teacher's speech mannerisms, yet it is doubtful that basic language patterns are learned merely from listening to a teacher.[6] On the other hand, the teacher who gives warm and encouraging counsel, who shows a democratic pattern of leadership, and who provides organized and stimulating direction is aiding pupils' self-confidence and

[5]*Ibid.,* p. 3.
[6]Frank B. May, "The Effects of Environment on Oral Language Development," in *Research in Oral Language,* p. 30.

their willingness to participate in oral language activities.[7] The importance of this kind of evidence to an instructional program cannot be minimized. Willingness to participate is the first step in all classroom learning, and self-confidence is essential for effective speaking.

A child's peers are also a major force upon his oral language expression, and beyond the primary grades a greater one than that of the teacher. While little research has been done on the effects of the speech of peers upon a child's basic language patterns or his articulation and pronunciation, the available evidence supports the general feeling of teachers that the effects are likely to be negative in the sense of improving speech.[8] Teachers and parents are aware that most children adopt the idiom of the school group. More importantly, however, children are influenced in their aspirations and values by the peer group. Just as the relationship of the teacher to the class group can provide support and foster willingness to participate, a child's peers can influence his attitude toward speaking and toward improving his skills.

As the research evidence suggests, teachers should evaluate their own voices and ways of speaking. They should also consider their personal relationships to children and any possible effects upon the children's oral language.

While most teachers recognize that oral communication is impeded by indistinct utterance, careless pronunciation, uninflected or improperly inflected speech, and incorrect phrasing, too few relate these faults to their own speech and the possibility that children are emulating a model who aggravates their problems. One teachers' bulletin in discussing this problem states:[9]

> Consider for a moment the effects of a too loud, harsh, strident voice on a class group. One of two reactions will ensue: the children will be frightened into submission; or they will become defiant, disorderly, and discourteous. Neither of these reactions is conducive to profitable learning. Contrast this behavior with the effects produced by a pleasing, well-modulated voice that gives evidence of strength of purpose with no hint of weakness. Almost at once there is a feeling of security evidenced by the

[7]*Ibid.*

[8]Dorothea McCarthy, "Language Disorder and Parent-Child Relationships," *Journal of Speech and Hearing Disorders*, 19:514–523, December, 1954.

[9]*Toward Better Speech: A Manual for Teachers of all Grades*, Curriculum Bulletin, 1952–53 Series, Number 5 (New York: Board of Education of the City of New York), p. 7.

relaxed and responsive attitude of the children. This reaction can be traced directly to the teacher's poise, friendliness and self-discipline, which are reflected in her voice.

The teacher may consistently encourage good enunciation, pronunciation and articulation by making sure that he himself is using a pleasing, friendly voice; speaking distinctly, enunciating clearly and naturally; and pronouncing words in a conventional and easy manner. Further, he should encourage children to feel free to talk at proper times and provide many opportunities for children to talk freely.

A teacher should also attempt to build upon the influences of the peer group on a child's speech. The possibility of doing this hinges largely upon the rapport the teacher has with the class, although making the program one based upon genuine communication needs in a setting that is interesting and stimulating to pupils will also help. The discussion in the remainder of this chapter will expand upon this basic premise of a good program and make other suggestions.

The Importance of Good Speech Habits

It is important to keep the oral language teaching in the elementary school closely related to natural and spontaneous speaking situations whenever possible. True ease in speaking can result only from constant practice in all of the various types of situations in which the individual, as a child or as an adult, will find himself called upon to speak. However, in learning to speak effectively, a child needs more specific help than simply the opportunity to talk. That is, "the oral language proficiency of children [will] be enhanced by instructional programs which offer specific practice in articulation, voice control, usage, and other elements of oral expression."[10] In addition, opportunities to talk must be guided into the types of situations important to society.

In developing oral language skills and proper attitudes toward their use, the teacher should constantly remember that in all matters of oral presentation, he must set a good example. Frequent and varied oral language situations must be provided, and the atmosphere of the classroom must be happy, friendly, and accepting, so that reticent children will not be afraid to speak. Above all, criticism should be friendly and constructive, and be based upon standards for speaking set up cooperatively by the pupils with help from the teacher.

[10]May, "Effects of Environment," p. 36.

Articulation is the process of uttering speech sounds as distinct sounds, syllables, and words. It implies the proper separation and relation of the sounds within the words and between words. In the sentence, "Although May didn't *want* to go in the water, she *was swimming* in the lake," careless articulation might make it sound like this: "Although May didn't *wanna* go in the water, she *waswimming* in the lake." Careless articulation undoubtedly accounts for many common language faults, such as "cancha," "doncha," and "didja."

Enunciation, on the other hand, refers to the fullness or distinctiveness with which the utterance is produced. The typical American habit of dropping the final *d's, t's* and *g's* as the terminal sounds of common words is a matter of enunciation. In the sentence above, the omission of the *g* sound in swimming (swimmin') is an example of indistinct enunciation.

Pronunciation is related to articulation and to enunciation, but refers especially to the utterance of sounds in syllables and words. Further, a social connotation is attached to this skill in that the sounds must be uttered in an accepted order and with an accepted accent or emphasis. For example, the sounds which the letters *a, c, e, h, i, l* and *t* represent may be clearly enunciated by the speaker in saying the word "athletic," but adding an extra *a* sound between the *h* and *l* causes the word "athletic" to be mispronounced "athaletic."

Adequate mastery of these three closely related abilities is largely a matter of normal development, hearing words spoken repeatedly in an accepted conventional manner, and using them frequently enough to make them sound and feel right. If children have normal speech apparatus and normal hearing, they will tend to acquire the pronunciation and enunciation of their parents and others with whom they come into contact. In other words, they will imitate the models they have. The teacher, then, becomes an important model; he must be very sure that his words are correctly pronounced, clearly enunciated, and well articulated. Further, the children must have many opportunities to repeat what they hear from the teacher model.

Studies of the growth and development of children show considerable variability in the ages at which, and under what environmental conditions, children develop certain abilities. One study provided an interesting table of the ages at which most children are able to articulate certain sounds:[11]

11Mildred C. Templin, *Certain Language Skills in Children* (Minneapolis: The University of Minnesota Press, 1957).

Improving Articulation, Enunciation, and Pronunciation

3 years — *m, n, ng, p, f, h, w*
3.5 years — *y*
4 years — *k, b, d, g, r*
4.5 years — *s, sh, ch*
6 years — *t, th, v, l*
7 years — *th* (voiced), *zh, j*

This same study showed that children of upper socio-economic levels exceeded those from lower levels in maturity in articulating speech sounds. An earlier study reported that growth and maturation eliminate many articulation problems noticed in children in the first four grades but that growth and maturation do not affect noticeable improvement in the speech sounds of children in higher grades.[12] Thus it would seem to be of great importance that children be consistently encouraged to avoid routine causes of speech errors.

It is impossible to list all of the errors made by children in articulating sounds, since children can and do make sound substitutions, omissions, insertions, and distortions. Among the most common problems are these:[13]

w for *r* — wabbit for rabbit
y or *w* for *l* — yamp or wamp for lamp
th (voiceless) for *s* — Tham for Sam
th (voiced) for *z* — thoo for zoo
d for *g* — doat for goat; dough for go
t for *k* — tum for come; tea for key
f for *th* (voiceless) — fank for thank
b for *v* — balentine for valentine
t or *ch* for *sh* — too or chew for shoe
sh for *ch* — shoe for chew
w for *wh* — watt for what
l or *w* for *y* — less or wess for yes
omission of initial sounds — *es* for *yes*

It is sometimes difficult to separate dialect differences from articulation problems (e.g. *watt*). The same is true for enunciation. The expressions below are some that often need some attention to make certain that the speaker is not misunderstood.

[12]V. Roe and R. Milisen, "The Effect of Maturation upon Defective Articulation in Elementary Grades," *Journal of Speech Disorders,* 7:44, March, 1942.
[13]Louise Binder Scott and J. J. Thompson, "Good Speech," *The Instructor,* February, 1958, pp. 59–62.

did you	gave them	how are you
don't you	gave him	how do you do
why don't you	give me	would you
what did you	give her	let me
didn't you	came to meet you	let him
did he	could have	let her
she may have	shouldn't have	

Children from homes in which a foreign language is spoken often have difficulty with the inflections and rhythm of American English. A similar problem may be faced by children who speak a dialect considerably different from "standard." Possibly a few children in each classroom may not use their lips and other speech organs correctly when they talk. Special opportunities must be provided for the improvement of the speech of children with these difficulties.

Almost all children will profit from some types of direct help with speech. The child who comes to school from a highly favored home and speaks clearly and well is an exception. Many children, even from homes where the parents' speech is satisfactory, will need help with some speech skills. They may have no serious handicaps, but some emphasis on the learning of these skills will help them improve the quality of their speech. Often, too, there are entire neighborhoods or areas in which slurred or careless speech is characteristic. Therefore, teachers will do well to observe these points in connection with speech instruction:

1. The sounds which are taught should be those which represent real difficulties to the children in the class.
2. A given sound should be taught at the time or in the grade where the difficulty in its utterance occurs.
3. The teacher should continually strive to present examples of good articulation in his own expression.
4. Attention should primarily be given to the special difficulties of individual children rather than to a given sound that is supposed to represent a problem to every child in the class.
5. Motivation must be such that the children will realize that good articulation is important in all oral expression and is not to be confined to just those times when the problem is being directly attacked.

Children in the middle and upper grades who have persistent difficulty with articulation and enunciation should be brought to the attention of a person specifically trained in speech correction. However, some children may simply never have learned to make certain sounds correctly. In such cases the teacher should make a direct attack on the problem by:

1. Showing the child how the sound should be made by means of illustration and demonstration.
2. Forming the sound clearly while the child observes the action of the lips and tongue.
3. Having the pupil examine his own imitative attempts by use of a mirror.
4. Following this procedure in practice exercises which require the child to:
   (a) repeat the sound several times.
   (b) speak syllables that include the sound.
   (c) speak short sentences in which the sound is used with some repetition, including sentences made of words of high social utility which children actually use in their own expression.
   (d) utilize exercises which facilitate breathing and the use of lips and tongue.[14]

Differences in pronunciations based upon acceptable speech in various geographical areas should not be regarded in the same way as careless and slurring speech. However, differences in speech among educated persons are not so wide as those among persons with less education. No educated person from one state or area in this country should have difficulty in understanding an educated person from a different area. The teacher should encourage the child to use the cultivated pronunciations of the particular area in which he lives but to accept and respect the pronunciations of individuals from different regions.[15]

The child acquires many of his habits of pronunciation by imitating others. The pronunciation, of course, varies with the occupations and social standing of the people he encounters, as well as where they live. For many children this may cause confusion. Some persons may use definitely colloquial pronunciation and others may use the pronunciation of formal platform speech. A comparison may be made between the wearing of different kinds of clothes for different occasions and levels of pronunciation. The use of colloquial pronunciation, like

[14]See Charles Van Riper and Katherine G. Butler, *Speech in the Elementary Classroom* (New York: Harper & Brothers, 1955), and similar textbooks for additional suggestions.

[15]The classroom teacher should have some familiarity with a pronouncing dictionary such as *A Pronouncing Dictionary of American English* by John S. Kenyon and Thomas A. Knott (Springfield, Mass.: G. and C. Merriam Company, 1949).

informal or work clothing, is perfectly appropriate in many situations. But men also wear tuxedos and full dress suits, which may be compared to formal usage. The principal idea to get across is that most of the time people wear comfortable, everyday clothes, and most of the time people use the informal level of language. Informal dress and informal speech are comfortable and practical, but wide variations exist within the bounds of each.

Each child needs the following abilities and voice habits for the most effective speaking: (1) volume and voice control adequate for various communicative activities; (2) the ability to pitch his voice appropriately for different situations; (3) a clear voice tone, and (4) a speaking tempo which facilitates the reception of ideas by his listeners.

Improving Voice Quality

Some children always seem to speak too loudly, while others can scarcely be heard even when they are near. Many children have not learned to adjust their voices to the size of the room. Some children speak in a monotonous tone; others pitch all their speaking in a shrill one. Some voices are resonant, pleasant and clear; others are nasal, breathy, hoarse, or thin. Some children speak so rapidly that the meaning of the communication is lost; others speak so slowly the result is the same. These are a few of the problems the classroom teacher may encounter and must solve. If the problems appear to be serious, he should secure the help of specialists. Until such help is an actuality, or if the problems are such that he can handle them, the teacher is obligated to help each child learn to speak in a voice that is naturally pleasing, rhythmical, and clear.

The tone and quality of a child's voice may be as dependent upon mental and emotional attitudes as upon physical factors. A child who speaks freely and without fear and hesitancy generally has a voice which shows satisfactory quality and control.[16] When normal children are embarrassed or emotionally upset, however, they may speak in shrill or monotonous tones. Thus, as suggested earlier, there should be an emotional climate which is free from tension. When language activities are characterized by an atmosphere which invites spontaneous expression, children are likely to speak with the appropriate intonation called for by the activity. Except for those children who have speech difficulties of a physical nature, spontaneous speech is seldom of poor quality.

[16]Edith B. Mallory and Virginia R. Miller, "A Possible Basis for the Association of Voice Characteristics and Personality Traits," *Speech Monographs,* 25:296–304, November, 1958.

Successful solution of voice problems is largely dependent on the realization that a voice is unpleasant or that its quality interferes with communication. One procedure effective in calling a child's attention to his voice is to record his speech in different situations and permit him to listen to it.

In addition to making use of a recording instrument there are several other ways in which a teacher can make a child aware that he is talking too loudly, too harshly, or in an unpleasant voice. One way, of course, is for the teacher to say simply, "Let's keep the voice down," or "Speak softly this time." Sometimes this procedure is criticized as discouraging fluency of expression. Such a remark will not make the child self-conscious if spoken in an encouraging tone and accompanied by a warm and friendly smile. Another way is for standards to be established by the class for a speaking situation, with suggestions about voice tone included. The teacher may interject the idea of voice quality by playing parts of several recordings of speaking voices (not necessarily of children in the class). Then he might ask, "Which ones did you *like* to hear speak?" "Why do you suppose you liked his voice?" "Do you know someone whose voice you especially like?" After some discussion, he may ask "What are some of the things we might do to make our voices more pleasant when we talk to the class?" These points should be listed on the board to become the standards for the next speaking situation, which preferably should follow immediately. At the end of the speaking activity the class should evaluate themselves in terms of the standards they have set up and see if they need to add more points to the ones they have. These should be left on the board as a reminder, and after the list has been completed a chart might be made showing the complete list of standards.

Another procedure may involve having the child talk with other children to discover himself how he sounds. For example, the teacher might say:[17]

During the next three minutes, I want each of you to talk with as many others in the room as you can. Your job is to find the person whose voice sounds the most like yours. You've heard about people who look alike but are not twins; well, you won't find anyone whose voice is just like yours, but you'll find someone whose voice is more like yours than anyone else's in the room. As soon as you've found your "sound alike," come up to the front of the room. Let's see how many pairs we can get.

[17]Van Riper and Butler, *Speech*, p. 175.

The child whose voice has not developed the expected natural qualities will also profit greatly from participating in choral speech activities (discussed in a later section of this chapter). He will tend to modulate his voice, to control its pitch, tempo, and volume to blend with those around him.

Speech is often *visible* as well as *audible,* and both teachers and pupils need to be aware of this. The elementary school teacher is not concerned with developing highly accomplished platform performers who make full use of meaningful physical expression. However, he is responsible for the elimination of annoying mannerisms which detract from effective communication. It is almost impossible for anyone to speak without using some body movements; these movements should be natural and in harmony with the speaking activity. Physical mannerisms which should receive attention include fidgeting, head jerking, hand twisting, eye blinking; any twitching of mouth, face, or body; a constant and inconsistent changing of facial expression or its opposite, an unchanging facial expression; and, generally, any overdone physical movement.

Basic to the elimination of most annoying mannerisms is the development of a receptive and positive climate in the classroom. Without this kind of support a child's self-consciousness, the basis for most distracting physical movements, will not be eliminated. It simply is not possible for a child to stop certain muscular movements because the teacher asks or tells him to do so. His nervous movements are expressions of his emotional state. Physical activities are helpful in cases where the problem is one of lack of coordination. Particularly helpful activities for this purpose in the language program are rhythmic games, pantomime, creative dramatics, memorized plays, puppet and shadow plays, monologues, dialogues, imitations, and demonstrations.

Speaking is done to communicate. A pupil speaks because he has something to say, because he needs to express an opinion, because he wishes to present facts or information. He has something to say *to someone;* therefore an audience situation is implied. This audience may be a single classmate, a group of classmates, or any number of parents, friends, or other visitors. Oral communication quite obviously is not a one-way street. It requires not only that the speaker must have something to say, but that he must say it in a way that will evoke proper responses from his listeners. Children should be made aware of their double responsibility in oral language situations. The speaker

Avoiding Physical Mannerisms

Achieving Audience Sensitivity

must be conscious of his audience and sensitive to their needs, interests, and desires. The listener must give courteous attention to the speaker, and respond to what has been said in an acceptable way.

We should encourage children to think and possibly disagree with the speaker while at the same time showing tolerance and respect for his opinion. In addition, the program should include:

1. Giving quiet, courteous, and alert attention to the speaker.
2. Responding with appropriate facial expression to show interest.
3. Making other appropriate responses, including laughter and applause.
4. Asking pertinent questions in order to amplify or clarify the speaker's comments.
5. Observing common courtesies in questioning.

A basic element of audience sensitivity appears when the communication is deliberately planned in advance of the presentation to appeal to the special interests of the audience. This type of preparation requires no last-minute adjustments in content or in preparation to attract or to hold the audience. One fifth-grade textbook reminds the pupils to "keep your audience in mind when you give a report orally. Boys and girls who are listening like to have the speaker look at them when he is talking. . . . Speak clearly and distinctly so your listeners will understand each word."[18] The same textbook suggests that these points be remembered by speakers:

1. Choose a subject that will interest your audience.
2. Plan to tell the things that will interest others.
3. Tell things in the right order.
4. Speak clearly and distinctly.
5. Speak in a voice loud enough for the size of the room where you are speaking.

Children are born critics, and, consciously or not, judge the one who is speaking sometimes even before he has begun to speak. Their thoughts may not be expressed in words, but their inner feelings are evidenced by their emotional response to a speaker: bright, smiling face, attentive posture; noticeably inert posture; constant talking, etc. The effectiveness of speech, like that of TV programs, is gauged by audience reaction. This reaction is not the responsibility of the speaker alone but is shared by the audience. Since the classroom audience usually includes the teacher, he should consider his own reactions.

[18]Thomas C. Pollock and John J. Forester, *Using Language, Grade 5* (New York: The Macmillan Company, 1954), p. 127.

Developing Oral Language Skills in Special Situations

Learning to communicate effectively by speaking is a process of blending a knowledge of the skills, abilities, and attitudes important to oral expression with experience in using them. Provision of frequent opportunities for speaking for genuine communication purposes is one of the most productive procedures that can be used. A child learns to be at ease and to speak effectively by speaking, just as he learns to swim by swimming or to ride a bicycle by riding. The role of experience in learning has been emphasized by writers and speakers many times. No statement on the importance of experience, the importance of participation, is better than that voiced a number of years ago by Hatfield.[19]

> Experience is the best of all schools. Certainly no one learns so thoroughly, and few learn so rapidly, in any other. And experience need not be a dear school, if it is competently organized and is conducted by a capable teacher who illuminates each situation in prospect and in retrospect. . . . The school of experience is the only one which will develop the flexibility and power of self-direction requisite for successful living in our age of swift industrial, social, and economic change.

This report also gives an excellent summary of procedures to be followed by the teacher in developing all types of language abilities:[20]

> The actual experiences in communication which go into the curriculum should be representative of the present experience of most pupils outside the English class — in other school classes, in clubs, on the playground, at home, at the store. Many of these may depend for their reality upon the social situation in the English class itself, but they should parallel quite closely the experiences that do and will occur elsewhere.
>
> A curriculum of actual experiences in communications implies typical (not invariable) classroom procedures somewhat like these: (The order of the activities would vary with circumstances and pupils.)
>
> 1. Making the pupils conscious of a present, worthy occasion for communication. Sometimes this occasion must be created by the teacher; frequently it needs only to be brought to attention.

[19]W. Wilbur Hatfield, *An Experience Curriculum in English,* A Report of the Curriculum Commission of the National Council of Teachers of English (New York: D. Appleton-Century Company, 1935), p. 3.

[20]*Ibid.,* pp. 135–136.

2. Letting pupils attempt to meet the situation by speaking or writing.

3. Giving advice and assistance as the pupils prepare (if the occasion permits preparation) and as they write (if the occasion calls for writing). This includes helping them to perceive the techniques which they can use to advantage.

4. Helping pupils to realize that the excellence of their work must be measured in terms of the effect of their efforts upon their audience, and pointing out the causes of their (usually partial) success or failure.

5. Introducing at any favorable time specific practice in a skill which the pupils realize the worth of but which they may not have mastered.

6. Noting growth, chiefly by comparing success on this and previous similar occasions.

Conversation

In terms of social importance, conversation is the most fundamental speaking activity of both children and adults. As such, it should receive considerably more than the incidental attention frequently given it in the typical program. Apparently some teachers regard conversational activities merely as the source of minor disciplinary problems, since such activities call for individual freedom of expression. However, even if a teacher has no fear of losing control of the class, he may nevertheless be influenced by the possibility that his fellow teachers may misinterpret the freedom and noisy activity in his classroom. Every teacher should remember that the quiet class is not always the good class, and that the actively interested class, even though noisy, may readily be the best class.

Conversation is generally defined as an exchange of thoughts or ideas about one or more topics between two or more speakers. It is well to note in this definition the words *exchange* and *thoughts*. Qualities of a good conversationalist include the abilities to:

1. Think clearly.
2. Use English effectively.
3. Speak to the point.
4. Discuss without arguing.
5. Stimulate others to talk.
6. Discover common interests.
7. Describe situations and events.

The good conversationalist should also show good judgment, tact, conviction, a wide range of interests, originality, good memory, broadmindedness, adaptability, and sincerity. Certainly this is a big order and one which cannot entirely be filled in the elementary school.

When a child feels secure, is happy, and is spared situations which cause undue anxiety, he tends to speak with ease. Likewise, power over language aids emotional and social adjustment. The child who has developed the ability to participate effectively in conversation gets greater satisfaction from activities which involve other people and has better chances for satisfactory growth than the child who does not have this ability. In the primary grades, emphasis should be placed upon first helping the child to feel comfortable in the conversational group and then creating within him a desire to participate fully. Oral language teaching at this level, besides developing the child's ability to converse naturally and spontaneously, should include such skills as selecting the proper time to talk and the proper time not to talk, talking about something of interest, sticking to the subject, enunciating clearly, and showing consideration for the rights of others by taking turns in talking and listening.

In the middle and upper grades greater emphasis should be placed upon developing each child's sense of responsibility to the group and upon showing respect for and giving encouragement to others. It is reasonable, too, to expect the upper-grade child to be able to carry on a sustained conversation with considerable skill and assurance.

The elementary school does not have the responsibility for producing polished conversationalists, but the children should be given many opportunities to take part in conversation in many different forms, in order that they may develop to the maximum of their abilities. A program of instruction based upon the following principles should accomplish this goal:

1. Conversation is a two-way process between a listener and a speaker, who exchange ideas in turn.
2. Conversation involves listening to the contributions of others and reacting to them.
3. Conversation is not random talk but involves real interaction about a subject of mutual interest.
4. Courtesy should prevail in the behavior of the participants even though the conversation may be very informal.
5. Good conversationalists have a responsibility to themselves and others to be truthful and considerate in their remarks.
6. Good conversationalists at all times attempt to avoid aggressive or argumentative attitudes. After all, conversation is a friendly discussion, not a verbal battle.

In building a program based upon these principles, the teacher will help children to learn the value of being informed on suitable topics and of discovering sources of interesting material. They will learn also to be enthusiastic, to use vocabulary that is varied as well as fitted to the topic and the particular situation, and to avoid distracting mannerisms. And they will learn the proprieties associated with conversation: when and where it is appropriate *not* to talk, how to change the subject tactfully, how to suit topics to situations and people, how to follow an introduction with remarks designed to put everyone at ease, and how to be a good listener.

Particular emphasis needs to be given to the observance of courtesies in conversation. Among those deserving special attention are the following:

1. Knowing how and when to interrupt the person talking.
2. Knowing how to disagree with the speaker's statement.
3. Avoiding completing the speaker's statement.
4. Not being too demonstrative.
5. Not monopolizing the conversation.
6. Avoiding unpleasant topics.
7. Not whispering in the presence of others.
8. Including all members of the group in one's remarks.
9. Expressing likes and dislikes moderately.
10. Avoiding being too personal.
11. Speaking in a soft voice.
12. Avoiding futile arguments.
13. Knowing what to do when two people begin talking at the same time.
14. Showing consideration for persons entering the group after conversation has started.
15. Avoiding hurting the feelings of others.
16. Not listening to conversations not meant for one.
17. Not using unfamiliar language.
18. Avoiding unusual mannerisms and affectations.
19. Not repeating needlessly.

Since conversation is a more spontaneous activity than most other oral language activities, it should be exploited by the teacher. Throughout the school day many topics arise which arouse pupil interests and stimulate the desire to communicate ideas and thoughts to others. Usually these topics will be related to purposeful activities of the classroom program so conversing about them is the natural thing for the pupils to do. The teacher, therefore, should consider their appropriateness and whenever possible allow the pupils to develop this spontaneous conversational situation. When the conversational situation does not arise spontaneously, it may be necessary for the teacher to plan a more formal approach to the subject.

In either the spontaneous conversational situation or the planned approach, attention is centered first on the content of what is being said. For example, if the children are talking about where to store their art materials, attention is given first to answering the implied question. Answering the question is the purpose of the conversation. As the conversation progresses, however, attention may be diverted from the subject matter to the best ways of carrying on a conversation. The teacher may ask if any of the pupils have noted that some contributions are better than others and why this is so. Points appropriate to the ages of the children may be noted, discussed, and placed upon the board or upon a chart. The number of different points should be limited and only the key ones should be recorded, so that the purpose of the conversation will not become lost in concern about technicalities in conversational skill.

Children have so many interesting experiences both in and out of school that the teacher should never be at a loss to find opportunities for teaching and practicing the conversational skills. Sometimes, however, some of these opportunities are overlooked or are not examined carefully enough to determine whether there is real purpose in conversing about a particular topic. Situations occurring in most classrooms which may be utilized for conversation may spring from the need to make plans for class activities, either for a portion of a day or for some longer-range purpose such as "things we must do before visiting the Indian museum," or "what we'll need at our party." Someone may point out a picture in a book or bring in an item from a newspaper. Special interests such as hobbies, games, and TV programs can all become the focus of a class conversation; so can behavior in particular situations, such as working on a committee or looking after a class pet.

In the teaching of conversation it is well to remember that it is an activity of some intimacy and that such intimacy is difficult to achieve in a formal physical setting. The shy child who will not talk from the isolation of his seat may find it easy to talk in a conversational group of four or five children where it is possible to talk in a low voice and feel secure in the physical nearness of others. In addition, the desks and chairs may need to be rearranged so that the children will face one another. Even in a small group, a self-confident child may need to be chosen to keep the conversation rolling and to urge the participation of all members of the group.

Discussion   Discussion between teachers and pupils and among pupils is undoubtedly the most frequently occurring oral language activity in the classroom. Through discussion children gain information, learn to deal with facts and problems, and develop the ability to express themselves effectively. Discussion not only occupies a key position in the school program, but has a very prominent place in adult activities as well. When a group has a common interest that requires planning, a solution, or agreement, a discussion will develop naturally.

Discussion differs from conversation in that it has a more purposeful goal. This goal is generally understood and in school situations has been agreed upon by both teacher and pupils. In the lower grades, the goal is perhaps less apparent to the pupils than to the teacher but is still present.

The guiding principles and the courtesies involved in discussion should be much the same as those previously listed for teaching conversation. However, because discussion has a more definite goal, the emphasis should be slightly different. Pupils must still remember to be courteous listeners and speakers—that is, they must remember to allow others to speak, to respect the opinions of others, and to speak in such a way that all may hear—but they must also learn the specific skills required for discussion. Most important of these is staying on the topic and working toward a suitable conclusion. Related to this is the ability to make concise and worthwhile contributions, either by statements or by questions, which have been formulated as a result of listening to and thinking about what has been said by others. Such contributions are worthwhile only when children learn to support arguments with facts, to distinguish between fact and opinion, and to know the difference between relevant and irrelevant material.

Basic to instruction in the discussion skills is the clear recognition of the problem in all its parts by all the children. Each child, if he is actually to participate, must be conversant with the problem. This, of course, does not mean that he must know everything about the problem, but he must know enough so that he can make a contribution. Knowledge of the problem or topic implies that individual and class preparation is necessary. At this point the teacher will need to teach research skills, such as using the encyclopedia, dictionary, maps, and other reference sources. He will need to help children relate their experiences to the topic. He will need to stress that a problem is answered with facts, not emotions, and that facts must be collected and evaluated.

It is important for a teacher not to permit the more talkative children in the class to dominate the activities. In order to prevent this it may be useful to keep a "participation index" to indicate the distribution of children's contributions.[21] Such an index is simply a tabulation of the number of times each child contributes to a discussion. With a focus upon the quality as well as the frequency of participation, perhaps such an index could be kept by a pupil or by several pupils and could then serve as an added device for relating the discussion to previously established standards.

Discussional activities are important, too, in teaching cooperation. A discussion problem is solved or clarified by the participation of all. Discussion implies reaching a better understanding of a problem or solving it. It implies tolerance and good sportsmanship.

Leadership training is a part of the instructional program in discussion. Many, but not all, children in a classroom need practice in the leadership skills that are necessary for the discussion leader. Leaders must be taught how to open a discussion, how to draw out thinking and information through skillful questioning, how to summarize main points, and how to handle sharp differences of opinion in a tactful manner. These skills are taught by the teacher serving as a model, by discussing how they are done, and by reference to appropriate sections of the language textbook. In pupil-led discussions the teacher should remain in the background as much as possible and provide guidance only as needed.

There are many situations in the school day which may be utilized for teaching discussion skills. Some representative situations or problems include:

1. The program for Education Week.
2. How to raise money to buy a record-player for the classroom.
3. How best to organize the art show.
4. What things about a movie make it good.
5. Classroom housekeeping.
6. A book everyone in the group has read.
7. An experience shared by all.
8. How to converse, use the telephone, etc.
9. How different people talk.
10. What a fifth-grade pupil should know about the Constitution.

[21]Dorothy G. Petersen and Velma D. Hayden, *Teaching and Learning in the Elementary School* (New York: Appleton-Century-Crofts, Inc., 1961), p. 121.

The following is one teacher's report on a class discussion:[22]

When the boys and girls in our third grade class returned to the room after the lunch hour some were quite indignant because one of the boys had thrown a rock at another. Since we are very particular at our school about rock throwing, the children know it is something they shouldn't do.

I asked the accused if he really had thrown the rock. He said he had because the other boy had said a certain area on the playground belonged to him and no one else could walk there. Some of the children thought that was funny and laughed. I asked what seemed funny and they replied that the playground belonged to all and no one person could claim part of it as his alone.

This seemed a good opportunity to discuss property and belongings. One child said, "That is just like saying that the school cafeteria belongs to only one person and no one else could eat there." I asked if children should share their lunches just because they shared the cafeteria. They promptly replied that that was different. That each should eat his own lunch because a lunch is meant for only one child.

We continued our discussion by naming a number of objects, buildings, and other things, and deciding whether each was something which might be used by only one or should be shared by a number of people.

Later we talked about places where it would be proper and safe to throw rocks. One boy said that his father and he sometimes spent an hour or so throwing rocks into a river near their home. We agreed that it would be good exercise and training to throw rocks under some conditions.

Reporting   Oral reporting is a language activity used primarily in the middle and upper grades and is an outgrowth of the "telling" and "showing" activities of the primary grades. It is a major language activity of the elementary school, sometimes being used quite informally and at other times more formally. Oral reporting in the elementary school includes speeches or talks that are organized in advance of their presentation, which are given to convince or inform, and that show effective use of language for communication. Oral reporting in the elementary school is more than the reading of a written report, but it does not have the characteristics of the rather formal speeches emphasized in secondary school speech classes, particularly those of a somewhat traditional nature. Oral reporting in the elementary school is done for genuine

[22]As reported by Mrs. G. W. McCready, Sonora, California.

Group news stories and oral reporting can teach the need for effective planning, writing, speaking, and listening

communicative purposes. Oral reporting takes several forms. For example, giving reviews of books, TV programs, etc.; summarizing a science experiment or what was learned about some subject; telling about a record that has been kept; or giving directions for doing something.

Important school and life situations calling for giving reports include the following:

1. Providing information from sources or material not accessible to all.
2. Summarizing results of independent observation.
3. Providing an answer to a definite question raised in class.
4. Making available results of council or class government activities.
5. Summarizing results of individual or group excursions.
6. Announcing recreational activities—concerts, plays, games.
7. Evaluating books.
8. Selecting important current events.
9. Summarizing progress of science experiments.
10. Reviewing class newspaper progress.

In the teacher's planning for oral reporting, specific attention should be given to the teaching of the skills that will help make oral reporting a profitable language experience. Basically, these skills are (1) the selection of appropriate material, (2) the collection and organization of this material, and (3) the actual presentation of the material to a group. The development of these skills and their practice should, in general, follow the suggestions for teaching discussed in Chapter 2 and earlier in this chapter. Particular points for a teacher to keep in mind in teaching reporting are the following:

1. Encouraging the condensing of materials from sources.
2. Not allowing the direct copying of materials without giving credit.
3. Basing reporting activities upon the needs of the individual and the group.
4. Assigning topics according to individual interests.
5. Stressing the importance of good beginnings and endings of reports.
6. Supervising note-taking occasionally.
7. Training pupils to give full credit for ideas, materials, and quotations used in reports.
8. Using group and individual evaluation of reports.
9. Using reporting activities to discover individual pupil weaknesses in usage, organization of ideas, voice control, and other important oral skills.

Even though some reports are quite informal, children need to be taught the definite steps in preparing a report. In every case, however, it should be stressed that communication is the purpose of the report and that the effectiveness of communication is enhanced by good form. The pupil should usually follow these steps:

1. Making a list of questions which might be asked about the subject on which he is reporting.
2. Consulting reference sources and making notes for the answers to these questions.
3. Looking over his notes and deciding how the report should be organized. This includes first dividing it into main divisions and then preparing a complete outline in order that details may be arranged in their proper places. For many reports this outline may be very simple. In fact, throughout most of the elementary grades the teacher should stress the importance of a simple outline.
4. Thinking about the length of time required for giving the report; reorganizing or cutting the outline if necessary.
5. Giving particular attention to ways to begin and end the report with interesting statements.

What makes a good oral report is an appropriate topic for a class discussion, and the discussion itself, as was suggested earlier in this chapter, is an effective teaching technique. From an exchange of ideas, major points of agreement among the pupils appear and may be recorded. One class agreed on these requirements, which were written on a chart:

> Choose a topic.
> Find books and materials
> Select the information for the report.
> Organize the information.
> Make notes to use.

Sometimes reporting activities may be improved by the use of devices and materials which add to the content of the report or to the means of presentation. For example, pictures or cut-outs on a flannelboard may be helpful in showing the organization of the report, in adding to the verbal description being made, or in minimizing the self-consciousness of the reporter. The same kind of help might be provided by diagrams, charts, chalkboard drawings or an outline, etc. Having a partner help the reporter is also useful. This partner might pantomime what the reporter is describing, hold up charts or pictures, or otherwise simply act as an assistant. Reporting may also be assisted by the construction of charts, displays, etc., which can be seen prior to the report and hence arouse interest.

Using a telephone is an activity that most persons engage in often. How effectively each one does this is debatable, as is the question of teaching telephoning in school. Some persons believe that since most children use a telephone at home from an early age, there is no need for the school to teach anything about its use. Others recognize that while most children have some knowledge of the telephone some instruction in its use is necessary. Certainly many adults and some children use the telephone skillfully; others antagonize their listeners— and the telephone company. The importance of the telephone as a medium of communication is emphasized in the following statement:[23]

Telephoning

> More than forty-four million telephones form a voice highway over the entire nation. This fact indicates that the telephone is a very important medium of communication in which the school and home have a responsibility for developing habits of courtesy,

[23]The Commission on the English Curriculum, National Council of Teachers of English, *Language Arts for Today's Children* (New York: Appleton-Century-Crofts, Inc., 1954), p. 378.

for considering the rights of others by limiting conversations and by calling at appropriate times, for providing practice in using the telephone in case of emergencies such as calling the police, the fire department, or the ambulance, or in making long distance calls.

Attitudes and abilities important to everyday life should be emphasized in teaching the use of the telephone. Children should learn how to formulate messages, inquiries, orders, and other detailed information as concisely as possible before making a call. They should be taught to identify themselves and their purpose in making the call both clearly and courteously. They should speak as graciously as in face to face conversation and know how to end a telephone call politely. They should also learn other courtesies related to using the telephone: the importance of returning calls, taking messages for others, avoiding placing calls at times inconvenient to the person called or monopolizing his time, and the necessity of asking permission to use someone else's telephone. They should learn also to consider whether or not others might wish to use the same phone.

In addition to the above social objectives, distinct speech, a well-modulated tone of voice, brevity, and pointedness are desirable language objectives. Certain specific telephoning techniques also must be learned, such as using the directory to find numbers, getting the operator or dialing a number, making emergency or special service calls, and placing long-distance calls.

Most of the actual situations involving the use of the telephone generally arise outside of school. In fact, many schools place definite restrictions on the use of the school telephones. More often than not a teaching situation in the use of the telephone at school is a dramatized or imaginary situation, depending upon the maturity of the pupils.[24] Typical telephoning situations which may be recalled or dramatized for teaching purposes include the following:

1. Answering a call intended for oneself.
2. Answering a call for another member of the family.
3. Calling a message to a friend.
4. Telephoning a message for someone else.
5. Giving a tradesman an order.

[24]Telephone companies usually have a kit of materials on the use of the telephone that they will make available to schools. This kit usually includes the film "Adventures in Telezonia."

6. Making emergency calls to fire station, police, hospital, or other special services.
7. Conversing with a friend over the telephone.
8. Calling a business firm where a secretary answers.

Language textbooks may include telephoning activities. For example, a fourth grade textbook suggests the following:[25]

> Choose a classmate to work with you. Plan telephone conversations for two of the situations below. Act out your conversations when it is your turn.
>
> 1. You call Bob to ask him to go rollerskating. Bob's mother answers. Bob is sick.
> 2. You are going on a short trip with your mother. You call your dentist. You ask to change the time of your appointment.
> 3. Your class is having an exhibit. You call your aunt to invite her to the exhibit.
> 4. Mr. John Adams, an insurance salesman, calls to speak to your father. Your father is at his office. The office telephone number is 426-3587.

In the primary grades, learning about telephoning provides a meaningful opportunity to teach (1) the courtesies of "please," "thank you," taking turns, and listening; (2) self-confidence and spontaneity of expression; and (3) creativeness in oral expression. In the middle and upper grades, instruction on telephoning provides opportunity to teach (1) further courtesies of conversation; (2) the informational or research skills of alphabetizing and getting specific help through the use of the Yellow Pages of the telephone directory; (3) calm reaction in emergencies, such as calling the police, the fire department, a hospital; and (4) the speech skills of articulation, enunciation, pronunciation, pleasing voice, and correct word usage.

In considering the teaching of telephone skills and behavior—particularly the courtesies which facilitate communication as well as making the exchange more pleasant—the atmosphere of the classroom, including the use of courtesy by the teacher, has far greater impact than *telling* pupils what to do. This basic fact is reiterated here also in regard to the teaching of conversation, discussion, and other speaking activities.

---

[25]Thomas C. Pollock, and others, *The Macmillan English Series,* 4, Third Revised Edition (New York: The Macmillan Company, 1967), p. 35.

Storytelling

Storytelling is an ancient art which was once almost universal. Today few people are good storytellers, a fact not difficult to understand, considering the demands of modern life. Ability to tell stories develops through use, and use responds to demand. The many readily available books and radio and TV programs leave little time for the children to listen to stories except in school and even less time to learn to tell stories themselves. The time left for the storyteller to practice his art is extremely limited. Something very important in the lives of both children and parents is lost when the radio, TV, and hi-fi are allowed to displace the bedtime story.

There is no one way to tell stories. Successful storytellers have their own ways of telling their favorite stories. They may even vary their methods to meet the demands of different types of stories.[26] Similarly there appears to be no single best way of teaching storytelling. Some of the following general suggestions may be helpful to the teacher and the class in a story hour.

1. The practice of relating the story closely to the experiences of the storyteller and his audience is a sound and widely-used principle. A child cannot be expected to tell a story well unless he is fully informed about the events, situations, and content of the story. In the first place, he would not *want* to tell it if it didn't interest him and if he didn't feel that his audience, because of a background of similar experiences, would be equally interested.

2. The general atmosphere of the place in which the story is told is an important factor in successful storytelling. Outside distractions should, in so far as is possible, be eliminated; the room should be quiet; the audience should be comfortably at ease. Since storytelling is intended to be a thoroughly enjoyable experience—one in which all pressures and cares are laid aside—a calm air of informality should prevail in the room. The children will generally prefer to sit in a circle, perhaps on the floor, grouped closely around the speaker. Children enjoy watching the speaker closely during these story hours, and then, too, the good storyteller likes to be able to look directly at everyone in his audience.

3. The pleasure of a storytelling experience depends so completely upon the masterful presentation of the story that the importance of a careful preparation prior to telling the story cannot be overemphasized. The story must be so well known to the teller that every

[26] A good aid to teachers is Dewey W. Chambers, *Storytelling and Creative Drama* (Dubuque, Iowa: Wm. C. Brown Company, 1970), 92 pp.

detail can be seen in his mind's eye. He must sense the mood of the story and plan ways to convey that feeling to his audience. The words he will use must be well chosen. Sometimes these will be his own words, and at other times they will be the words of the characters in the story.

4. Realistic standards and friendly criticism should be part of every storytelling experience but they should never be so exacting as to mar the pleasure of the occasion. Standards are needed to serve as reminders to the storyteller. They should, of course, be ones that he has helped prepare, and must be easily possible of attainment. Criticism should be used, too, but in a friendly, sensible manner. The prime objective of this activity is to develop successful storytellers and to encourage them to be willing to tell stories. Finding too much fault with a child's storytelling efforts is a poor way to encourage him to try again.

5. As is the case with all other language abilities, the storytelling skills must be established through actual learning of the skills and repeated practice in lifelike activities.

Brief guides to storytelling are helpful. These should be formulated by the teacher and the children. For example:[27]

Speak clearly.
Speak so all can hear.
Do not string sentences together with "and-uhs" or "so's."
Stand still.
Look at your audience.
Use colorful words.
Have a good beginning and ending.
Talk naturally.
Be interested in your story!

Not all of these need be presented at once. Perhaps only one or two points can be emphasized at a time and others can be dealt with later. There is a great deal to be said for a child storyteller "catching" techniques from the teacher storyteller.

To teach storytelling to children successfully, a teacher must have a real love of stories and some ability in telling them. The teacher is the model, and the one who, because of whatever pleasure he gets from telling and listening to stories, instills this feeling in the children. The number one item in importance for the teacher and the children is the

---

[27]Robert Whitehead, *Children's Literature: Strategies of Teaching,* © 1968, p. 107. Reprinted by permission of Prentice-Hall, Inc., Englewood Cliffs, N.J.

selection of the story to tell. In doing so, a distinction must be made between stories for the teacher to tell and those which children can tell. Stories which the teacher can tell abound in literature. Whitehead suggests the following as storytelling fare for different age groups:[28]

> *Preschool through kindergarten*—For this age group the stories must be short and to the point. Stories should be of familiar things: animals, children, home, machines, people, toys. Humorous and nonsense story poems, jingles, Mother Goose rhymes, and the accumulative tales are especially apt choices. Typical stories would include those in The Three Series: "The Three Billy Goats Gruff," "The Three Little Pigs," "The Three Bears," and the "Adventure of Three Little Rabbits." Others: "Little Red Riding Hood," "Henny Penny," and "The Teeny Tiny Woman."
>
> *Ages 6 to 10*—Animal tales, stories of child life in other lands, and the ancient and modern fairy tales are types of stories that appeal to this group. Among the many tales to be recommended we would include "The Elves and the Shoemaker," "Rumpelstiltskin," "Slovenly Peter," "The Steadfast Tin Soldier," "Hansel and Gretel," "The Sleeping Beauty," "The Bremen Town Musicians," and "Jack and the Beanstalk."
>
> *Ages 11 to 14*—Children in this stage of development demand true stories, tales of adult life, hero tales, and stories that teach something about personal ideals. These children want stories of adventure, too. The 13- and 14-year-old youngsters seek out the myths, legends, and epics, along with those stories of a biographical and historical nature that teach patriotism and service to country. Tales for telling to this group would include "The Story of Aladdin," "How Thor Found His Hammer," tales of Robin Hood and King Arthur, "Pecos Bill," "Paul Bunyan," and various tales about sports heroes.

Stories that children may tell can be original ones or ones that they have heard or read. In most instances their storytelling should grow out of classroom activities that give them something to tell about. These activities may then lead to a story—made-up or real.

Storytelling activities in a classroom should primarily involve either the teacher or one of the pupils telling a story to the group. However, some attention needs to be given to the improvement of storytelling from one such activity to the next. Generally improvement is achieved by the teacher and pupils together deciding what is in need of improvement and then working on these needs cooperatively and again appraising the effort. If these procedures do not satisfactorily accomplish the purpose, special activities or other kinds of lessons may

[28]*Ibid.*, pp. 103–104.

be needed. For example, stories may be told in small groups rather than in the total classroom setting. The small group may be the best setting also to practice on particular points important to storytelling— gesturing, for example—for making plans for the next storytelling experience, for telling jokes and anecdotes, or for working on new standards.

Although storytelling is primarily for enjoyment, other goals of oral language may be inconspicuously injected into the experience without spoiling the fun. By first listening to the teacher tell a story and then telling it himself, a child learns how to put ideas in sequence, how to compose sentences, and how to emphasize meaning with his voice. Children who have had frequent opportunities for listening to and telling stories are better able to appreciate desirable techniques of telling a story than are children who have had no such experiences.[29]

Storytelling should be carefully planned, with special attention paid to the creation of the right classroom atmosphere. The children must feel relaxed, at ease, and expectant. They must feel that they are participating in an enjoyable activity. The stories selected may be realistic or fanciful; reproduced or original. They may be stories about friends, pets, things they have seen, places they have been; stories about imaginary characters; anecdotes, or "cuties" as the TV announcers call them, with a suitable point of wit; stories about things seen in movies or on television; stories based on pictures they have seen or books they have read. In order to tell about things—to tell stories—children need opportunities to hear stories, to read stories, to go places, and to do things. It is noticeable, too, that the one who tells stories well works at it constantly, trying his skill frequently on others.

It is wise to keep in mind that storytelling may be varied by using a flannelboard or felt board, puppets, or other regalia. The use of these aids will assist pupils in remembering the story, in establishing rapport with the audience, and in gaining enough self-confidence for telling the story. Any of these aids may be used by a teacher for building interest in storytelling.[30]

Children should be encouraged to be constantly on the lookout for stories to tell. Many excellent ones about Halloween, Thanksgiving, Rosh Hashana, Christmas, and other holidays and special occasions

[29]See Chapter 15 for further suggestions on the teacher as a storyteller.

[30]In addition to the Chambers and Whitehead references on storytelling, see Henry Bamman and others, *Oral Interpretation of Children's Literature* (Wm. C. Brown Company, 1964), Joseph Wagner and Robert Smith, *Teacher's Guide to Storytelling* (Wm. C. Brown Company, 1958), and Ruby E. Cundiff and Barbara Webb, *Storytelling for You: Handbook of Help for Storytellers Everywhere* (Antioch Press, 1957) for many other suggestions.

often appear in magazines. The children should also be encouraged to tell stories they have read in their supplemental reading. It is generally a good idea for the teacher to require a conference with the pupil concerning the worth and appropriateness of his story before he is permitted to tell it to the class. Sometimes a committee of pupils may assist the teacher with the screening of stories.

Dramatizing

Storytelling leads directly to dramatizing, for all children love to see stories acted out, and most want to take part in the acting. As was suggested in Chapter 4, dramatization in the primary grades should be very informal; that is, it is not a dramatic activity, as most adults think of it, but a play activity. Such dramatic play is inherent in many child activities. It provides the spontaneity and natural enthusiasm which move children to express feelings and thoughts. The preschool child or the child of the primary grades sits in the cockpit of his airplane built of blocks or orange crates. He *is* the pilot. He talks as he thinks the pilot would talk. He does the things he thinks the pilot would do. Through such activity the child furthers his learning of language. He seeks facts, information, and materials which provide new relationships and meanings for him. He experiments with new words, new ideas, and new ways of saying and doing things.

The teacher in the intermediate and upper grades faces a major problem, however, if the pupils have not experienced much informal play and creative dramatics in the preceding grades. The introduction of dramatization through charades, action songs, and choral speaking will help to break down undue reserve and will build interest in further dramatic activities. In the activities suggested the pupils are motivated by the rhythm of chant, song, or verse, and the action is focused upon pantomime. With enough of this preparation, and with a real mood of enjoyment, the reluctant pupils will become ready for the more formal dramatizations.

Dramatizations in the middle and upper grades include those calling for scripts and those calling for no scripts. The scripts may be commercial ones, or they may be written by the teacher or by the children themselves. The first productions should consist simply of acting out very well-known stories without formal scripts. Beginning with no script is a fundamental technique used by teachers in producing more formal dramatizations, too.

The following is a suggested procedure for teaching dramatization:

1. The dramatization should be based on material thoroughly known by the children. The teacher and the class should discuss each

character in the dramatization: how each character feels toward each other one, and why he feels so; how each character looks, walks, talks, etc.; what each scene is like; what the dramatization is saying.

2. The children should cooperate in planning the setting, the costumes (if any), and the stage scenery. Whenever possible this planning should be extended to include the actual making of the costumes and scenery. These activities offer valuable opportunities for the development of responsibility and ingenuity, the use of special talents, and the "drawing-out" of the shy child.

3. After children thoroughly understand the dramatization, the first rehearsal should be begun without script. Various children should be tried for the different characterizations. Emphasis should be upon the way the child creates the character. What the child has the character do should be based upon his understanding of the dramatization and the part he is playing. The words and actions should be those of the child.

4. The next step is the actual casting of the characters. Since most productions may be repeated several times, it is generally possible to plan for several complete casts. The children who are interested in stage management, scenery design, or costuming should be put in those positions. Of course, the emphasis as far as language arts is concerned is upon language expression, but in the average classroom there will be enough jobs necessary to present a play so that each child can do several things that he wants to do.

The planning for somewhat formal dramatization should in no way be permitted to interfere with the continuance of the creative, spontaneous dramatic play of the lower grades. All such creative endeavors should be encouraged, but many can be channeled into dramatizations that are more planned. The creativity of many children can be capitalized upon and guided through careful planning into activities that are even more satisfying to them than their spontaneous efforts.

In addition to the dramatization of stories, including those written by the children themselves, there are many situations which may be dramatized and thus provide a means for teaching speaking and listening skills. Situations such as the following are excellent for dramatization: introducing people, answering telephone calls correctly, eating different kinds of food, delivering a message, entertaining visitors, going on a shopping tour, holding a club meeting, extending greetings or saying good-bye, or giving someone directions.

Puppetry is another form of dramatics that is very popular. Children often express themselves more freely through puppetry than through other dramatic activities. Since they are manipulating dolls, they have little opportunity to become afraid of the audience. Then, too, the activity seems more "make-believe" and the children may become more thoroughly a part of the story.

Puppets include *stick puppets* which are made of cardboard and fastened to long sticks, *shadow puppets* which are made the same way as stick puppets but are not colored and have holes in the faces of the figures for eyes, and *hand puppets* made from solid, three-dimensional materials such as paper bags, socks, and papier-mâché.[31]

A marionette is a string-controlled doll with head, body, legs, and arms worked from above. Upper-grade children enjoy making these figures and planning performances for them. The skilled storyteller may use marionettes as aids in getting his story across to his audience. Using puppets and marionettes calls forth much creativity on the part of children. Much of the dialogue is spontaneous and this is to be preferred over a written script.

Interviewing

Increasingly attention is being given to interviewing as an oral language activity that enters occasionally into the lives of both children and adults. The interview as a method for securing information is being stressed in social studies and science; the interview has a prominent place in television programs of news and information; interviewing, of which the panel presentation is one variation, is used in club programs. Interviewing not only calls for the use of many speaking and social skills; it also shows the importance of careful listening. The necessity for schools to provide a direct program of instruction in the various aspects of this activity was pointed out by Broening over thirty years ago:[32]

> The interview has become a very useful technique with the present-day emphasis on the students' having actual contact with the activities about them. . . .
>
> Are we helping our students to ask important, direct questions, so that they can bring back the information desired? Are we stressing the necessity of quoting statements exactly as they were made? Are we insisting on courtesy at all times? Are we teaching students how to make a tactful and pleasing entree and introduction to the person being interviewed?

[31]For directions for puppet making and use, see Mardel Ogilvie, *Speech in the Elementary School* (New York: McGraw-Hill, Inc., 1954), Chapters 2 and 3.

[32]Angela M. Broening, and others, *Conducting Experiences in English* (New York: Appleton-Century-Crofts, Inc., 1939), p. 128.

Many opportunities occur for children to conduct interviews. For example, they may interview the teacher who has taken a trip or has a special interest or hobby; they may interview a new child about where he formerly lived; they may interview parents who have special fields of interest, hobbies, or professions; they may interview school personnel about their work, or community workers like the grocer, postman, and fireman. Particular attention and practice should be given to the following:

1. Preplanning the interview, including researching the topic and the person to be interviewed.
2. Allowing the individual who arranged the interview to introduce the subject and close the interview.
3. Avoiding such trite opening statements as "Our teacher wants us to . . ." and "I have to. . . ."
4. Teaching the interviewer to stick to the topic of the interview.
5. Developing sensitivity regarding the amount of time used by the interviewer.
6. Creating a feeling about when an interview should be closed.
7. Discovering something about appropriate times for making appointments.

The interview should be conducted in a courteous and friendly manner, with the interviewer listening carefully, contributing worthwhile questions, taking notes, and expressing appreciation for the information being received. Further, the child conducting an interview must learn to plan ways to utilize the information he has received.

Daily classroom experiences offer opportunity to show children the need for orderly procedure. Many classrooms have class organizations or clubs and most pupils participate in organizations outside of school which have varying degrees of formality (and orderliness!), so there is a need to know how meetings should be conducted and participated in. Organization meetings call for a presiding officer and subordinates who have the oral language abilities and skills necessary to fulfill the duties of these positions. Children enjoy taking part in such organizations, and many worthwhile attitudes and understandings may be acquired in addition to those normally related to the language program.

Participating in Meetings

The teacher and pupils should discuss various ways of conducting meetings and the rules that may be appropriate. From such discussion the children will discover the value of rules in saving group time and energy. A wall chart or a mimeographed guide may be the outgrowth of such discussion. Often, rather formal parliamentary procedure is decided upon. One curriculum guide suggests the following as appropriate procedure for elementary school children to learn.[33]

Rules governing parliamentary procedure

1. The chairman calls the meeting to order.
2. The secretary reads the minutes of the previous meeting.
3. The chairman asks for corrections or additions to the minutes. After corrections or additions have been made, the minutes are then accepted.
4. The chairman calls for business to come before the meeting.
5. The group proceeds with the business of the day. (See making and voting on motions.)
6. The meeting is adjourned.

Making and voting on motions

1. The member who wants to make a motion rises and addresses the chairman by saying, "Mister (or Madam) Chairman."
2. The chairman recognizes the member by repeating his name.
3. The member proposes the motion by saying, "Mister Chairman, I move that. . . ."
4. Another member seconds the motion by stating, "I second the motion." (All motions must be seconded before they can be discussed or voted upon.)
5. After the motion has been seconded it is stated in full by the chairman as follows, "It has been moved and seconded that . . . ."
6. The chairman calls for discussion.
7. The chairman calls for a vote by saying, "All in favor say 'Aye.' Those opposed say 'No.' "
8. The chairman announces the result of the vote by saying, "The motion has been carried" or "The motion has been lost."

Needless to say, the teacher should know parliamentary procedure thoroughly in order to teach it. From this knowledge he will be in a position to teach habits of orderly procedure in all group activities. The form of the procedure should be suited to the age and ability level of the children but attention should be given to the development of advancing levels of skill in order to secure a degree of proficiency that will be useful to the child throughout his school and later adult life.

[33]*Toward Better Speech*, p. 77.

Choral speaking is an oral language activity which should be engaged in principally for pleasure. However, it also offers opportunities for introducing a variety of literature and for dealing with problems in oral expression. It provides a genuine opportunity for the input of linguistics into the program. Choral speaking can give children a real feeling for their language, a sense for the quality of words, an insight into the system of the language, and a recognition of the importance of stress, pitch, and juncture in the conveying of meaning and emotion. It may lead to (1) the improvement of voice quality, (2) the development of improved habits of enunciation and articulation, (3) the improvement of habits of pronunciation, (4) the freeing of children from unhealthy inhibition and excessive shyness toward expression, and (5) a recognition of the importance of the audience and group effort in such forms of communication.

Choral speaking can be used with children of all ages. It teaches them to listen, to remember, and to interpret words and word patterns. Most selections for choral speaking provide opportunity for learning to keep voices modulated—an important first step in developing good speaking habits. At about the third to sixth grade level the children become interested in choral speaking with themes of adventure or mystery. This interest can be directed toward improvement of diction, voice quality, vocabulary, and understanding of meaning.

A teacher can have little hope for success with choral speaking unless the children have a background of experience resulting from extensive listening to the reading and speaking of selected prose and poetry. Often as the children have listened to the teacher, particularly in the lower grades, they have been encouraged to join in saying some lines of a poem they have heard frequently. From this background the teacher can lead them readily into actual choral speaking. First selections are generally nursery rhymes that children know well.

Choral speaking involves much interpretation. Children should be encouraged to decide whether a line should be said rapidly or slowly, whether the voices should be soft or loud, and other factors which make for an interesting and pleasant experience for themselves and an audience. Different ways of speaking should be tried with each selection. Perfection in performance should not be expected at once.

With very young children whose voices are developing, no attempt should be made to group pupils according to voice quality. As children mature, and as they learn to enjoy a poem thoroughly, they will themselves often suggest some voice grouping. Voices in the elemen-

Choral
Speaking

tary school may be divided into two groups, light and heavy, or into three groups, light, heavy, and medium. A teacher who listens to his pupils talking and reading every day knows their voices—the high voices, the low, and the in-between. There should not be great difficulty in grouping them for the most effective speaking.[34]

After trying out and discussing various interpretations, the teacher and the children together set the pattern for interpretation of each selection. The teacher then has the responsibility, as the director, for indicating the rhythmic pattern, the starting and stopping points, and the tempo, and for keeping the voices in unison. The teacher and pupils talk over articulation, pronunciation, blending of voices, and the effect of their interpretation. All should remember that choral speaking is a cooperative, group communication activity.

Types of choral speaking have been identified by Abney as:[35]

1. *Refrain*—which requires a single soloist who reads the narrative, with the class joining in refrain.
2. *Two-part or antiphonal*—two groups balanced, one against the other; light voices versus dark; boys versus girls. Question-and-answer poetry, or poems of contrasting moods are good in this arrangement.
3. *Line-a-child or sequential*—interpretation of one or two lines by a number of individuals, leading up to a climax in which unison voices are often effective.
4. *Part arrangement*—in which maturing voices are grouped in choirs and blended somewhat as an orchestra.
5. *Unison*—in which all voices speak all lines as one.

Selections suitable for choral speaking are numerous. Some to try in the primary grades are "Hickory Dickory Dock," "Hippity Hop to Bed" (Leroy Jackson), "Hoppity" (A. A. Milne), "Little Jack Horner," "Rain, Rain, Go Away," "Blow, Wind, Blow," "My Zipper Suit" (Marie Louise Allen), "Sh" (James Tippett), and "The Purple Cow" (Gelett Burgess). At the intermediate level recommended selections include "A Farmer Went Trotting," "Shop Windows" (Rose Fyleman), "Susan Blue" (Kate Greenaway), "Autumn Woods" (James Tippett), "Poor Tired Tim" (Walter de la Mare), "Who Has

[34]*Oral Interpretation of Children's Literature* by Bamman, Dawson, and Whitehead has many useful teaching suggestions.

[35]Louise Abney, "Poetry—Interpretation," in *Guides to Speech Training in the Elementary School,* A Report of the Elementary Committee of the National Association of Teachers of Speech (Boston: Expression Company, 1943), p. 73.

Seen the Wind?" (Christina Rossetti), "Windy Nights" (Robert Louis Stevenson), "It Is Raining" (Lucy Sprague Mitchell), "Beulah" (Gwendolyn Brooks), and "Indian Lullaby" (Charles Myall). For the upper grades, the following may be tried: "The Coin" (Sara Teasdale), "The Flag Goes By" (Henry H. Bennett), "Afternoon on a Hill" (Edna St. V. Millay), "Do You Fear the Wind?" (Hamlin Garland), and "Trees" (Joyce Kilmer).

The making of announcements and the giving of directions and explanations are oral language activities frequently engaged in by both children and adults. School announcements are made by children about lost and found articles, school programs, exhibitions, and parties. Frequently children give directions for playing games or for performing some classroom task. They explain how they found a particular item or fact in a book. Outside of school, children make announcements at Scout meetings, club meetings, and parties. They give directions to one another in their play, and they explain their hobbies to anyone who will listen. Adults are called upon to make announcements at social gatherings and public meetings, to give directions to motorists, and to make explanations to employees or employers as a part of their work. Thus there are many occasions in which both children and adults are called upon to use directly the skills and abilities which are needed if announcements, directions, and explanations are to be effective.

Giving Announcements, Directions, Explanations

The skills and abilities necessary for making announcements and for giving directions and explanations are similar to those needed in other oral language situations. The language used must be properly organized and must be presented in terms which will be understood by the audience. All of the essential information relative to who, what, when, where, and how should be given. Correct language certainly should be used but attention must be paid to the particular language of the situation. Since these language situations are generally limited in time, specific attention must be paid to conciseness and clarity and the manner in which the communication is made.

Teaching the making of announcements and the giving of directions and explanations is best done through real situations. Children may be given opportunities to make announcements about programs, events, exhibitions, games, lost and found articles, rules, and other subjects to their own classmates, to other classes, in assemblies, and to neighborhood adult groups. Announcements may be made at school club meetings, and often one or more youngsters may be called upon to make announcements or to act as the master of ceremonies at school or club programs.

Teaching
Social
Amenities

Everyone should know something about how to extend and receive greetings, how to make introductions, how to give and accept compliments, how to show courtesy to others when speaking or listening to them, and how to apologize for breaches in social conduct. Learning to do these things is generally recognized by children as important, but sometimes outside motivation needs to be supplied. One way to stimulate interest in social conventions is by a discussion of customs of other people, periods, and places. For example, pupils become very much interested in greetings such as the following used in different parts of the world:

1. Eskimos rub noses when they meet.
2. French, Austrian, and some other European men kiss each other's cheeks.
3. In many European countries, men greet ladies by kissing their hands.
4. Japanese clasp their own hands and bow several times.
5. The Bakuba tribe in the Belgium Congo say "hello" and "goodby" by clapping their hands.
6. In this country it was once proper for girls to curtsy and boys to bow when greeted by another person.

Acting as a host or hostess is an important life activity that may profit from training. Occasions for gaining experience and confidence in these roles arise frequently in school. Visitors may come to the room and be greeted by a room host and hostess. The host and hostess may introduce themselves to the guests and in turn introduce the visitors to others in the room. Such activities, through careful teacher guidance, help the children become aware of the use and value of the commonly accepted forms of courtesy.

As an outgrowth of extensive discussion and practice, the child must become accustomed to observing the rather rigid conventions followed in making and in responding to introductions. He must learn the proper forms of expression to use in common social situations, such as being introduced to another child or to an older person, or having to introduce an older person to another older person. The most effective time to teach children about making introductions is just prior to a real occasion when they need to use the skills. This provides immediate and effective motivation for learning. Discussion of the skills is helpful, but will not give the child the needed experience and assurance. If numerous real situations are not available, imaginary social situations calling for many repetitions of the skills should be dramatized until the children develop the required feelings of ease and confidence.

The following general rules to be followed in making introductions should be learned by the boys and girls and practiced until each type of introduction is carried through with complete assurance.

1. Each person's name should be spoken plainly to avoid embarrassment to either party. It is not improper for either party to ask for names to be repeated if they are not understood at the time of the introduction.
2. In introducing two persons who are complete strangers, the person making the introduction should tactfully add some remark which may start a conversation.
3. If the individual is obliged to introduce himself to another he should be certain to tell his name and add some personal, identifying remark.
4. When introducing a relative, his or her last name should be given somewhere in the introduction.
5. One of the following formulas will help the individual to master the form of introductions:

_____, this is _____
or
_____, I'd like you to meet _____

In the first blank in each form, the child is to use the name of the person he wishes to honor. In the second blank he is to use the name of the other person.

The following rules may be used to help the one doing the introducing decide which person he wishes to honor:

1. In introducing a man and a woman (or a boy and a girl) the name of the woman or girl should be given first.
2. In introducing an older and a younger person, the name of the older person should be said first. If those being introduced are nearly the same age, either name may be given first.
3. In introducing an individual to your class or club meeting, mention the class or group first.

Many occasions arise naturally for using the social skills. Children may introduce friends and parents to the teacher and class. Many class groups appoint members to act as hosts and hostesses for special occasions or for a day or week; they answer the door, introduce visitors, and generally are in charge of the social obligations of the class. Sometimes one class may visit another and practice extending greetings and making introductions. Children may usher at school events. Other special occasions, such as class parties, call for the use of many social skills. Children may also practice courtesies in out-of-school activities by replying correctly to greetings on the street, responding to introductions at church, and greeting people and introducing themselves when engaged in such activities as collecting paper in the Boy Scout drive or selling Girl Scout cookies. Particular attention needs to be given to courtesy to older persons. Also, giving an apology in a gracious manner and receiving a compliment or congratulations simply and sincerely are difficult for many of us to do. Occasions for these activities do occur rather frequently, however, and learning to do them properly and easily is a responsibility of the language program.

Teachers themselves sometimes forget to practice many of the courtesies. The teacher should realize that in this area of the language program the most important teaching "method" is for him to practice what he preaches. Teachers will find many excellent special references on courtesies and the social conventions, as well as concrete hints and techniques for developing these skills, in the teachers' manuals of many language textbooks for the elementary school.

Evaluating Oral Language Skills and Products

In spite of the great social importance of oral expression and the increasing interest in teaching it, reliable standardized evaluative instruments suitable for the appraisal of either the skills or the products are not available. Doubtless the difficulties involved in securing normal samplings of oral language are largely responsible for the limited production and use of effective measuring instruments. Too, there are readily discernible difficulties involved in examining the intangibility of speech in an objective fashion.

While standardized instruments are not available, evaluation of oral expression is possible in a limited but important sense by teachers and pupils in informal ways. For example, tape recorders can be used to appraise the speech of individual children and the products of both individual and group expression. Further, language textbooks provide suggestions helpful for informal evaluation and diagnosis in other ways. The use of these materials and other suggestions regarding appraisal are discussed in the following sections.

Producing speech sounds requires extremely accurate coordination of all of the mental, physical, and emotional aspects of the speech mechanism. Thus, speech production should not be subjected to unskilled tampering. The most important function of the classroom teacher is to operate as an observer responsible for an immediate and nontechnical report on all individuals in his classes showing noticeable speech difficulties, leaving the technical examination and treatment to trained clinicians.

Determining Speech Disorders

The following guide to speech difficulties has been suggested by Eisenson and Ogilvie to help teachers determine speech disorders.[36] They suggest that when a preponderance of yes answers appear in relation to a particular pupil a speech correctionist should be consulted.

Analysis of Speech Defects

Articulatory Defects Does the child substitute one sound for another? Does he omit sounds? Does he distort sounds? Is he very hard to understand?

Stuttering Is the child disturbed by his dysfluency? Does he repeat sounds or syllables or words more than his classmates? Is his speech decidedly arhythmical? Does he block frequently? Does he have difficulty in getting his words out?

Vocal Difficulties Is the child's voice noticeably unpleasant in quality? Is his pitch higher or lower than most of his classmates? Is his voice monotonous? Is his voice light and thin? Is his voice husky? Is his voice too loud? Is his voice too weak? Is his voice difficult to hear in class?

Cleft Palate Speech Is there an obvious cleft of the teeth ridge or palate? Is his voice excessively nasal? Are his *p, b, t, d, k,* and *g* inaccurate? Are some of his other consonants distorted?

Cerebral Palsy Speech Does the child have obvious tremors of the musculature phonation and breathing? Is his speech slow, jerky, and labored? Is his rhythm of speech abnormal?

Delayed Speech Is his speech markedly retarded in relation to his classmates'? Does he omit and substitute sounds substantially more than his classmates? Does he use shorter and simpler sentences than his classmates? Does he use fewer phrases and prepositions than his classmates?

Language Impairment Is the child's comprehension of language markedly retarded? Does he seem to be inconsistent in his ability to understand and his ability to use language? Is the profile of his linguistic abilities uneven? (For example, can

[36]Reprinted with permission of the Macmillan Company from *Speech Correction in the Schools,* Second Edition, by Jon Eisenson and Mardel Ogilvie, pp. 10–12. Copyright 1957, 1963, by The Macmillan Company.

he read much better than he can spell? Is he surprisingly good in arithmetic and yet quite poor in either reading or writing?

Speech Defect Due to Impaired Hearing Does the child have frequent earaches and colds? Does he have running ears? Does he omit sounds or substitute one sound for another? Does he distort sounds? Does he speak too loudly? Does he speak too softly? Does he frequently ask you to repeat what you have said? Does he turn his heard to one side as you speak? Does he make unusual mistakes in the spelling words you dictate? Does he misinterpret your questions or instruction frequently? Does he do better when given written instruction than when given oral instructions? Does he seem more intelligent than his work indicates?

As this set of questions shows, many observable speech defects are largely the consequence of habits that have not been corrected or of not encouraging satisfactory speech. Conditions which reflect habits rather than physical or emotional problems are subject to instruction by the classroom teacher. Particularly, the teacher can provide retraining and can give a feeling of acceptance and security to the child with these habits. The training should be directed whenever possible by a trained speech correctionist but the fact should not be overlooked that the classroom teacher can provide a service and setting for instruction to the child with a speech disorder that a speech therapist alone cannot provide.

Correcting Speech Problems

One of the major ways a teacher can help the child with a speech difficulty is by assuming a direct, calm, objective attitude toward the problem. Much can be accomplished by building the child's self-concept, by helping the child adjust himself to the group, by keeping the child from any undue pressure of classmates, and by giving the child considerate but nonpampering attention. The chart below suggests possible causes of many speech problems and indicates possible remedial approaches to the problems. This should be used by a teacher who has no speech clinician available, or in instances in which the teacher is awaiting the clinician's services.

Appraising Oral Language Performance

All evaluation should be based upon objectives. In evaluating oral language performance the basis should be the skills, attitudes, and abilities the program of instruction has sought to develop. The list of functional objectives on page 230 is not exhaustive but it provides a framework for a teacher to identify other objectives with and to develop appraisal procedures for.

Diagnostic and Remedial Speech Chart

Observable Speech Disorder	Possible Causes	Suggested Remedial Treatment
1. Baby talk	Immaturity; home example; low mentality; defective hearing; inability to discriminate sounds accurately.	Set correct example and encourage home to do likewise; check hearing and discrimination; provide warm classroom climate.
2. Lisping	Malformation of teeth or jaws; loss of front teeth; hearing deficiency; immaturity.	Arrange for physical examination; teach formation of sounds; give breathing exercises.
3. Poor articulation	Carelessness; home background; defective hearing; inadequate knowledge of sounds.	Set correct example; give training exercises in making sounds; motivate class to set high standards in articulation; listen to recording of speech.
4. Excess nasality	Poor breathing habits; physical defects; home example.	Arrange for physical examination; give breathing exercises (panting, yawning, etc.), auditory discrimination exercises, exercises requiring blowing.
5. Breathiness	Emotional tension; improper breathing.	Give emotional security; prescribe deep-breathing exercises; check causes of excessive tension; arrange for choral speaking.
6. Stuttering	Physical defects; emotional problem.	Give security; avoid ridicule; arrange for physical examination; arrange for choral speaking.
7. Stammering	Feelings of inferiority; physical defects.	Give encouragement and security; join group activities; focus on the thought rather than on manner of speech.
8. High Pitch	Self-consciousness; insecurity; fatigue; faulty hearing and sound discrimination.	Prescribe adequate rest; give security; listen to recorded voice; do reading exercises.
9 Stridency	Poor social adjustment; home conditions; hearing defect; emotional problems.	Give security; listen to recorded voice; join in dramatization with need for soft voice, or choral speaking.
10. Low pitch	Physical defects; fatigue; emotional problems.	Arrange for medical examination; practice articulation and nonsense verse; provide security.

1. To converse with classmates and adults easily and courteously.
2. To participate in discussions, sticking to the point and respecting the opinions of others.
3. To organize information and report it effectively.
4. To plan an interview and carry it through courteously and effectively.
5. To use the telephone competently.
6. To conduct a meeting by means of parliamentary procedures.
7. To give clear directions, explanations, and announcements orally.
8. To tell a story or personal experience effectively and interestingly.
9. To greet others properly in various social situations.
10. To participate in choral speaking.
11. To make use of parliamentary procedures as a member of a group.
12. To take part in a dramatic activity.

Reference should be made to the listing of objectives for speaking in the various oral language situations identified earlier in this chapter. The objectives listed above, combined with those given earlier, can be the bases for checklists, statements of standards, and records of progress.

The following checklist for the evaluation of a discussion activity was proposed in a curriculum bulletin.[37] It is suggestive of checklists which might be devised for other speech activities.

1. *For the group*
   (a) Was the problem suitable for class discussion?
   (b) Was the problem stated clearly?
   (c) Were all the terms defined?
   (d) Was the topic of interest to all?
   (e) Did the members display attitudes of sincerity and co-operation by listening attentively, keeping to the point under discussion, requesting further information or clarification of information presented, permitting all members to participate?
   (f) Were all members qualified to discuss the problem intelligently on the basis of indirect and direct preparation?
   (g) Were the important issues discussed?
   (h) Did the discussion promote a better understanding of the problem and of the members of the group?
   (i) Were the voices audible and of good quality?
   (j) Were the speech patterns acceptable? Did they permit free and easy exchange of ideas?

[37] *Toward Better Speech,* pp. 81–82.

(k) Were the thoughts well organized and expressed in a convincing and concise manner?

(l) Was the discussion worthwhile in proportion to the amount and quality of information gained and the time consumed?

2. *For the discussion leader*

(a) Did the leader guide the discussion wisely?

(b) Did he encourage all members to participate?

(c) Did he discourage individuals or small groups from monopolizing the discussion?

(d) Did he keep the discussion on the point at issue?

(e) Did he keep the discussion moving forward by raising a new issue as soon as the one under discussion seemed to have been handled adequately?

(f) Did he focus attention on the important points by the use of a running summary?

(g) Did he summarize at the close of the discussion period?

Self-evaluation based upon standards that pupils set themselves should be an important part of the evaluation aspect of oral language teaching. For example, a class might adopt a list of "rules" for giving an oral report and use these as the basis for determining how effective their reports were:

1. Have an interesting topic.
2. Start with a good opening sentence.
3. Look at the audience.
4. Make your voice loud enough to be heard.
5. Organize your report carefully.
6. Stick to the topic.
7. Use good sentences.
8. Have a good closing.

Teachers also should give attention to self-evaluation. Questions such as the following help a teacher appraise his oral language program.[38]

Do I recognize the need for children to practice oral expression?

Do I consistently provide opportunities for children to communicate orally?

[38]George C. Bolz, "Promoting Oral Expression," *The National Elementary Principal*, 42:41–43, April, 1963.

Am I willing to work with children where I find them—willing to work patiently and understandingly with a shy child?

How can I improve my own skills in oral expression? Do I set a good example in my speech—enunciating clearly, speaking comfortably and easily, organizing my thoughts logically?

Do I listen to children? Do I give them my complete attention? Do I respond fully to their questions and comments?

Exercises for Thought and A

1. Record several children's speech in a natural communicative situa Evaluate the speech to determine teaching needs. Do you need other evidence?
2. Make a chart (suitable for the grade level of your choice) of standards to be observed in a specific oral language activity.
3. Suggest steps to make pupils more directly aware of the need for sensitivity to the demands of the audience situation.
4. Make a list of poems suitable for choral speaking at the grade level of your choice. Categorize these according to their appropriateness for refrain, antiphonal, line-a-child, unison, and voice parts speaking.
5. What should a teacher do about a child who stutters?
6. Make a plan for a correctional lesson in some phase of oral expression.
7. Examine several language textbooks for the grade level you are teaching or plan to teach. Evaluate these texts in terms of the suggestions in this chapter.
8. Devise a pupil's self-evaluation checklist to be used by a child for evaluating his speaking skills and products.

Selected References

Arbuthnot, May Hill. *Children and Books,* third edition. Chicago: Scott, Foresman and Company, 1964.

Batchelder, Marjorie H., and Comer, Virginia L. *Puppets and Plays: A Creative Approach.* New York: Harper & Row, 1956.

Bamman, Henry A.; Dawson, Mildred A.; and Whitehead, Robert J. *Oral Interpretation of Children's Literature.* Dubuque, Iowa: Wm. C. Brown Company, 1964.

Burger, Isabel. *Creative Play Acting.* New York: A. S. Barnes and Company, 1950.

Carlson, Bernice W. *Act It Out.* New York: Abingdon Press, 1965.

Crosscut, Richard. *Children and Dramatics.* New York: Charles Scribner's Sons, 1966.

Durland, Frances C. *Creative Dramatics for Children.* Yellow Springs, Ohio: The Antioch Press, 1951.

Early, Margaret J. "Communication Arts," *Encyclopedia of Educational Research,* third edition (Chester W. Harris, editor). New York: The Macmillan Company, 1960, pp. 306–311.

Eisenson, Jon, and Ogilvie, Mardel. *Speech Correction in the Schools.* New York: The Macmillan Company, second edition, 1963.

Munkres, Alberta. *Helping Children in Oral Communication.* New York: Bureau of Publications, Teacher's College, Columbia University, 1959.

Ogilvie, Mardel. *Speech in the Elementary School.* New York: McGraw-Hill, Inc., 1954.

Petty, Walter T. (editor). *Research in Oral Language.* Champaign, Ill.: National Council of Teachers of English, 1967.

Rasmussen, Carrie. *Speech Methods in the Elementary School.* New York: Ronald Press, 1962.

Sawyer, Ruth. *The Way of the Story-Teller.* New York: The Viking Press, 1962.

Siks, Geraldine B. *Creative Dramatics: An Art for Children.* New York: Harper & Row, 1958.

————. *Children's Literature for Dramatization.* New York: Harper & Row, 1964.

————, and Dunnington, Hazel B. *Children's Theatre and Creative Dramatics.* Seattle: University of Washington Press, 1961.

Tooze, Ruth. *Storytelling.* Englewood Cliffs, N.J.: Prentice-Hall, Inc., 1959.

Toward Better Speech. Curriculum Bulletin, 1952–53 Series, Number 5. New York: The Board of Education of the City of New York, 1953.

Van Riper, Charles, and Butler, Katherine G. *Speech in the Elementary Classroom.* New York: Harper & Row, 1955.

Ward, Winifred. *Playmaking with Children,* revised edition. New York: Appleton-Century-Crofts, 1957.

8

Teaching Written Expression

INTRODUCTION

Written expression is based upon oral expression. Thus the writing
program in elementary schools is conditioned by the program in oral
expression. If a child has been encouraged to explore his world, to
formulate his impressions, and to express these impressions orally,
then the foundation has been laid for teaching written expression.

Earlier chapters have discussed language learning, approaches
to organizing for instruction, and the beginning language arts
programs in the kindergarten and the primary grades. This chapter
extends the discussion of the curriculum content and teaching
procedures begun earlier. There are also a number of specific issues,
along with related skills and abilities—and activities fostering
their use—that must be considered in teaching all language
expression; these are primarily discussed in Chapter 10. In
addition, grammar is discussed in Chapter 11. Thus, because all
language activities are really related, the reader should reserve
his final judgments as to what should be included in a program for
teaching written expression until the entire book has been read.

Most writing programs in elementary schools identify two types
of writing. These are usually called *creative* and *practical,* with
factual, functional, expository, or *utilitarian* sometimes being
substituted for practical and *personal* less frequently
substituted for *creative.* The authors prefer not to make a marked
distinction between "creative" and practical," and do not do
so except for the organizational requirements of this book. We believe
children should be taught to do the writing that is important to
them and to their personal communication needs. We believe that all
such writing is personal and purposeful or practical. We believe
it is because it is the expression of the individual. We think all
writing can show style, imagination, and the elements of good
composition.

This chapter discusses the topics listed below. The chapter that
follows continues the examination of procedures for teaching written
expression, giving particular emphasis to "creative" activities.

234

1. Writing: Some Preliminary Considerations
2. Motivating Children to Write
3. Developing Writing Skills in Special Language Situations
4. Teaching the Conventions in Writing
5. Written Language Skills in Using Books
6. Self-editing and Proofreading
7 The Evaluation of Written Expression
8. Diagnostic and Remedial Procedures

Writing: Some Preliminary Considerations

A recent and useful book by Stephen Sherwin begins its chapter on writing with a quotation from Shakespeare: "to write . . . comes by nature." "However," continues the author, "schoolmen from Shakespeare's day to this have refused to leave the matter entirely in nature's care."[1] There is a good deal of food for thought in this statement, and in Sherwin's conclusion, reached after an examination of the research on three ways that have been tried for teaching writing—the study of traditional grammar, the study of linguistics, and writing—namely, that none of these can be defended. This conclusion might appear to leave teachers with no procedures to use that will effectively bear on the objective, yet many children do learn to write acceptably, if not well, and teachers surely are responsible for much of the growth. Therefore, there must be teaching procedures that are effective, as many wise teachers have discovered. They are not as precisely delineated as some would like, but there are basic activities and endeavors that are important and should be used by all teachers.

The former executive secretary of the National Council of Teachers of English stated a few years ago that, "Writing is the disgrace of American education."[2] While this may not be a point of view popularly accepted by teachers, the fact is that defenders of what is done about teaching writing in schools are not making contradictory statements—at least in their professional writing.

The State of Writing in Schools

In fact, Sherwin, in the book on research previously referred to, states that reports on writing instruction reveal many opinions and some facts, with the opinions covering the range from optimism to pessimism.[3] However, he goes ahead to say, "The facts, to the extent

[1]J. Stephen Sherwin, *Four Problems in Teaching English: A Critique of Research* (Scranton, Pa.: International Textbook Company, 1969), p. 109.
[2]James R. Squire, "The Teaching of Writing and Composition in Today's Schools," *Elementary English,* 41:3–14, January, 1964.
[3]*Four Problems,* p. 167.

that they are revealed by the status studies and error analyses, are almost uniformly discouraging." In a further statement—a commentary on the present state of research—he adds, "All the studies mentioned were published between 1929 and 1948," thus making it impossible "to speak in terms of hard facts about the current situation."[4]

The major problem in doing a really thorough study of the status of writing probably is due to the lack of agreement as to what is "good" writing and how writing should be judged.[5] In addition, as pointed out above, the principal general procedures tried as the means for teaching writing have not been proven effective, if one believes the accumulation of research evidence, but these approaches continue to be used. Thus, research comparing writing from different classes has the problem of evaluating that writing as well as that of making judgments about procedures used in the various classes if those procedures are already known to be unrelated to writing.

The Process of Writing

The discussion earlier concerning the names given to the types of writing that children do points up the inadequacy of pairs of terms as the basis for categorizing all writing. Labeling writing done for different purposes with different names fails to recognize the nature of writing, just as having students learn grammatical facts does.[6]

Writing is a personal act; it is an expression of the self. It is a process that is done for a purpose, which results in a product. It is a process of thought and emotion that requires certain skills and abilities to gain the product and accomplish the purpose. This product has certain qualities and conditions of form that can be judged in terms of the purpose. Because writing is personal, the individual himself determines the purpose and judges the product. As an expression of self, the process changes as the individual changes and as his needs for expression change. As his background of experience enlarges, as he

[4]Squire's comment, which was based on a study he did with Roger K. Applebee (*A Study of English Programs in Selected High Schools Which Consistently Educate Outstanding Students in English,* USOE Cooperative Research Project No. 1994. University of Illinois, 1966, 601 pp.) was possibly not considered by Sherwin in his review.
[5]Richard Braddock, "English Composition" in *Encyclopedia of Educational Research,* Fourth Edition, Robert Ebel, editor (New York: The Macmillan Company, 1969), p. 455.
[6]See Donald R. Ferris, "Teaching Children to Write" in *Guiding Children's Language Learning,* Pose Lamb, editor (Dubuque, Iowa: Wm. C. Brown Company, 1967), pp. 138–143 for a discussion of this point.

learns, his storehouse for expression becomes greater. In the same manner, as the child grows, his ability to express himself also grows, providing that he learns the skills he needs and his desire to express is not stifled.

All expression, written or oral, requires putting the words and larger units of that expression into a pattern or arrangement which accomplishes or seeks to accomplish the purpose of the expression. This arrangement is composition, and the effectiveness of it, whether it is good or poor, depends upon the thinking that went into it. Composition is essentially a thinking process, and one of the highest order. No written expression, not even a single sentence or a label or a short memorandum, will be effective expression unless it has good composition, unless it was thoughtfully done.

Composition and Writing

While composition hinges primarily upon clear thinking, the desire to express and the skills needed for the form of expression are also essential. Motivating children to express themselves in writing is discussed in this chapter, as well as some skills which are allied directly with written expression. Other compositional skills, especially those most directly related to organization, are discussed in Chapter 10, since they are a part of both writing and speaking.

Motivating Children to Write

Children do not learn to write by having writing tasks assigned them without regard to their interests, their experiences, and the value or lack of value they hold for the assignment. They may write—in the sense of simply putting words on paper, usually no more than necessary to "get by"—but they will not compose; they will not write from thought, from eagerness, from desire. All too often teachers rely on unmotivated assignments, on telling rather than teaching.

It is actually easy to stimulate the normal child to write if the assignment has an apparent, meaningful purpose and is an outgrowth of an activity and experience of his which has shown the need for expression. He will write when he has something to say, and when he feels that someone will read and appreciate or learn from what he has written. A child will write a report readily enough, for instance, if he feels that the information he will include in it is needed in a social studies problem and will be of interest to others in the class. He will

Stimulating a Desire to Write

gladly keep a record if he is convinced that this record will actually be referred to later and therefore there is a need to remember the details. He will write a summary of a science experiment if he enjoyed working on it and knows that the summary will be sent to his parents.

Oral discussion of situations which may call for writing must be related by teacher guidance to the activities of the class. Questions such as these may be used: "Do we know everything we should about life in an Indian village before we show the fifth-graders about it?" "Should different ones see what they can find out about Indian cooking, shelter, and ceremonies in the village?" "John, you visited the reservation at Tama last year; what do you remember about the ceremonies?" "Do you suppose you could write down those things and perhaps find others and prepare a report each of us could read?"

The key to all useful suggestions for stimulating written expression is the genuineness of the need for the writing. "Ever since we began expecting children to write only when they had a genuine need or the earnest desire to do so, we have found them eager to write well. In that mood they have been sensitive to our guidance and suggestion."[7] Children usually have much to write about; the teacher, through careful guidance and planning of class activities, must help them see the need.

Consider, for example, the needs for writing found by one child on a single day in a fifth-grade class:[8]

Put the plans for the day in the log book of the class.

Record the weather conditions on a chart.

Write arithmetic problems made from the information found in a supermarket advertisement.

Take notes from two reference books for a report in social studies on lighting in colonial times.

Make the bibliography for his reference sources.

List the characters and the properties needed for the dramatization of a reading story.

Compose an invitation to be sent to another class inviting them to the play.

Note the discussion topics in Student Council so that he could report back to the class.

Outline the main ideas found in a science article on the invention of the electric light bulb.

[7]Alvina Treut Burrows, and others, *They All Want to Write* (Englewood Cliffs, N.J.: Prentice-Hall, Inc., 1955), p. 3.

[8]*Using Language* (Wilmington, Del.: The Division of Elementary Education, Wilmington Public Schools, 1955), pp. 116–117.

Make a word picture of a person for the other children to guess
during a class game.

Ask permission from his parents to accompany his class on a trip
to the Town Hall.

Most of us would be appalled if we were called upon to write a report on the subject "Gas Dynamics." Even after considerable reading, we probably would be unable to write a paper that would be either of much interest to a reader or satisfying to ourselves. In the first place, many of us would not know how to find information on the topic; it is simply too far removed from our experience. Then too, many of us would not be much interested in the topic, since our lack of information may indicate little interest in this subject.

**The
Importance
of Experience
to Writing**

In evaluating the importance of experience in helping children to express themselves, it may be well for us to go back for a moment to a consideration of how children learn their language. Language is a set of symbols which represent concepts or ideas, with the meanings of these symbols possibly being different for different people. A commonality of meaning to two or more individuals depends upon the common elements in their experiences. The child in learning language has learned those symbols and their related concepts and ideas from other persons in his environment. He does not learn language—the words and the larger units—that he has had no occasion to use in his environment. He does not learn concepts that have no relation to his environment. He knows about those things that have been a part of his experience.

The experience background of each child is different from that of any other, though children of the same neighborhood and the same social and economic classes are likely to have had many similar experiences. Thus, how valuable a school activity may be in terms of providing experience to a particular child becomes very difficult to determine. Our best guess generally is that the interests a child shows are clues to his experiential background, and our best procedure is to extend these interests as far as possible.

Children at all age and grade levels have had many experiences. They have many interests. There is much they can write about. However, because of this fact we should not assume that it is not the school's business to provide activities which may extend their experiences. Even if a child comes to school with fluency and spontaneity of expression, or even if the school develops these abilities early, we cannot be assured that they will be maintained unless he has the opportunity to learn many things that he wants to tell others about and feels that he knows enough to do so. The words below, certainly as true today as when they were written, should be read frequently by every teacher, every textbook writer, and every other person propounding what the curriculum in the elementary school should be.[9]

> The further the child progresses in the elementary school, the greater is the danger that his language period may degenerate into one of exercise-doing, learning words in columns out of context, or studying language forms divorced from the use he is making of language the rest of the day. Special care, therefore, needs to be exercised to continue the kind of rich program of well-motivated enterprises common in the lower grades in order that the growth of language may continue in relationship to the development of meaning and that the challenge of a social purpose may motivate expression. Then the needed remedial drill and positive instruction in word knowledge and linguistic forms may be related directly to the problems which confront the pupil in his daily use of language.

Sometimes there is a mistaken tendency for teachers to think that providing activity is the same as providing experience. This may be due to a teacher's interest in having children "learn by doing." Of course, the principle of "learning by doing" is a valid one, but the kind and extent of the learning depends upon what is done. While every activity may have a purpose, this purpose may be unknown or meaningless to the child—and, we suspect, sometimes unknown and unimportant to the teacher. Activities do need to be provided, and sometimes it involves considerable contriving on the part of the teacher to relate these activities to the desirable experiences that society says the school should provide. Not all these activities need to be firsthand experiences; many should involve the use of books and other audio-visual materials. Again, though, they must be activities which are of interest to the children and are made meaningful to them by being related to experiences they have had earlier.

The importance of the classroom environment, the role of the teacher, and the effect of the audience have been identified in previous chapters as vital factors in sparking children's expression; they are further discussed with particular application to writing in Chapter 9.

[9] Dora V. Smith, "Growth in Language Power as Related to Child Development," *Teaching Language in the Elementary School,* The Forty-third Yearbook of the National Society for the Study of Education, Part II (Chicago: The University of Chicago Press, 1944), p. 59.

Developing Writing Skills in Special Language Situations

A vital writing program can only exist if the total program of a class-room is meaningful and challenging. Where ideas abound, expression of them comes freely, the idea of "assignments" becoming irrelevant. Writing may stem from the science class, a field trip in social studies, the need to establish rules for a game, the development of an imagina-tive story, the reading pupils have done, and numerous other genuine situations. This writing, while it should be an integral part of the lan-guage arts program, need not be haphazard and unplanned. Rather, it should be carefully planned so that children may learn the skills that they need and so that they may build upon earlier experiences to gain improvement.

The writing of letters is one of the most important written language activities of life and should receive major instructional emphasis in the elementary school. Many different types of letters need to be written, including such personal letters as those of invitation and reply, sympathy, regret, thanks, apology, congratulations, and friendship, and business letters dealing with requests, orders, applications, and com-plaints. Included also in letter writing are the special skills of writing business and personal telegrams and night letters, writing postcards, and addressing cards and envelopes.

Letter Writing

    Letter writing is most effectively taught as an integral part of an activity going on in the classroom. Children must understand the need for the writing of a letter and the importance of content, form, and courtesies before economical learning will occur. Teachers must be on the alert for opportunities which require the writing of real letters. Some frequently occurring opportunities that call for the writing of the various kinds of letters are the following:

Invitations:	To friends or parents to visit the classroom
	To another class or school to come to a play day
	To the principal or supervisor to observe an activity
Replies:	Of acceptance to an invitation from another class or a parent
	Of regret at not being able to come to a program
Sympathy:	To a sick classmate or teacher
	To a teacher or family of a classmate after a death or accident

Greetings:	To the principal, teachers, and classmates on birthdays or holidays
	To various friends on special occasions
Friendly letters and postcards:	To children in another classroom or school
	To a former classmate
	To last year's teacher
	To a student in a foreign land[10]
Thank-you notes:	To someone for talking to the class
	To friends and relatives for presents at Christmas
	To another class for the use of some books or to a parent for the loan of materials
	To the principal for some special favor
Requests:	To a company or individual for information
	To a shop keeper for materials
	To someone for permission to visit his business or home
	To the principal for permission to take a trip
	To the school custodian for doing some task in the room
	To the lunch room cook for a special item on the menu
Orders:	To a business for class supplies
	For a magazine subscription
Applications:	For a position on the school paper
	For a job in the school office
	For summer work or after school jobs
	For membership in a club
Complaints:	About an article in newspaper
	About a practice on the playground

The above are only a few suggestions. Most language textbooks give other suggestions and the alert teacher will think of many more. The important point is that there are actually many occasions for letter writing and that these occasions occur naturally in a classroom which has many activities under way.

It is most important that the children in all grades acquire proper habits and attitudes regarding letter writing. These will come largely through informal discussion and the teacher's wise use of real situations. Among the important habits and attitudes are the following:

[10]Sources of names are the following: The Christian Science Monitor, Boston, Mass.; Parker Pen Company, Janesville, Wisconsin; Youth of All Nations, 16 St. Luke's Place, New York, N.Y. 10014; School Affiliation Service, American Friends Service Committee, 160 North Fifteenth Street, Philadelphia, Pa.; The Canadian Education Association, 151 Bloor Street, W., Toronto 5, Ontario, Canada. Names may also be secured from columns in magazines such as *The Grade Teacher* and *The Instructor*.

1. Answering questions that have been asked.
2. Implying or expressing respect and esteem.
3. Expressing sympathy when needed.
4. Inquiring about matters of concern to the reader.
5. Expressing good wishes or congratulations.
6. Keeping the letter tidy.
7. Enclosing a stamped envelope when requesting a reply from uninterested parties.
8. Never reading another's letter except upon request.
9. Selecting appropriate materials (pen, paper).
10. Mailing letters promptly.
11. Both writing and typing the signature when the typewriter is used.
12. Placing the return address on the envelope.
13. Rereading letters before mailing.
14. Making social letters as interesting as possible.
15. Being concerned about the quality of writing and the correctness of spelling.
16. Answering invitations, and giving reasons when refusing invitations.
17. Not writing letters in anger.
18. Answering letters with relative promptness.

In addition, children need to develop certain abilities and knowledge which contribute to good letter writing. Among these are the following:

1. A realization that a letter is a means of communication.
2. A sensitivity to the situations in which a letter should be written.
3. A realization that a letter has different parts and a knowledge of the purpose of each part.
4. A knowledge of the relative position of each of the parts of a letter, and an ability to space the various parts properly.
5. A knowledge of the appropriateness of different types of salutations, addresses, and endings in terms of the addressee and the type of letter being written.
6. The ability to capitalize, punctuate, and place correctly the heading, salutation, ending, and signature.
7. The ability to spell correctly certain words of great importance in letter writing such as: dear, Mr., Mrs., Miss, gentlemen; names of cities, states, months; friend, sincerely, truly, sir, etc.
8. A knowledge of what it is appropriate to say in a letter in terms of the circumstances of the writing.
9. A knowledge of the factors that make a friendly letter interesting.
10. A knowledge of the appropriateness of writing materials to the purpose and type of letter.

11. A knowledge of how to fold a letter.
12. The ability to write and place both the address and the return address on the envelope, and an understanding of their importance.
13. A knowledge of how to enclose money in a letter, and how to write dollars and cents.
14. A knowledge of abbreviations to use in titles, addresses, etc.
15. The ability to write simple informal and formal invitations and acceptances.
16. A knowledge of what types of invitations deserve formal answers.
17. A knowledge of sources of information relative to correct procedure in regard to invitations.

Content. In the lower grades the teacher should spend considerable time with the pupils discussing the purpose of letters in general and more specifically the purpose of a particular letter that they are planning to write. The same practice should be carried on periodically throughout the middle and upper grades. Teaching the children about the purpose of letters in general and the specific purpose of a particular letter is naturally dependent upon the situation calling for its writing. The children must discover that in order to continue the interesting activity in which they are engaged, a letter must be written for the required information or material. They must understand that in another situation courtesy demands the writing of a letter of thanks or sympathy.

A discussion of letter writing should focus upon the content necessary to achieve the writer's purpose. Decisions should be made as to the details to be included. If the letter is an order for some material, the amount should be listed, and the use that will be made of free materials should be stated. The letter should also indicate when it is needed, and to whom it should be sent. These details should be organized into a logical sequence; in beginning letter writing they should be listed and organized on the board. Special attention will need to be given to good beginning and ending sentences. In the writing of friendly letters particularly, attention should be given to phrasing the thoughts in interesting and vivid ways. Other suggestions for developing ideas and attitudes about content in letters are the following:

1. Read to the class interesting letters recorded in literature, such as Roosevelt's *Letters to His Children.*
2. Analyze letters received as to their organization, why they are or are not interesting, and whether they do or do not achieve the purpose intended.
3. Encourage pupils in upper grades to plan what they want to say and possibly to make an outline of the content of a letter before writing it.

4. Help children to think of other interesting words and phrases to be used in place of the somewhat trite ones commonly used in both business and personal letters.
5. Have children exchange and analyze each other's letters.
6. Have children read letters aloud to the class. The children should then decide how certain ideas could be stated more clearly and interestingly.

Form. Children learn most about form in letter writing by seeing and studying good models. Most textbooks contain samples of different types of letters, but unfortunately a letter reproduced on the printed page of a textbook does not resemble the original letter in many respects. The content may be reproduced verbatim and in script, but the size of the paper stock, the widths of margins, the lengths of lines, the size of the writing, and the spacing between the lines must all be restricted to meet the specifications of the printer, not the standards of correctly written letters. As a supplement to or perhaps an antidote for these textbook models, the teacher and the class should develop correct forms of the several types of letters, with content dictated by the children. Following the class acceptance of each form, consideration should be given to the size, shape, and color of paper suitable for a letter of the type represented by the model. Proper paper should then be secured, and each child should produce a teacher-approved copy of the model letter for his personal use. Similar models can be prepared for envelopes. These, with the model letters properly folded and inserted in them, can be attached to textbook or notebook covers for convenient reference.

In addition to making their own models, pupils should see letters secured from business concerns, professional persons, and friends. The forms of letter writing actually in use may vary widely from the textbook models, and the pupils should be aware of this. However, the various forms have much in common in terms of heading, inside address, salutation, closing, and signature—these may have different placement on the page and may or may not have the identations the textbook shows, but they are included.

Typewritten letters, both business and friendly, should be given greater attention than most textbooks suggest, since more and more children in the elementary school have experience with typewriters.

Many of the activities in the classroom almost demand that reports be written or given orally. In social studies, science, and other areas of the curriculum there are almost unlimited opportunities for pupils to prepare reports that are purposeful to such study.

Writing
Reports

Written reports are closely related to oral reports because both require the same kind of planning and research. Thus, the discussion in this section should be related to that beginning on page 206.

As was suggested in earlier chapters, kindergarten and first grade children begin reporting activities by dictating to the teacher brief sentences and paragraphs that describe some experience they have had, a unit of work they have carried out, or the directions relating to some familiar procedure they have found interesting. In the second and third grades some of the report and summary work should be done by the children themselves. In the intermediate grades children should write summaries of an increasing number of paragraphs, recommendations of books read, reports on excursions taken or projects developed, and directions relative to classroom trips and activities.

The objectives for the various grade levels should be similar to the following:

Primary Grades

a. To begin to express observations in written form either by pictures or story
b. To learn to make accurate observations and reports
c. To develop the ability to note essentials clearly and in order
d. To learn the importance of definite, descriptive language
e. To see the value of concrete experiences as a means of learning
f. To learn habits of persistence in tasks of long duration

Intermediate Grades

a. To prepare summaries of increasing length
b. To learn the importance of planning in advance the steps in an activity
c. To learn the correct form for keeping minutes of a meeting
d. To train accurate observation and reporting, using as much descriptive language as possible
e. To learn to use a few key words which will recall data afterwards
f. To learn to organize for a particular purpose
g. To be able to use related materials to stimulate interest and achievement
h. To develop the habit of noting the source of material and giving credit for its use
i. To learn to select only appropriate material and to transfer it accurately

Upper Grades

a. To continue to refine and extend all previous objectives

      b. To acquire skill in taking notes that give a comprehensive record of a procedure, speech, or process
      c. To learn to take notes on important points while reading, listening, or observing

The writing of a report may serve as a challenge to the exceptional child, or to one who has developed some special interest or hobby. A child will painstakingly search for information about a topic that he is particularly interested in and that he thinks his classmates will want to read. Thus there must be a purpose for a report that is related to classroom activities.

Studies have been made of what children want to study when they have a choice. One study of the interests of pupils in the middle and upper grades showed three groupings or categories to be most popular, all of which lead naturally to report writing.[11] These groupings were: (a) periods of time (pioneer life, colonial days, and the like); (b) people (famous persons, persons doing particular jobs, children); and (c) cultural aspects of social studies (situations involving freedom, human rights, contributions by other people). However, the fact that such interests lead to report writing does not mean that children will automatically be interested in doing the writing. To repeat: there has to be a reason for writing a report, with that reason felt by the writer, to gain and maintain motivation for doing good writing.

Practice should be given to the entire class each year in defining and limiting the scope of a topic to be reported on, in planning the organization of a report, in using various sources to gain information, and in giving attention to the form and appearance of a report. As with other writing activities, standards should be developed in a classroom for the preparation and editing of reports. While these standards should be class-developed, the following illustrates what they might be like:

Writing a Report

1. Write the title on the top line and in the center of the page.
2. Skip a line after the title.
3. Capitalize the first word and each important word in the title.
4. Leave margins on each page.
5. Write legibly.
6. Use correct spelling and punctuation.
7. Organize your report carefully and make it interesting.

[11]Alvina T. Burrows, *What Research Says to the Teacher: Teaching Composition* (Washington, D.C.: National Education Association, 1959), p. 17.

Outlining   Outlining should be taught in the elementary school as an aid to study and the planning of expression. Outlines may be made of something read, of work to be done, of a story to be told, or of a report that is to be presented to the class. Simple beginnings in outlining may be made in the primary grades as a part of either language or reading instruction, thus introducing the children early to the idea of classification and organization. For example, in the kindergarten the children might dictate lists of items such as the following for the teacher to write on the blackboard:

Fruits	Vegetables
Oranges	Lettuce
Apples	Carrots
Grapes	Potatoes

Young children should make simple outlines of such things as a story to be told or dramatized, a trip that is to be taken or was taken, materials needed for a project. In the intermediate grades these types of outlining activities should be continued in greater detail.

The basis for outlining is clear thinking—understanding what is important and how it should be organized—the elements of all good composition.[12] While outline form should be taught, the emphasis should always be upon organization—order and relationships—rather than upon the details of indenting, upper and lower case letters, Roman and Arabic numerals, and the like. On the other hand, the significance of such details in providing organization and showing relationships needs to be demonstrated.

Outlining should be taught when it will be used; it should not be taught as an isolated skill. A good initial procedure (which may be necessary yearly until the skill is generally learned) is for the teacher and the pupils to prepare an outline based upon a selection all have read on some topic. This can be followed by the preparation of an outline for a report based upon information garnered from several sources. One of the best materials to outline in the beginning is a story that is well known to the pupils, so that they will have a good understanding of the sequence. Many stories are so written that the major and minor topics can be easily distinguished. The purpose of such an outline may be to dramatize the story for another class.

[12]See Chapter 10.

In teaching outlining, the teacher should stress the point that any task worth doing is worth planning in advance, and that outlining is valuable as an advance plan for the creative or practical expression of pupils as well as a way to glean meaning from the writing of others. The value of outlining must be demonstrated to pupils. One suggestion is to have them write stories, one without and one with an outline, and then compare the stories in a class evaluation period.

Outlines may be made in topical form or in sentence form. For the younger children the sentence form is undoubtedly easier to follow. If the sentence form is used, it should be pointed out that the period must be placed at the end of each sentence as in any other written work. The important thing for them to learn is to use one form consistently within the same outline. There is no one acceptable form for outlining, but some major principles such as the following may be used in developing the form for use in a particular school:

1. The outline should have an introductory and a concluding topic or sentence.
2. Each major topic should be of comparable importance and directly related to the subject of the outline.
3. There must be at least two subtopics under each major topic.
4. The same form for numbering, lettering, indenting, capitalizing, and punctuating should be used throughout the outline.
5. There should be no punctuation after the topics unless they are complete sentences.

The following outline form is offered as a general guide for either a topical or a sentence outline carrying three main topics with subtopics. If subtopics are indented, their subordinate value becomes apparent.

I. First main topic
   A. First subtopic
   B. Second subtopic
II. Second main topic
   A. First subtopic
   B. Second subtopic
III. Third main topic
   A. First subtopic
   B. Second subtopic

The first formal teaching of outlining generally comes in the fourth or fifth grade. One guide gives these directions for making an outline in the fourth grade:[13]

1. Pupils develop their outlines under the leadership of their teacher.
2. In answer to leading questions, the pupils tell the teacher which items are to be included in the one-paragraph report.
3. The teacher writes the items on the board, listing them in outline form.
4. The pupils copy the outline, observing the following points:
   a. The title is written on the second line. A line is skipped after the title.
   b. The first word and every other important word in the title begins with a capital letter.
   c. Each item in the outline is numbered to show the order in which it belongs. Either Roman numerals or Arabic numerals may be used.
   d. The number is written at the margin. It is followed by a period.
   e. The first word of each item in the outline begins with a capital letter.

Filling in Forms

As adults we are frequently called upon to fill in forms of one kind or another. We fill in the information called for on a test booklet, on the application for a driver's license, or on an order blank. There are many situations in day-to-day activities in school in which children are called upon to fill in forms. These situations should be utilized for language instruction. It is important, if forms are to be filled in accurately and completely, that children attain certain attitudes concerning these tasks. The following attitudes pertain particularly to filling in forms: (1) realizing the necessity of filling out blanks accurately and neatly; (2) realizing the necessity of following directions fully and accurately; (3) giving information in the *form* that is called for; (4) striving to give *all* the information called for; and (5) using every effort to make the completed work look attractive.

Situations in school which involve the filling in of forms may include the following:

1. *Writing a money order*
   a. To a picture company for pictures to be used in booklets

[13]*Language Handbook,* Houston Public Schools, Curriculum Bulletin, Number 53CBM15, 1953–1954 (Houston, Texas: Houston Public Schools), p. 99.

b. To a nursery for seeds for a school garden
c. To a manufacturing company for material to be used in social science
d. To a publishing company for a magazine subscribed to by the class

2. *Information blanks*
   a. Questionnaires regarding personal history or health
   b. Enrollment cards
   c. Library loan card
   d. Call slip for books at the library
   e. The heading of a standardized test
   f. An application blank for membership in a magazine club
   g. A book plate for textbooks

3. *Forms concerned with banking*
   a. A deposit slip for a school savings account
   b. An application card for a bank account in the school savings organization
   c. A withdrawal slip

4. *Mail order forms*
   a. A subscription blank
   b. A coupon for samples or free booklets as advertised in a magazine
   c. An order to a firm for books to be used in reference work

Skill in filling in forms with accuracy and neatness is taught principally through practice. In the primary grades children need oral drill in answering such questions as "What is your name?" "How old are you?" "How old will you be at your next birthday?" Later this sort of exercise may be expanded into a game in which children see which ones know all of the personal history a particular form, such as a standard test blank, may require. Of course, this activity should be introduced as a need occurs, but to give the proper kind of teaching the teacher may need to stimulate interest by preparing different types of forms to be completed. One teacher suggests this procedure for teaching the skills necessary for filling in forms:[14]

1. Introduce by pointing up situation in school where use of form is required, such as sending for material, absence excuse, or test form. In a discussion period set up questions.
   a. What kinds of forms are there and how are they used? Why are they used?
   b. What do we need to know to fill out a form correctly? Are there any special words we need to know the meaning of?
2. Have the children bring in as many forms as they can find. Discuss these and practice filling them out. The teacher may need to bring in forms that the children won't locate. The

[14]Reproduced with permission of Mrs. Mary Bowen, Folsom, California.

discussion emphasis should be on the use of the forms and the need for neatness and accuracy.

3. Have the children construct a form to be used, such as for a picnic to gather information about who will need a ride, who can provide a ride, what type of food they'll bring, which games they'll want to play, etc.

Announce-ments, Notices, Labels, Titles, Signs

A wide variety of writing activities are included under this heading, all of which have to do with concise, short-written phrases or statements. The objectives of the program are to learn to present information accurately, concisely, attractively, and as completely as required for the purpose of the communication.

The use of labels, signs, poster and chart titles, and announcements on bulletin boards should be widespread. The teaching emphasis should be upon clear, accurate, and purposeful statements but with special attention to neatness and essential details. Oral discussion of the wording of labels, signs, and notices, as well as of the appropriateness of places where these might be posted or placed should precede writing. Having children practice giving oral directions, making oral announcements, or orally suggesting titles, labels, and the wording of signs is also needed before these related written activities are engaged in. Another useful activity—particularly because it has natural appeal—is to have the children look for notices, signs, and labels in stores, along the streets and highways, and in school. Rewriting some of the weakest of these in class can be fun and a learning experience for the children.

Records, Rules, Minutes

Throughout the elementary school children have need to keep records of various types, to write rules for games and other activities, and to record minutes of meetings. Activities which may present opportunities for such writing include the following:

1. The making of a yearbook in which class and individual experiences and information learned are recorded.
2. Special topic books such as "Learning About Iron and Steel" or "Pioneers Travel West," which may include records of many types.
3. The listing of standards to receive attention during oral reporting.
4. Meetings of the class historical society for which minutes must be kept.
5. Listing of new words learned in various subjects, what they mean and how they may be used.
6. After seeing a film, the writing of particular points to remember.
7. The writing of the daily news on the chalkboard.

8. The writing of recipes for things made for social studies or science, such as "How We Made Butter," or "Making a Tin Can Telephone."

Elementary school children are particularly interested in nature and in science. It is not difficult to motivate them to keep records on such things as the following:[15]

> The time the sun sets at different seasons of the year
>
> When the birds go south; return north
>
> The dates of the planting and appearance of flowers and of different crops
>
> Changes in the amount of water in streams and ponds and the causes thereof
>
> The action of wind vane, thermometer, barometer, compass
>
> Weather calendars
>
> The changing position of the stars
>
> Relation of community industries to soil, climate, waterways
>
> Habits of wild animals and pets
>
> How animals and plants adapt themselves to their surroundings
>
> Height and weight records; the relation of these to proper food, sleep, exercise

The writing of such records offers excellent opportunity for instruction in written composition as well as in the basic value of the records themselves. The records that children keep should be accurate, definite, and written in the children's own words so they will be understood and be of actual value. The proper teaching of the use of records should convince the children of the importance of language and its correct use.

As was suggested earlier in this chapter, practically every situation or activity in the elementary school may provide opportunities for writing. For example, children may write autobiographies, biographies of friends and persons they meet in their reading and study, journals related to historical events, and descriptions of school activities. They may do research related to the content for such things as journals and diaries.

Other Writing Opportunities

Other opportunities that should not be overlooked include the writing of advertisements, radio or television scripts, book reviews, character sketches, news items, and jokes and riddles.

[15]*The Language Arts: A Handbook for Teachers in Elementary Schools,* Bureau of Elementary Curriculum Development, New York State Education Department, 1957, p. 26.

In addition to the teaching suggestions given earlier, the teacher should pay attention to the following principles when teaching writing:

1. Stress the importance of conciseness and clarity of expression.
2. Have children base all writing upon accurate research and observation.
3. Discourage the tendency to copy the writing of others without giving credit. Point out that this is plagiarism and is the same as stealing from someone else.
4. Help children choose important facts, arrange their material in a systematic and identifiable order (e.g. logical or chronological), and construct effective opening and summarizing sentences.
5. Cooperate with the children in discovering colorful and accurate words and expressions.
6. Encourage the making of accurate observations. Have the children practice this, for example, by seeing who can remember the most different objects, people, or incidents seen on a trip.

Teaching the Conventions in Writing

The conventions in writing include capitalization, punctuation, and manuscript form (the arrangement of writing on a page). Singling out these conventions does not mean that they are more important and should receive greater teaching attention than the content of what is written. Content is always more important than form but many judgments about writing are made on the basis of convention items; thus they must receive teaching attention.

Manuscript Form

A neat and attractive paper, whether it is a letter, a report, an announcement, or a story, is an implied courtesy to the reader and helps to increase the effectiveness of the expression. Because modern schools are very properly interested in developing the individuality of a child, some teachers let pupils present written expression without regard to established rules, neatness, or other factors which show consideration for the reader. However, working out with a group of children guidelines as to what constitutes a neat and acceptable paper by no means disregards individuality. Children generally appreciate understanding what is expected of them and in later school work and as adults they will appreciate even more having been obliged to learn how to prepare neat and attractive papers.

There are no set rules for manuscript form. There are some generally accepted ideas such as margins at top and bottom and at the right and left on the paper, but the width of these margins will vary with the person prescribing the form. To avoid needless confusion some schools have agreed on certain items of form to be followed within the system.

The following listing of items of manuscript form are suggested for consideration and agreement by the teachers in a school or school system. An excellent practice is for the school to compile a handbook on form, style, and usage for the guidance of the teachers and the pupils.

Agreement on items for a handbook does not mean that pupils cannot help set their own standards. The listing can be a guide to the development of classroom standards.

Kindergarten	The teacher should call the attention of the children to material which involves form. For example, attention could be called to the attractiveness of neat work, to margins in books and newspapers, to titles of stories, to attractive arrangements of work on paper.
Grade 1	a. Margin at left and right b. Spacing at top and bottom of page c. Writing done carefully and on one side of the paper
Grade 2	a. All given above for grade one b. First word of a paragraph indented c. Second line of paragraph brought back to the margin d. Placing the name and date correctly
Grade 3	a. All given for previous grades b. Spacing between title and body of a composition c. Avoiding crowding at end of a line
Grades 4, 5, and 6	a. All listed for previous grades b. Use of correct paper for particular writing occasions

Few current courses of study or curriculum guides make mention of such details regarding the form and appearance of written expression as those above. One exception, a guide for a county school system, includes the following:[16]

[16]"Language Arts Guide, Grades K–6," Jefferson County Schools, Lakewood, Colo., 1960.

HEADING FOR WRITTEN WORK

That a uniform heading be used for all written work by all pupils in the elementary schools the committee recommended that the following items be used:

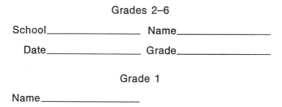

Grades 2–6

School_____ Name_____

Date_____ Grade_____

Grade 1

Name_____

Guides of an earlier period, which included lists such as the one below, reflect considerably more attention to manuscript form. Probably these are too arbitrary and too all-inclusive for the teacher who wants to work out standards for his class with the pupils. However, it is important for children to have standards of form and to observe them in their writing.

1. Leave at least a one-half inch margin at the left and at the right of all written work.
2. Leave a space of at least one inch at the top of a beginning sheet. Leave a space of at least one-half inch at the top of all other sheets.
3. Do not write on the last line of a ruled sheet, and on an unruled sheet leave at least one-half inch at the bottom of the page.
4. Write on one side of the paper only for all written work to be handed in or preserved.
5. Indent each paragraph from the left margin.
6. If a paragraph is numbered, the number should be indented.
7. No lines should be left unfilled at the right except at the end of a paragraph or in outline form.
8. Do not crowd writing at the end of a line.
9. Do not draw a line for the margin.
10. Put no periods after titles.
11. Do not capitalize words in the body of the material for the purpose of emphasizing something.
12. Abbreviations within a sentence should be avoided.
13. When it is necessary to begin a sentence with a number, use a word and not a figure.
14. All written work to be read by others should be spelled correctly and written legibly and neatly.
15. No paper containing untidy erasures should be handed in.

16. No written work should be posted which contains misspellings or other types of errors.[17]

While every teacher must be concerned not to suppress children's creativity or retard their willingness to express themselves, the authors believe that establishing standards neither suppresses nor retards. It is suggested, therefore, that teachers and supervisors within a school system should formulate statements of agreement on certain matters of manuscript form and appearance, such as position of name and date on the paper, placement of the title of a report or other written material, preferred size and type of paper to be used, use of one or both sides of the paper, and extent of top, bottom, and side margins.[18] Within the limits of the above school-wide agreements, the teachers and pupils should include matters of manuscript appearance in the statements of standards they establish for their own written work. Then, following the establishment of the standards of manuscript form and appearance, the children should be expected to observe them in all their written work. This practice is likely to have a more positive effect on the favorable development of the child's personality and his writing than the anything-goes policy of some teachers.

Errors in punctuation are the most frequently occurring type of error in conventions, or mechanics, of writing. Studies which have analyzed the writing of elementary and secondary school children and of adults show that errors in punctuation persist through all educational levels. These studies indicate that, in general, skill in punctuation is difficult to acquire, or it has not been well taught in schools.[19] Perhaps the greatest cause of this difficulty is that too little attention is given to the punctuation items of greatest social importance and too much effort is wasted upon items of little, if any, importance.

Punctuation

The task of determining the relative importance of punctuation items is to the classroom teacher like the selection of words for the basic spelling list. Exact information is difficult to come by and a "guess" may be wrong. An analysis of language textbooks is likely to be unreliable, since the authors of such books do not agree on the importance of various items.

[17]Adapted from Maude McBroom, *The Course of Study in Written Composition for the Elementary Grades*, Monographs in Education, First Series, No. 10 (Iowa City: State University of Iowa, December 1, 1928), pp. 100–101.

[18]Note: These statements should avoid conflict with matters of manuscript form suggested in the language textbooks in use.

[19]Robert R. Odom, "Growth of a Language Skill: Punctuation," *California Journal of Educational Research*, 15:12–17, 1964.

There is some mention in educational literature from time to time relating punctuation to intonations in speech.[20] Certainly punctuation at the end of a sentence is a major clue to the intonation pattern in reading that sentence. Other punctuation items may sometimes show the need for a change in pitch as well as indicating junctures. For example, "The two girls in the first row are close friends," will not be read orally the same way as, "The two girls, in the first row, are close friends." However, it is a fallacy to assume that any pause or change in pitch requires a punctuation mark. Thus, to teach children to punctuate sentences according to speech signals can be misleading. On the other hand, relating punctuation items to intonation patterns of speech is helpful to both oral and silent reading because they are often clues to meaning.

The following is a suggested list by grade levels of punctuation items that should receive instructional attention in the elementary school. The listing should not be held to rigidly since punctuation needs vary and each item should be taught as the need occurs.

Grade 1
  a. Period at the end of a sentence that tells something
  b. Period after numbers in any kind of list

Grade 2
  a. Items listed for grade one
  b. Question mark at the close of a question
  c. Comma after salutation of a friendly note or letter
  d. Comma after closing of a friendly note or letter
  e. Comma between the day of the month and the year
  f. Comma between name of city and state

Grade 3
  a. Items listed for grades one and two
  b. Period after abbreviations
  c. Period after an initial
  d. Use of an apostrophe in common contractions such as isn't, aren't
  e. Commas in a list

Grade 4
  a. All items listed for previous grades
  b. Apostrophe to show possession
  c. Hyphen separating parts of a word divided at end of a line
  d. Period following a command
  e. Exclamation point at the end of a word or group of words that make an exclamation
  f. Comma setting off an appositive
  g. Colon after the salutation of a business letter

[20]For example: Mary E. Fowler, *Teaching Language, Composition, and Literature* (New York: McGraw-Hill, 1965), p. 200; Paul C. Burns and Alberta L. Lowe, *The Language Arts in Childhood Education* (Chicago: Rand McNally and Co., 1966), pp. 183–185.

    h. Quotation marks before and after a direct quotation
    i. Comma between explanatory words and a quotation
    j. Period after numerals and letters in outlines

Grade 5 a. All items listed for previous grades
    b. Colon in writing time
    c. Quotation marks around the title of an article, the chapter of a book, and the title of a poem or story
    d. Underlining the title of a book

Grade 6 a. All items listed for previous grades
    b. Comma to set off nouns in direct address
    c. Hyphen in compound numbers
    d. Colon to set off a list
    e. Commas to set off transitional/parenthetical expressions (e.g. yes, no, of course, however)

Capitalization

Capitalization is also a mechanical element of written language about which considerable evidence has accumulated concerning children's needs at various grade levels.[21] These needs have been identified by examining examples of spontaneous and assigned writing and by examining the particular capitalization items for proper order of treatment and relative difficulty. Courses of study and textbooks in language are often quite definite in listing grade requirements in the area of capitalization. However, it is well to remember that such listings are merely guides for the introduction of drill upon the items and that within a classroom there will be considerable variation in skill in capitalization, as there is in language usage. This means, therefore, that items of capitalization called for generally in grades two and three should be mastered by an individual child before items which may be listed for grades five or six. (This principle should, of course, also apply in all other matters of form and convention.)

    The following list of minimal capitalization skills by grades is suggestive only, but it does take into account the needs of children in writing and the relative difficulty of the various items.

Grade 1 a. The first word of a sentence
    b. The child's first and last names
    c. The name of the teacher, school, town, street
    d. The word "I"

Grade 2 a. Items listed for grade one
    b. The date
    c. First and important words of titles of books the children read

[21]Robert R. Odom, "Sequence and Grade Placement of Capitalization Skills," *Elementary English*, 38:118–121, February, 1961.

        d. Proper names used in children's writings

        e. Titles of compositions

        f. Names of titles: "Mr.," "Mrs.," "Miss"

Grade 3

        a. Items listed for grades one and two

        b. Proper names: month, day, common holidays

        c. First word in a line of verse

        d. First and important words in titles of books, stories, poems

        e. First word of salutation of informal note, as "Dear"

        f. First word of closing of informal note, as "Yours" or "Your friend"

Grade 4

        a. All that is listed for preceding grades

        b. Names of cities and states in general

        c. Names of organizations to which children belong, as Cub Scouts, Grade Four, etc.

        d. "Mother," "Father," when used in place of the name

        e. Local geographical names

Grade 5

        a. All that is listed for previous grades

        b. Names of streets

        c. Names of all places and persons, countries, oceans, etc.

        d. Capitalization used in outlining

        e. Titles when used with names, such as President Lincoln

        f. Commercial trade names

Grade 6

        a. All that is listed for preceding grades

        b. Names of the Deity and the Bible

        c. First word of a quoted sentence

        d. Proper adjectives, showing race, nationality, etc.

        e. Abbreviations of proper nouns and titles

In addition to teaching the proper use of capital letters, attention should be given to eliminating unnecessary capitals. In particular, the practice of capitalizing words for emphasis should be avoided.

Teaching Capitalization and Punctuation

Instruction in the skills of punctuation and capitalization is most effectively given as the need for them arises. As children write, the need for particular punctuation and capitalization practices occurs. In the kindergarten and first grade, a child needs to know about capitalizing his first name when he writes it. When he first makes a weather calendar he needs to know that the names of the months and the days of the week are capitalized. With the help of the teacher, children will notice, as they read what they have written, that difficulties in understanding arise without the help of the capitalization of some words and the use of some punctuation marks. One course of study effectively expresses the functions of punctuation in this way:[22]

[22]*Using Language* (Wilmington, Del.: The Division of Elementary Education, Wilmington Public Schools, 1955), p. 121.

Children soon learn that punctuation marks act as traffic signals to help them on their way. The best learning for the use of these comes from having the child read his own work and find the places where they are needed for clarity. Periods, commas, question marks can be introduced when the need to use them arises. When added practice is needed, make that practice meaningful to the children.

From the initial discovery of need by the children the next step is the presentation of a model. That is, if a report has been written and contains many errors in punctuation and capitalization, the teacher should rewrite the material on the board or a chart, using correct punctuation and capitalization. This procedure emphasizes the need for the teacher himself to be careful in his own use of punctuation and capitalization.

An interesting presentation of appropriate and inappropriate capitalization is this example at the third-grade level.[23]

The children were keeping a diary on "Signs of Spring." At the top of each page (18 x 24 brown paper) was placed a picture and below it a title—"Robin Redbreast Returns," for example. Care was taken to show that in a title every important word began with a capital letter. After the children had chosen titles for their other pages, and written them on the back, the teacher said, "Did you begin the important words in your title with capital letters? Look and see!" Within the same project, the word April was repeated and the children reminded, "Names of months, also, begin with a capital letter."

One day one of the children drew the attention of the class to these two entries in the class diary:

> April 15—Today I saw a robin. It was sitting in the treetop and singing a song to me. (Barbara)
> April 17—I saw my friend Robin Redbreast. He flew to a tree. And then he flew away. (Rachel)

Tom: How does it happen that sometimes robin is written with a small *r* and sometimes with a capital?

Teacher: You are a boy, aren't you? If I write boy on the board, I write it with a small b. If you write boy in your stories, you write it with a small b. However, if I talk about a certain boy—Tom, for example—I write it with a capital letter. Or, if I were talking about any

[23]*Communication, A Guide to the Teaching of Speaking and Writing* (Minneapolis: Minneapolis Public Schools, 1953), p. 38.

robin, as Barbara was, I'd use a small letter. If I were talking about one particular robin that comes regularly to a tree in my yard, which I regard as a friend and to which I have given a name, as Rachel did, I'd use a capital letter.

Children need to develop habits of punctuation and capitalization. Since they do not ordinarily know how to write before coming to school, the school must take the responsibility for the habits children have in regard to their use of these mechanics. Emphasizing as few punctuation items and capitalization rules as possible will aid in motivating children to develop good habits. Much of the practice should be in writing situations that are for genuine communication purposes. However, some drill upon a troublesome item or skill is appropriate.

Language textbooks usually do not provide enough drill or practice exercises to be adequate for establishing punctuation and capitalization habits. The sentences below, from a fifth grade textbook, form an appropriate practice exercise.[24] This is the only such exercise on quotation marks in that particular book, however, and it includes only a few additional sentences for practice using commas.[25]

Quotation marks and commas

I hate to go to sleep Bob said.

I wish I could stay up twenty-four hours a day said Fred.

Their mother said Lights out up there.

The playground is being repaired today the guard explained to the boys.

Please keep your feet out of the aisle grumbled William.

Please look where you are stepping shouted Walter.

I wish you would both be quiet hissed Alice.

Guess what the Martian's wife was frying for breakfast Bob said.

It had to be unidentified frying objects said Fred with a guffaw.

You got it on the first guess said Bob.

The failure of textbooks to provide adequate practice material simply means that a teacher must construct his own. In many ways, of course, this is quite satisfactory since the ones constructed can be related directly to the needs that the children's writing shows.

[24]Andrew Schiller, and others, *Language and How To Use It, Book 5* (Glenview, Ill.: Scott, Foresman and Company, 1969), p. 104.

[25]The lack of practice exercises is not particularly unique to this textbook. All the language textbooks the authors have examined have only a few activities for practice on punctuation and capitalization matters. Some have none.

The following suggestions for developing capitalization and punctuation skills should prove useful to the teacher:

1. Observe all written work carefully, noting errors made, and perhaps tabulating the types of errors. This observation should be used as the basis for further teaching and review.
2. Use many proofreading drills which emphasize the types of situations that seem difficult for the pupil to handle.
3. Insist that pupils critically edit and proofread whatever they write.
4. Use dictation drills calling for the using of certain skills or for the avoidance of excessive punctuation and capitalization.
5. Give children work exercises which require them to use capitals or punctuation items.
6. Compile for each child (or mark and have him compile) a list of words which he frequently fails to capitalize, or which he frequently overcapitalizes. Give him exercises emphasizing these situations and acquaint him with the rules covering such situations.
7. Have each pupil edit his own or other pupils' papers with special reference to capitalization. Sometimes this can be done individually; at other times the child should work in a group.
8. Emphasize the importance of careful use of capitals and punctuation in all the pupils' work. Stress continually the importance of good form in writing.
9. Have pupils check their own writing after a dictation exercise. Emphasize self-diagnosis of difficulties.
10. Stress the relation of sentence structure to punctuation, and both to clarity and smoothness of expression.
11. Give special attention to handwriting if that is the cause of some capitalization faults.
12. Give frequent short diagnostic tests on the major capitalization and punctuation items. Have the pupils check their own work.
13. Make all drill and practice periods short and related to specific needs. For example, use a five-minute individualized drill period near the close of the day on errors observed during the day.

Written Language Skills in Using Books

Children in the elementary school need to learn about alphabetizing and indexing, both as aids to their reading and for preparing their own written materials. They need to learn that credit should be given to the writing of others when this writing is included in their own material; thus they need skills in footnoting and in using and preparing bibliographies. These skills are discussed in this section, and suggestions for teaching their uses are also made in other sections of the book (see Index).

The best way to learn alphabetical order and its uses is through practice in putting letters, and particularly words, in such order. Children also need practice in writing simple tables of contents, indexes, and headings for paragraphs. In all of these activities real situations should be utilized. When children put together a book of pictures they have collected, for example, they will need a table of contents and perhaps an index. In answering questions or preparing reports, children will need to use reference sources. From these genuine needs, then, the skills for the use of the sources are taught. Both reading and English or language textbooks suggest exercises for teaching these skills. For example:[26]

> A. Look at the page from a dictionary on page 70. Find the words *akin* and *Akron.* Why does the word *Akron* follow the word *akin?*

> B. Find the words *alack, alarm,* and *alas.* Notice that the first three letters of the words are the same. What is the fourth letter in *alack?* in *alarm?* in *alas?* Why do these words appear in this order?

An older textbook, as shown below, recognized the importance of children learning how to decide what they want to look for in an index.[27] Both of these types of exercises can easily be constructed by the teacher, since neither will appear frequently enough in textbooks to establish the pupils' skills nor be as closely related as desirable to the activities of a particular classroom.

> Pick out the key word in each question below.
> 1. How is radio important in flying?
> 2. For what are airships used?
> 3. Where is Randolph Flying Field?
> 4. How does radar help a pilot?
> 5. How are gliders used in flying?
>
> Make a list of the key words in the five sentences above. Talk over your lists in class. Did you all choose the same words?
>
> Now take the questions that your class raised.
>
> Decide in class which word in each question is the key word. Underline the key words.

[26]Thomas Clark Pollock, and others, *The Macmillan English Series,* 4, Third Revised Edition (New York: The Macmillan Company, 1967), p. 69.
[27]Harry A. Greene, and others, *Building Better English, Grade Five* (Evanston, Ill.: Row Peterson and Company, 1947), p. 22.

Children should learn to make and to use bibliographies as soon as they encounter books which contain them. They should learn acceptable bibliographical form for listing references in their social studies, science, and other reports. The following form may be taught in a systematic program as it is needed, using practice activities so that it will be thoroughly learned. These items should be stressed:

Bibliographies

1. To give completely and accurately all necessary information, such as author's name, page numbers, and date of copyright.
2. To use alphabetical order whenever suitable.
3. To write first the author's surname, followed by a comma.
4. To underline all titles of books or magazines.
5. To develop habits of absolute accuracy on references and forms.

A suggested bibliography form for grades one to six is the following:

Author, A. B., *Bibliography Form.*

For the upper grades and junior high school, the following form is recommended:

Books:	Author, A. B., *Bibliography Form as Practiced by the Publishers.* Boston: Hale University Press, 1962.
Magazine articles:	Author, A. B., "The Standardization of Bibliography Forms." *School Review,* 26:348–357, July, 1935.

Teachers in the lower elementary grades should begin to teach children the need for honesty in giving credit in their writing for ideas and information obtained from others. Many children develop a vague feeling that there is something wrong about using the ideas of others, with the result that they copy material and try to hide the fact that it is copied when actually the hiding is the only thing wrong with this practice. None of us, children included, can be expected to know all about everything. In fact, most people have very few completely original ideas. We simply learn many things from others and after a time are not able to identify the actual source of the idea or information. However, when we are able to identify the source we should do so, and this fact should be stressed to children at an early age.

Footnoting

Much of the instruction in how to quote the words of others and how to give credit for these words or for ideas will come about through the concern shown and the emphasis given by the teacher. He should have pupils practice these skills and plan for their use in their note-taking and information-gathering activities. No elaborate footnoting forms need to be used. At first only the author, title, and page numbers need to be given. Later, publisher and date of publication may be added. Most language textbooks make reference to footnoting and give models.

Self-Editing and Proofreading

An aspect of language teaching that too often is neglected is that of self-editing and proofreading. Children may recognize the need for writing in a special situation; they may be presented with a model and evolve their own standards; they may be cautioned about possible errors to be avoided; and finally, they may actually write and turn the product in to the teacher or perhaps to others to read and at no time reread it themselves or give thoughtful consideration to what they have written. Pupils who practice proofreading and self-editing are limited to those who have been forced into it by persistent teachers. From the beginning of instruction in written expression the pupil should be encouraged to depend upon himself, both in finding his own errors of expression and in correcting them. He should learn to examine carefully what he has written in terms of selection of the ideas or information, effectiveness of organization, clarity of expression, and courtesy to the readers, including legibility of writing, correct spelling, necessary punctuation, and acceptable usage.

From a genuine situation it is relatively simple to guide the pupil into an attitude of concern for achieving success in his writing. This is generally developed by reference to standards which have been established by the class, and later to standards the pupil himself has set. A child might develop these criteria, for example, which would serve as standards for his self-editing:[28]

1. Is my story told in good order?
2. Does each paragraph tell about one topic?
3. Is each sentence in a paragraph about the topic?
4. Are there any words I should change because they are un-interesting or don't say what I mean?
5. Is each sentence a good sentence?

[28]Walter T. Petty, *The Language Arts in Elementary Schools* (Washington, D.C.: The Center for Applied Research in Education, Inc., 1962), pp. 76–77.

In *They All Want to Write* a positive attitude toward editing and proofreading is advocated through attention to improvement in the writing after editing has taken place.[29]

> The contrast between the finished copy and the corrected rough draft, with its erasures, crossed out words, arrows and stars for insertions, was gratifying. The fourth-grade reporters were proud of their well-organized, accurate results and infinitely pleased with themselves and their new accomplishments.

Some simple proofreading skills should be taught when children first begin to write. In the first or second grade the child should be taught to read over what he has written; to check to see if the first words of his sentences are capitalized; to see if there is a period at the end of each sentence. It is not enough for the teacher to say, "Proofread what you have written"—an admonition meaningless to young children and ineffective to older ones without instruction in how proofreading is done. In the early stages of teaching proofreading the teacher and children may develop standards or lists of appraisal questions from which they may together select and correct errors. As children progress through the grades, however, they should be encouraged to develop for themselves criteria as suggested above for observance in proofreading and self-editing. The habit of depending upon the teacher to lead them through an evaluation of their work is almost as harmful as that of depending upon the teacher to make the corrections. Therefore, in spite of the fact that the teacher must give guidance in proofreading, attention should be directed toward developing habits that will enable the child to depend upon himself.

Class or individually developed criteria for proofreading should at first be limited to only one or two details. Later these may be expanded to include further items of organization, form, and mechanics. Group developed criteria which might be used at first should include such questions as:

> Have I written sentences?
> Have I capitalized the first word of every new sentence?
> Have I put a period at the end of each sentence?

Criteria to be used later might include such additional questions as:

[29]Burrows, and others, *They All Want to Write,* p. 65.

Have I indented the first word of each paragraph?

Have I left good margins?

Does each paragraph tell about one topic?

Does each sentence in a paragraph tell something about the topic?

Does each sentence begin and end correctly?

Checklists of criteria can usually be found in language textbooks. The following is one example:[30]

Checklist for Proofreading

1. Have you capitalized the first word, the last word, and all the important words in the title?
2. Do all of your sentences give complete thoughts?
3. Does each paragraph tell about one topic?
4. Have you indented the first word of each paragraph?
5. Have you capitalized the first word of each sentence?
6. Have you capitalized the word *I* whenever you have used it?
7. Have you used the correct punctuation mark at the end of each sentence?
8. Have you checked the spelling of each word?
9. Have you used *is, are, was,* and *were* correctly?
10. Have you left neat and even margins on the left side and on the right side of your paper?
11. Is your writing easy to read?

Pooley suggested the following procedure for use in the high school, which with modification is applicable in the elementary grades:[31]

A carefully worked out technique of proofreading can do a great deal to improve standards of written work and correctness in composition. For some reason it is very difficult to get students to reread their own work with a critical and corrective eye. The best procedure is one which is worked out with the group as a whole. When a set of compositions is ready to be handed in, the teacher should follow an accepted procedure of proofreading. The first step is to check the title of the paper, to make sure that it is correctly placed on the paper, has capital letters where capital letters are required, and that it is correctly punctuated. The next

[30]Josephine B. Wolfe, Adele J. Wright, Lillian E. Olson, *English Your Language,* Book 5, p. 25. Boston: Allyn and Bacon, Inc., 1963.

[31]Robert C. Pooley, *Teaching English Usage* (New York: Appleton-Century-Crofts, Inc., 1946), p. 232.

step is to scan the paper for paragraph form. Each paragraph should be properly indented; the first sentence in the paragraph should naturally begin with a capital letter; and there should be some kind of break in the composition to show the changes of thought. The next stage is to check the whole paper for accuracy in spelling and then for accuracy in word usage. Pupils that are dubious of the acceptability of certain phrases, or are unsure of the idiom they have employed should ask help of the teacher before handing the paper in. In some cases it may be advisable to have the reactions as a kind of double check on accuracy. This proofreading, if followed without fail at the time each paper is to be submitted, will have a vigorous effect, first in stimulating pupils to give their own papers a critical checking before they are handed in and in developing an attitude of respect for correctness and accuracy in all work.

The Evaluation of Written Expression

There are many standardized objective tests which purport to measure ability in written expression or some aspect of it. However, according to the report of a comprehensive investigation of studies upon which such tests have been based, their validity in actually measuring writing ability is questionable.[32] Knowledge of grammar can be measured, but as pointed out in this report, knowledge of grammar apparently has nothing to do with writing ability. Too, sentence sense (identifying good and poor sentences) and knowledge of usage (choosing the proper verb, etc.), can be measured, but ability shown on these measures appears to be little related to effective writing.

It is true, though, that the possibilities for the objective evaluation of pupil achievement and growth are much greater in written expression than in oral expression—a result natural enough, considering that the product of writing remains and can be examined. The difficulty comes about in deciding what is good writing and in separating *knowledge about* language, usage, and social conventions from *ability to use* the knowledge in producing written products. On the other hand, surely some things that children produce can be directly related to objectives of the writing program and evaluated accordingly. For example, samples of specific kinds of writing will show whether a child can do what was taught him or not. If he has to fill in a form, his ability to do this

[32]Richard Braddock, Richard Lloyd-Jones, and Lowell Schoer, *Research in Written Composition* (Champaign, Illinois: National Council of Teachers of English, 1963).

can be judged. If he writes a footnote, the correctness of this can be judged. If he writes a letter for a specific purpose, the extent to which this purpose has been achieved can be determined. Perhaps teachers need to better define the behaviors that they want children to exhibit. Lack of specificity of objectives always clouds evaluation.

Appraising
the General
Merit of
Written
Products

The difficulty in constructing standardized evaluative instruments which adequately measure writing ability has led from time to time to attempts to standardize appraisal procedures.[33] That is, ways have been sought to keep teachers' judgments constant from one writing sample to another. This is difficult to do, but some degree of objectivity and consistency can be held to if a guide to matters to be appraised is the basis for the judgment. The attempts referred to above have found form in scales and rating criteria, with each one reflecting beliefs about what is "good writing" by the weightings given to *organization, style, ideas, mechanics,* and so on.[34]

The value of a scale should not be underestimated because of shortcomings. Attempts to make evaluation procedures valid and reliable are needed because there is overwhelming evidence that teachers are capricious in judgment in evaluating student writing.[35] Validity of a scale hinges upon decisions about what is good writing but reliability can be increased by (1) securing an extensive series of samples of a pupil's written expression, (2) securing repeated ratings of the samples by a qualified judge, and (3) securing many independent ratings by qualified judges. By carefully collecting and scoring samples of the written products of his pupils under controlled conditions at the beginning and conclusion of a period of instructional time, the teacher can evaluate class and individual improvements as well as determine whether or not his pupils on the average are writing as well as they should at their present grade and maturity levels. If the teacher will remember the subjective character of the measures yielded by such procedures, and avoid the error of thinking of them as having the accuracy of objective test scores, these measures of general merit of written expression can be valuable aids in the classroom.

[33]A recent attempt was made by Vernon H. Smith. See Vernon H. Smith, "Measuring Teacher Judgment in the Evaluation of Written Composition," *Research in The Teaching of English,* 3, No. 2 (Fall, 1969), pp. 181–195.

[34]John C. Follman and James A. Anderson, "An Investigation of the Reliability of Five Procedures for Grading English Themes," *Research in The Teaching of English,* 1, No. 2 (Fall, 1967), pp. 190–200.

[35]The "capricious in judgment" is from Paul B. Diederich, "The Problem of Grading Essays" (Princeton, N.J.: Educational Testing Service, Research Bulletin RB61–15, 1961). Braddock, "English Composition," p. 455, says "It is common knowledge that the grading of compositions is notoriously unreliable."

Composition scales available commercially have received little use in recent years for the reasons cited above and because the requirement of standardized topics and control of writing conditions holds little appeal to English teachers and conflicts with philosophies concerned with the individual development of each pupil. There has been some resurgence of interest in scales in recent years, as shown by the publications of some universities and state councils of English teachers, but these are largely directed at helping secondary school teachers develop some commonality of practice in classroom grading of compositions.[36]

Using the older scales, the rater compared a pupil's paper with rated specimens of written expression and assigned a score to the pupil's written product based on the specimen most nearly similar.[37] Provision was made in the directions for minimizing the subjectivity of the rater.

The *STEP Essay Tests* represent the principal recently published instruments for measuring the quality of written products by rating procedures.[38] The test was devised for four ability levels ranging from the fourth grade to the sophomore year of college. Pupils are directed to write essays on particular topics in a thirty-minute writing period. Each pupil's paper is then matched with evaluated comparison essays on the same topic and assigned one of seven ratings. Each rating is weighted 50 percent for quality of thought and content, 30 percent for style, and 20 percent for mechanics of writing.

Evaluation of any writing is largely an appraisal of the quality of the product in terms of its purpose. From the beginning of instruction in written expression, self-evaluation by pupils should be encouraged. This may be done by providing each child with models, when possible and appropriate, for guidance and comparison. Self-evaluation will also be aided by check lists, such as the one below for appraising busi-

Evaluating Specific Writing Skills and Products

[36]For example: *A Scale for Evaluation of High School Student Essays,* published by the National Council of Teachers of English (1960) and prepared by the Joint Subcommittee on Composition of The California Association of Teachers of English.

[37]Early scales include the following: Edward L. Thorndike, *Thorndike Extension to the Hillegas Scale for the Measurement of Quality in English Composition by Young People* (New York: Bureau of Publications, Teachers College, Columbia University, 1914); M. H. Willing, *The Willing Scale for Measuring Written Composition* (Bloomington, Ill.: Public School Publishing Company. Reported as now available through ETSA, 120 Detzel Place, Cincinnati, Ohio); and Earl Hudelson, *Hudelson English Composition Scale* (Yonkers-on-Hudson: World Book Company).

[38]Educational Testing Service, Princeton, New Jersey. The essay segment has been omitted from the latest revision of the STEP test.

ness letters, and by the establishment of standards or guidelines.[39] As has been suggested many times in this book, such aids to self-evaluation can be made by pupils themselves. They might wish to put these standards in the form of questions:

1. Is my whole letter brief, courteous, and easy to read?
2. Is the spelling correct?
3. Did I write the heading correctly at the upper right side of my paper?
4. Did I block the inside address even with the left margin?
5. Did I write the name of the person or firm correctly?
6. Did I give the street address and the name of the town and the state?
7. Did I use a greeting suitable for a business letter, such as "Dear Sir:" "Dear Madam:" "Gentlemen:" or "Dear Mr. Blye:"?
8. Did I make my meaning clear in the body of the letter?
9. Did I indent the first word, and write the body of the letter in good paragraph form?
10. Did I use a suitable closing, such as "Yours truly," or "Sincerely yours"?
11. Did I sign the letter correctly?
12. Did I use paper suitable for a business letter?

Evaluating and Marking Papers and Assigning Grades

Evaluation should be considered a principal factor in the total teaching process. From evaluation the teacher learns what needs more teaching attention, what should be taught next, and what knowledge, skills, and abilities the pupils possess. The marking of papers is also generally regarded as a part of teaching, though too often it is simply fault finding. Assigning grades, however, is something entirely different from evaluation. Grades are assigned for purposes of reporting—first to pupils and later to parents—and while the task is one that every teacher must perform, it should not be equated with evaluation.

The role of assigning grades is considered in Chapter 2. Some repetition of the suggestions made is appropriate here because most teachers base the major portion of their grades in Language Arts or English upon performance in doing the types of writing described in this chapter. First, however, the following principles governing the marking of papers should be observed.

□ **Marking Errors**

Covering a paper with marks indicating errors is of little value to anyone. Pupils do not learn from having the errors marked in this manner and the teacher is likely to gain little information of a specific

[39]Adapted from *Building Better English, Grade 5* (Evanston, Ill.: Row, Peterson and Company, 1947), p. 93. Courtesy of Harper & Row, Publishers.

nature concerning those things needing further instructional emphasis. He should call the pupil's attention to only the grossest errors and record these for his teaching use.

☐ Marking Good Points

The red pencil is a favorite teacher weapon, but the sight of red marks usually causes pupils to destroy their papers or at least conceal them from classmates. The teacher should use the red pencil to call attention to commendable aspects of the writing also—a good choice of words, an apt expression, a neat margin, well organized thought, etc.

☐ Using the Positive Approach

Every written product from every child has something about it that can be commended. Perhaps it may only be a better formed letter, fewer erasures, or greater promptness in turning it in, but whatever it is (or more hopefully: they are) this should be the focus of the marking. The teacher should use the positive rather than the negative approach to marking.

☐ Providing Reasons

Letter grades or numerical scores are cold symbols—and they actually say little. As adults we do not give a novel a "B" or a "C"; we say it was a good book or not as good as his last one. The book reviewer may find fault but he gives his reasons for doing so. The teacher should use written comments as much as possible.

☐ Knowing the Child

Evaluation of a child's writing should be done in the interest of teaching the child to write better. This is accomplished only if he wants to improve. In requiring written work, the teacher must know each child and something of his thoughts. Further, he should have personal discussions with pupils as frequently as possible regarding specific writing products.

Since a particular letter or number grade means different things to different persons, and since it is of so little value in any specific sense as a factor in teaching, the excessive grading practices that are often quite common should be avoided. This does not mean that evaluation procedures should diminish; they should, in fact, be used much more than they usually are. The teacher should ask himself if he is more interested in teaching—actually evaluating and analyzing a pupil's work—or in accumulating a row of marks in a book.

The authors of this book are not so far removed from understanding custom and practice in elementary schools as to think that grades can be eliminated. But most sensible people—including parents—agree that schools do not have to revolve around the giving of grades. When grades are given it should be done on the basis of substantial evidence, in terms of specific objectives, and in light of effects upon the individual child.

Diagnostic and Remedial Procedures

Corrective instruction in language expression will be effective only if pupils are made sensitive to the social and personal importance of good writing and are stimulated to make the individual effort to improve. Teachers will find that many existing tests of language skills and abilities will prove valuable in aiding pupils to develop the desirable self-critical attitude. The informal appraisal techniques suggested in the preceding pages will also be helpful. In addition, the following general diagnostic and remedial suggestions should be useful to the teacher.[40]

Capitalization

Possible Causes of Low Test Scores	Additional Evidence of Deficiency	Suggested Remedial Treatment
1. Lack of knowledge of capitalization situations.	Analysis of pupil's test paper and other written work to determine types of errors made.	Identify specific capitalization skills missed by pupil and teach these. Stress proofreading drills on skills in which pupil is weak.
2. Limited knowledge of exceptions and irregularities in capitalization.	Analysis of test paper and daily written work; tendency to over-capitalize.	Give direct practice on capitalization skills taught in this grade. Point out exceptions and irregularities in the use of capitals.
3. Tendency to over-capitalize.	High correction for over-capitalization in test.	Inspect test paper and written work for excessive use of capitals. Use dictation and proofreading designed to emphasize correct use of capitals.

[40]Adapted from *Manual for Interpreting the Iowa Language Abilities Tests* (World Book Company, Yonkers-on-Hudson, New York), with the permission of Harcourt Brace Jovanovich, Inc.

Capitalization (continued)

Possible Causes of Low Test Scores	Additional Evidence of Deficiency	Suggested Remedial Treatment
4. Lack of self-critical attitude toward capitalization. Poor proofreading ability.	Erratic and careless work in daily written expression in other subjects; limited ability to note errors in own or other written copy.	Emphasize need for self-critical attitude toward own written work. Use proofreading exercises designed to emphasize use of capitals.
5. Poorly developed sentence sense.	Low scores on sentence sense tests.	Use suggestions in remedial chart for sentence sense.
6. Carelessness in writing.	Analysis of handwriting characteristics in daily work.	Practice capital letters and small letters which analysis shows cause trouble.

Sentence Sense

Possible Causes of Low Test Scores	Additional Evidence of Deficiency	Suggested Remedial Treatment
1. Limited meaning vocabulary.	Low scores on vocabulary tests; pupil's use of words in oral and written work.	Teach new vocabulary. Develop different meanings of common words. Stress using words in sentences demonstrating differences in meanings.
2. Poor reading comprehension.	Low scores on information and reading comprehension tests.	Give practice on word meanings, sentence and paragraph meanings, and comprehension of total meaning of content suitable for the grade.
3. Inability to recognize subjects and predicates of sentences, and to sense what is missing in a fragment.	Presence of many fragments in pupil's speech and writing.	Use matching exercises made up of subjects in one column and predicates in parallel column.
4. Failure to think of sentence as complete unit of expression.	Sentence errors in pupil's spoken and written work.	Stress use of sentences in daily oral and written work. Point out that there are times when fragments may be used but that they must be recognized as such. Practice on completion of exercises in which either the subject or predicate is missing. Use exercises calling for identification of fragments and sentences.

Sentence Sense (continued)

Possible Causes of Low Test Scores	Additional Evidence of Deficiency	Suggested Remedial Treatment
5. Use of "run-on" sentences; loose *and.*	Analysis of pupil's expression for use of loose *and's* and "run-on's."	Explain and illustrate various types of incorrect sentences. Stress individual practice in writing good sentences. Practice on identifying poor sentence structure and in recasting poor sentences.

Punctuation

1. Lack of knowledge of specific punctuation skills.	Examination of test papers to determine types of skills missed; observation of daily written work.	Check punctuation items missed in test with textbook and course of study. Use proofreading drills on skills missed by pupil. Stress correct punctuation, avoiding over-punctuation, and self-editing of own copy.
2. Tendency to over-punctuate.	Analysis of test and daily work for evidence of over-punctuation, especially commas.	Use dictation and proofreading for the elimination of improper or excessive punctuation.
3. Lack of self-critical attitude toward own written work.	Careless punctuation in daily work; failure to note errors in own or in other written copy.	Emphasize self-criticism of own daily written work. Use proofreading exercises to emphasize correct use of punctuation marks.
4. Poor general comprehension in reading.	Low scores on comprehension tests; poor reading in other subjects.	Give attention to punctuation during oral reading. Use content from varied subject-matter fields.
5. Poor vision or hearing.	Observation of pupil at work; nurse's or doctor's examination.	Refer pupil to doctor for medical attention. Move pupil to front of room. Encourage pupil to make special effort to write carefully and to make punctuation marks distinctly.
6. Poorly developed sentence sense.	Observation of pupil's daily usage.	Explain types of sentences and the relation of sentence structure to punctuation. Stress practice in writing sentences and punctuating them correctly. Use dictation and proofreading exercises calling for punctuation.

Punctuation (continued)

Possible Causes of Low Test Scores	Additional Evidence of Deficiency	Suggested Remedial Action
7. Carelessness in matters of form in written expression.	Observation and analysis of characteristics of handwriting and punctuation.	Stress essentials of good form in written work. Insist that pupils edit and proofread all written work.

Exercises for Thought and Action

1. Make a list of situations or activities occurring in the elementary school which would offer opportunities for writing. Try to think of situations and activities different from those given in this chapter. Describe the types of writing which might occur.
2. How would you improve the content of children's letters? Outline your program.
3. Find examples of variations in practice in the use of different punctuation items.
4. Outline a program designed to stimulate your pupils to proofread and self-edit all of their written work for both content and form.
5. Prepare a series of concise statements which you might use as standards in your teaching of written expression.
6. Analyze the papers from a class for (1) the number and frequency of punctuation items used and (2) the capitalization and punctuation errors.
7. Secure models of letters, outlines, reports, records, and so forth which might be useful to use with a class.
8. Construct punctuation, capitalization, and indexing exercises appropriate to a particular grade level for practice and remedial teaching.

Selected References

Anderson, Paul S. *Language Skills in Elementary Education.* New York: The Macmillan Company, 1964, Chapter 8.

Applegate, Mauree. *Easy in English.* Evanston, Ill.: Row, Peterson and Company, 1960.

Braddock, Richard; Lloyd-Jones, Richard; and Schoer, Lowel. *Research in Written Composition.* Champaign, Ill.: National Council of Teachers of English, 1963.

Burns, Paul C., and Lowe, Alberta L. *The Language Arts in Childhood Education.* Chicago: Rand McNally and Company, 1966.

Burrows, Alvina T. *What Research Says to the Teacher: Teaching Composition.* Washington, D.C.: National Education Association, April, 1959.

Burrows, Alvina T., and others. *They All Want to Write*. New York: Holt, Rinehart and Winston, Inc., 1964.

Crossley, Alice. "Can We Help Children to Write?" *Journal of Education*, 139:3–32, February, 1957.

Dawson, Mildred, and others. *Guiding Language Learning*. Yonkers-on-Hudson: World Book Company, second edition, 1963.

Logan, Lillian M., and Logan, Virgil G. *A Dynamic Approach to Language Arts*. Toronto: McGraw-Hill Company of Canada Limited, 1967, Chapters 11 and 12.

Mackintosh, Helen K., and Hill, Wilhelmina. *How Children Learn to Write*. U.S. Office of Education, Bulletin 1953, No. 2. Washington: U.S. Government Printing Office, 1953.

Petty, Walter T. *The Language Arts in Elementary Schools*. Washington, D.C.: The Center for Applied Research in Education, 1962.

_____. *Issues and Problems in the Elementary Language Arts: A Book of Readings*. Boston: Allyn and Bacon, Inc., 1968. Chapters 9 and 10.

Strickland, Ruth G. *The Language Arts in the Elementary School*. Boston: D. C. Heath and Company, second edition, 1957, Chapter 13.

Tidyman, Willard F., and others. *Teaching The Language Arts*. New York: McGraw-Hill, Inc., third edition, 1969, Chapter 15.

Trauger, Wilmer K. *Language Arts in Elementary Schools*. New York: McGraw-Hill Inc., 1963.

When Children Write. Washington, D.C.: Association for Childhood Education International, 1955.

Fostering Creativity In
Language Expression

9

INTRODUCTION

This chapter extends the considerations of the preceding two chapters concerning the teaching of oral and written expression. The focus of this chapter is upon creativity and its role in expression. The principal topics discussed include the following:

1. Creativity and Creative Language Expression
2. Conditions Fostering Creative Expression
3. The Teacher's Role in Creative Expression
4. Getting Expression Started
5. Creative Written Expression
6. Creative Oral Expression

The content of this chapter is related also to the chapter which follows, in which the attention is upon problems of usage and composition, constructing sentences, building vocabulary, and using reference sources. This chapter is also directly related to much of Chapter 15, "Teaching Literature In The Elementary School," because of the importance of literature in fostering creativity in language expression.

Creativity and Creative Language Expression

Creativity has come into its own as an educational concern. Not long ago creativity was thought of as something that could be achieved by only a few persons. In a school only a few pupils were regarded as being creative, having gained this distinction from showing talent in painting or in some other aspect of what we generally call "art"; in rarer instances creativity was recognized in a pupil who showed unusual ability in modifying or making things of a mechanical nature. This narrow view is no longer widely held. Now creativity is regarded as being possessed by everyone but, of course, in varying degrees of development or suppression. Its importance in all areas of life is also recognized, with increasing effort now being made to foster its development.

What is
Creativity?

Creativity has been defined in numerous ways. Torrance says that it may be defined in terms of a process, a product, a personality, or an environmental condition, but chooses to define it himself as "the process of sensing problems or gaps in information, forming ideas or hypotheses, testing and modifying these hypotheses, and communicating the results."[1] Smith defines creativity as the "sinking down [of] taps into our past experiences and putting these selected experiences together into new patterns, new ideas or new products."[2] Rogers has also defined it as a process: the "emergence in action of a novel relational product, growing out of the uniqueness of the individual on the one hand, and the materials, events, people, or circumstances of his life on the other."[3]

Creativity has also been defined as the contribution of something of an original nature, as the opposite of conformity, as the putting of isolated experiences and ideas into new combinations or patterns, as the breaking away from the main track, and simply as the adapting of ideas and information to one's needs. The concepts associated with

[1]E. Paul Torrance, *What Research Says to the Teacher: Creativity* (Washington, D.C.: National Education Association, 1963), p. 4.

[2]James A. Smith, *Setting Conditions for Creative Teaching in the Elementary School* (Boston: Allyn and Bacon, Inc., 1966), p. 4.

[3]Carl Rogers, "Toward a Theory of Creativity," *Creativity and Its Cultivation,* Harold H. Anderson, editor (New York: Harper and Brothers, 1959), p. 71.

curiosity, imagination, discovery, innovation, and invention are usually mentioned in descriptions of creative products and processes.

In the fields of literature, music, painting, sculpture, and the dance the idea of creativity is readily accepted. But creativity is found in many activities not always recognized as requiring imagination, as needing innovation, as calling for discovery. Usually we think of the activities of the store clerk as being largely routine. Yet the store clerk may very well produce a new sales approach or a new method of displaying a product that represents genuine creativity. In a field like mathematics, new thinking shows a markedly changed point of view. Max Beberman is quoted as saying that "mathematics is as creative as music, painting or sculpture."[4] In our age, disturbed by nuclear power and man-made satellites with their potential for good or evil, all forms of creativity must be recognized and nurtured, no less in language expression than in the many other areas of human mental and physical activity.

Creativity and the Language Arts

Creativeness appears to be a peculiarly human characteristic not related to basic animal drives but to a seeking of satisfaction in discovery and exploration.[5] Because of its human uniqueness it is related to other human traits, of which language is perhaps the most human. In many ways creativity may be considered as synonymous with the human potential. Lowenfeld stated, "I believe that one of the outstanding differences between man and animal is that man intentionally creates and the animal does not. That implies that every individual is a potential creator."[6] This creative potential is shown early in the life of an individual as he interacts with his environment, particularly as he does so through interpreting what he has gained from this environment by experimenting with language.

As a child manipulates language he exercises this unique creative power. "By exercising this power more fully and more astutely a person comes gradually to greater mastery over his environment."[7]

[4]Helen Rowan, "The Wonderful World of Why," *Saturday Review,* November 2, 1957, p. 42.

[5]Jack Getzels and George F. Madaus, "Creativity" in *Encyclopedia of Educational Research,* Fourth Edition, Robert L. Ebel, editor (New York: The Macmillan Company, 1969), p. 268.

[6]Viktor Lowenfeld, "Basic Aspects of Creative Teaching," *Creativity and Psychological Health* (New York: Syracuse University Press, 1961), p. 130.

[7]Mary C. Rodgers, *New Design in the Teaching of English* (Scranton, Pa.: International Textbook Co., 1968), p. 41.

Thus, as a child learns to "make sense" out of his world the creative potential is being developed. At first, although the creative power is strong, the full potential is only barely tapped. The child must continue to discover and explore for his creativity to flourish.

"The language arts are peculiarly adapted to the development of creativity in children."[8] It is principally through language that an individual expresses his ever-changing relationships with his environment. It is also principally by means of language that this environment expands. Thus, the language arts provide both content and instrument for making the creative potential functional.

Creativity and the Disadvantaged

The child who has been deprived of experiences which would have given him a standard dialect and verbal confidence in dealing with the language of the school is sometimes regarded as having little creative ability, particularly in the language arts area. The type of language limitation this child has reflects his limited experiences with verbal interpretation—verbal interpretation of the kind most "middle-class" children have had. However, there is little reason for believing that the child disadvantaged in this fashion is not capable of creative activity. This child can use language to the extent that has been necessary to live in his environment. He can be and often is creative with this language. What he cannot do is conform in his language expression to the expectancies of some teachers in matters of vocabulary, grammaticality, and conventions of format (i.e. punctuation, capitalization, story plot form, and the like). Too, sometimes he cannot conform in terms of the content of the expression. Given the right kind of instruction and additional language experience, the child disadvantaged in this manner develops verbal competency and "high order creative verbal behavior like other children."[9]

Creativity in Language Expression

A problem encountered immediately in the consideration of creativity in language expression centers on the issue of whether or not the product of the expression has utility or is "practical." Some writers hold the point of view that expression which is creative usually does not have utility and that expression which is made for a practical or utilitarian purpose cannot be creative. Thus, the writing of a friendly or business letter would not be classed as a creative process or result in a creative product because it has practical and utilitarian value. The

[8]*Ibid.*
[9]*Ibid.*, p. 49.

same would be true for an oral report containing information of interest and benefit to an audience. Other persons, however, hold that whatever an individual says or writes in his own way is creative. Considered from this point of view, any individual expression that a person makes is creative, whether or not it has utility, when it is not merely a repetition of the words of someone else. And, in the final analysis, of course, any expression may be thought of as having utility even if it results only in giving emotional release to the expressor.

The point of view held by the authors is that creative expression does not necessarily lack utility and purpose. In fact, we believe that language expression which is the individual's own is creative. We agree with the writer who has said, "the term *creative writing* might well be dropped from the lexicon of useful terms in the teaching of English."[10] We think that the practicality and utility of any language expression may be heightened through the use of imaginative thoughts and constructions, and the form in which these are put. Thus, a letter may be so written that the imagination is used, the senses are stimulated, and a true and artistic word-picture is painted for the reader. This is creativity; it is also practical and very effective communication.

Some persons hold that creative expression must be spontaneous. While a considerable amount of expression is spontaneous, much of this is not particularly creative. For example, a spontaneous answer may be given in response to a question and yet this answer may be merely a parroting of another's words. A spontaneous note may be written to thank someone for a present or a favor and be without the sparkle and imagination associated with creativity. On the other hand, while some creative expression is done spontaneously, much that is creative is a product of careful and lengthy thought. Even the writer of a rhyme may be acting spontaneously, but he may also be acting after considerable preparation. Certainly there must have been some stimulation or motivation, direct or indirect. Spontaneity is closely akin to "voluntary," a criterion often stated as a measure of creative expression. Again, there is an element of truth here; much creative expression is voluntary. Yet if voluntary action could be depended upon to produce creative language expression there would be no need to devote a chapter to the teaching of it nor would the teaching of language expression emphasize to such an extent the importance of an "intake" of experience.

Creativity of expression hinges upon many things, including an abundance of ideas and thoughts to express, which in turn is dependent

[10]*Ibid.*

upon a rich background of meaningful, vital experiences upon which to draw. The letter writer without many thoughts or ideas will only write "Thank you for the pair of socks sent me at Christmas," while the writer with more imagination and broader experiences may write "The red stripes on the socks you sent are picked up in the faint stripes in my new suit. Of course, I have to cross my legs for this to be noticed, but I do that often since it seems so striking." Few would deny that the latter thank-you note is not only more creative than the first, but it is also more effective communication because it says "thank you" in a more appreciative way.

For language expression to be creative it is believed that it must be:

1. *Original.*   That is, it must be based upon thoughts and ideas which are the person's own. These thoughts need not necessarily be new, but they should be stated in a way that is new to the person and not expressed in the exact way someone else expressed them or told him to express them.

2. *Based upon a Real Desire and Feeling of Need of the Individual to Express Himself.*   This desire or need does not necessarily come about spontaneously or voluntarily; in fact, every voluntary action is prompted by something, however remote from the immediate. It will not be creative if it is in any sense forced or stimulated against resistance.

3. *Imaginative and Different from the Commonplace.*   Creative expression has the sparkle and vividness which show that thinking, imagination, and something of the individual's personality and feeling have gone into it.

Creative language expression may take many forms. It may appear as a poem, a story, a play, a letter, a report, the minutes of a meeting, an interpretation made of a character in a story, or an announcement of a lost article made in an assembly. It may have the utility of attempting to recover that lost article, or of entertaining an audience through the interpretation of the character. On the other hand, it may be as lacking in direct utility as a note in a private diary, or a poem written to be seen by no one but the writer, or a joke made up and told by the maker. It may be a stanza jotted down hurriedly, or it may be prose produced after many hard hours of thought, self-editing, and polishing. In every case, however, if the expression is the individual's, if it shows imagination and is not commonplace, it is really creative.

The primary purpose of all language expression is the communication of thoughts clearly and lucidly with the amount of emotion and feeling necessary to make such expression really effective. The major purpose of creative expression is no different. There are no hidden aspects; creative expression just goes further than the expression that is void of the personal feeling, emotion, and thinking of the individual. Clear and imaginative thinking, based upon real understanding, will lead to clear and creative expression if the opportunity is provided. Creative expression shows feeling and emotion to the extent that the thinking process has really been involved. The child who adequately understands something, who has involved his thinking processes because he is interested, will achieve satisfaction from this thinking and a desire to express it. The expression will really be his because it comes from within.

The forms which creative expression seems most often to take, by the very nature of creativeness, point to two other purposes or values which should be particularly emphasized.

1. Creative expression serves as a release valve for pressure and tensions which are in the make-up of most of us. Often we are confused about various thoughts we have with regard to external conditions and possible effects. The release of these thoughts through language expression may provide a satisfaction and sense of relief. The release is likely to be creative, individual, and original, in an attempt to meet, explain, and justify, if only to ourselves, these external conditions and effects. In general children, as well as adults, who suppress their feeling to too great an extent are often not happy and their personalities may not be developed to the potential possible. Perhaps this is a real justification for the keeping of a personal diary. It gives the individual a chance to unload, if only to himself.

2. Creative expression of a truly imaginative nature is a means of securing fun and adventure. There is real pleasure and satisfaction derived from doing something which is new and original. The expression bolsters the ego and sense of self-worth, with pleasure resulting from the achievement and inventiveness. John, for example, almost "glowed" as a result of the praise from his fellow third-graders for his poem written after the class had discussed pets.

> Tabby is our mother cat,
> She's going to have a litter.

With all those kittens at her side
She'll need a baby sitter.

Bill was equally appreciative because his sixth-grade classmates thought these paragraphs from a letter to a pen pal in Ohio were "sure good."

We have an ambitious class. Everyone has a Pen Pal and we write every week. Getting letters is the most fun, but telling about things is fun, too. Here's what happened yesterday.

Jim brought a snake to school! It was only a little garter snake but the girls screamed and wouldn't get close. Jim put it in a cage we have but it got out. That's when the fun started. It took about an hour to find it. It was under our notebooks in the cabinet. Jim had to turn it loose outside after that.

Content and Correctness Some authorities in the teaching of the language arts emphasize that attention to sentence construction, items of standard usage, and mechanical skills will cause creativeness to be lost. Certainly attention to these alone does not make a masterpiece; this is true for letter writing, poetry writing, giving an announcement, or any other form of language expression. Matters of form and correctness are not the ultimate goals in any expression. On the other hand, correct usage, mechanical skills, and content are so interwoven in normal expression that it is impossible to separate one from the other completely or to say that one is of such importance that the others can be disregarded. Emphasis should always be given to content first, but not to content alone.

Children who can write and speak with real creativeness will want to use acceptable language and form. Indeed, a child who does not have some confidence in his own mastery of the skills of language is not likely to express his thinking and feeling through language media. If he has great difficulty in writing legibly, if he has too much hesitation in spelling, or if he has trouble saying some sounds, his expression will be suppressed, and what does come forth is not likely to represent his own individuality.

Most people, when they first try to create something in written form, pay very little attention to spelling, punctuation, agreement of subject and verb, etc.; their first concern is to get the idea down. Later they correct errors and rewrite where necessary. This practice places emphasis upon content first, but does not disregard correctness and form. Thus, in creative expression attention must be given to correctness and form; not to do so means sanctioning techniques that must later be unlearned. But correctness and form are not the first qualities to be considered in judging attempts made by children to express themselves. The essential aspects are the ideas, the personal feelings and thoughts expressed, and the desire and urge for this expression. The child's ideas and his grasp of the content he is expressing are important elements in the quality of creative expression. Such a quality is more likely to be secured when children are free from the strain of consciously and continuously giving attention to correct usage and form. This aspect of strain will be absent if teachers will have children work on the essential skills in practice situations until these become matters of habit.

Conditions Fostering Creative Expression

A primary goal of all teaching is to help each student develop his personality to its greatest potential. As each individual develops, it is natural for him to desire to express, to give out of himself in some manner. It is natural for him to struggle to express ideas and reactions which are his. It is human nature for a person to strive to create in order to gain the approval of his fellows, the satisfaction of self-attainment, and the feeling of personal worth that are his due. Thus, the development of creative expression in children becomes a matter of permitting them to release inhibitions and fears and of providing satisfying acceptance for their efforts.

The environment in which each person daily functions is of major importance in determining his opportunities for creativity and the acceptance or rejection of it. If the school is to foster creativity, if teachers are genuinely to nurture and develop it, the classroom conditions must foster goodwill, respect, and friendliness on the part of both teacher and pupils. Every effort should be made to have each child feel relaxed, at ease, and an accepted and important member of the group. Such a climate respects each child's personality, his problems of adjustment to other members of the group, and the emotional and social effects of his out-of-school environment.

The Classroom Environment

The establishment of this desirable environment is not a simple matter. It is, of course, largely dependent upon the teacher, but other school personnel and their attitudes about how children learn and what school should be like are also important. The principal of the school must encourage a teacher to have a happy, busy, and interesting classroom; the custodian must be interested in what the class does and be willing to accept disarrangement of furniture as part of the day's work. Parents must realize that children in school need to be active and that these activities and interests are of great importance to real learning. Physical materials in the classroom are also important. Little creative stimulation will come from a classroom that does not have many shelves of colorful and interesting books. Wall decorations and displays that are interesting and thought-provoking, materials for science and social studies in abundance, attractive furnishings, and other lively and decorative touches are all important in making the classroom a stimulating place.

Classroom environment that is attractive to the adult eye will not necessarily draw forth a child's expression. Children are highly sensitive to sham or pretense. There must be an air of honest freedom in which children sense willingness and encouragement for them to follow desirable expressional impulses. This highly desirable classroom atmosphere will come chiefly from the children's feeling of freedom to think independently and to express their own thoughts and feelings without officious direction or criticism from their teachers or the other members of their classes.

Providing Experiences

A child can be creative only within the realm of his experience. He can draw his thoughts and feelings only from within. His expression is limited to his impression, to what has been called the "input" that has been supplied him. For example, after a discussion of the shape of the earth a group of fourth-grade children wrote about their observations. One child wrote as follows:

> The earth is round and full of bumps. The cars and buses have a hard time on the hills.

This expression was a natural observation for a child who had lived his life in a rugged section of the country where transportation over steep roads was the only lifeline to the rest of the world.

In another fourth-grade class, the children discussed places in the west to which they had been, looked at flat pictures, films, and filmstrips of mountains, deserts, and rivers, and read about the places which seemed the most interesting. After these experiences one child wrote:

> The desert is a lonesome place,
> Where abundant is the brush.
> Where big and little lizards pace,
> And all the winds say "hush."

Another child wrote:

> I saw a canyon narrow and deep,
> With colors dull and bright.
> I heard the water rush and leap.
> What a wondrous sound and sight.

Children must have an abundance of opportunities for gaining ideas and impressions, for relating these to previous experiences, and—as illustrated above—for learning words they may not ordinarily use.

To foster expression which shows real imagination and vividness, however, it is necessary to do more than provide activities and opportunities for experience. One thing that must be done, as was suggested above and as is illustrated later in a separate section, is to help children learn to use new words. Further, as Mauree Applegate has suggested, "If you want your children to write . . . , you must take plenty of time to appreciate the little things that happen every day."[11] Many children, as well as some teachers, are unobservant and may not note the significance of the commonplace in their lives. They may fail to notice the intricacies of the dew-covered spider web in the plant by the school yard fence, the design formed by the shadows of the flag pole and the oak tree on the corner, and the eager look of the puppy waiting for his supper. A teacher must constantly encourage children to be observant and appreciative of what they have observed. This is best accomplished by a willingness to recognize flexibility in the daily schedule, by urging relaxation rather than pressure toward observing, and by taking time to discuss the details of what has been seen or experienced.

The talking-over needs particular emphasis. Certainly we all may see, hear, taste, and feel things and yet gain only vague impressions. Discussing experiences will help to expand and intensify impressions, but it must be thought-provoking and related to other experiences the children have had. The teacher who calls the class's attention to a flight of geese in the gray October sky has been observant and has shown the children something to watch for during that time of the

---

[11]Mauree Applegate, *Helping Children Write* (Evanston, Ill.: Row, Peterson and Company, 1954), p. 17.

year. Perhaps starting a list of things of beauty and interest to be seen in the sky will bring forth ideas such as the following:

a streaking falling star
a floating, drifting balloon
a swooping swallow
the trail of a jet plane
the chugging, blinking of a helicopter
the circling of a hawk
the darting of sea gulls
a kite straining on a string
churning thunder clouds

This need not be the end, and it may not be the time to suggest the writing of a verse or story. It will be thought-provoking and is likely to lead to further observations and additions to the list by the children themselves, and may bring forth an expression like fourth-grade Susan's "Clouds":

I like to see the clouds
Floating all around.
Often they smile,
Sometimes they frown.

Not all experiences need to be firsthand. Vicarious experiences may lend themselves as readily to creativity as experiences in which the child has actually participated. Reading, looking at pictures, listening to music or speech, and watching other persons and things may all lead to creative expression. The key is not the participation but the relating of the experience to the individual and his thoughts, his ideas, and his impressions. Creative expression is a reaction by the individual to his own experiences.

The Role of Reading Language expression that is vapid and unimaginative is often an almost direct consequence of a background of little reading. Reading to children and encouraging children to read, avenues that every teacher should follow, will be immensely rewarding in the expression that will usually result. Through hearing and reading, good language expression insinuates itself into the mind, generates thinking, awakens ideas, and gives impetus to expression. A reader finds pleasure, excitement, awe—feeling itself—through the many sensations aroused by his reading. Reading brings to a child the inheritance of the ages and an interpretation of the world in which he lives. It challenges his imagination and enriches his experiences—both essentials to creative expression.

A child must want to read and must have the skill necessary to satisfy this desire. The achievement of this goal for each child is the principal purpose of the reading program in schools. However, even with desire and skill in word recognition and comprehension, the goal will not be achieved without an abundance of books and other reading materials readily available.[12] Neither will it be achieved without careful teacher guidance in stimulating interest, in relating what is read to the children's experiences, and in fostering personality growth through reading. Guidance may also be needed in directing reading to selections which provide input that inspires creative expression.[13]

The basic test of the effectiveness of reading instruction is whether or not a pupil reads. Reading will not be done if feelings are not engendered, and if emotional or thoughtful response does not result. A discerning teacher, therefore, will permit responses to surface. Time is needed for many children. In this and other ways the effective teacher will encourage children's reading so that it is satisfying, brings forth feelings, and leads to a desire to express.

One writer calls attention to the need in creative expression for words which sparkle and spin, suggesting that such expression needs words with brightness, vitality, and gleaming appeal and words which are skillfully chosen to build the expression as painstakingly as a spider builds its web.[14] Language expression is dependent upon words, but children do not automatically grasp the uses of words most satisfying to themselves and their audiences. For creative language expression to result from an input of experiences, the experiences must be translated or expanded through and by the use of language, through and by the use of words.

The Importance of Words

Building interest in words—in what they denote and connote, in care in their selection, and in the intrinsic appeal of many of them—will be rewarded by expression which truly shows sparkle and spin.

Many interesting projects involving words will lead to their better use and to better expression.[15] Here are some which appeal to children:

1. Complete sentences or phrases which call for the use of comparison words.
   a. The wind howled like _____
   b. As soft as _____
   c. As smooth as _____

[12]See Chapter 15 for suggestions.
[13]See the list of useful selections at the end of this chapter.
[14]Ruth Kearney Carlson, "Sparkling and Spinning Words," *Elementary English,* January, 1964, pp. 15–21, 55.
[15]See also Chapters 10 and 12.

     d. He ran like a ―――――
     e. As green as ―――――

2. Make charts of substitutes for "tired" words.
     a. *said*—called, urged, shouted, began, exclaimed, replied, sighed, giggled, etc.
     b. *funny*—amusing, odd, laughable, strange
     c. *real*—very, quite, actual, genuine

3. Find adjectives for lists of nouns, such as the following:
     happy song   *steep* hill   *lazy* dog
     curving sidewalk   *swaying* trees   *polished* desk

4. Find words which would be especially used by a particular person or group. For example: astronauts, a tennis player, an automobile salesman, a fisherman, a pioneer going overland to California.

5. Before stories are written, have the class list words and phrases appropriate for the particular settings.
     a. *jungle*—humid, filtered sunlight, chattering, rotting leaves
     b. *Christmas*—holly, sooty chimney, tinkling bells, tinsel, symmetrical tree, bitter wind
     c. *Spring*—popping crocuses, gay blooms, lashing rain, bursting

6. Make charts of different kinds of words. For example:
     a. *color*—pale blue, amber, violet
     b. *quiet*—soft, tinkle, hush, whisper
     c. *noisy*—roar, bang, clatter, thunder
     d. *weather*—rainy, foggy, drizzle, humid, changeable

An Appreciative Audience

Securing the approval of one's fellows is a basic human desire. Appreciation of creative expression by an audience is no exception. Children like an audience, preferably an immediate one, for all their speaking and writing. They will express themselves with more vitality and spirit if they are aware that the teacher, a fellow pupil, or the class is ready to receive their efforts in an appreciative manner.

    Of course not all children in every situation will desire an audience as we ordinarily think of it. Children should not be forced before an audience, but with proper nurturing even the extremely shy and sensitive child will come to seek the approval of listeners and readers. Sometimes the audience can be only the teacher or one or two classmates but, regardless of the size, it should be a receptive one. The teacher who has helped create a classroom climate of genuine friendliness and respect for each individual will have few children who do not want an audience.

The Teacher's Role in Creative Expression

In addition to his major responsibility for establishing conditions which foster creativity, the teacher has other responsibilities if each child's creative potential is to be developed. It has been said that "creativeness cannot be taught; it can only be released and guided."[16] Thus it is not possible for the teacher to treat creativity as he would long division, American history, or the word recognition skills. Since imitation is the child's method of learning to use language—not only its sentence structure and its vocabulary, but also its beauty, its power, and its elegance—the example the teacher sets in showing creativity in his own expression and appreciation of creativity in others is of utmost importance. Torrance speaks of "a willingness to embark over untraveled ways."[17] This willingness must show in the imagination, originality, vividness, clarity of organization, and response to genuine need in the teacher's own expression. It is likely, of course, that some of his pupils may be more creative since their expression has not suffered the suppression that most adults' has, but with true receptiveness of each individual, a classroom atmosphere that fosters creativity, he can provide the model, the encouragement, and the appreciation needed.

Marksberry suggests that the creative process consists of four definite stages or periods:[18] (1) preparation; (2) incubation; (3) insight, illumination, or inspiration; and (4) verification, elaboration, perfecting, and evaluation.

These stages, as they relate to creative oral and written expression, are discussed in the following sections along with specific suggestions for things a teacher can do.

As has been stated, each teacher has a responsibility for providing opportunities for experiences, for continuously replenishing each child's impressions, ideas, and thoughts. Experiences which are meaningful to the child provide him with the material for his expression. It is foolish to expect expression from a source that is dry of thought, of ideas, of words.

Probably the greatest deterrent to expression that is creative, and satisfying to pupil and teacher, is moving too rapidly into the act of production. Having children give oral reports, dramatize reactions to an experience, or tell a story without adequate preparation, without talking over their plans, the feelings they had during the experience, or what the story characters might do in particular kinds of situations, will not truly bring forth their feelings, ideas, and creative thinking. The same is true of writing, with such inadequate preparation probably occurring

Talking Things Over

[16]Applegate, *Helping Children Write*, p. 1.

[17]E. Paul Torrance and R. E. Myers, *Creative Learning and Teaching* (New York: Dodd, Mead and Company, 1970), p. 319.

[18]Mary Lee Marksberry, *Foundation of Creativity* (New York: Harper & Row, Publishers, 1963), pp. 17–21.

more commonly. Teachers often think that showing children a picture, writing a few words on the chalkboard that the children might use in writing about it, and then saying "Write a story" will produce creative writing. Usually, except possibly by a few pupils, this does not happen.

Talking things over means talking about the events immediately preceding the expression—what sounds are heard from a railroad train, how people feel during a fog, what might be the reason for the baby's crying in the picture, what the sky looks like just before a thunderstorm—but it also means much more than that. Talking things over means daily discussing ideas that arise, discouraging the use of vague words, listening and reacting to sounds, providing for both free and planned talking situations. Above all it means taking the time to really talk, to actually exchange thoughts, and to pursue ideas to some depth.

**Developing a
Sensitivity
to Words**

Talking things over will lead to noting new words, new meanings, differences in pronunciation, and proper use of words. It will lead to writing words on the board, to talking about them, to using the dictionary. Children enjoy words that rhyme, new words, words that say something unusually well; they enjoy "collecting" them for bulletin boards, for notebooks, or for use in particular assignments.

A group of third-graders encountered the word "dashed" in a story and the teacher seized the opportunity to discuss other words that "can tell about how people moved." The children suggested the following, and with some success dramatized their meanings: *skipped, darted, scampered, trotted, limped, charged.* The teacher added *leaped, glided, slid, coasted,* and *ambled,* and these were discussed. Another teacher, of a fifth grade, also took advantage of a similar situation to teach word meaning and appreciation of the language. These children had read the expression "at the foot of the hill" in a social studies text, and while the meaning was generally understood, one child mentioned that the names of parts of the body are often used in descriptions. This led to a discussion of figurative language and the listing of these expressions on the board:

face of the cliff	brow of the hill	arm of the law
eye of the storm	heart of America	leg of the journey

Similarly such attention might be given to relationship words, such as *over, above, near, among, down;* to judgment words, such as *cold, bad, beautiful, best, deep, good, great;* to indefinite words, such as *few, many, any, some, several;* to definite words, such as *all, always, certain, every, sure;* and to synonyms, derivatives, idioms, and so forth.

The following are some procedures of a more direct nature for helping children to learn about words:

1. Notice and bring to the classroom colorful phrases and apt words. For example: *walking in the moss-silenced forest, a car snarling away from a curb, the wind churning and ladling the snow.*

2. Have the pupils try defining common objects, such as *a window, a ball, chalk.*

3. Put "teasers" involving etymology on the board. Some to try are: Which is more, a million or a myriad? Who were the first glamour girls? How are a dentist and a dandelion alike? What is the relationship of noise, an upset stomach, and a ship?

4. Illustrate on the bulletin board word families (*port, portage, portable, import,* etc.), words for particular days (February 14—*heart, heartache, hearten, heartily, heartsick,* etc.) words with prefixes (*uninterrupted, reread*) or suffixes (*invitingly, stubbornness*).

5. Take trips for the sole purpose of "collecting" words, or have pupils bring words to class from watching TV, riding on the school bus, or visiting a shopping center.

6. Get the children interested in words from foreign languages that have come into our language with little or no changes in spelling and meaning. For example: *sombrero, chocolate, opera, petite.*

The providing of literary experiences is discussed in Chapter 15 but a special word is appropriate here since reading is such a fundamental source of experience. Certainly a teacher should provide many types of literary experiences for children, including reading aloud himself, telling stories, having children read orally and tell stories, and of course fostering their personal reading. Not all reading will lead to creative expression readily and one could hardly expect particular kinds of expression to be made without a background of having read or heard expression of the same kind. That is, if children are to write or tell "tall tales" they should have heard or read many; to write poetry they should have had an experience background in poetry.

Literary Experiences

While most literary experiences may lead to creative expression by some children, often the teacher must steer the experience into actual creative effort. One guide suggests that a teacher begin a lesson on "made-to-order" stories by saying:[19]

[19]Detroit Public Schools, *A Guide to Instruction in the Language Arts, Grades 4, 5, and 6.* The Board of Education of the City of Detroit, Copyright 1959, pp. 167–168.

We have read many stories and poems this term. We have had fun talking and listening. Today we might try to write some "made-to-order" stories. This is a story you make up from a list of words and phrases. On the board you will find the list of words. Listen while I read them to you.

A tinkling sound
Bright, inquisitive, blue eyes
A faint blue line
Whispering and swishing sounds
Clickety-clackety
A smooth round object

Now take this list of words and see how quickly you can get a story idea. Perhaps these words and phrases have already started you thinking. Remember, try to weave all the words and phrases into your story. Remember to start your story with a good opening sentence. Recall some opening sentences from the stories we have read this term. Don't let spelling or capital letters or periods interfere with your writing. Get your thoughts and ideas on paper. Remember your story must have a *beginning,* a *middle,* and an *ending.* In the beginning you start the action, in the middle part you develop the action, and the ending rounds the story off.

This much direction seems somewhat abrupt and perhaps is too much telling and too little "drawing forth" from the pupils, but it does illustrate the relating of what has been read to a specific writing effort.

Getting Expression Started

Getting creative expression started should not be long delayed in spite of the cautions stated and the need for experiences and oral language development. Creativity begets creativity; creativity is contagious. Get it started and build upon the start that was made.

This section presents many ideas for stimulating children's expression. Most are directed specifically at written expression but may also be used for oral expression.

Beginning
With Group
Expression
The role of cooperatively written statements and stories has been described in earlier chapters of this book. Captions for pictures, signs on science collections, memoranda, greetings for cards, letters to be sent home, and experience stories of many types are some of the opportunities that have been suggested for group expression with the teacher as the scribe. The principal emphasis in these suggestions, however, has been on this writing as an aid to children prior to their developing

spelling ability and skill in handwriting. Such composition need not be limited to fulfilling this need, though, since the group writing of a story, a poem, a summary, or a description is appropriate at any elementary grade level and, in fact, is a very desirable procedure to use before children move into individual creative expression.

One fifth-grade teacher wrote the children's description of the pet hamster in the classroom. To construct the description, each row in the class decided upon a descriptive sentence, telling these in order from one side of the room to the other. Each sentence was written on the board by the teacher, who asked occasional questions to clarify sentence construction. When all the sentences had been written, the children discussed whether they were in the most desirable order or not and what changes should be made. The order of one or two was changed and in minor instances some wording. The teacher then put the description on a chart and the class discussed why it was a good description.

While the group composition described above was appropriate for the particular group of children at the time, group compositions should move toward securing more pupil feeling and personal reactions and less factual content. A description, of course, needs to be factual, but had the children composed a story about what the hamster thought of various happenings, personal feeling and imagination would naturally have entered into the sentences.

In addition to being a desirable procedure to use for getting a group started doing individual creative expression, group composition has particular advantages for teaching some skills and attitudes.[20] The importance of thinking about an idea before actually putting it in the expressional form can be made meaningful to children. The talking that the group does before agreeing upon the best sentence shows the value of the "input" of discussion.

Children can be shown that correct spelling, proper margins, and faulty handwriting can be improved after the original draft has been completed. With the teacher making such corrections in a natural way, they learn that this is what writers do. The opportunity is present to show that more than just proofreading for mechanical errors needs to be done; group reading for organization, appeal, saying clearly what was intended, and so on can be emphasized and thus pupils are shown that this too is a natural and regular part of writing. It is also easier to criticize typical kinds of faults in expression without having to direct

[20]Patrick Groff, "Success in Creative Writing—for Everyone!" *Elementary English,* 40:82–89, January, 1963.

this criticism at particular pupils and their personal efforts.

Models for various kinds of writing products can be presented without specifically identifying them as models and without directing that the group effort should be regarded as a model. The teacher may also use this group effort to show children that it is permissible to use some words or expressions that they may have hesitated to use; that expression should be made of feelings and thoughts without pretense and unrealistic language forms.

The Use of Topics

The most common procedure for endeavoring to have children express themselves with imagination and personal involvement is simply to assign a topic. Quite often this procedure is also the least successful. Among the reasons for its lack of success are the habit of assigning one topic for all pupils, lack of appeal of the topics, and the limited help the topics give toward starting the pupils' thinking. Here are some topics to try; or better, these topics may suggest other topics:

What Birds Say to One Another	Having Fun at the Beach
The Robot Who Cried	Soup Again?
Why My Dog is Happy	The Life of an Apple Seed
Getting Up Early in the Morning	Throwing a Boomerang
How to Spend a Million Dollars	When I Slipped and Fell
Substitute Teachers	What a Bulldozer Reminds Me Of
My Sister's Boyfriend	A Snowy Day Indoors
Walking Barefoot in the Mud	The Baby Sitter and the Refrigerator
	The Biggest Fish in the Bowl
	The Puppy's Day at School

Lists of topics can be put on the board, on a chart, or in a file, with the children turning to the file or chart for ideas to write about.

Establishing a Framework

Extending the procedure of assigning topics or having topics available, the teacher may present a setting, or framework, from which a title and composition can develop. Here are some that have been used successfully:

1. You are a large oak tree on the corner of the school grounds. You have been standing there for many years—even before the school was built. Tell the story of some things you have seen and heard.
2. You are among a group of people going overland by covered wagons to California in the 1850's. Tell what might have happened on one day of the trip.

3. You wake up suddenly in the middle of the night. Everything is quiet except for a distant honking, honking of an automobile horn. Describe what you think about.

4. The puppy got out when the garage door was opened. He ran down the street. What do you suppose his adventures were?

5. There were five people at the table but places had been set for six. No one said a word but a knock at the door caused all five to look up. Then they heard running. What do you think happened next?

6. Christmas is a time for fun, for giving and receiving presents, for secrets and surprises, and for singing joyously. Think of some of the things you have done at Christmas time; perhaps that jolly fellow has made you especially happy or you have had a good time with all the family at home or at your grandmother's. Think too of the sounds of bells, of carols, of crunching snow; or of the glittering sight of a tree; or of the smell of mince pies and turkey. See if you can write a Christmas story that will really make us think Christmas is right here. Try to do this by including sights, sounds, smells, tastes, and how you felt.

Children enjoy finishing stories that have appealing beginnings. One way to start stories is to have the class work as a group inventing an opening, with each child finishing the story individually. Magazines for teachers and those for children often have story beginnings that may be used either as they are or with modifications for maturity levels. A teacher, too, can give story beginnings. The ones that follow have been used with children and illustrate that beginnings of different lengths can be used.

Adding to Beginnings

1. The lamp on the table wobbled as the door slammed. It continued to wobble as Bill dashed across the room.

2. At the back of the yard a large black and white cat crept carefully along the top of the fence.

3. I could hear the sound of water. It was louder than the gentle rushing sound of the stream as it poured over the rocks; it sounded like a waterfall. "But there is no waterfall here," I thought. "What could it be?" I looked carefully upstream and started threading my way through the hanging branches and the tall grass.

4. The air was crisp and cold, the sky pale, and even Mr. Smith didn't seem to be up. Shivering and yawning, I looked down the street. I could just spy Bill rounding the corner, hurrying and with his hands jammed deep into his pockets. Under one arm was his pole and under the other a paper sack that was being flattened. I put my sack down and started around the house to the garage.

5. The fire had raged all night. The announcer on TV had said that it was spreading to the east. One picture showed the animals running—a fox, rabbits, chipmunks and squirrels, and even a deer. I knew that Pokey could run fast but he was so friendly he might not start running

in time. With the fire going to the east there wasn't any reason to worry anyway.

6. Jim just stood there. His legs refused to move. The sweat broke out on his forehead.

7. Usually we have fun at Grandmother's. We go to the park and see all the animals. We play with the toys from the attic. We have good things to eat, especially cookies and candy that Grandmother makes. This time, though, I knew things would be different.

   As Mary and I got off the bus, Grandfather came hurrying up as always but he didn't pick Mary or me up and swing us about as he usually did. He wasn't even smiling very much. He did kiss us and then said, "Children, your grandmother is in the hospital. She isn't seriously ill but she'll have to stay there several weeks. I don't know how we'll get along without her."

8. I pounded and pounded but the door wouldn't open.

9. The wagonmaster gave the signal and the wagons began circling. I rode faster trying to keep up. Then I heard the shooting and the men began to shout.

10. There was a slight flutter as the ship settled. Peering through the thick glass, the captain ordered the ladder lowered. This was it! Who would be the first down? Since I was in the fifth grade I had hoped it would be me. I held my breath waiting for what the captain would say next. I looked at Dick. He was watching the captain, too.

Using Objects, Pictures, Situations

Showing children a picture and suggesting that they write a story about it is a common procedure used by teachers. This may be a successful procedure but it has the disadvantage, as pointed out by Marksberry,[21] of possibly causing children to look outside themselves for things to write or tell about rather than to think about their own experiences and see the possibilities in their everyday activities. (To perhaps a lesser extent, this disadvantage could be attached to many of the suggestions for getting children's expression started.) The key to overcoming this is the relating of the picture, or the object or situation, to the children's experiences by extensive oral preparation and "drawing out" of their thoughts.

Not all responses to seeing an object or a picture or to participating in an activity, such as a field trip, should be the same; in fact, creativity would be missing if they were. Showing children a picture or an object or recalling some experience with them does not mean that the resulting expression from each child needs to be particularly related in content to the subject used for stimulation. Each child's personality,

[21]Marksberry, *Foundation of Creativity*, p. 41.

ideas, and background of experience will produce widely varying results.

The following are suggestive of things other than topics, frameworks, and beginnings that can be used in getting creative expression started.

1. Objects to use can be as varied as a bent shovel, a battered suitcase, an oddly shaped rock, a kite, a ragged shirt, two left shoes, an old school textbook, an alarm clock, etc.
2. Pictures can be equally as varied but they should provoke feelings. Pictures of animals and people may be used most successfully, especially if they show action or expression.
3. A field trip or other situation can be used if it is narrowed somewhat. For example, talking about the sounds heard will be more successful than talking about the entire trip and will usually stimulate more personalized expression.
4. Films and filmstrips secure pupils' interest and foster thought. Using a film without the sound, for instance, will bring forth many ideas. Showing only part of a film is also a good procedure for stimulating interest in "what do you suppose happened next?"
5. A newspaper story may be used as the basis for retelling, for writing a letter to someone mentioned in the story, for writing a "follow up," or for remaking into an imaginative news story of local interest.
6. For bringing the senses into expression, such things as pickles, different cloth textures, objects hidden from sight in a bag, and flowers and spices which have different odors may all be used.

□ **An Example of a Direct Lesson**

Here is an actual account of direct teaching resulting in written expression.

1. The class was shown a picture of a costumed girl, standing next to a white picket fence and holding a jack-o-lantern lit by a candle. The picture was mounted on a piece of tag board with these questions written under it:

> What time of the year is it?
> What is the girl going to do?
> Have you ever seen a jack-o-lantern like this?
> What do you suppose this girl's name is?
> If we could look down the street, what else might we see?

2. This was followed by asking other questions about what might be heard on Halloween, what might be smelled, how people feel, what they say and do, and so on. As these were answered and, as the discussion continued, the teacher began listing words and expressions on the board.
3. The teacher then asked the children if they could classify the words and expressions she had written. After further discussion the children decided on the classification as shown below.

What we hear	What we see	What we smell	What we taste	What we feel
laughter	goblins	candy	candy	scared
strange noise	yellow pumpkins	apples	apples	funny
shouts	spooks	burning leaves	cookies	cold air
happy talking	blinking lights	candles	cider	leaves falling
footsteps running	leaves	burning	licorice	happy
	shadows			
	other children			

4. The teacher then suggested that each child try to add other words and to think of adjectives, adverbs, and verbs to "go with" the words on the chart (not referring to the parts of speech by names, however, but only by examples such as *buoyant* shouts, running *haltingly, glimpsed* a flitting shadow).
5. Finally the teacher suggested that the children write stories about Halloween, making them as vivid and realistic to a reader as possible, possibly writing of "imagined" experiences rather than relating in detail things that had happened to them on Halloweens.

This procedure, of course, may result in some children using only words listed by the group or taking ideas for stories from suggestions made by other children during the discussion. Therefore, this amount of teacher guidance directed at the production of stories on a specific subject should not be used frequently. Its major purpose is to help pupils get started and to teach them to think before writing. With adequate and continuous "input" this procedure is useful in securing writing related to special days and events; and of course it is useful early in the school year.

Commercial Materials

In recent years commercial materials directed at stimulating creativity in the classroom have been developed. These have not been widely used as yet, and research on their use has been done only by a small number of researchers. Getzels and Madaus report that while "independent creative activities may at times lead to creative growth, the mere provision of such exercises does not guarantee such growth."[22]

Materials known to the authors include the following:

Making It Strange (Harper and Row Publishers, 1968): a set of four workbooks—for grades 3, 4, 5, and 6—and a teacher's manual.

[22]Getzels and Madaus, "Creativity," p. 272.

Invitations to Thinking and Doing (Ginn and Co., 1964): A workbook and teachers' guide. No indication of grade level.

Imagine, Look and Talk (Basil Blackwell and Mott, Ltd., 1967): Two workbooks, grade levels not indicated, mainly directed at stimulating oral expression. The author, Wallace Eyre, and the publisher are British.

Imagine and Write (American Education Publications, 1967): A series of four workbooks and teacher's guides (grades 3 through 6) directed at promoting creative writing.

These materials are not all alike; they do have the workbook feature in common, and they all try to stimulate the pupils' imaginations.

In addition, many tape and disc recordings, as well as films and filmstrips, may be used to motivate creative expression. *Imagi/Craft* (Ginn and Company, 1965) are recordings directed at providing guided experiences in creative thinking. Since these are recorded dramas of "Great Moments," similar recorded dramatizations might also be used to stimulate children's creative expression.

Creative Written Expression

Since the writing of poetry and stories is most commonly thought of as creative writing, further suggestions for their teaching are given in this section, together with examples of children's efforts in these forms. Examples are also included of other, more "practical" forms of writing.

Mauree Applegate tells the story of the forgetful gardener who plowed and cultivated a plot of ground but forgot to plant any seeds. She notes than even though he was forgetful, some seeds did spring up as a result of having fallen from parent plants. She compares many teachers and the conducive climates of their classrooms to the plight of the forgetful gardener, noting that "Reading poetry to the children, appreciating things together, giving the daily invitation to write, having a quiet hour each week, and providing a poetry drawer will grow more and better poetry" and, further, that "one cannot travel to the stars in a wheelbarrow, or speak of his journey there in the words of the field."[23] Too often teachers turn children to the task of writing without enough oral limbering up with words and ideas first.

As other writers have said, verse to be read to children must be selected with care in order to avoid copying and establishing overawed

Poetry and Rhymes

[23]Applegate, *Helping Children Write*, pp. 29, 31.

feelings.[24] They further suggest that "child-made" poems be read often to help the children gain courage to express their own thoughts and feelings. For most poetry and verse writing, children need to be directed away from a preoccupation with rhyming and toward concern with the thought. Emphasis should also be given to the expression of feelings and to vivid imagery. Despite the fact that writing poetry and verse is a highly individualized act, much can be done to help children, as is illustrated in the examples below, which are taken from a number of different classes and schools.

A discussion of spring sights, sounds, and feelings by one teacher and her class brought forth such phrases as "a brisk wind," "driving rain," "exploring flowers," and "the peeping sun." This discussion resulted in the following for one pupil:

> The brisk March wind blows
> Spring ever nearer and nearer.
> The brisk March wind blows
> The shadows from the peeping sun.
> Spring is near, ever nearer.
> Make sure you're ready to play and run.

Another wrote:

> Hang onto your hat; hold it tight!
> The driving rain is after it.
> Hold onto your hat; hold it tight.
> Or the gulping wind will get it!

The second grade had been studying the circus and had seen the animals and the crowds and excitement of the circus which had come to town. It was the topic of all the talking at school, and Arnold wrote:

> When circus time is here,
> People come from far and near
> To see the animals dance and play—
> It makes their lives so bright and gay.

The fifth-grade class enjoyed hearing their teacher read "City Rain" by Rachel Field and then talking about other things observed along the streets of the city during a rain storm. Following this experience, Evelyn wrote:

---

[24]Alvina Treut Burrows, Doris C. Jackson, and Dorothy O. Saunders, *They All Want to Write* (New York: Holt, Rinehart and Winston, third edition, 1964), p. 119.

The wind blows,
Leaves fall,
Red, yellow and brown.
The rain,
From a gray sky,
Plasters them
To the wet ground.

A form of poetry which is particularly satisfying to children is Haiku, one of the oldest types of Japanese poetry. Haiku generally has three lines consisting of seventeen syllables—five in the first and third lines, and seven in the second—although sometimes this formula is modified.[25] One child wrote:

My tiny puppy,
How mournful shine his sad eyes
Seeking, seeking me.

A sixth-grader wrote:

Graceful butterfly
From blossom to brightest bloom
Flickering, darting.

Children also like to write couplets, triplets, and other verse forms. Cinquain, for example, has a structure that appeals—the first line is one word, the title; the second line is two words, describing the title; the third line has three words, which express action; the fourth line has four words, which express feeling; and the fifth line has one word, a synonym for the title. After the fourth-grade class had written some together, Billy wrote this:

Puppy
Warm, sleepy
Wobbling and sniffing
Lost without a mother
Doggy.

Even with a great deal of stimulation from the reading of poetry and encouragement from group poetry writing efforts, some children will do very little poetry or verse writing. They should not be forced. but the door should be kept open for them to try when they wish. Sometimes just observing things will bring forth words and phrases from even the most reticent that lead to almost spontaneous writing of verse. A

[25]Harold G. Henderson, *An Introduction to Haiku* (New York: Doubleday Anchor Books, 1958).

straight and sharp icicle, the activities in an ant hill or a hive of bees, the drip of a leaky faucet, and so forth, would all surely start words flowing.

Prose Writing   Story writing may be stimulated in many ways. One first-grade teacher read a poem about owls. The children drew pictures of what they heard, told simple stories to one another, and finally, as a class, decided they would all like to write out Christine's version of the story:

> Two baby owls were sitting in a tree. They could not see in the day time. They decided they should go home and go to bed.

In another first-grade class Garry wrote this story after the teacher's friend told about penguins, using Willie, the marionette penguin.

> Willie is a penguin.
> He likes water.
> He likes fish.
> He danced for us.

John, age eight, showed his maturity and his developing story writing ability as he told about the volcano.[26]

> One calm day in the jungle far away there was a village, and the village was very small.
> Behind the village was a volcano, and the villagers did not know that the volcano was a volcano. The reason they did not know that the volcano was a volcano was because the volcano had not erupted for eight hundred years.
> Days went by and after a while the volcano began to shake and then to throw hot rocks and lava down the volcano side.
> It was a sad time for the people. They ran for their lives, leaving all behind but what they could grab up on the run.
> Days later, after the eruption had stopped, the villagers returned.
> They found that the only two huts left were the one on the hill and the one in the tree.

David, in the sixth grade, demonstrates real imaginative power in his story of how the wind came to be.

> One day the Spirit of the Moon was walking along. He came to a large cave, and started to enter it. All of a sudden he felt that he had to sneeze! He went "Ah, ah, ah-choo" right into the cave. The

[26]*Guiding Growth in Written Expression,* Los Angeles County Schools, June, 1956, p. 122.

back force of the sneeze was so great that when repelled it knocked over Moon Spirit.

He was so angry that he called the force a bad name! "Wind!" he yelled.

The Indians too, were afraid and brought him presents. Since the wind came from the north they called it the North Wind.

As story writing skill increases, attention should be given to the improvement of organization, to better characterization, and to story beginnings. For example, children might be asked these questions in considering their stories:

1. Does your story have a good beginning?
2. Will your reader be aware of the characters, the setting, and the sequence?
3. Does your story reach a high point or climax?
4. Is there an adequate explanation of how the story problem was solved?
5. Do all the parts fit together at the end in a way that will satisfy a reader?

To help children focus upon the plot of the story and how well it was developed, have them write five sentences which outline it. For example:

1. Mother and I were sitting in the kitchen after dinner one quiet evening.
2. Suddenly we heard a scratching noise at the back door.
3. Mother screamed and jumped up on a chair as a gray mouse darted across the floor.
4. I stood there and laughed at the funny sight, while mother recovered from terror.
5. I imagine the mouse was more frightened than Mother was.

One group of children began noting how stories begin, and developed the list below. The result of their efforts, of course, was that their stories began to vary from the standard "Once upon a time."

Possible ways to begin a story:
1. With conversation to set the stage for action.
2. With the end of the story, then going back to the beginning.
3. With the middle of the story, then to the actual beginning.
4. With a descriptive sketch of the chief character or characters.
5. With a summary paragraph telling the point of the story.
6. With a description.
7. With a statement of time, place, or circumstance.
8. With a question.

Not all prose writing must be in the form of a story. For example, one teacher secured some creative and thought-provoking ideas from his sixth-grade children by having them write their interpretations of adages such as, "The best place to find a helping hand is at the end of your own arm," "The best way to climb a mountain is to begin at the bottom," and "A mind is like a parachute; it is useful only when open."[27]

Not to be overlooked in the writing of prose is the writing of autobiographies of historical and imaginary characters, imaginary diaries and journals, and parodies. Creativity will usually result from biographies of a huge fish that lives in the swimming hole, a sailor with Columbus, or the boyhood of Benjamin Franklin; or from making up the diaries of Santa Claus, Peanuts, or a child in the Massachusetts Bay Colony; or from writing new words to a well-known song.

Practical Writing As was stated previously in this chapter, all writing may have actual utility and any "practical" writing may show genuine creativity. Letters, invitations, minutes of meetings, reports, and records often require clarity, graciousness, brevity, and factual statements. But this does not mean that vividness of expression may not be used, that imagination should never be a part of them, or that originality should not be shown. In fact, clarity and effectiveness may be abetted through the use of humor, inventiveness, and attention to the interests of the reader.

Children in every elementary classroom have a genuine reason at one time or another to write to classmates at home, to a recent visitor to the room, or to a relative or friend. The child who wrote the following was trying to show his feelings, and to do so with courtesy and good form.

Dear Aunt Phyllis,

We had fun while you were here, and I hope you will be back soon.

My favorite time was the trip to the zoo. The monkeys were really funny. You made funny faces too.

Going out to eat was great! I liked the big hamburgers with everything. I could eat a hundred!

Thanks a lot.

Love,
John

The writing of announcements of various types provides excellent opportunities for children to be both "practical" and creative. For instance, the youngster selling his bicycle really created in writing this:

[27]Walter V. Ashworth, sixth-grade teacher, Orville Wright School, Sacramento, Calif.

For Sale: The fastest bike in the West! Reduced for the Spring Red Sale. Only $25 if you zoom in fast. It is red, has a chiquita banana seat, 5 speeds, and dual brakes. Demonstration rides at 223 Poinsetta Drive after school. Don't be late. Buy! Then get home fast!

Children have many occasions to write reports which share facts or experiences with their fellow pupils. Essentially these reports are aimed at conveying information, but they may convey something of the writer and his feelings at the same time. The pupil in the fourth grade who wrote about "Why We Celebrate Lincoln's Birthday" could have gotten his information directly from the encyclopedia and conveyed it to the class in about the same language as he found in the encyclopedia itself. Instead a creative approach was used, as is shown in this introductory paragraph.

Every time I lie by the fire and read, I think that one of America's greatest presidents did just that. That man was Abraham Lincoln. He hated slavery, but he wanted to keep the states together. He said that "someday this country will be friends again." If you take this country and cut it into two pieces you will no longer have one country but two half-countries. Try to join each half to another country. It would not stay on. So the halves will have to join together again.

Gilbert, in the third grade, stuck fairly closely to the facts in writing his report about a submarine, but it was creative for him.

The Story of Nautilus
The Nautilus traveled two years without refueling. It could stay under water for 60 days. It came back to get fuel. It got its power from atomic energy.

Children often have opportunities to do creative report writing if the teacher provides the chance to publish their own "newspaper." Karin was encouraged to go further and submitted her story to the city newspaper:

On November 10th, a wild deer decided to be educated in the Howe Avenue Elementary School shortly before 9 A.M.
A couple of teachers, a janitor, and several children saw the deer.
One boy tried to catch the deer and has a torn shirt and a bruised side to prove it.
Much to the school's regret, the deer got away through the south gate after running across the playground.

These are only some of the kinds of children's writing that may be genuinely creative. Children have the ideas; getting them released is the key. A recognition that all forms of writing present opportunities for individual inventiveness, imagination, and the outpouring of feelings is the starting point. On this teachers build the attitudes and skills necessary to produce the quality of creative writing satisfactory to both themselves and the children.

Creative Oral Expression

The procedures suggested in earlier chapters, as well as in the preceding sections of this chapter, should bring forth much creative oral expression. This section gives additional focus to opportunities for such expression in storytelling and dramatization.

Dramatic Play

Dramatic play is a natural activity of children long before they start to school. Young children love to live in a land of make-believe and they early play "house," "school," and other games based on aspects of life about them. Much of children's emotional and social growth occurs through this form of creative experimentation and expression. In school, dramatic play is used to continue this growth.

While dramatic play is usually associated in schools with primary-age children, it may also be used by middle- and upper-grade children if opportunities are provided and if the children feel free to utilize them. A sixth-grade class may give creative expression to "landing on the moon," "how a cowboy walks," "creeping up on the Indians."

Dramatic play is spontaneous and free of immediate adult suggestion and control. It calls for the shedding of the child's normal personality inhibitions and for living the role he is portraying. A particular use may be to help children with personality and social problems. The "bully" on the playground may take a different role in an informal dramatization, a shy girl may give vent to repressed expression by acting as the domineering mother, or the child lacking in social poise may be the mother supervising the party.

Dramatization

Dramatization may take many forms; there is no hard and fast line between many of these forms and dramatic play. Children are naturally interested in "acting out things" and will play their parts with fervor if they feel free to do so and understand the plot. Much dramatization may take place with little preparation if the plot or the object of the dramatization is simple and familiar. In such dramatizations, encouragement and full freedom should be given to the child to act and talk for the character he is portraying in the way he thinks the character would act and talk. Dramatizations that are longer or more complicated will call for more planning and perhaps the working out and memorization of lines. However, the pupils themselves should do much of this preparation if the real creative values are to be obtained.

Dramatizations usually are done for audiences and the audience is important. In the elementary school the audience may often be the other children in the reading group, the remainder of the class, or a neighboring class. The use of an audience in the sense of a "staged" performance should be limited, however, since that much preparation may cause some of the children to become overly self-conscious in their roles.

In creative dramatics the teacher should not become a director as he might in the presentation of a formal play. Instead he should show understanding and friendly guidance, encouraging the development of ideas into dramatizations, keeping the dialogue spontaneous and the action fluid, and fostering group and individual solutions to problems.

Teachers alert to opportunities for the children to dramatize stories, events, and ideas will find many. The following suggestions may be useful to a teacher in noting opportunities in his classroom.

1. Listening to music, stories, and poetry can often provide material for dramatizing. Music may be interpreted physically and through oral expression; stories may be "acted out"; lines of poetry may be interpreted. The dramatizing of an ending to an unfinished story is of particular interest to children.

2. Children may dramatize situations established by the teacher. For example, situations such as the following might be used:
   (a) You are waiting for your friends to pick you up to go to the park. You think you hear a car stop in front of the house. You rush to the window and are disappointed when it is not your friends.
   (b) You are walking barefoot on some pebbles which are hot from the sun. Quickly you get on some cool grass. Then you walk on the hot sand until finally you get your feet in cold water.
   (c) You are walking to school and see smoke on a roof. Soon you see a spark of fire. Run to the door and let the person who lives inside know about it.
   (d) You see some shoes in a store window that you would like to try on. Go in the store and try them on.
   (e) You are a cautious boy. You never take any chances. You meet another boy for the first time who is adventurous. With a friend, act out what happens and is said.

3. Plays or skits written or simply told by pupils may be dramatized. For example:
   (a) One pupil asks directions to a certain place; another pupil gives him the directions.
   (b) A family discusses a TV program.
   (c) A dentist tells about the importance of regular brushing of teeth.
4. Many social situations may be dramatized. These may vary widely and could include the following:
   (a) How to ask for a job.
   (b) How to sell tickets for a benefit party.
   (c) How to present a gift.
   (d) How to introduce a stranger.
5. Historical events are good subjects for dramatization. Reading about the events can lead to impromptu speaking and action or to dramatizations of skits written by the children. For example:
   (a) Men around a campfire at Valley Forge.
   (b) The Boston Tea Party.
   (c) A night on the Oregon Trail.
   (d) A stopover on the Underground Railroad.

In helping children with their creative dramatizations the teacher should discuss the use of voice and expression appropriate to a character and the plot, the showing of action, and the conveying of meaning by facial and body expression.

Puppetry

Stick, hand, and shadow puppets may give variation to dramatization and offer great opportunity for creative oral expression. Many shy children find it easier to project their ideas and their interpretations of characters through a puppet actor. Some dramatizations are easier to stage using puppets rather than the children themselves. Animal figures, folklore characters, and "talking" inanimate objects are sometimes easier to manage with puppets.

A stick puppet is the easiest type to make. It usually consists of an outlined figure drawn on cardboard and attached to a stick. Also easy to make are hand puppets. The simplest form is the paper bag with a face drawn on it. Other hand puppets may be made of papier-mâché or cloth.[28] Every puppet should be constructed and used so that it has a definite "personality."

Any story or event suitable for dramatization can be presented by puppetry—providing, of course, that the stage does not become so

[28]See the following for puppet construction and use: John Bodor, *Creating and Presenting Hand Puppets* (Reinhold Publishing Corp., 1967); Marjorie H. Batchelder and Virginia L. Comer, *Puppets and Plays: A Creative Approach* (Harper, 1956); T. Tichner, *Folk Plays for Puppets You Can Make* (Abingdon Press, 1959); Shari Lewis, *The Shari Lewis Puppet Book* (Citadel Press, 1958).

crowded that the puppets are difficult to maneuver properly. Children may also be encouraged to write original puppet shows. Individuals or a class may create puppet plays from many incidents of history, from health practices as they come up in lessons, from discussions of social occasions, and from imaginative stories written for fun.

Since storytelling has been discussed rather thoroughly in Chapter 7 and must be based so largely upon literature (see Chapter 15), little will be presented at this point. The storyteller, however, needs attention to his stories similar to that suggested for the story writer. That is, teaching is necessary for storytelling to improve from one experience to another. Furthermore, it is especially important to remember the value of spontaneity in a story. Advantage must be taken of this spontaneity, both to encourage the pupil and to help him develop his storytelling abilities. Certainly children like to tell stories that they have heard, and to do so is useful in teaching them good storytelling techniques, but children have a natural desire to tell their own stories, to relate experiences they have had, and to use their imaginations in embellishing stories they have heard. These should all be encouraged because they are often the most creative things children do.

Storytelling

Creative forms of storytelling that children enjoy in addition to the relating of personal experiences include the telling of chain stories in which the teacher or one pupil starts a story and after a time stops and asks another pupil to continue, the telling of endings of stories only partially heard or read, and the developing of a story based upon a title or a briefly described setting.

Exercises for Thought and Action

1. Recall an elementary school teacher you had as a student whom you regarded as a good teacher. Was this teacher a creative person? Did he or she foster creativity in children?
2. Do you agree with the criteria given for creative language expression? If not, what criteria would you suggest?
3. Make a list of all the ways you can think of to get pupils of a grade level of your choice to express their ideas creatively.
4. Find examples of genuine creativity in "practical" writing in such sources as newspapers, magazines, and letters.
5. If you are a teacher, survey your classroom as objectively as possible for the degree of creativity fostered by the environment. Ask yourself if children's ideas abound or if they have been suppressed. Does the classroom belong to the entire group or is it predominantly yours?
6. What do you do with the child who insists he simply cannot write poetry?

7. Add to the suggestions of projects involving words. Put all of your ideas in a file for later use.

8. Prepare an evaluation of one or more of the sets of commercial materials designed to promote creativity listed in this chapter. Identify strengths and weaknesses.

9. What other topics, situations, or story beginnings can you think of that might be used to get creative expression in language started? Collect all of the ideas in a file or some other usable arrangement.

10. Collect examples of children's writing. What signs of children's feelings and imagination can you find? What signs of teacher pressures do the writings show?

Selected References

Applegate, Mauree. *Easy in English*. Evanston, Ill.: Row, Peterson and Co., 1960.

————. *Winged Words*. Evanston, Ill.: Row, Peterson and Co., 1961.

Arnstein, Flora J. *Children Write Poetry: A Creative Approach*. New York: Dover Publications, Inc., 1967.

Bodor, John. *Creating and Presenting Hand Puppets*. New York: Reinhold Publishing Corp., 1967.

Burger, Isabel B. *Creative Play Acting*. New York: A. S. Barnes and Company, 1950.

Burrows, Alvina, and others. *They All Want to Write*. New York: Holt, Rinehart and Winston, third edition, 1964.

Carlson, Ruth Kearney. "Seventeen Qualities of Original Writing." *Elementary English*, 38:576–579, December, 1961.

————. *Sparkling Words: Two Hundred Practical and Creative Writing Ideas*. Berkeley, California: Ruth K. Carlson, 1965.

Curry, Louise. *Teaching With Puppets*. Philadelphia: Fortress Press, 1966.

Durland, Frances C., *Creative Dramatics for Children*. Yellow Springs, Ohio: Antioch Press, 1952.

Marksberry, Mary Lee. *Foundation of Creativity*. New York: Harper & Row, 1963.

Pease, Don. *Creative Writing in the Elementary School*. New York: Exposition Press, 1964.

Petty, Walter T., and Bowen, Mary. *Slithery Snakes and Other Aids to Children's Writing*. New York: Appleton-Century-Crofts, 1967.

Smith, James A. *Setting Conditions for Creative Teaching in the Elementary School*. Boston: Allyn and Bacon, Inc., 1966.

Strickland, Ruth G. *The Language Arts in the Elementary School*. Boston: D. C. Heath and Co., 1969, Chapter 14.

Torrance, E. Paul. *What Research Says to the Teacher: Creativity*. Washington, D.C.: National Education Association, 1963.

Walter, Nina Willis. *Let Them Write Poetry*. New York: Holt, Rinehart and Winston, 1966.

Wilt, Mariam E. *Creativity in the Elementary School*. New York: Appleton-Century-Crofts, Inc., 1959.

Wolfson, Bernice J. "Creativity in the Classroom," *Elementary English*, 38:523, November, 1961.

Some Books for Children Helpful in Developing Language Expression

Alexander, Arthur. *The Magic of Words*. Prentice-Hall, 1962.

Belting, Natalia. *The Sun is a Golden Earring*. Holt, Rinehart and Winston, 1962.

Bendick, Jeanne. *A Fresh Look at Night*. Franklin Watts, 1963.

Borten, Helen. *Do You Hear What I Hear?* Abelard-Schuman, 1960.

_____. *Do You See What I See?* Abelard-Schuman, 1959.

Boxer, Deborah. *26 Ways to be Somebody Else*. Pantheon, 1960.

Conger, Marion. *Who Has Seen The Wind?* Abingdon Press, 1959.

Denison, Carol. *Passwords to People*. Dodd, 1960.

Emberly, Ed. *The Wing of a Flea*. Little, Brown, 1961.

Epstein, Sam and Beryl. *The First Book of Words*. Watts, 1954.

Fitzhugh, Louise. *Harriet the Spy*. Harper & Row, 1964.

Hoban, Russell. *The Pedaling Man and Other Poems*. W. W. Norton Co., 1968.

Hubbell, Patricia. *Catch Me A Wind*. Atheneum Publishers, 1968.

Huntington, Harriet. *Let's Go Outdoors*. Doubleday and Co., 1939.

Lambert, Eloise. *Our Language*. Lothrop, 1955.

Lawson, Robert. *They Were Strong and Good. Viking Press,* 1940.

Livingston, Myra Cohn. *Whispers and Other Poems*. Harcourt, Brace and World, 1958.

McClintock, Mike. *A Fly Went By*. Random House, 1958.

McGrath, Thomas. *The Beautiful Things*. Vanguard, 1960.

Merriam, Eve. *It Doesn't Always Have to Rhyme*. Atheneum, 1964.

Norton, Mary. *Borrowers Afield*. Harcourt, Brace and World, 1955.

_____. *Borrowers Aloft*. Harcourt, Brace and World, 1961.

O'Neill, Mary. *Hailstones and Halibut Bones*. Doubleday and Co., 1961.

Reid, Alastair. *Ounce, Dice, Trice*. Little, Brown, 1958.

Schultz, Charlie. *Happiness Is A Warm Puppy*. Determined Productions, 1962.

Showers, Paul. *Find Out By Touching*. Thomas Y. Crowell, 1961.

_____. *The Listening Walk*. Thomas Y. Crowell, 1961.

Slobodkin, Louis. *Magic Michael*. New York: The Macmillan Company, 1944.

Skills And Abilities
Important To Both
Oral And Written Language

10

INTRODUCTION

There are many skills and abilities necessary to effective expression
in both oral and written language. The purpose of this chapter is
to discuss a number of these, partially as reinforcement to suggestions
made earlier but also to emphasize the fact that oral and written
expression are highly related. The topics included are the following:

1. Dialects, Usage, and Grammar
2. A Functional Approach to Teaching English Usage
3. Developing the Rhetorical Skills
4. Promoting Vocabulary Growth
5. Using Sources of Information

Included are suggestions about improving the organization
of composition—both oral and written—, sentence construction, and
the content of composition. Also included are suggested activities
for teaching dictionary skills, building vocabulary, and making
expression interesting.

Since the teaching of usage is of such importance in the
language arts program, this chapter is especially related to Chapter
4 and to the chapter which follows, "Grammar in the
Elementary School."

Dialects, Usage, and Grammar

The social, economic, and educational limitations which may be placed upon a person if his language is regarded either as illiterate or non-standard are a major concern of teachers and the public. Both groups generally feel that children must be taught to speak and write "correctly," although they are likely to have difficulty in defining just what is meant by "to speak and write correctly." Laymen usually believe that somehow teaching *grammar* will achieve the objective, and they are joined in this belief by some teachers. "Grammar" may also be difficult for them to define. Added to these problems are those of defining *usage* and *dialect,* and of understanding that "correctness" is a term that will remain elusive and should not be the focus in helping children to speak and write more effectively.

Misconceptions about correctness in language usage and what should be done about teaching it in language arts and English programs have led to "millions (billions? trillions?) of child-hours spent writing *was* or *were* in blanks; a feeling of inferiority in millions of persons because they have been made to believe that their English is not good; a contrasting snobbishness in many others because they are convinced that they are among the elite who use good English; a belief that 'right' and 'wrong' are absolute terms in language, as they may be in mathematics; a hatred of English on the part of those who have difficulty in making their language conform to the teacher's expectations."[1] Misconceptions about grammar and usage teaching have also led to the labeling of words, the diagramming of sentences, frustration on the part of students and teachers, and a failure to appreciate the values which might be gained from studying language history, dialectology, semantics, and other areas of linguistics.

Misconceptions and Definitions

    In the everyday language of the community and school, the term *grammar* is used to refer to the way people speak and write and includes their choices of words, their construction of sentences and phrases, and even the punctuation and capitalization abilities shown. The term *usage* is less frequently used and when it is, it is used synonymously with grammar. *Dialect* is not a new word in general parlance,

---

[1] J. N. Hook, Paul H. Jacobs, and Raymond D. Crisp, *What Every English Teacher Should Know* (Champaign, Ill.: National Council of Teachers of English, 1970), p. 3.

but its use has been largely confined to describing how "quaint old people in out-of-the-way places" talk.[2]

These terms should not be confused by teachers because their meanings are different, and confusion leads to poor teaching practices. *Grammar* is the description of a language. *Usage,* according to *Webster's Third New International Dictionary,* is "the way in which words and phrases are actually used (as in a particular form or sense) generally or among a community or group of persons: customary use of language." Grammar is based upon usage; the way people use a language is what is described by the grammar of that language. Dialect is also related to usage. A *dialect* may be defined as "a collection of usages (including not only words and phrases but also pronunciations) characteristic of a certain individual or group."[3]

Usages change to reflect changes in meanings of words, the introduction of new words and expressions, and the acceptability or nonacceptability of particular words and phrases to different groups at a given time. Dialects reflect similar changes, although pronunciations tend to linger for a more extended period. Grammar, of course, also changes as it seeks to describe the language used. The fact that language does change has always been difficult for some teachers to accept; yet this fact must be accepted to understand the terms *grammar, usage,* and *dialect* and to effectively provide instruction about language.

Problems in English Usage

Language usage was earlier classified by levels—formal, standard, colloquial, and illiterate—but linguists have found that to attempt such classification resulted in impreciseness, in a failure to recognize language change, and in stigmatizing many individuals whose language is classified in the lower status categories. Many of the same problems exist with the more recently applied labels of "standard" and "nonstandard," though they continue to be used. Gradually there has been a movement toward using the term *dialect* in referring to differences in usage, without attaching "correct," "incorrect," "good," or "bad" to any one.[4]

However, teachers cannot escape the fact that usages are associated with particular social or economic groups or with particular occasions. There is a "standard" (but with variations) language used

[2]Raven I. McDavid, Jr., "The Sociology of Language," in *Linguistics in School Programs,* Albert H. Marckwardt, editor. The Sixty-ninth Yearbook of the National Society for the Study of Education, Part II (Chicago: The University of Chicago Press, 1970), p. 94.
[3]Hook *et al., What Every English Teacher Should Know,* p. 11.
[4]See the discussion of dialects in Chapter 4.

in books. There is a generally "standard" language used in public communication (the school, television and radio, etc.). Teachers have the obligation to make children sensitive to and appreciative of the factors which influence usage choices and to help them learn to make these choices as they are appropriate. In most settings—including that of the school—there are acceptable and nonacceptable usages. In the school setting acceptable usage is "standard" English or the prestigious dialect of the speech community. Within the acceptable dialect or "standard" English there is considerable variety. This variety is the source of many teaching problems because it leads to differences of opinion as to the acceptability of particular items. *Standard English* simply becomes impossible to define in absolute terms. Teachers are likely to be more rigid in their definitions, in their acceptance of changes in usage within a standard English framework than are many other users of standard English.[5] An interesting comparison of teacher attitudes toward certain usages with the attitudes of a large group of editors and authors was reported in an article now some years old.[6] The directions given to the editors, authors and teachers, as well as their respective opinions, are reported below:

Here are nineteen expressions about which there is today a good deal of controversy, and we'd like your opinion as an educated adult of their acceptability in everyday speech.

Do not be influenced by whether these usages do or do not violate formal grammatical rules. Rather, indicate, by affirmative vote, that you would be willing to use the expression listed or that you believe such an expression has become sufficiently current in educated American speech to be labeled *acceptable* usage; by a negative vote, that the expression is *unacceptable* in educated circles.

	% Acceptable by editors and writers	% Acceptable by 107 teachers
1. His attitude makes me *mad*. (Synonym for angry)	68	45
2. I *will* pay your bill if you accept my check	90	93
3. The reason I am worried is *because* I think she's ill	48	61

[5]McDavid, "Sociology of Language," p. 92.
[6]Norman Lewis, "How Correct Must Correct English Be." Copyright © 1949 by Harper's Magazine, Inc. Reprinted from the March, 1949, issue of *Harper's Magazine* by permission of the author.

4. The work is different *than* mine	31	37
5. We had a *nice* time at the party	88	85
6. *Can* I have another helping of dessert, please?	40	24
7. I encountered *less* difficulties than I had expected	23	40
8. Everyone put on *their* coat and went home	45	18
9. How much money have you got?	65	37
10. *Due* to the storm, all trains are late ..	65	87
11. She has an *awful* headache	77	65
12. We *only* have five left. (Position of *only*)	44	41
13. Let's not walk any *further* right now ..	58	44
14. We must remember to *accurately check* each answer	53	51
15. He's one person I simply won't do business *with*	86	69
16. Go *slow*	86	55
17. It is *me*	62	36
18. She acts as if she *was* my wife	34	24
19. *Who* did you meet?	43	44

The results appearing in the two columns following the sentences indicate the percentage of each group of judges considering the statement acceptable under the conditions stated in the directions. It is evident from this study that the teachers are somewhat less willing to forget their grammatical prejudices than are the less grammatically inoculated judges. Teachers were noticeably more sensitive to usages such as are represented by sentences 1, 6, 8, 9, 15, 16, and 17. They were less sensitive to the questionable usages in sentences 3, 7, and 10.

A more recent study by Womack confirms the fact that the battle of levels of acceptable usage has not been won in spite of support given this approach in English journals, by the National Council of Teachers of English, and by published sources of authority.[7] Womack questioned over 300 randomly sampled members of the National Council of Teachers of English with regard to the acceptability in formal or informal speech and formal or informal writing of fifty items of usage. The usages selected are as follows:

[7]Thurston Womack, "Teachers' Attitudes toward Current Usage." *The English Journal,* 48:186–190, April, 1959.

The split infinitive
the case of the noun or pronoun before the gerund
seven items of agreement between subject and verb and pronoun
     and antecedent
one . . . he
. . . is when . . .
these kind
data is . . .
preposition at end of a sentence
either of three
shortest of two
dangling participle (not an absurd one)
myself used in the nominative
between you and I
who are you waiting for?
drive *slow*
as if he *was*
it is *me*
aren't I . . .
Jones was younger than *him*
building's roof
after discussing the heroine, most of the young women expressed
    no desire to be *her*
it looks *like* it will rain
the boy felt *badly*
can in the sense of permission
very *nice* people
fixed in the sense of repaired
different than
awful colds
New York is *further* east than Chicago
try *and* finish
due to in the sense of because of
has *proven*
raised instead of *reared*
Americans *have got* to make democracy work
some students do not know *if* they can . . .
divided *between* three
the *reason* . . . was *because* . . .
the students *enthused* about . . .
the state *hung* the murderers

the old man *laid* down on his bed . . .

. . . *cannot help but* . . .

the swimmers *dove* into the pool

the soldiers fulfilled the *dying wish* of the commander

Womack stated that an item-by-item comparison of the teachers' views with published information in such sources as Leonard's *Current English Usage,*[8] Marckwardt and Walcott's *Facts About Current English Usage,*[9] "Current English Forum" in *The English Journal* or *College English,* and *Webster's New Collegiate Dictionary* reveals that in general the majority of the teachers still reject most usages that published information tends to support as acceptable.[10]

Resistance to change and to accepting usage items which are really in widespread use as standard is still evident. Johnson, in a recent study of the opinions of one hundred high school English teachers regarding five usage items as well as their own use of these items, found condemnation of the items "even though published studies of the usage of educated people have established their reputability."[11] He found that "67 per cent of the teachers opposed the use of *reason . . . is because* in speech, while 88 per cent opposed its use in writing"; that "79 per cent of the teachers were opposed to the use of *everybody . . . their* in speech and 95 per cent opposed its use in writing"; that 78 per cent rejected the use of *myself* as an objective pronoun in speech and 96 per cent disapproved of this usage in writing; that 26 per cent judged the use of *will* to refer to the future in the first person as unacceptable and 42 per cent thought it unacceptable in writing; and that 69 per cent disapproved of *who* as an object pronoun in speech and 90 per cent disapproved of its use in writing. Johnson also discovered that "94 out of the one hundred teachers used at least one of the 'incorrect' expressions which they themselves disapproved of and which they said they would correct in the oral or written language of their students."

[8]Sterling A. Leonard, *Current English Usage,* English Monograph No. 1 of the National Council of Teachers of English (Chicago: National Council of Teachers of English, 1932).

[9]Albert H. Marckwardt and Fred G. Walcott, *Facts About Current English Usage,* English Monograph No. 7 of the National Council of Teachers of English (New York: D. Appleton-Century Company, Inc., 1938).

[10]Published information clearly supports all but two of the usages (between you and I and intransitive *laid*).

[11]Robert Spencer Johnson, "A Comparison of English Teachers' Own Usage With Their Attitudes Toward Usage," unpublished doctoral dissertation, Teachers College, Columbia University, 1968, p. 154.

A Functional Approach to Teaching English Usage

Current social acceptability—as broad in definition as that term is—is the principal criterion for what is acceptable or standard usage; only a small part of what is variously labeled as "standard," "correct," or "good" usage is justified by any historically grounded evidence or logical principle. Language usage is largely a personal matter, with each person using language to express his own thinking, but with the effective user of language recognizing that the way he uses language in any communicative act is dependent upon (1) the purpose of the communication, (2) the meaning to be communicated, and (3) the effect desired in the communication.[12]

The selection of usage items requiring instructional attention is a major problem for teachers as they seek to develop the desired sensitivity to language and as they try to help pupils mature without their intellectual capacities and ambitions becoming limited by a lack of language facility. Language authorities for some years have recommended that the number of usage items which should receive instructional emphasis in the elementary school be quite limited. Pooley has made these observations in support of limiting the number of items, and in doing so, indicates the basis for selection:[13]

Usage to be Taught

1. The constant repetition of a relatively small number of errors constitutes over 90 per cent of the usage problem in the elementary grades.
2. A large number of "errors" listed in textbooks and language workbooks are not errors at all, but are colloquial English appropriate to the speech and writing of young children.

Support for these statements has been provided by numerous early studies. For example, one showed that forty percent of the nonstandard usages of children were in the forms of fifteen common verbs, chiefly in the confusion of the past and past participle forms.[14] Since these

[12]Robert C. Pooley, *Teaching English Usage* (New York: Appleton-Century-Crofts, Inc., 1946), p. 27.
[13]*Ibid.*, p. 179.
[14]W. W. Charters and Edith Miller, *A Course of Study in Grammar Based Upon the Grammatical Errors of School Children of Kansas City, Missouri,* University of Missouri Bulletin, Vol. XVI, No. 2, Education Series 9, 1915.

verbs are *see, come, run, write, begin, break, drink, lie, do, go, give, take, ring, sing,* and *sit,* similar evidence would surely be found if such a study were conducted today.

A similar concentration of errors on relatively few usages was indicated in another early study of several hundred thousand running words of electrically-recorded oral compositions by school children;[15] this study found that nineteen items accounted for 90 percent of the total number of errors.

To help a teacher decide which usages may need instructional attention in the elementary school, the following list is included.[16] Not all of these items should be dealt with by a single teacher, nor should instruction in them take precedence over those aspects of the language arts program which promote creativity, good composition of expression, and interest in language. A teacher should select for concentrated attention those which, in his judgment, are the worst deviations from the standards of the community.

ain't or *hain't*	*hadn't ought*	*them* books
yourn, hern, ourn	he *give,* he *walk*	*this here*
hisen, theys	my brother, *he*	*that there*
youse	*her* and *me* went	*us* boys went
onct	there *is* four	we, you, they *was*
hisself, theirselves	there *was* four	with *we* girls
hair *are*	they *knowed*	have *went*
a orange	I, they *growed*	have *wrote*
have *ate*	haven't *no,* isn't *no*	the *mens*
they *eats*	*leave* for *let*	*learn* me a song
was *broke*	haven't *nothing*	*me* and *Mary* went
he *brung*	that's *mines*	she *taken*
he *come*	where *it* at?	I *likes* him
clumb	where is she *at?*	I *drunk, drunks*
had, have *did*	he *run*	can't hardly
she, he *don't*	have *saw*	*does* we have
it *don't*	I *says*	
didn't ought	he *seen*	

[15]T. Keith Goltry, "An Analysis of Sentence Structure in Oral Composition," unpublished doctoral dissertation, State University of Iowa, July, 1935.

[16]Sources: Pooley, *Teaching English Usage;* Pooley, "Dare Schools Set a Standard in English Usage?" *English Journal,* Vol. 49, March, 1960, pp. 176–181; Marckwardt and Walcott, *Facts,* pp. 27–31.

Of course a teacher may be fortunate enough to have a class whose members use none of these expressions. In the unlikely event that this should occur there will be other instances of lack of subject and verb agreement—or noun or noun equivalent with its antecedent —that may receive attention. In addition, there will be idiomatic expressions that can be subjected to instruction. The usages selected for instructional emphasis, however, should be those which represent the greatest deviation from generally accepted expression. Absent from the list above are usages illustrated in the sentences which follow, which should not receive instructional attention in the elementary school— even though they are included in some textbooks.

You'd better go slow.
Can I have a drink of water?
It is me.
We got home at noon.
Everyone hand in their papers.
Bill is taller than me.
None of us were there.
Who did you choose?
He walks like he hurt himself.
The heavy bat helped to better hit the ball.
The reason he failed was because he tried too hard.
I will go as soon as I'm ready.
Will you meet Mrs. Jones and myself after the show?
Our catch was pretty good.
I'm tired of him complaining.

It is not possible to indicate the specific items of usage to be taught at particular grade levels since the language backgrounds of children vary widely. Textbooks, of course, do provide exercises for specific usage items but these should be used by a teacher only if the children in his class have problems with these usages—and then only if these are the grossest deviations they make. Every teacher should survey the oral and written usage of his class to determine the specific emphasis he needs to provide. The following example of a survey record form shows how a teacher recorded usages for his class and indicates in a compact and concrete manner the direction his total class and individual instructional efforts should take.

Teacher Analysis of Teaching Needed

Usage survey for _October_					
	verb forms	pronouns	redundancy	double negatives	illit-eracies
John	he done	her + me	this here	don't have no	youse hisn
Harvey	they knowed brung	they's	this here		
Lucille	she don't				
Peggy	has took				onct
MaryAnn			John he		
Douglas	has took	it's			
Cynthia					

Another form for teacher recording of usages for instructional attention is the following, which focuses upon items previously selected and which provides an easy means of noting particular improvements by pupils.

	Harry	Chas	Harriett	Jo	Betty	Roy	Doris	Tom	Gus	Henry	Sally	Alma	Bob
we was	✓			✓	✓				✓	✓			
have saw	✓	✓		✓		✓	✓			✓	✓		
me and	✓			✓		✓							
brung		✓						✓					
haven't no			✓										
he don't	✓												
hisself	✓												

Surveys of instructional needs should be made by teachers several times during a school year, though some teachers prefer to keep a running record in a notebook, with a page for each child. The initial survey of a class may show many items of usage needing instructional attention, but a teacher should not attempt to change all of these. Thus, until the surveying procedure shows that change has occurred for the specific items selected, records need to be kept only for that limited number of usages, simplifying the record keeping considerably.

Teachers are generally aware that usage habits of children persist from year to year in spite of efforts to bring about changes. Moreover, those usage habits which are less acceptable tend to be most difficult to eradicate. Several reasons have been suggested for this: (1) the habits which the child has acquired in the five or six years of his life before school entrance have become firmly fixed; (2) these habits tend to be strengthened even after coming to school, since the child usually continues to live in much the same type of environment as that into which he was born; (3) the child whose usage habits are most in need of change is likely not to be interested in correcting them, since to do so would set him off from his social environment; (4) the school generally does not provide enough active language situations for real exercise of acceptable usage; and (5) many of the lessons on usage taught in the school are ineffectively motivated and taught.

The Role of Habit

In addition to these reasons, and perhaps of even greater importance as a reason, is the emphasis the school typically gives to changing usage through written drill, even though the particular usages may be more prevalent in the children's speaking than in their writing. The problem, of course, is to eliminate the undesirable usage habits and to substitute more desirable ones. This is a difficult task, considering the fact that the school can do little about the influences of out-of-school environment. However, the school—every teacher—can do something about the reasons for the persistence of undesirable usage habits that are related to instruction.

A teacher can provide many active language situations for the genuine exercise of desirable habits. Every teacher should understand, as Blair has pointed out, that "the chief cause of deficiency in oral and written expression is probably *lack of experience and practice in using correct forms.*"[17] He further stated that "evidence from the field of psychology clearly indicates that pupils *learn to do what they do.* If a

[17]Glenn Myers Blair, *Diagnostic and Remedial Teaching* (New York: The Macmillan Company, 1956), p. 343.

pupil learns a rule of grammar, he will be able to repeat that rule, but he will not necessarily be able to put the rule to use in his speaking and writing. Transfer of training takes place only between elements and situations which are approximately identical. *If pupils are to speak and write correctly they must be given practice in speaking and writing correctly.*"[18]

Every teacher must recognize, too, that it is a basic instructional principle to apply remedy to the exact fault. Thus it is imperative that the usages that are departures from acceptable language must be identified for each child. The surveying and recording suggested in the preceding section should provide the basis that is needed.

Basic Instructional Procedures

A teacher who recognizes the role habit plays in a child's usage, the importance of using language for genuine communicative purposes, and the need for a direct and systematic attack upon the usage items selected for instructional emphasis, can achieve measurable success by following the steps suggested in the succeeding paragraphs.[19]

1. The first step is to appraise the usage problems of the class and of each individual in it through the use of checklists and the cataloging of usages (as suggested above). This cataloging should be for both oral and written usages. With the completion of this survey, the deviations from standard usage found should be compared with those in such lists as the ones in this chapter to determine which require instructional attention and which are simply colloquialisms.

2. The next step is to select the most frequent and grossest departures from acceptability for consistent attack. After being selected, they should be made known to the children, along with the reason for their selection. From the time of their selection, the teacher should strive to allow no deviation or lapses from the acceptable forms, even though this will call for diligent effort. When the new habits have become reasonably fixed, other items may be selected for attack.

3. As many opportunities as possible should be provided for the children to use the usage items being taught in natural communication.

[18]*Ibid.,* p. 355.

[19]A number of linguists and others interested in language usage in schools hold that many "errors" and "deviations" need not be dealt with in an instructional sense as suggested here. Labov states that "In cold fact, the number of differences between most nonstandard dialects (especially those of middle class speakers) and standard English are relatively few. In one way or another, most students have gradually learned to approximate the teacher's style, more or less. More important, their dialects have not obviously interfered with the learning of reading and writing to any serious degree." (William Labov, *The Study of Nonstandard English.* Champaign, Ill.: National Council of Teachers of English, 1970), p. 4.

These opportunities should call for both oral and written expression and should appeal to children.

4. It may be of considerable help if parents are (tactfully) made aware of usages under attack and are asked for their cooperation. This may be done at a group conference, at a PTA meeting, or by letter. Pupils may also write letters to their parents explaining what they are trying to accomplish with respect to learning usage.[20]

5. As much responsibility for improvement as possible should be placed upon the children themselves. They may make individual lists of troublesome items and individual charts of usages that they have mastered.

6. An essential part of the process is building interest in words and expressions, and an enjoyment of the fitness of words in their uses (see the vocabulary section of this chapter).

7. Perhaps the most vital point involved in developing acceptable usage habits is motivation. Pupils must be stimulated to want to use English effectively, or little good will result from teaching efforts. Teachers must utilize every possible device to relate the activities of the classroom to the basic goals of each pupil. A child must be made to feel that working on his English usage will benefit him personally. He must be convinced that his communication is more effective when he uses acceptable English, that most people actually do use it, and that these are the people with whom he will be associated. Efforts of the teacher to motivate pupils will of course be geared to each pupil's individuality. It is true, too, that efforts to change or expand usages in the lower grades will not depend so greatly on the pupil's actually feeling a need to do so, for he may be too immature to realize their importance. At this level, major dependence must be placed on simply developing usage habits through continuous attention and the provision of genuine situations for speaking and writing.

In addition, a teacher must consistently be aware of the fact that if desirable habits are to be established, children must consistently *hear* acceptable usage. They must *hear* and *see* what their usage problems are. They must *learn* acceptable usage—both how the words *sound* and how they *look*.

Further, drills or practice upon usage may help to fix habits.[21] Written usage drills or exercises have definite limitations, since they usually include too much and are given to the children without proper motivation. However, if a written practice exercise deals with only one

[20]Care must be exercised that usages selected for attack do not represent those commonly used in the community and not regarded as "errors."
[21]See pages 102–104 for examples of oral drills.

usage and is not used until a child is properly motivated, benefit is more likely to occur. The effectiveness of usage drill or practice (both oral and written) may be improved through the observance of the following suggestions:

1. Practice exercises are most effective when pupils feel a genuine need for their use.
2. Children must clearly understand the purpose of any drill and explanatory material that is a part of it.
3. Material for the content of drills should be familiar to the children whenever possible. For example, it might be related to a recent field trip or some seasonal interest.
4. The value of practice comes from repetition of the usage to be established; therefore, there must be enough repetition within an exercise to be of benefit.
5. Practice should be of short duration with each period stressing a specific usage.
6. The time of day devoted to usage practice should vary.
7. Individualization of practice may be provided by working with single pupils or by placing pupils in small groups making the same types of errors.
8. A child or group should concentrate on a limited number of usage items until some degree of success has begun to be achieved.

The difficulty encountered most often in teaching usage is caused by undue reliance on grammar. Pooley states with respect to such reliance as a means of correcting pronoun usage that "this fallacy arises from the assumption . . . that a pronoun error (him and me went home) is corrected by teaching the declension of the pronoun."[22] Similar statements might be made concerning the assumption that a verb usage may be changed by conjugating its forms, that the choice of an adjective form is affected by learning rules for the formation of the comparative and superlative, or that learning to use adverbs is aided by determining that many end with *ly*.

The solution to the problem of establishing an acceptable usage form is not found in "authority"—in the knowledge of grammar or in the application of its rules. Rather, it is found in genuine and purposeful communication, in the use of meaningful practice, and in making certain that children actually hear what they are saying, how this differs from the acceptable form, and how the acceptable form is necessary for the language situation in which it is used to be most effective.

However, both teacher and pupils should be aware that there are levels of language usage and that both the choice of words and

[22]Pooley, *Teaching English Usage*, p. 181.

the level of usage should be suited to the occasion on which they are used. Teachers sometimes become too pedantic about niceties in language expression. They need to remember that colloquial language is the comfortable, clear, idiomatic, forceful type of expression used in the informal situations of life, whether in school or not, which in general should be accepted without too much pressure. They should also recognize that there are occasions when a bit of expressive slang may be appropriate and can give "punch" to expression. On the other hand, teachers must guard against crude and illiterate expressions that are unquestionably provincial or unacceptable.

It is equally true, of course, that there are occasions in the lives of both children and adults that call for the use of formal expression, both oral and written, and children must be prepared for these. Such occasions as assembly programs, some reporting activities, and business letter writing are the most common examples. Perhaps the most important task of the teacher in connection with teaching language usage is to help children learn to suit their language to the occasion in which it is used and to use effective expression on both the formal and informal levels. In accomplishing this, as has been noted many times before, his own example is of prime importance. In addition, unusually apt expressions and well-used words may be selected from literature to show the value of the careful choice of words. In the process, of course, many of these words may be added to pupils' vocabularies.

As has been suggested, a teacher should evaluate the language usage of his class through informal surveys, either continuously or at frequent intervals. In addition, many of the usage items ordinarily requiring instructional emphasis in the elementary school appear on standardized language and general achievement tests. These tests, of course, are written so they do not measure a child's spoken usage. They may also be as unrealistic as some textbooks in their choices of usage items to test, particularly in that some choices may be far removed from the gross kinds of nonstandard usages many teachers must deal with. Further, the number of items tested are generally so few that, while the general level of a class as compared with other classes may be determined, little help is provided in diagnosing individual pupil needs.

*Evaluating
Usage
Teaching*

In spite of the shortcomings of standardized measures, however, a teacher should use them in a planned program of testing and should make use of the information provided by the tests in his subsequent teaching. The following chart should assist a teacher in analyzing the results from standardized testing.

Language Usage[23]

Possible Causes of Low Test Scores	Additional Evidence of Deficiency	Suggested Remedial Treatment
1. Failure to comprehend testing technique.	Misunderstanding of method of recording responses to items.	Prepare and use drill exercises similar to those used in test. Work with pupil until he understands technique.
2. Poor control over special language usages.	Observation and check on daily habits of oral and written expression.	Check pupil's test paper to identify types of usages missed. Check with text and course of study for grade emphasis. Emphasize individual drill on specific errors. Contrast correct forms with those to be avoided. Supplement with oral drill.
3. Poor language background.	Careless, inaccurate usage in oral and written expression.	Corrective instruction is the only remedy here. Select a limited number of usages and proceed as in No. 2 above.
4. Foreign language in the home.	Observed foreign accents. Evidence of two languages in the home.	Use direct corrective instruction here. Follow suggestions in No. 2 above.
5. Poor general reading comprehension.	Erratic response to test items; poor reading ability in other subjects.	Drill on sentence and total meaning comprehension as required for general improvement in reading.
6. Low mental ability.	Difficulty in following directions; erratic response to difficulty with common usages; low MA and IQ shown by reliable mental test.	Follow general procedure as outlined in Nos. 2 and 3 above. Have pupil prepare and memorize a key sentence for troublesome usages.
7. Careless language habits.	Erratic responses to test items; carelessness in informal expression.	Develop self-critical attitude toward usage errors. Bring pressure to bear favoring correct usages. Stress proofreading all written work.
8. Confusion caused by emphasis on formal rather than functional usages.	Inaccurate responses to items emphasized mainly through rules.	Emphasize individual drills; stress definite habits of correct response to important usages.

23From the *Manual for Interpreting the Iowa Language Abilities Test* (World Book Company, Yonkers-on-Hudson, New York, 1948), reproduced with the permission of Harcourt Brace Jovanovich, Inc.

Developing the Rhetorical Skills

One of the true weaknesses of elementary school language arts programs—perhaps even the greatest weakness—is the lack of attention given to the rhetorical skills of expression. Webster defines rhetoric as "the art of expressive speech or discourse: the study of principles and rules of composition formulated by ancient critics (as Aristotle and Quintilian) and interpreted by classical scholars for application to discourse in the vernacular." Thus rhetoric, along with grammar and logic, was part of the "trivium" of medieval days. Rhetoric, however, fell into disrepute because of attention given in its study to nomenclature and form rather than content, but there is evidence that we are witnessing a rebirth that is significant to teachers.[24] The new rhetoric gives attention to writing as well as speaking and to exposition and evocative and creative writing as well as argumentation and persuasion. The new rhetoric requires that attention be given to the selection of content, to organization and style, to sentence construction, and to consideration of the reader or audience.

Children must recognize that the best way to present an idea or thought clearly is to organize the expression so that it sticks to the point and presents information in proper and interesting sequence. Essentially the problem of organization is inherent in composition. While composition requires other skills and abilities, the fundamental factor is organization. The problem of organization occurs in the construction of sentences, paragraphs, and extended discourse. No expression—oral or written—is effective unless it is well organized, unless it has been properly composed.

Teaching Organization of Expression

When a child begins to recognize relationships he is beginning to organize. Activities such as telling a story in proper sequence, putting together a puzzle, making a list of things seen on a field trip, or making an outline are all organizational activities. Organizational ability as a part of the thinking process must be developed before the child can become skilled in arranging the order of his facts in his written or spoken expression.

Primary in importance in organization is sticking to the point. In oral language situations this means limiting the scope of a topic of discussion, the content of an announcement, or the theme of a report, and relating the ideas and thoughts expressed to that limited scope. An-

[24]Hook, *What Every English Teacher Should Know,* p. 33.

other feature of good organization is the presenting of material in the most effective sequence. Such sequence may involve a series of events in which time is a factor or events in which there is a cause and effect relationship.

The problem of organization is related to outlining, and ability to outline correctly indicates maturity in organization. Organizing ideas should be taught, however, before the mechanics of outlining. That is, children should learn early to make lists, to classify, to organize. From this experience, skills in outlining and more formal organizing will develop quite naturally.

☐ Sequence of Ideas Within the Sentence

No set formula can be stated for the presentation of ideas within the sentence. Many dull and uninteresting sentences are the result of always placing the subject first and following it with the predicate. Actually almost any word or phrase may be used for the beginning of the sentence or for the ending of it so long as the resulting sentence makes sense and fully and clearly expresses the intended idea. Simple sentences may be made interesting by varying the ways in which they begin. Children should be encouraged to transpose an appositive to the beginning of a sentence, to place a word or phrase modifier at the beginning, and to use increasingly complex and compound-complex sentences. It is not expected, of course, that the children learn these terms or receive direct teaching on their use, but rather that they should be encouraged in these and other natural ways to make their sentences interesting, varied, and meaningful.

☐ Connectives

The run-on sentence construction appears far too frequently in the expression of children at every grade level. Young children often have difficulty in keeping their ideas distinct, while older children are not always sure of their punctuation and thus tend to run simple sentences together in a monotonous pattern. Children should be advised that although *and* and other connectives are perfectly good words, they should not be used too frequently. A positive approach to the problem of using too many connectives seems to be the best teaching procedure. The teaching emphasis should be upon the natural use of connectives as they are needed for clearly expressing the meaning intended. Children learn the use of other connectives than *and* or *but* by practicing such forms as *for, which, if, when,* and *because* when opportunity arises.

Some suggestions for teaching the proper use of connectives follow.

1. Select and read to the class stories of generally equal interest; one in which all of the sentences are short, one in which all of the sentences are long, and one in which the sentences vary in length. Have the children decide which story they like best and why.
2. Select and write on the board several paragraphs having short choppy sentences. Have the children decide which sentences to combine and how to combine them.
3. Compile a list of connectives, such as:

and	if	until	which	that	as soon as
so	who	where	wherever	because	unless
but	since	when	whenever	although	then

4. Have each child bring to class some sentences from his own writing showing how he used good connectives in rewriting them.
5. Select a sentence, such as: "John was happy, *and* he began to laugh." Discuss the relationship of the two parts of the sentence, leading from the selection of some other words for *and* to a complete reorganization of the sentence.
6. Through such exercises as the above, lead children to discover that:
    And is used to join ideas of equal importance.
    So, therefore, since, because show cause or reason.
    When indicates time.
    Whenever indicates time and repetition.
    But is used when there is something unexpected to follow.
    Who, which, that are good substitutes for *and he, and it.*

□ **Order of Sentences Within Paragraph**

In order for children to use good paragraphing habitually, it is necessary to develop a feeling for the paragraph in much the same manner as sentence sense is developed. Children should learn about paragraphs as the need arises; that is, when they need to include a number of distinct topics within a single unit of expression. Actually this is not too difficult to teach in the primary grades if they have first learned to write single sentence paragraphs and later paragraphs of two and three sentences with the emphasis always being on the idea of beginning a new paragraph when a new idea or unrelated information is introduced. Teaching the single-sentence paragraph and later the paragraph of two or three sentences leads children to recognize that a paragraph has a main idea, or, as someone has expressed it, that sentences are like the branches of a tree—they all lead to the trunk, or main idea.

One teacher taught the organization of material into a report and at the same time developed the idea of good paragraphing by using the following procedure:[25]

1. I took the information one child had obtained and wrote the statements on the board.
2. They read the statements.
3. They decided which statements belonged together.
4. They decided which group of statements should come first, second, etc.
5. They read the report with statements in correct order.

Points to remember in teaching good paragraphing include the following:

(a) Emphasize the function of the paragraph as an aid to clarity of expression.
(b) Stress the importance of putting sentences in logical or sequential order.
(c) Inspect and analyze each pupil's writing for improved sentence sequence.
(d) Encourage children to watch for ways in which professional writers move skillfully from topic to topic and use paragraphs in their writing.
(e) Demonstrate to children that the beginning sentence should be interesting enough to get the reader's attention and let him know what the paragraph is about and that the ending sentence is actually needed in the paragraph.

☐ **Note-taking**

As children read, study, carry on experiments, participate in field trips, conduct interviews, listen to programs and reports, and watch films, there is an almost constant demand for note-taking. Note-taking is not something that is learned incidentally. It is an activity that calls for the use of organizational skills that are a part of logical and sequential thinking processes. Usually the development of these skills begins in the kindergarten and first grade when the teacher writes lists of things to do, things to watch for on a trip, things seen on the trip, and things to be remembered. Other activities for the primary grades which begin the teaching of note-taking are (1) drawing pictures to show ideas or facts, (2) building sand, block, and clay representations of ideas, (3) having children dictate descriptive labels, and (4) having children find pertinent passages. In the intermediate grades these activities are ap-

[25]*Using Language* (Wilmington, Del.: The Division of Elementary Education, Wilmington Public Schools, 1955), p. 63.

propriate: (1) building more complex replicas, such as models, pictures, diagrams, and illustrated maps; (2) individual or group dictation of memoranda or sentences based upon observation or reading; and (3) oral discussion of ideas and things to look for before individual note-taking is done. An illustration of this latter suggestion is given in one curriculum guide.[26]

> In a study of "Modern Press and History of Records" a group of children planned a study trip to a large city newspaper office. They discussed the important questions they wanted to ask and noted the things they wished to observe. These were listed on the board and included:
>
> Who gives the reporters their assignments?
> How does a linotype operate?
> How many papers are printed in a day?
> How does news come over a teletype machine?
> How are pictures printed in a paper?
> Where is the city desk located?

Children should be taught to take accurate notes. In their reading they should learn to take exact notes but *not* copy the exact words of the writer except as quoted material. Encouraging children to copy the exact words of a selection into their notes, as is suggested in some sources, may really lead to unintentional plagiarism in their writing.[27] Certainly children should exactly understand the idea, fact, or opinion of the writer, but copying the exact words can be done with little or no thought. Teachers should insist that the children indicate in their notes the exact source of the information.

□ Outlining

From the time children first learn to write independently, they can be helped to jot down their ideas and organize them in sequence. This is the beginning of outlining and may be as simple as:

> I went to the park.
> I saw the animals.
> I had a balloon and ice cream.
> I came home on a bus.

[26]*Arts and Skills of Communication for Democracy's Children,* Vol. II (San Bernardino, Calif.: San Bernardino County Schools, no date), p. 280.

[27]See, for example, Alvina Treut Burrows in Chapter 8 of *Social Studies in the Elementary School,* Fifty-sixth Yearbook of the National Society for the Study of Education, Part II (Chicago: The University of Chicago Press, 1957).

Outlining should be taught in the context of specific purposes. Each occasion calling for the making of an outline should accomplish the maximum with the minimum of time spent on actual outline making. Thus the idea will become established that the making of an outline is an aid to another activity. The first teaching of outlining should be done on a group basis with the pupil activity being oral and the teacher doing the writing. The children should work out composite outlines together, and as needed, copy them individually. Some pupil activities in organizing facts and outlining that can be handled cooperatively are the following: (1) the dictating of a story which the teacher writes on a chart, after which the story is cut into strips and the pupils arrange the sentences in outline form; (2) the listing of events that happened on an excursion in the order of their happening; and (3) the outlining of some process in either logical or chronological order.

The teacher should always stress the fact that any task worth doing is worth planning in advance, and that outlining is valuable as an advance plan for many activities, even those in which language expression is not involved. Outlining should be developed thoroughly when it is introduced and reviewed occasionally throughout the year. Of course, the initial teaching of formal outlining is much more meaningful and acceptable to children if they have had an adequate background of training in organizing their own thinking, planning and recording.

One curriculum guide suggests developing the concept of outlining through a particular experience, such as the cooperative planning of an oral report for an assembly program following a class visit to the International Airport.[28]

Discussing highlights of the visit

Selecting main ideas to be presented in oral report

Writing these main ideas on the chalkboard as topic headings

Listing the important facts related to each of the topics as a series of notes under each heading

Developing, according to standard form, a cooperative outline from the information recorded by arranging topics in order of importance, as determined by class, and organizing the related facts under each topic

Using the completed outline as a guide for presenting the oral report

[28]*A Guide for the Teaching of Language Arts* (San Francisco: San Francisco Public Schools, 1955), p. 19.

Providing additional cooperative experiences in developing both
sentence outlines and topic outlines

Stressing the correct use and placement of Roman numerals, sub-
headings, capital letters, Arabic numerals; capitalization and
punctuation

Encouraging children to use language texts and chart models as
reference aids in proofreading their outlines

What really determines whether or not a group of words is a sentence
is not easily answered. Textbooks often define a sentence as follows:
"A sentence is a group of words that in itself gives a whole thought."[29]
The textbook from which this definition was taken continues with the
statement: "A sentence is understood when read apart from the sentence that preceded it." This, of course, is not entirely true, since
many statements are perfectly good sentences but have little or no precise meaning apart from the remainder of the expression. The best
examples are the sentences of one word each such as "Yes," "Go," or
"Good."

    Defining a sentence as a group of words expressing a whole or
complete thought should be avoided. Rather, a sentence should be
thought of as a device for expressing an idea. With this in mind attention should be given to the idea and to expressing that idea in a way
that is clear and exact with no thought of a definition. In fact, a substantial number of children generally speak in sentences, thus showing
considerable knowledge of the grammar of the language—though, of
course, they do not know the grammatical terminology nor can they
express grammatical rules.[30] For the children who use partial communication units the provision of many opportunities for expression,
with the teacher carefully guiding the expression to its greatest effectiveness, will bring about an understanding of the sentence. These
children, and others who initially have greater control of language, will
very early discover that a sentence always has at least a subject and
a complete verb, either expressed or implied. They learn that there is
always a word or several words present or implied which makes the
group of words state something. They also learn that another word
or several words are present or implied about which something is
stated. They come to realize, also, that sometimes other elements must
be present or implied to express the idea with clarity and exactness,

*The
Construction
of Sentences*

[29]Harold G. Shane, Florence K. Ferris, and Edward E. Keener, *Building
Good English* (River Forest, Ill.: Laidlaw Brothers, 1956), p. 304.

[30]Walter D. Loban, *The Language of Elementary School Children* (Champaign, Ill.: National Council of Teachers of English, Research Report No. 1,
1963).

and that the inclusion in a sentence of too many elements may lead to lack of clarity.

Certainly a degree of sentence mastery must be developed before ideas and feelings can be expressed in effective and meaningful ways in either written or oral form. It is a common criticism that far too many pupils pass through the entire language program without gaining a clear conception of what a sentence is. Many of these pupils can recite a memorized definition of a sentence taken from a textbook, but their real understanding of the elements that make up a sentence or that determine sentence quality is either extremely vague or non-existent. Thus they are unable to construct good clear sentences of their own or to examine and edit their sentences critically.

Too often the problem of teaching pupils to form good sentences in both their oral and written expression is approached without an adequate understanding of what is involved. Sentences that are clear, concise, and interesting are indicative of clear thinking. A clumsy, awkward sentence is likely to be the result of a struggle to express a vague idea or feeling that has been poorly thought out. Before starting to write or speak a child should give thought to *what* is to be said and *how* best to say it.

One guide gives these suggestions for developing ability in sentence construction:[31]

> Sentence growth can be furthered at any time during the day and in any subject.
>
> The teacher should speak or read to the children in a voice that shows "sentence sense."
>
> The child should give one statement at a time and pause at the close of it. Use the word "sentence" informally at first.
>
> Show how a sentence can be recognized by starting with a capital letter and closing with a mark of punctuation.
>
> Help the child to recognize a sentence by dictating a sentence, reading it in a story or by having the child give a sentence in answer to a question.
>
> A child may tell one thing about an experience.

Faults in Sentence Construction
Control of the sentence is closely related to the fluency a child possesses in the use of language, which, in turn, is affected by the size and extent of his vocabulary and the experiences he has had. The principal

---

[31]*Child Growth Through Language Experience,* The Language Arts Committee, School City of South Bend, South Bend (Indiana: The South Bend Board of Education, September, 1952), p. 149.

faults in sentence construction common in the elementary school are the following:

☐ Omissions

Children's thinking sometimes runs ahead of their writing and speaking with the result that vital points are omitted from their sentences. Then, too, children often lose sight of their reader or listener or they assume that what has been omitted is known to everyone. The result of such thinking is the omission of parts of the sentence necessary for complete understanding. For example, the words *The wind blew* may express a complete thought, but they also omit elements needed in the development of the essential idea. *The cold wind blew the snow into deep drifts* may better express the intended thought. The pupil using the first sentence may have used it because he had not thought about the details of what he wanted to say, or he may simply have neglected filling in the essential details for the reader or listener.

☐ Loose "And's"

The word *and* is a conjunction which is used to connect words, phrases, or clauses. The overuse of *and, but,* or any conjunction, a common practice of young children, detracts from effective sentence structure. A conjunction should be used to connect words, phrases, and clauses of *equal* importance; it should not be used to simply tie together a series of simple sentences in the manner common to young children. The otherwise interesting little story which follows is an example of this error.

> Yesterday was my birthday and I was eight years old and my mother and father gave me an electric train and we had a birthday cake.

While all sentences need not be simple sentences, children should be encouraged to express only one idea at a time in a sentence until they have firmly grasped the idea of sentence construction. This problem of loose "and's" is a part of the total problem of good sentence structure.[32]

☐ Run-ons

A common type of error in sentence structure is that of expressing a series of more or less rambling and complete statements unseparated by adequate pauses or by proper punctuation and capitalization. This type of error, quite common in the early elementary grades, decreases

---

[32]See also pages 334–335 for activities in using connectives.

as children get older and as purposeful language expression is a part of the curriculum.

☐ Unnecessary Words

Another common type of sentence fault in the expression of children in the elementary school is the use of words as primers or launchers (well, see, you know, etc.) which contribute nothing to meaning and do not function as transition elements. In a related sense, children often repeat words in speech, a habit which is sometimes regarded as stuttering but is more often simply an attempt to clarify thinking and a search for words.

☐ Misplaced Sentence Elements

The location of modifiers and antecedents in a sentence very often has much to do with making the meaning clear. All of us have been confused by lack of clarity in such sentences as: "John told Harry that the postman had brought a letter for him." Not only confusing, but also often amusing, is the misplaced modifier. The sentence, "John said that the letter had been brought by the postman which he found in the mailbox," cannot help but conjure up a view of the postman's head sticking incongruously from the letter slot of a mail box. Such sentences as "He counted three beautiful paintings coming down the stairs," or "She dropped the letter she was carrying to her mother in the mud," are intriguing to pupils because of their humorous aspects but may lead to a serious consideration of word order. Children need to learn that whether a sentence is in natural or inverted order, whether it begins with its subject or with a modifying clause or phrase, its meaning will be clearer if modifiers are placed next to, or as close as possible to, the words they modify, and if pronouns are so placed that they clearly indicate their proper antecedents.

Teaching
Sentence
Sense

There are no shortcuts to skill in sentence construction. The desired control of sentences, including the understanding that is necessary, occurs only through constant and conscious teaching and learning effort on the part of the teacher and the pupil. The pupil must learn that his sentences must make "sense"; that is, that they must not be vague or incomplete and that they must not try to tell so much that the meaning is confused or lost. A focus upon the development of sentence sense should eliminate most sentence construction errors. The following suggestions for developing sentence sense should be helpful with most pupils:

1. Provide children with ample opportunity for oral composition, especially in the primary grades.

2. Encourage pupils in their oral expression to form habits of using sentences that make sense, and that are clear and concise.

3. Begin by emphasizing one-sentence statements, with the child understanding that his sentence must tell one thing and only one thing.

4. From the one-sentence composition move to the two-and three-sentence composition as sentence skill develops.

5. Continually expose pupils to good sentences that are read well by a good oral reader. This generally means that the teacher will read well-written materials frequently to the children in a voice that portrays "sentence feeling."

6. Encourage pupils to do considerable group composing and dictating of letters and other forms of written expression in the early grades.

7. Provide exercises in which each child tells one thing about some personal experience, such as an excursion, a project, or a picture.

8. Make frequent use of dictation exercises which require punctuation and capitalization.

9. Encourage children to answer questions with the expression of one complete thought.

10. Provide exercises in which pupils are required to distinguish between fragments and sentences.

11. Insist on pupils' proofreading their own writing.

12. Provide exercises for making sentences out of nonsentence groups of words.

13. Use matching exercises made up of short lists of complete subjects in one column and complete predicates in another.

14. Provide exercises for breaking up "run-on" sentences into correct sentences.

15. Develop the sentence concept through the use of contrast. Brief stories told by children may be written twice by the teacher in such ways that both good and poor sentence sense is shown. The two compositions should be compared, discussed, and evaluated, and the poor form should be reconstructed.

16. Provide exercises for the organization of sentence elements into their proper relationships.

17. Give careful explanations of the various types of incorrect sentences with illustrations of each.

18. Make certain that the child is able to recognize verbs (really the core of every sentence), around which all the other words are grouped as subject or predicate modifiers. Next see that he learns to find the subject of a verb and to see how a verb and its subject form the framework of a sentence. After this, pupils can advance to the study of words which modify the subject and verb.

Particular attention should be given to helping children relate their sense of the sentence as evidenced in their speech to their written expression. Although a child may include unnecessary words, excessively use "and," and do a great deal of rambling, his speech is likely to show the drops in voice indicating sentence separations. A teacher may have a child who has written run-on constructions read his expression and note that the junctures he uses do not coincide with his punctuation and capitalization. Often the first reading by the child will not result in his noting the run-on sentence in his writing, but if the teacher asks for a re-reading and then calls attention to the drop in his voice, he will begin to be more aware of his oral sentences.

Clarity in Sentence Construction

Concise, well-constructed, and sharply defined sentences are the product of clear thinking. Teaching children to clarify their thinking should begin in the kindergarten by encouraging expression and by helping children to talk about specific objects and events. Instruction should continue at each grade level by similar encouragement and by providing time for thinking before oral or written expression is required. Certainly clarity of expression will not occur if a child is confused about what he is attempting to express.

A child should be encouraged and helped to rewrite his sentences so they express in a clear and interesting way exactly what he wishes to say. Particular attention needs to be given to the use of modifiers to help to build up an idea or to create a colorful picture, as the following example shows.[33]

The children had returned from a study trip to the harbor. They wanted to write about their experiences, but many of them were not satisfied with the sentences they could write and asked the teacher for help.

Teacher: Perhaps we could write a sentence on the board and then see how we can make it different and better.

John: Here's one of mine. It's a sentence, but it doesn't tell much—"We saw the waves on the beach."

Teacher: Yes, that is a good sentence to work on. Perhaps someone can make the sentence tell more about the waves.

Patty: The waves tumbled over each other.

Sally: The waves rushed to the shore.

[33]*Arts and Skills of Communication for Democracy's Children,* Vol. II (San Bernardino, Calif.: San Bernardino County Schools, 1954), p. 263.

Teacher:	Could someone put those two ideas about waves together?
John:	The waves tumbled over each other as they rushed to the shore.
Martin:	I know another way to describe the waves— sometimes they're lazy.
Patty:	Lazy, lapping waves.
Sally:	The waves lazily lapped at the white sands of the beach.
Teacher:	That has a nice sound and makes a good picture. Anyone else have ideas?
Pete:	Sometimes the waves are noisy—they thunder and pound on the rocks.
Teacher:	Would we say that noisy waves lapped at the shore?
Martin:	No, they dash and splash.
Patty:	The roaring, tumbling, pounding waves dashed against the rocks.
Louisa:	I think the waves look like they're dancing.
Margaret:	Little bent-over dancers with white lace caps.
Polly:	And the dancers just vanish and more keep coming.
Teacher:	Those are lovely ideas. Can someone put them together in a sentence?
Martin:	The white-capped waves danced to the shore and —and—
Polly:	Vanished in misty spray.
Teacher:	I've written those sentences in my notes and I'll put them on the board so you can see them and use them if you wish.

This example shows the importance of group composition—the talking together about an idea or event before individual writing is done. It also illustrates how time spent in thinking results in better expression than that which would have been produced if expression had been the first activity following the field trip.

Variety in word order comes from flexibility in thought and expression. Smith suggests that it be taught by appealing to the interest achieved by saying the same thing in different ways.[34] She gives these examples at the primary grades level:

Variety and Word Order

[34]Dora V. Smith, "Growth in Language Power as Related to Child Development," in *Teaching Language in the Elementary School,* Forty-third Yearbook of the National Society for the Study of Education, Part II (Chicago: The University of Chicago Press, 1944), p. 68.

There was a tiger walking around his cage at the zoo. There was a monkey hanging on a swing and jumping around. There was a polar bear splashing in the water.

There was a tiger walking around his cage at the zoo. A monkey was hanging on a swing and jumping around. Splashing in the water was a polar bear.

Children should be encouraged to take an idea and see how it may be expressed in differently arranged sentences, such as:

I saw the fishing boat leaving the harbor as I came down to the dock.

As I came down to the dock, I saw the fishing boat leaving the harbor.

The fishing boat was leaving the harbor as I came down to the dock.

This activity could be followed by a discussion of which sentence various children liked best and why. Language textbooks contain practice exercises for the development of sentences with changed word order which suggest that each sentence be rewritten by inverting the subject and predicate.[35]

1. The deer sped away into the forest.
2. The deep voice of the clock boomed solemnly over the sleeping town.
3. A tiny, red-roofed hut could be seen far down the valley.
4. A herd of buffaloes thundered across the plain.
5. A footsore and weary dog straggled behind the rickety cart.

Children come to school with knowledge of word order in English. That is, through their experience with language they have sensed the grammar of the language system. Presented with the following frames for inserting the missing words, they would have no difficulty in choosing nouns for them.

I saw_____.
He hasn't any_____.
The_____was interesting.

Likewise, they should have no difficulty correctly inserting verbs in these frames:

---

[35]Mildred A. Dawson and others, *Language for Daily Use, Grade Six,* Fourth edition (Yonkers-on-Hudson: World Book Company, 1959), p. 144.

You_____quickly.
He_____it.

Or in inserting adjectives in this sentence:

The_____boy is very_____.

Most children do have this knowledge; most children also understand that some parts of sentences cannot be moved while other parts
can. For example, "Bob hit the ball hard" cannot become "The ball
hard Bob hit," nor can "She laughed" become "Laughed she." On the
other hand, "They looked up eagerly" can be changed to "Eagerly,
they looked up" or "They eagerly looked up."

Variety in expression can be developed by having children experiment with language as follows:

1. Substituting nouns for other nouns in sentences.
2. Replacing verbs in sentences with more vivid ones.
3. Replacing adjectives in sentences with more descriptive ones or ones
   which more accurately modify the nouns.
4. Changing the positions of movables in sentences.
5. Adding words, phrases, or clauses to the subjects of sentences.
6. Modifying the predicates of sentences by adding words, phrases, or
   clauses.

A simple way for children to do this is for the teacher to write
words on individual tagboard cards and place them in the chalkboard
tray or hang them on a string stretched across the front of the room.
Children can then move the words about as they change word order and
make expansions and transformations.[36] New words can be written on
blank cards as they are needed. For example, the sentence "Men in the
jungle hunt" can be expanded to "Men in the jungle hunt with primitive weapons" and to "Men in the jungle hunt their daily food with
primitive weapons." Similarly transformations can be made with the
focus upon interest and variety rather than upon a formal learning and
use of grammatical terminology. For example, "Bill bought a bicycle"
may become the passive "A bicycle was bought by Bill," the negative

[36]See Chapter 11 for examples of sentence construction activities related
to transformational grammar. Such transformational activities may be in formal
settings, but they also may be done informally and functionally as suggested
here.

"Bill did not buy a bicycle," or the exclamatory "What a bicycle Bill bought!"

Making Expression Interesting

Children must learn of the important role that interest plays in the communication process. They must come to realize that a listener or reader cannot be expected to maintain interest in what is written or said unless the writer or speaker is himself vitally interested and desires to convey this interest to his audience. By listening to interesting stories and by reading them, children can become more aware of the importance of interest in general and of factors which make for interest in their own expression. One language textbook suggests that children select stories they like from such collections as *Arabian Nights* and *The Jungle Book* and then discuss reasons why they enjoyed the stories. Points suggested for the children to consider are:[37]

> It tells about interesting characters and events.
> The words in the story make me see and feel all that happens.
> There is plenty of action.
> The characters seem alive.
> The characters converse.
> No part is dragged out too long.
> It has a surprise ending.

Similar lessons can be used to show the importance of various factors that help to make oral and written expression interesting.

There are many factors which affect interest. Some are taught in incidental ways and some are developed through specific lessons, as suggested above. The factors of content, concreteness, and the use of examples and similes are sufficiently important in all expression to justify special emphasis here.

□ Content

The first consideration in expression should be given to the selection of the topic. Expression should not be attempted unless the person attempting it has something to say, something about which he is informed and about which he can speak or write with authority and confidence—confidence and authority usually based upon experience. In developing the importance and use of interest factors the teacher must give attention to sources of content. In most instances, this means providing opportunities for children to enjoy direct or indirect experiences.

[37]Dawson *et al., Language,* p. 230.

On the basis of the background of each child, the teacher can guide him in the selection of the topic and the content that will result in expression that is both interesting and appropriate.

☐ Concreteness

Words are either *concrete* or *abstract.* A concrete word is one whose referent can be touched or seen, while an abstract word refers to an idea. Not all words, of course, can be or should be concrete, and not all concrete words are of like definiteness. The word *ship,* for example, is less definite than is *cruiser.* In expression, interest and meaning may be improved through the use of words and phrases which are concrete and thus give the child greater opportunity to build interest and variety into his sentences. One curriculum guide includes the following as activities for developing sentences based upon concrete words and ideas.[38]

> Present to the children a series of pictures of story characters whose facial expressions indicate feelings of happiness, sadness, or surprise. Have the children suggest exact words which describe the expressions, such as: *laughing, crying, smiling, surprised.*
>
> Have the children write a sentence, using one of the words and describing the expression, such as:
>
> > The man is surprised.
> > The girl is crying.
>
> Now have the children write a sentence which describes the expression in more detail, such as:
>
> > The man's mouth is open in surprise.
> > Tears are coming down the girl's face.

The importance of concreteness in stimulating interest can be demonstrated to children through the comparison of materials. Exercises that call for listing words in order of their definiteness or concreteness are helpful, too, as is the use of a dictionary to determine the exact meaning of a word. Particular attention should be given to the exact meanings of synonyms in order to use the one that expresses the meaning most definitely and concretely. However, the most effective means of developing skill in the use of concreteness in expression is by actual construction of sentences and paragraphs and by critical editing and revision of the product.

[38]*English Language Arts, Experimental Material: Composition Section.* The University of the State of New York, The State Education Department, 1965, p. 12.

☐ Examples and Illustrations

Expression is made interesting through the use of examples and illustrations—a fact that children often recognize by drawing pictures to accompany their writing. Certainly this should not be discouraged, but they should also be helped to discover that the use of an appropriate example can draw a "word picture" for the reader. For instance, the child who in a letter to his grandmother wishes to tell her that his puppy is getting fat should be encouraged to write something like this: "Our puppy is getting fatter every day, and now is fatter than that red pig of Grandpa's."

☐ Similes

The use of similes is another way by which interest may be added to expression. The purpose of similes is to give enriched meaning to composition by expressing comparisons or likenesses which are themselves interesting and readily understandable. Similes are always announced by such words as *like* or *as*. Children should learn to use the simile idea as a means of adding interest and meaning to their oral and written expression.

These suggestions for teaching the use of similes, examples, and figurative expressions are representative of procedures teachers can follow to encourage variety and interest in expression.

1. Encourage children to list interesting comparisons they encounter in their reading, in assembly programs, in television and radio programs, and at home, and to share them with other members of the class.
2. Encourage children to watch for opportunities to use examples, figures of speech, and interesting comparisons in their written and oral expression.
3. Have the children maintain a column on the bulletin board similar to the "Patter" in the *Reader's Digest.*
4. Have the children practice completing sentences such as the following with the most interesting phrase:
   The boat rocked as_____.

Promoting Vocabulary Growth

A major teaching concern at all grade levels is that of helping children to acquire and use vocabularies of sufficient breadth and depth to make their receptive and expressive language as effective as it should be in terms of their maturity and intellectual levels. Too many adults are able to use only a limited vocabulary, with the result that their expression is colorless, often boring, and sometimes not clearly understandable. This fact reflects the foundation they secured in their early years, including those spent in the elementary school. Further, many children learning to read are handicapped by inadequate vocabularies and this handicap often continues into adulthood.

By the time the average child enters school he has acquired a considerable understanding of a fairly large number of words. Early studies of the preschool child placed the total of words known at about 2,500, while more recent studies indicate that the figure may be nearly ten times that number.[39] It would seem that if a child "knows" such a large number of words he would surely have a large speaking vocabulary, though limitations in his writing and reading vocabularies might be understood. However, "knowing" a word often does not mean understanding in the sense of being able to use it. The school must at all times emphasize understanding by teaching the proper use of words. Promoting the growth of writing, speaking, reading, and listening vocabularies is a most important function of the language program in every classroom.

The best means for giving breadth and depth to a child's vocabulary is the provision of many opportunities for new, life-like, and interesting experiences. For example, kindergarten or first-grade children may be taken to visit a farm. From such an experience, the following words and perhaps many more might be added to their vocabularies:

The Role of Experience in Vocabulary Building

milking machine	pasture	harvest	flock
tractor	manger	cattle	irrigate
barn	grain	orchard	
silo	crop	well	

Opportunities for direct experience may be given children in many ways and in all areas of the curriculum. All such experiences should provide for a heavy emphasis on the enrichment of the children's vocabularies. Here are some ways often used, particularly in the primary grades:[40]

[39]Mary K. Smith, "Measurement of the Size of General English Vocabulary Through the Elementary Grades and High School," *Genetic Psychology Monograph*, 24:311–345, 1941.

[40]Adapted and expanded from list by Mildred A. Dawson, *Promoting Vocabulary Growth*, Language Arts Notes, Number 5 (Yonkers-on-Hudson: World Book Company).

1. Manipulative activities that involve handling various materials, tools, and equipment; learning new names and understanding directions; discussing plans and results.
2. Social experiences within the classroom, such as the "show and tell" period, the daily news period, committee work that calls for planning and discussing, free conversation periods, or general class discussion.
3. Developing the children's social responsibility for receiving and greeting guests, extending courtesies, and helping one another.
4. Developing children's interest in the natural environment and in community activities by means of field trips that entail preliminary discussion of plans, training in observation, and eventual discussion of the total experience.
5. Having children observe and handle specimens and articles brought into the classroom in connection with science or social studies.
6. Setting up a class science museum or hobby display that involves classification, organization, and the making of appropriate labels.
7. Encouraging children's interest in words and urging them to be more and more curious about words.

Unquestionably it is possible that many activities which school children engage in hold possibilities for vocabulary growth but may not accomplish this growth. Definite guidance in word study is necessary if these activities are to result in large vocabularies. On this point Smith says:[41]

Merely setting the stage is not enough. Conscious attention to the meanings of words and to their usefulness for the expression of ideas is imperative. The teacher is in a position to lead children to a precision and extension of language which, without her assistance, they could not achieve for themselves. Sometimes the problem is to learn words new to the child's experience. Sometimes it is to give specific application to general terms, as in the case of *water,* now applied to *river* and now to *lake.* Sometimes it is to build generalizations out of specific experiences. Often it is to derive new meanings for old words previously met in different contexts, as in the instance of the "tow" rope and the call for "succor." Frequently, also, it is to help redefine the child's use of language by seeking the most *exact* or the most *concrete* word to express an experience which he has just had or shared with others. For example, first-grade children, stroking a bunny which was visiting school at Easter, were asked to tell what the bunny *felt like.* "It feels nice," "It feels fine," "It feels swell" were the immediate responses of the children. Without the teacher's urging that they help us to understand still more clearly *what* the bunny *felt like,* they would never have achieved the "It feels soft" or "It feels like silk," which came triumphantly in the end.

[41]Dora V. Smith, "Growth in Language Power," pp. 54–55.

Words and their meanings can be brought to the attention of children through provision of experience. In addition, there are many other procedures that can be used which have appeal to children and which develop a consciousness of the meanings and uses of words. Some of these procedures are the following:

Vocabulary
Building
Activities

1. Listing on the board and on charts new words encountered in classroom activities, in reading, and in out-of-school experiences. Following the listing these should be discussed and examples of their use shown.

2. Keeping individual lists of new words that the pupils like and want to use. This should not be an assignment of so many words a day, or anything of the sort that becomes drudgery, but something a child wants to do because he is interested in the words.

3. Making charts of "quiet" words, or perhaps "sound," "gay," "sad," or "musical" words. Charts may also be made of words to use instead of commonly overworked words, and of words for special occasions or special interests, such as football games, space travel, and camping trips.[42]

4. Finding words and phrases that prompt images, such as "dancing leaves," "a pacing tiger," "a shining beach."

5. Building words from root words by adding various prefixes and suffixes. For example, the root word *port* might be used and as many prefixes and suffixes as possible added to it. Some would be: *report, transport, portable, portage, porter, reporter, export.*

6. Noticing alliteration and rhyme in posters and slogans, in picturesque and descriptive phrases, and in reading in general.

7. Suggesting ideas and topics for written compositions and oral reports which will bring forth new words and words used in new ways. Topics such as the following may do this:

    > The Freshness of Spring
    > Across the Nation by Jet Airliner
    > Sounds at Night
    > What I Saw in the Park
    > What a Duck Sees as He Flies South

8. Playing word games such as scrabble, rearranging letters of a word to make new words, changing the suffix of a word, finding a word that begins with the letter that ends the preceding word, etc.

9. Finding words whose meanings have shifted or for which new meanings have been added. For example: junk, phone, splurge; stage, capsule, pad, bird, clean (in space jargon).

10. Having vocabulary building campaigns, such as learning a new word each day, the word of the week, new words from social studies, etc.[43]

[42]Marguerite P. Archer reports in "Building Vocabulary with a Fourth Grade Class," *Elementary English,* 37:447–448; November, 1960, that the class found 104 words that could be used instead of *said.*

[43]See Chapter 12 for other suggestions.

Reading as a
Means of
Building
Vocabulary

The practicality of developing vocabularies through actual experiences is limited. One of the best answers to this limitation lies in extensive reading. One language authority describes reading as a means of developing vocabulary as follows:[44]

> Reading, reading, reading. The more the children read the more meanings they learn.
> Reading things one is interested in
> Reading easy things for fun
> Reading anything and everything that adds to the value of the things one is doing or studying
> Reading to build new interests
> Reading newspapers, magazines, books, catalogs—anything that adds interest to living.

Reading as a means of vocabulary development is limited, of course, by the pupil's skill in reading, his interest in reading, and his skill in getting genuine meaning from such context. Teachers must realize that reading as a means of developing vocabularies depends heavily upon the guidance they give. Consideration should be given to these "principles of context operation" as stated by Deighton:[45]

1. Context reveals the meaning of unfamiliar words only infrequently.
2. Context generally reveals only one of the meanings of an unfamiliar word.
3. Context seldom clarifies the whole of any meaning.
4. Vocabulary growth through context revelation is a gradual matter.

In addition, what the context of the reading material reveals to a particular reader depends upon his previous experience, the clarity of the relationship between an unknown word and the context which reveals its meaning, and the physical proximity of such context to the unfamiliar word.

This suggests that a teacher needs to do much more than provide time for children to read (as important as this is) if he expects them to strengthen their vocabularies by this means. Guidance in the choosing of reading materials is needed so that what the children read will

---

[44]Ruth G. Strickland, *The Language Arts in the Elementary School* (Boston: D. C. Heath and Company, Third edition, 1969), p. 250.

[45]Reprinted with the permission of the publisher from Lee C. Deighton, *Vocabulary Development in the Classroom* (New York: Teachers College Press, 1959), p. 3 © 1959 by Teachers College, Columbia University.

be understood and will build upon earlier experiences they have had. Children will also need to be taught to use the dictionary with many reading activities and to use all the clues to meaning that are in the context of the material itself. Such clues will include examples which may explain unknown words, restatements which are really definitions, and modifying clauses or phrases which reveal meanings. In addition to learning to use these clues which clarify the meanings of words and phrases, children need to learn to make inferences, to "read between the lines." Direct attention should be given to particular categories of words; for example, children can be taught the meanings of (1) words often used figuratively, such as *eye, face, hill, river;* (2) judgment words, such as *fine, great, heavy, long;* (3) relationship words, such as *across, over, under, still, among;* (4) indefinite words, such as *some, several, most, much;* and (5) common idioms, such as *clear up, hold out, make do, bring down.*

With proper teacher guidance it is possible for each book or article that a child reads to reinforce his reading vocabulary and give him confidence and a sense of mastery in using words which he recognizes and understands but has hesitated to use in his expression.

Sometimes, also, children read fluently but without discrimination or feeling. These pupils need to be taught to note words or phrases which seem particularly well chosen and appropriate. They should be stimulated to discover and think about the feelings that various words arouse and to note the difference between vivid and colorless expression in their reading.

A word does not become a real part of a child's vocabulary until he uses it repeatedly with confidence. A basic part of the language program dealing with vocabulary, then, must be the development of the child's confidence in using new words. A language program which focuses upon genuine communication activities will provide the opportunities needed. In addition, direct attention to specific words will foster the desired confidence in their use. This is illustrated in the following report of a kindergarten class: [46]

Using New Words and New Meanings

> After the first snowfall the children brought a bowl of snow into the room and watched it melt and *evaporate.* They learned the word as they observed the fact.
>
> Next day Linda said, "My daddy doesn't believe that water *evaporates,* but I'm proving it to him. I put some water in a glass and each day some has *evaporated* until it will be all gone.

[46]*Communication: A Guide to the Teaching of Speaking and Writing* (Minneapolis: Minneapolis Public Schools, 1953), p. 26.

Real understanding of the meaning of a new word is shown in this report:[47]

> Ronnie shared his prized guinea pigs with the class. The children watched the little animals eagerly as they gnawed and nibbled. They held them close to feel the soft warm bodies. They listened to the characteristic "conversation" of the guinea pigs. They heard the scratching and digging of tiny claws.
>
> When the young guinea pigs were born and were less than an hour old, excited voices called, "See how tiny his claws are!" "Feel the soft velvety fur." "The babies are really miniature guinea pigs, aren't they?"
>
> This last comment came from Joe, who had been working on a miniature adobe house and had been fascinated by the new word miniature. He was eager to experiment with it in many situations.

Since many words have several connotations, it is necessary for children to learn to use words as accurately as possible if they are to convey the meaning intended. Children must be taught precision in the choice of the words used in their expression, as these words act as a bridge for understanding between themselves and their reader or listener. At the kindergarten and first-grade levels the teacher may begin by teaching the correct names of familiar objects such as parts of the body or school equipment. The same practice should continue at every grade level.

Children should also be taught to understand that many words have similar but not identical meanings and therefore should be selected with care. For example, in describing the idea of eating too rapidly, a teacher asked the children to express more clearly the sentence, "He ate much too quickly." Some of the results were:[48]

> He gobbled his food like a young turkey who hadn't been taught his manners.
>
> He gulped whole pieces of bread. They almost choked him.
>
> He swallowed so fast, the milk just wouldn't go down and he had to wait to catch a little breath.

Pronunciation and Vocabulary Development

Young children's problems of usage or pronunciation are very often the result of hearing and imitating nonstandard language. Pronunciation difficulties may also result from a lack of careful attention to the use of the word, difficult sounds within the word, or misunderstandings about the word; for example, a child may use *brang* as the past tense

[47]*Arts and Skills of Communication*, p. 234.
[48]*Developing Children's Power of Self-Expression Through Writing* (New York: Board of Education of the City of New York), pp. 79–80.

of *bring,* believing it should match with the past tense of *ring* or *sing.* If a child is hesitant about the pronunciation of a word due to any of these or other reasons, he will frequently avoid using the word in his speech and writing. He will simply use a word that he is confident he knows and make no attempt to master the use of the new word.

The teacher's own example in matters of pronunciation is especially important. Children soon become aware of the teacher's desire for them to use standard, acceptable pronunciation and, if the teacher-pupil relationship is as it should be, children will develop a sense of obligation to use the standard form.

Although teaching the use of a dictionary is discussed later in this chapter, it should be listed here as a tool for vocabulary building. However, it should be noted that this use of a dictionary demands the ability to find and select the information needed for a particular purpose and to ignore other unrelated information. For example, a child may need to check the spelling of a familiar word. He may want to know how a word is divided into syllables. At the upper grade levels he may want to select the applicable meaning from the several meanings listed. The pupil should be taught to regard the dictionary as a reference source that contains much more information than may be needed at any one time.

Using the Dictionary

Whenever a new unit, a new topic, a new country, or a new problem in science or social studies is being studied, the words of that particular problem, many of which are new to most of the children, should be put on the board or on a chart, pronounced, and called to the attention of the children in as many ways as possible. No opportunity should be overlooked for using these words in meaningful sentences in both oral and written expression. In a new area of study, children should never be allowed to stumble and mumble over words or to avoid using the exact and specific words. The words should be left in view on the board or chart in order that the children may refer to them as often as necessary.

Teaching the Vocabulary of a Subject

Using Sources of Information

Skill in using the library and its materials as well as other sources of information is of great importance to both oral and written expression. Children in the middle grades, particularly, find themselves in a new world of experiences in contrast to those encountered in the primary grades. Their environments have expanded; they encounter many new facts and practices. They need to be correct and specific about information. It is essential that they learn how to use the valuable printed resources of this new world.

Instruction in the skills of properly using different sources of information involves several principles worth noting. The teacher should:[49]

1. Provide for individual differences in pupil's abilities, interests, and needs wherever possible by small-group instruction and by using instructional materials of varying levels of difficulty.
2. Deal with individuals or small groups selected on the basis of common needs.
3. Be sure that the pupils understand the purpose of the instruction. They need to know exactly what technique is being stressed and how it will contribute to effective independent study and research.
4. Lead the pupils to acquire feelings of responsibility for really understanding what they study. He should discourage rote repetition of words not fully understood, a practice which leads to verbalism or answering in the words of the book.

The Library   Carefully planned instruction in the use of library materials is essential if children are to make use of a library effectively for school activities and later as adults. The amount and type of instruction depend upon the library facilities available, both school and public, and the degree of familiarity the children already have with libraries.

Elementary school children should learn that:

1. Books are arranged in a systematic fashion (either Dewey Decimal or Library of Congress classification) and that this classification system is an aid to the user of the library.
2. The card catalog is an index of all books in the library, arranged by name of the author, title of the book, and subject of the book.
3. Books are shelved numerically from left to right, section by section.
4. Fiction is arranged alphabetically by the names of authors.
5. Other materials, such as filmstrips and records, picture files, atlases, etc., are in special areas.

In addition to the necessary knowledge suggested above, children need to know how to check out and return books to the library; find directions for locating books by use of the card catalog; use diction-

[49]Adapted from Mildred A. Dawson, *Training Pupils to Study,* Language Arts Notes, Number 3 (Yonkers-on-Hudson: World Book Company, 1955), p. 2.

Children can assist in making books available in the classroom

aries, encyclopedias, atlases, and similar reference sources; use special reference sources such as *Reader's Guide;* make use of bibliographies; and—one of the most important points of all—take accurate notes.

Behavior in the library, and care and appreciation in handling books are the result of direct instruction, supervised practice, and good example.[50] Speaking softly, walking quietly, and asking for help from the librarian when needed are all important to efficient use of a library. Teachers should also teach young children to handle books only when their hands are clean and to turn pages carefully. Insistence upon these practices with older children is not out of order.

Since the card catalog is the fundamental guide to materials in a library, particular attention should be given to teaching the following:[51]

1. An understanding of the purpose, contents, and value of the card catalog.

[50]Numerous films and filmstrips are available for use in teaching library skills. For example: *Library Series* (McGraw-Hill), *Using the Library* (Encyclopedia Britannica), and *Library Services* (Eye Gate House).

[51]Paul McKee, *The Teaching of Reading in the Elementary School* (Boston: Houghton Mifflin Company, 1948), p. 429.

2. An understanding of the meaning of the letters on the drawers.
3. Skill in finding a word in an alphabetical list.
4. Skill in using guide cards.
5. An understanding of the arrangement of cards in the drawers.
6. An understanding of the meaning of each piece of printed matter on each of the following types of cards:
   a. the author card
   b. the title card
   c. the subject card
   d. the author-analytic card
   e. the title-analytic card
   f. the subject-analytic card
7. An understanding of the meaning and use of "see" and "see also" on cross reference cards

In teaching children to use the library an elementary teacher should depend upon instructional help from a trained librarian. This instruction should always be followed by assignments by the teacher which require the use of the skills the children have been taught.

The Dictionary Most people are intrigued by words and it is natural for children to be attracted to the book that tells so many interesting things about so many words. Children also seem to have a natural affinity for names and pictures of objects arranged in alphabetical order. The dictionary is such a basic source of information that if it were possible to teach the use of only one reference source, it probably would be the dictionary.

Skill in using a dictionary develops slowly and requires the guidance of sympathetic and wise teachers over a period of years. While dictionary teaching is the responsibility of every teacher encountered by the child in his school career, particular attention needs to be given to its introductory teaching. Often the fourth-grade teacher has the task of really introducing the dictionary to children, but with the widespread availability of picture dictionaries for primary grade children, many dictionary skills can be introduced earlier. First-graders can be taught beginning alphabetizing, the use of a dictionary to find the spellings and meanings of words, and the importance of the dictionary as a source of new and interesting words. With the introduction of the beginning types of dictionaries in the third and fourth grades, most of the dictionary skills given below may be taught.

Basic to dictionary teaching is their availability. Each child should have his own dictionary at the fourth-grade level and above. In addition, each intermediate grade classroom should have other dictionaries available, including an unabridged one. It is important to remember that children should not be expected to go to another room, look on a closet shelf, move a pile of books, or ask the teacher's permission to get a dictionary.

☐ Dictionary Skills to be Taught

Often dictionary skills are taught only in connection with the reading program as a means for checking pronunciations and clarifying meanings. However, as pointed out by Trabue, "Dictionary training for the interpretation of reading materials will not necessarily enable the individual to use the dictionary effectively in facilitating his own expression."[52] Using the dictionary as an aid to expression must be taught deliberately, definitely, and specifically for this purpose.

The following is a list of the dictionary skills which should be taught, with the approximate grade levels at which they should be introduced.[53]

1. Learning the names of letters, recognition of each (Grade 1)
2. Learning alphabet, consecutive arrangement of letters (Grades 1, 2)
3. Learning location of letters in alphabet with relation to each other (Grades 1, 2)
4. Finding in any alphabetical arrangement words beginning with certain letters (Grades 1, 2, 3)
5. Arranging words alphabetically; beginning with different letters; beginning with the same letters (Grades 1, 2, 3)
6. Appreciation of dictionary as a tool and interesting source of much information (Grades 1–6)
7. Understanding that the dictionary is built on alphabetical order by first, second, third letters, etc. (Grades 1–4)
8. Familiarity with relative position of letter sections; *d's* come in first third of the dictionary, *y's* in final third, etc. (Grades 4, 5)
9. Using guide words to locate material on a page (Grades 3, 4, 5)
10. Understanding that words are listed by root forms (Grades 4, 5)
11. Using the dictionary to find the correct spelling of a word (All grades)
12. Learning the use of diacritical markings and key words as aids in pronunciation (Grades 4, 5)

[52]M. R. Trabue, "Use of the Dictionary," in *Teaching in the Elementary School,* (Nelson B. Henry, ed.), Fifty-third yearbook of the National Society for the Study of Education, Part II (Chicago: University of Chicago Press, 1944), p. 187.

[53]Adapted from listing in Iowa Elementary Teachers Handbook, Vol. 2, *Reading* (Des Moines: Iowa State Department of Public Instruction, 1944).

13. Learning the meaning and use of accent (Grades 4, 5)
14. Learning the meaning and the use of respelling to show pronunciation (Grades 4, 5)
15. Learning the meaning and the use of syllabication (Grades 4, 5)
16. Using the definition best suited to the context (Grades 4, 5)
17. Using the dictionary for determining the correct use of homonyms (Grades 4, 5)
18. Using the dictionary as a key to various meanings of a common word (Grades 4, 5)
19. Understanding abbreviations in the dictionary (Grades 5 and above)
20. Using synonyms and antonyms to clarify meaning (Grades 5 and above)
21. Using the dictionary to get related forms, irregular plurals, irregular verb forms (Grades 5 and above)
22. Using cross references for additional information (Grades 5 and above)
23. Understanding significance of word derivation, prefixes, suffixes, etc. (Grades 6 and above)
24. Learning about special features of the dictionary; e.g., table of measure, atlas, etc. (Grades 5 and above)

□ **Alphabetizing**

Some knowledge of the alphabet is acquired by many children even before they come to school. When the child starts school, he soon learns the letters in his name, if he has not known them before. As he learns to read and to write, he learns all the letters and learns more about their order in the alphabet. Learning the alphabet involves more than simply memorizing the order of the letters. It should mean knowing instantly where a letter comes in the alphabet, and which letters immediately precede and follow it. Some suggestions for teaching these skills are:

1. Asking questions at various times throughout the day which call for remembering the position of letters. Questions such as the following are appropriate:
What letter is before *i*, after *i;* before *y*, after *y*?
Is *f* near the first or the last of the alphabet?
2. Turning to words beginning with certain letters in a telephone directory, glossary, or dictionary.
3. Pointing to or saying any letter and asking the children to say the alphabet forward or backward to some other letter.
4. Arranging lists of words alphabetically. The first lists should be those in which each word begins with a different letter. Later exercises may be given which call for alphabetizing based upon the third or fourth letters of words.

5. Making alphabetical lists of children's names, names of cities, or names of objects. At first, attention should be given only to the first letter.
6. Arranging lists of words in which all words begin with the same letter.
7. Giving the children time to turn freely through dictionaries and explore for themselves.
8. Dividing the dictionary into quarters and learning what letters are in each quarter.
9. Practicing opening the dictionary to certain letters.
10. Practicing on such exercises as "If you are looking for *j* and open the dictionary to *h,* which way should you turn to find *j?*"

□ Guide Words

After children become acquainted with the dictionary and have developed considerable skill in alphabetizing, they are ready to learn to use the guide words at the tops of the pages in the dictionary. They may be shown the value of these guide words by such questions as: "Are there any words which come after the righthand word?" Children must be shown that to use the guide words efficiently they must have a thorough understanding of alphabetical order so that they can tell quickly when looking at a word if it would come before or after the guide word at the beginning of the page. The following two sample lessons should be helpful in teaching about guide words:[54]

> *Directions:* Notice the two words at the top of each page in your dictionary. The one on the left side is the same as the first word on the page. The word on the right is the same as the word which appears last on the page. These words are called *guide words.* Turn to a page in your dictionary and read the guide words. Look up the word *insect.* Between what two guide words is it?
>
> *Directions:* You may read the words below when studying about *airplanes.* Each word in the list is in your dictionary. Find each of the words and write the two guide words on that page.

Word	*First guide word*	*Second guide word*
propeller	————————	————————
hangar	————————	————————
aviation	————————	————————
airdrome	————————	————————
wing	————————	————————
beacon	————————	————————
ceiling	————————	————————
goggles	————————	————————
parachute	————————	————————

[54]Iowa Elementary Teachers Handbook, Vol. 2, *Reading,* pp. 173–174.

The line below represents page 472 in a certain dictionary. *Nest* and *new* are the guide words on the page. Underline the words in the following list which would be found on this page of the dictionary:

nest	**472**	*new*
lake		nerve
net		Negro
neutral		nail
neglect		nettle
nesting		next
nestling		

☐ **Other Dictionary Skills**

One of the principal uses of the dictionary by middle- and upper-grade children is for help in pronouncing words. These children need to be taught to use pronouncing keys and diacritical marks and to understand syllabication and accent marks. Diacritical marks are of value only as they help pupils with pronunciation. These skills should be taught in situations that call for their use.

Children need to be taught also to find meanings of words. In most instances, a child looks up a word not merely to learn the meaning, but also to determine the meaning in a particular context, or to use the word in a particular way. The following is a sample lesson for teaching this skill:[55]

> *Directions:* The dictionary often lists many meanings for one word. The use of the word in the sentence tells you which one to choose. Before each sentence below put the number of the meaning which fits that sentence. Make up four other sentences, using the word with each of these same four meanings.
>
> sup-port' (su-port'), v. 1. To hold up; to keep from sinking or falling; as pillars support the porch roof. 2. To bear. 3. To take sides with; to back up; as, to support a candidate. 4. To provide with food, clothing, shelter, etc.; as, he supports his mother.
>
> 1. He could not support the suspense any longer.
> 2. Many people must support a man to get him elected to office.
> 3. He helped to support his family by working after school.
> 4. The shelf was supported by braces.

Other Reference Sources   The use of an encyclopedia, atlas, almanac, biographical dictionary, or similar reference source involves many of the same skills needed for effective use of the card catalog or dictionary. In addition, the use of most reference books involves the ability to locate within the topic the

[55]*Ibid.*, p. 175.

particular section, paragraph, or sentence that will give the child the specific information he is seeking. Such an ability involves the skill of skimming, which is taught in relation to the basal reading program, but should be reinforced here and used in connection with gaining new ideas for use in expression.

Specific items to be taught concerning the use of an encyclopedia, the most commonly used reference source, are listed by McKee as follows:[56]

1. An understanding of the contents, purpose, and value of an encyclopedia.
2. An understanding of the form in which the material in an encyclopedia is arranged.
3. Skill in finding a word in an alphabetical list.
4. An understanding of the location of the index in an encyclopedia.
5. An understanding of the meaning of guide letters on covers of volumes.
6. An understanding of the placement of topics made up of compound words.
7. An understanding of the different types of encyclopedias.
8. Skill in using pronunciation keys.
9. Skill in locating on the page the particular information needed.
10. Skill in using cross references.
11. Skill in using guide words.
12. An understanding of the purpose of bibliographies given at the close of articles.
13. An understanding of the meaning of certain marks such as boldface type, parentheses, italics, etc.
14. An understanding of how to keep an encyclopedia up to date.
15. The attitude of depending upon the encyclopedia as one of the more valid sources of printed information.

As children use books as sources of information—as well as sources of pleasure—they often have need to use the table of contents, the index, and the glossary. The table of contents should be taught with the child's introduction to reading in the first grade. Teachers should give assignments which require pupils to turn to the table of contents or the index rather than simply giving page numbers. Many children's books have a glossary of new words used in the stories or lessons. A glossary is used in the same way as a dictionary. It is a help with the pronunciation and the meaning of the new words which are found in

[56]McKee, *Teaching of Reading*, p. 429.

that book. In doing research, children should learn to look for a glossary and to use it when they encounter a word which is unfamiliar to them.

The index of a book should be taught as a tool for research in that book; that is, a pupil should learn to use the index as a means of locating information on a given topic. In written expression, the pupil should learn to prepare an index for a record, report, or summary he has made.

The following skills and information concerning the use of an index should be taught:

1. The difference between topics and sub-topics.
2. What the different punctuation marks in the index mean.
3. How maps, graphs, tables, or diagrams are shown in an index.
4. The use and significance of the key or direction at the beginning or the end of the index.
5. Different types of arrangement of sub-topics.
6. How the pages of the most important discussions on the particular topic are shown.
7. Whether or not pronunciation is indicated in an index.
8. How to look under more than one topic if necessary to find the information wanted.

Exercises for Thought and Action

1. Evaluate the suggested program for teaching usage in terms of disadvantaged children and their language. What modifications can you suggest for the teacher in an inner-city slum?
2. Listen to your friends—including teachers—as they talk. Do they use words and grammatical constructions that violate your ideas of "standard" usage?
3. Suggest a series of exercises for giving children practice in separating sentence fragments from sentences.
4. State clearly the distinction between the so-called "loose *and*" and the "run-on sentence."
5. Illustrate ways in which the proper use of introductory words and connectives adds interest through improving the organization of the paragraph.
6. Visit an elementary classroom and list and tabulate the usages you think the instructional program should attack.
7. Suggest a number of devices which you as a teacher might use to improve the construction of sentences in the written expression of your pupils.

8. Without looking at the two columns at the right, record your personal reactions to the suitability of the usages in the Lewis study. Do the same for the usages in the study by Womack.
9. Devise a series of exercises designed to give your pupils practice in organizing sentences in an effective order within a paragraph.
10. Develop a series of exercises designed to give your pupils practice in alphabetizing, using the index, or using guide words in the dictionary.

Selected References

Arts and Skills of Communication for Democracy's Children, Vol. II. San Bernardino, Calif.: San Bernardino County Schools, no date.

Dale, Edgar. "Vocabulary Development of the Underprivileged Child," *Elementary English,* November, 1965, pp. 778–785.

Blair, Glenn Myers. *Diagnostic and Remedial Teaching.* New York: The Macmillan Company, 1956.

Dawson, Mildred A. *Teaching Correct Usage.* Language Arts Notes, Number 6. Yonkers-on-Hudson: World Book Company, 1956.

————. *Training Pupils to Study.* Language Arts Notes, Number 3. Yonkers-on-Hudson: World Book Company, 1955.

Deighton, Lee C. *Vocabulary Development in the Classroom.* New York: Bureau of Publications, Teachers College, Columbia University, 1959.

Evans, Bergen, and Evans, Cornelia. *A Dictionary of Contemporary American Usage.* New York: Random House, 1957.

Labov, William. *The Study of Nonstandard English.* Champaign, Ill.: National Council of Teachers of English, 1970.

Loban, Walter D. *The Language of Elementary School Children.* Champaign, Ill.: National Council of Teachers of English, 1963.

Mahoney, Sally. "Basic Study Skills and Tools," *Elementary English,* December, 1965, pp. 905–915.

Marckwardt, Albert H., and Walcott, Fred G. *Facts About Current English Usage.* Monograph No. 7, National Council of Teachers of English. New York: D. Appleton-Century Company, Inc., 1938.

Newsome, Verna L. "Expansions and Transformations to Improve Sentences," *The English Journal,* May, 1964, pp. 327–335.

Petty, Walter T. "A Composition Foundation in the Elementary School," *California English Journal,* Spring, 1966, pp. 66–69.

Pooley, Robert C. *Teaching English Usage.* New York: Appleton-Century-Crofts, Inc., 1957.

Rodgers, Mary C. *New Design in the Teaching of English,* Chapter VI. Scranton, Pa.: International Textbook Company, 1968.

Tidyman, Willard F., Smith, Charlene W., and Butterfield, Marguerite. *Teaching the Language Arts,* Third Edition, Chapter 13. New York: McGraw-Hill, Inc., 1969.

11

Grammar In The Elementary School

INTRODUCTION

This chapter is concerned primarily with the place of grammar in the elementary school language arts program. It traces briefly the historical development of grammar, presents the findings of research in connection with its use as a teaching method, discusses recent developments in the study of grammar, and suggests ways in which they may have application to the language arts program. Principally it is concerned with the presentation of a viewpoint toward the goals of the language arts program and the manner in which they may be accomplished. Naturally, any consideration of grammar as it concerns the elementary school is closely connected with concern over matters of usage in oral and written composition; particularly, the reader should refer to Chapter 10, "Skills and Abilities Important to both Oral and Written Language."

Special considerations of this chapter include the following:

1. Grammar and Linguistics
2. Developments in the Teaching of Grammar
3. Values Attributed to the Teaching of Grammar
4. Grammar for Today's Classroom

Grammar and Linguistics

Some teachers in recent years have adopted the term *linguistics* to identify what they formerly called *grammar*. Others, however, have recognized that *linguistics* describes a much wider area of study and have broadened their language arts programs to include semantics, dialectology, and the history of the English language. Still others have broadened the content of their teaching to include greater attention to phonology and morphology but with their programs still reflecting a grammar study rather than a language study emphasis.

Earlier sections of this book have defined *linguistics* (and the newer related terms) and *language* (Chapter 1); *dialects* and *non-standard English* (Chapter 4); and *usage, dialect,* and *grammar* (Chapter 10). Grammar is further defined in the following sections, and the newer grammars are briefly described.

The way grammar is defined is apparently dependent in large part upon the identity and the purpose of the one defining it. Grammar is variously defined in dictionaries—six different meanings being listed in the college edition of Webster's New World Dictionary. The first two are those most commonly used by language scholars—that is, that grammar is "that part of the study of language which deals with the forms and structure of words (morphology) and with their customary arrangement in phrases and sentences (syntax)," or that it is actually "the system of word structures and word arrangements of a given language at a given time." For the educated person who is not a language expert, one of two further meanings might come more readily to mind: grammar is "a system of rules for speaking and writing a given language, based on the study of its grammar (as a system) or on some adaptation of Latin grammar" or "a book containing such rules." The average man on the street might prefer still another: grammar is "one's manner of speaking or writing as judged by conventional grammatical rules." This last meaning is commonly used by students and teachers of the English language to refer to *usage* rather than *grammar,* while they would probably accept all of the others, possibly preferring the second—that is, that grammar is the system of word structures and word arrangements of a given language. This is the meaning which will be used in the present discussion.

The Meaning of Grammar

In addition to the various meanings attached to the word *grammar* and the distinction between grammar and usage, there are a number of adjectives frequently attached to the word which may also add to the

Types of Grammar

confusion. For instance, most teachers have heard of *traditional* grammar, *functional* grammar, *structural* grammar, *generative* grammar, and *transformational* grammar. The term *traditional grammar* refers to that description of the English language which is based upon the rules of Latin grammar; this is the type of grammar which was learned in the elementary and secondary schools by most American adults who are over twenty-five or thirty. That portion of the rules and generalizations concerning the English language which may be considered to be most useful in influencing important items of usage is called *functional grammar;* for example, the rule that the subject of a sentence agrees with its verb in number and person is an item of functional grammar. This term came into use in the early middle years of the twentieth century as language experts became convinced that a thorough knowledge of the principles of grammar does not necessarily bring about fluency—or even correctness—in speaking and writing. It should be emphasized at this point that the adjective *functional* refers to methodology rather than to a description of the language. That is, it is not parallel in meaning to *traditional, structural, or generative* but may utilize any of these systems for describing the language in the effort to teach children to *use* the language effectively.

Several decades later, the term *structural grammar* came into use —though it was not new: scholars had been working on this idea since the late nineteenth century. This term means the description of the language based on the way it is used rather than on the rules of Latin grammar; it was the structural linguists who first recognized that, while all languages have system, not all languages have the same system, so they set about describing the English language in terms of its own system. It was during this period in the development of the "new" grammar that such terms as *intensifier* and *class 1 words* came into being. More recently, however, a fourth term has come into use. This is *generative grammar*—more frequently called *generative-transformational* or simply *transformational.*[1] This system for describing the language is based upon a theoretical model or description of the way language works rather than upon a corpus from the language as is the case with structural grammar. The principal identifying characteristic is a belief in the ability of a speaker to produce an infinite number of sentences he has not heard before. That is, given a basic

[1]For a dicussion of structural and generative grammars see J. Donald Bowen, "The Structure of Language" in *Linguistics in School Programs* (Albert H. Marckwardt, ed.), The Sixty-ninth Yearbook of the National Society for the Study of Education, Part II (Chicago: The University of Chicago Press, 1970), pp. 36–63.

sentence pattern, an individual can generate endless variations of this pattern by moving, substituting, and/or adding specific parts.

Developments in the Teaching of Grammar

The teaching of grammar in the elementary school has been the subject of much controversy for many years. The controversy has continued in spite of the accumulation of research evidence negating its value in improving oral and written expression and the failure by its advocates to establish other valid reasons for teaching it to the exclusion of other subject matter. These facts merit the following discussion of the historical antecedents of present circumstances.

The rise in the eighteenth century of a wealthy middle class of merchants led to the writing of systematic grammars. Aspiring to social prominence, these newly wealthy families employed tutors to help them gain refinement of diction and usage. These tutors knew that English had no rules, no authority, upon which spellings, style, or usage could be based. Thus, they based their judgments of correctness and elegance upon the system of grammar they knew best—that of Latin. That this should have happened is not surprising. Latin was the language of learning, since it was the language of the church, which had preserved and perpetuated learning throughout the Middle Ages; and it was also the ancestor of French, considered to be the most elegant of languages since it had once been the official tongue of the English court. Therefore, since the eighteenth century was an age of elegance and formality, its scholars set about formulating rules for the use of the English language based upon Latin grammatical structure and on usage found in formal literary works and language which had traditionally been considered learned and elegant. Great credit must be given to their work, but notice must also be given to its weaknesses. First, while recognizing that language has system, they erroneously presupposed that all languages have the same system. Second, they failed to realize that language is a living, growing, changing thing; therefore, being true products of their century, they attempted to *prescribe* what correct usage should be rather than to *describe* what it was even in their own day.

Traditional Grammar Backgrounds

This formalized approach to the study of language thus became the rule. With the recognition of composition as a school subject about the middle of the nineteenth century, grammar continued to occupy a prominent position in the language curriculum. Because Latin and the other formal and disciplinary subjects still actively dominated the curriculum, it was natural for composition and language instruction to be considered a content subject rather than a skill subject, with the study of grammar as its chief content. Instructional emphasis in the English classroom was devoted almost entirely to learning the tenses of verbs and the cases of nouns, diagramming and analyzing sentences, and memorizing rules. What little opportunity for oral or written expression the pupils enjoyed was in the form of memorized orations or declamations and the writing of formal themes and compositions. Long after the need for such activities as letter writing, reporting, and taking minutes of meetings was recognized, correct form was still considered a matter to be taught separately from production by means of drill and the repetition of rules.

Opposition to the imposition of such arbitrary standards has been expressed from the time of Shakespeare to the present, and every observant student has noticed that reputable writers and speakers do not always follow the rules laid down by grammar books. Many examples could be cited here, but one is sufficient to illustrate the point. For years, traditional grammar books insisted that a sentence may not begin with *and* or *but*. Fortunately, some realistic English teachers have now abandoned this rule, but far too many still cherish and perpetuate it. Yet even in Latin, upon which the rules are supposedly based, one frequently finds sentences beginning with *et;* the King James translation of the Bible, so often praised for the beauty of its language, contains numerous verses beginning "And it came to pass"; while examples from twentieth century literature are legion—a capitalized *and,* not intended to show interrupted conversation, actually begins a short story often included in high school literature texts.[2]

The Influence of Research Toward Change

Despite such empirical evidence of the failure of traditional grammar to describe the English language accurately, the teaching of this grammar remained in a secure and almost unchallenged position in the school curriculum until psychology developed as a science in this country around the turn of the century. At that time many school subjects—such as Latin, algebra, geometry, and natural history—were studied for two reasons. First, the knowledge of these fields was considered the mark of an educated man. Second, mastery of these and other generally difficult subjects was believed to strengthen certain men-

[2]Katharine Mansfield's "The Garden Party."

tal faculties and thus provide the desired mental discipline, a primary educational objective. The accomplishment of this objective was dependent upon general learning, not upon the acquisition of specific skills. That is, the study of grammar, Latin, or mathematics was believed to develop the mind as well as to provide mental discipline and develop the power to think in an orderly and logical fashion in any similar field of activity. Specifically, it was assumed that the study of grammar would transfer directly to the individual's abilities to express himself verbally—that the ability to define and identify nouns, verbs, participles, conjunctive adverbs, etc., or to correctly diagram any given sentence would ensure fluency and correctness in writing and speaking.

As early as 1906 research reported that pupils in the seventh and eighth grades with no training in formal grammar did as effective work in writing compositions or in interpreting literature as did those with two years of drill on formal grammar.[3] A few years later, Briggs conducted a carefully controlled teaching experiment designed to reveal the extent of the transfer of grammatical skills to language abilities of seventh-grade pupils. He concluded that "these particular children after the amount of formal grammar that they had, do not, as measured by the means employed, show in any of the abilities tested improvement that may be attributed to their training in formal grammar."[4] This study offered conclusive proof of the failure of formal grammar to transfer to such readily identifiable language skills as the ability to state a definition, to apply a definition, or to correct errors.

In the next two decades Rapeer,[5] Boraas,[6] and Asker[7] in three independent studies corroborated the earlier findings of Hoyt and Briggs and led to the general conclusion that "knowledge of formal grammar influences ability to judge grammatical correctness of a sentence and ability in English composition only to a negligible degree."[8] This conclusion has been confirmed many times; two of the

[3]Franklin S. Hoyt, "Studies in English Grammar," *Teachers College Record,* 7:467–500, November, 1906.
[4]Thomas H. Briggs, "Formal English Grammar as a Discipline," *Teachers College Record,* 14:251–343, September, 1913.
[5]L. W. Rapeer, "The Problem of Formal Grammar in Elementary Education," *Journal of Educational Psychology,* 4:125–137, March, 1913.
[6]Julius Boraas, "Formal English Grammar and the Practical Mastery of English," unpublished doctoral dissertation, Department of Education, University of Minnesota, 1917.
[7]William Asker, "Does Knowledge of Formal Grammar Function?" *School and Society,* 17:109–111, January 27, 1923.
[8]*Ibid.*

most recent studies having been carried out by Kraus[9] in 1957 and by Harris[10] in 1960–62. The latter is of particular interest since it avoided two criticisms often leveled at such studies: that results are based on objective test measures rather than actual writing and that they are conducted over too short a period. Harris carefully validated his criteria in a pilot study, then conducted his experiment over a two-year period and based results on frequency counts of actual writing done by the pupils before and after the two-year period. One group was taught traditional grammar, while the other studied grammar only in connection with needs demonstrated in their own writing. Results of the study significantly favored the second group.

The use of graphic analysis or sentence diagramming was for many years a favorite teaching device of upper-grade teachers; its justification was that it illustrated the relationship between the various parts of the sentence and helped children to understand these relationships better. Two different studies led unquestionably to the conclusion that while diagramming responds nicely to training and is readily learned, it has very slight value insofar as production of sentence mastery is concerned. Barnett, for example, demonstrated that children could be taught to diagram sentences rapidly and correctly, but that the skills thus acquired did not contribute in any significant degree to an improvement in pupils' language usage or in their abilities to read and comprehend sentences.[11] Stewart also examined this problem in a comprehensive investigation involving twenty different school systems, with classes selected and balanced in all essential respects.[12] Again the children in the experimental group demonstrated that they could be taught to diagram, while those in the control group showed slightly more improvement in sentence mastery than did those who learned diagramming.

Fortunately, the use of diagramming as a teaching technique is disappearing; few recently published texts advocate it, though some

[9]Silvy Kraus, "A Comparison of Three Methods of Teaching Sentence Structure," *The English Journal,* 46:275–281, May, 1957.

[10]Roland J. Harris, "An Experimental Inquiry into the Functions and Value of Formal Grammar in the Teaching of English, with Special Reference to the Teaching of Correct Written English to Children Aged Twelve to Fourteen," unpublished Ph.D. dissertation, University of London, 1962.

[11]W. W. Barnett, "A Study of the Effects of Sentence Diagramming on English Correctness and Silent Reading Ability," unpublished master's thesis, State University of Iowa, 1942.

[12]J. Reece Stewart, "The Effect of Diagramming on Certain Skills in English Composition," unpublished doctoral dissertation, State University of Iowa, 1941.

teachers still assert its efficacy. To the writers of this text, however, there is good reason to question whether the patterning of sentences or the use of formulas for performing transformations which are found in the texts based on structural and transformational grammars may not be merely a modern substitute for sentence diagramming.[13] No evidence is presently available concerning this possibility, but it is to be hoped that research will be forthcoming. Teachers should watch for such research and evaluate its results carefully in relation to the goals of the language program.

The role of society in the development of the language arts curriculum cannot be omitted. For, as English-speaking nations became industrial rather than agrarian, as education became more widespread, and as new means of communication drew people closer together, the ability to speak and write effectively and correctly became increasingly an economic necessity rather than a social grace. Psychology had shown that one learns by doing, and research had demonstrated that the study of grammar does not teach a child to punctuate, spell, or write effective sentences. It would seem to follow, therefore, that he could learn to speak clearly and acceptably by having much experience in speaking; that he might learn to write, not by analyzing sentences and memorizing rules, but by writing and rewriting sentences of his own. Since a true learning experience demands that the activity be purposeful, the learning of the skills necessary to produce effective usage must take place in meaningful situations. That is, they must be taught as they are actually needed in the expressional experiences of the individual. Thus the functional approach to the study of language began.

Beginnings of the Functional Approach

The functional study of grammar is not concentrated at any grade level, presented in a series of lessons isolated from speaking or writing, or concerned only with traditional grammar. The functional approach is essentially the building of a body of concepts and understandings throughout the elementary school years. These concepts and understandings are developed inductively, again over a period of years. Foundations of understanding are built in the lower grades, with the formulation of principles extending into the junior and senior high school years.[14] The specific matters to be taught depend on the lan-

[13]See, for example, Paul Roberts, *The Roberts Language Series* (New York: Harcourt, Brace, and World, 1966), and *English Syntax* (New York: Harcourt, Brace, and World, 1964).

[14]Willard F. Tidyman, Charlene W. Smith, and Marguerite Butterfield, *Teaching the Language Arts* (New York: McGraw-Hill, Inc., third edition, 1969), p. 315.

guage experiences and the needs of the children. The teaching procedure is that suggested in Chapter 2. That is, the evaluation of the speaking and writing done in genuine communication situations provides the focus for remedying faults in expression through the teaching of grammatical (as well as other) factors making for more effective expression—agreement of subject and verb, verb tense, pronoun-antecedent agreement, etc. None of the teaching is formal; it all centers upon the improvement of the particular expression.

Critics of functional grammar, as well as many who simply misunderstand its intent, draw the implication that, when this approach to the study of language is used, children learn no grammatical terminology and skills are taught only incidentally, as and if the need happens to occur. Nothing could be further from the truth. It is true that class hours are not devoted to the identification of parts of speech or grammatical structures, but these are called by their proper names, and it should be presumed that the child will learn them, insofar as he needs to, just as he learns the names of the other children in his class. The skills needed for effective use of language are developed through a carefully planned program of meaningful activities which call for the use of these skills, and needed practice for the correction of errors is provided in the same way. The approach is perhaps best understood through an examination of its aims. At the inception of language instruction in the schools, its purpose was to develop in the pupil a complete mastery of the elements of formal grammar. Those who advocate the functional approach believe that today the primary goal of language instruction is communication—communication in all its aspects of reading, writing, speaking, and listening.

Structural
Grammar in
Schools

At about the time that scientific study of learning was beginning, scholars also began to study language scientifically. First to appear were historical and comparative linguistics; and, as scholars studied the history and development of languages, a number of important truths began to emerge. Of particular value to those interested in the teaching of the English language were these: first, that while there are families of languages, each has its own system, and the system of English is not the system of Latin; and second, that language is not static but changing. As long ago as 1891, the English grammarian Henry Sweet wrote that teachers generally fail to realize "how unsettled grammar still is,"[15]

[15]James Sledd, "Grammar or Gramarye?" *The English Journal,* 49:298, May, 1960.

and in 1894 Otto Jesperson proposed the thesis that change in language is improvement, not corruption.[16] Thus the necessity for descriptive linguistics was born.[17]

> The linguists learned to work inductively and to describe each language in and for itself, to distinguish speech from writing, to avoid rash value judgments and uncontrolled speculation, and to reject the easy circularities and evasions of pseudodefinitions in grammar. They came to demand at least two things of everyone who wished to lay down laws for the use of language: first, a precise knowledge of how people actually do speak and write; second, a reasoned justification for statements of how people *should* speak and write. Since most schoolroom grammars did not meet these standards, they fell into disrepute among competent linguists.

Replacements for these grammars, however, were slow in arriving, probably for two major reasons. First, the description of a language based upon "a precise knowledge of how people actually do speak and write" is certainly no easy task; one must discover how people do speak and write, differences in socio-economic and regional usages must be taken into account, definitions of terms must be agreed upon, and innumerable other problems must be satisfactorily solved. Second, many of the scholars were not interested in the problems of the elementary (or secondary) language arts teacher, but only in the pursuit of the task itself. Perhaps this is not a just criticism, for certainly the task of arriving at a satisfactory description of the language would have to be completed before it could be passed on to the schools. It is quite likely, too, that the influence of the linguists helped to bring about the recognition, even by confirmed traditionalists, of the different levels of usage as well as the initiation of studies of the actual usage of people concerned with writing and speaking such as those conducted by Marckwardt and Walcott.[18]

Leonard Bloomfield's *Language,* published in 1933, gave some immediate impetus to the linguistic movement in the United States. It was not until several decades later, however, that its impact began to

---

[16]The Commission on the English Curriculum of the National Council of Teachers of English, *The English Language Arts* (New York: Appleton-Century-Crofts, Inc., 1952), p. 275.

[17]Reprinted from *A Short Introduction to English Grammar* by James Sledd. Copyright © 1959 by Scott, Foresman and Company, Glenview, Illinois.

[18]Albert H. Marckwardt and Fred C. Walcott, *Facts about Current Usage* (New York: Appleton-Century-Crofts, 1938).

strike the curriculum, largely because of the work of such men as Trager and Smith,[19] Fries,[20] and Roberts.[21] After its slow start, the study of structural grammar gained advocates with amazing speed and moved at a steady pace from the university classroom, to the secondary school, and finally to the elementary level. The major drawback to its use during the 1950's lay in the fact that there was still much dispute over such matters as the number of phonemes in the English language and how they should be symbolized graphically, whether terminology should be entirely new or at least partly based on traditional names for the various types of structural elements, and even how these elements should be defined or described.

Not all of these disputes have been resolved, but terminology has become more nearly uniform. For example, in the sentence "The dog barked," the word *barked* may be called a *verbal* or a *verb phrase,* but is no longer referred to as a *class two word; dog* is a *noun, the dog* a *noun phrase,* and *the* either an *article* or a *determiner.* In other words, there seems to be a return to much of the traditional terminology, though some new terms and certainly new definitions have been added. It should be pointed out, however, to those who use this disparity as a criticism of the new grammars, that traditional terminology and definitions have not always agreed, either—for example, in the sentence "This is my hat," is *my* an adjective or a pronoun? Structuralists further add that no description of the English language, or any other, can be regarded as closed and fixed and that there is still much to be learned about the nature of language and of the English language in particular. Since language is a living thing, its description cannot be finalized, and the directions which linguistic study may take cannot be entirely predictable.

The Rise of Generative-Transformational Grammar

In the opinion of many grammarians and other students of language, the most promising grammar to appear in the past decade or so is one that is called transformational or generative-transformational and is based upon a theory about the operation of human abilities that are thought to underlie the production and recognition of sentences.[22] The theory appeared with the publishing of Noam Chomsky's *Syntactic*

[19]George L. Trager and Henry Lee Smith, *An Outline of English Structure,* (Norman, Okla.: Battenberg Press, 1951).

[20]Charles C. Fries, *The Structure of English* (New York: Appleton-Century-Crofts, 1952).

[21]Paul Roberts, *Patterns of English* (New York: Harcourt, Brace, and Co., 1956), also *English Sentences,* 1962, and *English Syntax,* 1964.

[22]Bowen in *Linguistics in School Programs,* p. 44.

Structures in 1957. Its basis is the belief that language capacity is a biological endowment. Thus if there is an inborn capacity for learning language, then a human should be able to use and diagnose a language to a far greater extent than might be possible simply from exposure to that language through his home and other environmental experiences.[23] This means that a user of a language can generate expressions which are utterly new to him—that he has not heard, that he has not read. The theory also asserts that the ability to learn and process language impulses is universal among human beings; all humans have this capacity for language—but not for a particular language. This would seem to mean that all languages have much similarity, though observation would lead even a novice at language study to believe otherwise. The transformationalist, however, would explain that the similarity is at the "deep structure" level rather than at the "surface structure" level that can actually be analyzed.

Grammars—descriptions of the structure of a language—which are based upon generative-transformational theory begin with a small "kernel" of sentence types and a larger number of rules for transforming these types by substitution, reordering, and combining of parts. The sentence types are limited in number and include the following:

Subject-verb:	The boy laughed.
Subject-verb-object:	The dog bit the man.
Subject-verb-predicate nominative:	The girl is pretty.
	Mary is a girl.

Transformations are applied to such kernel sentences, not indiscriminately, but in accordance with the almost illimitable number of formulas obtained through observation of the ways in which the English language is used. That is, one may not simply decide to move the determiner *the* to a position following its noun to produce "Boy the laughed," since this is not a grammatical utterance according to observed language behavior. He may, however, produce a question by removing the *ed* morpheme from the verb and placing the auxiliary *do* (plus the *ed* morpheme, to get past tense[24]) before the noun phrase: *Did the boy laugh?* Or, with the second type of kernel, he may perform a passive transformation by reversing the positions of the noun phrases,

[23] Richard W. Dettering in *Linguistics in School Programs,* p. 281.

[24] In this system any past tense (regular or irregular) is defined as the present tense plus the *ed* morpheme. In this particular case the spelling of the present plus the *ed* morpheme becomes *did.*

placing *by* in front of the second, and adding an auxiliary plus the *en* morpheme to the verb, thus: *The man was bitten by the dog.* These, of course are the simplest kinds of transformations; there are also formulas for adding adjectives, adverbs, phrases, and clauses, and for producing compound and complex sentences, etc., as well as rules governing such matters as the formation of plurals and tenses, the combination of various kinds of sentence elements, and the order in which these elements may be placed.[25] The study of the English language has shown that native speakers of it know most of these things, though they usually are unable to verbalize their understanding—that is, for example, they know without being told (or "discovering" anew) that the determiner goes before the noun rather than after it. In spite of this fundamental understanding, however, some linguists believe that by bringing this understanding to the verbal level and extending it, by studying the sentence itself and the many ways in which transformations may be applied to it, children can be led to produce in their own writing and speaking more varied and interesting sentences.

Values Attributed to the Teaching of Grammar

The value of teaching grammar has long been a debatable issue. Various claims have been made over the years as to the value of its inclusion in school programs, with theory rather than research evidence as the basis of most of these. Essentially the differences in regard to the value or lack of value of grammar teaching result from differences in beliefs about the purposes for the instruction provided and the way children learn.

Grammar Study to Improve Composition and Usage

As has been stated, the study of grammar in schools was initiated on the assumption that, through such study and the development of understandings about the grammar of the language, pupils would learn to write and speak more acceptably and effectively. Earlier in this chapter it was shown that neither knowledge about learning nor empirical research evidence substantiated this assumption. Some persons interested in the preservation of grammar teaching have discounted earlier re-

---

[25]Some examples of transformations are given later in this chapter, and were given in the preceding one. However, an adequate understanding of generative-transformational grammar requires considerable study; see references in *Linguistics in School Programs, op. cit.*

search in light of the development of "new" grammars. Yet there is no body of evidence supporting the teaching of structural or transformational grammar as a means for improving composition and usage.[26]

It would appear that the formal study of grammar, either old or new, will not automatically produce the ability to use language well. It is, however, already evident that many teachers are seizing upon one of the new grammars as "the" solution to their language teaching problems. It is probable that most linguists do not intend this interpretation, yet often their statements lead to the inference that such transfer does indeed take place. Roberts, for example, stated that "a student motivated to improve his writing will find a conscious understanding of the syntax an obvious help,"[27] and further, that "a knowledge of the grammar will bear not only on the writing the student does but also on the reading he does."[28] Such statements may well be used to support the teaching of a grammar as formalized as any of a century ago.[29] Teachers would do well to keep in mind the following principles, stated in the *Handbook of Research on Teaching* prepared by the American Educational Research Association:[30]

1. There are more efficient methods of securing *immediate* improvement in the writing of pupils, both in sentence structure and usage, than systematic grammatical instruction.
2. Improvement of usage appears to be more effectively achieved through practice of desirable forms than through memorization of rules.

Probably few linguists really claim any transfer of knowledge of grammar to fluency in writing or speaking, even though they sometimes appear to imply it. Roberts, for example, in the article previously quoted, went on to say:[31]

The Study of Grammar as an End in Itself

[26]Roy C. O'Donnell, "Does Research in Linguistics Have Practical Applications?" *English Journal,* 59:410–412, March, 1970.

[27]Paul Roberts, *English Syntax* (teacher's edition) (New York: Harcourt, Brace and World, Inc., 1964), p. 2.

[28]Paul Roberts, "Linguistics and the Teaching of Composition," *The English Journal,* May, 1963, p. 335.

[29]See the criticism of such formal study by Wayne A. O'Neil in "Paul Roberts' Rules of Order: The Misuses of Linguistics in the Classroom," *Urban Review,* Vol. 12, No. 7, June, 1968.

[30]*Handbook of Research on Teaching,* N. L. Gage, editor (Chicago: Rand McNally and Co., 1963), p. 981.

[31]Roberts, "Linguistics."

It is not to be expected that study of the grammar, no matter how good a grammar it is or how carefully it is taught, will effect any enormous improvement in writing. Probably the improvement will be small and hard to demonstrate and for the large number of students who lack the motivation or the capacity to learn to write, it will be nonexistent. But even these students can learn the grammar, and it is valuable for them to do so. For grammar is the heart of the humanities, and like other humane studies its ultimate justification is that it informs the mind and teaches its own uses.

In other words, some linguists (to the extent that this statement is representative) accept the premise that certain things are valuable to know in and for themselves. If, in the words of Pope, "the proper study of mankind is man," then surely the language of mankind is also a proper study. The truth of such a statement would seem irrefutable. But the body of knowledge which it would be interesting and valuable to know is enough to consume a lifetime of study without reaching its end. The questions the elementary teacher must ask himself are these: What learnings are most important to the child? Is a knowledge of grammar valuable or necessary to all pupils at every grade level? Considering the time available, should such knowledge take precedence over the ability to read with understanding and appreciation; to use the skills of spelling, punctuation, and capitalization; to listen thoughtfully and courteously; to speak intelligently and interestingly; and to write clearly and correctly?

Should grammar be taught then? The answer, of course, depends largely upon the answers to the questions above. Certainly pupils and classroom groups will vary greatly in abilities and needs. Certainly, too, the attempt to teach a detailed and formal grammar can be frustrating to both teacher and pupils, often disregards interests and needs, and usually is done at the expense of genuine communicative activities.

This, however, does not mean that usage should not be taught, that appropriate grammatical terminology should not be used in referring to elements of sentence structure, or that explanations should not be given regarding usage or the conventions of punctuation and capitalization. It does mean that as grammar is taught, it should be taught in connection with writing or speaking. The teaching must not be haphazard, however, but must be carefully planned to provide for the presentation of those skills, conventions, items of usage, and techniques that the child will need in his writing and speaking, both in school and out. The grammar taught should be functional rather than theoretical and learned inductively rather than deductively.

For many years elementary teachers have been prodded into teaching grammar by the complaints of secondary teachers of English that the pupils who come to them are unable to identify the parts of speech or to tell a subject from a predicate. Such complaints frequently exaggerate the supposed deficiences and often result from (1) a lack of understanding of the functional teaching that has been done—which, for example, would have been directed at helping children choose the best verb or the proper tense and person; (2) a failure to recognize the role of the elementary school in the total program; and (3) perhaps also a mistaken belief in the theory of transfer along with ignorance of research. Certainly one of the goals of the elementary school is to prepare its pupils for the secondary school, just as preparing its students for college work is a function of the high school. Again, every teacher should carefully re-examine the goals of the total language arts program. Are these goals centered around the learning of grammar or are they centered around the acquisition of the skills of communication in both its expressive and receptive aspects?

The Study of Grammar to Satisfy Future Educational Needs

Until quite recently, one of the reasons given for the teaching of grammar in the elementary schools was to prepare pupils for the study of foreign languages in the secondary school. Some foreign language teachers vociferously asserted the necessity for a thorough understanding of grammatical principles as a preparation for the study of French, Spanish, or any other language taught in the secondary school. In the past decade, however, foreign languages have not only moved into the elementary school in many areas, but have converted almost universally to the use of the oral-aural method of teaching. Presumably the makers of foreign language programs have recognized the truth of what experimental psychology has long been proclaiming: that language is learned through it use. Perhaps it is time for the teacher of the English language to take a leaf from the notebook of the French or Spanish teacher. Programs for disadvantaged youth are already utilizing this technique, and it seems probable that the nondisadvantaged might profit from it as well.

Grammar for Today's Classroom

As has been demonstrated in the preceding sections, the teaching of traditional grammar failed to improve the quality of children's speech and writing. Equally, the teaching of a linguistically-oriented grammar has resulted in the same failure. But, as one writer points out,[32]

> . . . perhaps some of us have had unrealistic expectations of what linguistics should do. A knowledge of linguistics should reasonably be expected to have one major result, i.e., an enlightened understanding of how our language system works. If this is true, then the criterion for evaluating the merits of instruction in generative grammar, or structural grammar, or traditional grammar should be simply, "How well does it enable the student to understand how language works?" This question may be a very different one from that of how well it aids a student in writing, or speaking, or reading. It may very well be that the latter question is not a fair question at all.

Such a statement should lead the teacher to re-examine the objectives of the language arts program. Surely some understanding of language and the way it works is a laudable goal, but the primary objective is to help each pupil to achieve his optimum level of development in the use of the tools of communication—reading, writing, speaking, and listening.

Grammar and the Textbook

As suggested above, a considerable amount of grammar teaching continues to be done in the elementary classroom. A primary reason for this is surely that the textbooks used generally include various items of grammatical information for teaching. Further, usage items presented for teaching, even in recently published texts and those purporting to be based on linguistic principles, are frequently outdated or unimportant. For example, nearly all language series published in the 1960's contain exercises teaching the distinction between *can* and *may,* despite the fact that this distinction was shown to be disappearing as long ago as the 1930's[33] (Few writers observe it currently.). Similarly, these same texts teach the use of the nominative pronoun after *be* (e.g., "That is he," "It is I") although observation and research demonstrate conclusively that this is a usage seldom observed in oral language and virtually never called for in writing.

In view of such incontrovertible evidence, the teacher should be constantly aware, as suggested in Chapter 10, that the textbook is a tool, not an arbiter to be religiously followed. It should be used as needed and with discrimination, according to the needs of a particular class or of particular children.

[32]O'Donnell, "Research in Linguistics," p. 411.
[33]See studies by Leonard (cited in Chapter 10) and by Marckwardt and Walcott (cited earlier in this chapter).

The foregoing should not be interpreted as meaning that the study of grammar does not have its uses. Language scholars have provided much valuable information—and some equally important attitudes— about language. The teacher of language arts should become acquainted with this knowledge and these attitudes; the more he knows about language, the better able he will be to help children learn to use it. The pitfall he must avoid is attempting to teach grammar to children, either in and for itself or as a means of improving their ability to write and speak. Marckwardt has said:[34]

> . . . we may speak about and even hope for some influence of new concepts of language in textbooks and in the classroom, but this is a far cry from the direct teaching of a hitherto unknown or neglected body of subject matter. The impact of linguistics is likely to be greater in terms of the way the teacher and the textbook writer think about language than in any specific body of procedural gimmickry.

The way a teacher thinks about language is almost certain to be dependent upon what he knows about language. If that knowledge is limited to what he was taught in elementary and secondary schools, it is highly likely that his attitudes about such matters as dialects and levels of usage may be influenced by prejudices of an earlier day and that he may think of grammar as prescriptive rather than descriptive. The teacher should seek out courses in structural and/or generative-transformational grammar that are offered by most colleges and universities and should read as widely as possible on the subject. The reasons for this are two-fold: first, the science of linguistics is a subject of much interest and discussion in educational circles, so the teacher should not be ignorant of it; and, second, the teacher must himself understand the workings of language if he is to help children learn to use it effectively. The attitudes which he may be hoped to develop as a result of this study may do much to influence the language arts program of his classroom.

1. He will recognize that grammar is descriptive rather than prescriptive. This should lead him to teach usage inductively rather than deductively, letting pupils learn through observation rather than through memorizing rules; to help pupils see that the language used by educated people is more effective because it is more acceptable to those people, not because "the book says it is right."

2. He will understand, and communicate to his students, the fact

[34]Albert H. Marckwardt, in *Linguistics in School Programs*, p. 325.

that language grows and changes. He will learn to observe the language of those about him, will become more aware of what constitutes acceptable usage, and will be better able to select from the textbook and other sources those items which are relevant to the needs of his class.

3. He will recognize that there are levels of usage, suitable to different places and occasions. Equally, he will understand that dialects and colloquialisms are not necessarily substandard; these understandings should aid him in helping children who come to the school using nonstandard English.

4. He will see language as a part of man's culture, rather than as merely a vehicle for its transmission—as a manifestation of man's (or a society's) needs, interests, aspirations, and activities. As a result, he will be more likely to create in children a desire to learn about words, to understand the purposes for which and the ways in which they may be used, and to be able to use them more effectively.

5. He will learn something of the ways in which children learn language and the relationship between language learning and child development; therefore, he will be better equipped to help children learn to use language acceptably and effectively.

A Language
Arts Program
for Today

Experimental psychology has shown that all learning takes place most readily when the motivation is strong. The functional approach in teaching usage, the common conventions, and essential language structure utilizes this principle by presenting the socially important skills for instruction as the need for them arises in the classroom. For example, there is the simple matter of using capital letters. In most instances there is little question of which words should be capitalized. There are, however, many rules that cover these kinds of words; at least the number would seem considerable to the child if all were presented to him at one time. Yet the rules may be mastered without undue effort if the various needs are introduced as they arise in meaningful situations. For example, when the child first learns to write his own name, he learns that its first letter is capitalized—and shortly he discovers that the other children's names also begin with capital letters. When he begins to read, he observes that each sentence begins with a capital letter. This is called by its proper name, not designated as a "big" letter, and thus the children's acquaintance with terminology is begun. If an alert pupil notices that the word which begins the sentence is not necessarily a name, this is an excellent opportunity for the teacher to begin building the concept of the sentence. At this point, certainly, no detailed grammatical explanation should be given; it is enough merely to explain that each new sentence begins with a capital letter and to point out sentences in the book. Opportunities for strengthening the concept will arise as the class dictates stories for the teacher to write on the chalkboard and on many similar occasions.

One of the earliest forms of written expression introduced in the language program is the writing of letters. Letter writing is a valuable activity not only because of its high social utility but also because it can be pleasantly motivated. Furthermore, it introduces or reinforces a surprising number of language skills, particularly those of capitalization and punctuation. The child has already observed that people's names and new sentences begin with capitals; as he writes his first letter, he has these concepts reaffirmed by the teacher, and he also discovers that such titles as Miss, Mrs., Captain, or Doctor are capitalized when used with names, as are Dear in the salutation and the first word of the complimentary close. As he addresses the letter (for in a properly motivated situation the letter will certainly be mailed) he learns that the names of the street, city, and state to which it is to be sent are also capitalized. No rules have been learned, and these learnings will need to be reinforced through other experiences, but the concept of common and proper nouns has begun to be established. In grade four when the social studies program includes the study of people of other lands, the child discovers that names of countries and the people who live in them are capitalized, as are place names such as those of rivers and mountains.

This is the fundamental concept behind the functional approach to grammar. No formal grammar is taught in the first six grades. Rather, the emphasis is upon increasing the child's experiences and understandings, his abilities in securing and sharing information, his competence in meeting the usage needs of his life in school and out. Such grammatical elements as are mentioned are not presented in isolated form. The program consists in the development of language concepts beginning in grade one and growing continuously throughout the elementary school. Rather than beginning with the study of nouns and verbs, subjects and predicates, the child begins by writing first sentences and then paragraphs. Emphasis is placed upon saying a thing clearly, completely, and interestingly.

Here the results of linguistic study can be particularly helpful. Generative grammar is principally concerned with the varying ways in which sentence elements are arranged, and certainly one of the major ways in which the teacher may help children to express their ideas in interesting ways is by encouraging them to experiment with phraseology, word order, and ways of combining sentence elements. This need not be done in a formalized way, through the application of complicated formulas for performing transformations. Rather, it should be accomplished informally through the encouragement of experimentation with word order, the giving of praise when something is well said, and the provision of many models of good writing.

A further use of linguistic knowledge in the elementary school might be the use of pitch in teaching punctuation. It appears quite probable that if children were taught to listen for the lowering of pitch, the number of run-on sentences could be appreciably lowered. Certainly studies are needed in this area, as well as in many other areas where approaches suggested by linguistic study might be helpful.

The matter of teaching acceptable usage is also treated in Chapter 10, and further teaching suggestions may be found on pages 101–104. The important fact to be emphasized here is that grammatical usage, like other language skills, must be established gradually and as the need is demonstrated. Also like other language skills, usage is a matter of habit and must be established by practice, not by learning rules. Generalizations may, of course, ultimately be formulated, but only *after* observation and practice. In teaching usage, too, the teacher should pay particular attention to studies of language and to observation of the language that is actually used by educated people in writing and speaking instead of relying entirely on what is presented in language texts.

It is important to remember also that the functional approach does not leave the learning of language skills entirely to unplanned, incidental teaching. On the contrary, the program is carefully planned so that opportunities for motivated teaching and learning will arise, and activities are designed that will call for those skills which it is desirable for the child to learn. The needs of individual children or groups may be discovered through the use of both standardization and teacher-made tests, as well as through informal evaluative devices, as suggested in Chapter 10.

The following principles, as summarized by Tidyman, Smith, and Butterfield, provide the fundamentals of the functional approach:[35]

1. Grammar is taught as needed in expressional activities.
2. New concepts and rules are learned inductively through the study of live language and therefore have meaning for the learner.

[35]Tidyman and others, *Teaching Language Arts,* p. 317.

3. Terms and statements of rules follow ideas and understandings.
4. The observation of language plays an important role.
5. Familiar generalizations, recalled and applied as needed in meeting new problems, gain increasing clarity and breadth of application.
6. The direction and rate of growth are determined by the teacher according to plan; development is orderly, systematic, and planned.

Exercises for Thought and Action

1. Distinguish between grammar and linguistics. How many variations in definitions for each term can you find?
2. Examine an elementary school language arts textbook for its grammar content. Does the book distinguish between grammar and usage items? Does the textbook attempt to teach grammatical principles through an inductive approach?
3. Examine research reports on the results from teaching a "new" grammar. See issues of *Research in English* and the *American Educational Research Journal*.
4. Present arguments for and against the teaching of grammar in the elementary school.
5. Prepare a lesson for some other grade level, showing how you would help children to improve sentence structure.
6. Plan a lesson in letter writing for a third-grade class. Show how the need might arise, outline procedures to be used, and suggest follow-up activities.
7. Find several definitions of the noun, verb, adjective, or adverb. Compare them, and decide which you prefer, giving reasons for your choice.
8. React critically to the statements of attitudes a teacher should have toward language given on page 385. Would you change this statement and, if so, how?
9. List ways in which the concepts of pitch and stress might be useful in the elementary classroom.

Selected References

Braddock, Richard, and others. *Research in Written Composition.* Champaign, Ill.: National Council of Teachers of English, 1963.

Cameron, Jack R. "Traditionalists, Textbooks, and Non-English Grammar," *Elementary English,* 41:143–148, February, 1964.

Carlson, G. Robert. "Conflicting Assumptions in the Teaching of English," *The English Journal,* 49:377–386, September, 1960.

Corbin, Richard. "Grammar and Usage: Progress but not Millenium," *The English Journal,* 49:548–555, November, 1960.

DeBoer, John J. "Grammar in Language Teaching," *Elementary English,* 36:413–421, October, 1959.

Gleason, H. A., Jr. *Linguistics and English Grammar.* New York: Holt, Rinehart, and Winston, Inc., 1965.

Hook, J. N., Jacobs, Paul H., and Crisp, Raymond D. *What Every English Teacher Should Know.* Champaign, Ill.: National Council of Teachers of English, 1970.

Joos, Martin. *The Five Clocks.* New York: Harcourt, Brace and World, 1967.

Lambert, J. J. "Basic Concepts for Teaching from Structural Linguistics," *The English Journal,* 49:172–176, March, 1960.

Lenneberg, Eric H. *Biological Foundations of Language.* New York: John Wiley & Sons, 1967.

Linguistics in School Programs. The Sixty-ninth Yearbook of the National Society for the Study of Education, Part II, Albert H. Marckwardt, editor. Chicago: The University of Chicago Press, 1970.

MacCampbell, James C. *Readings in the Language Arts in the Elementary School.* Boston: D. C. Heath and Co., 1964.

Marckwardt, Albert H., and Walcott, Fred G. *Facts about Current English Usage.* English Monograph No. 7, National Council of Teachers of English. New York: D. Appleton-Century and Co., Inc., 1938.

Roberts, Paul. *English Syntax.* New York: Harcourt, Brace and World, Inc., 1964.

————. "Linguistics and the Teaching of Composition," *The English Journal,* 52:331–335, May, 1963.

Sledd, James. *A Short Introduction to English Grammar.* Chicago: Scott, Foresman and Co., 1959.

Thomas, Owen, "Generative Grammar: Toward Unification and Simplification," *The English Journal,* 51:94–99, February, 1962.

The Teaching Of Spelling

12

INTRODUCTION

The teaching of spelling has long been a concern of teachers. This concern is a result of the easily observable fact that many children seem unable to spell words they commonly need to write. This concern is not new, nor are complaints about the effectiveness of spelling instruction. Worries about poor spelling have persisted since the thirteenth century and present-day complaints about instruction have their counterparts prior to the middle of the nineteenth century.[1]

In spite of the concern and complaints, there appears to be evidence that instructional practices continue to be influenced far more by habit than by research evidence.[2] In this chapter the research evidence is examined, with specific recommendations made for establishing an effective spelling program. The features of the program are discussed under the following major topic headings:

1. Spelling in the School Curriculum
2. Goals of the Spelling Program
3. The Instructional Program
4. Special Considerations in Spelling Instruction
5. Measuring the Results of Spelling Instruction
6. Diagnosis and Correction

[1]Thomas D. Horn, "Spelling" in *Encyclopedia of Educational Research* Fourth Edition, Robert L. Ebel, editor (New York: The Macmillan Company, 1969), pp. 1282–1299.

[2]Arnie E. Richmond, "Children's Spelling Needs and the Implications of Research," *Journal of Experimental Education*, 29:3–21, September, 1960.

Spelling in the School Curriculum

Spelling programs in elementary schools vary from the informal and incidental to those in which time is set aside for specific instruction and the use of textbooks which structure the program. While spelling is important only to writing and spelling instruction must be integrated into the total curriculum, an entirely incidental program cannot be defended.[3] Good instruction requires a definite and systematic program.

The Problem of Spelling

As children record and exchange their ideas and information by writing, they need to spell correctly the words they are using. Writing is done for the purpose of transferring thought from a writer to an audience. While it is possible to communicate in writing without all of the words used being correctly spelled, such communication lacks something in effectiveness. Too, spelling all words correctly in many instances is crucial. Correct spelling not only gives the individual confidence and independence in his writing and is often essential to his success in a vocational or social sense, but it also represents a reasonable if not necessary courtesy to extend to readers.

Although the teaching of spelling may be regarded as a relatively simple matter in comparison to instruction in such areas as social studies and science, the recurring expressions of concern, complaint, and even frustration indicate that the attainment of desirable instructional results is apparently not a simple matter. The difficulty seems to be that too little knowledge of the research on spelling instruction is possessed by teachers and too little is reflected in the commercial spelling materials that so greatly affect teaching practices. Certainly much research has been done, with a recently published comprehensive review of this research listing 244 studies in its bibliography.[4] Not all of the spelling research has been good research, nor are all questions answered. However, a thorough critique of this research by Sherwin indicates that there are many instructional practices that should be followed.[5]

Of course, no instructional procedures can ever alleviate frustrations traceable to the complexity and illogicality of the spelling of our language. However, excessive concern with the hybrid nature of the

[3]Carl Personke and A. H. Yee, "A Model for the Analysis of Spelling Behavior," *Elementary English*, 43:278–284, March, 1966.

[4]T. Horn, *Encyclopedia of Educational Research*, 1969, pp. 1294–1299.

[5]J. Stephen Sherwin, *Four Problems in Teaching English: A Critique of Research* (Scranton, Pa.: International Textbook Company, 1969), pp. 29–108.

English language, with the fact that it is studded with words lifted bodily or adapted from other languages, or with the lag in changes in spelling as compared to changes in pronunciation will not solve the instructional problems.[6] It is highly unlikely that it will ever be possible to change spelling to conform to pronunciation, and some authorities argue that this is not desirable even if it were possible.[7] Nor does it seem profitable to attempt to alleviate frustration regarding an inconsistent sound-to-letter relationship by teaching many generalizations about how sounds are represented. This would appear to be primarily the substitution of one source of frustration for another, though this conclusion is disputed by some spelling authorities, as will be shown later.

Frustration is largely eliminated through the instilling of confidence in spelling or in anything else. In spelling instruction confidence can be instilled in each child by (1) providing him with a definite and efficient method of learning; (2) providing words to be learned that are most needed in his writing activities; (3) making him aware of his skill in spelling and the progress he is making in learning new words; (4) making the spelling instruction period meaningful and interesting; and (5) developing in him an interest in his language and a desire to spell and use each word correctly.

Research has shown that spelling ability is related to abilities in reading, handwriting, speech, and written composition.[8] Correlations between scores on reading and spelling tests have been reported at, for example, .48, .51, .61, and .63, so it is not unexpected that children learn to spell many words by reading them.[9] However, the act of meeting a new word in reading does not automatically mean that its spelling will be learned. Words must be met frequently through reading for this to occur, and even then one study showed that 63 of the 222 most frequently misspelled words are among the 1,000 words of highest frequency in reading.[10] Thus, while there is a good deal of transfer of learning between spelling and reading, to teach spelling through reading activities interferes with the process of getting mean-

Spelling and the Other Language Arts

[6]Jean S. and Paul R. Hanna, "Spelling as a School Subject: A Brief History," *The National Elementary Principal,* May, 1959, p. 9.
[7]William J. Stevens, "Obstacles to Spelling Reform," *English Journal,* February, 1965, pp. 85–90.
[8]T. Horn, *Encyclopedia of Educational Research,* 1969, p. 1289.
[9]*Idem.*
[10]James A. Fitzgerald, *A Basic Life Spelling Vocabulary* (Milwaukee: Bruce Publishing Co., 1951).

ing by reading and is not the most effective way to teach spelling. Furthermore, there is little evidence to suggest that spelling instruction promotes growth in reading.[11]

Speed and legibility in handwriting are factors that are commonly mentioned as affecting spelling achievement. Certainly in many spelling tests in which time is a factor, a faster writer obviously has an advantage over a slower one, just as it is also obvious that an illegible word must be considered incorrectly spelled. Handwriting practice emphasizing legibility and speed will aid spelling instruction by enabling pupils to write with greater facility, which in turn should expand their written vocabularies and, ultimately, will increase their potential for scoring higher on spelling tests. Most commercial spelling materials make provision for handwriting practice, and most handwriting programs provide for the writing practice to be upon words which are most frequently written.

Speech problems also affect spelling achievement, with improvement in pronunciation and articulation and the development of the use of standard English resulting in growth in spelling ability.[12] Again, while the relationships between the language skills exist and a program which seeks to foster their mutual development is desirable, neither the relationships nor the integrated program will take the place of direct instruction in each area. This does not mean that spelling, or any other language skill, should be taught in a meaningless and rigid environment. Systematic instruction does not preclude a teacher's capitalizing upon the important role the interrelatedness of the language arts can play in the total curriculum.

Goals of the Spelling Program

In most schools the instructional program in spelling centers in the use of a textbook or a workbook; in some of these the teacher supplements the instruction suggested in these materials. In a few schools the spelling program (largely the selection of words to learn) is taken from the daily work of the children. However, regardless of the materials or the basis for the selection of the words, too often the spelling instruction is limited and not really correlated with the general program in language. The basic goal in spelling is, of course, to teach

[11]Gus Plessas and Walter T. Petty, "The Spelling Plight of the Poor Reader," *Elementary English,* 39:463–466, May, 1962.
[12]Jon Eisenson and Mardel Ogilvie, *Speech Correction in the Schools* (New York: The Macmillan Company, 1963), p. 200.

children to spell the words they are most likely to need to spell in their life activities as children and as adults. This goal sets only the general pattern for the spelling program, however, and must be expressed in more specific objectives if it is to be achieved. The following basic objectives should be a part of every spelling program:

1. To develop in each child an attitude that
   (a) recognizes that correct spelling is important to effective communication
   (b) creates a desire to spell correctly all the words he writes
   (c) instills a desire to spell correctly an increasing number of words and to understand and use words more effectively
2. To develop in each child the ability to
   (a) recognize all the letters of the alphabet in capital and lower case forms in both printed and handwritten materials
   (b) write all the letters of the alphabet in a legible manner in both capital and lower case forms
   (c) alphabetize words
   (d) hear words accurately as they are spoken
   (e) pronounce words clearly and accurately
   (f) see printed or written words accurately
   (g) group and connect the letters of a word properly
   (h) use properly any punctuation elements important to spelling
   (i) use a dictionary, including the use of diacritical markings and guide words
   (j) use phonetic aids in arriving at the proper pronunciation of unfamiliar words
   (k) use applicable knowledge of sound and symbol correspondence
   (l) use the most effective spelling rules
   (m) use effective procedures in learning to spell new words
3. To develop in each child the habit of
   (a) proofreading his writing carefully
   (b) using reliable sources to determine the correct spelling of unknown or doubtful words
   (c) following a specific study procedure in learning the spelling of new words

Research has established that 3,000 to 4,000 words are so frequently written that they may be considered basic for every child to learn. In addition, there are words of particular cruciality to writing and those which are frequently misspelled. These are also included in a basic list. Most commercial spelling programs provide a basic list in their books for the elementary grades, with some adding other words to it in attempts to teach generalizations about sound representations and structural patterns.

A Basic Vocabulary

Early in the language program children need to learn to spell the words they are currently using in their writing activities in school.

To some extent, then, the specific spelling words to be learned must be determined by local curricular emphasis. Children should learn the words specifically required for their individual needs as they arise. However, the teacher or local school staff should not be responsible for the compilation of the basic vocabulary forming the heart of the spelling program. Not only is this an expensive and technical task, but it might lead to grave omissions in words chosen. Moreover, the results of extensive research in this area are not readily available to the teacher, yet most commercial spelling materials have utilized this research.

The total number of words to be taught in the spelling program is perhaps not so important as is the stress upon spelling in all writing activities and upon the supplemental spelling skills of proofreading, using the dictionary, and learning to apply spelling generalizations. Furthermore, teachers must make adjustments in the list of words to be taught, unless the spelling books they are using do so, in order to care for the needs and abilities of slow and gifted learners. When such adjustment is needed, it should be done on the basis of evidence of the relative importance of the words in the basic list for a specific grade level or for the school. Teachers should turn to research reports for this help and not attempt to decide subjectively the importance or suitability of a particular word.[13] As Horn says: "It is important to remember that it is impossible to teach all the words which children need in their writing, much less all words needed by adults."[14] It should be noted that Horn mentions the impossibility of *teaching,* not the impossibility of a child or an adult *learning,* the words needed in his writing.

The Importance of Attitudes

Being a good speller is not simply a matter of ability to spell a basic core of words correctly, or even to spell many words. Certainly it is not a matter of making a perfect score on a spelling test. The good speller is the person who recognizes the importance of correct spelling, who endeavors to spell correctly each word that he writes, and who is equipped to learn how to spell new words independently. He knows

[13]For example: Ernest Horn, *A Basic Writing Vocabulary,* University of Iowa Monograph in Education, No. 4, 1926; Harry A. Greene, *The New Iowa Spelling Scale* (University of Iowa, 1954); Fitzgerald, *Basic Life Spelling Vocabulary;* Walter T. Petty, *Improving Your Spelling Program* (San Francisco: Chandler Publishing Co., 1959); and Henry D. Rinsland, *A Basic Vocabulary of Elementary School Children* (New York: The Macmillan Company, 1945).

[14]Ernest Horn, *What Research Says to the Teacher: Teaching Spelling* (Washington, D.C.: National Education Association, 1954).

that correct spelling will improve the quality of his written expression. He believes that the spelling words he is called upon to learn are important words that he will need to use frequently in his written work. In other words, the good speller has an attitude conducive to learning to spell socially useful words both through direct instruction and incidentally. Thus, while an important objective of the spelling program is to teach children to spell the words in a basic vocabulary list, that is not the sole major objective. The development of a favorable attitude toward spelling is also of great importance.

To develop in children a good attitude toward spelling, the teacher himself must regard spelling as important, as something that really matters. He should endeavor to spell correctly all words that he writes; when he has doubt as to the spelling of a word, he should use a dictionary to check himself. He should show children that the words they are learning to spell are words that they consistently use in writing and have need to spell. Simple investigations directed at their own and their parents' and friends' writing will show this.

Each child should learn to use a specific and efficient method of learning to spell a word, and should be required to study only those words which spelling tests and actual writing situations have shown that he is unable to spell. Asking pupils to study words they already know is a major deterrent to the development of favorable attitudes.

The teacher should require a high standard of neatness and accuracy in all written work. The standards should be developed cooperatively by teacher and pupils and should be consistently observed. Developing these standards will encourage in the class a spirit of mutual pride and cooperation in spelling achievement. To further this spirit, children should be allowed to help one another study and proofread for spelling errors and to give encouragement to those needing it.

The teacher should immediately attack any negative attitudes by encouraging and stimulating the children's efforts. Fault-finding should be eliminated in favor of determining the cause of spelling failure. Negative attitudes are also discouraged if the achievement of the class is emphasized and if individual pupils can see their own progress. Records of progress may be kept by the pupils themselves and any achievement appraised in the light of earlier efforts.

A good attitude toward spelling is basic to a successful program, but merely desiring to spell correctly will accomplish little unless certain habits such as those described below have been established.

The Role of Habits

1. *Being Concerned About the Spelling of Words Used in Written Expression.* For the child, this means teaching him to think "Is this word spelled correctly?" and "Am I sure?" This habit is established by the development and maintenance of standards in written work and by the teacher's repeatedly calling attention to the standards.

2. *Carefully Proofreading All Written Work.* This means examining each word carefully to see if it is spelled correctly. The teacher must insist that a misspelled word is a mistake in spelling, whether the child knows better or not, and that the only way to avoid the making of such mistakes is to proofread for spelling errors.

3. *Checking the Spelling of All Words About Which the Child Is In Doubt.* The pupil should ask the teacher the spelling of such words, or when skill in use of the dictionary is developed, he should consult that authority.

4. *Using a Specific Procedure for Learning the Spelling of New Words.* Such a procedure may vary from child to child (as is discussed later) but the particular steps a child follows should be thoroughly known by him.

The Instructional Program

As suggested above, spelling is most often taught in periods set aside for the purpose and with a spelling book which largely determines the words taught and the teaching techniques used in those periods. For this instruction two general plans have been identified and one or the other is typically used. These are the *test-study* and the *study-test* plans. Sherwin says ". . . the evidence is fairly consistently in favor of test-study. The poorer studies are the ones on the other, study-test, side."[15] In teaching spelling by the test-study plan, the teacher tests the pupils first to determine the words that each pupil does not know how to spell. Thus interest in spelling is not lost by those pupils who know how to spell all or many of the words in the spelling lesson, nor is instructional time wasted. The test-study plan of spelling instruction consists of these features:

1. A preliminary term or monthly test is given to determine the general level of spelling achievement of the class and of the individuals within the class.

[15]Sherwin, *Four Problems,* p. 107.

2. A test on each weekly (or other instructional period) assignment is given before instruction is begun on that assignment. Sometimes the test is preceded by the teacher's pronouncing each word as the pupils look carefully at it. Following this the pupils pronounce the words themselves. The pretest procedure may also be modified prior to the first testing by the teacher's explaining the meanings of words which in his judgment pupils may not know. Usually the first step of the test-study plan should not be modified, however, since both meaning and pronunciation of properly chosen words will probably be known.

3. The words that each pupil misspells on this pretest are identified by the child and become his study list for the lesson.

4. In learning to spell each word, each child uses the steps that have been worked out by the class, or by the teacher and himself if modifications have been necessary to fit his particular needs.

5. A mid-lesson test is given to determine progress made since the pre-test. A final weekly or lesson test shows the total progress made during the lesson and identifies words for later review.

6. Each child keeps his own record of spelling achievement on a chart or similar device.

7. Any words that the child misspells on the final test are recorded by him in a special review word list.

8. Each child studies the words in his review list in the same manner as he studied them in their original presentation.

9. At regular intervals testing of the review words for each child is done until all such words are mastered.

10. A final term or monthly test is given to measure the progress made since the administration of the first test.

The major difference in the study-test plan is that no pretest is given. The pupils begin the study of the words as the first step in the lesson. Thus all words in a lesson become the study list for each pupil whether he needs to study them or not. Also, usually only two tests are administered—a mid-lesson and a final one.

Many spelling textbooks or workbooks present the weekly list of words in context; that is, the words are introduced by their inclusion in a story or paragraph. This procedure, within limits, has value in making sure that pupils know the meanings of words to be learned. However, research has shown that the most efficient and economical method of presenting spelling words is by a list.[16] This does not imply that meaning is of no concern; but it is well to remember that if the words are carefully selected, they will be words whose meanings are known to children or which may be readily learned since they will be used in

The Spelling Lesson

[16]*Idem.*

the child's writing. Too much attention to a contextual presentation may simply be a waste of the pupil's time.

As to the amount of time to devote to spelling lessons, principles of learning and research in spelling indicate that no more than 75 minutes per week should be devoted to the spelling period.[17] Time allotment is related, of course, to objectives of the total program sought to be accomplished by spelling periods, to the abilities of the pupils, and to the efficiency of the instruction. With a favorable attitude on the part of t..e pupils and a spirited attack upon the learning of the words in the lesson, as little as 60 minutes per week may be allotted to learning these words. Certainly efficient procedures and good attitudes and habits prevent dawdling and loss of interest.

A typical weekly spelling program, which has taken into account research evidence regarding instruction, has these features:

First Day.   Administering the pretest on the words in the lesson. (See the form of test below.) Checking the tests, each pupil checking his own. Making individual study lists of words misspelled. Discussing the words as necessary—their meanings and use, any unusual spellings, the application of any spelling rules, or etymological matters that are appropriate and of interest.

Second Day.   Visual and auditory study of structural and phonemic elements in the words. Study of the words on the individual spelling lists.

Third Day.   Administering of a test (usually including all words in the lesson as a means of insuring that guessing did not account for some correct spelling on the pretest). Checking the test, again each pupil checking his own. Studying the words misspelled.

Fourth Day.   Continued practice in visual-aural analysis of the words. Learning new meanings for the words. Extending word knowledge through practice in using linguistic principles. Studying words misspelled on the third-day test.

Fifth Day.   Administering the final test. Checking the tests, still each pupil checking his own. Writing words in a review list. Marking achievement on a progress chart.

In addition, most programs provide for handwriting diagnosis and practice, practice in using a dictionary, and various word building activities. Newer spelling textbooks provide listening and writing ac-

---

[17]Walter T. Petty, "Handwriting and Spelling: Their Current Status in the Language Arts Curriculum" in *Research on Handwriting and Spelling,* Thomas D. Horn, editor (National Conference on Research in English, 1966), p. 2.

tivities, the study of word origins, spelling games, and special exercises and activities for the less able and more able children.[18]

Modern spelling programs incorporate the findings of research in presenting the steps in learning to spell a word. The steps involve visual, auditory, and kinesthetic imagery as well as an emphasis on recall. Most of the children will need to follow all the steps, although many of the best spellers will learn the word primarily by visual imagery, and thus quite rapidly. The poorer spellers will need extra help and encouragement in learning the steps; they may also need to have the steps individualized, such as adding extra ones to help them say the words properly or to gain better auditory or kinesthetic impressions. The poorer achievers in spelling should be particularly encouraged to use the systematic study steps, with special attention being given to those which require recall since recalling a spelling is the principal ability needed to spell words correctly in actual writing.

Study Steps

In spite of the fact that most spelling books list the steps in learning to spell a word and suggest that pupils refer to these steps often, the best procedure is for the teacher and the class to learn the steps and use them without reference to the book. Teachers can guide children into thinking about how a word should be studied and from this guidance and the resulting discussion the children can themselves state the necessary steps. The statement of the children can then be written on a chart and hung in a place in the room where it can be readily referred to. Through their experience in studying words, the children may want to modify or revise their statement from time to time. This should be encouraged if any of the steps generally suggested have been omitted in the children's statement or if local conditions or individual problems seem to warrant some change. Each child should be encouraged to determine for himself whether the steps listed by the class are those he should follow or if some modification would be an aid to him.

The following method of studying the spelling of a word is suggested to the teacher as a model for guiding the class to develop its own statement of steps.

1. Look at the word carefully and pronounce it correctly. If you are not sure of the pronunciation, look it up in the dictionary or ask someone who is sure to know. Say the word slowly, naturally, and clearly, looking at the word while it is being said.
2. Cover the word or close your eyes, pronounce it, and think how it

---

[18]For example, see Walter T. Petty and Gus P. Plessas, *You Can Spell,* Grades 1 through 8 (Boston: Allyn and Bacon, Inc., 1964, 1966).

looks. Try to visualize just the way the word is written as you repeat each letter in sequence to yourself.

3. Look at the word again to be sure that you said it and spelled it correctly. If you did not, start over at 1.
4. Cover the word and then write it, thinking carefully how the word looks. Check the accuracy of your spelling. If you misspelled the word begin again at 1.
5. Repeat this again without looking either at the book or at your previous attempts.

The Lesson Test

In life situations words are seldom spelled orally or written in a list or columnar form. Aside from situations in school, spelling needs invariably arise when an individual is writing connected discourse in which he chooses his words and writes them without giving undue thought to the correctness of their spelling. Because of this fact many educators favor some teaching and testing of spelling words in contextual form. That is, the words to be learned or to be tested appear in connected discourse—sentences and paragraphs—as they are introduced in lessons and as they are given to children as a test. This practice is defended on the ground that it provides training in handwriting, punctuation, capitalization, and the form or appearance of a manuscript as well as making spelling more natural. Procedure of this sort, however, should be used sparingly. The experimental evidence favors a column or list presentation and testing of the words.[19] The list approach is also less time consuming and the other skills which are reputed to be taught along with the spelling are taught more effectively when specific focus is given to each of them.

Ernest Horn summarized the evidence on the question of the form in which spelling words should be presented in the following statement:

> Written tests are to be preferred to oral tests. . . . Recall tests are superior to and more difficult than recognition tests. The evidence indicates that the most valid and economical test (in spelling) is the modified recall form, in which the person giving the test pronounces each word, uses it in an oral sentence and pronounces it again. The word is then written by the students.[20]

However, the instructional program in spelling certainly should not ignore the pupil's need to spell words in context in all his normal

[19]Sherwin, *Four Problems,* p. 107.
[20]Ernest Horn, "Spelling" in *Encyclopedia of Educational Research,* Third Edition, Chester W. Harris, editor (New York: The Macmillan Company, 1960), p. 1340.

writing activities in other school subjects. This suggests that a combination of list and context dictation activities may provide the most effective teaching.

Particular attention should be given in spelling instruction to the correction of the tests. In the first place, tests should be regarded as learning activities as well as a means for measuring spelling achievement. The most important aspect of the testing is the "correcting" or evaluating that takes place after the test has been given. This evaluating should be done by the pupils—each pupil evaluating and correcting his own paper. Ernest Horn stated that "when corrected by the pupils and the results properly utilized, the test is the most fruitful single learning activity per unit of time that has yet been devised."[21]

To utilize the testing procedure most profitably as a learning activity, the teacher should show the children how testing identifies the words they need to learn to spell, how it is a learning procedure in that it calls their attention to the way they have misspelled a word and what they need to do to spell it correctly, and how it forces them to recall either the actual spelling of the word or those associations which are useful in spelling it. As stated above, pupils should correct each of their own tests and record their own scores, with only an occasional rechecking by the teacher to see that the checking has been carefully done.

Observations of the authors and others lead to the following suggestions concerning practices in spelling instruction that some teachers use but which should be avoided.

Practices to Avoid

1. The teacher should probably not waste time calling attention to known hard spots in words. While known hard spots for many words have been determined, a more positive approach is needed. Attention should be focused upon looking carefully at the word as it is pronounced, noting the structure of the word, the sequence of the letters, and the letter representations given to sounds, rather than upon watching for a particular place of possible error.

2. The practice of writing words in the air is of doubtful value. This practice takes time and does not give the child a realistic image of the word. Supposedly this practice is to give a kinesthetic impression of the word, but the result is questionable, since the arm and hand movements are generally not the same as in writing a word. A kinesthetic impression is useful to a few very poor spellers but this practice

---

[21]E. Horn, *What Research Says to the Teacher*, p. 17.

does not provide it. A tactile-kinesthetic impression can be gained through finger-tip impression in sand or on the chalkboard.

    3. Children should not be required to make repeated writings of words without intervening attempts at recall. The practice of having a child copy a word five times, or ten times, encourages poor habits and attitudes.

    4. The teacher should avoid condemning children for asking how to spell a word. Of course, this does not mean fostering the habit of some children who always ask, particularly for the spelling of words that have been in their spelling lessons. However, asking how to spell a word is an expression of concern with spelling correctly and should lead to using the dictionary and other sources for checking spelling.

    5. When a word is spelled by the teacher for a child, this spelling should be given in written form on a slip of paper or on the chalkboard —rather than orally. The effort of the teacher should always be to get the child to look at the word and thus gain a visual impression.

    6. The teacher should not use the studying or writing of spelling words as a form of punishment. This practice will certainly not aid the spelling program, and it is even highly doubtful if it serves as a very meaningful punishment.[22]

Special Considerations in Spelling Instruction

Perhaps the greatest area of controversy "centers on the question of whether competency in spelling can be obtained through a general use of spelling generalizations (rules) or not."[23] This is not a new issue since reports by Turner in 1912 and Archer in 1930 showed generally negative results from rule teaching, while Lester in 1917 and Watson in 1926 reported positive results.[24] Opinion at the present time is probably reflected in Sherwin's statement that, "After examining the studies and weighing their methodological virtues and defects, it appears that rules offer limited help in the teaching of spelling."[25] It should be added, however, that some spelling researchers today emphasize the *learning* of sound-to-letter generalizations rather than the *teaching* of rules. This question is discussed further in the following section.

[22]Adapted from Walter T. Petty, *Improving Your Spelling Program,* pp. 24–25.

[23]Albert H. Yee, "The Generalization Controversy on Spelling Instruction," *Elementary English,* February, 1966, p. 154.

[24]*Ibid.,* p. 155.

[25]Sherwin, *Four Problems,* p. 106.

Linguistics
and Spelling

Before the advent of the interest in linguistics the question of the regularity or irregularity of sound and written symbol correspondence was generally associated with "phonics" rather than with "linguistics." Hanna and Moore reported from a study of a 3,000-word vocabulary, for example, that "Nearly three-fourths of the vowel phonemes are spelled by their regular representations from about 57 percent to about 99 percent of the times they occur."[26] Horn reported from the study of a larger list of words that "The sound of long *a* (a) . . . was found 1,237 times, with 601 exceptions to the commonest spelling; the sound of *k* was found 2,613 times, with 932 exceptions; and the sound of *s* in *sick,* 3,846 times, with 1,278 exceptions."[27] From these studies and the conclusions of the investigators, differences in the interpretation of results and their implications for classroom instruction is clearly shown. On the one hand, it was suggested that the degree of "regularity" was great enough to warrant "grouping words about a phonemic family for a week's lesson and teaching the pupil inductively to *hear* the phoneme, then to *write* that phoneme with alphabetical letter or letters . . ."[28] Horn, on the other hand, stated that "One is hardly justified in calling spellings 'regular' or in teaching the commonest spellings as principles or generalizations when the exceptions are numbered not merely by the score but by hundreds."[29]

More recently, researchers at Stanford University have conducted extensive studies involving the computerized analysis of a vocabulary of 17,000 words. From this analysis these investigators report "that the great majority of individual phonemes of oral American-English are indeed consistently represented in writing by particular graphemic options when the main components of the phonological structure underlying the orthography are taken into consideration. Without regard to their occurrences in respective positions in syllables, consonant phonemes collectively were represented by an equal number of graphemic options over 80 percent of the time in the selected list of words."[30]

As a second phase of this study, the investigators devised a set of

[26]Paul R. Hanna and J. T. Moore, "Spelling—from Spoken Word to Written Symbol," *Elementary School Journal,* February, 1953, pp. 329–337.

[27]Ernest Horn, "Phonetics and Spelling," *Elementary School Journal,* May, 1957, pp. 424–432.

[28]Jean S. and Paul R. Hanna, "Spelling as a School Subject," p. 16.

[29]E. Horn, "Phonetics and Spelling," p. 430.

[30]Paul R. Hanna, *et al.,* "Linguistic Cues for Spelling Improvement," Report to U.S. Office of Education on Project Number 1991 for the period January 2, 1963, to December 31, 1964 (Mimeograph), p. 4.

rules for spelling the 17,000 words. This programming took into account "1) the simple phoneme-grapheme relationships, 2) the effect of position of a phoneme in a syllable, and 3) the effect of syllabic stress upon choice of graphemic option." A fourth factor, identified as "internal constraints"—such as a particular phoneme following another in a word—was also used. Results from this computerized spelling were reported as 49 percent of the words being spelled correctly, 37.2 percent with only one error, 11.4 percent with two errors, and 2.3 percent with three or more errors.[31]

From these studies the investigators report that "even a limited knowledge of the phonological relationships between the sounds and the letters of the orthography can provide the power to spell literally thousands of words. . . ."[32]

Certainly these newer studies represent constructive and substantial evidence which may prove useful to instruction in spelling. However, as pointed out by Fries and others, spelling patterns (i.e. consistency of sounds and symbols relationships) to which *readers* must respond is something different from spelling patterns to be produced by writers.[33] Too, it is well to remember that any analysis of how a phoneme is represented in writing usually does not recognize dialect differences in speech, that the same individual varies his pronunciation of many words depending upon their context (e.g. *and* in snow and ice, head and arm, man and beast, rod and gun), and that decisions as to the graphic representations of sounds call for a great deal of subjective judgment which may vary from investigator to investigator.[34]

There has been little investigation of the success from actually teaching children to arrive at linguistic principles which may aid them in spelling, even though a good many commercial spelling materials present words chosen for their consistency of pattern and organized into lessons which presumably teach children to arrive at generalizations regarding these patterns.[35] One study directed at the question does report that the "use of generalizations for spelling instruction

[31]Richard E. Hodges and E. Hugh Rudorf, "Searching Linguistics for the Teaching of Spelling," *Research on Handwriting and Spelling,* Thomas D. Horn, editor (National Conference on Research in English, 1965), p. 34.
[32]*Ibid,* p. 532.
[33]Charles C. Fries, *Linguistics and Reading* (New York: Holt, Rinehart and Winston, Inc., 1963), p. 170.
[34]Walter T. Petty, "Research Critiques—II," *Elementary English,* May, 1965, pp. 584–587.
[35]For example: Theodore E. Glim and Frank S. Manchester, *Basic Spelling Keys* (Philadelphia: J. B. Lippincott Co., 1967); Paul R. Hanna and others, *Power To Spell* (Boston: Houghton Mifflin Company, 1967).

appears to be less useful than Test-Study methods."[36] Other research on the question obviously should be done, but the perceptive comment of the late Ernest Horn a number of years ago that "the limited success in attempts to teach pupils to learn and apply even a few spelling rules suggests that we should not be too optimistic about the practicability of teaching the more numerous and complicated rules or principles . . ." is likely to be substantiated.[37]

On the other hand, children do make generalizations, in the same manner as all of us have learned to do as we transfer spelling knowledge of some words to new words that we encounter. In many spelling programs the children also learn to be cautious about the applicability of these generalizations, a fact that most adults learned in spelling programs in which there was no great emphasis upon spelling patterns. Of course, for years teachers and programs have taught children to note sound and symbol relationships by teaching word "families," the adding of suffixes, the building of compound words, the analysis of words into syllables, and the influence of context (as in choice among homonyms). Too, spelling authorities have long stressed the importance of careful pronunciation and the need for sight, sound, and taction in gaining images of words. The crucial aspect of teaching a program as suggested by these linguistic studies, however, comes in determining the actual procedures for helping children to discover phoneme-grapheme correspondences and to make these discoveries in an efficient, economical manner that results in ability to spell correctly the words they need in their writing.

The extent to which spelling rules should be taught is, of course, related to the issue of the regularity of sound representation. It is true that the inductive development of some understanding of the degree and kinds of grapheme-phoneme correspondence may lead to generalized understanding and not necessarily to the formalized stating of rules. On the other hand, the numerous spelling rules advocated by some textbook writers twenty years or so ago for teaching to children became formalized, and they were based upon generalizations about how sounds in certain circumstances should be represented. This kind of rule teaching proved to be of little value because of the many exceptions, particularly with respect to the words children most often

The Teaching of Rules

[36]Albert H. Yee, "Is the Phonetic Generalization Hypothesis in Spelling Valid?" *The Journal of Experimental Education,* 37:91, Summer, 1969.
[37]Ernest Horn, "Phonics and Spelling," *Journal of Education,* May, 1954, p. 235.

need to spell. The rules listed below have been shown to have few exceptions in application, and thus are of practical value.

1. Words ending in silent *e* usually drop the final *e* before the addition of suffixes beginning with a vowel, but they keep the final *e* before the addition of suffixes beginning with a consonant (*make-making; time-timely*).
2. Words ending in a consonant and *y* change the *y* to *i* before adding all suffixes except those beginning with *i*. The *y* is not changed to *i* in adding suffixes to words ending in a vowel and *y,* or when adding a suffix beginning with *i* (*busy-busily; carry-carrying; stay-stayed; enjoy-enjoying*).
3. Words of one syllable or words accented on the last syllable, ending in a single consonant preceded by a single vowel, double the final consonant when adding a suffix beginning with a vowel (*run-running; begin-beginning*).
4. The letter *q* is always followed by *u* in common English words (*quite; quart*).
5. English words do not end with *v* (*believe; give*).
6. Proper nouns and most adjectives formed from proper nouns should always begin with capital letters (*France; French*).[38]

In teaching these rules the following procedures should be utilized. (1) The teaching should be inductive; that is, the teacher should permit its development from the examination of words to which the rule applies. (2) Only one rule should be presented at a time. (3) Exceptions to rules should be shown to children. (4) Rules should be systematically reviewed and applied. And (5) emphasis should be upon the use of the rule rather than upon the memorizing of a verbal statement.

The brighter children, at all grade levels, learn to make generalizations rather easily, often without direction from the teacher. The slow learning child, however, does not do this easily. For this child it is simply much easier to teach the spelling of each word separately than to try to teach enough examples of the application of a rule to give it meaning for him.

Spelling Readiness A major contribution of the study of linguistic principles as they apply to the graphic representations of the words of our language is the surge of interest in teaching children to perceive sounds accurately and to discriminate properly among similar ones. Too often little recognition has been given to aural-auditory abilities in readying children for instruction in skills needed in reading and writing. Recently developed

[38]See E. Horn, *Encyclopedia of Educational Research,* 1960.

language and spelling programs, however, recognize this past deficiency and provide for increased attention to rhyming, to discriminating among beginning and ending consonant and vowel sounds in words, to associating sounds and letters, and to recognizing and identifying letters.[39]

Certainly the readiness concept is as important in spelling as in any other aspect of learning, and many teachers have in the past recognized this. Time and effort spent on readiness training in the kindergarten and first and second grades will provide dividends throughout the child's school life. A child who cannot recognize that *ball* and *tall* do not begin with the same sound, and that *him* and *men* do not rhyme, and does not know what letter begins *mouse* is not going to succeed in spelling; neither, of course, is he ready for beginning reading instruction.

Activities which help to develop readiness for beginning spelling instruction include the following:

1. Showing pictures of objects, two or more of which have names that begin with the same sound, and having the children identify those with the same beginning sounds. For example, show pictures of a *bear,* a *baby,* a *ball,* and a *lion.*

2. Doing the same for ending sounds. For example, *sled, bread, bed,* and *cap.*

3. Saying words and having the children hold up their hands when pairs of words begin with the same sound (or have the same end or internal sound—e.g. big-boy, fill-ball, live-give).

4. Saying pairs of words and asking the children whether they rhyme.

5. Having objects named and asking children to give other words which begin with the same sound (or end, etc.).

6. Saying a key word followed by several other words, with the children holding up their hands for each one that begins (or ends, etc.) with the same sound as the key word. For example: *soft,* followed by *dot, sit, sing, bought, fan, song.*

7. Giving much practice in careful and accurate pronunciation by having the children name many objects, identify pictures, give words which relate to other words the teacher or they have said, and—most importantly—actually talk about things of interest to them.

8. Having the children match pictures with letters which begin their names.

9. Doing the same for ending or medial sounds and the letters which represent them. Caution will need to be exercised with these activities since the letters representing some final sounds are definite (as in *men, bad, top*) while in others the representation is less clear (e.g. *sing, cake, ball*).

[39]See, for example, *You Can Spell,* Book 1.

10. Having children think of words which begin with the same letter and then say these words to compare beginning letters and sounds.
11. Introducing exercises similar to those above but which relate to consonant clusters rather than single consonants.
12. Practicing visual perception and discrimination by finding like and different objects, words, and word elements.

Readiness for spelling, as for other school subjects, differs with individuals. When children enter the kindergarten and first grade they are at various stages of development in their abilities to express themselves orally. They also listen with varying degrees of effectiveness. Recognition must be given to the fact that while language development does not proceed through distinct stages, children do pass through certain obvious phases. The first discernible phase is the ability to use and understand spoken language. This phase, as well as the others, is extended by the proper environment throughout a child's years in school, but it should be discernible before instruction is given which requires abilities beyond it, such as those needed for reading and writing. The second phase is that of relating spoken language to printed symbols—at first, particularly to those symbols which represent the words in the child's speaking and listening vocabularies. The third phase is that of written expression, including spelling. No phase is ever completely terminated, and the development within each is never the same for two individuals, but the sequence is there and must be respected to achieve instructional success.

Caring for Individual Needs and Abilities

Any successful spelling program should give attention to the individual needs of pupils and challenge each according to his ability. This is not as difficult a problem as it is often thought. Pupils should study only those words of actual written communication usefulness that they cannot spell. Thus if the list of words has been carefully selected, and if a child can correctly spell these words on the pretest, he need not study the words of a particular lesson. When a child has great difficulty with spelling, the number of words he is asked to spell should be reduced from the total presented to the majority of the class in order to develop the proper attitude toward spelling and to teach him how to study.

Children may be grouped for spelling instruction in a manner similar to the grouping for reading and mathematics instruction. The first step in instituting groups should be the administering of a quarterly, semester, or yearly pretest of 25 to 75 words (depending upon the abilities of the children to handle the mechanics of writing.)[40] The

[40]See *Construction of Tests* section further on in this chapter.

words on this test should be randomly selected from the words to be taught for the particular quarter, semester, or year. Children misspelling none or very few of these words may be considered the high achievers, those misspelling 10 to 50 percent should be labelled the average group, and those children misspelling more than 50 percent of the words may be considered the slow spellers.

The high and average groups may be tested for each lesson on all the words of a lesson, though some enrichment words may be added to the list for the high group if they are carefully selected for their needs in writing. For the slow group, one-half or fewer of the lesson words should be selected. The actual number chosen should be sufficient to challenge but not so great as to frustrate these pupils.

Testing pupils in groups with varying numbers of words assigned may be done in several ways. One possibility is to give the enrichment words to the high group, then give the regular lesson words to the high and average group. Have the slow group begin as their words in the lesson are reached in the testing procedure. Another possibility is to treat each group separately with the test being given to one group at a time and the other groups doing independent work. A third method involves pronouncing all the test words in the manner suggested with the high group writing each word, the average group every other word, and the slow group every third word. Or one can administer the test to all by simply saying, for example, "Group 1, hygiene—A good hygiene practice is to brush one's teeth after every meal—*hygiene.* Group 2, *during*—Be quiet during the test—*during.* Group 3, *idea*—I have no idea where he is—*idea.*"

For the child who learns spelling words easily and who has few spelling mistakes in his writing, enrichment activities should be provided. Of course, fundamentally such a pupil might be allowed to read or otherwise spend his time independent of teacher direction without any harm to his spelling achievement. Many teachers, though, feel that every child should be doing something related to spelling. Therefore, activities such as the following may be given to the "good" spellers:[41]

Activities for the High Spelling Achiever

1. Selecting synonyms and antonyms from words in a list
2. Using words in sentences to show varied meaning
3. Learning plurals, particularly of troublesome words as they are encountered

[41]Taken from *A Guide to the Teaching of Spelling Grades Two to Six* (Long Beach, Calif.: Long Beach Public School, 1951), p. 8. See also Walter T. Petty and Gus P. Plessas, "Challenging Superior Spellers," in *The Elementary School Journal,* 58:154–157, December, 1958.

4. Finding root words in large words
5. Adding prefixes and suffixes to root words and noticing their effect on meaning
6. Studying history of interesting words and reporting in class
7. Using words in some form of creative writing
8. Making titles or slogans for the bulletin board
9. Doing purposeful dictionary exercises
10. Making individual spelling graphs
11. Making word charts: synonyms, antonyms, homonyms, contractions, abbreviations
12. Forming derivations from weekly list
13. Listing words in early lessons for practice in alphabetizing
14. Learning words from local unit list
15. Studying library card catalog and telephone books to discover importance of correct spelling
16. Proofreading compositions to find spelling errors
17. Building compound words
18. Collecting samples of homonyms and interesting word usage from other sources in the school, such as library books, readers, newspapers
19. Adding to individual dictionaries words which are of special interest

Other activities which may be given to the high achievers—and to the others for motivational purposes at times—include the following:

1. Finding substitutes for overworked words such as *awful, funny, scared, pretty, good, glad, got*
2. Rewriting trite sentences using more interesting and specific words
3. Adding prefixes and suffixes to root words and explaining differences in meaning. Prefixes that are parts of names, as *Mac, Van, O'*, may kindle special interests in words
4. Forming plurals for irregular words, such as *wife, tax, foot, valley, mouse*. Listing groups of words that illustrate various ways of forming plurals
5. Finding the histories of words such as *desperado, digit, festival, vocation*
6. Finding and discussing the origins of new words, such as *radar, jeep, videotape, astronaut, backlash*
7. Making lists of words which may be spelled correctly in more than one way (*theatre* and *centre*, for example)
8. Having children bring to class lists of words grouped by similar sounds, roots
9. Providing crossword puzzles and the making of these puzzles by the children
10. Playing word games such as scrabble and anagrams

Perceptual development is helped by teamwork

11. Presenting words with scrambled letters and having the children un-
scramble them
12. Providing riddles which may be answered with words from a list

Children may prepare many of the products of these activities on
charts which will be useful to the entire class. Many of the activities
can be worked on by children working in pairs.

The child who has difficulty in learning and retaining the spelling of
the words at his grade level is often retarded in other areas of the language arts. The teaching problem is not insurmountable, however;
considerate thought given to his frustrations should lead to the conclusion that he "may best be accommodated through attention to relevant
factors conditioning spelling ability, such as particular disabilities, and
by a reduction in the number of words to be studied."[42] Particular focus
should be upon readiness factors (see page 408), even though the
child may be beyond the normal beginning stages of spelling instruc-

Helping
the Slow
Speller

[42]T. Horn, *Encyclopedia of Educational Research*, 1969, p. 1288.

413

tion, and to building favorable attitudes and good study habits. The suggestions below are useful in teaching a slow speller:

1. Emphasize the importance of the words to be learned. Teach only a minimum list and make certain that the words taught are important.
2. Teach no more words than the pupil can successfully learn to spell. Success is of major importance and the poor speller has probably had much experience with failure in learning to spell the words in the weekly lessons. Difficulty in spelling a word is not necessarily determined by its length or by the frequency or infrequency of its use. For assistance in determining the difficulty children have with common words, and in selecting those with which they may have success, the teacher should turn to a source such as *The New Iowa Spelling Scale*[43] in which the results of hundreds of actual spelling attempts by children are reported.
3. Give more than the usual amount of time to oral discussion of the words to be learned. In addition to making certain the meanings of the words are known, ask questions about structural aspects of the words. For example, ask what word begins with a particular letter, which word has a vowel sound like that in another word, which word has these two letters together, etc.
4. Pay particular attention to pronunciation, making certain the pupil can pronounce each word properly and naturally. Provide listening lessons calling for perception and discrimination skill.
5. Provide exercises for strengthening visual perception and discrimination. Such activities as inserting missing letters in words, substituting letters to make new words, putting syllables together into words, fitting words into outlined word shapes, and categorizing words according to some structural element are useful.
6. Strengthen the pupil's images of words by having him trace their forms with his index finger as they are written on the board.
7. Note any bad habits of study the pupil may reveal. He must be shown that the bad habit is harmful and may be preventing him from achieving success in spelling.
8. Check and perhaps modify his method of individual study. Have him study at the board.
9. Provide many varied writing activities which call for using the words he has learned to spell.

Spelling Games

The use of spelling games is advocated by some spelling authorities and criticized by others. Certainly games should not be substituted for direct instruction but they may be used to stimulate and maintain pupil interest.[44] Games which may be used include the following:[45]

[43]Greene, University of Iowa, 1954.

[44]T. Horn, *Encyclopedia of Educational Research,* 1969, p. 1289.

[45]See the teachers' editions for *You Can Spell,* for many other games. See also Paul S. Anderson, *Resource Materials for Teachers of Spelling* (Minneapolis: Burgess, 1959).

1. One child begins by saying, "Who can spell the word which means (for example) more than one shoe?" One child goes to the board and writes it. If he spells it correctly, he asks the next question.
2. Start with one child saying, "I am thinking of a word that begins with *gl* (or some other letter or combination of letters)." Children who think they know raise their hands. The child called on writes his guess on the board. If he is correct and the word is spelled correctly, he thinks of the next word.
3. One child starts the game by writing a base word on the board, such as *write*. He then asks for a volunteer to spell a new word which has this word as its base (*writing, writer*). One child writes the new word on the board. If he is correct he writes the next base word.
4. Write a number of words to which the endings *ed, er,* and *ing* can be added and see who makes the longest list.
5. Divide the children into teams of equal size. Pronounce a word and have the first member of each team write the first letter of the word on the board. As soon as a child writes his letter he runs to the second member of his team and gives him the chalk. The second member of the team then writes the next letter. This continues until one team completes the word correctly. The team finishing first receives one point and the highest score wins.
6. Write each syllable of each spelling word that has two or more syllables on separate slips of paper. Put all the slips of paper in a box and shake it. Divide the class into two teams. Have a member of one team draw a slip from the box and write on the board the spelling word which contains that syllable. If he writes it correctly, his team scores one point. Continue this, alternating from team to team, until all the slips have been drawn.
7. One child begins the game by spelling a word he knows. He asks another child to spell a word which begins with the last letter of his word. Continue in this manner, giving a point to the opposite team when a pupil cannot think of a word or misspells his.
8. Write two lists of identical words on the board (not in the same order), but with one letter of each word missing. Have a child from each team go to the board and put in the missing letter in the first word in his team's list. The second child in each team writes the letter for the second word, etc. The first team to do all words correctly wins.
9. Three children from each of two groups go to the board. Pronounce a word to each child, alternating between the teams and pronouncing the words as quickly as possible. The first group to say they have their three words spelled correctly halts the writing. The spelling of the words is then checked and if the group finishing first has all three words spelled correctly, their team receives five points. Subtract one point for each word missed. The other group scores one point for each word correctly spelled.
10. Divide the class into five or six equal groups. Give each child in a group a number. Have the 1's go to the board and write as you pronounce several words. Correct their spelling and tally the number of misspelled words. Have the 2's go to the board and attempt to spell the

same number of words as the 1's tried. When every child has had a chance to write, and the scores are totaled, the lowest scoring group wins.

The Spelling Demons

It is not at all unusual to find journal articles which identify and list spelling "demons," the words most frequently misspelled by children in their written expression. Too, school systems often present such lists to teachers, suggesting that these words be given special attention in teaching and review. The following categorization of many of these words into lists of those which represent similar problems is presented as an aid to teaching them more successfully.

☐ Phoneme-Grapheme Irregularity

Many words in frequent use are spelled in ways that include the representation of one or more sounds in them by a letter (or letters) that is not the most common representation of the particular sound. These words require direct teaching, particular attention to gaining visual impressions, and frequent review. Teaching them also requires that children learn the limitations of generalizations about sound and symbol correspondence as well as the benefits that may result from knowing the generalizations. Commonly written words which fall into this category include the following:

ache	believe	enough	they
across	birthday	friend	tonight
again	build	guess	thought
afraid	color	heard	very
already	could	mother	wait
among	cousin	one	want
any	dead	school	were
beautiful	decide	sure	when
because	does	the	women
	doesn't		you

☐ Homonym Problems

Many words frequently and persistently misspelled are homonyms. Some of these also are spelled with letter representations that are less commonly found and they, thus, might also be categorized with those above. Teaching these words successfully requires that the pupils clearly understand their meanings, know the meaning and spelling of the other word that sounds the same, and gain visual images of the words that can be recalled. The homonyms most frequently misspelled include the following:

there	hear	your
their	here	you're
they're	buy	write
two	would	piece
to	for	know
too	our	some

☐ **Failure to Apply Rules**

Many words are misspelled that would not be if the pupils knew and applied the rules suggested earlier in this chapter. Others would not be misspelled if they understood the function of the apostrophe, how words are compounded, and which words should be capitalized. The most persistently misspelled of these words are the following:

coming	its	Sunday
didn't	it's	that's
don't	getting	tried
I'll	sometimes	truly
I'm	studying	writing

☐ **Other Causes**

Improper pronunciation is a frequent cause of spelling errors. Words such as the following are often misspelled, in many instances probably because of improper pronunciation: *and, going, third, today, Saturday, pretty, hundred, kept, been, library, children.* Silent letters, of course, are a major source of spelling difficulty. Problems with the spelling of words containing such letters (and about half of the words in a dictionary do have "silent" letters) are related to those identified as having phoneme-grapheme irregularity and their solution requires that teachers make certain that pupils look closely at the words, identify specifically the letter representations of the sounds, and associate the generalizations that have been learned in reading class that are helpful in determining pronunciations. Some of the words with silent letters most persistently misspelled are the following: *February, Christmas, time, have, fine, like, are, safe, half.*

Measuring the Results of Spelling Instruction

There is much more to being a good speller than merely being able to do well on weekly spelling tests. The good speller is one who recognizes the social importance of correct spelling in all of his written expression, makes a special effort to spell correctly each word he writes, and equips himself to learn independently how to spell the new words he encounters. A child does not just learn spelling; he learns to spell specific words. Naturally such factors as superior mental capacity, outstanding vividness in imagery, ability to relate sounds and symbols properly, and an unusually retentive memory may all contribute to success in learning to spell. Thus it is obviously impossible to secure objective measures of all of the elements that contribute to spelling success.

The nature of spelling ability makes it extremely difficult to construct valid spelling tests. In the first place, the words tested should be selected from those which have been taught. This places a burden on a standardized test-maker since from classroom to classroom there is considerable variation in the words in specific lessons, to say nothing of the grade level variances in commercial spelling materials.[46] In the second place, the form of the spelling test should be as much like an actual spelling situation as possible. That is, actual spelling requires recalling a spelling or association of sounds and letters, so asking a child to recognize the correct spelling among several spellings given to a word is not the same skill. All of this means that the most useful means for measuring spelling achievement are tests constructed by the classroom teacher, if the construction is done properly.

Construction of Tests   It is important that the content of a spelling test be chosen from properly validated writing vocabulary lists comprised of words that are now and will be ultimately of greatest usefulness to the pupil's writing. Many early sources of such word lists, such as the one compiled by Anderson and used by Ashbaugh in constructing the *Iowa Spelling Scales,* Horn's *Basic Writing Vocabulary,* and Bixler's *Standard Elementary Spelling Scale,* have been used in the development of commercial spelling textbooks.[47] A valuable source of socially-evaluated and difficulty-rated spelling material for this purpose is *The New Iowa Spelling Scale.*[48] The 5,507 words comprising this list were screened from eight different valid vocabulary sources. If the direc-

[46]See Douglas F. Dickerson, "Misleadings vs. Actualities in Spelling," *American School Board Journal,* 120:33–34, February, 1950.

[47]W. N. Anderson, *Determination of a Spelling Vocabulary Based Upon Written Correspondence.* Studies in Education, Vol. II, No. 1 (Iowa City: State University of Iowa, 1917); E. J. Ashbaugh, *The Iowa Spelling Scale* (Bloomington, Ill.: Public School Publishing Company, 1919); Ernest Horn, *A Basic Writing Vocabulary,* Monographs in Education, First Series, No. 4 (Iowa City: State University of Iowa, 1926); H. H. Bixler, *The Standard Elementary Spelling Scale* (Atlanta: Turner E. Smith and Company, 1940).

[48]Greene, *The New Iowa Spelling Scale.*

tions accompanying the scale and those in the following paragraph are followed, this scale can be used as a source of material for spelling tests that will provide valid and reliable measures of spelling efficiency.

Teachers who are using no spelling textbooks or who are using texts which include words of unknown social importance will find these spelling scales valuable sources for use in selecting valid content for their own spelling tests. Words included in a spelling test should, of course, be selected from those comprising the list studied by the pupils.

Words selected from a socially validated vocabulary source such as *The New Iowa Spelling Scale* should be in the list studied by the pupils and should be selected in terms of their known spelling difficulty.[49] Common sense dictates that the words included in a test for any grade should be adapted as closely as possible to the average ability of the group to be tested. Some theoretical considerations suggest that test words ranging in difficulty from 14 to 86 percent standard scale accuracy with a mean of 50 percent tend to give a distribution of scores approximating the normal frequency curve with the pupil scores grouped closely around the mean.

The principle of sampling commonly used in all other testing applies equally well in the field of spelling. The number of words required for reliable results depends largely upon the purpose the test is to serve. For a survey of the status of spelling in an entire school system, a list of twenty-five carefully selected words may be sufficient. A much larger list of words is required in a test intended to reveal the spelling ability of individual children, while fifty words may be adequate for use with a complete class group.

The form of the spelling test has been presented earlier in this chapter in consideration of the weekly lesson. The following statement adapted from the introductory pages of *The New Iowa Spelling Scale* shows how a spelling test in the form suggested may be prepared and administered.

Let us assume that a fourth-grade teacher has checked the words presented in the local spelling textbooks against the vocabulary of *The New Iowa Spelling Scale*. This check has revealed that the following words taught in this grade appear in the alphabetical list of this scale with the spelling accuracies given immediately following each word.

[49]Throughout this discussion, *spelling difficulty* should be understood to be best represented by the percent of times a word is misspelled in a given grade without regard to, or from any information about, the previous opportunity the pupils may have had for learning the words. The quality as defined here is really "persistence of error" and should not be confused with "learning difficulty" as such.

List A				List B			
grade	67	month	50	luck	67	inch	50
floor	57	army	48	miles	57	copy	48
able	56	evening	45	unlike	56	fighting	45
track	54	gloves	40	party	54	meetings	40
boots	50	office	35	mails	52	program	35

In practice, there would certainly be many more words common to both the spelling text and the scale, and naturally many more than ten words would be included in the spelling list. Lists A and B are shown simply to indicate how two parallel and approximately equal word lists may be compiled. The words from List A are presented in the sample dictation test below. The score expected on these words prior to study would be approximately 50 percent for beginning fourth-graders.

Directions: Write the following words as I read them to you. First you will hear a word, then a sentence in which the word is used, and then the word. Do not begin writing until you have heard the sentence and the word repeated. *Write only the word.* Do not write the sentence. Be careful of your writing and your spelling.

1. grade	I am in the fourth grade this year.	grade
2. floor	The floor of the room was covered with mud.	floor
3. able	Jim was able to work the puzzle.	able
4. track	A broken rail on the track caused the wreck.	track
5. boots	How did you get your boots so muddy?	boots
6. month	School started a month ago today.	month
7. army	My brother was in the army two years.	army
8. evening	Every evening Father reads me a story.	evening
9. gloves	You may wear your gloves to school today.	gloves
10. office	My sister works in an office in the city.	office

The rate at which spelling words should be dictated depends upon the writing rate of the children. The proper dictation rate for spelling lists is easy to determine from observing the children at work.

The material should be dictated at a rate approximating the standard rate of writing for the grade. The rate of dictation is dependent upon (1) the rate at which children of the grade normally write; (2) the number of letters in the exercises to be written; and (3) the time required for the examiner to dictate the exercise. Experience has shown that the addition of 10 percent of the writing time will compensate for the dictation time. The accompanying table, based on standard writing rates per letter *adjusted for the time required for dictation,* gives the time allowance in seconds per letter for the different school grades.

Grade	2	3	4	5	6	7	8
Time in seconds per letter, adjusted for dictation time	1.84	1.38	1.18	1.0	.92	.83	.73

For tests in which entire sentences are dictated for children to write, the same attention should be given to timing and directions. In the sample test below the time factors in the preceding table have been utilized to show the rate of dictation. In dictation tests each sentence should be read only once. In beginning the test do not suggest that it is a spelling test. Something like the following is a good approach:

> I am going to read to you some sentences which I wish you to write down. The sentences are not long and you need not hurry. Listen carefully and then write each sentence or word as I have read it. Be careful of your writing and spelling.

In scoring this type of spelling test, only the words in italics are considered critical. In constructing the dictation exercises, the critical words should not be placed at the beginnings or ends of sentences since the child may not hear or understand the first word, or may not be able to complete the writing of the last word within the time limit.

Specimen Dictation Exercise and Spelling List

Start with watch at — **50 Word Spelling Test for Grade 7**

Start with watch at	
60	He is *evidently entitled* to the money.
26	Write a *brief description* of the man.
51	I *prefer* this *proposition* myself.
14	We have an *excellent commercial* club here.
43	We are *studying science* and *literature* today.
14	The city *council* will not *interfere* with the work.
48	We *acquire literary appreciation* through study.
22	The *annual agricultural demonstration* was held here.
59	The *university* is *altogether* too *crowded* this year.
35	The *superintendent authorized athletics* in the school.
14	Stop.

Now have the children write the following words on the blank side of the paper. Pronounce these words as you would an ordinary spelling lesson at the rate of about one word every 12 seconds.

Spelling List

bargain	league	absence	pitcher	handkerchief
regardless	salmon	unusual	confident	magazine
remedy	quarrel	pleasant	whirl	operate
assure	scenery	graduation	carnival	kindergarten
equipment	opposed	positive	charity	temperature

Standardized Tests   The best standardized spelling tests are those found as subtests of achievement test batteries.[50] These spelling tests are a means for comparing one school or classroom with another in terms of spelling achievement, but they do have the serious shortcomings suggested on page 269. They usually call for some kind of recognition of the correctness or incorrectness of spelling. For example, the test might ask the child to choose the incorrect spelling among several words or to mark words as right or wrong. Some variation of this is provided by at least one test at the primary and intermediate levels in that the test examiner reads the words for the child to spell.[51]

  A few attempts have been made to develop diagnostic spelling tests. The best known of these is the *Gates-Russell Diagnostic Tests* which purports to measure children's abilities in oral spelling, pronunciation, giving letters for sounds, spelling one syllable, spelling two syllables, recognizing reversals, learning to spell hard words, auditory discrimination, and study methods.[52] Provision is also made for recording handwriting speed and quality, vision test results, and hearing, handedness, and speech factors.

Diagnosis and Correction

The discovery from the results of repeated observation and testing that a pupil is seriously below his age and grade expectancy in spelling achievement may be of considerable value, but to have real value the test must also reveal the causes of his poor showing. The following information, which may be secured through observation and measurement, is helpful in identifying the pupil's disabilities and in analyzing his spelling habits:

☐ General Capacity
Measures of general learning capacity are secured from giving group and/or individual mental tests or using results from such tests if they are available.

---

[50]For example: *Iowa Tests of Basic Skills* (Houghton Mifflin Company), *Metropolitan Achievement Tests* (Harcourt, Brace and World), and *Stanford Achievement Tests* (Harcourt, Brace and World).

[51]*Stanford Achievement Tests.*

[52]A. I. Gates and D. H. Russell (Teachers College, Columbia University, 1937).

□ **Attitude toward Spelling**

Attitudes are revealed most readily from the children's previous records in spelling and by their scores on a series of carefully validated spelling tests.

□ **Reading Ability**

Reading ability is determined from silent reading comprehension tests emphasizing words and word meaning. In addition, oral reading tests should reveal superficial speech defects as well as deficiencies in pronunciation and enunciation.

□ **Handwriting, Legibility and Speed**

Handwriting difficulties arise through slow and faulty letter formation. Previous school records on handwriting as well as speed and quality ratings on standardized scales are useful.

□ **Visual Defects**

Visual defects are found by observation and superficial tests of binocular vision and visual acuity. If deficiencies are suggested, immediate medical examinations should be secured.

□ **Auditory Defects**

Observation and superficial tests may be made. If necessary, secure medical examination.

□ **School Attendance**

Records secured should include complete school history of attendance and age-grade progress data.

□ **Speech Defects and Maturity**

Speech problems may be noted from testing suggested in item 3. If needed, supplemental speech data may be secured.

□ **General Health**

General health information may be secured from school medical or nursing service data.

□ **Personality Characteristics**

Data from observations of pupil's industry, aggressiveness, independence, attentiveness, exactness, etc., may be collected and analyzed.

One of the most encouraging modern approaches to the identification of the causes of spelling deficiency seems to be the careful observation and testing of the work habits of the pupils. The failure of pupils to learn and utilize approved methods of learning to spell new or difficult words is one of the chief causes of poor achievement in spelling. Certainly, this is not always the fault of the child. Frequently he is not taught how to study, or the methods he is taught are not effective. Frequently little more than general observation is required to reveal whether or not the child makes a systematic attack on his learning of new or difficult words. Does he definitely center his attention upon the word; does he try to visualize the word, i.e., close his eyes and attempt to recall its appearance; does he say the letters of the word softly to himself; does he pronounce the word correctly syllable by syllable and try to recall how each syllable appears; does he compare the word with the correct written or printed copy; does he watch for silent letters, double letters, different vowels having the same sound, and for different combinations of letters; does he recall the word repeatedly until he has mastered it; does he develop the meaning of the word by using the dictionary, and fix it in his experience by using it in sentences?

Very frequently, words are misspelled because they are spelled the way they are heard or pronounced. Improper pronunciation by the pupil himself is more likely to result in misspellings than is mispronunciation by the teacher either in teaching or in testing. Imperfect hearing or improper pronunciation or enunciation of the words by his associates thus becomes a contributing cause. It is therefore imperative that children form proper habit of pronunciation and enunciation.

The lack of a spelling conscience or a critical sensitivity to correct spelling is a frequent cause of poor spelling in normal written expression. Pride in spelling ability and a sensitivity toward spelling errors must be developed to the point that it carries over into all of the normal writing activities in school and life. Pupils must come to feel a deep dissatisfaction every time a word is misspelled in their written work.

Informal
Diagnostic
Measures
The abilities and disabilities which condition learning to spell are many and varied. They range from mental and physical disabilities to attitudes toward learning. Horn reports the following as having been shown to be amenable to instruction or remediation: motivation; work habits; and special abilities and disabilities in vision, hearing, and speech.[53]

Spelling ability has long been shown to be strongly related to

[53]T. Horn, *Encyclopedia of Educational Research*, 1969, p. 1287.

visual perception, discrimination, and memory. Therefore, if a pupil transposes the order of letters, doubles the wrong letter, substitutes an incorrect letter, or inserts or omits silent letters, practice on accurate visualizing of words and recalling them (see page 401) will help. A simple check list in which the teacher records the exact kinds of errors a child makes will generally indicate the kind of remedial instruction that should be given.

Tests of auditory discrimination are relatively easy to devise. For example, a teacher may simply ask the children to record the letter representing the first sound in *jump*, the last sound in *sat*, etc.[54] Another approach is to pronounce pairs of words (*tag-rag, bag-bat*) and have the pupils indicate whether they begin with the same sound, have the same medial sound, etc. Any informal test of auditory perception or discrimination should be given to pupils individually to discover the auditory problems they may have.

Having pupils individually pronounce words as they are looking at them will aid in determining whether there are speech problems that may be related to spelling ability.

While special teaching attention can be given to some words, the main differences between the good speller and the poor one are actually to be found in (1) the study technique each uses, (2) their mental and personality characteristics, and (3) the emphasis each gives to the subject. These, of course, are strongly affected by the teacher and the spelling materials used.

Further Diagnostic Aid

The accompanying chart provides a summary of the many causes of spelling deficiency as well as remedial suggestions which the classroom teacher may profitably follow.

Diagnostic and Remedial Chart for Spelling[55]

Possible Causes of Low Test Scores	Additional Evidence of Deficiency	Suggested Remedial Treatment
1. Lack of experience with the testing technique.	Low score on test contrasted with high score when words are given on dictation test.	Drills on choosing correct spellings from lists of errors of same word; choosing correct forms from long lists, some correct, some incorrect; proofreading own written work.

[54]Wayne Otto and Richard A. McMenemy, *Corrective and Remedial Teaching* (Boston: Houghton Mifflin Company, 1966), p. 218.

[55]Adapted from the *Manual for Interpreting Iowa Language Abilities Tests* (World Book Company, Yonkers-on-Hudson, New York, 1948), pp. 24–25 with the permission of Harcourt Brace Jovanovich, Inc.

Diagnostic and Remedial Chart for Spelling (continued)

Possible Causes of Low Test Scores	Additional Evidence of Deficiency	Suggested Remedial Treatment
2. Emphasis on different or wrong vocabulary.	Low scores on test in contrast with good record for daily work	Check words not taught in your course with lists of known social utility.
3. Failure to develop a critical attitude toward spelling.	Indifference to spelling errors in daily written work.	Emphasize proofreading of own work. Drill on choosing correctly spelled forms in lists. Check pupil's certainty of his judgment of correctness of spelling.
4. Lack of teaching emphasis on individual's own spelling difficulties.	Observation of pupil's misspellings in daily work.	Have pupils keep lists of misspellings in daily work as basis for individual study. Focus on pupil's own errors. Try for transfer to all written work.
5. Specific learning difficulties: **a.** Faulty pronunciation by the teacher.	Observation of speech habits; informal pronunciation tests based on spelling vocabulary.	Look up word in dictionary. Pronounce it distinctly for pupil. Have him repeat it while looking at word to associate sight and correct sound.
b. Limited power to visualize or "see" word forms.	Observation test. Have child try to visualize a 3-in. cube painted red. Ask questions: number of faces; number of planes necessary to cut it into 1-in. cubes; number of small cubes; number painted on one side, two sides, three sides, not painted, etc.	Emphasize the practice of looking at the word, closing eyes, and attempting to recall the word, as part of every spelling study period.
c. Difficulties in seeing or in hearing.	Observation; doctor's or nurse's examination.	Refer to nurse or medical service. Move child to front of room near window and blackboard. Stand near him in tests and spelling exercises. Make special effort to speak and write clearly.

Diagnostic and Remedial Chart for Spelling (continued)

Possible Causes of Low Test Scores	Additional Evidence of Deficiency	Suggested Remedial Treatment
d. Failure to associate sounds of letters and syllables with spelling of words.	Individual interview; analysis of spelling errors in tests and in daily work.	Go over words with child while he studies them. Teach him to analyze words himself.
e. Tendency to transpose, add, or omit letters.	Analysis of spelling papers; observation of daily work; pronunciation tests.	Emphasize visual recall of words. Have child practice writing the words, exaggerating the formation of the letters. Underline individual hard spots.
f. Tendency to spell unphonetic words phonetically.	Note types of errors made in spelling tests, especially insertion or leaving out letters.	Show that all words are not spelled as they sound. Each word must be learned individually. Emphasize steps in learning to spell. See *h* below.
g. Difficulties in writing; letter formation.	Observation of daily written work and spelling papers. Check writing with writing scales.	Practice difficult letter formations and combinations. Emphasize need to avoid confusing letter forms, as *i, e, r,* and *t.*
h. Failure to master method of learning to spell.	Low scores on daily tests; observe the child's method of study in spelling; test on steps in learning to spell.	Check child's method of learning spelling. Teach steps in learning to spell until he uses them. Steps: (1) look at word, (2) listen as teacher pronounces it, (3) pronounce it by syllables, then say the letters, (4) use it in a sentence, (5) close eyes and visualize it, (6) write it, (7) close eyes and recall, (8) write word. Repeat steps as necessary.

Exercises for Thought and Action

1. What are the critical techniques in teaching spelling? Review this chapter and list them.
2. How would you develop attitudes of concern for correct spelling among pupils in a class?
3. Consider how you attempt to recall the spelling of a word. Do you write it several ways and decide which spelling "looks right"?

4. Examine several pages, selected at random, in a dictionary for "regular" representations of sounds. What percentage of words include "silent letters"?

5. Compare words included in a commercial spelling textbook with a listing of highly useful words such as Greene's *New Iowa Spelling Scale,* Fitzgerald's *A Basic Writing Vocabulary,* Rinsland's *A Basic Vocabulary of Elementary School Children,* or Horn's *A Basic Writing Vocabulary.* Were the words selected on the basis of their social utility?

6. Find different viewpoints from those presented in this chapter on such issues as oral testing of spelling, calling attention to hard spots in words, teaching phonetic generalizations, and using the study-test lesson procedure.

7. Consider how you would inductively teach a spelling generalization. Specifically, what would you do?

8. Add to the activities suggested for enriching the spelling program.

9. Read in *The Sixth Mental Measurements Yearbook* (Highland Park, New Jersey: The Gryphon Press, 1965, Oscar K. Buros, editor) reviews of published spelling tests.

10. Construct a spelling test as suggested in this chapter for a grade level of your choice.

11. How would you teach children to proofread for spelling errors? How would you establish the habit of careful proofreading?

Selected References

Fitzgerald, James A. *A Basic Life Spelling Vocabulary.* Milwaukee: The Bruce Publishing Company, 1951.

Greene, Harry A. *The New Iowa Spelling Scale.* Iowa City: Bureau of Educational Research and Service, University of Iowa, 1955.

Groff, Patrick. "Research on Spelling and Phonetics." *Education,* November, 1968, pp. 132–135.

Hahn, William P. "Phonics: A Boon to Spelling?" *The Elementary School Journal,* April 1964, pp. 383–384.

Hanna, Paul R., and Jean S. "Spelling as a School Subject: A Brief History," *The National Elementary Principal,* May, 1959, pp. 8–23.

Hildreth, Gertrude. *Teaching Spelling.* New York: Henry Holt and Co., 1955.

Horn, Ernest. *What Research Says to the Teacher: Teaching Spelling.* Department of Classroom Teachers and American Educational Research Association. Washington, D.C.: National Education Association, 1967.

Horn, Thomas D. "Some Issues in Learning to Spell," *Education,* December, 1958, pp. 229–233.

————. "Research in Spelling," *Elementary English,* March 1960, pp. 174–177.

_____. editor. *Research on Handwriting and Spelling.* Published for the National Conference on Research in English by the National Council of Teachers of English, Champaign, Ill., 1966.

Montebello, Mary. "Evaluation" pp. 294–295 in *Guiding Children's Language Learning* (Pose Lamb, editor). Dubuque, Iowa: Wm. C. Brown Company Publishers, 1967.

Personke, Carl and Lester Knight. "Proofreading and Spelling A Report and a Program." *Elementary English,* November, 1967, pp. 768–774.

Petty, Walter T., and Plessas, Gus P. "The Spelling Program," *Education,* October, 1961, pp. 80–82.

Sherwin, J. Stephen. *Four Problems in Teaching English: A Critique of Research.* Scranton, Pa.: International Textbook Co., 1969.

Yee, Albert H. "The Generalization Controversy on Spelling Instruction," *Elementary English,* February, 1966, pp. 154–161.

_____. "Is the Phonetic Generalization Hypothesis in Spelling Valid?" *The Journal of Experimental Education,* Summer 1969, pp. 83–91.

13 Improving Children's Handwriting

INTRODUCTION

The teaching of handwriting has long been a part of the school curriculum—one of the "Three R's." Historically it has been taught as a separate subject, yet handwriting obviously enters into all written language activities. In the early part of this century handwriting instruction was dominated by specialists advocating particular systems—Spencerian, Roman, Palmer—with an emphasis upon specific forms of letters and precise movements in forming them. Since the 1930's the early formalism has decreased and greater freedom in individual styles has been substituted.[1]

The later emphasis resulted from a recognition that children often had difficulty with the movements required for particular systems, an increasing awareness of the differences in the growth and development of children, and the difficulty in reading the script produced by some of the systems. Also, the fact that handwriting cannot be thought of as a skill separate from the occasions which demand its use for practical purposes had a bearing upon the change in emphasis.

This chapter considers the handwriting programs in elementary schools and presents specific suggestions for teaching and evaluating. The topics discussed are the following:

1. Handwriting Today
2. A Program for Handwriting Instruction
3. Instructional Considerations
4. Issues and Problems in Handwriting
5. Evaluative and Remedial Procedures

[1]Wayne Otto and Dan W. Andersen, "Handwriting" in *Encyclopedia of Educational Research,* Fourth Edition, Robert L. Ebel, editor (New York: The Macmillan Company, 1969), p. 571.

Handwriting Today

With the use of electric typewriters, tape recorders, computers, and mechanical reproducing equipment steadily increasing, many persons may question the need for handwriting instruction. However, with further thought comes the recognition that most change is slow—a fact particularly true in educational endeavors. Before the need for handwriting instruction is eliminated, machines will have to replace handwritten communications—both business and personal—much more extensively than they have to date. Furthermore, even the strongest advocate for minimizing or eliminating handwriting instruction will surely admit that nothing has so far replaced handwriting in terms of ready availability for day-to-day incidental written communication.

To study the extent to which handwriting is used, Templin surveyed 454 adults regarding their weekly writing activity, the types of handwriting instruments used, and the amount of writing done.[2] She concluded that (1) the typewriter has not replaced the pencil, (2) the ball point pen seems to have wide acceptance, and (3) handwriting legibility is still important to efficiency in both the business and social worlds.

There exists a widespread belief that the quality of handwriting has decreased in recent years—a statement that probably could have been made at many times in our history and about other aspects of the school curriculum as well. The evidence does not seem to support the opinion that handwriting quality has deteriorated. One study compared samples of script prevalent in 1912 with others written in 1959 and found no appreciable difference in the legibility of the samples.[3] On the other hand, there is some contrary evidence and certainly not everyone is willing to accept legibility as the sole factor in determining quality; in fact, "quality" is difficult to define.[4] Thus, handwriting instruction will probably continue to be attacked, and as one observes children in many classrooms sitting in all sorts of positions at their desks, with pencils and pens clutched in various ways, and with the

Public Concern About Handwriting

[2]Elaine Templin, "How Important Is Handwriting Today?" *The Elementary School Journal,* 61:386–389, October, 1960.

[3]Adrienne Erlebacher and Virgil E. Herrick, "Quality of Handwriting Today and Yesterday," *The Elementary School Journal,* 62:89–93, November, 1961.

[4]Erick A. Enstrom, "Print—Handwriting Today," *Elementary English,* 41:846–850, December, 1964.

papers upon which they are writing at varying angles, he may feel that there is some reason for public concern.[5]

The importance of handwriting in daily activities of most children and adults is readily apparent to most observers, although fortunately not everything we write has to be done by hand. We do take notes, write grocery lists, address letters, and write checks. Such writing needs to be legible to the reader and public concern will increase if it is not.

Handwriting in Schools Most schools teach handwriting. A nation-wide survey in 1960 found that 96 percent of the schools responding teach handwriting, with typically five periods per week being devoted to its instruction in the primary grades.[6] A survey in four mid-western states showed that 70 percent of 680 school systems had formal handwriting programs, with 59 percent of them offering a minimum of 50 minutes per week of handwriting instruction.[7]

The surveys of practices also reveal that handwriting programs are largely tied to commercial handwriting materials.[8] As many as sixteen commercial programs were shown to be in use, but with a substantial majority of the users selecting among the better known commercial materials.

The influence of habit, custom, tradition, public opinion, or whatever one may choose to call it in handwriting programs is often suspected and was revealed to some extent by Groff.[9] He questioned the directors of elementary education in seventy-two metropolitan areas and found that they based much of their programs upon such influence rather than upon research evidence.

A Program for Handwriting Instruction

One language arts methods book states that "Handwriting is all too often the most neglected, the least understood, and the poorest taught

[5]Robert O'Brien, "The Moving Finger Writes—But Who Can Read It," *Saturday Review,* July 18, 1959, p. 8.

[6]Virgil E. Herrick and Nora Okada, "The Present Scene: Practices in the Teaching of Handwriting in the United States—1960," *New Horizons for Research in Handwriting,* Virgil E. Herrick, editor (Madison: University of Wisconsin Press, 1963), pp. 17–38.

[7]Fred M. King, "Handwriting Practices in Our Schools Today," *Elementary English,* 38:483–486, November, 1961.

[8]Walter T. Petty, "Handwriting and Spelling: Their Current Status in the Language Arts Curriculum," *Elementary English,* 41:841, December, 1964.

[9]Patrick J. Groff, "From Manuscript to Cursive—Why?" *The Elementary School Journal,* 61:55–62, November, 1960.

subject in the elementary school."[10] Yet, if we are to believe the surveys of school practices, handwriting is taught in the great majority of schools. Perhaps the difficulty occurs because of poor teaching and from poorly formulated and understood objectives for what teachers surely spend time doing.

The major reason for teaching handwriting is its necessary role in communication. Handwriting remains the principal tool of written expression; for this reason it must be legible. Thus the principal objective of handwriting instruction is making the handwriting legible.

The Objectives
of Handwriting
Instruction

Considering this objective, a teacher should not stress meaningless drill on handwriting but should strive mainly to have pupils produce legible copy. The misapplication of the principle of use and need that is so frequently evident is a result of the neglect of sound procedures in instruction. The principal factor that is overlooked is that handwriting is a developmental process that requires more than just a few years of the child's total period of growth. Simply permitting children to write as they have the need is not giving handwriting instruction nor can handwriting be taught once and then dropped from the instructional program. Production of legible writing at a reasonable speed can be achieved and maintained only as a result of constant and meaningful practice. Thus the handwriting program should be built around these basic goals:

1. Encouraging pupils to use handwriting as a means for effective expression.
2. Helping each child to discover how skill in handwriting will serve his needs.
3. Having all pupils strive for neatness and legibility with moderate speed in their writing activities.
4. Establishing practice periods of adequate length at all grade levels.
5. Analyzing the handwriting faults of individual pupils and seeking their correction.
6. Developing in each pupil a sense of personal pride and self-appraisal and a desire for self-improvement.
7. Developing correct posture and the proper use of writing tools.

Such goals are directed at the development of attitudes which foster the learning of the skills of handwriting. More specific objectives

[10]Lillian M. Logan and Virgil G. Logan, *A Dynamic Approach to Language Arts* (Toronto: McGraw-Hill Company of Canada Limited, 1967), p. 451.

of the actual mechanical skills are suggested by the definition of good writing in one curriculum guide.[11]

Good writing must be legible; it must have:
1. Correct letter formation
2. Good spacing between letters and words
3. Uniform slant
4. Satisfactory alignment
5. Correct size letters

Good writing must make a pleasing appearance; it must have:
1. Careful arrangement of work
2. Neatness
3. Smooth, even line quality

Good writing must be easily written; to write easily, one must have at all times:
1. Good posture (body, arms, hands)
2. Correct position of materials (pen, book, paper)
3. Free movement (not exclusively arm movement)
4. Rhythm (properly stressed strokes and pauses)

Good writing must show life and dash in quality of line and spacing; this is accomplished by:
1. Making strokes rapidly
2. Decreasing the duration of pauses, letters, and words

The Handwriting Program

Surveys have shown that a majority of schools teaching handwriting do so in special periods; some, however, have no special period assigned to handwriting but give attention to individual problems as the need arises. Certainly handwriting, like all the other language arts, should be given attention throughout the school day. But—again like the other language arts—it needs more than incidental attention. A combination of both approaches, then, would appear to be the best solution.

Each child must be given opportunity and encouragement to develop his individual style, to detect his own illegibilities and poor writing habits, and to practice systematically and efficiently those aspects of writing in which he shows his greatest need. He must learn how letters are formed and how they are connected into words, and he must be able to refer to suitable handwriting models in his practicing. In most schools this teaching is done through the use of a handwriting workbook. The handwriting workbook should be used by the pupil as a reference source giving information about how to make letters, how to join them, how to hold the hand, and the like. The teacher should

[11]Language Arts Guide, Grades K-6," Jefferson County Schools, Lakewood, Colorado, 1960, pp. 127–128.

refer to the manual which usually accompanies the workbook for suggestions to help each child.[12]

The handwriting period should be spent mainly in practice upon the specific problems of the different children. One teacher built her year's handwriting program upon "a tripod of (1) diagnostic procedures, (2) remedial work, and (3) motivation."[13] Her first step was to evaluate the children's writing, using standardized rate and quality scales. From this evaluation and the use of a chart for diagnosing handwriting faults, problems of slant, uniformity of alignment, letter formation, and spacing were identified for each child. The next step was to attempt to determine the causes of the handwriting faults. Such items as poor posture, improper paper position, inadequate lighting, and other factors were established as some reasons for the handwriting defects. Other defects were determined to be the result of psychological causes, including lack of interest, desire for affection, and lack of confidence. The greatest number of causes as determined by this teacher, however, were related to improper and inadequate teaching. The remedial work she attempted consisted of frequent comparisons of pupil writing rates and quality of product with the scale norms for the grade; the writing of timed sentences; close attention to posture, manner of holding the pen, pressure on the paper, and position of the paper; and regular inspection of written products for evenness of spacing, slant, and size of letters. The greatest amount of teaching was devoted to showing children how to make letters that have to be closed, that are half-space size, that require over- and under-curves, and that have to begin and end in certain positions in order to connect properly with adjoining letters.

As the teacher in the program described above discovered, the most important element in the instructional program is motivation. The motivational approaches she used included:

1. Emphasizing the value of legible and rapid writing.
2. Using handwriting functionally through a school program calling for much writing for genuinely communicative reasons.

[12]Commercial materials for use by both teacher and pupil vary rather widely in suggestions to teachers and pupils, including how to form letters. See Virgil E. Herrick, *Comparison of Practices in Handwriting Advocated by Nineteen Commercial Systems of Handwriting Instruction* (Madison: University of Wisconsin, 1960).

[13]Sister M. Laurentia, "Teaching Penmanship in the Fourth Grade," *Catholic School Journal*, 59:27, March, 1959.

3. Periodic comparison of handwriting products with hand-writing scales.
4. Keeping charts and graphs showing individual and class progress.

Some teachers might regard the foregoing program as one of too much rigidity. However, evidence from research favors individualized analysis and remediation.[14] The degree of competition implied might be questioned also. Again, as Freeman pointed out, competition in itself is neither good nor bad—used in moderation it has a place in motivation.[15] Chief attention should be given to the competition the child may have with himself in striving to write well because the skill is needed.

Both research evidence and modern practice do not hold children to a particular form of handwriting but insist that each child be allowed to develop individuality in style. Little teaching effort should be spent having each child make letters according to particular models and by specific movements. This does not mean that a child does not need to be taught letter forms, how to connect letters, and to make the movements which are economical of time and effort. In addition, studies of handwriting quality point out that poor handwriting is the result of lack of attention to factors in uniformity which make for legibility.[16] The most commonly cited factors causing poor handwriting are these:[17]

1. Improper position of the hand in writing.
2. Improper position of the paper.
3. Improper position of the body for writing.
4. Poor letter formation, such as poor habituation in letter form, wavering or angular letters, and lack of distinct strokes.
5. Poor control of the arm, hand, and finger muscles.
6. Poor alignment and spacing, including inconsistent slant, cramped or scrawled writing, and lack of uniformity of lines.

[14]See, for example, Marlow Ediger, "Essentials in Teaching Handwriting," *Education,* 86–37–39, 1965; and Beatrice A. Furner, "An Analysis of the Effectiveness of a Program of Instruction Emphasizing the Perceptual-Motor Nature of Learning in Handwriting," *Elementary English,* 47:61–69, January, 1970.

[15]Frank N. Freeman, "Teaching Handwriting," *NEA Journal,* 43:482, November, 1954.

[16]Leslie Quant, "Factors Affecting the Legibility of Handwriting," *Journal of Experimental Education,* 14:297–316, 1946.

[17]Virgil E. Herrick and Leland B. Jacobs, *Children and the Language Arts* (Englewood Cliffs, N.J.: Prentice-Hall, Inc., 1955), p. 275.

Instructional Considerations

As with the teaching of other skills, the teaching of handwriting is most effective when both the teacher and the children have attitudes which are favorable to its learning. Handwriting must be regarded as an important skill—one that is necessary for effective expression and one which must be learned. The teacher can help instill this attitude in the children by setting a good example. He will help the children by making certain that his own letters are formed correctly and neatly, by showing good posture while writing at the desk or at the chalkboard, by writing smoothly and rhythmically, and by holding the pen, pencil, or chalk correctly.

The Role of Attitude

Children will learn that handwriting is important if they recognize that what they have written cannot be read, and therefore their attempt at communication has failed. In addition to a favorable attitude, favorable conditions for learning are important. Children learn to write best when:[18]

They write something that is meaningful to them and have definite ideas they want to convey;

They are permitted considerable liberty in making handwriting adjustments;

They advance to each new step in the writing process without too great an expenditure of time and effort as they show readiness to succeed in it;

They have a strong personal incentive to improve their writing;

They are physically comfortable, emotionally secure, and have proper materials with which to work;

They have thorough teaching as it is needed and ample opportunity to practice under continuous supervision;

They progress at their own rate of speed, and instructional procedures are individualized;

They are encouraged to evaluate their own progress in terms of their previous achievements and present needs.

The same consideration that is so commonly given to readiness for beginning reading instruction is necessary for handwriting. There should be many readiness experiences provided for the child whose muscular coordination shows that he is not yet ready to make letter

Readiness for Writing

[18]*Practices and Problems in Handwriting,* Educational Research Bulletin of Bureau of Reference and Statistics, No. 9 (New York: Board of Education of the City of New York, Sept., 1947), p. 22.

forms. All kinds of body coordination exercises, especially those of a rhythmic nature, are helpful and needed by most children entering school. The child should gradually be led to gain a sense of rhythm and balance. The child also needs to explore, feel, taste, touch, and see many things during the readiness process. These activities help him to be ready to see the differences between letters, to note how they are made, to follow his teacher's directions, to make the movements called for in beginning handwriting, to hold the writing instrument easily and properly, and to feel secure and positively motivated when instruction begins.

More specifically, the child is ready for the introduction of manuscript writing if he shows:[19] (1) a facility in the use of crayons, scissors, brushes, and pencils in a variety of activities; (2) a persistent interest in learning to write his own name; (3) the ability to copy simple shapes; (4) the establishment of hand dominance; and (5) an interest in writing and reading messages.

Building readiness for handwriting, as for reading, is not something that is applied and then dropped. It must be continued as the children write first on the chalkboard, then on large unlined paper, and even as they are taught to use the ordinary writing instruments and materials.

Posture and Movement

Undoubtedly one of the most important *physical factors* affecting the individual's handwriting is the matter of his desk and his position with respect to it. The desk-seat and writing-top should both be adjusted to permit the pupil to sit comfortably with both feet touching the floor and both arms resting in a relaxed position on the writing-top. He should face the desk squarely, bending slightly forward at the hips. In the case of the *right-handed individual,* the right arm and hand should be placed in the proper writing position while the left should be used to hold the paper and to move it upward and to the left as the writing progresses. There are wide differences of opinion about the position of the writing arm, the angle of the hand and wrist, and the use of arm and finger movements. There is rather close agreement on the recommendation that the paper be placed at such an angle with the body that the wrist of the writing arm is perpendicular to the line of writing.[20] Most teachers of handwriting recommend that the writing instrument be held lightly by placing the forefinger nearer the point

[19]Adapted from Logan and Logan, *Dynamic Approach,* p. 454. See also the readiness sections in Chapters 5 and 14.
[20]See section below for recommendation for left-handed writers.

Paper Position for Writing

The relaxed angle of the forearm across the desk and the maximum convenience of the forearm and fingers to the paper decides the position of the paper. Usually the angle of the bottom of the paper with the edge of the writing surface should be 30 degrees.

For manuscript writing the paper is usually perpendicular to the edge of the desk. Some authorities suggest an angle of about 10 degrees.

than the thumb, with both at least one inch above the writing point. They also agree in general that rapid and legible writing is the result of the smooth coordination of whole arm, forearm, wrist, and finger movements.

Myers, in a comprehensvie survey of research and practice in handwriting, says: "Probably the most scientific studies on position as applied to handwriting have been made by Freeman."[21] She then cites Freeman's findings:

1. Statistical investigation indicates:
   (a) The writers should face the desk squarely—side position causes spinal curvature.

[21]Emma Myers, "A General Review of Handwriting Instruction," unpublished master's thesis, State University of Iowa, 1954.

    (b) Both forearms should rest on the desk for approximately three quarters of their length—if one elbow is unsupported, spinal curvature is produced.

    (c) The paper should be directly in front of the writer—paper on one side of the middle line requires different adjustment of the two eyes, causing eye strain, twisting of the head and body, which produces curvature.

    (d) Paper tilted so the lower edge makes about a 30 degree angle with the edge of the desk.

2. Statistical and experimental evidence indicates:

    (a) The forearm should form a right angle with the base line of the letters—this position is more common among good writers than poor writers.

    (b) The hand should be held with the palm down—good writers do not incline the hand with more than a 45 degree slope to the wrist. Poor writers tend to rest the hand on its side (flat wrist produces strain).

    (c) The hand should rest on the third and fourth fingers.

    (d) Forefinger should rest lower down on the pen or pencil than the thumb.

    (e) Penholder should be grasped loosely, with the fingers moderately curved.

    (f) The writing movement should be a combination of arm and fingers, the arm for the forward progress, the fingers for the individual letters.

    (g) The writing movement, particularly in the early stages should be divided into a series of units of movement, separated by very slight pauses. It is not continuous and uniform in speed.

3. Experimental and observational evidence indicates:

    (a) Downward strokes should be toward the body or nearly perpendicular to the edge of the desk. The slope produced will thereby correspond to the angle of the tilt of the paper—forward for right-handers, backslant for left-handers.[22]

Legible letter formation is developed through practice in the making and connecting of the letters, comparison of the results of this practice with acceptable models, and the establishment of rhythm movements in writing. Smoothness of movement is also related to speed of writing, and both are highly correlated with age. The question of rhythm in writing has been of concern for some time but in most schools the use of rhythmical exercises set to music or counting has

[22]This last phrase is subject to considerable question, since many left-handed writers do not have a backslant. See also figures on next page from E. A. Enstrom, "The Relative Efficiency of the Various Approaches to Writing with the Left Hand," *The Journal of Educational Research,* 55:573–577, August 1962.

Paper and Arm Positions for the Left-Handed Writer

I-D₂

Reverse of right-handed position. Arm axis is 90° with paper ruling. Slant strokes are directed downward and outward (leftward). Slant is generally forward and uniform.

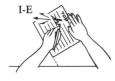

I-E

Paper is turned more to the right (clockwise) than the reverse of right-handed placement. Arm axis angle with paper ruling is greater than 90°. Slant motion is a sideward (leftward) push of the writing arm. Slant is uniformly forward.

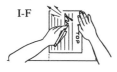

I-F

Extreme turning of the paper. Paper ruling is 90° (plus or minus 5°) with the front edge of the desk. Slant motion is a sideward (leftward and upward) push of the writing arm. Slant is generally forward and uniform.

The positions for writing with the left hand shown above are reported in the study as the most efficient adjustments to take into account (1) quality, (2) rate, (3) freedom from smearing, and (4) posture. Of these three, 1-E was rated the most desirable, I-D₂ the second most desirable, and I-F the third, among some fifteen positions found being used by left-handed writers.

Source: See footnote 22.

been discontinued. Hildreth says: "The employment of rhythmical aids is increasingly discounted. The length of time taken to write different letters of the alphabet in any form varies with letters. The use of a uniform rhythmical count for all children fails to recognize the needs of individual children.[23]

However, Myers, commenting on this statement, says "the point and purpose of counting (may) have been lost to many teachers of handwriting. It seems quite clear that guidance in finding the rhythmical movement for each letter is needed. Once the timing of the different parts of a letter is worked out, some counting to regulate the repetition of the rhythm of the letter can be used to encourage speed or rate of writing."[24]

[23]Gertrude Hildreth, *Learning the Three R's* (Minneapolis: Educational Publishers, Inc., 1947), p. 604.
[24]Myers, "Handwriting Instruction."

Andersen says that the evidence is unclear as to the part that rhythm plays in handwriting.[25] From his review of research, he concludes that because there is no common definition of rhythm and no clear data regarding its role, further clarification of its possibilities in instruction must be sought. The Hildreth and Myers statements point up differences in definitions, yet with an element of truth probably present in each. Certainly not all children should be expected to write at the same rate (rhythmic count), but every child should write with a smoothness that implies a rhythm.

Handwriting Materials
The materials for handwriting instruction include chalk, chalkboard, paper, crayons, pencils, pens, and usually commercial handwriting manuals. Herrick's study reported considerable variation in the use of these materials in so far as advocacy by commercial systems is concerned.[26] Most such programs call for the use of chalk and crayons in the primary grades, as well as large beginners' pencils. As to the latter, however, there is less emphasis today upon a larger diameter for the pencil than normal, but rather it is recommended that the pencil lead should be larger, since the essential feature is for the beginning pupil to make an easily seen line. The use of ink is generally suggested for grades three or four and beyond, with the ball point pen the instrument generally used.

The use of the chalkboard is helpful at all grade levels, though regrettably chalkboard space is decreasing in many classrooms. There are differences in the characteristics of the paper suggested for handwriting instruction. For grade one, 12-inch by 18-inch newsprint usually should be used first. In the beginning this may be unlined with lines of widths appropriate for each child later made by folding. Still later one-inch ruled paper may be used. In grade two, paper with ¾ to ½ inch lines is suggested. The ½ inch line is also generally recommended for grade three, with ⅜ inch suggested for children in grades beyond the third.

A teacher should remember always, however, that materials suggested, or actually provided, for a particular grade level must not result in the regimentation of the children. Differences in the maturation of children and their abilities in writing must be recognized in the paper or writing instruments selected for each child. To have all first-grade children write on paper of 1-inch line size all year is certainly not recognizing the differences among children.

[25]Dan W. Andersen, "Handwriting Research: Movement and Quality," *Elementary English,* 42:48, January, 1965.
[26]Herrick, *Comparison of Practices in Handwriting,* pp. 88–89.

As has been mentioned, most schools purchase commercial handwriting teaching materials and use these for the lessons taught. Usually these suggest practice exercises and include suggestions to teachers for their use. However, these materials may not provide completely for an adequate handwriting program, particularly one that gives full consideration to the needs of the children of a specific class. As a further aid to teachers, some school districts provide supplemental instructional help with curriculum guides. The following is a suggested lesson from one guide.[27] It illustrates an approach which recognizes the individual differences in a total class setting. It also focuses upon a common handwriting problem, relative sizes of letters.

Planning a
Handwriting
Lesson

Suggested Approach

To do good writing you need to remember only four letter heights.
Loop letters and *capitals* are almost a space tall.
Intermediate letters (d, p, t) are ⅔ of a space tall.
Small letters (a, c, e, etc.) are ⅓ of a space tall.
Lower loop letters go half a space below the line (f, p, g, etc.)
Let us check the writing we did for Lesson VII. Using the two sentences, we shall draw a line that touches the top of the *capitals* and *loop letter*. A ruler will help us to do this easily. Do the same thing with the *intermediate letters*. Now draw a line along the top of the *small letters*. Check to see if all capital and loop letters touch their line. Check the other letters to see if they touch their lines. How well did you do?
Excellent_____ Good_____ Fair_____ Poor_____
Put the correct heading on your paper, and then write each of the following words twice
    little   baby   all   bill   kick   hall
Use your ruler to check the height of the loop letters. Then write:
    did   tied   pit   tipped   test   top
Use your ruler to check the intermediate letters. Then write:
    am   or   seem   mice   saw   size   was
Use your ruler to check the small letters. Then write this sentence carefully to check all four sizes:
    Everyone expected that the judges would quickly decide to award the beautiful prize for excellent work to Mary.
Now use the check sheet on the sentence you just wrote. How well did you do?

	Excellent	Good	Fair	Poor
Loop letters:	_____	_____	_____	_____
Intermediate:	_____	_____	_____	_____
Small letters:	_____	_____	_____	_____
Lower letters:	_____	_____	_____	_____

Look at all the writing you did today. What is the one main thing you need to work on to improve? Check it.

[27]Nathan J. Naiman, *A Handwriting Blitz for Grades Five and Six* (San Diego: San Diego City Schools, 1964), p. 8.

Slant of writing   _____
Size of letters   _____
Finish strokes   _____
Letter formation   _____

Such a lesson can lead to grouping of the pupils for specific aspects of handwriting practice. For example, a class might be grouped as follows:

Group 1—Children needing further development of coordination. These might work on the formation of the letters of the lesson.

Group 2—Children needing practice upon relative size of letters and letter slant. These children might work on writing words with various sized letters.

Group 3—Children who form letters well but who need practice in writing smoothly. These children might practice by writing sentences.

Group 4—Children who write smoothly and relatively easily, with well-formed letters, but who should write more rapidly. These may practice writing sentences, timing their efforts while retaining quality.

Suggestions for Handwriting Practice

In addition to guides and textbook materials, practice should grow out of the needs of the pupils in practical writing situations. However, these practical writing situations should be under the teacher's guidance, with handwriting receiving attention in accord with other writing goals but never neglected.

The following suggestions may be useful for helping the teacher with the actual teaching of handwriting:[28]

1. Practice periods should be provided; practice during these periods should be upon individual needs.
2. Practice should be of short duration but usually should be frequent.
3. A checklist which keeps account of individual needs should be kept by the teacher.
4. Writing periods should follow periods of quiet activity rather than periods of strenuous movement.
5. Whenever possible practice should grow out of the needs shown in purposeful writing situations such as:
   (a) writing names, signs, and labels
   (b) writing stories, poetry, and reports
   (c) keeping a class diary or log
   (d) writing short stories or letters with the teacher.

[28]Adapted from *Handwriting, A Guide for Elementary Teachers* (Downers Grove, Ill: Downers Grove Public Schools, April, 1956), pp. 2–4.

6. Children should learn to evaluate their own performance. Comparison may be made with levels of achievement shown on commercial scales as well as with their own previous writing efforts.

7. Samples of children's writing should be collected at intervals for analysis of their errors by other pupils, the teacher, and other school authorities.

8. Too much stress on details—such as, the tail of the "q" is too long, or the "o" is not round enough, or the "t" is too tall—tends to make handwriting less interesting to your pupils. Rather than stress these difficulties, ask the child to refer to the wall charts to make his own comparison.

9. Handwriting should have speed enough to enable children to express themselves as they think.

10. Each child's handwriting should be displayed on the bulletin board sometime during the semester.

While doing handwriting for genuine communication purposes is the best motivation for children to learn to write well, some extra activities, related simply to providing practice and to building interest, may be useful. The following are some things that may be used:

Motivational Activities

1. Lists of spelling words may furnish writing exercises. Many spelling "errors" are actually handwriting errors. Sentences may be composed using the spelling words.

2. Research activities can give practice in writing proper names. From source materials such as the World Almanac or an encyclopedia, have children list the ten largest cities in the U.S.; the ten largest cities in the world; the five highest mountains; the longest rivers; or any groups that will have meaning in the class's social studies.

3. Occasionally, show pupils' papers with the opaque projector (or overhead if a machine for copying papers on transparencies is available). Discuss the good qualities of each paper and then how the handwriting and the appearance of the paper might be improved. Encourage children to refer to standards they have established in their critiques.

4. Two teachers with pupils of the same grade level can plan a handwriting lesson together and have papers written without names on them so that they can be exchanged for the children's evaluation and comparison. The principal focus should be upon building class pride.

5. For helping children with spacing, turn lined paper sideways and have words written with one letter for each space.

6. Good handwriting is not only writing legibly, but doing it quickly and easily. Tape record a paragraph or two, speaking slowly but evenly, and paying strict attention to the number of words per minute. Play the recording and have the class copy it. Let each child be his own critic. Could he have done better? Another day, play another recording with dictation at a slightly faster speed.

7. Assignment of classroom "jobs" may occasionally be made on the basis of letters of application submitted by the students. The selection should be governed in good part by the neatness of the application and by the appearance of the handwriting. Selection might be made more objective if "applicants" use fictitious names. Selections may be made by class officers or by a committee appointed for the occasion.

8. Draw from children check points they should think about: slant, uniformity, size, roundness, spacing, and closed letters. Check one point each day. Then practice correcting that point. "Before" and "after" handwriting samples will show what improvement has been made.

9. Pupils can make a poster of good handwriting with pockets where children may insert their daily writing activities, evaluating the handwriting as they file. The pockets may be labelled "Excellent," "Good," "Unsatisfactory."

10. Using riddles may be worthwhile. For example: I fly.
                                                    I sing.
                                                    What am I?_____

11. Filling in blanks may be useful:
    I am _____years old.
    I have _____sisters.
    I have _____brothers.

12. Individual mailboxes by each child's desk can be made of bags or envelopes in which the pupils place daily notes to each other. Legible notes are read and filed in a pupil folder; illegible notes are sent to the dead-letter office where a committee of pupils acts as postman to study (and report) weaknesses of the writing.

The Role of Parents

Parents exert a great influence upon their children's attitude toward handwriting and consequently upon the resulting quality and speed. Parents should be informed about the handwriting that is to be taught in the school at each grade level. Copies of the forms of letters—both manuscript and cursive—may be sent to parents, including instructions on how the letters are formed. Particular problems may be encountered with parents in the teaching of manuscript form, since often they have taught their children block printing at home. They may regard manuscript as not really writing or they may not understand the why and how of the transition to cursive.

A teacher can keep parents informed through a series of group conferences. In addition, letters may be sent home (often written by the children) explaining things of concern. As one curriculum guide suggests, parents can reinforce the school's handwriting instruction when they:[29]

[29]Reprinted from *Teaching Handwriting* (New York: Board of Education of the City of New York, 1961), pp. 34–35.

Realize that, in order to write well, children need a clean, smooth writing surface in a well lighted place and suitable writing materials—well sharpened pencils, free flowing pens, smooth paper.

Encourage the use at home of the style of writing children are learning and using at school.

Give opportunities at home for children to write telephone messages, shopping lists, thank-you notes or other communications in which clear, easily-read writing is important. Help children to understand that legible handwriting is a courtesy to the reader and a source of personal satisfaction in a job well done.

Issues and Problems in Handwriting

Surveys of handwriting programs and instructional practices have identified particular problems and unsettled issues. Not all of these are discussed in this section, since many of them call for the conducting of research and others have been identified earlier in the chapter. The fact that not all handwriting matters have been decided was emphasized by Horn. He listed some twenty-one questions requiring research to discover their answers.[30]

Left-handed writers seem to be a perennial classroom problem to many teachers. Much of this concern is unwarranted, however, and due to a lack of understanding of how to help the left-handed child adjust to a skill that is performed by most children with the right hand, for which instructional material is geared. There is often confusion as to whether a left-handed writer should be changed to a right-handed one.

Handedness

The first thing for the teacher to realize is that no one is entirely left-handed or entirely right-handed. Freeman stated that "by the usual test five or six percent of the children are found to prefer the left hand over the right or to be more skillful in using it."[31] A lesser number are ambidextrous; that is, they do not favor either hand. The rest, 90 percent or more, are right-handed. Of those who are classed either as right- or left-handed, some have stronger preference than others. They range all the way from extreme right-handedness, ambidexterity, and mild degrees of left-handedness to extreme left-handedness.

Freeman further pointed out: "There has been some dispute among psychologists as to whether right- or left-handedness is inborn or is learned by imitation or precept. The burden of evidence is that it

[30]Ernest Horn, "Questions for Research on Handwriting," *The Elementary School Journal,* 62:304–312, March, 1962.

[31]Frank N. Freeman, *Solving Handwriting Needs* (Columbus, Ohio: Zaner-Bloser Company, 1960), p. 24.

is inborn. This is indicated by the fact that preference appears very early, that the superiority of one hand or the other is frequently great and that there exists a small group who are more skillful with the left hand, contrary to all examples of teaching."

Most authorities agree that hand dominance is fairly well established by the time children reach school age. They further recommend that the child who is dominantly left-handed be trained to use the left hand for writing and not changed to the more common right-handed pattern. There are some children, of course, who will come to school with a wavering dominance. For these few children it is recommended that encouragement be given to use the right hand, since this is largely a right-handed world. A teacher should make certain that dominance has not been established, however. Such determination should not be left to casual observation; tests, such as throwing, putting pegs in holes, locking and unlocking a padlock, or cutting with scissors, should be used.

Teaching the Left-Handed Child

The left-handed pupil encounters daily confusion in a world of right-handed people, usually including a right-handed teacher. Because the pupil cannot imitate the teacher as other right-handed classmates do, he feels different, perhaps peculiar. It is important that the teacher be aware of this possible lack of self-confidence and be prepared to provide for his particular needs.

A left-handed child, like his right-handed counterpart, will learn to write with greater ease, legibility, and speed under favorable conditions. Drummond suggests the following to help the "lefties."[32]

> Provide lots of writing on the chalkboard. It is practically impossible to use the upside-down style at the board.
>
> Make sure the paper is properly placed on the desk. For manuscript, paper should be square with the desk. For cursive, the bottom right corner should be pointed at the body. It is hard to write in the upside-down position if paper is placed properly. Also, less hand smearing occurs.
>
> Permit lefties to continue manuscript writing indefinitely. Their writing is almost always more legible before they learn to write cursive than afterwards. As the left-handed children begin to change to cursive, though, watch the placement of the paper like a hawk.
>
> Encourage children to hold pencils or pens so that the top of the writing instrument is pointing over the shoulder of the same arm.

[32]Harold Drummond, "Suggestions for the 'Lefties,'" *The National Elementary School Principal,* Vol. XXXVIII, No. 5, Feb. 1957, p. 15. © 1957, National Association of Elementary School Principals, NEA. All rights reserved.

Encourage lefties to develop a writing slant which feels natural and good. The slant will, undoubtedly, be a bit backhand compared to generally accepted handwriting styles because it is natural that way. A *consistent* slant makes writing legible, and a lefty is not likely to be consistent using a slant which is natural for right-handers.

Furnish lefties with pencils which have slightly harder lead than that used by right-handers. Harder lead will not smear as easily, thus providing less reason for twisting the wrist so that the hand is in the upside-down position.[33]

When ink is used, be sure that all lefties have a good non-skip ballpoint pen which has a high quality non-smear cartridge.

Encourage lefties to learn to type. Most classrooms should have typewriters to encourage children to write creatively. With lefties, the need for typewriters is even greater.

Questions concerning the relative value of teaching manuscript (print script) or cursive forms of handwriting have persisted since the introduction of manuscript form over forty years ago. The questions center principally around these issues: (1) Can manuscript writing be done as rapidly as cursive writing? (2) When should children be changed from using manuscript form to using cursive form?

The Manuscript-Cursive Issue

Most modern schools have accepted the practice of teaching manuscript writing for the child's initial writing experiences, but the extension of manuscript form as the only or principal means of writing throughout the grades and high school is still a topic of considerable debate. Some schools continue to teach manuscript writing throughout the grades and give no instruction in cursive writing. Other schools continue instruction on manuscript after beginning the teaching of cursive writing. However, the actual number of school systems following either of the latter two practices is at this time limited.

It is generally agreed that manuscript is easier to learn than cursive, particularly by young children who have problems in coordinating their physical movements. The arguments for using manuscript writing are best summarized by the following list of values:[34]

1. It is easy for children to learn because of the simple strokes.
2. Children can obtain satisfactory results early without drill on movement or form.

[33]This adjustment should not be necessary if the paper is placed correctly and the pencil held properly.

[34]Dorothy H. Stewart, "Handwriting Up to Date," *Elementary English,* 29:408, November, 1952.

3. The letter forms are so simple that each child can see his difficulty and correct it.
4. The child learns one alphabet for both reading and writing.
5. Even a child with poor muscular control can produce readable results.
6. Manuscript writing facilitates children's work in beginning reading.
7. Children who have written manuscript for a number of years can equal the speed of those using cursive writing and in most cases exceed it.

This last value is debated by many. However, the volume of evidence that manuscript may be written with as much speed as cursive is increased. Groff reported that a Brookline, Massachusetts, study found "in all cases manuscript writing was as fast as cursive writing, and in some instances faster. In every case the legibility of the manuscript papers was far superior."[35] Studies have shown, too, that manuscript writing seems to favor the development of fluency of expression in the primary grades. Since fluency of language expression is a major goal of the language program, the extension of the use of manuscript form, particularly into the third and fourth grades, has become the major item of the current controversy.

Groff believes that there is no point in changing children from manuscript to cursive form and that reasons given for changing are largely opinions rather than facts derived from research investigations.[36] He adds that "no research evidence available suggests that children like cursive handwriting better than manuscript or that cursive is preferred for written material of greater length or of better literary quality. There is substantial evidence that contradicts the notion that cursive handwriting is easier to learn, easier to write, and that errors made in cursive are easier to correct."

However, tradition, regardless of whether it is based upon any real evidence or not, is certainly a major controlling factor in all that is done in schools and cannot be minimized—and handwriting instruction is no exception. Therefore, school handwriting programs will continue generally to provide for a transition from manuscript to cursive form. When this should be done is definitely a current issue.[37] Freeman attempted to settle this issue by examining practice and asking handwriting authorities. The preponderance of opinion and prac-

[35]Patrick J. Groff, "From Manuscript to Cursive—Why?"
[36]*Ibid.*
[37]Frank Freeman, "The Transition from Manuscript to Cursive Writing," *Elementary English,* 35:366–372, October, 1958.

tice reported favored grade three; there was, however, particularly in some states, strong favoring of grade two. As Freeman recognized, this is not a scientific way to decide an issue. Some language authorities substantiate their views for extending the use of manuscript by relating them to child development. To these the second grade appears too early to add cursive handwriting for two principal reasons:[38] first, children still have not developed the muscular skill to do cursive writing easily, requiring an excessive amount of time spent in learning it at this level; second, children have just reached the stage in which they can genuinely use manuscript writing as a tool for doing imaginative and other types of writing.

It is particularly short-sighted for any school system, classroom, or set of handwriting materials to suggest that a transition should be made during a specified semester, particularly for all children. Surely no one would suggest that all the children are ready at the same time for such instruction. Also, confronting a child with a new form of writing at a time when he is intent upon writing his ideas and using his imagination seems equally short-sighted. On the other hand, as most second- and even first-grade teachers know, many children do want to learn "real writing," and some of course can do so without great difficulty or loss of writing interest. There is growing opinion that reasonable mastery of both styles of handwriting is needed for optimum skill in meeting varying written communicative needs. However, considering the volume of information that is pressured to be taught and the increasing number of skills children need to know, one wonders if children have the time to learn and maintain two sets of skills, both taught essentially for the purpose of permitting an individual to record his expression in written form. And, since the majority of children now learn to use a typewriter, three forms of writing are actually taught. Perhaps educators need to reject many of the pressures brought upon the selection of curriculum content, to firmly establish a valid position, and then to hold to this position regardless of tradition or other pressure.

Evaluative and Remedial Procedures

Since instruction in handwriting has as its major objectives the development of the skills necessary for writing legibly with speed and

[38]E. A. Enstrom, "After Manuscript Writing—When Shall We Begin Cursive?" *The Elementary School Journal,* 61:24–27, October, 1960.

ease, evaluation of the program requires that the factors of quality and speed must be measured. Skill in handwriting depends upon a very complex type of mental-visual-muscular coordination. If the written product is to possess the desired legibility, speed of production, and general aesthetic qualities, a high level of this coordination must be developed. The close dependence of language expression in recorded form upon handwriting speed and legibility makes it important that a functional program of handwriting instruction be coordinated with the total elementary school program. Legibility and physical appearance are both important elements affecting the quality of written expression. The teacher is thus confronted with a real need for instruments to appraise the results of instruction in handwriting, as well as to diagnose the difficulties of individual pupils in writing.

Selecting Samples for Evaluation

Handwriting samples or specimens selected for evaluation on a quality scale and for deriving rate scores are affected by three factors which must be considered when they are being collected. The first of these is the suitability or the difficulty of the copy pupils are asked to write. If a scale calls for the writing of material that may be difficult—for example, the Ayres scale asked for sentences from the Gettysburg address[39]—it may not be appropriate to use with children in the primary grades. More recently developed scales have recognized this problem and now one suggests the following for the third grade: "My name stands for me. I want to write it well." For the fifth grade it suggests: "I live in America. It is good to live where you have freedom to work and play. As an American, I support my country and what it stands for."[40] The sample should contain very few spelling or vocabulary difficulties and should be understood by the pupils. The selected copy should be written on the blackboard several days prior to the test where it can be studied and where it can be seen during the writing test itself.

A second factor is the care with which the instructions for the writing test are given. Children are easily influenced in the quality and the rate of their writing by the wording of the directions and the manner of giving the test. The following directions are suggested: "When I say begin, start to write as well as you can and at your usual speed the copy you have read and memorized from the blackboard. Write your copy over and over until I say stop. When I say stop, you are to

[39]Leonard P. Ayres, *A Scale for Measuring the Quality of Handwriting of School Children* (New York: Russell Sage Foundation, 1912). (Now reported to be out of print.)

[40]*Guiding Growth in Handwriting: Evaluation Scale,* 1966 edition (Columbus, Ohio: Zaner-Bloser Company).

quit writing at once, even though you are in the middle of a letter."

The third factor which must be controlled in the collection of handwriting samples is the time allowance. Scale directions indicate the amount of time to be allowed (usually two minutes) and these directions must be followed.

The quality of a pupil's handwriting may be determined by comparing the specimens to be evaluated with samples of established or known value. At one time this meant the comparison of the samples of the child's writing with the copy-book model. This procedure naturally resulted in an overemphasis on the shape, size, and shading of the letters—made largely for decorative purposes. Under these conditions, quality and rate certainly were not the main objectives of writing instruction or measurement. With the appearance of scales for the evaluation of handwriting merit and legibility, the teaching emphasis moved away from writing as a decorative art to writing as an effective tool of written communication. The speedy production of handwritten copy at a socially acceptable level of legibility quite properly became the major goal of instruction in handwriting.

Quality or Legibility

Handwriting scales are not generally in current use. The Herrick and Okada study showed that only about a third of the schools used a scale in evaluating children's handwriting.[41] Some of these scales were ones developed within the school systems and others were those appearing in some achievement tests.[42] Andersen reports that the Freeman (Zaner-Bloser) scale is the one most commonly used, with the West and Ayres scales receiving some use.[43]

Handwriting scales definitely have a place in instruction, if we are concerned with the legibility and speed of children's writing. Some kind of standard or norm as the basis of comparison is always useful to evaluation. The fact that a scale does not take into account each pupil's stylistic inclinations does not mean that a measure of quality and rate cannot be achieved.

Scales used for evaluating handwriting may be divided into two groups in accordance with the purpose each serves: (1) general merit scales, and (2) analytical and diagnostic charts and scales.

Scales for Measuring Handwriting Quality

The *Thorndike Scale for the Measurement of Merit of Handwriting* consists of 16 specimens of handwriting arranged in ascending order of merit from a low scale value of 4 units above zero to a high

[41]Herrick and Okada, "The Present Scene."
[42]For example: *California Achievement Test*.
[43]Andersen, "Handwriting Research," p. 51.

of 18.[44] The unit of measurement used in this scale was based upon the consensus of a large number of persons presumably qualified by training and experience to discriminate between minute levels of quality in handwriting specimens. These specimens, selected and described as being one unit apart, are arranged in order from poorest to best to constitute the rough scale. The poorest specimen is somewhat arbitrarily designated as representing a quality four judgment units above zero, zero representing just no handwriting quality whatever. A second specimen approximately one judgment unit better is assigned a scale value of 5.

The scaled specimens reproduced here represent scale values of 8 and 9 on the Thorndike Scale, and are defined as being one scale unit apart. According to the standards provided with the scale, quality 9 is approximately normal for fifth grade.

8

moved along down the driveway. The audience of passers by which had been gathering about them melted away

9

Then the carelessly dressed gentlemen stepped lightly into Warren's carriage and held out a small card, John Vanished behind the

The *Ayres Handwriting Scale,* the second scale to be developed, was standardized on the basis of legibility alone. Ayres believed that the judgment unit used in the *Thorndike Scale* introduced many undesirable subjective elements and proposed to measure legibility in terms of the speed and ease with which samples of handwriting could be read by trained and competent readers. This scale, known generally as the *Gettysburg Edition* because the specimens were based on the first four sentences of Lincoln's Gettysburg Address, has been one of the most widely used handwriting scales.

---

[44]Neither the Thorndike nor the Ayres Scale is used today except in handwriting research. Their description is included here to illustrate scales and the possibilities as instructional aids.

The accompanying sample represents quality 60 from the Ayres Scale. This quality, according to modern standards, is approximately normal expectancy for sixth-grade pupils at the end of the year.

> *Four score and seven years*
> *ago our fathers brought for*
> *theupon this continent a*
> *new nation, conceived in*
> *liberty, and dedicated to*
> *the proposition that all*
> *men are created equal*
> *Now we are engaged*
> *in a great civil war, test-*
> *ing whether that nation,*
> *or any nation so con —*
> *ceived and so dedicated*

Quality 60 of the Ayres Scale

The American Handwriting Scale, one of the most comprehensive of the general merit scales, provides a number of distinctive features, of which at least two deserve special mention: (1) a separate scale is provided for each grade from two to eight; (2) the specimens have been scaled for both quality and rate, taking into account the fact that the better writing is usually done at a more rapid rate and the poor writing at a slower rate.[45] The provision of separate scales for each grade from two to eight makes possible a somewhat more accurate evaluation of quality of writing in its relation to the grade in which it is produced than is possible in a single scale.

The *Guiding Growth in Handwriting Evaluation Scales* provide five specimens of handwriting for each grade level and suggests that

[45]Developed by Paul V. West. Published and copyrighted by A. N. Palmer Company, 1951.

samples compared be rated as good, medium, or fair.[46] The scale for each grade level suggests a numerical score for each of the five specimens.

Reproduced here are several specimens from the scales. These undoubtedly show more accurately than the earlier developed scales the general quality of handwriting nationally.

Specimen 3—Medium for Grade 5

Similar cursive handwriting may be marked 75. The standard speed for this grade is about 60 letters per minute.

I live in America. It is good to live where you have freedom to work and play. As an American, I support my country and what it stands for.

Specimen 5—Poor for Grade 5

Similar cursive handwriting may be marked 65, and writing poorer than this may be evaluated accordingly.

My name stands for me. I want to write it well.

Specimen 2—Good for Grade 1

Similar manuscript writing may be given a mark of 80.

We love our flag, red, white, and blue.

Scoring Handwriting Specimens

Before attempting to use a quality scale for evaluating handwriting samples, the teacher should make a very careful study of the scale itself, the directions for its use, the norms, and the special functions which the scale is designed to perform. Differences in quality apparent in the low value, average, and superior samples in the scale should be

[46]See footnote 40.

especially noted. The quality of the specimen being evaluated is determined by comparing it with the scale samples and moving it along the scale until a scale sample is found that closely matches it in appearance, quality, or legibility. The quality value of the matching scale sample is then assigned to the pupil's handwriting sample. As experience with the scale gives the user confidence, he may wish to increase the accuracy of his scoring by assigning intermediate values.

Because of the nature of the scale and the way in which it is used, objective and highly accurate ratings of handwriting samples are difficult to secure. However, research shows that through the use of a training period spent in study of the scale samples, study of the grade norms and other evaluator's scores as a basis for adjusting the scorer's own levels of expectancy, and directed practice with samples of known quality, the average teacher can learn to rate handwriting samples with sufficient accuracy and objectivity for survey use.[47]

The accuracy with which handwriting rate scores may be obtained is largely determined by the care with which the samples are collected. Rate of writing may be expressed in either seconds per letter or in letters per minute, but the latter is the form most commonly used. The rate score is obtained by counting the total number of letters written by each child and dividing this number by the number of minutes allowed for the writing.

According to the *Guiding Growth in Handwriting* scale, rates for the different grade levels in words per minute should be as shown below. The rate norms for grade one and two are for manuscript form and the others are for cursive.

Grade	1	2	3	4	5	6	7
Rate	25	30	45	50	60	67	74

Directions for this scale suggest that the sentences to be evaluated be written on the board by the teacher, that the children be permitted to practice writing them several times, and that the writing to be ·scored be done for two minutes.

Today, the location of specific faults in handwriting centers on informal procedures devised and utilized by teachers or such published materials as the *Handwriting Faults and How to Correct Them* chart.[48] This chart, like related ones published by other commercial concerns,

Diagnostic Charts

[47]Leonard S. Feldt, "Reliability of Measures of Handwriting Quality," *Journal of Educational Psychology,* 53:288–292, December, 1962.

[48]Zaner-Bloser Staff, *Handwriting Faults and How to Correct Them* (Columbus, Ohio: The Zaner-Bloser Company).

is designed to reveal whether or not the child's specimen of handwriting violates one or more of the following essential qualities: (1) uniformity of slant, (2) uniformity of alignment, (3) quality of line, (4) letter formation, and (5) spacing. Three levels of quality—excellent, mediocre, and poor—are shown for each trait.

In addition to illustrating these qualities, the chart contains the following excellent suggestions on ways to test a child's handwriting copy for each quality. The chart is particularly helpful because it enables both the teacher and the pupil to discover specific handwriting weaknesses that are in need of remedial treatment and makes helpful suggestions for correcting the defects.

How to test legibility: Make a letter finder by cutting a hole a little larger than the letter in a piece of cardboard. Place the hole of this finder over each letter in turn and mark the letters which are illegible. Have the pupils practice these letters separately, then write the word again and test as before.

How to test slant: Draw slanting lines through the letters and mark all letters which are off slant.

If the slant is too great, the paper is tilted too much. If the writing is too vertical, the paper is too upright, and if the slant is backward, the paper is tilted the wrong direction.

How to test for spacing: Draw parallel lines between letters (see diagram). Place the paper in front of you and mark all letters and words which are unevenly spaced.

correct   *incorrect*

spacing   *spacing*

| How to test alignment: | Alignment and size are closely integrated and should be studied together. Use a ruler (a diagnostic ruler is best) and draw a base line touching as many of the letters as possible. Also draw a line along the tops of the small letters. Mark the letters above or below these lines. |

Correct alignment   *Incorrect alignment*

| How to test size of letters: | Draw lines along the tops of the letters. Remember the minimum letters i, u, v, etc., are ¼ space high; d, t, p are ½ space; capitals and l, h, k, b, d, are ¾ space high. All the lower loop letters extend ½ space below the line. |

Comparative size of letters

| How to test for quality of line: | Make a letter finder by cutting a hole a little larger than the letter in a piece of cardboard. Place the hole of this finder over each letter in turn and mark the letters which are illegible due to the quality of line. Have pupils practice these letters from their writing books separately until the letters are perfectly legible. Then have them write the whole word again and test as before. |

A particular value of diagnostic charts is that pupils become interested in using them. Children like the "scientific" approach to their problems and are motivated by it.

The fact that only 7 percent of the schools reported upon in one survey had a planned program for diagnosis and remediation of handwriting difficulties supports the statement made near the beginning of this chapter that poor teaching occurs.[49] The evidence is simply overwhelming that much handwriting instruction should be based upon diagnosis of handwriting faults and to ignore these faults and the remedial measures that might be taken compounds the difficulties.

An early investigation of the writing of children and adults found approximately 3,000 different causes for illegibilities.[50] While the kind of analysis done in that study may be too detailed for the greater freedom permitted in styles of writing today, more recent studies do support the fact that there are many malformations of letters that ought to be remedied.[51] The following summary, adapted from the extensive tabulation in the early study, provides significant information for remedial teaching.

Important types of letter malformations

a	made like	*u*	*l*	made like uncrossed	*t*
a	made like	*o*	*m*	made like	*w*
c	made like	*e*	*n*	made like	*u*
c	made like	*i*	*n*	made like	*v*
d	made like	*cl*	*o*	made like	*a*
e	closed		*r*	made like	*i*
g	made like	*y*	*r*	made like	*s*
h	made like	*li*	*r*	made like	*n*
i	made like	*c*	*s*	indistinct	
i	with dot right		*s*	made like	*r*
i	with dot left		*t*	made like	*l*

The following list of seven of the most common defects in writing, with the suggested contributing causes, should provide additional diagnostic and remedial assistance.

[49]Dan W. Andersen, "Handwriting Research: Style and Practice," *Elementary English,* 42:123, February, 1965.

[50]L. C. and S. L. Pressey, "Analyses of Three Thousand Illegibilities in the Handwriting of Children and Adults," *Educational Research Bulletin,* 6:270–273, September 28, 1927.

[51]Edward R. Lewis and Hilda P. Lewis, "An Analysis of Errors in the Formation of Manuscript Letters by First-grade Children," *American Education Research Journal,* 2:25–35, 1965.

Defect	*Causes*
1. Too much slant	a. Writing arm too near body
	b. Thumb too stiff
	c. Point of nib too far from fingers
	d. Paper in wrong position
	e. Stroke in wrong direction
2. Writing too straight	a. Arm too far from body
	b. Fingers too near nib
	c. Index finger alone guiding pen
	d. Incorrect position of paper
3. Writing too heavy	a. Index finger pressing too heavily
	b. Using wrong type of pen
	c. Pen too small in diameter
4. Writing too light	a. Pen held too obliquely or too straight
	b. Pen too large in diameter
5. Writing too angular	a. Thumb too stiff
	b. Pen too lightly held
	c. Movement too slow
6. Writing too irregular	a. Lack of freedom of movement
	b. Movement of hand too slow
	c. Pen gripping
	d. Incorrect or uncomfortable position
7. Spacing too wide	a. Pen progresses too fast to right
	b. Excessive sweeping lateral movement

In addition to charts on handwriting which give levels of quality and which point up particular faults, teachers should make use of the opaque and overhead projectors for showing children's handwriting for total class appraisal and comment. Pupils may also project their own papers and through the medium of enlargement and the focusing of specific attention may note their own errors.

As with every school subject, corrective work in handwriting can be applied effectively only on an individual basis and following a careful individual diagnosis. With far too few exceptions, programs for teaching handwriting in schools have been designed to instruct but not to measure the growth resulting from that instruction or the specific areas in which the instruction has not been successful. Programs need to be supplemented by time and effort devoted to diagnosis and remediation.

Exercises for Thought and Action

1. From the discussion in this chapter what aspect of handwriting instruction would you judge will take the greatest proportion of the time set aside for handwriting teaching?
2. Practice your handwriting at the chalkboard. Can you tell a child the difference between the way a piece of chalk should be held and the way a pencil should be held? How can you keep your chalkboard writing horizontal?
3. Look at several commercial handwriting systems. What differences are there in the forms of the letters?
4. What would you do about a child entering your fifth-grade classroom who formed letters differently from the way your handwriting program called for? Would you have him change the way he made the letters?
5. Use a handwriting scale or diagnostic chart and evaluate your own handwriting. Identify specifically the practice you need.
6. Find examples of poor handwriting among adults and consider how great a handicap to their vocational and social lives this handwriting is.
7. Describe specifically the particular practices you would use in teaching a left-handed child.
8. Present to the class the several procedures suggested in commercial handwriting systems for making a transition from manuscript to cursive form.
9. There is some advocacy for using a combination of manuscript and cursive forms, most often identified as an italic style, as a single form to be taught. Find out all you can about this advocacy.
10. How would you proceed in informally determining the quality and the speed of handwriting that are acceptable in the community in which you live?

Selected References

Berry, Winifred, "Italic Writing," *Education Digest,* 26:50–51, April, 1961.

Ediger, Marlow, "Essentials in Teaching Handwriting," *Education,* 86:37–39, 1965.

Enstrom, E. A., "After Manuscript Writing—When Shall We Begin Cursive?" *Elementary School Journal* 61:24–27, October, 1960.

Erlebacher, A., and Herrick, V., "Quality of Handwriting Today and Yesterday," *Elementary School Journal,* 62:89–93, November, 1961.

Feldt, Leonard S., "The Reliability of Measuring Handwriting Ability," *Journal of Educational Psychology,* 53:288–292, December, 1962.

Freeman, Frank N., "On Italic Handwriting," *Elementary School Journal,* 60:258–264, February, 1960.

Gray, William S. *The Teaching of Reading and Writing: An International Survey.* Columbia University: Monograph on Fundamental Education, No. 10, 1956.

Groff, Patrick J., "From Manuscript to Cursive—Why?" *Elementary School Journal,* 61:55–62, November, 1960.

Herrick, Virgil E. *Comparison of Practices in Handwriting Advocated by Nineteen Commercial Systems of Handwriting Instruction.* Madison: University of Wisconsin Press, 1960.

————. (ed.) *New Horizons for Research in Handwriting.* Madison: University of Wisconsin Press, 1963.

Hildreth, Gertrude, "Manuscript Writing after Sixty Years," *Elementary English,* 37:3–13, January, 1960.

Horn, Thomas D. (ed.) *Research on Handwriting and Spelling.* Published for the National Conference on Research in English by the National Council of Teachers of English, Champaign, Ill., 1966.

King, Fred M., "Handwriting Practices in Our Schools Today," *Elementary English,* 38:483–486, November, 1961.

Myers, Emma H. *The Why and Hows of Teaching Handwriting.* Columbus, Ohio: The Zaner-Bloser Company, 1963.

Otto, Wayne, and Anderson, Dan W., "Handwriting," *Encyclopedia of Educational Research,* Fourth Edition, Robert L. Ebel, editor. New York: The Macmillan Company, 1969.

Templin, E. M., "Research and Comment: Handwriting, the Neglected R," *Elementary English,* 37:386–389, October, 1960.

14 Basic Reading Instruction

INTRODUCTION

Reading and listening are the two receptive language arts. It is through reading and listening, coupled with the basic ability to observe, that information and ideas are received and become the substance for the expressive arts of speaking and writing. This chapter presents an overview of the elementary school reading program and examines instructional problems and issues. The following major topics are discussed:

1. Reading and Language
2. The Objectives of Reading Instruction
3. A Modern Reading Program
4. Approaches to Reading Instruction
5. The Reading Lesson
6. Practices and Issues in the Teaching of Reading
7. Materials for Reading Instruction
8. Evaluation in Reading Instruction

The teaching of reading, which has a unique place in the elementary school curriculum, is a complex activity that involves a more detailed consideration than can be given here. Therefore, it is recommended that textbooks devoted exclusively to the teaching of reading (see Selected References) be used to supplement the discussion in this chapter. The reader is also advised to check the index of this volume for discussion of teaching reading in the sections devoted to the disadvantaged, the primary grades, literature, and so forth.

Reading and Language

The ability to speak with some assurance and proficiency and to listen to and understand speech is essential for a child before he can learn to read, since from such ability he has learned to comprehend ideas formulated into sentences, to determine word meanings from the context of sentences, and to interpret ideas expressed by means of word symbols. Getting meaning from print is relatively easy for the child who has skill in speaking and listening and who has had much experience in using these skills. Many of the difficulties children encounter in reading are highly related to their inadequacies in using language. When the language to be read is too far removed from the child's experiences, largely expressed through his use of language, problems in recognizing and understanding symbols are apt to arise.

A child's first sounds are without meaning; they are purely reflexive responses to stimuli, but they include phonemes which later will be parts of words. Gradually, as various combinations or clusters of phonemes are sounded, meanings become attached—perhaps first by the child and later by other persons in his environment (although they may not be the same; his "da-da" may mean "This is fun" but to his father it means that he has been recognized). As these combinations of phonemes begin to resemble words of the language of his environment—the "ba-ba," "ma-ma" sorts of babbling—meaning relationships really begin to be established. Thus, the child early learns to associate meaning with patterns of sounds. He learns of the relationship between words and meanings. The child entering school can speak several thousand words; for many of these, and others, he has some meaning attachment. For some words that he can speak he will have vague or false ideas as to their meanings. This condition does not change while he is in school (or as an adult, for that matter)—though, of course, the number of words he speaks and the meanings he knows will increase. Language learning is a continuous process. Human beings are always learning new words and the meanings attached to them, new meanings for words they already know, and new ways to combine words in expressing ideas and relating knowledge.

A child's learning to read is largely based upon the teacher's understanding that:[1] (1) reading is related to most language activities in the curriculum; (2) learning to read is related to, and built upon,

[1]Adapted from Arthur W. Heilman, *Principles and Practices of Teaching Reading* (Columbus, Ohio: Charles E. Merrill Books, 1961), p. 38.

past linguistic experiences; (3) learning to read should be a natural outgrowth of these past language experiences; (4) learning to read is a developmental process that involves years of guided study; and (5) different methods of teaching reading may be justified but the one criterion a method should meet is that it builds logically and systematically.

To these understandings should be added another: that reading provides a major avenue for the further development of power in using language—for learning new words, new concepts. Thus initial language ability is needed in learning to read and reading is a tool for extending this ability.

It is possible, of course, for a child to be proficient in language—or reasonably so—upon coming to school and still fail to learn to read. It is possible also, after he has begun to learn to read, for him to have considerable language ability and yet develop difficulties in reading. Problems associated with visual perception, emotional blocking, skill deficiencies, and so forth, may prevent reading success. However, without adequate proficiency in language, no matter how well he can perceive word forms and perform other functions related to effective reading, true reading will not occur since the content will be unintelligible to him.

The Objectives of Reading Instruction

The fundamental objective for teaching reading in schools is to develop in each child the attitude, abilities, and skills necessary for him to use reading as a means of securing information, fostering and reacting to ideas, developing interests and tastes, and deriving pleasure. The school must make each child as able and as diversified a reader as his capabilities and the instructional time will allow. The first task is to help him to acquire the skills needed for bringing his experiences to bear upon the written symbols in order that he may properly interpret them and to use those skills efficiently and effectively. The second task is to teach him to appreciate reading and to use it to grow as a person. The fundamental objective of teaching reading is not achieved until *both* of these tasks have been accomplished. Particular stress needs to be given to the second task, since experience has shown that schools successfully teach the reading skills to most children but fail to develop these children into adults who actually read.

To accomplish the tasks suggested, a reading program should be thought of as consisting of three parts—which in a modern program are intertwined rather than built one upon another. These parts are (1) the development of recognition and comprehension skills, (2) the functional use of reading in learning, and (3) the use of reading for recreation.

The specific goals of reading instruction which give attention to the three parts of the program are the following:

1. The development of fundamental reading skills in
   (a) recognizing words
   (b) securing word meanings
   (c) comprehending and interpreting what is read
   (d) reading silently at speeds appropriate to the material and purpose of the reading
   (e) reading orally
   (f) using books efficiently
2. The provision of opportunity for rich and varied experiences through reading
3. The development of enjoyment through reading
4. The development of lasting interest in reading voluntarily
5. The acquisition of ability for using reading in resourceful ways to meet particular needs and interests

A Modern Reading Program

Reading in a modern school program is not taught in isolation; children use reading for gaining information and ideas and for enjoyment as they are taught the skills of reading. The use of reading as a tool for learning thus receives emphasis from the very beginning of reading instruction. Reading naturally is a part of many school activities, and in a modern program its use is fostered and its skills are practiced whenever possible. The reading program also takes into account the many differences among the children in a class as to interests and abilities. This recognition, along with the use of reading throughout the school day, calls for a program which is considerably expanded from one which merely "has" a child "in" a reading textbook.

It is fairly common to hear that there is no one best way to teach reading and, of course, this is true in a very literal sense.[2] However, recognizing that reading instruction is a vital part (but only a part) of the total and interrelated program in all of the language arts does

The Bases
of the
Program

[2] Mary C. Austin and Coleman Morrison, *The First R* (New York: The Macmillan Company, 1963), pp. 220–223.

eliminate some "ways" or "procedures" that are sometimes used in reading instruction programs. In a like manner, acceptance of particular objectives for reading instruction precludes the use of "ways" that are without merit in achieving these objectives. In other words, while there is no "one best way," there are procedures that are not sound and there are some procedures that are better than others.

1. A modern reading program is based upon conditions which facilitate reading. Such conditions include an abundance of attractive reading materials in the classroom, a well-equipped and well-managed library easily accessible to every child, attention to reading in all school activities, physical equipment in the classroom which is attractive and appealing to children, and a vital interest in reading on the part of all teachers in the school.

2. The principal basis of a modern program, ordinarily provided through basal reading instruction, is the systematic and sequential development of skills, including the skills which provide readiness for initial instruction. The basal reading program is built around the use of a series of textbooks which have been planned for the sequential development of vocabulary and the various reading skills. These books are supplemented by manuals or guide books for teachers, books which provide content enrichment and additional practice in using the skills taught, and workbooks. An adequate program provides for:

a. Continuity of growth in reading habits, skills, and attitudes
b. A wide variety of reading activities closely related to the interests and needs of children at the various grade levels, including their needs in other school subjects
c. A rather complete organization of the total reading program, including the incorporation of reading other than basal reading into that program
d. The presentation of information and ideas of importance to many activities of children, both within and outside of the school

3. Essential, too, in a modern program is the provision for using reading under the teacher's guidance in the content fields of the curriculum. This instruction should include the reading of textbooks in these content fields, as well as the reading of encyclopedias and other reference materials. Particularly important are the skills of learning to interpret maps, charts, tables, and graphs.

4. Independent reading of supplementary reading textbooks and other books under occasional teacher guidance must also be provided for. There are many occasions in the classroom for this type of reading, including the gathering of information in other subject areas, reading for pleasure, and practicing the use of reading skills.

5. Guided literature reading, including the reading of prose and poetry by the teacher, is also a part of a modern reading program. This aspect of the total program is developed more fully in Chapter 15.

6. Perhaps the ultimate phase of the reading program is the provision for free and voluntary reading by the students. In free reading the students read, often outside of class and without teacher guidance, materials of particular interest to them. This reading is largely for recreational purposes, but the functional aspect enters into recreational reading. Reading for recreation is not always just for enjoyment; much recreational reading includes the seeking of information and the development of ideas.

The author of a major textbook on the teaching of reading stated that "reading problems in American schools are due less to the teachers' lack of knowledge than to their disinclination or inability to follow the sound principles of teaching which they already know."[3] He further identified a number of principles as basic rules from which all teaching practices should evolve.

Principles of reading instruction are based upon the results of study of the intellectual, physiological, and emotional growth and development of children. They are not infallible laws but they do provide a sound basis for teaching reading at all levels of instruction.

Principles of Reading Instruction

☐ Arousing Interest

The reading program must be stimulating, yet free from too much or the wrong kind of pressure.   Most children want to learn to read; they come to school eagerly and are willing to devote the time, effort, and energy necessary to learn. If the material used in the reading program is interesting in content and style, a major step toward learning to read will have been taken; a similar step is taken at each level of instruction with such materials. Materials—the books—are not all that is needed for the program to be stimulating. The total classroom environment must be rich and vital, reading must be useful and important to the total curriculum, and the teacher must be capable and understanding.[4] Often the teacher, other forces in the school, and the parents—either together or singly—exert overt and subtle pressures on the child. Goals set beyond the child's capabilities, achievements compared with norms

[3]Heilman, *Principles and Practices*, p. 2.
[4]One investigator (Robert Dykstra, "Summary of the Second-Grade Phase of the Cooperative Research Program in Primary Reading Instruction," *Reading Research Quarterly*, 4:49–70, 1968) recently suggested that the entire instructional setting was involved in the effectiveness of a particular program rather than the method or materials alone.

which do not take into account all factors, "getting through" the material rather than teaching, and the showing of disappointment and disapproval are sources of pressure which do not foster learning and growth.

☐ Helping the Individual

Learning to read is an individual process calling for adjustment of procedures and materials for each individual.   Each child should be able to expect his teacher to provide for his rate of learning, to study him as an individual, and to help him when he is in difficulty. Dividing a class into three or four groups for instruction may be useful to instruction but this will not teach children how to read; it will not necessarily properly recognize the individuality of any child in any of the groups. The need is for an attitude on the part of the teacher which genuinely seeks to meet the child's expectations.

☐ Preventing Frustration

No child should experience repeated failure.   No one can thrive on never succeeding; confusion and frustration can only result. When a child experiences difficulty with reading he tends to avoid attempting to do it, and the more difficulty he has the more he will seek to avoid failing again. Certainly such action may have serious personality and social consequences as well as preventing him from learning to read. This principle does not mean that children should not be challenged, that difficult tasks should be avoided. It does mean that there is a place in the developmental process of learning to read for each child—a place that provides opportunity for growth without failure.

☐ Organizing Sequentially

Reading instruction should be sequentially organized.   The learning of every skill or ability depends upon the previously learned skills and abilities. This is as true in reading as in other learning. While there may be differences in the opinions of reading experts and classroom teachers as to the order of specific elements in certain aspects of the total program (word analysis, for instance), there is agreement about much of the program. For example, before a child can effectively find words in a dictionary he must know alphabetical sequence. All good teachers recognize the importance of organization to lessen the hazard of omitting essential skills or of overemphasizing them. The reading programs outlined in basal reading series generally provide the sequential organization that is desirable.

☐ **Getting Meaning**

Reading is a process of getting meaning from written language. It is not a process of getting *the* meaning since the meaning any reader obtains depends upon the experiences he brings to the reading act; neither is reading a mechanical process of word-calling or "decoding." Of course, the reading process is not simple and, in fact, has never been defined to the satisfaction of all reading authorities, but certainly to simply say words (or to just recognize them in silent reading) is only a first step. Therefore a child must be taught more than word recognition skills.

☐ **Maintaining Readiness**

The concept of readiness should be respected at every level of reading development. Although the major emphasis regarding "reading readiness" has traditionally been placed upon its relationship to beginning reading, it should not stop there. Readiness achieved at one level of development does not mean that readiness is maintained at a further level. There needs to be as much concern with readiness in the third, fourth, or sixth grade as in the first.

☐ **Encouraging Independence**

Reading instruction must teach each child independence in reading. The instruction must develop in each child the skills needed for recognizing words without being dependent on another person, for following through with tasks without continual direction, and for achieving the purposes of his reading without teacher guidance. Of course, the development of such independence will have to be guided and fostered, and it will occur gradually.

☐ **Appraising Progress**

Systematic and continuous diagnosis and evaluation should be provided in the program. The developmental nature of reading instruction makes it axiomatic that skills and abilities taught at each level should be appraised before progression to the next level. Much appraisal can be informal, by the teacher and by the child, but more formal evaluation is also needed at regular intervals. Most importantly, evaluation should be for the purpose of guiding instruction; that is, it should be diagnostic and should be used to determine the reteaching necessary and the subsequent skills and abilities to be taught.

Approaches to Reading Instruction

There are many methods for or approaches to giving children instruction in reading. These range from those which seek to instruct children individually to those which seek to simplify in some manner the problem of the irregularity in symbols used to represent the same sounds in our language. Some of the approaches are relatively new, some are old approaches in new apparel, and some have been in use for many years. Some of the differences in these involve actual procedure, so they may rightly be labeled differences in method, but the majority simply involve different types of materials, different ways of grouping, or variations in handling the progress of a child from one achievement level to another.

The Basal Reader Approach
The basal reader approach is the one most widely used in teaching reading and the one that has been in longest continual use in schools. The basis of the approach is the belief that the skills needed to recognize words, gain understanding from written language, and use reading as a means for learning must be organized systematically and as completely as possible, with full recognition of the relationships among the skills and the developmental nature of learning. The approach requires a set of textbooks (and usually workbooks, filmstrips, supplemental books, etc.) which are written to present the skills and vocabulary systematically and in a sequential and developmental fashion. In other words, the program or approach is in the textbooks and related materials, which include, as a fundamental part of the program, teachers' manuals in which specific directions are given for developing skills, vocabulary, and related attitudes and abilities; for organizing the class to provide the instruction effectively; and for evaluating achievement and diagnosing difficulties.

While the instructional designs of various basal reading series (of textbooks) are not alike, they do generally provide for (1) preparational activities—introduction of new vocabulary, setting purposes for reading, establishing experiential backgrounds; (2) silent reading to get the sense of the story; (3) oral reading to check on use of specific skills; (4) introduction to and practice on particular skills; and (5) enrichment activities—supplemental reading, related arts, building additional background, etc.

The basal reader approach is used in at least ninety percent of elementary schools.[5] It has been criticized—particularly for such things as the extent of the control and repetition of vocabulary, awkward sentence construction in some beginning instructional materials, and the content of the stories included in the books—but the values it has in presenting an organized program usually overcome the criticisms. On the other hand, complete reliance on a basal program often limits reading instruction for some pupils and may be a too easily found crutch for the lazy teacher.

The language-experience approach utilizes the experiential backgrounds of the pupils and their abilities in expressing themselves orally for the content and form of the reading material. The basic premise of the approach is that children need to understand the relationship between speaking and writing—and, hence, speaking and reading—and that this understanding will make all reading instruction easier for them. Pupils write what they read, either by writing directly themselves or by dictating to the teacher. From the time of the child's first experience at school, he is encouraged to tell about things that are of interest to him. These are written on charts by the teacher as experience stories; following the writing, the child shares what has been written by telling his classmates what the story says. This is followed by encouraging the child to write his own stories; thus writing receives an earlier emphasis in this approach than it is given in conventional basal programs.[6] The objective is to stress the interrelationships among the language skills, particularly between writing and speaking.

The Language-Experience Approach

There are many aspects of this approach that are little different from practices good teachers have always used in teaching reading. The principal uniqueness is that reading skills are taught as they emerge from the story writing and reading. The responsibility for the program thus rests heavily upon the teacher.

While the value of relating all of the communicative skills is not questioned, the language-experience approach has been criticised for the assumption of similarity and ready transfer among the vocabularies the child has in listening, speaking, writing, and reading; for the incidental approach to the learning of skills; and for its emphasis upon beginning reading without adequate attention to the transition from a

[5]Lillian M. Logan and Virgil G. Logan, *A Dynamic Approach to Language Arts* (Toronto: McGraw-Hill Company of Canada Limited, 1967), p. 251.

[6]Dorris M. Lee and R. Van Allen, *Learning to Read Through Experience* (New York: Appleton-Century-Crofts, 1963).

child's reading his own writing to reading the writing normally found in books he must read.[7]

The Individualized Approach

Since children learn at different rates and in different ways, there is reason to believe that learning is more effective and more efficient if the learner is allowed to progress at his own pace and to the extent of his capacity. Because of this belief and the fact that motivation to learn is a significant factor in success, there has been vacillating interest for a number of years in an individualized approach to reading instruction. The basis for individualized reading programs is the selection by the pupil himself of books to be read, with the expectation that as a result the child will pursue his interests and read extensively. While teaching practices in this approach vary widely, all emphasize that the pupil and the teacher have conference time together every few days at least, to discuss what has been read and to check skill development progress. However, as Durkin points out, these conferences need not be extended to a full-scale tutoring program, with an undue amount of time devoted exclusively to teaching reading skills.[8] The aim of the conference is to give instruction a more personalized basis and to more accurately assess pupil growth.

Durkin also very properly says that teachers should keep in mind that individualized reading is not a method but is an expression of a "philosophy about classroom organization and materials." Furthermore, perhaps "approach" is not an accurate term. In some programs initial instruction is given by a language experience approach, while in others beginning instruction is in the first books of a basal series. In still others, simply written books from various sources are used to teach the first reading skills. From the beginning skills are developed on the basis of needs (the development might be done in small groups), with the teacher keeping records of each child's progress. Good record keeping is an integral part of effective individualized programs.

A major factor in the effectiveness of this approach is the accessibility the children have to many books. Interests must be discovered and fed. To have a pupil fail to find a book that he has not read and that is of interest to him will destroy the motivation that is the key to the approach. Sharing of what has been read is also important and leads to the extension of the reading interests of pupils.

[7]George D. and Evelyn B. Spache, *Reading in the Elementary School*, Second Edition (Boston: Allyn and Bacon, Inc., 1969), pp. 170–185.

[8]Dolores Durkin, *Teaching Them to Read* (Boston: Allyn and Bacon, Inc., 1970), p. 170.

This approach is not a method or set of procedures *per se* but is a set of materials which make use of a special alphabet for writing the words in the books rather than the traditional one. The Initial Teaching Alphabet (abbreviated i.t.a. or i/t/a) contains 44 symbols, adding 20 to the conventional alphabet (and not using *g* and *x*), with all of the symbols being in lowercase form. The objective is to achieve a closer grapheme-phoneme correspondence than is ordinarily possible. Thus the child has a symbol for each sound (if he speaks a "standard" midwestern dialect) and learns to make only one symbol rather than both capital and lower case (the capital letters are simply larger than lower case ones).

The symbols added to make up the 44 in the augmented alphabet are similar to the conventional symbols; thus the material is not difficult for a mature reader of English to comprehend. For instance, *ieland* represents *island,* ∫hær wos a fa∫her bær is *there was a father bear.* The alphabet does not provide for variations in pronunciation in the printed books, though presumably a teacher printing in i/t/a could take into account the local dialect. Emphasis is placed in using i/t/a for early writing by the children since they can spell words as they sound.

Results from using i/t/a have generally shown that children do learn to read early and that transition can be made to reading conventional material. However, studies have shown no particular advantage from using i/t/a over other approaches.[9]

Programmed instruction provides for the presentation of subject matter in small units, each calling for a response from the pupil. Each unit is followed by an answer to the student as to whether his response is right or wrong. The objective of programmed instruction is to permit each child to learn at his own rate, and the basis of programming in reading is that the various skills can be broken into small units and taught sequentially.

Proponents of programming state that while a pupil may or may not become involved with the content of a conventional book, he must become involved in a program. They also stress the value of reinforcing learning at each step and the opportunity to correct mistakes im-

The Initial
Teaching
Alphabet
Approach

Programmed
Instruction
in Reading

[9]See studies by Cartwright and Jones, Milne and Fyfe, Fry, and Dykstra in Samuel Weintraub, Helen W. Robinson, and Helen K. Smith, "Summary of Investigations Relating to Reading, July 1, 1968, to June 30, 1969," *Reading Research Quarterly,* Vol. V, No. 2, Winter, 1970, pp. 256–260.

mediately. Critics of programming are disturbed by its impersonal approach and question the extent to which all of the skills necessary for effective reading can be achieved by it.

There are many unanswered questions regarding all programmed instruction, and that in reading is no exception. Undoubtedly the careful analysis of reading skills and abilities which is necessary for writing effective programs will benefit all reading instruction. Too, the recognition given to differences among pupils in learning rates and interests will prove helpful in gaining better insights into pupils' needs and ways of learning. On the other hand, the mechanical nature of programming is not likely to have sustained appeal to instinctively creative teachers and pupils.

There are many other approaches which have some acceptance with teachers. Some of these require different methods or procedures (because the philosophies upon which they are based are different) but most are different in approach merely because the materials used are different. For example, "Words in Color" codes each of 48 sounds with a different color. In other words, a particular sound (phoneme) is always in the same color even though represented by various letters. Another approach often referred to is one labeled "linguistic," which now usually "refers only to those [materials] which reflect the recommendations of linguists."[10] Linguists generally recommend using words in the beginning stages of reading which fit particular spelling patterns (e.g. van, fan; sad, Dad, had), although it is only fair to say that linguists tend not to agree with one another to any greater extent than do reading "authorities."

Actually, defining an approach or method results in a great deal of ambiguity, since the characteristics of one approach tend to merge with those of one or more of the others. For example, one report on reading research identifies all of the following (and more) as approaches to reading instruction, in addition to all of the ones previously identified in this chapter, but without defining any of them except in the language of the particular researchers reporting on them: "perceptual-motor activities," "visual," "auditory," "conventional," "conventional basal," "synthetic phonics," "phonics-first basal," "Diacritical Marking System," and "highly personalized."[11]

Regardless of the name given to the approach or method used by a teacher, the program should be built upon the bases for a modern program stated earlier and be compatible with those principles of read-

[10]Durkin, *Teaching Them to Read*, p. 135.
[11]Samuel Weintraub *et al.*, "Summary of Investigations."

ing instruction outlined. The key to effective instruction in reading is the teacher rather than the approach or method. Thus the responsibility for developing a program based upon sound principles is clearly upon the teacher.

The Reading Lesson

Knowing what to do and when to do it is essential to effective reading instruction. This requires a great deal of knowledge about the reading process, the sequential development of reading skills, the materials available for use, and the children to be taught. To utilize this knowledge in the best manner possible also calls for long-range and daily planning. Much of the planning is directed at specific lessons, but attention is also given to working out a general procedure that is effective and with which the teacher is comfortable.

The teacher in a modern reading program should be flexible in instructional methods and techniques used from day to day and from one particular teaching situation to another. The focus, however, should always be upon reading to gain meaning and to interpret and use the ideas presented in print. Most methods give attention to this goal, although those which appear to give excessive focus to "word calling" perhaps do not give it the proper amount of attention. Methods generally, however, tend to be built around a fundamental instructional plan for all directed-reading activities. The essentials of such a plan are the following:

Essentials of a Reading Lesson

1. Developing readiness for the reading activity
   (a) Through a discussion of experiences which are related to the content to be read
   (b) Through the introduction of new words and new concepts and the relating of these to words and concepts which are already known
   (c) Through stimulating interest in what is to be read and establishing purposes for the reading
2. Guiding the first, or survey, reading of the selection
   (a) Through motivating questions related to the purpose or purposes
   (b) Through noting the organization of the selection
3. Rereading for specific purposes, such as
   (a) Answering specific questions
   (b) Interpretive oral reading
   (c) Finding specific words or explanations of particular concepts

4. Developing important habits and skills
   (a) Through direct instruction and practice in using word recognition techniques, comprehension skills, and so forth
   (b) Through the use of workbook and teacher-prepared materials
   (c) Through evaluation of progress and the establishment of further instructional goals
5. Providing for enrichment
   (a) By following up on activities begun during rereading
   (b) Through relating what has been read to interests and needs in other curriculum areas
   (c) By suggesting supplemental reading and other activities

Teaching children to use picture cues

Examples of Reading Lessons   A reading lesson is usually a segment in a larger unit. It may deal with a complete story, a part of a story, a particular skill or set of skills, or the use of certain skills and abilities for special purposes. The following are examples of reading lessons which show the general content (but omit many details) of several types. They illustrate that a fundamental plan is the basis for all of the lessons.

☐ **A Second-Grade Lesson**

This lesson uses a story, "Oswald Makes Magic," from *On We Go,*
the second level reader for the second grade in a basal series.[12] The
children have read the first part of the story in a previous lesson.

A. *Building Readiness.* The teacher asks the children if they remember
the trick Agnes (Oswald the magician's wife) tried to play on Oswald.
They discuss whether it worked or not and other things that happened
in the first part of the story. The teacher then tells the children that they
are going to read about some really big magic that Oswald made; that
he made something with his magic that was supposed to have come
from a land far away and that the name of this land is China.

B. *Introducing New Vocabulary.* The teacher writes the new words
wrong and *frightened* on the board and beside them these sentences:
"It is wrong to take something that doesn't belong to you. The sound
of the airplane frightened the baby." He then reads the sentences and
asks the children to give other words which begin the same as *wrong*
and *frightened*. Words suggested are *wrist, write, friend, front,* and *free.*
The teacher also asks for words that mean the same as *wrong* and
frightened. Naughty and *scared* are suggested. The teacher next asks
individual pupils to say the words. The other new words to be met in
this part of the story—*Chinese, dragon, blow, pet, loud, ears,* and *hind*
—are not introduced since the children should be able to get their
meanings independently.

C. *Setting Purposes for Reading.* The teacher asks the pupils to turn to
page 140 and to look for the title of the next part of the story. He then
suggests that pages 140 and 141 be read to find out what magic gift
Oswald got for Agnes. He suggests, further, that if the pupils come to
a word they do not know they try to get the meaning by using the words
around it and the sound it begins with. He asks the pupils to think how
a good storyteller would say the lines on those pages if he were telling
the story.

D. *Discussing the Content Read.* The teacher asks different children
(permitting time for answering and additions the children want to
make) these questions: What did Oswald get for Agnes? What did
Oswald use to get the dragon? Did dragons, like the one Oswald got for
Agnes, ever really live in China?

E. *Reading to Answer Specific Questions.* The teacher tells the children
that one sentence on page 140 tells why Oswald tried to think of something to put in the garden. He then asks one pupil to find and read
orally that sentence. In the same manner he asks for sentences to be
read that tell where Agnes lived as a little girl, how big Oswald was,
and what the dragon did when he saw Agnes.

[12]Paul McKee and others, *Reading for Meaning* series (Boston: Houghton
Mifflin Company, 1963).

In a manner similar to that described above the teacher has the pupils read the remainder of the story. After the lesson is completed an assignment is made in the workbook which is related to the story. In a subsequent daily lesson attention is given to the reading skills suggested in the teacher's guide as appropriate for the unit.

□ A Third-Grade Lesson

This lesson is the second lesson (second day) based on the story "Snowed-in Hill."[13] The entire story has been read in a "guided reading" session.

A. *Setting Purposes for the Lesson.*   The teacher writes the title of the story on the board and asks the children to review the plot of the story. He next writes the word *problems* on the board and asks the children to *skim* the story to find problems created by the blizzard.

B. *Development of Skills.*   From the skimming the teacher asks the children for the problems they found. These are listed on the board. After these have been listed he asks different pupils to tell how the problems were finally solved.

C. *Practice Activity.*   The teacher distributes copies of the exercise (as suggested in the teacher's manual), directing the children to underline the correct ending for each statement. A sample of the exercise is as follows:

> 1. The milk truck did not come through, so—
>   Jack had no milk to drink.
>   Father took the milk to Mr. Mack's.
>   Father did not milk the cows.
> 2. The telephone worked again because—
>   the men worked on the lines.
>   the snowplow went through.
>   the blizzard had stopped.

After the exercise is completed the teacher has the sentences read orally and the answers justified.

D. *Enrichment Follow-up.*   The teacher shows the film "Winter on the Farm" which provides further opportunity for discussion and stimulation for reading other stories about living on farms in the winter.[14]

□ A Fourth-Grade Lesson

The purpose of this lesson is to teach the prefix *re*. The lesson is not from any particular reading book, although the skill development programs in basal reading series have similar lessons. The steps in the lesson are as follows:

---

[13]*Friends Far and Near,* pp. 32–42. Ginn Basic Reading Series (Boston: Ginn and Company, 1961).

[14]Encyclopedia Britannica Films, 1150 Wilmette Avenue, Wilmette, Ill.

A. The teacher reminds the children that earlier they had to write letters over again in preparing them to be sent home to parents. He asks for another way to say "wrote again." They suggest *rewrote*.

B. The teacher asks for another way to say "We addressed our envelopes again." If the children have difficulty he tells them *readdressed*.

C. The teacher writes *rewrote* and *readdressed* on the board and asks the children to tell him their meanings. He writes "wrote over again" and "addressed over again."

D. The teacher writes the following words on the board: *retell, return, reappear, reappoint, rearrange*. The children are asked the meanings and these are written beside the words.

E. The children are asked the meaning of *re*. They respond *again* or *back over again*. The children are asked if they know what kind of syllable *re* is. If no one knows, the teacher tells them and writes *prefix* on the board.

F. The teacher asks the children for other words beginning with the prefix *re*. Those suggested might include *rebuild, recall, refill, replace, restate, resell, retype*.

G. The teacher asks for sentences using the words *retold, redirect*, and *reorganize*, which have been added to the children's list. The meaning of *re* as it is affixed to each word is discussed.

H. The children are asked to write five sentences, using any five words from the list on the board.

Practices and Issues in the Teaching of Reading

As has been suggested, instruction in learning to read and guidance in the use of reading skills should be built upon certain principles. However, methods or approaches vary and with their related activities may depart in some respects from some of the principles outlined. Issues of a controversial nature, as well as practices which should receive particular attention, are discussed in the following sections. The reader is reminded that for a complete discussion he should examine recently published textbooks devoted strictly to the subject of reading instruction.

Attention has been directed in many places in this volume to the extent of the differences among children of the same grade or chronological age, particularly differences in language development. The discussion here of reading readiness is fundamentally related to what has been said regarding pupil differences and specifically supplements the discussions of readiness in Chapters 3, 4, and 5.

Reading
Readiness

Reading readiness is not an all or none proposition, nor does the term mean the same thing to all persons. Some regard readiness (in reading or any skill area) as a stage in maturation—physical, mental, and emotional. Others regard it as an expression of desire, purpose, or interest. Still others emphasize that readiness hinges largely upon information and abilities learned through previous experiences.[15] However, the evidence indicates that readiness for initial reading instruction is dependent upon (1) physical factors such as the child's ability to see and hear words clearly, (2) mental factors such as the ability to follow directions or to relate the sequence of events in a simple story, (3) social factors such as the ability to work with a group and to accept a teacher's direction, (4) psychological factors such as appearing well adjusted to schoolwork or showing interest in reading, and (5) experiential factors such as knowledge of the concepts and information which will be met in the reading experiences.

Reading readiness is actually only an expression of the old teaching rule that the teacher must begin at the child's level—the level of what he knows or can do—and build upon this. Reading readiness functions at all grade levels and in all reading activities. Progress in learning to read, or progress in achieving the next stage in reading skill, is most rapid and has the greatest chance for success when all factors affecting the readiness are optimum. At any stage in reading instruction many of these factors can be improved and developed; a teacher cannot just wait for the readiness to be achieved. Instruction can be provided through systematic programs to develop readiness factors in the areas of personal and social adjustment, visual and auditory discrimination, language facility, habits of attention and work, eye movements, interests, and concept building through experiences.

There is some controversy concerning reading readiness, though most criticism comes from persons who are uninformed or have made "snap" judgments based upon chance observations.[16] Readiness programs simply recognize that a child has to be taught from the foundation of what he already knows and what he can already do. Programs in readiness for beginning reading endeavor to aid in the development of factors important to the first steps in learning to read.

Critics of beginning readiness programs have often voiced the complaint that some children are ready to learn to read, or perhaps

[15]Gertrude H. Hildreth, *Readiness for School Beginners* (Yonkers, N.Y.: World Book Company, 1950).

[16]For example: Charles C. Walcutt, *Tomorrow's Illiterates: The State of Reading Instruction Today* (Boston: Little, Brown, 1961).

may even be able to read, when they first enter school. It is true, of course, that some children are able to read when they enter school, but these are few in number. Durkin, for example, found that about one percent of children entering the first grade in one California city were able to read.[17] Most kindergarten and first-grade teachers would attest to the fact that a majority of children are not ready to read when entering the first grade and that these children benefit from a readiness program. Criticism directed at the much-too-common practice of having a six-week "readiness" period at the beginning of the year in the first grade and then instructing all the children in beginning reading is nevertheless justified. This practice simply does not recognize the purpose of reading readiness programs.

Both vision and hearing are important factors in reading success. Seeing accurately is obviously important to reading but it is equally obvious to most teachers that children, at any grade level, have difficulty in making fine visual discriminations, such as between *ch* and *th*. The relationship of the accurate perception of sounds to reading is perhaps less obvious since most reading is not done orally. However the fact that reading is so highly dependent upon language development establishes the relationship.

Perceptual and Discriminatory Development

Children entering school have developed considerable ability in seeing and noting likenesses and differences, and these experiences have not all been with large objects. However, they usually have not had enough experience in perceiving letters, combinations of letters, and words and in discriminating among them. While readiness workbooks typically provide ample practice in noting likenesses and differences among geometric figures and drawings of animals and other objects, this kind of practice is too removed from the perception and discrimination needed for reading. Extra attention must be given by teachers to practice with words and letters. Such practice does not require that either the letters or the words be named; the focus should be upon the likenesses and differences in the same manner as is done with objects or drawings. This kind of practice needs to be continued beyond the time that the child first learns to read, especially for children who progress slowly in reading.

Auditory discrimination is a fundamental part of word recognition, particularly that aspect which is usually labeled phonics. Again,

[17]Dolores Durkin, "The Precocious Reader: A Study of Pre-School Reading Ability," *California Journal for Instructional Improvement,* 2:24–28, December, 1959.

it can be said that most children come to school with considerable ability in auditory discrimination (since they have learned their language), but they have difficulty in isolating and reproducing sounds and in discriminating among similar ones as they need to in order to use auditory analysis in identifying unknown written forms of words. Teachers must give children practice in hearing differences in sounds in the several parts of words, in hearing similar sounds, in relating sounds to letters, and in accurately pronouncing words that they use in their speech.

The Question of Phonics

Phonics is an adaptation of phonetics, the science of speech sounds. Phonic analysis is one of the most important of the ways by which unknown words may be recognized. This is a well-documented fact; as Heilman states, "there are no non-phonetic methods (in the teaching of reading) in use in America today."[18] In spite of this, however, the controversy continues, much of it resulting from misunderstandings and from the development of certain myths about phonic instruction. This controversy, and the vagueness of many who write and speak on it regarding the real issues, have often caused confusion among teachers concerning many of their instructional practices about which there should be no question. For example, first-grade teachers may feel hesitant about deliberately teaching the names of the letters of the alphabet to children, when the real issue is the teaching of the alphabet in sequence and in ways unrelated to the first-grade curriculum.[19] Children obviously need to know the names of letters and to recognize letters quickly and accurately. Another myth is built around statements concerning how many words a child must know by sight before he makes use of word-recognition techniques, including phonics. Often instructions to teachers in basal reading series and in textbooks on the teaching of reading will state that a child needs 75, 150, 50, or some other number of sight words before he is introduced to phonics. While the principle is true that ability to recognize some words at sight is needed before aids to word recognition may be used (since such aids or techniques call for the relating of an unknown word or a part of a word to a known word), it is not true that even in beginning reading instruction such knowledge and techniques may not be put to use. For example, the child who can recognize at sight the words *can* and *mother* can be taught that *man* begins like *mother* and rhymes with

[18]Heilman, *Principles and Practices,* p. 241.
[19]*Ibid.,* p. 215.

can. Instruction in helpful methods of recognizing words should begin with even the earliest of reading lessons.[20]

Actually instruction in phonics begins in the readiness program with activities which call for discriminating between common sounds, similar words, beginnings of words, and rhyming elements. With the beginning of actual reading this instruction is expanded to the combining of visual and auditory perception of and discrimination between words and elements in words. Later, various principles concerning the sounds of vowels, consonants, blends, digraphs, and diphthongs are introduced inductively and made a part of the tools which a pupil has to use in recognizing words.[21]

The question is not "Should phonics be taught?" Nor is it even "When should phonics instruction begin?" These questions are easily answered: phonic analysis is a useful aid and must be taught, and instruction should be given whenever it will aid in recognizing graphic

[20]Arthur I. Gates, "The Teaching of Reading—Objective Evidence Versus Opinion," *Phi Delta Kappan,* 43:197–205, February, 1962.

[21]See the teachers' manuals of basal reading series for listings of principles.

Applied phonics provides meaningful self-directed activity

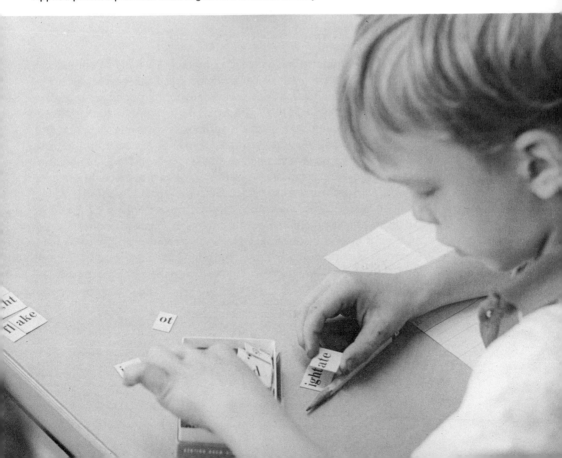

symbols which represent words. The real questions center upon the approaches used for teaching phonic generalizations. Questions arise from such practices as extensive drills on the "sounds of letters"; isolating "sounding out" from meaning; teaching children the "sounds" of consonant letters in isolation, such as *buh, cuh, duh,* and *tuh* for the sounds represented by *b, c, d,* and *t;* and instruction prior to actual reading in the sounds assigned to letters or combinations of letters. While there is some disagreement as to the answers which might be given to questions related to these practices, many reading authorities agree that these are poor, misleading, or false approaches.[22] Certainly gaining understanding from graphic symbols is the reason for reading and no more drill on phonic techniques should be given than is necessary for learning to use principles helpful in gaining meaning. Many distortions in pronunciation—and a failure to then "recognize" a word in the reader's speaking vocabulary—result from "sounding" isolated letters. As Durkin has said, "When consonants are sounded alone, in isolation from other letter-sounds, the result is an impure sound."[23] It is generally agreed also that the teaching of phonic generalizations prior to actual reading does not recognize the purpose of reading and what the act is as a total process. The synthetic approach of teaching sounds is a mechancial procedure that results in facility in word calling rather than in reading.

Linguistics and Reading

A number of linguists have recently proposed a variety of approaches to reading instruction which depart somewhat from procedures advocated generally. Other linguists have advanced principles regarding language that they believe should receive attention in reading instruction. One difficulty with linguists' proposals is the limited amounts of teaching materials and suggestions of method that conform to these principles which have been made available. A second difficulty present, as far as most teachers are concerned, is the lack of research evidence at this time supporting the proposals and advocacy.[24]

While not all linguists agree on what part of linguistics should be taught in reading (some regard reading as a process of relating structural units of oral language to their graphic representations and others regard it as a process of translating phonemes into words), they all tend to object to the isolation of speech sounds, the overstressing of

---

[22]H. A. Robinson, "A Study of the Techniques of Word Identification," *The Reading Teacher,* 16:238–242, January, 1963.
[23]Durkin, *Teaching Them To Read,* p. 275.
[24]Spache and Spache, *Reading in the Elementary School,* pp. 170–185.

learning individual words rather than learning larger contextual units, and the unnatural language patterns present in some reading materials. Too, there appears to be great reliance upon meaning being gained through the process of oral reading, with the structure of the language as it is voiced providing the necessary clues. Generally the programs that have been developed use grammatical sentence structures but the emphasis upon using words with regular spellings (*bat, cat, mat,* etc.) causes the context to have little meaning. The later books do progress to using sentences with semiregularly spelled words and finally to ones with irregular spellings.

The linguists are making a contribution to reading instruction by stressing the importance of the syntactical structure of language, by using a scientific approach to the study of graphic representation of sounds, and by suggesting that there needs to be a sequential introduction of sound and structural elements based upon analysis of language learning.

Teachers should keep in mind, however, that learning to read may be accomplished with deaf children who have no speaking ability or who have no auditory memories as a source of reference. Too, children without deafness have been taught to read without ever reading orally and without reference to "sounding out" words. Such evidence, though, while indicating that the need for an oral approach is not absolute, does not mean that auditory perception and discrimination are not important and helpful in reading. As to the structural elements—the grammatical quality of the language structure—it is well to recognize the differences between the expressive language acts of writing and speaking and the receptive act of reading. While children obviously use a greater number of language patterns in their speech than they meet in the first reading instruction texts, and these spoken patterns are more advanced and diversified, it has yet to be proved that children have an advantage in learning the essential skills needed for independence in reading from having read only language which corresponds to their spoken expression. At the same time, it seems likely that structuring the language in the first readers to correspond more closely to spoken language is sensible.

Word recognition involves analyzing unfamiliar printed or written symbols for clues to their meaning. Essentially the word recognition skills are of two kinds—structural and phonetic—although a type of analysis may occur as a word is recognized through such aids as pictures, the context itself, the configuration or appearance, and the

Word Recognition Skills

recognition of familiar parts. Word recognition also occurs through looking for a word's pronunciation and meaning in the dictionary.

Structural analysis relates to the recognition and use of word parts or the visual characteristics of words as contrasted to the phonetic characteristics. For example, a compound word such as *football* may be recognized through first noting that the word *ball* is a part of it. Structural analysis also involves using knowledge of prefixes, suffixes, roots, inflectional endings, the division of words into syllables, and the effect of accent.[25] Structural analysis is useful in that it is based upon two fundamental facts about language: first, that a root word retains its basic meaning in derived and inflected forms and in compounds; and, second, that affixes to the root have meaning themselves or add to the meaning of the root in specific ways. Thus, by adding *s* to *boy* a specific meaning is denoted; the adding of *un* to *like* combines the meaning of the root and the meaning of the prefix to give the meaning of the new word; the meaning of the compound word *horseback* is easily determined from the meanings of the words which have been put together.

Phonetic analysis is done for the purpose of pronouncing an unknown word. If the word can be pronounced it often is a word that a child knows. Of course, even if the word is correctly pronounced, if it is not known to the pupil phonetic analysis has accomplished nothing of aid to reading. It is important to remember, however, that children ordinarily come to school knowing several thousand words. That is, they have heard many thousands of words, have related meanings to many of them, and are able to use several thousand in their own speaking. Thus analyzing a word whose written form may be unknown is often helpful since possibly the sound of it is known.

Phonetic analysis often provides only an approximation of the proper pronunciation but this is often enough to enable the reader to derive the correct word as he makes use of other word recognition aids. For example, if a child encountered the sentence, "The oar fell out of the boat," and the only unknown word were *oar,* phonetic analysis would provide at least a close approximation of its pronunciation. Then, if the child knew about oars—having seen them or heard them referred to in stories—this knowledge and the context of the sentence should give him the correct pronunciation and the meaning of the word.

The use of context clues is extremely important in reading. The accomplished reader uses his skill in combination with structural and

[25]E. A. Betts, *Foundation of Reading Instruction* (New York: American Book Company, 1954), p. 645.

phonetic clues; he also uses context clues alone since this is the most rapid technique for gaining the meaning of an unknown word in the majority of circumstances. For example, in the sentence "Bill climbed to the_____of the tree" a reader would have no difficulty recognizing *top* if this were the unknown word, and thus would have no need to pause and use structural and phonetic clues. Of course, if the word were *apex, crown,* or *pinnacle*—though the likelihood of this would not be great—the context might or might not be enough and there would be need to combine other clues or perhaps, because such words are not frequently used, a dictionary would be needed. The more difficult the total context is to the reader, the less likely it is that the immediate context alone will provide adequate clues to recognizing unknown words. However, to use context clues properly, more than the immediate context is used. Infrequently there is a need for recognizing several unknown words in a single sentence. Context aid is usually provided from several preceding sentences and also from succeeding ones.

It is important for teachers to remember that the attainment of skill in using word recognition techniques is not an end in itself. The purpose is the determination of what words mean. Pronouncing a word may do this if, when it is pronounced, it is known to the child. Knowing the meaning of a structural element may provide enough aid to determine the meaning. However, the gaining of the meaning of a word—by any of the word recognition skills, or various combinations of them—is only a necessary basic step in reading.

The good reader is versatile in the use of clues to word identification and does not slow his reading down by dwelling on either phonetic or structural analysis when he is able to determine the word quickly through an understanding of the context in which it is used, its configuration, the construction of the sentence it is in, an accompanying diagram or picture, the paragraph or section heading, or some other means. Careless or unskilled use of any word recognition technique can lead to guessing and to mistakes and loss of meaning. However, the skillful reader uses the most appropriate technique and exerts the degree of caution in using any technique relevant to the purpose of his reading.

Facility in word recognition, combined with wide experiences and the relating of those experiences to language symbols, usually leads to understanding. As was implied in the preceding section, however, there is a danger present in many reading programs that overconcern with word recognition may retard the child's attainment of reading

Teaching
Compre-
hension

maturity. Particularly, there is danger that undue emphasis on word recognition will lead to inattention to reading skills which aid understanding.

Comprehension, which is the ultimate goal of reading, is a complex activity. Comprehension comes from the reader's relating his own background of experiences to the words of the writer. The printed page itself contains no meaning; as someone has said, "It is just ink on paper." Meaning comes from the mind of the reader. Thus, the problem in teaching children to read with understanding becomes one of providing many and varied experiences, selecting reading materials which relate to experiences they have had, and making use of certain skills which facilitate the relating of the language on the printed page to their experiences.

A comprehensive reading program provides for instruction in reading to:

1. Get the main idea of a sentence, paragraph, or longer selection
2. Select important details
3. Follow directions
4. Determine the organization of the selection
5. Secure visual or other images from the material
6. Draw inferences
7. Anticipate meaning and predict outcomes and conclusions
8. Summarize what has been read
9. Discriminate between fact and opinion
10. Gain information from specific kinds of materials such as encyclopedias, atlases, maps, graphs, etc.

Basal reading programs include activities for developing skill in reading for the purposes listed above. However, the teacher should have children use these reading practices for learning in all subject areas. The instruction in the basal programs is only a foundation and cannot possibly give the amount of practice necessary to make a mature reader.

Not to be overlooked in the teaching of comprehension are the skills directly related to word meaning. Every teacher knows that it is possible for a child to recognize a word as one he has seen before and to say the word without faltering and yet not understand clearly and correctly what it means in the setting in which it is used. The causes of this of course vary. Certainly some reading content is too abstract to gain meaning from it easily. However, the principal reason is the willingness to accept merely the reproduction of the symbols; that is, to accept saying the words as reading. To eliminate this kind of willingness requires that the teacher better understand the meaning of reading and that he learn how to help students go beyond such verbalism and genuinely read with understanding. Procedures such as the following should be used:

1. The teacher should give the children experience backgrounds for understanding the reading they are to do. This should include field trips; looking at objects, films, pictures; listening to records; discussing experiences they have had and relating them to the reading; and telling about events related to the content of the reading, along with giving the meanings of words which may be beyond their range of use or which are used in unusual ways in the reading.[26]

2. The children must be helped to recognize and interpret punctuation marks. This requires the meaningful teaching of punctuation in written expression and oral reading practice which gives attention to thought units and the relation of punctuation to reading by such units.

3. Children should be encouraged to raise questions regarding a selection to be read prior to reading it. Also teachers should encourage questioning during and after reading; the focus should be upon *meaning* rather than words or manner of reading.

4. The teacher should ask questions which go beyond the recalling of facts or the reading of sentences orally in response to factual questions. He should not merely ask "What did Father do first when the car stopped? Read the sentence which tells what he did." This type of question is helpful in teaching skimming, in appraising general understanding of the selection, for providing practice in reading orally, and for possibly noting word recognition difficulties, but the student might be able to answer it and yet have little real understanding. Judgment questions should also be asked. For example: "What kind of day was it? What would you have done first?"

5. Children may be asked to paraphrase or tell in their own words what has been read. In order for a student to do this he must grasp the meaning as he reads, seeing relationships between the various parts and how they fit together for the total effect sought by the author. Related to the ability to paraphrase is understanding of the organization of sentences, paragraphs, and larger units. There should be deliberate effort made to teach sentence and variations in sentence and paragraph order.

[26]It is particularly important to build background prior to children's reading of assignments in social studies and science.

6. The most effective learning about a topic results from wide reading on that topic rather than from intensive "digging" in only one source. Thus, perhaps fewer topics should be assigned for study to assure the comprehension desired.

7. Exercises should cause pupils to deal with figurative language, bias, and analogy.

Oral Reading

While there is a current revival of interest in oral reading due to the linguist's emphasis upon oral language, the general trend has been to de-emphasize children's oral reading since silent reading has greater social utility and because many poor reading habits may develop when all members of a class silently "follow along" while "turns" are taken in reading aloud. Modern reading programs, however, recognize that oral reading is a form of communication and does have a place, though a less emphasized one, in the total reading program.

Oral reading may be of two types: (1) sight reading in which no preparation has been made for the oral presentation, and (2) prepared oral reading for communication and/or enjoyment. The first type is used by a teacher to determine a pupil's ability in recognizing words, in phrasing, and in enunciation, and the attention he gives to punctuation in his reading. This type of oral reading is done individually, without an audience in the usual sense except the teacher, and without the other children "following" the reader's efforts. The second type of oral reading calls for preparation and is used for true communication. There are many opportunities for such reading: proving a point in a discussion; sharing an exciting, happy, or sad part of a story; answering specific questions; reading reports, directions, announcements, and creative products; and reading in choral and dramatic situations.

Oral reading is a complex skill demanding that the reader not only recognize the words and understand what he reads, but also convey this understanding to an audience. Because of this complexity, silent reading (except as noted above) should always precede oral reading. Difficulties with vocabulary and with meaning can thus be worked out prior to facing the audience. A child who stumbles through unfamiliar material feels confused and inadequate, and not only fails to interpret the material to the audience but will likely be less willing to read or speak before the group again.

Oral reading has a particular place in the teaching of literature. The teacher reads orally to develop interest in reading, to develop appreciation, and to provide stimulation and excitement. Poetry, of course, should always be read aloud and the rhyme and rhythm savored and enjoyed. Many stories, too, are more effective when read aloud and accompanied by sound effects and changes in tone and speed. Every teacher should spend at least a few minutes each day reading aloud something which the children will enjoy. Generally for this reading the selection should be above the reading level of the class, but not above the comprehension level. For example, though few third-grade children would read *Rabbit Hill* for themselves, they will enjoy hearing it read.[27] Too, a child might read a selection from a story which he has particularly enjoyed but which others have not read. His choice might be appreciated by the other children, and some would be influenced in their reading by his presentation. It is a good practice to establish standards for oral reading in the same manner as standards are set for other oral and written language activities. One fifth-grade class developed these standards and a pupil wrote them on a chart:

When Reading Aloud
1. Make sure you have a good reason.
2. Prepare ahead of time.
3. Read carefully and clearly.
4. Be certain everyone hears you.
5. Pay attention to punctuation.
6. Try to read with expression.

There are many ways to organize an instructional program in reading, but the traditional plan is to group the children within one classroom into two to five groups. The composition of the groups is determined by the students' reading levels as measured by standardized reading tests, plus informal appraisal of reading ability by the teacher, with the reading ability of all of the children in any one group being approximately the same. The principal advantage of this plan is that the range in abilities that the teacher must deal with at any one time is considerably narrowed from that which would be faced in teaching the entire class. In addition, provision of material that each child may succeed in reading is facilitated, for each group can receive instruction in a book different from those used in the other groups.

Grouping for Instruction

The traditional plan has a number of limitations, however, which have led to the advancement of other plans for instruction. One limitation is that such grouping does not really mean that the children in a group have the same reading ability, and thus the teacher is still faced

[27]Robert Lawson, *Rabbit Hill* (New York: Viking Press, 1944).

with the problem of dealing with wide differences. Another is that the standardized reading tests and other means of appraisal may not reveal the various levels of reading abilities which the pupil may use, but rather gives only a composite picture which is not too meaningful for specific instructional purposes. The traditional plan has been criticized, too, because of the feeling that the stigma likely to be attached to those in the lower groups, or the lowest group, may retard instruction.

Other plans for instruction include grouping on the basis of interests rather than ability and grouping on the basis of social preferences. Both of these plans allow a teacher to deal with fewer children at a time, just as does the traditional plan. Both are likely, however, to result in an even wider range in reading abilities than would have been the case in the traditional plan.

An organizational plan that has received considerable recent attention is the individualized approach, discussed earlier in this chapter in "Approaches to Reading Instruction." According to this plan each child reads a book of his own choosing, at his own rate, and keeps his own records. The advantages claimed for the plan are that each child is truly instructed at his own level, that he is more interested in reading since he has chosen what he wants to read, and that such attributes as self-direction and self-confidence are fostered. Advocates of the plan also emphasize the elimination of competition among groups, though they admit to increased competition among individual pupils. Criticism of the individualized approach centers around the apparent lack of a systematic plan for teaching the various reading skills. It is obvious that a limited supply of books, an inexperienced teacher, and the number of pupils the teacher has in the average classroom would all reduce the effectiveness of the plan.

It would appear that the best teaching plan makes use of features from all of the plans described above. Dividing a class into groups, with as much attention to homogeneity as possible, is the most systematic way to teach the reading skills. The particular groupings may be modified from time to time to take care of special interests and specific problems. Such modification should prevent any stigma being attached to membership in a low group, for it would be recognized that a single pupil's abilities in reading may range rather widely. Under this plan individualized reading instruction can occur in the supplemental reading program and in the free reading and literature programs.

In planning for instruction in reading it is important for the teacher to recognize the purposes of such instruction and the range of differences among children. No simple plan will achieve these purposes, recognize these differences, and be compatible with every teacher's personality. As Betts has said, "To find one plan of class organization to be executed effectively by all teachers with all children is as difficult as finding a word to rhyme with *orange.*"[28]

Materials for Reading Instruction

A reading program designed to meet the objectives of reading instruction must be broadly conceived. This broadness must extend to the materials used in instruction as well as to teaching procedures and to the organization of the program.

☐ Basal Readers

The principal materials of instruction in the large majority of reading programs are the basal readers, series of books structured for use in developmental sequence. They are designed to teach a basic vocabulary of words, present the various reading skills in an organized manner, and maintain pupils' interest in learning to read. Basal reading programs also include workbooks, teacher's manuals, related supplementary books, word and phrase cards, wall charts, and appraisal materials.

☐ Other Books

While all reading programs should extend beyond the books in the basal program (including those identified as supplemental in the series), particular emphasis on the need for a library of circulating books is required in individualized programs. The "self-selection" program simply cannot function without many books on various ability levels and dealing with varied interests. Most advocates of self-selection instruction state that a minimum of ten trade books per child (suitable to his ability and interest) is needed in the classroom.[29] In addition, self-selection programs as well as basal programs require dictionaries, appropriate textbooks in all curriculum areas, reference books, and supplemental books for the various textbooks.[30]

[28]E. A. Betts, "Developing Basic Reading Skills Through Effective Class Organization," *Education,* 78:571, May, 1958.

[29]Shelley Umans, *New Trends in Reading Instruction* (New York: Teachers College, Columbia University, 1963), p. 100.

[30]See Peggy Brogan and Lorene Fox, *Helping Children Read* (New York: Holt, Rinehart and Winston, Inc., 1961) and Jeannette Veatch, *Individualizing Your Reading Program* (New York: G. P. Putnam and Sons, 1959) for teaching procedures in self-selection.

☐ **Teacher-prepared Materials**

Teacher-prepared materials include experience charts and stories, parallel stories (written by the teacher and using the same vocabulary as the story in the reader), duplicated worksheets, and word and phrase cards to meet specific needs.[31] Many of the materials (particularly charts) can be made by the teacher and pupils working together.

☐ **Child-prepared Materials**

Teachers often find that having children write and illustrate materials is quite effective. At the middle and upper grade levels these materials take the form of a class newspaper or yearbook. Child-prepared materials may present difficulties in preparation unless the teacher can enlist the aid of someone to help with typing, although certainly not all such materials must be typed.

Many teachers have children in the primary grade prepare a picture dictionary.

☐ **Classroom Materials**

Other materials necessary for effective instruction in reading include the chalkboard, pocket charts (to hold word and phrase cards), charts, flannelboards, tape and disc recorders, film and filmstrip machines, overhead projectors, and the recordings, pictures, and films for them. In addition, television can be used for building background and interest and possibly for direct instruction, and programmed books may individualize and supplement instruction.[32] Games are also useful in teaching word recognition skills and the meanings of words.[33]

Evaluation in Reading Instruction

Measuring the skills and abilities necessary for effective reading has not encountered the problems in development of satisfactory instruments that have plagued the other receptive language art of listening. On the contrary, measuring instruments and evaluative techniques have been developed further and are more readily available in the area of reading than perhaps in any other area of the school curriculum.

[31]See Chapter 5 for making and using experience charts.
[32]See Umans, *New Trends,* for a discussion of programming, the use of the overhead projector, etc.
[33]See Spache and Spache, *Reading in the Elementary School,* at the end of each chapter for references to games, charts, and programmed materials.

For this reason, and because the teaching of reading is not the principal concern of this book, only a survey of evaluation in reading instruction is presented here.[34]

Since a major purpose for teaching reading is to enable children to understand and react intelligently to those things they have occasion to read in ordinary life situations, reading must be regarded as an important tool for learning and for gaining pleasure. In order to plan and implement an instructional program in reading which fits the needs of individual children, it is necessary to measure and appraise the various skills and abilities at particular times and intervals, and in particular areas of concern. Evidence of growth in reading abilities and skills is determined by (1) observation by the teacher of the pupil's reading; (2) informal tests, inventories and checklists of material in readers and similar textbook materials; (3) standardized reading achievement tests; and (4) examining the pupil's work in other subject areas and records which have been kept of his reading. The informal aspects for appraising growth are usually dealt with in the teacher's manuals that accompany the textbooks in a basal reading series; therefore, principal consideration will be given here to standardized tests.

As has been pointed out, readiness is an important factor in reading, not only at the first-grade level, when instruction in reading is first given, but throughout the elementary school as children progress from one level of ability to the next. Readiness may be thought of as the maturity achieved or the specific ability acquired which is necessary for successfully learning a new skill or attaining a further goal. The belief that a pupil should be ready for any learning situation with which he is faced has long been an accepted principle of teaching and is neither unique to beginning reading instruction nor to any other aspect of reading instruction.

Measurement
of Reading
Readiness

Readiness for a reading task is dependent upon many factors, among them: (1) intelligence, (2) the ability to perceive written and oral symbols accurately, (3) physical health and vigor, (4) background of experience, (5) an understanding and use of language, (6) emotional and social stability, and (7) interest in reading and learning. Equal or comparable development of each of these factors—and others —is not vital for attainment of success in every new reading task, but sufficient development in most factors is necessary. Certainly the fac-

[34]An excellent collection of papers on evaluation in reading programs is Roger Farr's *Measurement and Evaluation of Reading* (New York: Harcourt, Brace and World, Inc., 1970).

tors making for success at each successive stage in reading must be appraised, and if deficiencies are found, they must be remedied. Appraisal is sometimes made by checklists but more often through the use of standardized tests which focus upon specific skills and abilities. The standardized tests usually measure abilities in visual discrimination, auditory discrimination, word meanings and concepts, listening comprehension, visual-motor coordination, rate for learning words, number concepts, and word-picture relationships.[35] While most reading tests can be thought of as diagnosing reading skills and therefore indicating readiness for certain reading tasks, the teacher's greatest concern about reading readiness is concentrated at the beginning reading stage, for which specific reading readiness tests are available.

The *Harrison-Stroud Reading Readiness Tests* employ testing procedures which are representative of most such tests.[36] Instructions are given orally by the teacher, and readiness is measured by the pupil's ability to (1) use symbols, (2) make visual discriminations, (3) use context, (4) make auditory discriminations, (5) use context and auditory clues, and (6) give the names of letters.

The *Gates Reading Readiness Test* deals with picture directions, word matching, rhyming, and the identification of letters and numbers.[37] The *Lee-Clark Reading Readiness Test* is also widely used and measures (1) recognition of likenesses, (2) discrimination of differences, (3) experiential background, and (4) ability to discriminate among similar but different forms of letters and words.[38]

Measurement of Oral Reading Abilities Oral reading tests, such as the *Gray Oral Reading Paragraphs,*[39] the *Gray Standardized Oral Reading Check Tests,*[40] and the *Gilmore Oral Reading Test*[41] are effective means for evaluating efficiency in the use of word-recognition clues and techniques. In addition, oral reading

[35]Thomas C. Barrett, "Predicting Reading Achievement through Readiness Tests," *Reading and Inquiry* (Proceedings of the International Reading Association), J. A. Figurel, editor, 1965, pp. 26–28.

[36]Lucille Harrison and James B. Stroud, *The Harrison-Stroud Reading Readiness Tests* (Boston: Houghton Mifflin Company).

[37]Arthur I. Gates, *Gates Reading Readiness Test* (New York: Bureau of Publications, Teachers College, Columbia University).

[38]J. Murray Lee and Willis W. Clark, *Lee-Clark Reading Readiness Test* (Los Angeles: California Test Bureau).

[39]William S. Gray, *Gray Standardized Oral Reading Paragraphs* (Indianapolis, Ind.: Public School Publishing Co.).

[40]William S. Gray, *Gray Standardized Oral Reading Check Tests* (Indianapolis, Ind.: Public School Publishing Co.).

[41]John V. Gilmore, *Gilmore Oral Reading Test* (New York: Harcourt, Brace and World, Inc.).

tests measure accuracy of oral reading, comprehension of material read, and rate of reading. Types of errors made by the child are usually recorded by the teacher, who is thus enabled to gain a concise picture of a child's particular difficulties with word recognition and pronunciation. The scores made on these tests and the teacher's analysis of errors do not, however, show certain factors which are important to reading aloud to an audience. Such factors as phrasing, volume, expression, voice quality, poise, and rhythm generally are best appraised by careful and systematic observation by the teacher.

Silent reading serves a number of purposes, not all of which are subject to testing. The two major types of silent reading tests are work-study tests and vocabulary, or word-knowledge, tests. While at the secondary level there are some standardized tests which purport to measure the outcomes of teaching literature, the literature focus at the elementary school level is such that evaluation is done by the teacher through informal procedures.

Measurement of Silent Reading Skills

Tests such as the *Gates Primary Reading Tests* and the *Gates Advanced Primary Reading Test* purport to measure word recognition and understanding paragraph meaning.[42] The *Gates Basic Reading Test,* for use in Grades 3 to 8, has five separate booklets designed to measure (1) appreciation or general comprehension, (2) understanding directions, (3) noting of details, (4) vocabulary, and (5) level of comprehension. The *Iowa Silent Reading Test,* elementary edition, measures rate and comprehension, directed reading skill, word meaning, sentence meaning, paragraph comprehension, and skill in locating information.[43] The *Nelson-Lohmann Reading Test* is a paragraph test for Grades 4 through 8 which uses multiple-choice questions to measure the grasp of central ideas, word meanings derived from context, details, and the pupil's ability to integrate ideas.[44] In addition to these and other similar tests specifically designed to measure reading skills, achievement tests such as the *California Achievement Tests* have sections which measure vocabulary, ability to follow directions, and the use of reference and interpretative skills.[45]

[42]Arthur I. Gates, *Gates Primary Reading Tests* (New York: Bureau of Publications, Teachers College, Columbia University).

[43]Harry A. Greene and Victor H. Kelley, *Iowa Silent Reading Tests* (Yonkers, N. Y.: World Book Co.).

[44]Educational Test Bureau, *Nelson-Lohmann Reading Test* (Minneapolis: Educational Publishers, Inc.).

[45]Ernest W. Tiegs and Willis W. Clark, *California Achievement Tests* (Monterey, Calif.: California Test Bureau).

1. Examine several books of a basal reading series. What values do you see in the controlled vocabulary? Do you find evidence of the "sequential nature" of the reading skills? Do the books have appeal for children?
2. Report to class on the operation of a reading program which emphasizes "self-selection."
3. Look up reports on materials and methods of instruction used with disadvantaged children. For a particular subculture make a list of reading instructional materials which are most appropriate.
4. Outline a weekly plan for teaching reading at a particular grade level, making use of three reading groups.
5. Make a list of filmstrips, records, games, and charts useful to teaching word recognition. Include information as to where they may be secured.
6. At the grade level of your choice, make a list of the phonetic and structural generalizations appropriate for teaching. Make use of teacher's manuals for basal reading series in making your list.
7. Examine several basal reading programs for their diagnostic and evaluative suggestions. Bring to class examples of checklists and other informal devices proposed.
8. Prepare several exercises which could be used for practicing finding the main idea, selecting details, determining the organization, summarizing what has been read, etc.

Selected References

Bond, Guy L., and Wagner, Eva Bond. *Teaching the Child to Read,* Fourth Edition. New York: The Macmillan Company, 1966.

Cutts, Warren G. *Research in Reading for the Middle Grades.* Washington, D.C.: Superintendent of Documents, Government Printing Office, 1963.

Dawson, Mildred A., and Bamman, Henry A. *Fundamentals of Basic Reading Instruction.* New York: David McKay Company, 1963.

DeBoer, John J., and Dallmann, Martha. *The Teaching of Reading.* New York: Holt, Rinehart and Winston, Second Edition, 1964.

Durkin, Dolores. *Phonics and the Teaching of Reading.* New York: Bureau of Publications, Teachers College, Columbia University, Revised Edition, 1969.

Fries, Charles C. *Linguistics and Reading.* New York: Holt, Rinehart and Winston, Inc., 1963.

Gunderson, Doris V. *Research in Reading at the Primary Level.* Washington, D.C.: Superintendent of Documents, Government Printing Office, 1963.

Heilman, Arthur W. *Principles and Practices of Teaching Reading.* Columbus, Ohio: Charles E. Merrill Books, Second Edition, 1967.

Lefevre, Carl A. *Linguistics and the Teaching of Reading.* New York: McGraw-Hill, Inc., 1964.

McKee, Paul, and Durr, William K. *Reading: A Program of Instruction for the Elementary Grades.* Boston: Houghton Mifflin Company, 1966.

Russell, David H. *Children Learn to Read,* Second Edition. Boston: Ginn and Company, 1961.

Smith, Nila Banton. *American Reading Instruction.* Newark, Delaware: International Reading Association, 1965.

Spache, George D. and Evelyn B. *Reading in the Elementary School,* Second Edition. Boston: Allyn and Bacon, Inc., 1969.

Stauffer, Russell G. *Directing Reading Maturity as a Cognitive Process.* New York: Harper and Row, Publishers, 1969.

Strang, Ruth. *Helping Your Child Improve His Reading.* New York: E. P. Dutton and Company, Inc., 1962.

Umans, Shelley. *New Trends in Reading Instruction.* New York: Bureau of Publications, Teachers College, Columbia University, 1963.

15

Teaching Literature In The Elementary School

INTRODUCTION

The teaching of literature is one of the more important tasks of the elementary school teacher—and should be one of the more enjoyable, for both teacher and pupils. Yet Squire reported in the 1969 edition of the *Encyclopedia of Educational Research* that "Concern has continued to be expressed over the need to strengthen the curriculum in literature in the elementary school," adding that the Committee on the National Interest of the National Council of Teachers of English had criticized the fact that "only a small percentage of time was devoted to literature in conventional elementary programs."[1] It is possible, of course, that the definition of the term *literature*—or even a subjective evaluation of what is meant by "good" reading—might enter into the formation of such a conclusion, but it is also possible that teachers and makers of school curriculums have sometimes forgotten the ultimate objectives of education in their concern for the teaching of needed skills and information. However useful the skills of reading, writing, listening, and speaking may be, surely one acquires them for purposes other than those that are strictly utilitarian. Even with the omnipresent television set occupying much leisure time for both children and adults, publishers insist that more books are being sold today than ever before. Guiding children's tastes in reading and helping them to discover the pleasure to be found in books should, then, become a vital aspect of the language arts program.

Oral interpretation is, of course, an important aspect of the literature program, and this is more fully discussed in Chapter 7. Creative writing, too, often grows out of the literature program; further suggestions in relation to this may be found in Chapter 9. Considerations particularly stressed in these pages are the following:

---

[1]James R. Squire, "English Literature" in *Encyclopedia of Educational Research,* Fourth Edition, Robert L. Ebel, editor (New York: The Macmillan Company, 1969), p. 464.

1. Objectives of the Literature Program
2. The Teacher and Literature
3. Children's Reading Interests
4. Techniques in Teaching Literature
5. Special Considerations in the Teaching of Poetry
6. Evaluation in the Literature Program
7. Aids in Book Selection
8. Books for Particular Purposes

Objectives of the Literature Program

The objectives of any literature program are necessarily stated in some-what general terms; therefore, the individual teacher may find many ways of implementing them to suit the needs of particular pupils or classes. Almost invariably, a statement of objectives revolves around four major purposes: enrichment of the individual, development of insights and understandings, transmission of the culture, and develop-ment of taste in reading. Whitehead states these in terms of eight goals which the teacher of literature should have in mind:[2]

1. To help the child understand himself and his present problems.
2. To provide opportunities for escape from routine.
3. To provide a focus for leisure time activities.
4. To develop an appreciation of country and American ideals.
5. To increase the child's knowledge and understanding of the problems of others.
6. To discover and develop ethical standards.
7. To utilize literature as a source for further creative endeavor.
8. To promote an appreciation of the English language.

Logan and Logan, on the other hand, prefer to think of objectives in terms of questions.[3]

In developmental reading the teacher is concerned with the ques-tion, "What is Johnny doing in reading?" In literature he is con-cerned with the question, "What is reading doing for Johnny?" The teacher must ask himself, "Can I teach so enthusiastically, so effectively, so creatively that Johnny will under my guidance:

[2]Robert Whitehead, *Children's Literature: Strategies of Teaching*, © 1968, pp. 6–7. Reprinted by permission of Prentice-Hall, Inc., Englewood Cliffs, N.J.
[3]Lillian M. and Virgil G. Logan, *A Dynamic Approach to Language Arts* (Toronto: McGraw-Hill Company of Canada, 1967), p. 502.

1. Share the real and imaginary experiences of the author
2. Extend and enrich his own experiences
3. Broaden the scope of his interests by bringing him into contact with a wide range of literature in a wide variety of situations
4. Develop insight into his own personality and problems
5. Develop discriminating taste and a permanent love for literature
6. Express creativity through literature?"

Whether he prefers questions or statements, the teacher should be sure that he has specific goals in mind. He should be equally sure that these goals are suited to the needs and abilities of his pupils; that they are child-centered, not teacher-centered; and that they are broad enough to provide for individual differences. He must not make the error of attempting to force a set of preconceived standards upon his class or expecting all pupils to respond to a particular story or poem because it is considered a "good" one. If one accepts the thesis proposed in Chapter 1 of this book that the goals of a program determine the selection of subject matter needed to achieve them, then he must examine these goals carefully in selecting the content of the literature program. Objectives of a literature program are stated in terms of attitudes, insights, and understandings; such objectives cannot be achieved through a previously established content, with students being told what they are to like and what they are to gain from it. Children must be guided and encouraged to find pleasure in reading, for unless it is a pleasurable experience for them, they will read little but what is required, and thus the goals of the program will be lost. Therefore, the teacher must study his class; discover their needs, interests, experiences, and abilities; and then take the time and trouble to plan a program around these.

The Teacher and Literature

"The acid test of any reading program," wrote David Russell, "is whether or not the children in it or graduated from it read for themselves."[4] Even though the reading habits of parents and other members of the family influence the child to a certain extent, it is the teacher whose influence is most felt during the years when the child is learning to read. The teacher, then, is really the heart of the literature program.

[4]David H. Russell, *Children Learn to Read* (Boston: Ginn and Company, 1961), p. 362.

First, the teacher must himself like to read. If he does not feel that reading is important enough to set aside a portion of his own day for reading, then he cannot hope to inspire his pupils with a true love for reading. Enthusiasm is catching: studies and reports of teachers' observations have shown that pupils like best those areas of the curriculum that the teacher himself most enjoys teaching. Surely it follows, then, that if the teacher does not truly enjoy reading, the pupils will not be motivated.

Second, the teacher should become as familiar as possible with what is best in children's literature. One recent text suggests that "A course in children's literature is a must for any elementary school teacher."[5] Certainly such a course is invaluable, but it is not sufficient in itself, nor is this the only way in which the teacher may inform himself about children's books—as the authors of the aforementioned text recognized. In addition, there are a number of excellent books about children's literature, and numerous listings of books recommended for various age and grade levels; these will be discussed in a later section of this chapter. Further, the school and public librarians can offer valuable help. But none of these is sufficient, though all are helpful, for the teacher who is to inspire a real love of reading in his pupils must himself be familiar with children's books. The beginning teacher should consider it a prerequisite to spend several days in the children's section of the library, getting to know what is available and noting books which seem particularly suitable for oral reading as well as those suited to the grade level which he is to teach. And every teacher, either new or experienced, should visit the library regularly, so that he may become acquainted with new additions and discover selections suited to the needs and interests of particular children in his class. An excellent aid here is a packet of index cards, on which useful reminders might be written. These should be kept simple and should be made only for books the teacher feels he may want to remember and find later (see example on next page).

Another requirement is that the teacher must know his class. Many studies have provided helpful information concerning children's interests in reading and their findings are discussed in the succeeding section, but no good teacher fails to remember that the pupils in his class are individuals, with individual interests, individual abilities, and individual needs.

A final essential for the successful teacher of literature is that he

[5]Iris M. and Sidney W. Tiedt, *Contemporary English in the Elementary School* (Englewood Cliffs, N.J.: Prentice-Hall, Inc., 1967), p. 303.

```
Animal Stories, age 3-6

     Horton Hatches the Egg
     by  Dr. Seuss
delightful fantasy - elephant hatches egg
good for reading aloud (1 sitting)
     verse form
many pictures, large enough to show to
     group
                         Norton Library
```

be able to read aloud well and that he should enjoy reading aloud. Some time for reading to the children should be allowed in the schedule for each day. This is particularly necessary in the early years when the children cannot read much for themselves, but it should not be neglected in the upper grades, when other activities become important and the value of reading for relaxation and enjoyment needs to be re-emphasized. Students who read well may wish to participate and should certainly be encouraged to do so, but the teacher should furnish the model. All selections for reading aloud, of course, should be carefully selected and prepared; if the teacher feels that he does not read well, he should practice—perhaps even take a few speech lessons, if necessary—so that the experience will be a happy one for both himself and the pupils. This aspect must not be omitted or neglected, since reading aloud is the primary way in which the teacher may communicate his enthusiasm for books to the children.

Children's Reading Interests

Authorities are agreed that any successful program aimed at getting children to read and improving their tastes in selecting reading materials must start at the children's level and include a carefully planned program for broadening their interests and raising the level of their tastes. This means simply that the teacher should begin by discovering what kinds of subjects the children are interested in and providing a wide variety of materials suited to these interests and to the reading ability of the particular children involved. Obviously as mentioned

An informal atmosphere adds pleasure to stories

above, each child has individual interests and abilities; however, numerous studies of children's interests have established a few guidelines which may prove helpful to both the beginning and the experienced teacher.

For the prereader or the child who is just beginning to read, illustrations and pictures are naturally of prime importance. Small children like bold colors rather than muted ones; the pictures should be simple rather than complicated, and of objects, animals, or people that can be easily identified by the children. This does not mean that they must be photographic in quality, for children are perceptive and imaginative —in fact, a simple line drawing may be much more meaningful than an actual photograph, which would probably include far too many distracting details. Further, the pictures should tell the story, so that

Kindergarten and Primary

after the book has been read to him—and the pictures shown at the same time, of course—the child may enjoy "rereading" the book himself by looking at the pictures. For these beginners, also, pictures should occupy most or all of the space in a book, with very few words appearing on any single page.

In subject matter, the primary child needs stories which provide him with assurance and a sense of achievement.

> The youngest children in our schools, the prereaders and beginners in reading, just because they are small and inexperienced, are uncertain, insecure, and generally find themselves in the wrong. Someone is always saying, "Don't do that," or "No, you aren't old enough for that." So, of course, these young pilgrims need lots of reassurance about their place in the world, that they are loved, needed, and capable of doing things on their own.[6]

Since these children are imaginative and because they also love stories about animals and mechanical objects, they can easily identify with such characters as the Happy Lion in the series by Louise Fatio. They will shiver through the winter with poor Horton as he faithfully sits on his egg, and struggle manfully up the hill with *The Little Engine that Could.* The child of a minority group may find special solace in a story like *Whistle for Willie,* by Ezra Jack Keats, and the Caucasian child will find no difficulty in identifying with Willie, for children have no prejudice and they all know the agony of being unable to do the things that older boys and fathers can do easily.

Folk and fairy tales are also popular with young children and should be included generously in the literature program for two reasons: because they are a vital part of the heritage of literature for children *and* grownups and because they pave the way for acceptance and enjoyment of the world of imaginative literature which lies ahead.

Middle Grades By the middle grades the interests of the child will have broadened since he has come to experience more of the world around him. Informational books such as the *First* books and the *All About* books will help to satisfy and encourage his curiosity about this world. And, as he learns about other lands in social studies class, he will be attracted to stories about children of these lands, as well as those of the many sections of his own country. History, too, with its colorful adventures of heroes and explorers, is a popular subject for this age group and can often be used to open up a new field of literature, the biography.

[6]May Hill Arbuthnot, "Developing Life Values Through Reading," *Elementary English,* January, 1966, p. 11.

This will correlate well with the current trend for using biography in social studies at the fourth and fifth grade levels. Animal stories continue to be popular with both boys and girls of this age group, and by about the fifth or sixth grade boys will probably develop an interest in sport stories.

It must not be presumed, however, that because the middle-grader is interested in real people and the real world about him, he has lost his taste for the imaginative, and it is particularly important that his interest in the real should not be encouraged to the point that the imaginative is crowded out. Paul Bunyan is as much a part of the story of the expanding frontier as the first railroad, and the child of this age will delight in tall tales and folk stories of all lands. Further, he is quite as willing to accept that Peter Pan can fly through the air as he is to demand that this same delightful boy should shiver at the approach of Captain Hook or feel the universal need for a mother's love and care.

Children of the middle grades will also enjoy humor, and this quality should be carefully nurtured, since laughter is an invaluable weapon against the tensions and cares of modern life. Mary Poppins and Henry Huggins will delight these children, as will the huge but friendly dinosaur hatched from Oliver Butterworth's *Enormous Egg.*

Nearly all of the interests of the middle grades are carried into the upper elementary years. Perhaps the major change at this level is that the sexes begin to differ more markedly in their choices of subject matter. Since they mature more rapidly, the girls begin to show interest in stories with some love interest, while the boys' preference for sports and adventure grows more marked. Children of this age are active and full of life, so they want plots that move rapidly; they love mystery and adventure of all kinds. At the same time, however, they are experiencing the first pains of approaching maturity, and they are well aware that there are problems in the adult world which they must soon face. They not only want but need to be exposed to stories in which people like themselves face problems and attempt to find workable solutions.

Upper Grades

Techniques in Teaching Literature

Often the young teacher, fresh from college literature courses, is so impressed with his newly discovered knowledge of symbolism, literary allusion, onomatopoeia, and the many other techniques of the writer's craft that he feels such knowledge is necessary to the children's appreciation of fine literature. Such a teacher needs to re-examine his objectives in teaching literature. Seldom is the objective of teaching pupils to analyze a piece of literature to be found among these goals. The Nebraska *Curriculum for English,* for example, specifically warns teachers away from such practices:[7]

> ... the teacher should not deliver lectures and ready-made literary analyses to elementary school children. She should not deliver the background material in the units to students but lead them when and as they can to perceive what a work is about. She should not ask children to recognize and apply the technical critical terminology of the interpretive analyses given in these sections of the units: the primary purpose of the curriculum is to create understanding, not conventional bourgeois citizens or polite little boys, however desirable the creation of these may be.

Perhaps the temptation to analyze is at least partly rooted in the fact that such knowledge *can be tested,* whereas it is difficult indeed to test appreciation or whether a child's self-understanding has increased. The teacher must content himself with the knowledge that most of the true values of literature simply *cannot be tested,* and that whatever grading he must do is bound to be arbitrary and highly subjective. Even the number of books read, or the number of pages, is no measure since the relative values of what was read or of what the pupil got from it are not subject to measurement.

All this is not to say that the teacher may not ask "Do you know who Apollo was?" or "What do you like about the sound of this poem?" but he should remember not to spoil enjoyment by prolonged analysis and explication.

In a similar vein is a second "don't" for the teacher of literature. The enjoyment of reading should not be negated by the necessity of filling out standardized book report forms or writing long, formal book reports. The purpose of making a book report is not to prove that the student has read a book but to allow him to share it with others in some way that is suitable to him and to the book. Certainly the written report has value and should not be eliminated, but there are many other excellent ways in which a pupil may show what he has acquired from reading a particular book, and these will be discussed in a later section.

[7]*A Curriculum for English,* Grade 5, Units 45–57 (Lincoln: University of Nebraska Press, 1966), p. xiv.

A final "don't" concerns memorization. Undoubtedly requiring the memorizing of lines or poems is not so common as it once was, but many teachers still cling to this custom. No one would say that children should *never* memorize poems. A child who is going to read a poem to the class should certainly be urged to know it well enough that he will neither stumble over words nor have to look at the page so much that he loses eye contact with his audience. He may even decide that he wants to memorize it, but he should not be required to. Similarly, the members of the class may decide that they should memorize a poem they are going to recite as a verse choir, but this should be a decision made by the group, not by the teacher. On the other hand, the teacher who truly loves words and the sounds of words and himself enjoys memorizing favorite phrases or poems will often communicate this feeling to his pupils, so that they will choose to memorize their own favorites. However, memorization should never be a "blanket" assignment or one that is looked on simply as a chore by the pupils.

Much has already been said about children's interests at various age levels, and a fairly successful program could probably be built around the suggestions which have been furnished by research in this area. However, children are individuals, and they can be reached more effectively if we know their individual likes and dislikes, as well as their capabilities. The shy child who has never opened up before may be drawn from his shell when the teacher takes the trouble to find him a book about his special hobby, astronomy, or the reluctant reader in the seventh grade may actually enjoy a book for the first time because it is a true story of his favorite baseball hero.

Finding Children's Interests

There are a number of ways in which the teacher may fit the selection of materials to the needs of a particular class. Perhaps the simplest is a card file in which a card for each child lists his reading level, interests, and perhaps the names of the books he reads during the year. Information for the cards may be obtained informally by talking with the children as they browse or by the use of a short questionnaire asking such questions as the following:

1. What person do you most admire?
2. What is your favorite TV program?
3. Name one book that you especially liked.
4. What do you like best to do after school or on Saturdays?
5. What place in the world would you most like to visit?
6. If there were only one book in the room, what would you want it to be about?

Armed with this type of information, the teacher may make a list of kinds of books to look for when he seeks new materials for the room library. Such information is also helpful in broadening interests and raising levels of taste or ability, for a student may be led from one field to an allied area or may be challenged to read a more difficult book because it is of particular interest to him.

Many books must be available if children are to learn to enjoy reading

Room Libraries

Books must be available to pupils if reading is to be encouraged. Every elementary classroom should have a book corner, where pupils may go to browse both at a regularly provided time and when they have finished assigned work with which the other children are still busy. The book corner should be bright and attractive, with tables and chairs so that pupils may take time in selecting the books they wish to read. Books should be attractively displayed, not just filed on shelves, and they should be changed frequently so that children will not feel that they have "run out" of anything to read. The library corner may also be a place where models, pictures, dioramas, etc., which pupils have made in lieu of book reports, may be displayed. A bulletin board provides a place for pictures or written reports by the children, colorful book jackets, announcements about new books in the school or room library, or pictures cut from magazines and attractively mounted by the teacher to illustrate a particular book or group of books.

Reading Aloud
by the
Teacher

In addition to merely providing books and a place to put them, the teacher should actively participate in the children's discovery and enjoyment of books. If he obviously likes to read, the children will be encouraged to read also. However full the schedule may be, some time should be set aside each day for reading aloud by the teacher or by a member or members of the class. Perhaps the reading may be only a short poem or a paragraph or page from a story; perhaps it may be an entire story or chapter from a book. In any case, it should be carefully selected and prepared so that everyone can enjoy it.

This reading can serve many purposes. At the kindergarten and primary levels, of course, it is necessary for the teacher to read because the children can read so little for themselves. At this level particularly —but at all other levels, too—the teacher should show the pictures as he reads and allow the children time to examine them. Afterward, the children may look at the book and enjoy remembering the story, and later, of course, read it and other stories for themselves. As children grow older, there are many books which are extremely interesting but somewhat difficult in reading level and which the teacher may wish to select for oral reading. Dialect sometimes poses difficulty for children, too, yet it frequently furnishes great enjoyment for oral reading, especially if done well. The teacher should be warned, however, that reading dialect well requires a great deal of practice.

Sometimes the teacher may want to read only a section of a book as a sort of "sales pitch" to interest pupils in reading it. What seventh grader, for example, could resist the opening of Emily Neville's *It's Like This, Cat:*[8]

> My father is always talking about how a dog can be very educational for a boy. This is one reason I got a cat.

And surely the primary child would wish to go further if the teacher read these lines:[9]

> One evening Harold got out of bed, took his purple crayon and the moon along, and went for a walk in an enchanted garden.

Other stories might provide exciting incidents which can be used to provoke interest. At any rate, reading may be used as a means of selling books to children. This should not be overdone, however, for

[8]Emily Neville, *It's Like This, Cat* (New York, Harper & Row, 1963).
[9]From *Harold's Fairy Tale* by Crockett Johnson. Copyright © 1956 by Crockett Johnson. Reprinted with permission of Harper & Row, Publishers.

the children will tire of it. And some stories simply demand to be read aloud in their entirety because they are so delightful, so beautifully written, or so powerful in their message that they need to be shared. Too, the excitement which accompanies holiday time can be alleviated by a story, while at the same time a greater awareness of the meaning of this particular season can result. Every teacher should have a ready supply of stories and poems for holidays. Most libraries have a special shelf for such materials, but it would be wise for the teacher to have his own private collection of favorites as well. In fact, a subject file of stories and poems and where they may be found will prove invaluable.

Perhaps a special word should be added about Christmas, since numerous court cases have resulted from its celebration in the schools, and school boards are plagued annually by calls from honestly concerned parents during the Christmas season. This is perhaps the most important holiday in the Christian calendar, and it is often celebrated also by those who are not Christians; it is therefore difficult to ignore. However, religious freedom is guaranteed by the Constitution of the United States, and no teacher in the public schools should attempt to teach religion or to interfere with students' religious beliefs. This does not mean, though, that the teacher may not share with his pupils the beauty of a Christmas story or poem. For example, he might preface the reading of Henry Van Dyke's "The Other Wise Man" with the observation that this is a story based on the Christian belief about the birth of Jesus and that it is a beautiful story of love and devotion, whether one shares that belief or not.

The teacher should keep in mind that one of the objectives of the literature program is to promote understanding of self *and others.* Surely one way to accomplish this is to help children to learn about each other's religious holidays. Stories about such Christian holidays as Christmas and Easter have long been available, for American literature has largely followed the White-Anglo-Saxon-Protestant tradition, and fortunately some excellent books about Jewish holidays are now appearing. For young children (third or fourth grade), the story "Joel is the Youngest" by Ish-Kisher tells about several Jewish holidays, while information for upper grades may be found in Zelligs' *Story of Jewish Holidays and Customs* (Bloch Publishing Co., 1954) or Gilbert's *Your Neighbor Celebrates* (Friendly House Publishers, 1957).[10]

[10]In addition to the above, the Thomas Y. Crowell Company has a series called *The Crowell Holiday Books,* including such titles as *The Jewish Sabbath, The Jewish New Year, Hanukkah,* and *Passover;* The J. B. Lippincott Company has *Jewish Holidays,* which explains the history of sixteen Jewish holidays and includes suggestions for activities and crafts.

A more complete discussion of storytelling may be found in Chapter 7, but no discussion of literature would be complete without reference to it. In addition to being able to read well, it is extremely helpful if the teacher can also tell stories effectively. This is particularly true in the primary grades, where children's attention span is short, since the maintenance of eye contact helps to keep attention.

Storytelling is also a good technique when:

1. The teacher wishes to show the pictures in a book while telling the story.
2. The illustrations in a story are not particularly appealing, and the teacher wishes to use puppets or flannel board figures.[11]
3. The story itself is an excellent one, but its vocabulary is too difficult for the children.
4. The story is too long for reading, but may be shortened for telling without losing meaning.
5. The story contains lengthy descriptive passages which might cause children to lose interest.

Under no circumstances should the storyteller attempt to memorize his story; however, if certain words or phrases are repeated throughout the story or if specific wording is important to the denouement, these words should be carefully learned, or the story may be spoiled. But if the way it is told is a part of its charm—as, for example, with Thurber's delightful fables[12]—then it should be read, not told. Chambers suggests that the teacher should keep a set of cards for each story on which are noted important details of the setting, a list of characters, and a brief sketch of the plot. These may be reviewed quickly before each telling so that the story will be fresh in his mind. The same author suggests the following criteria for selecting a story to tell:[13]

1. Is the story one that personally excites the teller? Is it a tale he wants to share with others?
2. Is it a tale that he *can* tell? Perhaps the content and the mood of the story are not compatible with the personality of the teller.
3. Is the tale one that lends itself to telling? Or would the story be better served if it were read orally to the children, rather than told?

[11]Excellent suggestions for preparing to tell stories with the aid of flannel-board figures can be found in Paul Anderson's *Flannelboard Stories for the Primary Grades* (Minneapolis: Dennison, 1962).

[12]*The Thirteen Clocks, The White Deer,* and others.

[13]Dewey W. Chambers, *Storytelling and Creative Drama* (Dubuque, Iowa: William C. Brown Company, 1970), p. 16.

4. Is it a tale that will appeal to the age group of the listeners?

5. Is the length of the tale correct for the audience? Is it too long for young children . . . too short for those in the middle and upper grades?

If the teacher can answer these questions positively, and if he prepares thoroughly so that he will not spoil the story by omitting important details or forgetting at a crucial moment, he will find storytelling a delightful and rewarding experience, both for himself and for his pupils.

Reading Time

In addition to providing time for reading and telling stories himself, the teacher should allow time in each day for pupils to browse and read or, at the primary level, look at books and become used to handling them. This may also be a time in which children share books and give book reports, but the time should not be entirely taken up by these activities. The teacher, during this time, can help pupils in selecting books or in preparing book reports, and in doing so, he can find out more about their interests and discover ways of encouraging them to read at higher levels or in other areas. Reading is perhaps the most valuable leisure time activity in which a person of any age can indulge; therefore, the school should do everything possible to foster the reading habit and should never find the schedule too busy to allow time for it.

Room Atmosphere

Learning in any area, of course, is more apt to occur when the atmosphere of the classroom is pleasant and free from pressures, but this is particularly true during the periods devoted to reading and sharing literature. This is a time which should be pleasurably anticipated by both teacher and pupils. In the lower grades, for example, the children may be grouped in a circle around the teacher when a story is to be read or told; such a grouping is not only more relaxed and informal, but it is also better for showing pictures or other illustrations. Questions and comments by the children should not be discouraged at these times, though of course they should not be prolonged to the point where the thread of the story is lost. Similarly, when children are in the library corner, they should be allowed to share an amusing illustration, to help each other find books, or to work together on a group report. This does not mean that the library corner should be allowed to become a "gossip corner"; such a situation can easily be avoided if the teacher moves about the room and knows what students are doing and if the atmosphere of the room at all times of the day is one in which children are encouraged to move about freely but quietly and to respect the rights of others.

Even though the classroom has its own library corner, the school library and librarian should be an integral part of the literature program. The teacher and the librarian should work together, not separately. Most librarians welcome suggestions from teachers as to what books might be purchased or how many copies of a particular book are needed; further, since the librarian has many book selection aids at hand, he or she can often be invaluable in finding just the right book for a reluctant reader, a book about a particular subject for a hobbyist, or a selection of books for the room library.

Libraries and Librarians

Since the librarian is a person with whom the children do not come into regular contact—except by arrangement—many children grow up actually afraid to ask for information or help in a library. Even college students frequently do not know how valuable and willing a helper the librarian can be. To avoid this kind of situation, the librarian can be invited to the classroom, sometimes as a guest when a special activity has been planned for the literature period and sometimes to show the children new books or tell them a story. The children should go to the library, too, and become familiar with its arrangement and its many sources of information. Perhaps in the early grades several children could go to the library with the teacher to select books for the room library; in the middle grades, the entire class should visit the library and learn where different kinds of books are kept and how to use the card catalog, and of course individuals or small groups may be permitted to go to the library at any time when they do not find the books they want in the room library. The latter is not intended to supplant the school or public library, but simply to make books readily available to the pupils and encourage them to form the reading habit.

The public library may be used in much the same way as the school library. If there is a story hour at a local library, arrangements should be made to attend it as regularly as possible. Arrangements should be made to have the class visit the library, learn how it is arranged, get acquainted with the librarian and other staff, if any, and obtain library cards. This is particularly important for children of the inner city who may not have access to many books at home and whose parents may not have made arrangements to go with them to the library. Many such neighborhoods have special libraries set up for these children; the teacher should know about these and go with the children to visit them.

If two heads are better than one, surely several working together can make a literature program that is vital and exciting and that can entice even the most reluctant reader to find pleasure in books.

Book Reports   Book reports are often considered by children to be onerous tasks which do much to destroy the pleasure of reading. They need not be, and the teacher who can erase this impression—or see that it never gets established in the first place—will do much to enhance the literature program.

First, it should be said that there is no rule which requires that every book read must be reported on. If the sole purpose of the report is to discover whether or not a child actually read a book, if pupils are required to read a specific number of books or pages, or if they are urged to compete in number of books read, they will find many ways of making reports without reading books. However, much has been said in these pages about *sharing* books, and if a person has enjoyed an experience, he also enjoys sharing it. The question the teacher must ask himself, then, is "How can a particular child share with others his enjoyment of a particular book?"

For the imaginative teacher, there are many answers to this question. Perhaps a young artist might illustrate a scene from a story, draw a picture or caricature of one of the characters, or draw a comic strip depicting one of the scenes. A girl might like to draw costumes of another era or another country or perhaps even dress a doll in an appropriate costume. Maps showing the locale or topography of a story's setting; mobiles; models of ships, forts, weapons, or different types of habitation; dioramas depicting battle scenes; even pictures cut from magazines and neatly mounted and titled to illustrate a story—all these will not only add variety but also help to make the library corner more attractive and inviting.

Oral activities could include describing the relation to the book of one of the objects mentioned above, reading or telling an exciting incident, describing the character one would most like to be, composing and giving for the class a speech one of the characters might have made in a particular situation, or, if several children have read the same book, enacting a scene from the story. With any of these, the teacher should supervise the preparation and make sure that it is meaningful to the class. For example, if a student is going to give a speech one of the characters might have made, he should tell something about the circumstances which led up to the speech. Variety should also be planned for; nothing could be deadlier than fifteen such speeches, all given on the same day, and interest will be much greater if only two or three oral presentations are given in a single period. Presentations should also be complete in themselves (neither student nor teacher should read up to an exciting point and then conclude by saying, "If you want to find out what happens next, read the book"), but neither should they encompass the entire story so that there is no need to read the book. That is, one incident from the book can be told or read in its entirety, and the speaker can tell the class, "This is just one of the amusing incidents which befell Peter in his journey—there are many more." Thus interest is piqued, and that is one of the purposes for sharing.

Written reports have their place, too, since excellence in written expression is one of the objectives of the total language arts program. One type of report which should be discouraged is the simple recounting of the plot. Children should learn almost from the beginning to tell in a few sentences what the story was about, since this will help them to organize their thinking about the book and prepare them for discovering the theme, but they should not be allowed to write pages and pages, detailing every event; such a report is both dull and purposeless. Other topics which can be much more varied and interesting include the following:

1. Write a character sketch of the most admirable character (or the most unusual or least admirable).
2. What did you learn from this book that you did not know before?
3. Describe the setting of the book. What did it look like and what kind of place was it—happy, gloomy, lonely, or what? Was it suitable for the story?
4. Did the characters in the book behave like real people? Give examples to prove your answer.
5. Write a different ending that would fit the events of the story and the way the people in it behaved.
6. Write dialog for one of the incidents in the story as though it were a scene from a play.
7. Write a poem that shows how the book made you feel, or about the setting or one of the characters.
8. Write a letter to one of the characters in the story, discussing an event or situation that occurred.
9. Write a portion of a diary that might have been kept by one of the characters. (This could be an entry for a single day or it could cover a period of time during which a particular incident occurred.)

Results of such assignments can be posted on the bulletin board or made into an attractively covered notebook which is kept in the library corner to help children in selecting books. Another kind of aid which the children can make themselves is a card file of books particularly liked by members of the class. Cards should be at least 5 by 8 inches in size, perhaps even larger, and can be filled out by the students as they read books they would like to recommend to others. For greater uniformity, the cards may be duplicated, if desired, in a form similar to the following:

Recommended by ....

Name of book ....

Name of author ....

Principal characters (not just a list—tell who they are):

Where and when does the story take place?

What is the book about (not more than three sentences)?

Why did you particularly like this book?

The making of such cards can be an excellent preparation for the writing of book reviews, which children should learn to do in the upper grades. Writing a good review is difficult and requires careful preparation. A first step is for the teacher to bring to class several reviews of different kinds of books—for example, a collection of stories, a novel, a non-fiction selection, and a book of pictures, photographs, or maps. These should be duplicated or placed on transparencies so that all pupils can see them at the same time. Similarities and differences can be noted by the pupils, and they can discuss which ones they think are best and which of the books described they might be encouraged to read. Following the discussion, the class may draw up a list of questions which a good review might answer—a list which will probably include such questions as these:

1. What is the name of the book?
2. Who wrote it?
3. Who are the main characters? What kind of people are they?
4. What is the story about?
5. Is the author trying to prove something about people or life?
6. Does he succeed in his purpose? That is, did he persuade you that he might be right?
7. Are the illustrations appropriate and interesting?
8. What is the setting of the story? Is it suited to the characters and the purpose of the story?
9. Is historical information, scientific data, etc., accurate?
10. What kind of people would like this book?
11. What are the particular strengths and weaknesses of the book?
12. Are there any special features of the book that make it unusual—illustrations, language used, relation of author to content, etc.?

After questions have been formulated, the class might discuss whether all of them are suited to every type of book; members of the class could suggest specific books which most of the pupils know and decide which questions might be appropriate to answer in a review of each. The teacher might then duplicate the list, with a heading such as the following, and keep copies for the pupils to use when they write.

This is a list of questions which might be answered by a book review. When you are ready to write a review, decide which of the questions ought to be answered for the particular book you have read and arrange them in the order in which you think they should be answered. Under each question, briefly list the things which need to be said. This is the outline for your paper; use it to write a first draft and then decide what corrections and improvements need to be made. Select a suitable title and write the final draft neatly in ink.

This plan avoids dull, stereotyped reports; teaches organization of material; and helps pupils to see that, though there are general principles which can be followed, each book, like each individual, needs treatment suited to its own nature. The children will, of course, need assistance in learning to select the questions and the information to be used; an excellent preparation would be to have pupils again select a story or book which they have read together—perhaps even a textbook—decide which questions should be answered, and choose the items to be included in the answers. This outline might then be turned into a composition, with the entire class working together and the teacher writing on the chalkboard or a transparency. This should help prevent the children from falling into the error of beginning each section with the question it answers. In addition, some of the better reviews written by pupils can be posted on the bulletin board or made into a booklet so that other children may use them as models.

Group Reading   Since individual children have individual needs, interests, and abilities, much of the value of the literature program is obtained as the children read those books which they have selected for themselves. But insights and understandings are also developed through exchanging ideas about a common experience in reading. From the very beginning, selections which the teacher reads to the class can be a springboard for discussion of ideas and the ways in which they are presented, for group composition, or for individual creative efforts centered around a common theme. In the middle and upper grades, groups, or the entire class, may read the same selection. The teacher should use great care in choosing material for such reading; it must not be too difficult for the slower readers nor lack challenge for the more advanced, and under no circumstances should a teacher use a particular selection simply because enough copies are available or plan to have a class read *every* selection in the literature book. Even a difficult book may be successful if the pupils have a purpose for reading it, and a simple one may capture the most precocious if its theme is prepossessing and its language pleasing. Should the class be particularly diversified in interests and abilities, it might be wise to choose several stories with some common element; such a procedure could lead to group presentations for the entire class—perhaps a panel discussion about the ideas presented or a dramatization of a particular episode of a story—or the groups could meet individually to discuss their common experience. In any case a selection for group reading should meet these criteria:

1. Is it suitable to the interests of the group?
2. Is it suitable to the reading ability of the group?

3. Does it have a theme or purpose which is of value?
4. Can it lead to some activity—either oral or written—which will call for skills and abilities needed by the pupils involved?

Special Considerations in the Teaching of Poetry

Poetry is—or should be—a vital part of the literature program, yet too often it is neglected or badly taught in today's schools. Some teachers simply do not know how to present poetry to children; others feel it has little place in the modern science-oriented world; a few, unfortunately, spoil children's appreciation by poor reading or prolonged analysis of form and style. Yet children love rhythm, rhyme, and the sounds of words. As toddlers, they repeat advertising jingles heard on TV; on the playground, they tease each other in verse—"Mary's mad, and I am glad, and I know what will please her"; in the classroom they write rhymes in memory books or school yearbooks—"Roses are red, violets are blue, sugar is sweet, why aren't you?"; they play games like "London Bridge is Falling Down" or "Farmer in the Dell" and even jump rope to rhythmic chants; they respond with pleasure to words like "hippity-hop," "galumph," and "the great gray-green greasy Limpopo River."

In the adult world as well, poetry has been a part of the daily life of man since recorded history began—and probably before. Primitive savages sang their chants to the gods of nature; the ballad was one of the earliest forms of storytelling; the first great literary work in the English language, *The Canterbury Tales,* was in poetic form; audiences stood for hours in the pits to watch *Hamlet* and *Othello.*

In more recent years successful poetic dramas have been produced on Broadway, musicals like *Hello, Dolly* have broken box office records, TV jingles have made fortunes for advertising agencies, and folk songs have become the language of protest. In every age lovers have written rhymes of varying degrees of excellence to their sweethearts, and mothers have sung lullabies and recited nursery rhymes to their children. Poetry, then, is a natural way in which man expresses his emotions—and perhaps is more needed than ever in the tension-filled world of today.

The examples cited above suggest one important key to the teaching of poetry: with very few exceptions—and these primarily not suitable for elementary grades—poems are meant to be *heard.* Poetry's oral nature is clearly indicated by the fact that so many of its techniques are

The Presentation of Poetry

concerned with its sound and by the frequency with which poems have been set to music. The teacher, then, becomes the primary avenue by which an aversion or a love for poetry is transmitted to the children. Even more than with other forms of literature, the teacher's own attitude is of first importance.

But perhaps the teacher himself has had poor experiences with poetry; perhaps he has embarrassing memories of struggling to recite before a class of sniggering adolescents the entire prolog to *The Canterbury Tales* in the original Middle English; perhaps he believes that he does not really like poetry. The first step is to discover some poetry that he does like, and there are many ways in which this can be accomplished. Attending a well done Shakespearean performance can erase the effects of countless hours of classroom boredom. A volume of twentieth century poetry may amaze the reader who was overexposed to the eighteenth century— or that same reader may discover that, after a few more years of living, he finds wisdom and artistry in Pope's *Essay on Man*. For some, getting to know more about poetry may be the answer, but whatever the means of discovery, the search will be well rewarded, both for the teacher and for his pupils, by the addition of a new dimension to literary enjoyment.

This does not mean, of course, that young children should be expected to appreciate Shakespeare, Eliot (except for *Old Possum's Book of Practical Cats*), or Pope; rather, it is recommended that the teacher find appreciation on his own level before attempting to select poems for the children. The next step for the teacher is to explore the world of children's poetry and provide himself with a store of poems suitable for many occasions. These should be poems which he likes himself, but they should also be selected with the children's backgrounds in mind. For example, children of the inner city slums will probably find little meaning in such lines as "Over the river and through the woods, To Grandmother's house we go," but these same children might be surprised and delighted with Rose Fyleman's "I think mice Are rather nice[14] or Rachel Field's "Skyscrapers":[15]

> Do skyscrapers ever grow tired
> Of holding themselves up high?
> Do they ever shiver on frosty nights
> With their tops against the sky?

[14]Rose Fyleman, *Fifty-One New Nursery Rhymes* (Garden City: Doubleday, Doran & Co., 1932).

[15]Reprinted with permission of The Macmillan Company from *The Pointed People,* by Rachel Field. Copyright 1924, 1930, by The Macmillan Company.

Do they feel lonely sometimes
Because they have grown so tall?
Do they ever wish they could lie right down
And never get up at all?

From areas of immediate understanding, pupils may be led to other interests and greater appreciation, but, as with any other facet of the program, the children must start where they are. Perhaps this is especially true of poetry, since it is an expression of emotion and no one can be expected to appreciate something of which he has no understanding. Experience can be vicarious, however, and literature is one of the vehicles for such experience, but a background for understanding must first be created. Pictures, records, and movies can help to create this background, and the addition of a poem brings new depth to understanding.

If poetry is a natural outgrowth of man's daily experience, then it should also be treated in the classroom as one of the ways in which people express the way they feel, not as something indulged in only by artists and intellectuals. For example, during a study of Indians, the teacher will surely wish to tell some of the enchanting Indian legends and introduce the children to their songs and chants of worship; only in this way can the children truly come to understand what the Indians were like. A cold morning when the classroom windows are frosted over is a perfect time for David McCord's "Frost Pane,"[16] perhaps even accompanied by the drawing of a Nalphabet or a Nelephant. Or newly fallen snow might prompt these lines:[17]

Last night there walked across our lawn a beast we didn't know—
We saw his little footprints marked quite plainly in the snow.
It might have been an ocelot, or perhaps a grizzly bear—
We *hoped* it was a dragon, come out walking from its lair;
We didn't want a grown-up one, all fire and scales and foam,
But just a baby dragonlet that we could carry home;
We'd keep him in the nursery and give him a nice name,
And have him for a fam'ly pet, with ribbons on, quite tame.

This does not mean that no poem can be presented unless the proper situation arises or can be created; if this were true, much

[16]David McCord, *Far and Few, Rhymes of the Never Was and Always Is* (Boston: Little, Brown, and Co., 1952).
[17]From *Little Girl and Boy Land* by Margaret Widdemer, copyright, 1924, by Harcourt Brace Jovanovich, Inc.; renewed, 1952, by Margaret Widdemer Schauffler. Reprinted by permission of the publishers.

pleasurable experience would be denied the children. Neither should poetry gush forth with clocklike regularity at every possible opportunity until they become satiated with it. Rather, the teacher should strive to create a climate in which poetry is accepted as a unique and delightful way in which one may express how he feels about the world and all that is in it. An ordinary day in the classroom might, for example, call forth Myra Cohn Livingston's "Whispers:"[18]

> Whispers
>   tickle through your ear
>   telling things you like to hear.
> Whispers
>   are as soft as skin
>   letting little words curl in.
> Whispers
>   come so they can blow
>   secrets others never know.

As was noted earlier, poetry is meant to be heard. Therefore, in addition to liking poetry and creating an atmosphere for its appreciation, the teacher must learn to read it well. Reading anything well requires practice, but a poem demands special preparation so that its sound and rhythm may create the desired effect. The children, too, should be shown the need for practice when they are going to read poems to the class—and they should be encouraged to read aloud often, for the pleasure of poetry comes from reading and hearing it. Pupils may sometimes like to share poems they find especially pleasing with other members of the class, or the group may wish to prepare a choral reading of a poem.[19] This adds particularly to appreciation since preparation provides the oportunity for experimenting with different speeds, voice levels, and intonations so that the children discover readily how much the sound of poetry contributes to meaning and enjoyment. Reading aloud, either singly or together, also helps them to begin to recognize the difference between good and bad poetry.

Another variation on reading by teacher or children is the use of records. The teacher should be warned, however, that, just as he would prepare to read a poem to the class, so should he preview any recording before using it. Although there may be value at times in hearing a poet

[18]From *Whispers and Other Poems*, © 1958, by Myra Cohn Livingston. Reprinted by permission of Harcourt Brace Jovanovich, Inc.
[19]A discussion of techniques for choral reading may be found in Chapter 7.

read his own work, unfortunately some poets do not read well, even from their own work, and do little to inspire appreciation; professional actors often furnish much better renditions. Most libraries have record collections, so the teacher may preview at no cost before making purchases.

Although the presentation of poetry should be almost exclusively oral, visual aids cannot be omitted altogether. The teacher should be constantly on the watch for pictures which will make suitable illustrations of poems; these may be used when a poem is presented orally, or occasionally a bulletin board may be made up which is centered around a few lines or a short poem, either new or already known to the children. Once in a while, a bulletin board display may honor a poet whose work the children have particularly liked, but these should be few in number; attention should be centered primarily on the poems themselves.

No teacher should feel any compulsion to teach particular poems because they are in the suggested course of study, because they are in the anthology available to the class, or because they are reputed to be classics. There are enough "good" poems to suit anyone's taste. An invaluable asset is a file of titles, with notations as to where the poems may be found. These may be arranged by subject (or in whatever manner the teacher finds convenient) and they should include a generous assortment of poems suitable for holidays, the seasons of the year, and any other subjects which seem appropriate to the grade level and backgrounds of the children.

The primary purpose of teaching poetry is enjoyment and appreciation; this is the one end to be desired. However, if it is achieved in any measure at all, a number of activities may develop almost as natural outgrowths of the program. For example, a poetry bulletin board may inspire the children to seek out pictures which illustrate poems they particularly like. Or they may wish to make their own personal poetry scrapbooks, with illustrations they have drawn themselves or cut from magazines. And, just as pictures may be used to inspire writing, so poems may inspire drawings, which should, of course, be displayed. Further, if the children really come to enjoy poetry, they will want to try writing poems themselves. Choral and individual reading are an integral part of the program rather than follow-up activities, though the planning of a "Poetry Day" for parents or for another class might be considered a culminating activity.

*Follow-up
Activities*

Evaluation in the Literature Program

This chapter has repeatedly emphasized that the objectives of the literature program are—and should be—most frequently stated in terms of qualities which are difficult to measure. This fact makes any objective evaluation of achievement in literature virtually impossible. However, as one writer has pointed out:[20]

> It is difficult to resist the assumption that those attributes which we can measure are the elements which we consider most important.... The behavioral analyst seems to assume that for an objective to be worthwhile, we must have methods of assessing progress toward these goals. Goals are derived from our needs and from our philosophies. They are not and should not be derived primarily from our measures.

Therefore, if the teacher accepts this philosophy—and the objectives of the literature program—he must also accept the fact that evaluation in this area will necessarily be highly subjective. He must, of necessity, avoid such considerations as the number of books (or pages) a child has read or how many reports he has written. Rather, he might think in terms of questions such as the following:

1. Has this child appeared to enjoy reading any book(s) during the year (or other grading period)?
2. Has he written *anything* creative as a result of this reading?
3. Has he recommended any book, poem, or story to another pupil?
4. Did he read anything which might be considered more difficult or a "better" book at the end of the year (grading period) than at the beginning?
5. Did he seem to gain in understanding of himself or others or of the world about him as a result of the literature program?

It is easy to see that answers to such questions are not easily arrived at and that grades reached in this fashion are almost certain to be at least "satisfactory." In fact, if these questions cannot be answered in the affirmative in a large majority of cases, the teacher should re-examine his literature program to discover whether it is really directed at its proper goals. One authority suggests that the teacher evaluate himself and his program by asking these questions:[21]

[20]Myron Atkin, "Behavioral Objectives in Curriculum Design: A Cautionary Note" in *Current Research on Instruction*, edited by Richard C. Anderson and others (Englewood Cliffs, N.J.: Prentice-Hall, Inc., 1969), pp. 64–65.

1. Do I have a planned literature program as part of an integrated language arts curriculum?
2. Does my classroom reflect a well-planned, thoughtfully organized body of literature experiences?
3. Do I focus on literature as literature as well as using tradebooks to enhance and enrich studies in other curriculum areas?
4. Is "pleasure" present in my literature program?
5. Is there a balanced program between instruction and the encouragement of individual free reading?
6. Is time for independent reading schedules provided?
7. Is time available regularly?
8. Do I guide youngsters into the delights of reading for enjoyment as well as for information?
9. Do I read aloud to the youngsters as a way of introducing them to the best in literature?
10. Does the reading aloud occur in intermediate grades as well as in primary grades?
11. Do I go beyond the literature stories in the readers?
12. Are enough tradebooks sufficiently accessible to youngsters in my classroom?
13. Do those tradebooks reflect the diversity of interest present in my classroom?
14. Are my feelings for books reflected in the behaviors I exhibit toward and about books?
15. How many new tradebooks have I read this year?

Aids in Book Selection

□ **Anthologies of Children's Literature**

A number of excellent anthologies and books about children's literature are available to help teachers choose selections for reading to children and to help them guide the children's individual reading. Many of these list sources in which teachers can find additional information about books. Such books include the following:

May Hill Arbuthnot, *Children and Books* (Scott, Foresman and Company, 1964) and *The Arbuthnot Anthology* (Scott, Foresman and Company (1961).

---

[21]Mary S. Montebello, *Children's Literature In The Curriculum* (Dubuque, Iowa: William C. Brown Publishers, 1970).

May Hill Arbuthnot, Margaret Mary Clark, and Harriet Geneva Long, *Children's Books Too Good to Miss* (Press of Western Reserve University, 1966).

Miriam Blaton Huber, *Story and Verse for Children* (The Macmillan Company, 1965).

Charlotte S. Huck and Doris A. Young, *Children's Literature in the Elementary School* (Holt, Rinehart, and Winston, 1968).

International Reading Association Publications Committee, *Children, Books, and Reading* (International Reading Association, 1964).

Leland B. Jacobs (ed.), *Using Literature with Young Children* (Teachers College Press, Columbia University, 1965).

Edna Johnson, Carrie E. Scott, and Evelyn R. Sickels, *Anthology of Children's Literature* (Houghton Mifflin Company, 1959).

Nancy Larrick, *A Teacher's Guide to Children's Books* (Charles E. Merrill Books, Inc., 1963) and *A Parents' Guide to Children's Reading* (Doubleday, 1964).

☐ **Lists Published by Professional Organizations and Publishers**

The most complete listing of children's books is found in *The Children's Catalog,* published by the H. W. Wilson Company (950 University Ave., New York, N.Y.) every five years and kept up to date with annual supplements. The R. R. Bowker Company also publishes an annual listing called *Best Books for Children* (1180 Avenue of the Americas, New York, N.Y.). The American Library Association (50 E. Huron Street, Chicago, Ill. 60611) publishes *Subject Index to Books for Primary Grades, Subject Index to Books for Intermediate Grades, Subject Index to Poetry for Children and Young People, Subject and Title Index to Short Stories for Children,* and *Basic Book Collection for Elementary Grades.* This association also publishes booklists, as do the Association for Childhood Education International (3615 Wisconsin Ave., N.W., Washington, D.C. 20016), the Child Study Association of America (9 East 89th Street, New York, N.Y. 10028), and the Children's Book Council, Inc. (175 Fifth Ave., New York, N.Y. 10010). The National Council of Teachers of English has published *Adventuring with Books,* a graded, annotated list organized according to subject.

☐ **Reports and Reviews**

A number of periodicals report on books published and review many of them:

Childhood Education Magazine, published by the Association for Childhood Education International, has reviews in each issue.

The Horn Book (Horn Book Inc., 585 Boylston Street, Boston 02116, Massachusetts) is published six times each year and is devoted entirely to children's literature.

Elementary English has a monthly "Books for Children" section and often has additional articles on authors, illustrators, and special books.

Parents Magazine (Parents Institute, Inc., 52 Vanderbilt Ave., New York 10017, N.Y.) regularly reports on children's books.

The New York Times has a column each week "For Younger Readers" and in the fall and spring of each year devotes one issue of its book review section to children's books.

Bulletin of the Children's Book Center, published monthly (except August) by the University of Chicago Press.

School Library Journal, published monthly September through June by R. R. Bowker Co., (1180 Avenue of the Americas, New York, N.Y. 10036).

The Saturday Review several times a year devotes a section to new books for children. Usually in one of the pre-Christmas issues there is a special review.

The Reading Teacher, published by the International Reading Association, has a monthly "Literature for Children" section.

The American Library Association Bulletin annually has a section on "Notable Children's Books" in its April issue.

The National Education Association Journal annually discusses children's books in its November issue.

The Instructor, published monthly, has a section called "Books for Children."

□ **Newspapers and Magazines**

There are many magazines and newspapers designed for children that are good sources of supplementary reading material and have special appeal for some readers in that they are different from books. A few of these are:

Child Life (Child Life, Inc., 1100 Waterway Blvd., Indianapolis, Indiana) K-5.

Ideals (Ideals, Milwaukee, Wisconsin) K-8.

American Girl (The Girl Scouts of the USA, 830 Third Ave., New York, New York) 5–8.

Boys' Life (The Boy Scouts of America, New Brunswick, New Jersey) 5–8.

Ranger Rick's Nature Magazine (National Wildlife Federation, 1412 Sixteenth St., N.W., Washington, D.C. 20036).

Calling All Girls (Better Reading Foundation, Inc., 52 Vanderbilt Ave., New York, New York) 4–8.

Children's Digest (Better Reading Foundation, 52 Vanderbilt Ave., New York, New York) 1–6.

Highlights for Children (Highlights for Children, Inc., 2300 W. Fifth Ave., Columbus, Ohio) 1–6.

Humpty Dumpty's Magazine (Better Reading Foundation, Inc., 52 Vanderbilt Ave., New York, New York) 1–3.

Jack and Jill (Curtis Publishing Co., Independence Square, Philadelphia, Pennsylvania) 1–6.

☐ **Paperback Books**

Paperback books are fast becoming an integral part of the school's literature program, since they make possible the purchase of a greater number of books—or of multiple copies of a single book. Nearly every major publisher of books for schools has begun publication of its own series of paperbacks for use in the literature program, and these should surely add variety and vitality to the literature program. In addition, paperback book clubs are making possible the purchase of books by pupils at little cost. Teachers, administrators, and others concerned with the literature program should make it a point to visit regularly the publishers' displays at meetings of professional organizations, since it is virtually impossible to keep up with the number of new titles appearing regularly.

Listings of paperbacks for children may be found in:

Lucile Boylan and Robert Sattler, *A Catalog of Paperbacks for Grades 7 to 12* (Scarecrow Press, 257 Park Ave., S., New York, N.Y. 10010).

Recommended Paperback Books for Elementary Schools (Book Mail Service, Box 363, Jamaica, New York).

Paperbound Books in Print (published monthly by R. R. Bowker Co., 1180 Avenue of the Americas, New York, N.Y. 10010).

☐ **Book Clubs**

Many children will become interested in literature through the incentive of membership in a book club. Sometimes a club may be only for the purpose of exchanging personal books the children have. Other clubs center around commercial distribution of books. The following are the names of some clubs, their addresses, and details of the age levels for which they are intended.

Arrow Book Club, Scholastic Book Services, 904 Sylvan Ave., Englewood Cliffs, New Jersey 07632. Ages 9–11.

The Bookplan, 921 Washington Ave., Brooklyn, N.Y. 11225. Ages 8 months–11 years.

Catholic Children's Book Club, 260 Summit Ave., St. Paul, Minn. Ages 6–16.

Junior Literary Guild, 177 Park Ave., New York, N.Y. 10017. Ages 5–16.

Lucky Book Club, Scholastic Book Services, 904 Sylvan Ave., Englewood Cliffs, New Jersey 07632. Ages 7–9.

Parents' Magazine Book Club for Little Listeners and Beginning Readers, 52 Vanderbilt Ave., New York, N.Y. 10017. Ages 3–8.

See Saw Book Club, Scholastic Book Services, 904 Sylvan Ave., Englewood Cliffs, New Jersey 07632. Ages 5–7.

Teen Age Book Club, Scholastic Book Services, 904 Sylvan Ave., Englewood Cliffs, New Jersey 07632. Ages 12–14.

Weekly Reader Children's Book Club, Education Center, 1250 Fairwood Ave., Columbus, Ohio 43216. Ages 4–10.

Young America Book Club, 1250 Fairwood Ave., Columbus, Ohio 43216. Ages 10–14.

Young Folks Book Club, 1376 Coney Island, Brooklyn, N.Y. 11230.

Young People's Book Club, 226 North Cass Ave., Westmont, Ill. 60559. Ages 4–10.

Young Readers of America (Division of Book-of-the-Month Club), 345 Hudson St., New York, N.Y. 10014. Ages 9–14.

☐ Books for Particular Purposes

If children are truly to develop a greater understanding of themselves and others, then those who select books for the literature program must be more realistic in their attempts to accomplish this goal than they have been in the past. For many years, literature programs have included units designed to help pupils learn more about children in other lands—and rightly so, of course—as well as stories about the ways in which individuals have met and solved personal problems. But little has been included to help create better understanding among the various groups within our own country. Some attention has been given to the American Indian and his heritage, largely due to the social studies program, and more than a few stories in our literature center around the theme of understanding those who are "different" in some way. But American schools and American literature have developed largely in the WASP tradition. Fortunately, however, changes are beginning to appear. Illustrations in many of the newer books picture children of different races, stories by and about blacks are appearing in some quantity, and, as mentioned earlier in this chapter, some excellent books about Jewish customs and beliefs are now available (see p. 514).

Particularly noteworthy are books which show similarities rather than differences among children of different races. *Whistle for Willie*[22] about a small boy's efforts to whistle for his dog, reveals only through its illustrations that Willie is black, while in *What Happens When You*

[22]Ezra Jack Keats, *Whistle for Willie* (New York: The Viking Press, Inc., 1964).

Go to the Hospital,[23] Karen—also black—goes to the hospital to have her tonsils removed and experiences the usual interests, fears, and pleasures of a child's first experience of this type. Equally important are such books as *The Way It Is,*[24] which shows life as it is in a slum neighborhood and features photographs by fifteen black and Puerto Rican boys. An excellent bibliography of books about blacks or featuring black characters has been published by the National Council of Teachers of English;[25] it is annotated and lists books under such headings as "Picturebooks and Easy-to-Read Books," "Fiction," "Sports," and "Biography." A listing of this type would be a valuable addition to the library of any teacher and is a *must* for teachers who have black children in their classes.

Exercises for Thought and Action

1. Memorize and tell a story using flannelboard figures or puppets for illustration.
2. Compile for a grade level of your choice a file of stories and poems suitable for a particular holiday.
3. Compile a poetry file for a particular grade level.
4. Present a poetry lesson for a grade level of your choice.
5. Select a book you like and "sell" it to the class.
6. Assume that you have a class of a particular grade level. Select three stories, one for slow, one for average, and one for advanced readers, and show how you would use these for group reading.
7. You are teaching in a new school. Select a particular grade level and compile a list of the books you might place in the room library at the beginning of the year, before you have become acquainted with the pupils. Be sure to identify what kind of community the school is in—suburban, inner city, etc.
8. Compile a list of books by or about black, Puerto Rican, Mexican-Americans, etc., which might be useful if your class needed help in building self-confidence or a self-image. Select a particular grade level.
9. Prepare a literature bulletin board for a particular grade level.
10. Assume that you are a fifth-grade teacher, beginning his first teaching assignment. What activities would you plan in the first week to begin a literature program?

[23]Arthur Shay, *What Happens When You Go to the Hospital* (New York: Reilly and Lee, 1969).

[24]John Holland (ed.), *The Way It Is* (New York: Harcourt, Brace, & World, 1969).

[25]Charlemae Rollins (ed.), *We Build Together* (Champaign, Ill.: National Council of Teachers of English, 1967).

Selected References

Anderson, Paul. *Flannelboard Stories for the Primary Grades*. Minneapolis: Dennison, 1962.

Arbuthnot, May Hill. *Children and Books*. Chicago: Scott, Foresman and Company. Third Edition, 1964.

————. "Developing Life Values Through Reading," *Elementary English*. 43:10–16, January, 1966.

————, Clark, Margaret Mary, and Long, Harriet Geneva. *Children's Books Too Good to Miss*. Cleveland: Western Reserve University Press.

Arnstein, Flora J. *Poetry in the Elementary Classroom*. New York: Appleton-Century-Crofts, 1962.

Bammon, Henry A., Dawson, Mildred A., and Whitehead, Robert J. *Oral Interpretation of Children's Literature*. Dubuque, Iowa: William C. Brown Company, 1964.

Brewton, John E. and Sara W. *Index to Children's Poetry*. New York: H. W. Wilson Company, 1942. First Supplement, 1954, Second Supplement, 1965.

Chambers, Dewey W. *Storytelling and Creative Drama*. Dubuque, Iowa: William C. Brown Co., 1970.

Children, Books, and Reading. Perspectives in Reading No. 3. Newark, Del.: International Reading Association, 1964.

Colwell, Eilsen. *A Storyteller's Choice*. New York: Walck Publishing Co., 1964.

Development of Taste in Literature. Champaign, Ill.: NCTE, 1963.

Doyle, Brian (ed.). *The Who's Who of Children's Literature*. New York: Schoeken Books, 1968.

Eakin, Mary K. *Good Books for Children, 1948–1961*. Chicago. University of Chicago Press, 1962.

Eastman, Mary Huse. *Index to Fairy Tales, Myths, and Legends*. Boston: F. W. Faxon Company, 1926. First Supplement, 1937, Second Supplement, 1952.

Guilfoile, Elizabeth. *Books for Beginning Readers*. Champaign, Ill.: NCTE, 1962.

————, and others. *Adventuring with Books*. Champaign, Ill.: NCTE, 1966.

Haviland, Virginia. *Children's Literature, A Guide to Reference Sources*. Washington, D.C.: U.S. Government Printing Office, 1966.

Horn, Thomas D., Fisher, Audrey, and Lanman, James L. "Periodicals for Children and Youth," *Elementary English* 43:341–358, April, 1966.

Huber, Miriam Blanton. *Story and Verse for Children*. New York: The Macmillan Company, 1965.

Huck, Charlotte S., and Young, Doris A. *Children's Literature in the Elementary School*. New York: Holt, Rinehart, and Winston, 1968.

Jacobs, Leland B. (ed.). *Using Literature with Young Children.* New York: Teachers College Press (Columbia University), 1965.

Johnson, Edna, Sickels, Evelyn R., and Sayers, Frances C. *Anthology of Children's Literature.* Boston: Houghton Mifflin Company, 1959.

Ladley, Winifred C. *Sources of Good Books and Magazines for Children.* Newark, Delaware: International Reading Association, 1970.

Larrick, Nancy. *A Teacher's Guide to Children's Books.* Columbus: Charles E. Merrill Books, Inc., 1963.

Mahoney, Bertha E., and Field, Elinor Whitney. *Newberry Medal Books, 1922–1955.* Boston: Horn Book Company, 1955.

Montebello, Mary. *Children's Literature in the Curriculum.* Dubuque, Iowa: William C. Brown Co., 1970.

Palovic, Lora, and Goodman, Elizabeth B. *The Elementary School Library in Action.* West Nyack, N.Y.: Parker Publishing Co., 1968.

Rollins, Charlemae. We Build Together. Champaign, Ill.: NCTE, 1967.

Smith, Dora V. *Fifty Years of Children's Books.* Champaign, Ill.: NCTE, 1963.

Tooze, Ruth. *Storytelling.* Englewood Cliffs, N.J.: Prentice-Hall, Inc., 1959.

———. *Your Children Want to Read.* Englewood Cliffs, N.J.: Prentice-Hall, Inc., 1957.

Whitehead, Robert. *Children's Literature: Strategies of Teaching.* Englewood Cliffs, N.J.: Prentice-Hall, Inc., 1968.

Textbooks and Workbooks

16

INTRODUCTION

The textbook is an important ingredient of practically every
language arts teacher's program. For most teachers it is a basic
guide to the content of the program, to the methods of teaching
and to the evaluation that should be done. The fundamental nature
of these things points to the central role of the textbook—and
to a lesser extent the workbook. The foregoing statement might cause
the reader to wonder why this chapter was not placed near the
front of the book rather than at the end. The reason for the placement
is that the authors appreciate the place of the textbook but feel
that teachers should learn to rely upon their own beliefs and
knowledge to a far greater extent than they generally do. At least
they should not rely solely on a textbook for their programs.
We believe the textbook is a useful guide and aid; it should not be
the program for any teacher.

Textbooks must be chosen carefully, and they must be used
wisely and effectively. Both selection and use need to be considered
by every teacher and this should be done on the basis of evidence
and philosophy. The discussion in this chapter seeks to give attention
to these factors by focusing on the following topics:

1. The Textbook in the Program
2. Using Textbooks in the Language Arts
3. The Selection of Language Arts Textbooks
4. Workbooks in the Language Arts Program
5. The Selection and Use of Workbooks

The Textbook in the Program

Without question the textbook is the most readily accessible instructional aid for a teacher. Many important considerations in language arts teaching revolve around the textbook.

The Textbook Today

School textbooks have been given a great deal of attention in recent years by professional groups of teachers, by governmental agencies, and by the public. This attention has been a reflection of the general concern with educational problems and is an attention that will continue. Yet much that is voiced about textbooks—to say nothing about all that is said about education in general—is based upon opinion rather than upon research. Hilton, in reviewing the history of textbooks and the research upon their functions, selection, and influence makes the following points:[1]

1. Textbooks change in response to various pressures. These include changes in educational purposes, in learning theory and practice, in subject matter, and in printing technology.
2. There is little research to support statements as to the direction and extent of textbook changes.
3. Textbooks seeking to incorporate new learning about content and methods sometimes go to extremes.
4. A textbook's influence is modified by how a teacher uses it.
5. The idea of a single textbook is increasingly giving way to one in which the textbook is used with supplemental materials, including other textbooks.
6. "Nontextbook teaching" is not necessarily good teaching.
7. Textbook selection is largely done on a subjective basis.

Textbooks in the Language Arts

In an ideal language arts program the curriculum would be developed from a modern philosophical foundation as this applies to teaching and learning. This foundation would be one grounded in experience and research evidence. The learning situations would be set up in accordance with sound principles of learning. The class activities would be planned and directed by a superior teacher, well trained in methods of teaching and a master of the subject matter. The children would come from home environments in which language is appreciated and used

[1]Ernest Hilton, "Textbooks" in *Encyclopedia of Educational Research,* Fourth Edition, Robert L. Ebel, editor (New York: The Macmillan Company, 1969), pp. 1470–1478.

well. The school itself would be attractively furnished, artistically decorated, and properly equipped. Facilities for cultural contacts with the best in art, music, and literature would be available. The school library would be stocked with many interesting volumes of fiction and poetry suitable for children. The book shelves would be filled with colorful volumes on art, literature, music, science and other subjects. Encyclopedias, world almanacs, yearbooks, dictionaries, atlases, globes, and reference sources of all types would be available when needed.

In such a school the world of language and all it encompasses would be so completely available to each child that there would be little need for textbooks. Material needed for activities to stimulate language expression would be accessible in almost every area of interest. It would seem that in such an environment the child might acquire an adequate mastery of the skills of language expression and reception without ever realizing that he had been studying at all.

The difficulty with this lovely picture lies in the fact that few such ideal schools, curriculums, teachers, and libraries exist except in our professional dreams. After all, schools are built and operated by typical citizens in typical communities. Most teachers are typical in their mental abilities, scholastic achievements, professional interests, and backgrounds of training and experience. Unfortunately, this "typical" teacher is often overloaded, and has only a sketchy outline for a course of study along with an inadequate library. This teacher stands in real need of ready-made instructional help. The textbook becomes almost an absolute necessity.

While there are wide differences in the quality of textbooks, it may not be too much to expect that in general the textbook should represent the highest levels of curriculum development in the subject. In the language arts curriculum the basic textbook should serve the following functions:

Functions of the Language Arts Textbook

1. Reflect a defensible and modern point of view on language teaching and demonstrate its application in the instructional material presented.
2. Provide a well-organized and properly graded source of the expressional skills which bear the burden in communication.
3. Present a rich, readable, and varied source of subject matter, geared to children's interests and needs, as the basis for suggested activity programs in which expressional skills are acquired under lifelike conditions.
4. Present, with its accompanying manual, teaching methods and means for motivating children.

5. Provide the necessary initial fixation and maintenance practice exercises.
6. Provide evaluation and remedial materials.

Every teacher should know and understand the several functions of the language textbook as he develops his instructional program. He should consider these functions, relate them to his own viewpoints and knowledge, and learn how to use the book properly. The following sections discuss the functions listed above, emphasizing the importance of the textbook in the program and the need for most teachers to depend heavily upon it as an instructional aid.

□ Reflecting a Point of View

An examination of sets of language texts with copyrights in each of the eight decades from 1890 through the present reveals in a striking manner the changes in point of view that have taken place in the teaching of receptive and expressive abilities and skills. In general, the trend has been away from the abstract and formal toward the functional, although in certain periods (including the present) there have been surprising reversals in this general trend. Some of the recently published elementary school English textbooks reflect the present differences in viewpoints. A few, for the purpose of teaching a grammatical system, present content very formally.[2] Others seek to develop a genuine understanding and appreciation of language in a functional manner. Thus, it would appear that the likelihood of substantial movement away from the functional is remote.

For the teacher who has not crystallized his own thinking on a point of a view regarding language arts teaching, the textbook may give the assistance he needs in objectifying his own philosophy.

□ Serving as a Source of Content

The language arts or English program includes so many specific skills that only a highly trained subject matter specialist could possibly keep them all in mind. For the typical teacher, overloaded with many other subjects, the textbook provides an organized and cataloged source of information on the curriculum considered suitable for instruction in the particular grade. One writer has aptly described the textbook as "an assistant teacher in print."[3]

[2]For example: Paul Roberts, *The Roberts English Series* (New York: Harcourt, Brace and World, Inc., 1966).
[3]Malcolm E. Melliott, "What to Look For in Choosing a Textbook," *N.E.A. Journal,* 44:158–159, March, 1955.

☐ Presenting Suitable Subject Matter

Skill in the use of language is not developed economically by talking about language but by using language in genuine communicative and expressional activities. The textbook should provide suggestions for worthwhile classroom activities requiring the use of language, though because of page limitations information of this sort is not as abundant as it should be. What is included however, is generally suggestive of the kinds of activities pupils should engage in to make possible teaching based upon actual need. Some of the newer textbooks have considerable content which deals with the language—its structure, history, and manipulation—which may serve as suitable subject matter if it is approached functionally and in connection with the on-going activities of the classroom that appeal to children. If it is approached formally and the focus is largely upon learning about language rather than using it, then there is little reason to expect a child to write or speak more effectively as a result.

☐ Serving as a Source of Teaching Methods

Unless he has been fortunate enough to have had considerable training in methods of teaching elementary school language arts, the classroom teacher is compelled to depend almost entirely on the textbook for suggestions about teaching specific types of lessons. While the instructions are written into each textbook lesson for the guidance of the pupil, they are often very frankly pointed in the teacher's direction. In addition to these indirect hints on methods of handling the lesson, the teacher is usually given extensive and timely suggestions about methods in the teachers' manuals prepared by most textbook publishers. These manuals are usually well written, and in many cases contain the benefit of the extensive knowledge and experience of successful teachers and supervisors. The teacher who, through his own indifference, does not secure and use the manual is not only making a costly blunder but is missing an effective means of simplifying his teaching problems. In numerous surveys of special groups of teachers in this field, the authors have been amazed to learn how many teachers have not been made aware of the existence of these teacher guides for the textbooks they were using, or if they knew about them did not consider them important enough to study and use in their teaching.

☐ Providing Fixation and Maintenance Practice

Economy of time is of such great importance to the teacher that all available sources of material for the fixing of skills at the time of initial learning should be utilized. In the language arts a great deal of such practice is required, and the textbook should supply much of it. Modern textbooks in language attempt to provide exercises, practice materials, and suggestions for activities in adequate amounts; yet in the opinion of many teachers few texts provide sufficient amounts of fixation and maintenance materials. The teacher, then, must supplement the practice material with material he has made himself, or with workbooks which are designed to accompany the textbooks.

□ **Providing Sources of Evaluation Material**

The textbook should supply the teacher with the materials for evaluating the results of the instructional program as well as with directions for their effective use in corrective instruction. Some recognition of the importance of teacher-made informal objective tests and standardized tests in language should be given in the textbook or in the teacher's manual, though only a small part of evaluation in the language class consists in the use of such tests. The use of inventory devices, either in the form of objective exercises or class-made standards, is recognized as a good technique for focusing the individual pupil's attention on specific skills, and for identifying the pupils who are in need of instruction on the skills involved.

Below are sample items from a check test in a fifth-grade language textbook.[4]

A. Read these sentences silently. Then copy them on paper. Use capital letters where they belong.
   1. linda swam in lake michigan last summer.
   2. susan and tom told the class about the horseback riding they did in colorado last summer.
   3. have you read *the little house on the prairie* by laura ingalls wilder?
   4. john saw the soapbox derby in akron, ohio.
B. Proofread the paragraph below. Then write the paragraph correctly.
   what fun we had camping by the lake it was so cozy sleeping in the tent. when it rained. we swam and went horseback riding during the day. we liked to eat our food cooked over a campfire. we used our boat when the lake was calm. we can hardly wait until next summer.

[4]Josephine B. Wolfe, *et al., English Your Language,* Book 5 (Boston: Allyn and Bacon, Inc., 1963), p. 37.

C. Turn to the title page of your language book. Write the following:
1. The title
2. The names of the authors
3. The publisher
4. The date of publication

Write this information in the order in which it is listed above.

Using Textbooks in the Language Arts

For a teacher to begin on the first page of a language arts textbook and continue page by page through the entire book is a procedure which fails to take into account the language abilities and needs of a particular class, to say nothing of the varying needs and abilities of the individuals in the class. Textbooks, in language arts as well as in other subject areas, should be used in a variety of ways. As has been suggested, perhaps an extremely capable teacher, teaching in a unique situation and with adequate resources, does not need to use a textbook. But most teachers do not have the teaching resources and experience for teaching without the textbook. This does not mean, however, that a teacher needs to be a slave to the textbook and show no initiative or professional competence. It does not mean that the language assignment from day to day should consist merely of listing page numbers in the textbook.

The teacher should understand the functions of a language textbook, as developed in the preceding section. The competent teacher also knows that a textbook has limitations:

1. By itself it does not teach (although some learning may be achieved by reading it).
2. The content presented as settings for language activities is bound to be artificial for a particular class.
3. The practice exercises are likely to be inadequate because of limitations in the size of the textbook and because so much language practice needs to be done orally.
4. The teaching suggestions are also brief because of spatial limitations.
5. The evaluation aids are only suggestive and do not evaluate with the completeness required.

In addition, textbooks may not perform the functions suggested. For example, some language arts textbooks make no provision for evaluation; some have no practice activities. Others, as has been suggested earlier in this book, may have no provision for teaching listening, proof-reading, or some other area or aspect of the language arts. There are shortcomings in many of the textbooks, and these should be recognized by the teachers using them. With such recognition the textbook generally becomes useful.

Classroom Activities and Textbook Use

There are innumerable occasions for genuine language activities in the classroom as the teacher and children work, play, and study together. The teacher who has difficulty in recognizing the opportunities for language teaching in these activities may turn to the textbook for guidance. For example, if as the children return from recess they are discussing (perhaps arguing about) a misunderstanding of the rules of a game they were playing, this may be the ideal time to teach the giving of directions. The children may look in their language textbooks for information on how to give directions. This act should lead to the reading of the content in that particular section of the book and to following the suggestions concerning practice for giving directions, for setting standards, and for learning special usage items.

In another instance the teacher may have observed that many of the children regularly used the expression, "We was going," and can then suggest referring to the textbook concerning this usage. This in turn might lead to an examination of the textbook's examples, practice upon the exercises for illustrating the usage, and use of the given drills for helping establish a more acceptable habit of expression.

The Textbook as a Guide

Teachers should also make use of the textbook as a guide to the language skills, abilities, and knowledge that should be taught and developed, and to the determination of the sequence of their presentation. While the activities of a classroom are not likely to coincide with the sequence of the ones presented in the textbook, and thus page by page use is inappropriate, it is true that the content, activities, skills, and abilities suggested in the textbook for teaching at a particular grade level have been carefully selected and planned and should not be ignored. A prudent teacher carefully and regularly checks his language teaching against the program in the textbook and plans for activities which will call for using those sections of the textbook which he has not already used and for which there is need with his group of children.

The following example illustrates the type of material included in a textbook to supplement the language teaching opportunities which occur naturally.[5]

[5]Harry A. Greene, *et al., The New Building Better English,* Fourth Edition (Evanston, Ill.: Harper and Row, Publishers, 1965), Grade 7, p. 235.

Guides to Using Vivid, Exact Nouns

1. Go over written work that you do, at home or at school. Think about each noun. Ask yourself, "Can I find a more exact, or definite, word? Can I find a word that makes a clearer picture?"

2. In your reading, learn to notice the author's choice of nouns. Being aware of what words good writers choose can help you in your own oral and written expression.

3. As a rule, avoid weak nouns like *sound, noise, light, motion.* Find, for example, a noun that names the *special kind* of sound: the *splash* of waves, the *trickling* of a stream, the *rattle* of hail.

4. Avoid a general noun when a specific (exact) one fits.
   General: Ann was wearing red *shoes.*
   Specific: Ann was wearing red *sandals.*
   General: A tall *tree* shades the front of our house.
   Specific: A tall *elm* shades the front of our house.
   Be as specific as you can. For example, *food is* general; *dessert* is more specific; *pie* is still more specific.

The Selection of Language Arts Textbooks

The widespread use of textbooks in the several language arts areas, reflecting their virtual indispensability as teaching resources, requires that great care be given to their selection. The selection process should consist of critically examining several competing books or series of books and evaluating them as objectively as possible in terms of the teaching objectives, the children to be taught, and the other resources that are available.

The more important general factors determining textbook quality are discussed in this section. This material should be of assistance to teachers and others in the selection of textbooks to meet their instructional needs.

Quality
Factors for
Consideration

☐ Appeal to Child Interest

One of the most important factors determining the suitability and usability of a textbook in a given grade is the appeal it makes to the children who are expected to study it. While it may be doubtful if all children opening a textbook for the first time expect to find a series of sugar-coated morsels about using language, most children feel the importance of having a textbook in their hands. They know that grown-ups use textbooks so they are expecting the books to be useful. They rightly should expect the textbook to take into account their backgrounds of experience, their values, and their interests. If a child lives in the core of a city, the textbook should show him that his life and interests are understood. The same may be said for children who live in other environments and have had other experiences. The wide differences in children's experiences make the task of appealing to all children who may use a textbook a difficult one.

☐ **Motivation**

Another important element in the text is the manner in which it presents devices and procedures for stimulating each child to take an active personal interest in each of the new language activities undertaken by his group. The child must be made to feel that his ideas and opinions are important to the members of his group. He must be given experiences of such richness, novelty, and interest that he feels a need to communicate his feelings and ideas to others.

The most important motivating forces for effective language expression arise from the well-planned class activity. The many group discussions in which the plans for the activity are developed, the committee meetings in which important decisions are reached, the class meetings in which standards of usage or personal conduct are formulated all stimulate the individual to carry his share of the responsibility. To do this he must organize and present his ideas, criticize and disagree tactfully, assume leadership in areas in which he is qualified to lead. Textbooks in the language arts should place a great deal of emphasis on the importance of the activity program in motivating language use and in providing opportunities for the effective mastery of language skills in lifelike situations.

☐ **Illustrations**

Colorful and attractive illustrations scattered through the book add to the interest of the presentation and may prove to be important motivational devices. The more physical activity the illustrations demonstrate, the more the children seem to like them. Children are attracted to the book with a colorful binding and like to turn through the pages talking about the children and activities portrayed and relating them to their own lives. The illustrations should, of course, relate to the instruction to be given and should not be included simply to provide color or show other children. In addition to pictures, charts and diagrams may be included to better illustrate activities or otherwise motivate children.

☐ Linguistic Considerations

The language in a textbook should be clear and natural. Explanations should be simply written, without appearing to talk down to the child. Technical or special words must be defined and illustrated in the context in which they appear. However, there is much more to understandable language than a simple vocabulary. Often it is difficult to discover just what makes the presentation in one textbook interesting and that in another boring. The answer probably lies in the individuals who do the writing. Some authors write in a style pleasing to children; others are unable to do so. The language arts textbooks is not designed to provide light and entertaining reading for the school child, but it must have enough interesting facts, activities, and bits of information scattered through its pages to keep the child hunting for more.

☐ Relation to Other Subjects

One of the very important advances found in most of the language arts textbooks of today over earlier ones is that the instructional effort seeks to relate language to practically all other school subjects and activities. Today the language arts program as presented in the best of the modern textbooks overlaps with practically every subject. It is in these other subject-matter activities that the real motivation for the language mastery is developed. Language skills are made habitual through use in all school activities. The use of good oral and written expression is just as important in the science, mathematics, music, art, and social studies classes as it is in the class in which language is supposed to be the central activity.

☐ Stimulation of Personal Activity

The value of the language arts textbook is strengthened by the stimulation it provides for the individual child to become personally active. Language structure may provide interesting topics for class discussion, but it is primarily through individual and personal activity in which language is *used* that knowledge about language becomes important. The extent to which the text stimulates the child in creative oral or written expression is one of the best measures of the quality of the book.

☐ Vague and Unusual Concepts

A common fault in the presentation of instructional material in textbooks is the introduction of words and concepts which are often meaningless to the child. For example, what do expressions such as *several times a day, a high wind, a few miles away,* mean? How many times is *several* times? How strong is a *high* wind? How far away is a *few miles?* In Maine a few miles might be two; in Ohio it might be twenty; in Texas it might be one hundred. The child of seven or eight has sufficient difficulty in comprehending instructional material written in concise language without being further confused by the introduction of vague and uncertain terms. In the examination of language textbooks under consideration for adoption, a careful check should be made for suitability of vocabulary and freedom from terms with vague and uncertain meanings.

☐ **Point of View**

Authors and publishers of different language arts textbooks may disagree as to the specific language skills and subject matter to be presented. If the textbook under consideration does not make clear its general point of view on subject matter in its introductory statement, a careful check should be made of the teacher's manual for this information. In the event that the philosophy of the school interested in choosing a language arts textbook is in disagreement with the point of view of the text under consideration, a reexamination of the philosophy may be in order to see that it is actually held to. A further examination of the text may also be necessary.

☐ **Consistency in Emphasis on Child and Adult Values**

The textbook should present a program in which both the child's immediate language needs and his ultimate language needs as an adult are given proper instructional emphasis. Some books appear to take an adult view, looking completely past the child's present school needs. They seem to assume that the needs for both ages are identical or that the child's school needs for language training will be met automatically in his other school activities. This is not the case. Although many of the needs of the two groups are similar, in many other cases they may be quite different. The effective language program is one in which instructional emphasis is adjusted to maturity of the pupils as well as to their language needs.

☐ **Recognition of Individual Differences**

Authors of textbooks usually are forced by the limitations of space to adapt the content of the book for a specific level to the abilities and interests of the large middle or average group of children. Some supplementary help must be provided for the rather sizable group that will not be able to work as rapidly as the average pupils. A satisfactory textbook should provide this. Another problem is what to do with the very active group of superior children who encounter little or no difficulty with the routine activities and lessons and are frequently bored by the useless waste of their time. They surely cannot be asked to do more of the same types of exercises. The superior texts make a definite attempt to aid the teacher by providing individualized enrichment activities designed for the use of pupils who have met all minimum and average requirements.

Evidence of the quality of a textbook or series should be determined as objectively as possible.[6] Such matters as the reputation of the authors as scholars and teachers, the reputation of the publisher in publishing quality materials, the extent of use of the particular book or books, and the quality of the paper and printing should be appraised. Further, score cards which list factors that are important to quality should be devised and used. In addition, reputable publishers should make available objective evidence about their books. For example, the publisher of a reading series should make available a detailed tabulation showing the exact words comprising the basic vocabulary on which the reading program is based, the new words introduced at each successive level in the program, and the sequence followed in the introduction of skills. Likewise a spelling textbook publisher should present the facts about the source of the vocabulary comprising his program. Distributions showing frequencies of appearance of practice exercises on particular items should be secured.

Securing Objective Evidence of Quality

Workbooks in the Language Arts Program

The part that workbooks and other practice materials should play in the language arts program needs examination in the light of the answers to two broad but important questions. First, is there a real need for the kind of instructional material which workbooks and practice lessons purport to supply? Second, if this need is critical, do these instruments meet that need satisfactorily?

[6]Score cards or outlines of points to consider in selecting language arts textbooks appear in some professional textbooks. For example, there is an outline in Paul C. Burns and Alberta L. Lowe, *The Language Arts in Childhood Education* (Rand McNally, 1966), pp. 344–346; in an earlier edition (1963) of the present book a scorecard for language arts textbooks appears on pp. 446–448. In addition, the handbook by Kenneth S. Goodman and others, *Choosing Materials to Teach Reading* (Wayne State University Press, 1966) gives psychological, sociocultural, educational, linguistic, and literary principles, many of which need to be considered in selecting language arts textbooks.

Workbooks and supplementary practice lessons in language have tended to emphasize the readily identifiable mechanical features of expression, such as punctuation, capitalization, form, and some matters of usage—reflecting definite points of view concerning "correctness." For the teacher who believes that the development of such skills and habits should not be a distinct phase of language teaching, but feels that they will be best developed through systematic emphasis in connection with much oral and written expression, the workbook has little or no appeal. Another large group of teachers, however, while perhaps not denying the importance of the functional development of these skills in connection with expressional activities, considers that supplementary practice and drill are not only desirable but necessary to effective learning. Thus for this rather large and important group of teachers, the problem is not one of deciding whether or not to *use* practice material for certain learning purposes, but one of determining *which* materials appear most promising. As has been suggested, a properly trained teacher ideally should assemble or produce all of the material he needs for his teaching, if heavy teaching schedules and crowded classes do not place a severe strain on his time and energy. However, even under the best of conditions the preparation of suitable practice material is a complicated and time-consuming process, often calling for the abilities and experience of the specialist. Under such circumstances, it is quite natural for the teacher to turn to workbook exercises.

Limitations of and Arguments Against Workbooks

Although there is widespread disagreement regarding workbooks, there is general agreement that all learning is the result of personal and purposeful mental activity on the part of the learner, and that it takes place most readily when the individual is motivated and has a clear understanding of what is expected of him. Most teachers agree that one of their most important instructional tasks is the providing of interesting situations which call forth these personal and purposeful mental activities and responses on the part of their pupils. The point on which they do not agree is the question of whether a workbook, an actual communicative activity, or some other device offers the best way to attain the objectives. It is unfortunate that much of the argument on both sides of the question appears to rest more heavily on subjective opinions than on the results of research. Furthermore, the picture is clouded by the fact that the available evidence is inconclusive and often contradictory.[7]

[7]Miller J. Stewart, "Workbooks: Help or Hindrance?" *Elementary English,* 43:477–479, May, 1966.

Criticisms of workbooks fall into two general categories, those related to the content and the organization of the material, and those concerned with the manner in which the material is fitted into the total instructional program.

Workbooks restrict the educational program.   Teachers may come to rely on the workbook and cease to use their own initiative in planning a stimulating instructional program. Thus the use of workbooks may limit the initiative of the teacher and reduce the amount of planning in which children may participate. Too often the workbook becomes a controlling force rather than a supplemental aid.

Arguments regarding the restrictive nature of workbooks can generally be applied equally to textbooks, the major difference being that the quality of authorship and materials in workbooks may not be equal to that of textbooks. Certainly either workbooks or textbooks can be misused; if they are misused they restrict the instructional program.

Workbooks are not educationally sound.   Pooley attacked workbooks some years ago.[8] His criticisms appear to be as valid today in that habits of usage are established in meaningful communication activities rather than by exercises or by learning a grammatical system. Pooley was not attacking workbook exercises that call for practice on mechanical skills such as punctuation or capitalization. He said, "The workbooks in language are generally unsound in method, in that the type of practice given is the filling in of blanks and the crossing out of alternative forms. Such practice may aid the brighter pupil to discover certain distinctions in usage, but it has very slight effect in the establishing of good habits or the breaking of undesirable habits. Such practice for the slower pupil often reinforces bad habits, as he tends to supply the familiar but undesirable form, or to cross off the desired form. Above all, such practice is futile because it is silent and detached from genuine communication." In an implied criticism of the tendency of workbooks to call for a written response in practice exercises designed to correct errors in oral usage, Pooley pointed out that "usage practice must be heard and spoken to be effective, and it should always be in a setting of normal and natural use of language for a purpose recognized by the pupil."

Workbooks become "crutches" for the poor or lazy teacher.   The ready availability of workbook exercises often tempts the poorly prepared teacher to make more use of these materials than is justified in the instructional program. According to Kerr, some administrators feel

[8]Robert C. Pooley, *Teaching English Usage* (New York: Appleton-Century-Crofts, Inc., 1946), pp. 183–184.

that "the use of workbooks is not professionally defensible because workbooks are often regarded as a kind of busywork that is relied on by inexperienced and lazy teachers. Frequently the children are required to work at more or less mechanical tasks which are not too closely related to their other learning activities."[9]

The continuous use of workbooks on every occasion and at every excuse or the use of workbooks in too many different subjects may cause them to become ineffective. Unpleasant or monotonous experiences with workbooks may readily make the teacher as well as the child allergic to them.

Workbooks fail to produce expected improvements in language as shown by scores on language tests.   The effectiveness of certain practice materials and workbooks has been questioned as the result of contradictory evidence from numerous studies of their use in classrooms.[10] The specific nature of learning in the language arts should make it obvious that growth toward mastery of skills as a result of practice exercises would be revealed in the language test only if the same skills were involved. A check of the overlap of emphasis in commercial workbooks with the content of standardized language tests indicates a lack of common content and emphasis. Obviously there is need for greater cooperation on the part of the authors of language workbooks and language tests in the selection of content.

Workbooks fail to produce superior ability to write complete sentences.   This statement seems to be justified by the evidence reported some years ago by Curtin.[11] According to Curtin's data, workbooks produced only average gains in teaching sentence sense and word meaning, but showed some superiority in teaching such mechanical skills as capitalization and punctuation. To this indictment of the workbook as a device for the development of skill in constructing sentences, Madden, without offering supporting evidence, adds the statement that workbook-trained children "are often poor in written expression in general."[12]

Workbooks add unnecessarily to the outlay for instructional equipment.   Whether the workbooks are purchased by the parents or

[9]Margaret Kerr, "Teaching with Workbooks," *Elementary School Journal,* 48:218–221, December, 1947.

[10]Robert L. Docter, "Reading Workbooks: Boon or Busy Work," *Elementary English,* 39:224–230, March, 1962.

[11]James Curtin, "Evaluation of Certain Language Workbooks," unpublished master's thesis, State University of Iowa, 1950.

[12]Richard Madden, "Workbooks! Tool or Crutch?" *NEA Journal,* 49:94–95, February, 1956.

by the school, their cost is an important item. The objection is not so serious if workbooks in many different subjects are not involved, but if a disproportionate share of school funds available for textbooks and library facilities goes for workbooks so that other important materials cannot be acquired, it becomes serious.

Workbooks fail to provide adequately for individual differences. In spite of the large amount and variety of practice material typically presented in workbooks, those opposed to their use hold that little or no differentiation in assignment of practice activities actually takes place. In fact, many workbooks make no more differentiation between exercises for brighter children and exercises for those needing special work than many teachers do.

Those who favor the use of language workbooks naturally question the validity of many of the arguments presented by those opposed to their use. They insist that the criticisms apply equally well to textbooks and other related instructional materials, and that the comments are not all unfavorable. The following points are among those most frequently presented in defense of their use:

Values of and Arguments for Workbooks

Workbooks are useful educational tools; they need not be misused. The effectiveness of workbooks depends largely upon the teachers using them. According to Stewart, ". . . it seems fair to conclude that workbooks in the hands of thoughtful teachers are valuable so long as they are kept in proper perspective—are not misused and are seen as helpers rather than dictators."[13]

Workbooks result in time-saving in securing pupil responses. Whether classes are large or small, the teacher can secure only one oral recitation at a time. When workbooks are properly used, with individual assignments given as needed, the teacher can secure as many responses as there are individuals in the class at that moment.

Workbooks encourage the establishment of good work habits. By setting a specific task, a definite plan of attack, and a time to complete the task, workbook exercises aid pupils in establishing habits of thoroughness in their school work.

Workbooks aid in class control. The readily available test and practice materials provided in the modern workbook enable the teacher to keep his class active and under control, thus discouraging disciplinary problems.

Workbooks provide meaningful practice. If the content of workbooks has been carefully selected in terms of pupils' needs, meaningful

[13]Stewart, "Workbooks," p. 479.

practice is provided. Frequently, the practice material found in workbooks is not available commercially elsewhere. Practice on punctuation items, capitalization needs, dictionary activities, and the like is needed to establish habits.

Workbooks provide material for individual instruction. One of the chief values of a satisfactory workbook lies in the amount and character of the practice material, in the advantage it offers in making individual assignments, and in its adaptability to individual instruction through material for individual practice. Workbooks provide a practical means of supplementing group instruction with individual instruction.

Workbooks provide a means of adjusting for individual differences. Workbook exercises of suitable content and difficulty give the slow student an opportunity to gain confidence in his own ability to improve his language skills.[14] Controlled vocabulary and simple and clear directions enable him to proceed independently. He is directed to a wide variety of material designed for different types of needs. Adjusting instruction to the superior pupil is a more difficult problem to solve. While there is little point in rewarding the superior child with more practice on skills he has already mastered, workbooks, through a wide variety of exercises and supplementary drill, may help the teacher to meet this problem satisfactorily.

Workbooks provide a means of preserving pupils' work for review. According to many teachers, principals, and supervisors, the opportunity which the workbook offers for the preservation of their earlier work in convenient and attractive form has a very definite appeal for children.

Workbooks are useful in diagnostic and remedial work. Some modern workbooks in the language arts contain or are accompanied by excellent inventory and mastery tests which if carefully analyzed will give the teacher a clear picture of the strengths and weaknesses of his pupils in many different aspects of language ability. They are not to be treated as substitutes for an adequate analytical testing program, but they do provide valuable supplementary diagnostic information for the teacher's guidance.

Workbooks add variety and supplement instruction. Interesting activities and practice exercises that frequently are crowded out of the textbook itself find a useful place in the workbook. Such materials, often written by the textbook authors themselves, are likely to be

[14]Harry W. Sartain, "Do Reading Workbooks Increase Achievement?" *Elementary School Journal*, 62:157–162, December, 1961.

organized like the textbook and compare favorably with the quality of exercises in the book itself.

Workbooks save the teacher's time and energy.   The time saved from preparing and duplicating teacher-made practice exercises may be used profitably in planning activities that will much more greatly enrich and extend the children's experiences as a basis for expression. The child's time is also saved by avoiding the endless copying of exercises from the textbook or from the chalkboard.

Workbooks provide savings on cost.   The use of a workbook largely does away with mimeographed sheets, scratch pads, notebooks and the like. It provides each child with his own individual book at a cost probably below that of similar teacher-made materials.

In a discussion dealing primarily with the value of workbooks in reading, Gray stated for the guidance of authors and teachers the following principles which, if carefully followed, would make workbooks valuable instruments in any skill area.[15]

1. Make each exercise fit the total skill program necessary for each level.
2. Provide varying types of exercises to fit the needs and interests of the child. Then supplement the materials with teacher-made material. It will prevent boredom.
3. Never let the material become an end in itself. Practice on skills should be a means to an end. The end is to use the skill in a functional situation. . . . A transfer of learning takes place only when the teacher deliberately attempts to make it take place.
4. The material should be the basis for additional teaching. Every page should be checked so that the difficulties will be noted and removed through further teaching and practice. Every practice lesson should be a diagnostic lesson.
5. The children must be able to understand what, how, and why they are to do each thing they do. Seeing a reason facilitates a transfer of learning.

The Selection and Use of Workbooks

If it is decided that a workbook or several workbooks are desirable for a classroom, two additional problems confront the teacher: (1) How can I select a good workbook or practice material? (2) How can I use this material most effectively to help children learn?

[15]W. S. Gray, *Basic Instruction in Reading in the Elementary and High Schools* (Chicago: University of Chicago Press, October, 1948), pp. 149–151.

The following questions should be considered in the selection of workbooks:

1. Does this type of material support and strengthen the objectives of the program?
2. Is the content organized to help the children attain these objectives?
3. Is it interesting to the pupils?
4. Is it attractively arranged?
5. Does it supplement and enrich the class activities?
6. Will the pupils gain a feeling of success in using this material?
7. Are the exercises varied and well motivated?
8. Does the material utilize sound principles of learning?
9. Is the vocabulary suitable for the pupils with whom it is to be used?
10. Are the directions simple, clear, and concise enough to permit pupils to work independently?
11. Does the material provide drills of the types needed by most pupils?
12. Does it provide practice material of a suitable range of difficulty?
13. Does it contain material capable of stimulating written expression in other than a mechanical manner?
14. Does it indicate that proper regard was given to scientific findings in the selection of content?
15. Does it provide adequately for review?
16. Does it stimulate self-appraisal by the pupil?
17. Does it contain suitable inventory, check, and master test material for pupil guidance?
18. Can the material be objectively and rapidly scored to save the teacher's time for the preparation of other valuable learning activities for the children?
19. Is it economically priced?

If a teacher is to realize fully the advantages of these materials as instructional aids, he must give special attention to the manner in which they are used. As a first and general principle, caution should be exercised concerning the use of many different workbooks in many different subjects, and the use of any one too often. Leaning too heavily on such materials may lead to failure to do the best job of teaching of which a teacher is capable. The following statements summarize concisely a number of other important principles which should be observed in this connection:

1. Before using any supplementary practice material, the teacher should determine just what he wants it to accomplish and then plan his teaching so that it can be used to help reach this objective. Each

particular practice lesson should be outlined with as much care as any other lesson.

2. At the outset, the workbook or other practice material chosen should be carefully evaluated in terms of criteria such as those suggested in this chapter. Acceptability of point of view, suitability of content, adequacy of methods, and desirable physical and mechanical features should all be considered. Special attention should be given to the ways in which accepted pedagogical and psychological principles are utilized.

3. Each workbook test or practice lesson should be checked as soon as possible, preferably by each child checking his own. The children should always know exactly what errors they made and why they are errors. Furthermore, the pupils should correct their wrong answers.

4. Practice exercises are important in aiding the pupil to acquire needed skills that he has not already developed. A pre-testing program consisting of informal tests made by the teacher or objective inventory tests such as accompany many workbooks provides a practical and economical means of identifying the individual children in need of further practice as well as the areas in which the practice is required.

5. Since great individual differences in abilities and needs exist within every class, there is no justification for assigning the same practice or workbook lesson for all pupils unless it is clear that it is actually needed by all.

6. Since adequate and permanent mastery of a skill cannot be expected to result from a single lesson, carefully chosen and properly distributed practice must be provided if the teaching and learning program is to be effective in producing the desired results.

7. The assignment of a carefully chosen lesson or practice exercise from the workbook does not in any sense conclude the teacher's responsibility. Its use must be properly motivated by showing the pupil the evidence of his needs and by convincing him that the proposed practice is not a punishment but an interesting experience which is almost certain to help him individually in the development of habits of expression that are valuable and permanent social assets.

8. The interest of the pupil in the potential values of workbook and practice material may be aroused by a frank explanation, discussion, and demonstration of an easy sample lesson. This initial interest must be maintained for those children whose records indicate that they need considerable practice. The best way to accomplish this is by making sure that the child's experience includes a variety of types of practice (lest he grow into a bored "blank-filler"), that the materials

are as functional as possible in relation to his needs, and that he is constantly aware of the progress he is making through their use.

9. In addition to the basic exercises, the better workbooks have many associated contributions to offer. These include inventory devices in verbal or test form, checklists and tests to measure progress, guide sheets for further practice, mastery tests, explanatory materials for teacher and pupil reference, suggestions for follow-up activities, progress charts, record blanks and the like. Both teacher and pupils should become familiar with all of these and be prepared to use them on every legitimate occasion.

10. In attempting to individualize the use of workbooks in the language arts class, the teacher is certain to encounter a number of problems of classroom management. Since many of these can be anticipated, time spent in developing a systematic plan for the handling of administrative details will be well rewarded. Administering the inventory tests, carrying out diagnostic procedures, individualizing the actual assignments, checking and recording test scores and results, and handling the physical materials of the program can all be coordinated into a workable system by any competent teacher. Without such planning, workbooks are likely to degenerate into merely another set of instruments in the regimentation of instruction.

Exercises for Thought and Action

1. Consider teachers you know and their use of textbooks. To what extent are the recommendations of this chapter followed?
2. Examine English, reading, spelling, and handwriting textbooks available to you. Are they of the quality suggested? How would you improve them?
3. Suggest a procedure for selecting and adopting a series of language textbooks for a school system in which you are a teacher.
4. How could you determine (1) the comprehension difficulty of directions, and (2) the vocabulary range of content in the textbook?
5. Discuss the major functions of workbooks as presented in this chapter. Do you agree with them?
6. What are the chief factors which have stimulated the development of the workbooks in language arts now available?
7. Outline what you consider a proper method of using a workbook to supplement the basic language textbook.
8. Which of the arguments advanced here in favor of the use of workbooks presents the strongest case for their use?

Selected References

Black, Millard H., and Whitehouse, LaVon Harper. "Reinforcing Reading Skills Through Workbooks." *The Reading Teacher:* 15:19–24, September, 1961.

Cronbach, Lee J., *et al. Text Materials in Modern Education.* Urbana, Illinois: University of Illinois Press, 1955.

Docter, Robert L. "Reading Workbooks: Boon or Busybody?" *Elementary English,* 39:224–230, May, 1962.

Dresden, Dorothy. "Use and Misuse of Workbooks and Teachers' Guides in Kindergarten Through Grade Three." *American Conference on Reading,* 19:75–78. Chicago, 1957.

Durrance, Victor R. "Public Textbook Selection in Forty-eight States." *Phi Delta Kappan,* 33:262–266, January, 1952.

Eibling, Harold H. "Textbook Selection: How to Be Sure the Right Ones Are Picked." *School Managment,* 8:81–86, 1964.

Felton, Wilma. "The Values of Workbooks in a First Grade Reading Program." *Elementary English,* 34:377–382, October, 1957.

Giannini, Bernadette. "Workbooks for Slow Classes." *Clearing House.* 33:160–162, November, 1958.

Goodman, Kenneth S., Hans C. Olsen, Jr., Cynthia M. Colvin, and Louis F. VanderLinde. *Choosing Materials To Teach Reading.* Detroit: Wayne State University Press, 1966.

Harlow, G. C. "Silent Teacher: The Workbook." *Childhood Education,* 41:84–86, October, 1964.

Hilton, Ernest. "Textbooks." *Encyclopedia of Educational Research,* Fourth Edition, Robert L. Ebel, editor. New York: The Macmillan Company, 1969, pp. 1470–1478.

Kerr, Margaret. "Teaching with Workbooks." *Elementary School Journal,* 48:218–221, December, 1947.

Kliger, Samuel. "Workbook and the Programmed Text." *English Journal,* 52:674–676, December, 1963.

Madden, Richard. "Workbooks! Tool or Crutch?" *NEA Journal,* 49:94–95, February, 1956.

Mattingly, E. H. "Meet the Modern Workbook," *Illinois Education.* 38:191, January, 1950.

Melliott, Malcolm E. "What to Look for in Choosing a Textbook." *NEA Journal,* 44:158–159, March, 1955.

Sartain, Harry W. "Do Reading Workbooks Increase Achievement." *Elementary School Journal,* 62:157–162, December, 1961.

Stewart, Miller J. "Workbooks: 1930–1964." *Elementary English,* 43:149–153, February, 1966.

Stewart, Miller J. "Workbooks: Help or Hindrance?" *Elementary English,* 43:477–479, May, 1966.

Textbooks in Education. New York: The American Textbook Publishers Institute, 1949.

Index

A

Abilities (see Skills)
Ability grouping (see Grouping)
Activities:
  and linguistics, 31–32,
    346–347, 377–380
  and textbooks, 544
Activities for:
  bilingual children, 114–117
  disadvantaged children,
    110–113
  identifying language needs,
    44–45
  primary grade children, 75–76
  reading readiness, 148–149
  vocabulary development,
    352–353
Activities for developing skill in:
  choral speaking, 221–222
  creative writing, 298–303
  discussion, 205–206
  filling in forms, 250–251
  handwriting, 445–446
  letter writing, 241–242
  listening, 140, 174–175
  oral reporting, 206–208
  report writing, 252–253
  spelling, 409–412
  storytelling, 214–216
  telephoning, 211
Activity planning, 53
Aids to textbook selection,
  529–534

Alphabetizing, 264, 362–363,
  470
Aims (see Objectives)
Announcements, making, 223,
  252
Anthologies of children's
  literature, 529–530
Anxiety and speech, 201
Articulation, 191–192, 221
Articulatory defects, 227
Assignments, 49–50
Attitudes, role in teaching:
  the disadvantaged, 98–101
  handwriting, 433, 437–438
  spelling, 396–397
  telephoning, 210
  usage, 318–322
  writing, 242–243
Audience, importance in:
  creative writing, 292
  expressional lessons, 53–54
  listening, 138
Audience sensitivity, 197–198
Auding, 154
Audiovisual aids in:
  creative expression, 301
  language arts teaching, 57
  listening, 177–178
  oral reporting, 209
  reading instruction, 496
Auditory acuity, 154, 165
Auditory discrimination, 105,
  108, 154–155, 422–425,
  483–484

Auditory perception, 76–77, 149

B

Basal reading instruction,
　472–473
Basic instructional procedures,
　51–58
Basic spelling words, 395
Bibliography, teaching of, 265
Bilingual children, 114–117
Biloquialism, 101
Book clubs, 532–533
Book lists, 530
Book reports, 518–522
Books:
　as aids to listening, 178
　aids to selection, 529–534
　basal reading, 472–473
　for developing language
　　expression, 315
　text, 537–558

C

Capitalization:
　activities, 259–263, 343
　evaluating, 274–275
　teaching, 260–263
Charts, experience, 113
Checklists:
　handwriting, 444
　proofreading, 268
　in usage teaching, 328
　use of, 45
Choral speaking, 137, 197,
　221–223, 526
Classroom organization, 40–43
Composition:
　in creative writing, 306–308
　and grammar study, 380–381
　group, 80, 296–298
　and rhetorical skills, 333–350
　and writing, 237

Comprehension skills in:
　listening, 159
　reading, 489–492
Content in:
　expression, 348–349
　reading, 488–489
　writing, 286–287
Conversation:
　and discussion, 204
　in primary grades, 128–129
　teaching, 200–204
Correct usage (see Dialects,
　　Usage)
Correctional lessons, 55–58
Courtesy in:
　discussion, 204–205
　interviewing, 219
　social amenities, 224–226
　telephoning, 211–212
Creative expression, 283–284,
　296–315
　purposes of, 285–287
Creativity:
　conditions fostering, 287–296
　defined, 280–281
　process of, 293
Creativity in:
　disadvantaged children,
　　281–282
　dramatization, 216
　Kindergarten, 80–81
　literature, 503
　primary grades, 144–145
　rhythmic movement, 125
　sentence construction,
　　344–345
　storytelling, 131–133
Culturally deprived (see
　　Disadvantaged children)
Curriculum:
　determination of, 7, 10–16
　Kindergarten, 78–83
　and textbooks, 538–542
Cursive writing, teaching of,
　438–442

D

Defective speech, 191–196
Diagnosis in:
  correctional lessons, 56–67
  handwriting, 457–464
  reading, 471
  spelling, 422–427
  workbooks, 554
Diagramming sentences,
  374–375
Dialect study, 32
Dialects (see also Usage):
  and books for children, 32
  and the disadvantaged, 95–98
  and grammar, 317–318
  and pronunciation, 192–193
  and usage, 317–318
Dictated stories, 143–144
Dictation:
  in primary grades, 143–144
  in punctuation teaching, 263
  test in spelling, 421
Dictionary teaching, 357,
  360–364
Differences, pupil (see
  Individual differences)
Directions, instruction in
  giving, 223
Disadvantaged children:
  creativity of, 282
  dialects of, 96–98
  and grammar, 383
  identified, 88
  and language development,
  91–95
  and listening activities,
  109–110
  strengths of, 90–91
  teachers of, 89–101
Discussion:
  in primary grades, 128–129
  teaching of, 204–206
Dramatic play, 79, 310
Dramatization:

and creative expression,
  310–312
in primary grades, 133–134
and storytelling, 212
teaching of, 216–218
and telephoning, 210–211
Drills:
  punctuation, 263
  in standard English, 102–103
  in workbooks, 553–554

E

Early language learning, 64–68
Education:
  and curriculum content, 7
  purposes of, 5–7
Emotions and speech, 195–196
English:
  and language arts, 2
  nonstandard, 318–320
  standard, 192–195, 319–322
Enunciation, 123, 191, 221
Enrichment:
  of experience backgrounds,
  121–122
  of language experiences,
  101–102
  in reading lesson, 478
Environment and:
  the disadvantaged, 89–93,
  107–108
  dramatization, 134
  expression, 75
  language development, 91–94
  literature study, 516–517
  speech training, 188–190
  written expression, 287–288
Errors:
  instruction to remedy, 57
  punctuation, 257
  usage, 124, 323
Evaluating:
  handwriting, 444–445,
  451–461

Evaluating *(cont.)*
  language needs, 44–45
  listening, 178–182
  oral language, 228–232
  reading instruction, 471,
    496–499
  spelling, 417–422
  textbooks, 542–543
  usage teaching, 331
  written expression, 269–277
Evaluation:
  defined, 9
  in expressional lessons, 56
  and grading, 60–61, 272–274
  in language programs, 58–61
  in the literature program,
    528–529
  procedures for, 44–45
  and purposes of education,
    8–9
Exercises (see Activities)
Experience and:
  beginning reading, 143–144
  creativity, 288–291
  the disadvantaged, 89–90,
    111–113
  individual differences,
    121–122
  oral language, 199–200
  poetry teaching, 524–526
  reading, 490–491
  vocabulary development,
    351–356
  writing, 239–240, 288–291
Experience charts, 113
Experiences in nursery schools,
    105–108
Experiential limitations, 92–94
Expressive language arts, 3
Expressional lessons, 51–55

F

Filling in forms instruction,
    250–252

Films and filmstrips, 177–178
    (see also Audiovisual
    aids)
Footnoting, 265–266
Form:
  bibliography, 265
  for footnotes, 265
  in letter writing, 245
Frustration, prevention of, 470
Functional grammar, 375–376
Functional language arts
    programs, 36

G

Games, language arts, 49, 73,
    77, 110, 414–416
Generative grammar, 378–380
Goals (see Objectives)
Grades and evaluation, 272–274
Grading, 60–61
Grammar:
  defined, 317–318, 369
  and dialects, 96–98, 317–318
  functional, 37, 375–376
  generative-transformational,
    378–380
  and language development,
    65–67
  and linguistics, 24, 369–371
  of nonstandard English, 97
  research, 372–375
  and sentence construction,
    339–341
  structural, 376–378
  teaching, 371–380
  transformational, 370–371
  types of, 369–370
  and usage, 327–328, 382–383
  values of teaching, 380–383
  and writing, 235, 269
Grapheme-phoneme
    correspondence, 407
Group expression, 296–298

Group stories, 143–144
Grouping:
  ability, 46–47
  in handwriting, 444
  in literature programs,
    522–523
  in spelling, 410–411
  for reading instruction,
    493–495

H

Habits:
  and dialects, 95–98
  and instruction, 57
  speech, 190–198
  spelling, 397–398
  usage, 327–328
Haiku, 305
Handedness, 73–74, 447–448
Handwriting:
  faults, 435
  motivation, 445–446
  objectives, 433–434
  in primary grades, 141–142
  and public concern, 431–432
  readiness, 437–438
  and spelling, 394
Hearing and speech, 228

I

Individual differences, 43–45
Individual deficiencies, 56
Individualization in:
  listening instruction, 176–177
  reading, 470, 474, 495
  spelling, 410–411
  textbooks, 548–549
Individualized activities, 48, 51
Individualized reading, 474–475
I.T.A., 475

Instructional procedures
  (see also Activities):
  basic, 51–58
  in capitalization, 260–263
  in listening, 168–176
  in primary grades, 126–145
  in standard English, 101–104
  in usage teaching, 328–331
Integration of language arts,
  35–40
Intelligence and:
  language, 68
  listening, 157–158
Interests:
  children's, 247, 511–512
  grouping for, 494
  reading, 469–470, 506–509
  textbook provisions for,
    545–546
Interrelatedness of the language
  arts, 3, 157–162,
  186–187, 393–394
Interviewing, 218–219
Introduction teaching, 225

K

Kindergarten:
  and the disadvantaged,
    107–111
  language arts programs, 72–83
  objectives, 122–126
  reading, 147–149
  storytelling, 130–133

L

Laboratory instruction, 48
Language:
  activities, 31–32
  activities for bilingual,
    114–117
  bilingual, 114–117

Language *(cont.)*
  characteristics, 17–19
  and creativity, 281–282
  defined, 16–18
  and disadvantaged, 85–118
  and intelligence, 68
  in Kindergarten, 72–83
  and the language arts, 3, 5
  learning, 15–16, 386–388
  and linguistics, 16–27
  needs, 11–14
  in nursery schools, 104–107
  preschool, 71–72
  purposes for, 1, 20–21
  and reading, 464–466
  and speech, 39–40, 186–187
  study, 24–26
Language ability:
  and self-image, 113
  differences in, 43–45
Language development:
  and articulation, 191–192
  of the disadvantaged, 91–95
  factors influencing, 67–70
  in Kindergarten, 78
  in preschool years, 64–67
  of young children, 123
Language experience in
        reading, 473-474
Learning:
  by doing, 52–53
  difficulty in spelling, 416–417
  language, 64–70
  and language arts, 15–16
  and reading, 467–471
Left-handed children, 447–449
Lessons:
  capitalization, 261–262
  handwriting, 443–444
  listening, 168–174
  reading, 477–481
  spelling, 399–401
  written expression, 301–302
Letter writing, 241–245

Libraries:
  and librarians, 517–518
  room, 512
Library skills, 358–360
Life needs and the curriculum,
        11–13
Linguistic activities, 31–32,
        346–347, 377–380
Linguistic insights needed,
        30–31
Linguistic objectives, 31
Linguistics and:
  creative writing, 294
  defined, 16, 22–27, 317
  descriptive, 376–377
  elementary school programs,
        27–32
  grammar, 24, 369–371
  language, 16–27
  language development, 64–67
  reading, 486–487
  spelling, 405–407, 412–413
  textbooks, 28–29, 547
  usage, 318–319
  utility of studying, 28–29
  vocabulary study, 27,
        353–354
  writing, 235
Linguists:
  definition of language, 17–18
  structural, 25
  transformationalists, 26
  views on grammar teaching,
        381–382
Listening:
  activities in primary grades,
        109–110, 140, 174–175
  and creative expression,
        311–312
  defined, 153–154
  and language, 38
  in primary grades, 124–125,
        138–140
  standards, 180–181

Listening *(cont.)*
  teaching, 139, 164–177
  types of, 162–164
Literature:
  children's interest in, 506–509
  in the primary grades,
    134–137
  teaching, 509–523
Literature and:
  choral speaking, 221–223
  creativity, 295–296
  creative writing, 304–305
  Kindergarten programs, 72
  language arts programs, 502
  oral reading, 492–493
  reading instruction, 467
  and teachers, 504–506

M

Magazines for children, 531–532
Manuscript form in writing,
  254–255
Manuscript writing, 141–142,
  449–451
Materials:
  for handwriting, 442
  for reading instruction,
    495–496
  useful for motivating writing,
    302–303
Measurement (see Evaluation)
Meetings, conducting, 219–220
Minutes, instruction in writing,
  252–253
Minority groups and language
  arts, 88 (see also
  Disadvantaged children
  and Bilingual children)
Models:
  for letter writing, 244–245
  in expression, 54

in oral reading, 506
teachers as, 106
Morpheme, 25
Morphology, 25, 369
Motivation:
  and handwriting, 435–436,
    445–446
  in textbooks, 546
  and usage teaching, 329
Motivating:
  children to write, 237–240,
    293–296
  correct spelling, 393
  oral expression, 199–200

N

National Conference on
  Research in English, 11
National Council of Teachers of
  English, 11, 164, 235, 320
Nongraded schools, 47
Nonstandard English, 91, 98
Notetaking, teaching of,
  336–337
Nursery Schools:
  and the disadvantaged,
    104–107
  and the language arts, 71–72

O

Objectives and evaluation, 8–9
Objectives for instruction in:
  conversation, 202
  creative expression, 285–286
  grammar, 382–384
  handwriting, 433–434
  language arts, 5–8, 10–12
  linguistics, 28–29

Objectives for inst. *(cont.)*
  listening, 168–169
  literature, 503–504
  preschools, 70–71, 105
  primary grades, 121–126
  reading, 466–467
  reading poetry, 527
  report writing, 246–247
  spelling, 395
  storytelling, 214–215
  written expression, 140–141,
      236–237
Oral language:
  activities, 126–137
  and creative writing, 293–294
  and listening, 161–162
  objectives, 122–124, 194–195
  situations, 199–228
  and voice quality, 195–196
Oral reading:
  and literature, 505
  measuring abilities in,
      498–499
  by the teacher, 513–514
  teaching, 492–493
Oral reporting:
  in literature, 518–520
  in primary grades, 129–130
  teaching, 130, 206–209
Organization of:
  classrooms, 40–43
  expression, 333–336
  meetings, 219–220
  paragraphs, 335–336
  reports, 145
  sentences, 334–335
  stories, 213
Organizing for:
  instruction, 35–42
  reading instruction, 470,
      493–495
Outline teaching, 248–250,
      307, 337–339

P

Paperbacks in literature
      program, 532
Paragraphing, 335–336
Parents and handwriting,
      446–447
Parliamentary procedure
      teaching, 220
Pen pals, 242
Perception (see Auditory and
      Visual)
Personality characteristics,
      187–188, 423, 425–426
Phoneme, defined, 24
Phoneme-grapheme
      correspondence, 416
Phonemes:
  in language learning, 64, 158
  representation, 405, 416, 476
Phonics, 483–486
Phonology defined, 24
Physical mannerisms and
      speech, 197
Planning:
  language activities, 129
  language arts instruction,
      34–62
  oral reporting, 207–208
  storytelling, 212–213
Play and activity periods,
      126–128
Poetry:
  in the primary grades,
      134–137
  teaching, 523–527
  writing, 303–306
Point of view:
  social utility, 11–15
  in textbooks, 540
Posture and handwriting, 436,
      438–442

Practice:
  corrective, 57–58
  handwriting, 444–445
  materials in textbooks, 400
  patterns in English, 115–116
  usage, 329–331
Practical writing, 283, 308–310
Preschool:
  guidelines for programs, 107
  language development, 64–67
  language programs, 70–72
Principles for teaching:
  conversation, 201–202
  dramatization, 216–217
  listening, 168
  oral reporting, 130, 206–209
  reading, 469–471
  writing, 254
Programmed instruction, 50–51,
    475–476
Programs for language arts
    (see Organization)
Pronunciation and:
  choral speaking, 221
  dialects, 96–97, 192–194
  disadvantaged, 108
  spelling, 407, 417
  vocabulary development,
    356–357
Proofreading, 49, 266–267,
    297, 398
Prose writing, 306–308
Psycholinguistics, 23
Punctuation:
  activities, 343
  evaluating teaching of,
    276–277
  and linguistics, 31
  skills, 144–145
  teaching, 257–263
Puppets, 217–218, 312–313
Purposes of education (see
    Objectives)

Q

Questioning in reading
    instruction, 491

R

Readiness:
  for handwriting instruction,
    141
  maintaining, 471
  measuring, 497–498
  reading, 147–148, 471,
    477–479, 481–483
  spelling, 142, 408–410
  writing, 437–438
Reading:
  beginning instruction in,
    147–150
  and creative writing, 290–291
  and experience charts, 113
  interests, 113, 469–470,
    507–509
  in Kindergarten, 81–83
  and language, 38–39, 464–466
  and linguistics, 486–487
  and listening, 38, 158–160
  oral, 487
  questioning in lessons, 491
  readiness, 83, 481–483
  and spelling, 393–394
  tests, 498–499
  textbooks, 110, 472–473,
    478–481
  and vocabulary, 354–355
Records as listening aids, 177
    (see also Audiovisual
    aids)
Reference source teaching,
    364–366
Remedial procedures:
  in handwriting, 458–461
  in speech, 228

Remedial procedures *(cont.)*
  in spelling, 426–427
  for writing, 274–276
Reports:
  on books, 530–531
  oral, 112, 206–209
  written, 144–145, 245–247,
    309–310
Rhetorical skills, 333–350
Rhythm in handwriting,
    440–441
Rules:
  for making introductions,
    225–226
  for parliamentary procedures,
    219–220
  spelling, 404–408

S

Scales:
  composition, 270–271
  handwriting, 453–456
  written expression, 270
Schedules, 41–43
Selection of textbooks, 545–549,
    555–558
Self-editing, 49, 55, 266–269
Semantics, 26, 334–335
Sentences:
  construction, 339–349
  diagramming, 374–375
  patterns, 98, 108–109
  sense, 275–277, 342–350
Sex factors in language
    development, 69–70
Sharing experiences, 78
Show and Tell, 129
Skills:
  capitalization, 259–260
  dictionary, 361
  discussion, 204–205
  in filling in forms, 250–252

letter writing, 243–244
  listening, 156–157
  locational, 357–358
  needed, 7, 12, 45
  oral reporting, 208
  perceptual, 76–77
  punctuation, 257–259
  rhetorical, 333–350
  spelling, 395
Social amenities, 224–226
Socialization as a language
    objective, 123
Social utility:
  limitations, 13–15
  principle, 11–13
Society and the disadvantaged,
    86–91
Socio-economic factors, 68–69
Sociolinguistics, 23–24
Speech:
  characteristics, 193
  correction, 193–194
  defects, 227–230
  of disadvantaged, 97–98
  and handedness, 74–75
  and hearing, 226
  in Kindergarten, 72, 74–75
  in language arts programs,
    39–40, 186–187
  and linguistics, 17
  and listening, 161–162
  and punctuation, 258
  and reading, 487
  remedial, 228–230
  silent, 197
  and spelling, 394
Spelling:
  evaluation, 417–422
  instruction, 398–404
  objectives, 395
  and other language arts,
    393–394
  rules, 407–408

Spontaneity of expression,
122–123, 239
Standard English, 193–195
Standardized tests (see also
Tests):
listening, 178–179
spelling, 422
writing, 271
Standards:
evolving, 54–55
listening, 138
oral reading, 493
proofreading, 266–268
pupil developed, 180–181
storytelling, 213
writing, 255
written reports, 247
Storytelling:
books about, 215
creative, 313
in Kindergarten, 79–80
in literature programs,
515–516
in primary grades, 130–133
and puppets, 218
purposes of, 214–215
standards, 213
teaching, 212–216
Story writing, 143–144, 306–308
Structural analysis in reading,
488–489
Structural grammar, 376–378
Study steps in spelling, 401–402
Subject matter organization,
35–37
Syntax, 25, 369

T

Tapes, 177 (see also
Audiovisual aids)
Teachers:

and the disadvantaged,
98–101
and individual differences,
45–51
and language arts, 4
listening habits, 165
and literature, 504–506
and prejudice, 99
role in creative expression,
292–296
speech, 231–232
Telephoning, instruction in,
209–211
Test-study in spelling, 398–399
Tests:
constructing, 418–420
handwriting, 458–459
listening, 178–180
reading, 498–499
spelling, 398–399, 401–403,
410–411
writing, 271
Textbooks:
for bilinguals, 117
and disadvantaged, 110–111
and grammar, 384
informational skills in,
264–265
language arts, 538–539
linguistic study in, 28–29
and listening, 178
and oral language, 198
and punctuation, 257, 262
reading, 110, 472, 495–496
selection, 529–534
and social amenities
teaching, 226
spelling, 394, 399–400
telephone activities in, 211
Thinking and:
conversation, 200
language, 21
listening, 157–158

Thinking and *(cont.)*
outlining, 248
writing, 237
Topics for writing, 298–299
Transformations in language
    drills, 103
Transformational grammar, 26,
    378–380
Types of listening, 162–164
    (see also Listening)

U

Usage (see also Dialects):
acceptable, 319–322
defined, 318
and dialects, 317–318
functional teaching of,
    323–331
and grammar, 369, 381–382
levels, 383
practice, 113
standard, 318–322
teaching, 127, 323–331

V

Visual perception, 76–77, 466
Vocabulary development:
activities, 27, 108, 125–126,
    138, 291–295, 348–357
and dialects, 96
of disadvantaged, 93–98, 111
and environment, 92–94
and listening lessons, 170–171
in nursery schools, 104–105
and poetry, 137
in preschool years, 65,
    125–126

and reading, 39, 354–355, 479
and spelling, 409–410,
    412–413
Voice:
control, 123
quality, 195–196

W

Word recognition skills, 487–489
Words in Color, 476
Words, spelling, 395–396,
    407–408
Workbooks:
in language arts program,
    549–558
for spelling, 399–400
stimulating creativity,
    302–303
Writing:
activities, 241–242, 250–253,
    298–303
conventional forms in,
    254–256
dramas, 216
environment, 287–288
and grammar, 373–376,
    380–381, 383–384
in literature programs,
    519–521
motivation for, 237–240
outlines, 248–250
reports, 245–247
and spelling, 392–393
Written expression:
evaluation of, 269–277
by groups, 142–143
in primary grades, 140–147
situations, 241–254